第十二届中国城市住宅研讨会论文集

Proceedings of The 12th China Urban Housing Conference

可持续高密度人居环境建设的智慧化与创新

INTELLIGENTIZATION AND INNOVATION OF SUSTAINABLE HIGH-DENSE HUMAN HABITAT TRANSFORMATION

主　编：邹经宇　李秉仁　孙一民　龚兆先
Chief Editors: Tsou Jin-Yeu, Li Bingren, Sun Yimin, Gong Zhaoxian

中国建筑工业出版社
CHINA ARCHITECTURE & BUILDING PRESS

图书在版编目（CIP）数据

第十二届中国城市住宅研讨会论文集 可持续高密度人居环境建设的智慧化与创新= Proceedings of The 12th China Urban Housing Conference INTELLIGENTIZATION AND INNOVATION OF SUSTAINABLE HIGH-DENSE HUMAN HABITAT TRANSFORMATION / 邹经宇等主编 .—北京：中国建筑工业出版社，2017.6

ISBN 978-7-112-20910-1

Ⅰ.①第… Ⅱ.①邹… Ⅲ.①城市—住宅建设—中国—学术会议—文集 Ⅳ.①F299.233.5-53

中国版本图书馆CIP数据核字（2017）第133740号

责任编辑：率　琦　白玉美　王莉慧
责任校对：王宇枢　李欣慰

第十二届中国城市住宅研讨会论文集
Proceedings of The 12th China Urban Housing Conference
可持续高密度人居环境建设的智慧化与创新
INTELLIGENTIZATION AND INNOVATION OF SUSTAINABLE HIGH-DENSE HUMAN HABITAT TRANSFORMATION
主编：邹经宇　李秉仁　孙一民　龚兆先
Chief Editors: Tsou Jin-Yeu, Li Bingren, Sun Yimin, Gong Zhaoxian
*
中国建筑工业出版社出版、发行（北京海淀三里河路9号）
各地新华书店、建筑书店经销
北京京点图文设计有限公司制版
北京圣夫亚美印刷有限公司印刷
*
开本：880×1230毫米　1/16　印张：37½　字数：135千字
2017年6月第一版　2017年6月第一次印刷
定价：200.00元（附光盘）
ISBN 978-7-112-20910-1
　　　（30549）

版权所有　翻印必究
如有印装质量问题，可寄本社退换
（邮政编码 100037）

主 编　Chief Editors

邹经宇　教授　　　　　香港中文大学中国城市住宅研究中心主任
Prof. Tsou Jin-Yeu　　香港中文大学建筑学院教授
　　　　　　　　　　　Director, Center for Housing Innovations, The Chinese University of Hong Kong
　　　　　　　　　　　Professor, School of Architecture, The Chinese University of Hong Kong

李秉仁　教授　　　　　中华人民共和国住房和城乡建设部专家委员会主任
Prof. Li Bingren　　　中华人民共和国住房和城乡建设部科学技术委员会副主任（常务）
　　　　　　　　　　　Director, Committee of Experts, Ministry of Housing and Urban-Rural Development, PRC
　　　　　　　　　　　Deputy Director, Committee of Science and Technology, Ministry of Housing and Urban-Rural Development, PRC

孙一民　教授　　　　　华南理工大学建筑学院常务副院长、教授
Prof. Sun Yimin　　　亚热带建筑科学国家重点实验室常务副主任
　　　　　　　　　　　Deputy Director-General and Professor, School of Architecture, South China University of Technology
　　　　　　　　　　　Deputy Director-General, State Key Laboratory of Subtropical Building Science

龚兆先　教授　　　　　广州大学建筑与城市规划学院院长、教授
Prof. Gong Zhaoxian　Director and Professor, College of Architecture and Urban Planning, Guangzhou University

编 辑　Editors

邓毅　教授　　　　　　广州大学建筑与城市规划学院副院长、副教授
Prof. Deng Yi　　　　Deputy Director and Associate Professor, College of Architecture and Urban Planning, Guangzhou University

苏平　教授　　　　　　华南理工大学建筑学院建筑学系副系主任、副教授
Prof. Su Ping　　　　Deputy Director and Associate Professor, Department of Architecture, School of Architecture, South China University of Technology

李响　女士　　　　　　香港中文大学建筑学院博士研究生
Ms. Li Xiang　　　　 PhD Student, School of Architecture, The Chinese University of Hong Kong

赵明君　女士　　　　　香港中文大学中国城市住宅研究中心副研究员/研究拓展及管理室主任
Ms. Chao Mingchun　Research Associate/Unit Leader of Research Development & Administration Unit, Center for Housing Innovations, The Chinese University of Hong Kong

主办单位　Organizers

香港中文大学中国城市住宅研究中心
Center for Housing Innovations, The Chinese University of Hong Kong

广州市科学技术协会
Guangzhou Association for Science & Technology

华南理工大学建筑学院
School of Architecture, South China University of Technology

广州大学建筑与城市规划学院
Colleague of Architecture and Urban Planning, Guangzhou University

广州中山大学地球环境与地球资源研究中心
Center for Earth Environment & Resources, Sun Yat-sen University, Guangzhou

协办单位　Co-organizers

京港学术交流中心
Beijing-Hong Kong Academic Exchange Centre
广东省土木建筑学会
Guangdong Society of Civil Engineering and Architecture

指导单位　Advisory Organizers

中华人民共和国住房和城乡建设部专家委员会
Committee of Experts, Ministry of Housing and Urban-Rural Development, PRC

中华人民共和国住房和城乡建设部科学技术委员会
Committee of Science and Technology, Ministry of Housing and Urban-Rural Development, PRC

支持单位　Supporting Organizers

香港中文大学社会科学院
Faculty of Social Science, The Chinese University of Hong Kong
香港中文大学香港亚太研究所
Hong Kong Institute of Asia-Pacific Studies, The Chinese University of Hong Kong

中国城市住宅研讨会论文评审办法
Paper Review Method of the China Urban Housing Conference

1. 邀请国内外城市规划、城市设计、建筑设计、建筑技术、房地产、城乡发展政策、空间规划等领域的知名学者，具有长期实践经验的产业界专家，担任本届中国城市住宅研讨会论文评审委员会委员。

2. 所有作者要求在截止日期前，于线上论文提交系统提交800～1000字的摘要，并另附一份参考文献列表。由中国城市住宅研讨会秘书处将所有摘要及相应的参考文献列表，按研究领域与方向进行分类，再以匿名方式发送给三位（或以上）论文评审委员，进行评审。

3. 论文评审委员需在截止日期前，于线上论文提交系统完成评审并且填妥中国城市住宅研讨会论文评分表，根据论文的贡献性、接纳性分别给出0～10之间的某一数字作为该论文摘要的贡献评分、接纳评分，同时给予必要的评语。所有提交的论文摘要，将获得三位（或以上）论文评审委员的匿名评分及评语。

4. 中国城市住宅研讨会秘书处在收齐所有论文摘要评审结果后，将每篇论文的所有分数加以统计，并分别取贡献评分、接纳评分的平均值作为贡献评分结果、接纳评分结果，进行由高到低排序。完成初步评分统计后，上报中国城市住宅研讨会学术委员会。

5. 中国城市住宅研讨会学术委员会在综合考虑贡献评分结果、接纳评分结果、评委评语及评分详情基础上，确认获得被本届中国城市住宅研讨会论文集录取的论文摘要。

6. 中国城市住宅研讨会秘书处根据中国城市住宅研讨会学术委员会有关论文摘要录取决议，以电子邮件形式向摘要被录取的作者发出录取通知，邀请撰写论文全文，并于论文全文提交截止日期前于线上论文提交系统提交。最后将被录取的论文摘要标题、论文编号公布于本届研讨会网站。

第十二届中国城市住宅研讨会论文评审委员会委员
Review Panel of the 12th China Urban Housing Conference

（以英文姓氏排序 In alphabetical order of the last name）

安关峰总工程师
Dr. An Guanfeng
广州市市政集团有限公司
Guangzhou Municipal Engineering Group Co.Ltd.

鲍莉教授
Prof. Bao Li
东南大学建筑学院
School of Architecture, Southeast University

Henco Bekkering教授
Prof. Henco Bekkering
代尔夫特理工大学建筑学院
Faculty of Architecture and the Built Environment, Delft University of Technology

Stephen Cairns教授
Prof. Stephen Cairns
新加坡-瑞士苏黎世联邦理工学院研究中心未来城市实验室
Future Cities Laboratory, Singapore-ETH Centre

郑炳鸿教授
Prof. Chang Pinghung, Wallace
香港大学建筑学院
Department of Architecture, The University of Hong Kong

陈永勤教授
Prof. Chen Yongqin, David
香港中文大学地理与资源管理学系
Department of Geography and Resource Management, The Chinese University of Hong Kong

陈上元教授
Prof. Chen Shangyuan
逢甲大学建筑专业学院
School of Architecture, Feng Chia University

Wolfgang Dokonal教授
Prof. Wolfgang Dokonal
格拉茨技术大学
Graz University of Technology

丁沃沃教授
Prof. Ding Wowo
南京大学建筑与城市规划学院
School of Architecture and Urban Planning, Nanjing University

福田知弘教授
Prof. Fukuda Tomohiro
大阪大学大学院可持续能源与环境工程学部
Division of Sustainable Energy and Environmental Engineering, Graduate School of Engineering, Osaka University

冯宜萱女士
Ms. Fung Yin Suen Ada
香港特别行政区房屋署（发展及建筑）
Development & Construction Division, Housing Department, Hong Kong SAR

范悦教授　　　　　　　　　　大连理工大学建筑与艺术学院
Prof. Fan Yue　　　　　　　　School of Architecture & Fine Art, Dalian University of Technology

何明锦教授　　　　　　　　　中国科技大学（台湾）建筑系暨建筑研究所
Prof. Ho Mingchin　　　　　　Department/Graduate Institute of Architecture Design, China University of Technology(Taiwan)

谢尚贤教授　　　　　　　　　台湾大学土木工程学系
Prof. Hsieh Shang-Hsien　　　Department of Civil Engineering, Taiwan University

郝琳教授/执行董事　　　　　　香港中文大学中国城市住宅研究中心/
Prof. Hao Lin　　　　　　　　Integer绿色与智慧设计事务所/欧华尔顾问有限公司
　　　　　　　　　　　　　　Center for Housing Innovations, The Chinese University of Hong Kong/Integer Intelligent & Green Ltd./ The Oval partnership Ltd.

黄一如教授　　　　　　　　　同济大学建筑与城市规划学院
Prof. Huang Yiru　　　　　　 College of Architecture and Urban Planning, Tongji University

韩继红教授　　　　　　　　　上海市建筑科学研究院（集团）有限公司
Ms. Han Jihong　　　　　　　Shanghai Research Institute of Building Sciences Group

姜中桥女士　　　　　　　　　中华人民共和国住房和城乡建设部科技与产业化发展中心
Ms. Jiang Zhongqiao　　　　　Center of Science and Technology of Construction, Ministry of Housing and Urban-Rural Development, PRC

邝君尚教授　　　　　　　　　香港科技大学土木及环境工程学系
Prof. Kuang Junshang　　　　 Department of Civil and Environmental Engineering, The Hong Kong University of Science and Technology

郭琼莹教授　　　　　　　　　中国文化大学景观学系
Prof. Monica Kuo　　　　　　 Department of Landscape Architecture, Chinese Culture University

龚书章教授　　　　　　　　　台湾交通大学建筑研究所
Prof. Kung Shu-Chang　　　　 Graduate Institute of Architecture, Chiao Tung University, Taiwan

李振宇教授　　　　　　　　　同济大学建筑与城市规划学院
Prof. Li Zhenyu　　　　　　　College of Architecture and Urban Planning, Tongji University

梁以德教授　　　　　　　　　中国绿色建筑与节能（香港）委员会
Prof. Leung Yee Tak, Andrew　China Green Building（Hong Kong）Council

林拓教授　　　　　　　　　　华东师范大学现代城市研究中心/中国行政区划研究中心

Prof. Lin Tuo	Center for Modern Chinese City Studies, East China Normal University/Research Center of Administrative Divisions in China, East China Normal University
李迅教授 Prof. Li Xun	中国城市规划设计研究院 China Academy of Urban Planning and Design
刘崇教授 Prof. Liu Chong	青岛理工大学建筑学院 School of Architecture, Qingdao Technology University
吕斌教授 Prof. Lü Bin	北京大学城市与环境学院 College of Urban and Environmental Sciences, Peking University
李保峰教授 Prof. Li Baofeng	华中科技大学建筑与城市规划学院 School of Architecture and Urban Planning, Huazhong University of Science and Technology
梁伟雄教授 Prof. Liang Weixiong	广东省土木建筑学会 Guangdong Society of Civil Engineering and Architecture
吕伟娅教授 Prof. Lü Weiya	南京工业大学城市建设学院 College of Urban Construction, Nanjing Tech University
李彦颐教授 Prof. Li Yenyi	树德科技大学建筑与室内设计研究所 Graduate School of Architecture and Interior Design Department, Shu-Te University
马欣伯博士 Dr. Ma Xinbo	中华人民共和国住房和城乡建设部科技与产业化发展中心 Center of Science and Technology of Construction, Ministry of Housing and Urban-Rural Development, PRC
孟玟廷教授 Prof. Maing Minjung	香港大学建筑学院 Faculty of Architecture, The University of Hong Kong
Jurgen Rosemann教授 Prof. Jurgen Rosemann	新加坡国立大学设计与环境学院 School of Design and Environment, National University of Singapore
Francesco Rossini教授 Prof. Francesco Rossini	香港中文大学建筑学院 School of Architecture, The Chinese University of Hong Kong
饶戎教授 Prof. Rao Rong	清华大学建筑学院 School of Architecture, Tsinghua University

沈建法教授
Prof. Shen Jianfa
香港中文大学地理与资源管理学系
Department of Geography and Resource Management, The Chinese University of Hong Kong

宋昆教授
Prof. Song Kun
天津大学建筑学院
School of Architecture, Tianjin University

沈粤教授
Prof. Shen Yue
广州大学建筑设计研究院
Architectural Design & Research Institute, Guangzhou University

孙澄教授
Prof. Sun Cheng
哈尔滨工业大学建筑学院
School of Architecture, Harbin Institute of Technology

沈杰教授
Prof. Shen Jie
浙江大学建筑工程学院
College of Civil Engineering and Architecture, Zhejiang University

孙多斌先生
Prof. Sun Duobin
北京诚慧恒绿色科技有限公司
Beijing Chenghuiheng Green Technology Ltd.

邹经宇教授
Prof. Tsou Jin-Yeu
香港中文大学中国城市住宅研究中心
Center for Housing Innovations, The Chinese University of Hong Kong

汤羽扬教授
Prof. Tang Yuyang
北京建筑大学建筑遗产研究院
Academy of Architectural Heritage, Beijing University of Civil Engineering and Architecture

Hendrik Tieben教授
Prof. Hendrik Tieben
香港中文大学建筑学院
School of Architecture, The Chinese University of Hong Kong

王秋元博士
Dr. Wang Chiuyuan
国际城市论坛
International Forum on Urbanism

王承慧教授
Prof. Wang Chenghui
东南大学建筑学院城市规划系
Department of Urban Planning, School of Architecture, Southeast University

王昌兴教授
Prof. Wang Changxing
北京清华同衡规划设计研究院有限公司
Beijing Tsinghua Tongheng Urban Planning & Design Institute

王绍森教授
Prof. Wang Shaosen
厦门大学建筑与土木工程学院
School of Architecture and Civil Engineering, Xiamen University

王文安教授 Prof. Wang Wen-An	淡江大学建筑系 Department of Architecture, Tamkang University
温雅先生 Mr. Wen Ya	广东省住房和城乡建设厅 Guangdong Provincial Department of Housing and Urban-Rural Development
吴光庭教授 Prof. Wu Kwang-Tyng	成功大学建筑系 Department of Architecture, Cheng Kung University
吴永发教授 Prof. Wu Yongfa	苏州金螳螂大学建筑学院 Gold Mantis School of Architecture and Environment, Soochow University
徐腾芳教授 Prof. Xu Tengfang Tim	香港中文大学中国城市住宅研究中心/太平洋瓦电公司 Center for Housing Innovations, The Chinese University of Hong Kong Pacific Gas and Electric Company
肖军先生 Mr. Xiao Jun	广东省建筑设计研究院 Architecture Design and Research Institute of Guangdong Province
徐雷教授 Prof. Xu Lei	浙江大学建筑设计与理论研究所 School of Architecture and Civil Engineering, Zhejiang University
夏海山教授 Prof. Xia Haishan	北京交通大学建筑与艺术学院 School of Architecture and Design, Beijing Jiaotong University
严汝洲先生 Mr. Yim Yu Chau Stephen	香港特别行政区房屋署（发展及建筑） Development & Construction Division, Housing Developmen, Hong Kong SAR
杨建荣教授 Prof. Yang Jianrong	上海市建筑科学研究院 Shanghai Research Institute of Building Sciences Group
叶青教授 Ms. Ye Qing	深圳市建筑科学研究院股份有限公司 Shenzhen Institute of Building Research Co.,Ltd
袁磊教授 Prof. Yuan Lei	深圳大学建筑与城市规划学院 School of Architecture and Urban Planning, Shenzhen University
喻肇青教授 Prof. Yu Chao-Chin	中原大学景观学系 Department of Landscape Architecture, Chung Yuan Christian University

| 赵锂教授 | 中国建筑设计院有限公司 |
| Prof. Zhao Li | China Architecture Design Group |

| 周燕珉教授 | 清华大学建筑学院 |
| Prof. Zhou Yanmin | School of Architecture, Tsinghua University |

| 张路峰教授 | 中国科学院大学建筑研究与设计中心 |
| Prof. Zhang Lufeng | Center of Architecture Research and Design, University of Chinese Academy of Sciences |

| 曾卫教授 | 重庆大学建筑城规学院 |
| Prof. Zeng Wei | Faculty of Architecture and Urban Planning, Chongqing University |

| 张玉坤教授 | 天津大学建筑学院 |
| Prof. Zhang Yukun | School of Architecture, Tianjin University |

| 张颀教授 | 天津大学建筑学院 |
| Prof. Zhang Qi | School of Architecture, Tianjin University |

| 詹庆明教授 | 武汉大学城市设计学院 |
| Prof. Zhan Qingming | School of Urban Design, Wuhan University |

| 曾捷教授 | 中国建筑科学研究院建筑设计院 |
| Prof. Zeng Jie | China Academy of Building Research Architectural Design Institute |

| 周荃女士 | 广东省建筑科学研究院集团股份有限公司 |
| Ms. Zhou Quan | Guangdong Provincial Academy of Building Research Group Co., Ltd. |

序　言

　　住宅伴随着人类文明的出现而出现，并且共同繁荣、协同发展。从史前聚落到传统民居，从工人新村到高层公寓，从一砖一瓦精雕细琢到构件预制化和住宅产业化，住宅不仅是每个人的居住场所，也是城市文化的载体，是科技创新的践行者。50年前，勒菲弗（Henri. Lefebvre）在纪念《资本论》发表一百周年之际，发表《城市的权利》（Right to the City），提出了居民有进入城市和参与活动、使用及创造城市空间的权利。"进入城市的权利"包括居住、生活、工作等。居住的权利是进入城市的权利中最基本的构成。然而城市居住问题的产生是一定空间范围内的资源配置、人口变迁和就业等社会问题的综合化结果。为了探讨这一复合型的城市问题，亟须不同学科知识的融汇整合，以及对不同视角下的住房问题解决策略，进行通用性和地域性的归纳和演绎。

　　20世纪末，中国进入传统意义上的快速城市化发展时期。住宅伴随着城市建设力度的加强，开始了多样化和开放式的发展，也衍生了更为复杂和综合性的问题。中国城市住宅研讨会（下文简称"研讨会"）值此背景下创办，以期广泛团结海峡两岸和国际间的学者、专业人士和青年学生，共同探讨当前最具代表性的住房研究议题，并作为一个平台推动不同研究领域间的交流和多学科合作。首届研讨会暨中国城市住宅研究中心成立仪式，于1998年12月在当时国家建设部（现为住房和城乡建设部）主楼301会议室举办，由时任部长的俞正声先生亲自主持，获得了许溶烈院士在内的多位专家亲临指导和支持。历届研讨会均遵循严格的匿名评审方式，由中国城市住宅研讨会论文评审委员会执行，确保每篇论文至少获得三位以上的评委进行匿名审阅，最终由中国城市住宅研讨会学术委员会讨论决定入选的论文名单。时至今日，研讨会已成功举办十一届，见证了中国城市住宅快速发展的二十载春秋。

　　当前的中国随着人口激增与资源紧张，城市化进程呈现出相对纠结和矛盾的情况。住房问题也随之日渐复杂和多样。这一现象是社会、经济和文化问题的综合体现，不同于任何超越传统和结构单一的供求、舒适问题。当前的住宅问题，既有的小康住宅、经济适用房等模式已不再适用，也难以通过户型、住型、居住区设计等方法独立解决。而是需要打破学科的界限，跳出传统的思维，探索前瞻性的理念，并进行交叉学科的知识整合。因此，本届研讨会以"可持续高密度人居环境建设的智慧化与创新"为主题，希望通过国际学术会议的模式，增进不同研究领域间的交流讨论和相互启发，共同探索在高密度城市化这一普遍存在的大趋势下如何提升未来人居环境质量。

　　承蒙海峡两岸专家学者、业界人士和青年学生的支持与贡献，本届研讨会收到大量优秀的论文投稿。研究议题涉及城市规划、建筑设计、建筑技术、公共政策、人文地理以及社会科学等多个学科范畴，覆盖了住区规划设计、住宅类型学研究、绿色建筑、装配式住宅、城市规划与更新改造、包容性社会、文化认同、保障性住房、长者友善人居环境、智慧城市与智慧住宅等多个专题。考量图书出版的页数限制，本届研讨会论文集以纸质书籍附加光碟形式出版。纸质书籍将收录部分论文全文；光碟中包含了所有论文的全文电子文档。研讨会组织方根据评审委员会的建议，结合论文全文的完成情况确定收录方式。所有获得论文集收录的文章，均已被列入研讨会纸质论文集附录中，并安排本届研讨会进行论文宣讲。

　　在此，本人谨代表第十二届中国城市住宅研讨会组织委员会诚挚感谢中华人民共和国住房和城乡建设部专家委员会、中华人民共和国住房和城乡建设部科学技术委员会，以及共同主办本届研讨会的广州市科学技术协会、华南理工大学建筑学院和广州大学建筑与城市规划学院以及京港学术交流中心等单位的专家领导对本届研讨会各项准备工作的大力支持。同时感谢中国建筑工业出版社的各位同仁于本届研讨会论文集出版过程中的倾力协助。在本书出版发行之际，希望本书不仅可以成为住房相关领域学者、业界人士及青年学子的一本有用的参考资料，同时借助本书收录论文所探讨的研究议题，推动海峡两岸及国际间更广泛的讨论和交流，从而促进大中华地区乃至其他具有相似高密度城市肌理的国家和地区在人居环境优化上的进步与发展。

邹经宇

2017 年 6 月 11 日于香港

Preface

Housing emerges with the birth of human civilization, and co-develops and prospers together. From prehistory settlements to traditional residential housing, from workers' villages to high-rise apartment, from hand-made to modular prefabrication and house industrialization, housing is not only the residential place of everyone, but also the plate of urban culture, practitioners of new science and technologies. 50 years ago, in honor of the centennial anniversary of "Das Kapital" authored by Kari Marx, Henri Lcfcbvre published the "Right to the City", claimed that people has the right to access the city, participate public activities, utilize and create urban space. Among the rights to the city, i.e. residential, life, work, etc. The residential right is the fundamental element. However, the emergence of urban residential problems is the compound result of multiple social problems, i.e., resource distribution, population migration, employment, etc. To investigate this complex issue, it's high time to integrate multi-disciplinary knowledge and think about housing strategies from different angles for the generalized and localized induction and deduction.

In the end of 20th century, China entered the era of rapid urbanization in the conventional sense. With the intensification of urban development, the China urban housing began its diversified and open development. Meanwhile, the issues entailed with housing development were also becoming more complex and compound. The China Urban Housing Conference (abbreviate as CUHC as below) was established under this background. As a platform to promote the academic exchange and interdisciplinary collaboration, the CUHC aims to widely unite the scholars, professionals and students from cross-straits area and internationally for the most representative cutting-edge housing topics. The first CUHC and Opening Ceremony of Center for Housing Innovations was organized in December, 1998, in Room 301 of the Major Building of Ministry of Construction (now the Ministry of Housing and Urban-Rural Development), PRC, convened by Mr. Yu Zhengsheng, the then Minister of Ministry of Construction, PRC. Prof. Xu Ronglie, Senior Consultant, Science and Technology Committee of the Ministry of Housing and Urban-Rural Development, PRC, and a number of other specialists offered great supports and attend the event in person. Each session of CUHC adopts strict blind-review procedure on abstracts, which guarantees each abstract will be anonymously reviewed by at least 3 reviewers. This procedure is undertaken by the Paper Review Panel of the China Urban Housing Conference. The selection result is up to the decision of the Academic Committee of the China Urban Housing Conference. To date, the China Urban Housing has been organized in 11 sessions, witnessed the over-20 years of housing development in China.

The urbanization progress is becoming unprccedentedly fast. Resulting from the population booming and resource scarcity, the rapid urbanization co-exists with tangled and contradictory situations. Housing problems are as well becoming more and more complex. However, this is the concurrent phenomenon of the diversified social, economic and cultural problems, distinct from any of the conventional and single-structural problems.

Preface

The existing housing strategies, e.g. Xiaokang Housing and affordable housing, are no longer adaptive to the current housing situation, which can't be solved independently by unit design, housing typology studies, residential design, etc. Instead, we need to step over the stereotype of disciplinary boundary and jump out of the conventional mindsets to integrate knowledge, embrace innovation and enlighten wisdom. Hence, the 12th China Urban Housing Conference is themed by "Intelligentization and Innovation of Sustainable High-dense Human Habitat Transformation", by which the Organization Committee expects to improve the inter-disciplinary exchange and mutual enlightenment on the way to investigate methods to optimize the quality of future human habitation under the trend of high-dense urbanization.

Thanks to the wonderful work of all authors from cross-straits and international areas, we have received many excellent abstracts that concerns a wide range of disciplines including urban planning, architectural design, and technology, public policy, human geography and sociological subjects, and cover the topics like residential planning and design, housing typology studies, green building, precast housing, urban planning and renewal, inclusive sociology, cultural identity, affordable housing, age-friendly habitation, smart city and housing, etc. In response to the limitation to pages for binding, the 12th CUHC proceedings is published via a combination of printed book and CD-ROM. The printed book includes a portion of the accepted papers; while the e-publications (CD-ROM) attached to the book contain the electronic text of all the accepted papers. The publication media is decided by the Organization Committee based on the suggestion of Peer Review Panel and the actual situation of full paper submission. All included papers will be catalogued and arranged presentation in conference.

On behalf of the Organization Committee of the 12th China Urban Housing Conference, I hereby extend our great appreciation to the supports from the Committee of Experts and the Committee of Science and Technology, Ministry of Housing and Urban-Rural Development, PRC, as well as Guangzhou Association for Science & Technology, School of Architecture, South China University of Technology, Colleague of Architecture and Urban Planning, Guangzhou University and Beijing-Hong Kong Academic Exchange Centre, etc. Meanwhile, our gratitude also goes to the editors of China Architecture and Building Press, who have exhausted every possibility to enable the timely publication of this proceedings. At the time when we hold this book, we hope it could not only serve as a reference book for people who are scholars, professionals and students in the housing research areas, but also realize the broader reflections amongst the cross-straits areas and international regions on the housing topics that discussed by the papers presented in the 12th CUHC and in that way to promote the advance and development on research and practices to optimize human habitation in the Greater China and where spreads the similar high-dense urban context.

Prof. Tsou Jin-Yeu,
11 June 2017, from Hong Kong

目 录
Table of Contents

中国城市住宅研讨会论文评审办法 ··· V
    Paper Review Method of the China Urban Housing Conference

第十二届中国城市住宅研讨会论文评审委员会委员 ··· VI
    Review Panel of the 12th China Urban Housing Conference

序　　言 ··· XII
    Preface

特 邀 论 文
Invited Paper

共享、特色、节约：保障性住房创新设计的探索 ·· 3
    Sharing, Characteristic and Saving: Exploring the Innovative Design of Affordable Housing
    李振宇　孙二奇
    Li Zhenyu, Sun Erqi

我国既有住区建筑居住品质问题研究与实践概观 ··· 11
    The Conspectus of Research and Practices on Residential Building Qualities in China
    范　悦　董　丽　李翥彬
    Fan Yue, Dong Li, Li Zhubin

多元文化视角下的城市回族社区居住空间形态研究：以济南北大槐树回族社区为例 ··················· 17
    Study on the Living Space of Urban Hui Nationality Community from the Perspective of Multiculturalism: Taking Jinan Beidahuaishu Community as An Example
    曾　鹏　李若冰　浦　钰
    Zeng Peng, Li Ruobing, Pu Yu

传统村落人居环境营建的生态智慧探讨 ·· 26
    The Ecological Wisdom on the Construction of the Human Settlements for the Traditional Village
    曾　卫　朱雯雯
    Zeng Wei, Zhu Wenwen

中美城市居住区步行友好性比较研究——武汉与奥斯汀的六个居住区实证研究 ·························· 35
    Comparative Study on Neighborhood Walkability between Chinese and American Cities——Empirical Study on Six Neighborhoods in Wuhan and Austin
    彭　雷
    Peng Lei

隔热涂料在建筑中应用的节能评价方法探讨 ··· 46
    Discussion on the Energy Saving Evaluation Method of Heat Insulating Coatings Used in the Buildings
    范宏武
    Fan Hongwu

Building E-pathy City from an Age-friendly Unit ··············· 53
从长者友善单元建立同理城市
Chang Ping Hung Wallace
郑炳鸿

Travel in Tin Shui Wai as A Housewife ··············· 62
师奶的天水围之旅
Wang Danning
王丹凝

基于BIM的主动式防灾通知系统之即时通信架构设计 ··············· 73
Communication Framework Design for a BIM-based Proactive Security Messaging System
郭韦良　李秋明　吴轩竹　谢尚贤
Kuo Wei-Liang, Lee Chiu-Ming, Wu Hsuan-Chu, Hsieh Shang-Hsien

SENS project: A User Experience Approach for Smart Energy Environment ··············· 82
SENS：以使用者经验探讨智慧电能环境之互动体验模式
Chang Teng-Wen, Huang Hsin-Yi, Sambit Datta
张登文　黄馨仪　Sambit Datta

建筑屋顶绿化对于顶楼空间降温效益的评估研究：以高雄市建筑为例 ··············· 91
The Evaluation of the Roof Greening Benefits for the Roof Space Floor Cooling: A Case Study of the Building in Kaohsiung City
程达隆　李彦颐　张七斗　林嘉雄
Cheng Da-Long, Li Yenyi, Chang Chi-Tou, Lin Chia-Hsiung

住区规划、设计与住宅类型研究
Residential Planning, Design and Housing Typology Research

上海围合式住宅理想模型设计研究 ··············· 103
Research on the Ideal Model of Shanghai Enclosed Housing
卢　斌
Lu Bin

北方家属楼的特征性演变：以哈尔滨职工住宅为例 ··············· 110
Characteristic Evolution of Northern Family Building: Cases of Harbin Staff Housing
顾　闻　李振宇
Gu Wen, Li Zhenyu

住宅通用化设计之课题与实践——以台北市兴隆公共住宅为例 ··············· 117
The Subject and Practice of Universal Design in Residential Projects: Taking Taipei Xinglong Public Housing Project as An Example
高文婷　郑人豪　陈雅芳
Kao Wen-Ting, Cheng Jen-Hao, Chen Ya-Fang

从开放社区到三维都市：中国当代社会住宅建筑设计趋势与方法研究 ··············· 124
From Open Community to Three-dimensional City: Research on the Tendency and Methods of Social Housing Design in China

孙二奇
Sun Erqi

以 Upside-down 体系为核心的住宅适应性设计研究 ··············130
Research on the Adaptability Design of Residential Buildings Based on the Upside-down System

欧阳文　甘振坤　张　超　陈婉蓉　倪晨辉　陈　旭
Ouyang Wen, Gan Zhenkun, Zhang Chao, Chen Wanrong, Ni Chenhui, Chen Xu

外廊式集合住宅中外廊空间邻里交往研究——广州深圳 6 个典型案例的比较分析 ··············137
Residential Neighborhood Communication Space in the Veranda Style House——A Case Study of Six Typical Gallery House in Guangzhou and Shenzhen

郭　萌　杜宏武
Guo Meng, Du Hongwu

中外文化的交融在近代闽南侨乡民居中的体现 ··············144
The Blending of Chinese and Foreign Culture in the Houses of Overseas Chinese in South Fujian

卢汀滢　边如晨
Lu Tingying, Bian Ruchen

共享园林"园中园"创意与营造实践 ··············150
Creative Concept and Practice of Shared Garden Space

吴永发　张　玲
Wu Yongfa, Zhang Ling

基于空间布局形态的住栋环境要素分类研究 ··············157
Research on the Classification of Environmental Factors Based on the Layout Pattern between Buildings

张明科　范　悦　高　莹　赵　涛
Zhang Mingke, Fan Yue, Gao Ying, Zhao Tao

北京四合院建筑形制和气候适应性中阴阳关系的解读 ··············164
The Interpretation of Yin Yang of the Forms and Climatic Adaptation in Beijing Courtyard House

郭　聪　王惜春　戴　俭
Guo Cong, Wang Xichun, Dai Jian

维也纳社会住宅的可持续整合性设计策略：以 Mautner-Markhof 为例 ··············171
Sustainable Integrated Design Strategies of Social Housing in Vienna

胡裕庆　李振宇
Hu Yuqing, Li Zhenyu

既有住区底层开放空间的功能构成及布局研究 ··············178
Research on the Function Composition and Layout of the Bottom Open Space in the Existing Residential Area

王轶鸥　范　悦　赵　涛　李汀蕾
Wang Yiou, Fan Yue, Zhao Tao, Li Tinglei

密度视角下城市住区公共空间环境特征研究初探 ··············183
Research on the Public Space's Environmental Features of Urban Residential Area Based on Density Perspective

鲍　莉　湛　洋　詹佳佳
Bao Li, Zhan Yang, Zhan Jiajia

碎片整理：针对未来租赁住房的开放建筑新模式 ··············189
Defragmentation: Open Building as A Strategy for Future Rental Housing

姚严奇　李振宇
Yao Yanqi, Li Zhenyu

寒地城市住区室外公共空间居民使用受限情况改善——以沈阳浑南新区新建居住片区为例············196
The Improvement of the Situation that the Use of Outdoor Public Places Restricted by Residents in Cold Urban Residential District ——A Case Study of A New Residential District in Shenyang Hunnan New District
张东潇　高智慧　刘玥彤　胡　帅
Zhang Dongxiao, Gao Zhihui , Liu Yuetong, Hu Shuai

城市交界空间激活策略初探···204
Study on the Activating Strategy of Interface Space between Urban Quarters
袁成龙　鲍　莉
Yuan Chenglong, Bao Li

城乡规划与人居空间设计
Urban-Rural Planning and Human Habitat Design

洮南市城市收缩的表现特征及精明成长策略研究···213
Research on Performance Characteristics and Smart Development Strategy of Shrinking Cities——Taonan City as An example
何邕健　杨　琳
He Yongjian, Yang Lin

城乡关系重构背景下村落人居环境提升策略研究：以柳州环江村为例·····························220
The Integrated Strategies Research for Improving the Rural Human Settlements Environment under the Reconfiguration of Urban-Rural Relation：A Case Study in Huanjiang Village of Liuzhou City
张　恺　李　乘　沈　杰
Zhang Kai, Li Cheng, Shen Jie

Village Planning Adapted to China Planning System and Urban Rural Integration ·····················227
适应中国规划体系和城乡统筹的村庄规划
Zheng Shujian
郑书剑

From Gentrification to Studentification: A Case Study of HEMC in Guangzhou, China ···············234
从绅士化到学生化的演变——基于中国广州大学城的案例研究
Liu Yongshen
刘永深

EPC-PPP 模式下建构小城镇全域旅游体系的探索与实践：以开化县域的整体营造为例·············242
Exploration and Practices through Reconfiguration of Region-based Tourism System in Small Towns under the EPC-PPP Model：A Case Study of Comprehensive Construction in Kaihua County of Zhejiang Province
李　乘　沈　杰　唐玉田
Li Cheng, Shen Jie, Tang Yutian

Pro-growth Coalition of the Local Political Economy and the Contemporary Upsurge of Sustainable Urbanism in China: Three Cases in Shenzhen··249
城市增长联盟与可持续城市化策略：以深圳三个新城建设为例的研究
Fu Yang, Zhang Xiaoling

符 阳　张晓玲

Communities Inside the Ruins: A study of the Nature of Communities in Abandoned Buildings in Manila as An Alternative Housing Solution for Urban Areas ··················256

　　废墟内的社区：作为城市地区替代住房解决方案的马尼拉废弃建筑物性质研究

　　Mar Lorence G. Ticao

　　Mar Lorence G. Ticao

绿色建筑与可持续环境设计
Green Building and Sustainable Environment Design

A Study of the Energy Conservation Potentials of Earth Sheltered Housing for Purposes of Urban Scale Developments ··················265

　　覆土建筑的节能潜力在城市开发尺度的研究

　　Jideofor Akubue, Liu Suya

　　安　赛　刘素雅

应对雾霾——人口结构变迁下的城市旧有住宅的弹性转型与有机更新··················273

　　Responding to the Fog —— The Elastic Transformation and Organic Renewal of the Old Residential Buildings under the Changing Population Structure

　　田　昊　周　博

　　Tian Hao, Zhou Bo

基于家庭尺度的混合形态社区居民碳排放影响因素研究：以天津为例··················279

　　Study On Influencing Factors of Family Carbon Emissions from Mixed Form Community

　　亢梦荻　杨　琳　陈　天

　　Kang Mengdi, Yang Lin, Chen Tian

基于最小干预度原则的既有多层住宅节能改造模式研究··················286

　　Energy-efficient Mode of Existing Multi-story Residential Based on the Minimum Interference

　　常　艺　宋　昆

　　Chang Yi, Song Kun

基于 LEED ND 绿色社区认证体系的新区慢行交通系统构建：以成都天府新区科学城为例··················293

　　The Construction of Walkable Streets in New District Based on the Certification Standards of LEED ND: Take Chengdu Tianfu New Area Science City as An Example

　　曾　晶　郝桐平　吴亚芯

　　Zeng Jing, Hao Tongping, Wu Yaxin

小区型高楼住宅配置水绿规模改善热岛效应策略之仿真研究··················300

　　Simulation Study on the Strategy of Equipped with Water and Green Areas on Alleviating the Heat Island Effect of the Scale of Residential Buildings

　　王文安　董思伟

　　Wang W.-A., Tung S.-W.

低层住宅改变楼板与开口规模对通风降温舒适度效益之研究··················307

　　Study on the Effect of Changing the Floor and Opening Scale on the Comfort of Ventilation and Cooling in Low-rise Residential Buildings

王文安　董思伟
Wang W.-A., Tung S.-W.

Comparison of the Guidelines for Heat Island Countermeasures in China and Japan ……… 314
　　中日城市热岛应对技术标准的比较分析
　　Li Qiong, Yoshida Shiji
　　李　琼　吉田伸治

热带城市私人住宅的被动式设计方法研究：以越南岘港市为例 ……… 321
　　Passive Design Methods of Private House in Tropical Climate: Danang City, Vietnam
　　鲍　莉　Duc Vien LE
　　Bao Li, Duc Vien LE

Thermal Profiles of A High Density City ……… 328
　　高密度城市热剖面
　　Maing Minjung
　　孟玟廷

Urban Heat Island Effect (UHI) Analysis of Hangzhou Based on Remote Sensing ……… 335
　　杭州市城市热岛效应初探
　　Wang Siqiang, Xiang Meng, He Yanan, Zhang Yuanzhi
　　王思强　向　萌　何亚男　张渊智

人居环境更新、改造与历史活化
Renewal, Transformation and Activation of Human Habitat

重庆抗战时期名人旧居选址特征研究 ……… 345
　　The Site Selection Research on Chongqing Celebrities' Former Dwellings during War of Resistance Against Japan
　　何　媛
　　He Yuan

自下而上的城市更新与居住形态演变：以田子坊为例 ……… 350
　　Bottom-up Urban Renewal and Residential Morphology Development: A Case Study of Tianzifang
　　朱晓宇
　　Zhu Xiaoyu

Land Readjustment as A Solution to the Dilemma of Urban Village Redevelopment in China: A Case Study of Yiwu ……… 357
　　以义乌为例探讨解决中国城中村改造困境的方案：土地调整模式
　　Yuan Dinghuan, Yau Yung, Li Ruoshi
　　袁定欢　邱　勇　李若诗

日本长期优良住宅认定制度对我国既有居住建筑改造的启示 ……… 365
　　The Inspirations from Japanese Long-life Quality Housing to Chinese Residential Building Renovation
　　李翥彬　兰凯斐
　　Li Zhubin, Lan Kaifei

存量背景下上海老旧社区更新的价值导向与规划实践 ……… 371
　　The value Orientation and Planning Practice on Old Residential Renewal of Shanghai in the Background of Inventory Planning

匡晓明　陆勇峰　丁馨怡
Kuang Xiaoming, Lu Yongfeng, Ding Xinyi

触媒理论引导下的社区更新模式探讨：以可食地景为例 ··· 378
Research on Community Sustainable Renewal Based on City Catalyst Theory: A Case of Edible Landscape Construction
徐晓岛
Shyu Shyaodao

"城中厂"的紧凑型居住化改造探索：嘉兴市民丰造纸厂、冶金机械厂的改造经验 ····················· 385
The Re-habitation of Town Factories and the Construction of High Density Life: the Experience on the Regeneration of Jiaxing Min Feng Paper Factory and Machinery Factory
邝远霄　李振宇
Kuang Yuanxiao, Li Zhenyu

基于领域行为理论的既有住区公共空间改造研究：以苏州为例 ·· 392
A Study on the Transformation of Public Space in Existing Residential Area Based on the Theory of Field Behavior: Taking Suzhou as An Example
胡　莹　汪文韬
Hu Ying, Wang Wentao

语用思维下长影旧址街区的保护与更新 ··· 398
The Context of Pragmatic Thinking Projected Changchun Site Blocks' Protection and Renovation
刘　岩　高雁鹏　付艳华　刘生军
Liu Yan, Gao Yanpeng, Fu Yanhua, Liu Shengjun

社会空间博弈下城市与住房的转型机制研究——以苏州山塘街为例 ·· 405
A Study on the Transformation Mechanism of Cities and Housing under the Social Space Scramble——A Case Study of Shantang Street
郑　玥　胡　莹
Zheng Yue, Hu Ying

保障性住房与房地产市场管理
Affordable Housing and Real Estate Management

台湾地区面向青年人的社会住宅模式供给模式探析——以新北市为例 ····································· 415
Analysis on the Mode of Supply of Social Housing for Youth in Taiwan——A Case Study of New Taipei City
郭净宇
Kuo Chin-Yu

Hong Kong's Public Housing Policy and Social Problems——A Case Study of Tin Shui Wai New Town ··· 423
香港的公营房屋政策与社会问题——以天水围新市镇为例
Li Yi
李　益

开放住宅体系周期性共享租用模式探究 ··· 431
Periodic Renting Sharing Mode Research of Residential Open Buildings
王春彧　李振宇
Wang Chunyu, Li Zhenyu

Green Building Understanding Among Public Green Housing Residents: A Case Study in Hong Kong ······438
香港公屋居民对于绿色建筑认识：个案研究
 Ji Jie, Yin Huai
 季　洁　鄞　槐

Social Housing in Different Cultures——Comparative Study Western Europe and East Asia: A First Attempt ···445
不同文化背景下的社会性住房：西欧与东亚的初步比较研究
 Wolfgang Dokonal, Marlis Nograsek, Ernst Dengg, Tsou Jin-Yeu
 Wolfgang Dokonal　Marlis Nograsek　Ernst Dengg　邹经宇

台北都市区家户之居住安排特性研究······452
A Study on the Characteristic of Household Living Arrangements in Taipei Metropolitan Area
 徐国城　刘芷妤
 Hsu Kuo-Cheng, Liu Chih-Yu

对我国棚户区改造建设管理云平台的研究和实践······462
The Development of Construction Management in the Shanty Towns Cloud Platform and Application
 陆伟良　李学东　杜　昱　苏　俊
 Lu Weiliang, Li Xuedong, Du Yu, Su Jun

长者友善人居环境营造
Age-friendly Human Habitat

基于老年人行为的既有住区环境优化设计研究：以大连地区为例······471
Research on the Optimal External Environment Design of Old Residential Area Base on the Elderly Behavior——Take Dalian as An Example
 于文婷　周　博　周志伟
 Yu Wenting, Zhou Bo, Zhou Zhiwei

生产性适老社区的设计概念初探······478
A Primary Study on Concepts of Designing Productive Community for the Elderly
 吴浩然　张玉坤　贡小雷　郑　捷
 Wu Haoran, Zhang Yukun, Gong Xiaolei, Zheng Jie

长远老年建筑设计策略······485
Redesigning Long-term Senior Care Housing Strategy
 吕庆耀
 Bryant Lu

应对老年人走失的高密度住区转型研究······491
High Density Residential Transformation Research Dealing with the Old Lost Problem
 卢丹丹　周　博　周志伟　杨岸霄
 Lu Dandan, Zhou Bo, Zhou Zhiwei, Yang Anxiao

苏州姑苏区古建旧民居的适老化更新与再利用······498
The Regeneration and Reuse of Historic Residential Buildings Adapting to Ageing in Suzhou Gusu District
 曹修安　华振宁
 Cao Xiuan, Hua Zhenning

智慧城市与计算机辅助技术集成应用
Smart City and Computer-aided Technology Integration

BIM 平台架构下采光性能模拟的自适应性建筑立面策略与原型研究 ············· 507
  The Research of Adaptive Building Facade Strategy and Prototype Based on Daylight Performance Simulation
   陈上元 沈扬庭 何妍萱 吴念瑾
   Chen Shang-Yuan, Shen Yang-Ting, Ho Yen-Hsuan, Wu Nien-Chin

日本智慧型技术在城市住宅中的应用研究 ············· 513
  A Study on the Use of Intelligent Technology on the Field of Urban Housing in Japan
   伊藤增辉
   Ito Masuteru

An Innovated Smart Home Sensors Integration and Remote Control Solution and Implementation Based on the Mirror Touch Interaction ············· 519
  一种基于镜像交互技术的智能家居传感器集成与远程控制解决方案及实现
   Li Jixun, Qiu Shenping, Wang Hao, Ye Lei
   李佶逊 邱沈萍 王 浩 叶 雷

轻型钢结构模矩化设计方法论 ············· 526
  The Design Methodology of Light Gauge Steel Structure Modular
   陈上元 刘泰佑 蔡立伟
   Chen Shang-Yuan, Liu Tai-Yu, Cai Li-Wei

整合建筑信息建模参数编程引擎与嵌入式系统的智能化城市住宅研究 ············· 532
  The Research of Smart Urban Housing via Integrating BIM-based Parametric Programming Engine with Embedded System
   沈扬庭 吴念瑾
   Shen Yang Ting, Wu Nien Chin

以网络数据为主体的空间句法模型对城市中心的识别与分析——以吉林市轨道交通项目为例 ········ 539
  The Identification and Analysis of the City Center by the Space Syntax Model Based on Network Data——Jilin's Rail Transit Project
   杨振盛 盛 强 刘 星
   Yang Zhensheng, Sheng Qiang, Liu Xing

社区居民社会聚集的影响：对北京街区公共空间的空间句法分析 ············· 545
  The Influence of Outdoor Gathering of Community: Space Syntax Analysis on the Public Space in Beijing's Neighborhoods
   刘 星 杨振盛
   Liu Xing, Yang Zhensheng

探讨深度学习在智慧城市中的应用方法：以 AI 风水助手为例 ············· 553
  Customize Deep Learning for Smart City: AI-based Feng Shui Assistant as An Example
   杨金泽 李秋明 邱仁钿 谢尚贤
   Yang Jin-Ze, Lee Chiu-Ming, Chiou Jen-Dian, Hsieh Shang-Hsien

附 录 第十二届中国城市住宅研讨会论文全文收录列表 ············· 561
  Appendix List of Full Papers Included in the 12th China Urban Housing Conference

特 邀 论 文

Invited Paper

共享、特色、节约：保障性住房创新设计的探索

李振宇　孙二奇

（同济大学建筑与城市规划学院；高密度人居环境生态与节能教育部重点实验室）

摘　要：城市保障性住房设计面临着挑战。作为民生项目，保障性住房要做到为城市设计，为社区设计，为居民设计。本文以浦东三林回迁安置房设计方案为例，从共享、特色和节约三个方面，探索保障性住房设计的创新点。共享包括城市空间共享、组团院落共享和邻里庭院共享。特色包括造型特色、院落特色和平面布局特色。节约包括省用地、省公摊。

关键词：保障性住房，创新性，共享，特色，节约

1　背景

1.1　为人民设计

居者有其屋是社会和谐的重要保证，保障性住房的设计关乎国计民生。包豪斯第二任校长汉斯·梅耶认为，设计应该为人民服务，满足人民的需要是"一切设计行为的起点和目标"。在当代中国，保障性住房的设计也应该贯彻以人为本的理念，以为人民设计为宗旨。这其中包含三个层次的含义。一是为居住在其中的人民服务，这关乎居民的切身利益，要为他们提供功能合理、环境宜人、节省高效的居住空间。二是为周边的居民服务，要为他们提供一个环境友好、尺度舒适的街坊空间，形成具有归属感和场所精神的公共空间。三是要为城市居民服务，这种服务是偏向于城市意象和城市景观层面的，例如，对于路过这里的市民来说，设计项目应该呈现出一个具有城市感的面貌，形成优秀的城市界面。由此，保障性住房的设计也应该考虑城市 - 组团 - 邻里 - 单元多层次的需求。

1.2　浦东三林保障房项目介绍

随着城市转型发展的不断深入，黄浦江两岸地区作为承载上海城市功能提升和形象展示的重要发展轴，其开发建设呈现出由中心城核心区向南北两侧拓展的趋势。三林外环外地区是上海中心城的南部门户，也是城市生态廊道建设的重要内容。随着前滩和三林滨江南片地区等重要城市功能区的规划建设，地区的区位优势日益凸显。然而，该地区城中村人口及居住环境问题突出，动迁安置工作迫在眉睫。其中 $0.57 \times 10^6 m^2$ 动迁安置房布局在本次项目范围内。按照人均住宅建筑面积 $35m^2$ 计，约可安置人口约 1.6 万。

在此项目中，以下四个方面成为预期要达到的目标：

1. 在高密度居住环境中，探索动迁住房建设对城市风貌的价值，丰富中心城周边地区的空间形象，成为动迁住房创新设计的样本；

2. 创造生动有趣的住区生活空间，兼顾既有建成环境和规划发展愿景；在建成区、规划生态走廊等不同元素中形成良好的衔接，探索人居环境和生态环境的双提升；

3. 为居民提供满足功能要求的新颖住宅套型和室内外共享空间；

4.探索保障性住房设计多元化的工作模式。

本项目位于上海三林片区,属外环之外、浦东新区邻近闵行区的边缘处。基地一共分为三个片区,9个地块,紧邻城市主要干道上南路,如多片大小不一的树叶,挂在东西向城市干道南路上(图1)。我们本着为人民设计的宗旨,提出了"共享"、"特色"和"节约"的设计理念,着手于保障房创新性设计的探索。

图1 项目基地位置与城市干道位置关系

2 创新性设计实践与探索

2.1 共享的建筑

随着共享经济的方式逐渐渗透到日常生活之中,"共享"的概念也越来越深入人心,在城市与建筑空间设计上,我们也提出三个层次的共享概念。

2.1.1 城市公共共享空间

建筑的北侧界面成为面向城市干道的主要界面。因此,在方案中,我们结合规划的中心河港及绿带,重视建筑北向造型与立面处理,使建筑面向干道形成良好的城市界面。同时,小区组团之间采用开放式的设计方法,形成窄马路、密路网的社区肌理,将社区内部街道向市民开放,形成城市层面的公共共享空间。并且组团内的院落空间,通过开放的道路,在一定程度上也面向城市开放(图2)。

图2 三个片区总平面图

2.1.2 组团半公共共享空间

在组团层面,通过围合院落空间,形成面向社区内部的公共共享空间,为居民提供内部活动场所,形成具有场所感和归属感的社区空间。在部分社区院落之间，通过二层空中绿廊步道贯穿连接，加强院落联系，活化社区活动（图3）。

 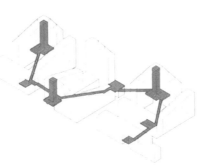 

图3　组团半公共共享空间意向图

2.1.3　邻里半私密共享空间

在建筑单体层面，我们更加关注社区内居民作为整体的交流和共享，打破传统保障性住房邻里之间相对封闭的状态。因此，我们在建筑中插入半公共的空中花园、活动平台等一些"虚空"的空间。这些虚空间，成为介于家庭空间和庭院空间之间的过渡，成为每幢建筑和外部城市环境沟通的场所（图4）。

通过对城市-组团-邻里三个层次的共享空间设计，形成参差多态的公共空间类型，将共享建筑的概念初步引入保障房设计领域。

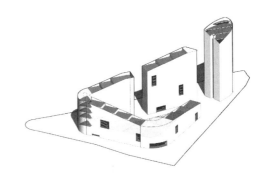

图4　邻里半私密共享空间示意图

2.2　特色的空间

2.2.1　造型特色

在建筑造型方面，拒绝千篇一律的行列式布局和板式高层的形式，另辟蹊径，采用了独特的形体和院落设计手法，力求在建筑单体形态和院落组团形态设计上寻求突破和创新。我们运用围合式布局，形成具有邻里感的院落空间；采用高低错落的体量，形成参差的形态；通过底层架空和顶层退台的方式，形成公共的特色空间；建筑实体庭院空间相互映衬；沿街、沿河立面形体，我们将之特殊化处理，形成标志性（图5）。

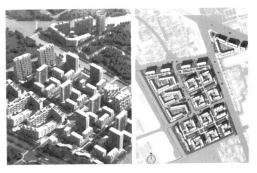

图5　整体造型意向图

2.2.2　院落特色

院落空间一直是中国传统居住形态的重要元素之一，它是居民公共生活的最基本载体。在三林保障房项目中，我们尝试将院落空间作为社区公共空间设计的核心，创造丰富多样的院落形态和空间。从图底关系来看，主要包含九种设计原型，分别为一字形、双L院、转角院、三合院、四方院、田字院、水滴院、椭圆院以及回字院（图6）。

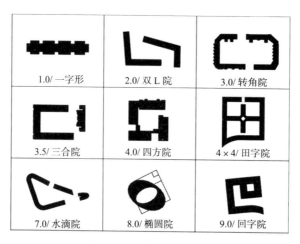

图 6　九种院落设计原型

一字形：一字形院可以说是似院非院，它更关注的是建筑形体和周边环境的互动，与周边建筑和环境共同围合成开放院。主要策略便是通过北向退台的方式，形成露天廊道，创造面向开放空间的公共活动空间，与此同时，也减少了公摊面积，可谓一举多得（图7）。

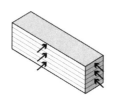

图 7　一字形形体生成

双L院：顾名思义，双L院是由两个L形体量围合而成的梯形半开放庭院。在梯形的一个对角上，形成开敞的入口；另一个对角上，通过建筑底部架空，使庭院面向河面开放，将临河景色引入到庭院之中，在视觉上为内部庭院注入更多外部景观因素。建筑的屋顶顺势形成台阶状空中花园，将公共空间，由地面二维引向空中三维，创造立体庭院（图8）。

转角院：转角院呈C形，由三部分组合而成：南边的9层、北边的24层以及中间的9层锯齿形廊式串联。之所以称之为转角院，除了形状之外，还因为建筑的转角处的特殊处理。为了致敬国际知名建筑师克莱胡斯，转角处借鉴克莱胡斯设计的手法，在架空的体量之下，削切转角，形成内部庭院开放的入口（图9）。

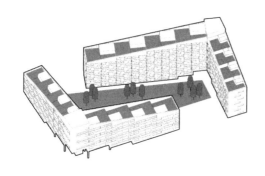 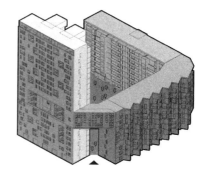

图 8　双L院　　　　　图 9　转角院

三合院：三合院之"三"在这里有两层含义。一是内部庭院三面围合，二是指三个院子之间通过空中步廊连接，形成一个三合院小组团。在这个组团内，不利的建筑转角和交通空间相结合，形成空中公共平台。空中步廊成为串联这些公共平台的核心元素，将一个个孤立的点连接成线，成为一个具有活力和流动性的统一整体（图10）。

四方院：四方院的设计根据我们研究的结果，设置外轮廓为55m见方、内院院为30m见方，若干个这样的四方院组合，形成密路网、窄马路的社区肌理，营造富有生活气息的社区街道空间。为了创造比较完整的沿街立面，庭院相对封闭，四面围合。四边建筑之间留出公共平台，成为建筑内与外交流的切口，也丰富了公共空间的层次（图11）。

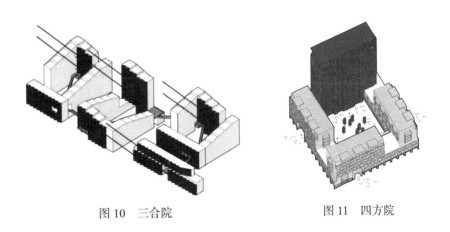

图10　三合院　　　　　　　　　图11　四方院

田字院：田字院在设计上致敬柏林里特大街住宅组群。整体呈108m见方的田字形，西南角根据地形走势作曲线状。大庭院内部分为四个36m见方的内庭院，通过建筑的架空，四个庭院之间相互连通，邻里氛围浓厚。屋顶部分根据造型和功能需要，设置台阶状空中平台，成为地面庭院空间的拓展（图12）。

水滴院：水滴院的成型是场地几何和建筑物理条件限制相互作用的结果。基地呈三角形，因此我们顺应地形走势，由南至北，形成连续上升状形体。这样的手法具有以下典型的优点：南低北高，有利于创造良好的日照环境；全体居民都拥有良好的视野，无遮挡；形体的开口和架空部分，形成对外开放的姿态；穿插其中的空中花园丰富邻里生活空间。形体的北侧里面紧邻城市主干道，因此特色鲜明的北立面，也成为市民共享的城市公共界面（图13）。

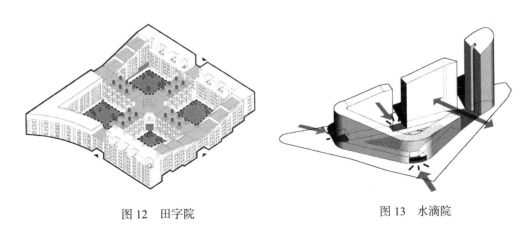

图12　田字院　　　　　　　　　图13　水滴院

椭圆院与回字院：椭圆院与回子院分别是社区中的两个配套设施——幼儿园和社区活动中心。椭圆院形体自由活泼，由椭圆形和方形嵌套而成，在两个形体嵌套、交叠的部分，形成现象透明性，空间体验丰富；回子院的形体溯源来自中国传统的纹饰，一波三折、层层递进的院落空间，是引导人们由开放到私密，进入社区中心的主要路径（图14）。

图14 椭圆院与回子院

由城市到院落，由院落到家庭，院落空间成为家庭空间和城市空间之间的连接和过渡。丰富的院落形态创造了多层次的共享空间，满足居民多样的功能需求，必将成为社区内最鲜明的特征和最活跃空间。

2.2.3 平面布局特色

户型设计是保障性住房设计最根本也是最关键的内容之一。为了满足回迁安置居民多样的家庭组织结构，我们设计了多样的房型。单元式、平层廊式和跃层以及中廊互越的房型组合使用，丰富了居住的可能性，家家有趣味性。

2.3 节约的理念

在三林项目中，我们不仅关注空间的共享设计、社区特色院落氛围的营造，而且，在创造多样丰富的空间同时，我们也关注如何能花最少的资源做最多的事情，创造最多的价值，能够更多地让利于民，还利于民。因此，我们提出了"节约"的设计原则。

2.3.1 功能混合节约用地

为了完善社区配套，同时解决部分用地条件不好等问题，我们在社区中间部分建筑组团内进行功能混合，在局部朝向不利以及沿街建筑底层引入商业功能，活化社区整体功能配置，便民利民。适度功能混合套裁的办法，一方面消化掉场地本身存在的不利问题；另一方面也不必再为社区配套功能另辟新地，节省了土地和空间资源（图15）。

2.3.2 组合交通节省公摊面积

如何减少公摊面积，一直是保障性住房设计的难点，也是居民关心的重点问题。我们在基本户型的基础上，尝试通过组合交通的方式，设计零公摊户型。通过北向退台，将每一层的廊道和垂直交通都见天，不算面积。在户型上，一至四层平面随着退台而减少进深，北向功能房间相应调整变化。最上面两层设计为跃层式，以满足户型和功能需求。这种通过去掉交通面积节省公摊的方式，是我们在三林保障房项目中进行的一种积极尝试（图16）。另一种省公摊的方式，我们采取了中廊互

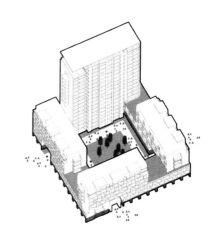

图15 底层引入商业功能

越的平面设计。将走廊设置在中间,每户人家分为上越和下越两种形式,三层共享一条中廊,节省公摊面积。

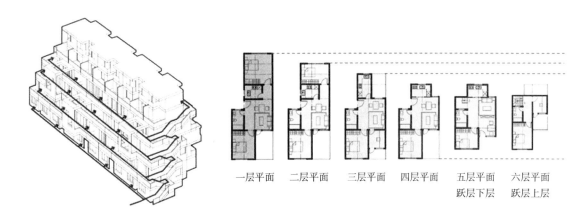

图 16　退台零公摊

3　总结

保障房的设计和建设,是政府解决人民住房问题的体现,是政府关注民生的体现,与人民的生活息息相关,是众多建筑类型中相对比较平凡的。而作为一个建筑师,做好这项平凡的工作对许多人却是意义重大,尤其是对居住在其中的居民。

在三林居民回迁安置房项目中,我们在实现保障房基本功能的同时,也希望加入一些独特的思考和实践总结的经验,在平凡的基础上做到具有创新性和独特性。在这个项目中,我们初步提出建筑共享的概念,从城市到院落到邻里三个层次,还空间于民;提出类型丰富的院落空间形态,由一字形到回字形,供乐趣于民;提出功能套裁省用地、组合交通省公摊的策略,节约土地、空间资源,让实利于民。我们在寻找统一中的参差多态。试图用共享的空间、多样的住宅建筑和高效率的套型平面,造就一个具有迷人的魅力的社区。这是我们放眼世界、立足当前的选择。

致谢

本篇论文的写作受到国家自然科学基金项目《长三角地区"城中厂"的社区化更新技术体系研究》的资助(编号:51678412)。参与本项目设计人员:李振宇、卢斌、宋健健、朱怡晨、束逸天、孙二奇、顾闻、王春彧、姚严奇。文中所有图片均为设计团队绘制。

Sharing, Characteristic and Saving: Exploring the Innovative Design of Affordable Housing

Li Zhenyu, Sun Erqi

(College of Architecture and Urban Planning, Tongji University; Key Laboratory of Ecology and Energy-saving Study of Dense Habitat, Ministry of Education)

Abstract: The design of social housing is facing challenges in the contemporaryera. As livelihood projects, the affordable housing should be designed for the city, the community and the residents. This paper takes Sanlin social housing project as an example to explore the innovation of social housing design from three aspects, namely sharing, characteristic and saving. The meaning of sharing includes city space sharing, group courtyard space sharing and neighborhood courtyard sharing. Characteristic means characteristics of shapes, courtyards and unit layout. The meaning of saving includes saving land area and saving public sharing area.

Keywords: Affordable housing, Innovation of design, Sharing, Characteristic, Saving

参考文献

[1] 克里斯蒂安·德·包赞巴克. 开放街区——以欧路风格住宅和马塞纳新区为例 [J]. 城市环境设计, 2015, 7.

[2] 布兰卡·列奥. 当代社会住宅的可持续性与交往空间 [J]. 时代建筑, 2011, 4: 62-69.

[3] 李振宇, 张玲玲, 姚栋. 关于保障性住房设计的思考——以上海地区为例 [J]. 建筑学报, 2011, 8.

我国既有住区建筑居住品质问题研究与实践概观

范 悦 董 丽 李翥彬

（大连理工大学建筑与艺术学院）

摘 要：随着存量时代的到来，社会需求的提高，城市居住建筑与环境的品质问题不断呈现，并且日益尖锐。本文综观我国既有住区环境与建筑更新历史与研究，重新定义住区建筑的内涵与品质问题，并通过概观住区建筑更新的理论研究与实践探索，梳理和总结了品质提升的现行更新模式，为今后从建筑学以及多学科角度展开既有住区建筑品质提升基础理论与优化策略研究奠定了基础。希望通过本文，引起各界对我国既有住区更新的关注与广泛探讨。

关键词：住区建筑，居住品质，既有住区，再生

1 存量时代既有住区建筑更新概况

随着近30年来城市化进程的快速推进，我国许多城市地区的大批住区建筑使用功能及环境品质严重滞后于时代需求。虽然功能寿命已到期，但设计寿命远未达到使用年限。对城市住区建筑的可持续使用造成严重挑战。在城市资源环境紧缩约束的背景下，寻求内涵增长与创新发展，实现提升居住功能，激发住区活力，改善人居环境，增强城市魅力，成为新常态下我国城市发展的重要方向。因此，在存量时代，对于建成环境的优化更新与品质提升，特别是既有住区建筑更新改造，成为新时期我国建筑行业的研究重点。

2015年12月20日，中央城市工作会议报告指出："要有序推进老旧住宅小区综合整治，推进城市绿色发展，提高建筑标准和工程质量，高度重视做好建筑节能"。[1]当前，老旧住区在我国所占比重较大，并随着年代的推进数量逐渐增加，全国各大城市已经针对自身特点开始不同层面的既有住区更新改造计划。北京市政府于2012年底印发《北京市老旧小区综合整治工作实施意见》，至2015年年底，将建筑面积 $58.5 \times 10^6 \mathrm{m}^2$ 的1582个老旧小区的综合整治工作全部完成[2]；天津市2015年既有居住建筑节能改造计划共计 $14.3662 \times 10^6 \mathrm{m}^2$，涉及全市13个区县，约24万户居民，共571片小区；"十二五"期间，上海已经累计实施各类旧住房改造 $70 \times 10^6 \mathrm{m}^2$，受益居民超过100万户。"十三五"期间，上海还将按照"业主自愿、政府扶持、因地制宜、多元筹资"的原则，实施 $50 \times 10^6 \mathrm{m}^2$ 的各类旧住房修缮改造[3]；大连自2013年起开展《大连市既有居住建筑节能改造工作》（"暖房子工程"）[4]，结合"大连市城市建设五个一工程"与《大连市住房维修计划"一二三"工程实施方案》，截至2015年年底，3年共完成既有住宅改造 $6.86 \times 10^6 \mathrm{m}^2$，累计投资23亿元。[5]

2 既有住区建筑内涵与品质概述

住区建筑在本文中指我国以住宅-组团-小区以及适当配套公建组成的住区居住建筑及环境。由于当时低设计标准以及低建造水平的限制，目前国内城市开展的节能改造绝大部分针对上述类型住区建筑。

既有住区的"品质"可从功能性、物理舒适性与场所性三个方面考虑，并体现阶段性特点。首先，居住功能的满足。即配套基础设施与生活服务设施建设，满足居民的基本生活需求；其次，居住物理舒适性的保障。即生态、可持续的住区室内外环境，能够为居民提供绿色低碳的住区生活；另外，场所人文关怀的营建。即结合当前既有住区地域环境、居民属性与生活方式的特点，进行场所精神与住区文化的营造。另外，住区健全的物业管理机制与运营模式，也成为全方面推动住区的维护、更新与持续发展的重要内容。根据以上定义和属性分类，当前我国住区建筑品质问题不同程度地表现在以下几个方面。

2.1 住区建筑与环境的功能缺失

新中国成立后，随着不同时期我国对居住要求的不同，全国住区规划建设大致经历了六个重要的阶段（图1）。[6] 总的来看，2000年以前的既有住区建筑主要包括以下几方面功能缺失问题：（1）住区基础设施较差，配套设施不全，难以满足便捷的生活需求；（2）以满足基本居住需求为主，住区室外的绿化率不高，环境综合质量较低；（3）受组团布局、规模的限制，住区环境单调雷同，缺少自由灵活的布局形式；（4）用地紧缺，难以满足日益增长的功能需求，如机动车停车位的严重不足，居民活动场地的缺失等。[7]

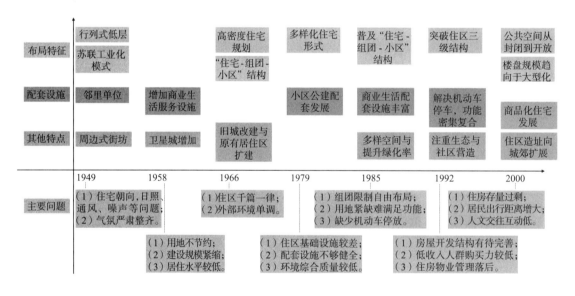

图1 我国不同时期住区（宅）的特点及问题

2.2 住区建筑性能退化带来的舒适性问题

随着时代的变更，住房出现机能老化，缺少完善的物业管理，甚至弃管，缺少必要性的维护修缮，导致住区与住宅的机能退化。另一方面，建造当时的设计及建设标准较低，也造成了保温隔热性能无法满足现阶段人们对于舒适性的要求。具体来讲，住区建筑的性能退化主要表现在以下几方面：（1）住宅机能老化，包括屋面、墙体等外围护结构以及基础、管网等由于建设标准低且缺少修缮维护导致的性能退化严重，无法有效保证室内基本的舒适度；（2）住区环境缺少养护、修复与管理，导致的绿地、场地、楼梯与铺装等出现大面积废弃，室外环境舒适度降低，进而影响到居民从事户外活动的积极性，住区活力下降；（3）由于缺少有效监管，部分既有住区道路、停车等基础设施陈旧，无法满足居民出行等的便利性要求，对居住品质产生了较大影响。

2.3 居民需求提升、生活方式转变引发的新需求

随着社会的进步、居民生活方式的转变与对生活水平要求的全面提升，既有住区主要包括以下几方面问题：（1）用地紧张，有限的场地难以满足多种使用需求，如机动车拥有率大幅度提升导致的停车位紧缺，居民健身活动场地缺少等；（2）老年人数占老旧住区60%～80%的人口比例[8]，并随着我国老龄化社会背景会逐年增加，缺少适老性设施影响老年人出行与休闲生活；（3）随着居民健康与审美意识的加强，以及对热舒适度要求的提升，绿色生态、通风遮阴等成为住区室外环境亟待提升的重要方面；（4）既有住区设施老化及环境品质低下，导致居民缺乏归属感、人文交往互动偏低等问题。因此，提升居民归属感、社会交往活动与地域场所精神的塑造与传承成为当前的迫切需求。

综上所述，从建筑学学科视角出发，如何解决既有住区建筑中存在的功能缺失、性能退化、物理舒适度降低、住区环境品质低下等问题，应对居民生活方式的转变与需求的提升，全面提升居住品质，成为新常态下既有住区建筑品质提升的重要研究内容。

3 既有住区建筑更新的理论与实践探索

既有住区建筑的更新主要指通过修缮、改造、加减建等方式，改善既有住区的机能与价值，从而提升既有住区的综合品质，延长其使用寿命与居民使用的舒适度与满意度。针对既有住区建筑的更新问题，近年来国内已经有较多的有益探索。

在理论研究层面，吴良镛院士的"人居环境科学"从"自然系统、人类系统、居住系统、社会系统与支撑系统"五大系统构建完整的住区环境；周燕珉教授、胡惠琴教授以"适老性"为出发点，提出住区及环境的更新设计策略；胡毅规划师、张京祥从空间生产与转型视角，对中国城市住区更新进行解读与重构；汪洋教授从城市系统及其更新动力学角度，分析城市机能衰退的原因和演变机理，为城市和住区建设协调发展提供科学决策依据。

在技术研究层面，范悦教授多角度介绍国外经典住区与建筑再生案例，研究存量时代的既有住区更新方法；饶小军教授针对南方地区的既有建筑进行绿色改造研究，而高宇波教授则对旧住宅性能进行评价及实践效用研究；作为国家重点研发方向，一系列国家科技支撑计划、国家自然科学基金重点项目均围绕既有住区、住宅领域开展，形成《城市旧住宅区宜居更新技术研究报告》、《城镇居住区景观绿化与热岛效应改善关键技术研究》、《城市社区绿色化综合改造技术研究与工程示范》、《既有建筑评定与改造策略和标准研究》、《既有建筑绿色化改造综合检测评定技术与推广机制研究》等多项技术与示范研究成果。

在实践探索层面，吴良镛院士以"菊儿胡同"为试点进行"有机更新"改造，提升居住品质的同时传承了历史文脉[9]；上海石库门里弄步高里的原生态改造模式，保持居住功能不变，修缮与增补基础设施，保持了原有的建筑风格与街区风貌；南京小西湖地区的旧居住区改造提出了由自上而下的政府主导转变为上下结合的政府引导、社区共建与公众参与的模式，并提出分层次、分阶段、强制性与弹性控制相结合的推进实施方案；上海在公众参与的住区改造实践中已有成效，新中国成立后重要的居住区代表"曹阳新村"通过"公众论坛"完善公共空间与设施，实现了城市微空间的激活。

在规范政策层面，各级政府为了促进既有住区的改造，颁布了一系列有效政策。住建部于2012年印发《既有居住建筑节能改造指南》，从基本情况调查、居民工作、节能改造设计、节能改造项目费用、节能改造施工、施工质量控制与验收方面提出详细指导意见；国家《既有建筑改造绿色评价标准》

GB/T 51141—2015 于 2016 年 8 月起正式实施；另外，各城市也同时推进相关政策，如《深圳市既有居住建筑绿色化改造技术规程》、《北京市老旧小区综合整治工作实施意见》、《上海市旧住房综合改造管理暂行办法》、天津市《中心城区散片旧楼区居住功能综合提升改造实施方案》、《大连市既有居住建筑节能改造工作技术要求》以及《老旧小区"6＋1"方式综合改造实施推进会》等；从专项内容来看，《绿色建筑评价标准》、《绿色住区标准》、《城市停车设施建设指南》、《海绵城市建设指南》与《智慧社区建设指南》等都为既有住区改造提供了有益的依据。

4 既有住区品质提升主要模式

针对既有住区不同类型的品质问题，近年来各级政府及主管部门进行了一系列的更新改造工程。主要包括以下几类模式。

4.1 以居住建筑节能改造为主的模式

既有居住建筑节能改造是指对不符合民用建筑节能强制性标准的既有居住建筑的围护结构、供热系统、采暖制冷系统、照明设备和热水供应设施等实施节能改造的活动。节能改造为主的更新模式是在有限的经济条件下快速满足居民基本使用功能的重要措施。我国自 2001 年起发布《既有采暖居住建筑节能改造技术规程》JGJ 129—2000，各省市地区均出台相应地方标准。2010 年，住建部引发《既有居住建筑综合改造技术导则》与《既有居住建筑综合改造技术集成》，以详细指标推动节能改造工作的贯彻执行。2008 年起，全国北方地区住宅节能改造工程全面展开，明确提出"十二五"期间完成北方住宅节能改造 $400 \times 10^6 m^2$，各省（区、市）要至少完成当地具备改造价值的老旧住宅的供热计量及节能改造面积的 35% 以上。[10]

4.2 以居住功能的综合改造为主的模式

居住功能的综合改造包括：住宅成套化改造、局部加减建工程、设备更新、环境整治与外墙修缮等多项内容，是当前我国既有住区更新最常见模式。例如，天津市作为综合改造工程的典型代表，执行：更新"一个箱"，安装"两道门"，改造"三根管"，实现"四个化"，完善"五功能"，整修"六设施"，基本涵盖了旧楼区的各项居住功能，2012～2014 年的三年间，累计提升改造旧楼区 1340 个，使 100.7 万户、310 万居民直接受益。[11] 居住功能的综合改造是对节能改造工程的范围扩展，从住区视角较为全面地解决既有住区的问题，提升居民的生活品质。

4.3 以社区营造与智慧社区建设为主的模式

社区营造指的是从社区生活出发，集合各种社会力量与资源，通过社区中人的动员和行动，社区完成自组织、自治理和自发展的过程。社区营造是充分了解居民使用需求，构建社区文化与场所精神，增加居民的住区活动参与，提升既有住区活力的重要内容。智慧社区是指充分利用物联网、云计算、移动互联网等新一代信息技术的集成应用，为社区居民提供一个安全、舒适、便利的现代化、智慧化生活环境，从而形成基于信息化、智能化社会管理与服务的一种新的管理形态的社区。智慧社区的建设将极大提升居民的生活满意度，是新时期推进住区更新与健康发展的有效模式。

4.4 以既有住区的适老化改造为主的模式

1999年起，我国进入老龄化社会，同时既有老旧住区的老年人比例相较新建住区更大。因此，对于既有住区的建筑与环境进行适老化设计是当务之急。在部分地区，对多层建筑加建电梯，甚至可放入担架的电梯工程已经展开；北京市海淀区仅在2012年就在50个居民小区实施了"无障碍"设施改造。在住区环境方面，更新注重从景观化向人性化转变，切实考虑不同年龄段老人的切实需求，从满足安全到适应老年人活动，再到鼓励老年人参与，逐步推动适老化改造的进程与力度。既有住区的适老化改造是应对当前老龄化社会的重要人文关怀。

5 既有住区建筑研究展望

面对既有住区建筑复杂的品质问题，相关学者及政府部门从不同侧重点，对既有住宅单体建筑或者居住组团改造的理论及实践进行了探讨，但是目前在以下几个方面研究依然缺乏。首先，对既有住区建筑退化机理的研究还比较少，缺乏多学科知识判断的标准和方法；其次，以往的研究中，对住区建筑的品质的关注度更集中在新建住宅小区，既有住区改造很少从功能性、舒适性、场所性等方面考虑其整体品质的提升；再次，目前既有居住建筑改造的特点主要集中在对单项指标的改造，如保温、平改坡、结构加固等单一方面，对住区建筑环境品质的优化研究依然不足。国家自然科学基金重点项目《北方既有住区建筑品质提升与低碳改造的基础理论与优化方法》，聚焦北方既有住区建筑"品质提升"和"低碳改造"问题，从功能性、舒适性、场所性等品质属性出发，研究住区建筑退化机理与品质、低碳的相关性。项目展开目标决策、设计方法、效能评价三个层次的研究，构建品质与低碳相互介入与耦合的理论体系。最终，尝试提出多目标整合的优化设计策略，以及支持品质提升与低碳改造设计的知识库与工具方法。

既有住区建筑更新是一项持久化工程，随着理论研究与实践探索的同步推进，将会形成更加精细化、综合化与科学化的既有住区建筑品质提升体系，促进相关研究、实践领域发展以及民生条件改善。

致谢

作者感谢国家自然科学基金重点项目（51638003）以及国家自然科学基金青年项目（51608091）对本论文研究的资金支持。

The Conspectus of Research and Practices on Residential Building Qualities in China

Fan Yue, Dong Li, Li Zhubin

(School of Architecture and Fine Art, Dalian University of Technology)

Abstract: The quality problems of residential buildings and urban environment have been raised, and become increasingly serious with the advent of the housing stock era and the growing demand for housing quality. This paper overviews the research literatures and design practices on the regeneration of residential buildings and environment, attempts to redefine the contents and quality issue of residential building, and summaries the regeneration methods for residential building quality improvements. This research aims at a solid foundation on theory and policy for future residential building quality improvement from an architectural study and a multi-disciplinary perspective. This paper also intents to attract extensive attentions and discussions on the residential regeneration in china.

Keywords: Residential building, Living quality, Existing building, Regeneration

参考文献

[1] 李克强. 中央城市工作会议 [R]. 北京：中国共产党中央委员会，2015.

[2] 北京市人民政府. 北京市老旧小区综合整治工作实施意见 [R]. 京政发〔2012〕3号，2012.

[3] 顾金山. "共享发展"新闻通气会 [R]. 上海：上海市住房和城乡建设管理委员会，2015.

[4] 大连市人民政府. 大连市既有居住建筑节能改造工作 [R]. 大政办发〔2013〕41号，2013.

[5] 大连市城乡建设委员会建筑节能管理处. 既改工作十二五总结 [R]. 辽宁：大连市城乡建设委员会，2015.

[6] 吕俊华，彼得·罗，张杰.1840~2000中国现代城市住宅 [M]. 北京：清华大学出版社，2003，8：105-276.

[7] 开彦. 中国住宅房地产60年历程与成就之三（住区规划下篇）[EB/OL]. http://blog.sina.com.cn/s/blog_4998f9280100fruh.html，2009-10-18/2015-12-27.

[8] 李睿. 新城市主义对我国城市老旧住区更新的启示 [D]. 天津：天津大学，2013：45.

[9] 方可. 探索北京旧城居住区有机更新的适宜途径 [D]. 北京：清华大学 2000：194.

[10] 古春晓，刘瑞芳，冯海峰. 财政部、住房和城乡建设部：进一步深化供热计量改革 [J]. 建设科技，2011，8：14-16.

[11] 人民网. 天津中心城区成片旧楼区居住功能综合提升改造三年综述 [EB/OL]. http://www.tj.gov.cn/jmjj/xmjj/jszs/201502/t20150206_259474.htm，2015-02-06/2015-12-27.

多元文化视角下的城市回族社区居住空间形态研究：以济南北大槐树回族社区为例

曾 鹏[1]　李若冰[1]　浦 钰[2]

（1.天津大学建筑学院；2.山东省城乡规划设计研究院）

摘　要：快速城市化进程中，回族聚落不断融入新的城市建设中，传统的族群宗教文化也逐渐与城市文化相融合。本文通过研究城市回族社区的结构演变、内部空间形态与建筑形式，探讨多元文化对"围寺而聚"的自足型社区产生的影响，揭示此类聚落的文化内涵及其生存发展的适应性，以期为城市回族社区建设发展的提供有益启示。

关键词：多元文化，回族，居住空间形态，北大槐树社区

1　引言

回族是我国分布最广和城市化程度最高的民族之一，也是我国最为典型的"世居 - 聚居型"少数民族[1]。回族聚集区"围寺而聚"的自足型聚居形态表达了回族居民与周围环境以及社会文化所建立起来的某种特殊联系，这种联系通过居住空间形态、建筑形式以及交往等方式存在。随着城市化进程的不断推进，城市回族社区的居住环境日渐恶劣，其社区感、归属感正在减弱，整个聚集区的文化正在走向衰落。

作为人们居住、生活、休息和进行日常交往活动的场所，居住空间是人类社会文化的一种空间状态和人文形态，目前学术界研究重点主要集中于居住空间分异、城市单位社区发展和农村传统聚落演变等方面，对于具有多元文化的城市中少数民族居住空间的研究尚有空白。

北大槐树社区特殊的地理位置和发展历程造就了其多文化交融的特色，使其成为一个既具特殊性又有普遍性的研究对象。本文采用实地调查与空间句法相结合的方法，探究城市回族社区的混合空间利用与建筑形式，重点剖析社区多元文化与居住空间形态之间的关联，从多元文化共生的角度对我国城市传统回族聚落改造更新与可持续发展提出有益启示。

2　北大槐树社区概况及多元文化特征

2.1　济南回族及北大槐树社区概况

在全国范围内，每一个省都有回族聚居区存在。其中以宁夏、甘肃、河北、河南、青海、山东、云南、新疆居住回族最多。[1]济南回族的迁入最早是在公元13世纪初，大都居住在历山顶附近的"乌满喇"巷一带，即今济南市历下区按察司街，济南市南关寺的《重修南关古礼拜寺碑记》记载："唐以来，迁居东街济南历邑乌满喇巷，立有清真寺"。[2]至明清时期，统治者镇压我国西北起义回族，被迫

东迁，在济南逐渐形成三大回族聚集区，北大槐树社区即为其中之一，其余两处分别位于回民小区和堤口庄。北大槐树社区位于济南市槐荫区，地处商埠区和东西城衔接的关键位置，津浦铁路从社区北侧穿过。社区东侧以纬九路为界，西至十二马路，北接津浦铁路，南至经一路（图1）。

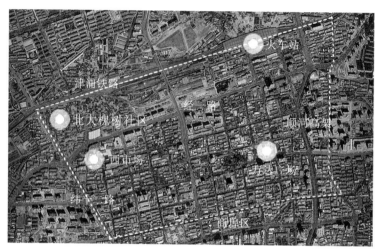

图1 北大槐树社区区位及实景图
资料来源：根据 Google Earth 截图自绘。

北大槐树社区是济南保存最为完整的老街片区之一，由明清时期北大槐树庄演变而来，是一个回汉杂居的社区，回族居民较多，占总人口的93%。清真寺位于社区西北角，占地0.08hm²，建筑面积394m²，门楼高悬匾额"清真寺"三个大字，以大门和礼拜殿为轴，南北对称（图2a）。

2.2 社区的多元文化特征

由于北大槐树社区特殊的地理位置和历史进程，在其发展过程中出现了宗教文化、商埠文化、槐文化和铁路文化等多元文化。

2.2.1 回族宗教文化

回族的家族观念较为薄弱，族群意识强，在信仰、文化、习俗和行为方式等方面有着高度的一致性。其核心是信仰安拉的独一性、《古兰经》的天启神圣性以及安拉使者穆罕默德的先知地位。[3]族群制度、回族礼拜、围寺而居、禁食猪肉及其制品以及善于经商等是其重要民族文化特征。

2.2.2 济南商埠文化

明清时期，济南是南北两京之间重要的工商业城市。清光绪三十年（1904年），济南自开商埠，创造了近代中国内陆城市对外开放的先河[3]，促进了社会发展及城市化进程，成为清末城市"自我发展"的重要典范。北大槐树社区地处济南市商埠区西北部，是西市场商圈的重要组成部分，商埠文化在很大程度上影响着北大槐树社区的经济、社会以及整个社区的空间形态。

2.2.3 槐文化

槐荫区原有8条以"大槐树"相称的街道，北大槐树街是其中之一。民间传这些"大槐树"与唐朝开国名将秦琼有关。这些参天古槐虬枝盘绕，历经岁月的沧桑而苍翠挺拔，为居民遮风挡雨（图2b）（图2c）。已成为北大槐树的文化象征之一，是居民生活中不可分割的部分，被打上了祥瑞的符号。

（a） （b） （c）

图 2 北大槐树社区实景图

（a）北大槐树清真寺；（b）北大槐树社区实景图；（c）北大槐树社区实景图
资料来源：（a）来自网络，（b）、（c）均为作者自摄。

2.2.4 铁路文化

津浦铁路的发展是济南近代产业和商埠发展的真实写照，从侧面反映了济南近现代发展史。1912年，津浦铁路通车，商埠区依临铁路迅速发展，北大槐树社区的规模也逐渐扩大。津浦铁路通车后，形成了建筑风格独特的天津巷，成为社区内唯一一条以城市命名的巷子。

3 北大槐树社区居住形态研究

3.1 北大槐树社区总体形态演变

北大槐树社区总体形态演变大体经历三个阶段：明清时期～20世纪初、20世纪初～20世纪40年代、20世纪40年代至今（图3）。

（a） （b） （c）

图 3 明清时期至今北大槐树社区形态演变示意图（作者自绘）

（a）20世纪初总体形态示意；（b）20世纪40年代总体形态示意；（c）21世纪社区总体形态示意

明清时期～20世纪初，部分迁入济南的回族在北大槐树街西首集聚，建清真寺，回族人十分重视清真寺在集聚区的核心地位，逐步形成"围寺而居"的居住雏形（图3a）。至1904年济南开埠，发展成为具有一定规模的聚居区。1912年，津浦铁路建成通车，1942年纬十二马路拓宽，聚居区西、北两个方向的发展受到阻碍，开始向东南方向沿北大槐树街扩散发展，清真寺不再是回族聚居区空间上的中心（图3b）。20世纪50年代，津浦铁路职工大量在北大槐树街东首安家，聚居区在空间上向东继续扩展，扩大形成城市居住区。后经填充式增长，现已发展成为以回为主、回汉居民杂居的居住社区（图3c），北大槐树社区的发展总体上经历了"集聚—扩散—填充"的发展过程（图4）。

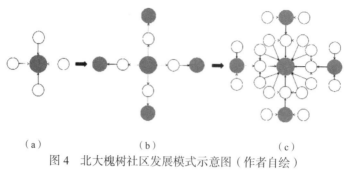

图 4 北大槐树社区发展模式示意图（作者自绘）
（a）集聚模式；（b）扩散模式；（c）填充模式

3.2 社区内部空间特征

本文采用空间句法（Space Syntax）中的轴线分析法对北大槐树社区内部空间特征进行分析。根据用最少且最长的轴线覆盖整个空间系统的原则，以北大槐树社区的道路网为载体，利用 Auto CAD 软件绘制社区轴线图（图 5）。将轴线图导入 UCL Depthmap 软件进行运算，根据整合度值的高低自动对于每条线段进行染色，色调越暖代表整合度值越高，色度越冷代表整合度值越低（本文以明亮度进行代替，即亮度越高代表代表整合度值越高，亮度越低代表整合度值越低），由此得到变量分析图。

3.2.1 全局整合度分析

由图 6 可知，北大槐树社区的整合度最高的是北大槐树街，党家巷、天津巷和纬十二路次之。北大槐树街是社区的中心街道，高整合度证明其高可达性，在回族人社区中的生活、空间、文化、交通等方面更具重要性。社区的全局整合度数值分布格局具有明显的"整合度核心"，即以北大槐树街为中心两侧约 20m 范围，这个区域集中了社区内 85% 的公共服务设施，是整个社区日常生活的中心街道（表 1）。

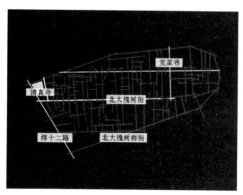

图 5 北大槐树社区轴线图
资料来源：根据社区 CAD 资料改绘。

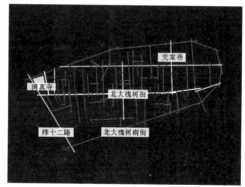

图 6 北大槐树社区全局整合度分析图
资料来源：根据 UCL Depthmap 软件生成改绘。

北大槐树街 20m 范围内社区公共服务设施一览表　　表 1

序号	名称	数量	占总量百分比
1	小卖部	7	77%
2	家庭旅馆	5	83%
3	北大槐树第二小学	1	100%
4	北大槐树幼儿园	1	100%
5	卫生院	1	100%

3.2.2 局部整合度分析

社区的局部整合度中心为北大槐树街和清真寺（图7），次级中心为社区扩展发展过程中主要依赖的道路和街巷。经上文分析北大槐树街作为局部整合度中心不难理解，而清真寺在回族人生活中承载着重要的族群意义，回族人日常生活中宗教仪式、婚丧嫁娶及学习交流等均在清真寺进行，因此成为局部整合度中心，即整个社区的公共活动中心。

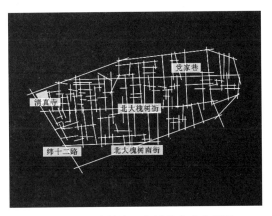

图7 北大槐树社区全局整合度分析图
资料来源：根据UCL Depthmap软件生成改绘。

3.3 居住结构特征

回族聚居区传统的院落布局主要有一字形、二字形、L形、U形、三合院形及四合院形六种[4]，主体居住建筑坐北朝南。在北大槐树社区，回族院落的面积、空间布局及建筑内部空间表现出较为明显的分异特征，主要分为以下四种（表2）。

北大槐树街社区院落形制一览表　　表2

序号	院落形式	家庭结构	占比	院落布局
1	一字形	一代人 两代人 三代人	49%	
2	三合院	二代人 三代人	39%	
3	L形	两代人 三代人	9%	

续表

序号	院落形式	家庭结构	占比	院落布局
4	四合院	三代人 四代人	3%	

3.4 社区建筑特征

3.4.1 清真寺特征

传统意义上的清真寺一般是大拱顶结构，多数是由分行排列的方柱或圆柱支撑的一系列拱门，拱门又支撑着圆顶、拱顶。而北大槐树社区的清真寺则采用了中国传统院落式布局，二进院落，木结构建筑，青砖灰瓦，建筑精美。院落形态与其他寺庙相似，唯一区别是采用绿色屋顶，西北侧的屋子在屋脊上装有三个立着的花柱，中间一个顶端有伊斯兰教新月标志。

3.4.2 民居建筑特征

在北大槐树街区回族民居建筑，呈现出伊斯兰建筑细部装饰风格、中国传统建筑风格与西方古典建筑元素相结合的特征。

部分民居保留着高大轩敞的中国传统式门楼，但绝大多数已简化为随墙门（图8a）、（图8b）、（图8c），采用红砖砌筑、水泥抹灰的西洋三段式构图。墙面大都为清水红砖墙，有三角形山墙和两端高起的不太正统的西洋式墙垛构成，由方形红砖砌筑，顶部砌两层并斜向上出挑，又层层向内收进，形成不太正统的西洋式墙垛，反映出社区居民对西洋建筑形式朴素的理解和简单的模仿。

回族民居的传统大门上常见悬挂和雕刻着由艺术阿拉伯文字书写的与伊斯兰教信仰有关的古兰经经文，如"清真言"或"太斯米"等（图8d）。建筑细部雕饰圆雕滑润丰满，浮雕行云流水，透雕玲珑剔透。雕刻集中了多种形式，除伊斯兰传统的内容之外，多以琴棋书画，花草瑞兽为主，其中又以"出泥荷花"的形象最为多见（图8e）。

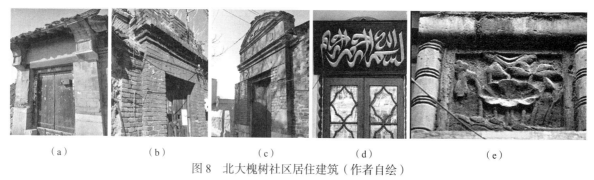

图8 北大槐树社区居住建筑（作者自绘）
(a)简式门楼；(b)山字门楼；(c)西式门楼；(d)大门古兰经文；(e)细部雕饰

4 文化对北大槐树回族社区居住空间形态的影响

4.1 文化对社区形态的影响

基于共同宗教信仰和文化认同，形成以清真寺为核心的族缘式聚居，是传统回族的社会组织形式。20 世纪前，北大槐树清真寺一直作为聚居区的中心，住宅圈层式布局于寺周围。济南开埠后，受到商业文化和西洋文化的冲击，聚居区逐渐由封闭发展为外向开放型居住区，并沿主要交通道路扩展，聚集程度有所降低。津浦铁路通车后，部分汉族人在铁路附近的天津巷定居，而回族人仍集中在北大槐树街两侧，彼此之间互不沟通也互不干扰，一定程度上体现了回族人强烈的自我保护意识。直至 20 世纪七八十年代，随着聚集人口的增多，北大槐树街区开始填充式发展，由一开始宗教为主导的聚集区发展成为以宗教信仰、生活、教育、就业为一体的复合型居住空间。

4.2 文化对社区内部空间的影响

由于城市发展对回族聚居区造成了发展方向上的限制，使得清真寺在空间上不再占据主导位置，回族聚落传统的"围寺而居"逐渐演变成"近寺而居"，但清真寺在精神和文化上的核心地位不容动摇，仍是回族人重要的活动节点。1904 年济南开埠后，商业繁荣发展，回人善经商的特征逐渐被激发出来，社区开始沿商业型道路——北大槐树街发展，寺坊制的发展核心演变为社区内重要的街坊通道。这是社区居民在心理上建立秩序的中心，社区的建筑多以这条街为中心展开布局，构建此核心的轴线延伸至南北各处，创造出格网式的街巷布局，形成内敛式的空间布局，这对于社区使用者是有文化上的庇护领域意义。也就是说，城市回族人社区提供组构来传递文化和社会本性，而文化也对空间的实体形态产生了影响。

4.3 文化对民居建筑的影响

4.3.1 宗教文化对民居的影响

回族的建筑形式大多随整个民族或社区的迁移而逐渐融入本地建筑当中，在伊斯兰教义的基础上对济南本土建筑进行改良，演绎出地域特征明显、回族文化特色突出的伊斯兰建筑。北大槐树街区住宅通过建筑造型创新、细部装饰的民族化、色彩运用的规范化等手法，在老济南商埠区创造了回族特色的民居建筑形态。

4.3.2 开埠后西洋文化对民居的影响

开埠后的济南，与西方国家在文化及物质方面的交往明显加强，西方建筑文化逐渐融入商埠区的各类建筑，使北大槐树街区的回族传统民居发生了较多变异。回族传统的屋面形式在建筑形象中所起的控制作用逐渐淡化，立面构图中开始使用券拱和柱式等西方古典建筑的构图元素，使得传统回族民居出现了中西合璧的立面形象，充分反映了开埠后西洋文化对北大槐树街区建筑形制的影响。

4.3.3 津浦铁路文化对民居的影响

津浦铁路通车后，部分天津铁路职员在此安家，形成建筑风格独特的天津巷，巷子内住宅风格的差异体现出职员的级别不同（表 3）。

表 3　天津巷高级别住宅一览表

序号	级别	特征
1	高级别住宅	中国传统门楼，雕饰精美，院落开阔，具有传统四合院的布局特征
2	低级别住宅	门楼简化为随墙门，上段为半圆山花和繁复的水平线脚，山花中嵌有巴洛克式花饰，以蘑菇石作为毛石底座；院落狭小，初具联排式住宅特征

4.3.4 济南文化对民居的影响

济南文化对北大槐树社区民居产生过重要影响。位于北大槐树街东首邵家巷的邵家大院，正房与西厢房均为三开间的硬山屋顶，屋顶正脊为叠砌的瓦脊，两端对称翘起、斜伸向天，体现出典型的济南民居风格。"四面荷花三面柳，一城山色半城湖"，便是形容济南古城风貌的名联佳句，而北大槐树社区建筑细部雕饰常见"出泥荷花"的形象，是济南精神文化的象征。

5　结论与建议

5.1　结论

回族社区的演进一方面与城市的社会、政治、经济状况相关；另一方面与文化形态的更替有着密不可分的关系。北大槐树片区共生的多元文化对回族传统的"寺坊制"产生了深远影响，使其在发展过程中形成了"入乡随俗，因地制宜，和而不同，融而不化"的规则特征，更加注重精神的体现与情感的表达。由于北大槐树社区文化的复杂性与融合性，社区中的清真寺不再通过可见的模式传达其所具有的"权力"，而更多通过不可见模式比如可达性与文化崇尚等来体现回族人的文化归属感。回族传统的"生活-信仰"型的单-空间[5]开始向"生活-生产-信仰"型的经济空间和"宗教传承-有机更新"型的文化空间过渡。

5.2　建议

在对城市回族社区的更新建设过程中，政府和规划部门应正确认识、尊重回族的宗教信仰，充分满足社区穆斯林宗教生活和日常生活的需求。政府还应发掘和保护社区的多元文化，唤起社区居民对多元文化的重视和继承。建立高效循环的"信息共享-社会参与"型社会空间、"生活-生产-信仰"型经济空间和"文化传承-有机更新"型文化空间，使回族聚落能够在社会环境复杂的城市中平衡各种矛盾，顽强地生存发展下去，实现回族社区更新与城市发展的双向互动。

Study on the Living Space of Urban Hui Nationality Community from the Perspective of Multiculturalism: Taking Jinan Beidahuaishu Community as An Example

Zeng Peng[1], Li Ruobing[1], Pu Yu[2]

(1.School of Architecture, Tianjin University; 2.Shandong Urban and Rural Planning Design Institute)

Abstract: In the process of rapid urbanization, the traditional culture of the Hui nationality has gradually merged with the urban culture. This paper explores the influence of multiculturalism on the self-contained community of "enclosing the temple" by exploring the structural evolution, the internal space and the architectural form of urban Hui community, revealing the cultural connotation of this kind of settlement and the adaptability of its development, so as to give some suggestions for the construction and development of urban Hui community.

Keywords: Multiculturalism, Hui nationality, Residential space patter, Beidahuaishu community

参考文献

[1] 朴龙虎. 我国城市中民族聚居区的居住模式研究 [D]. 天津大学, 2007.

[2] 徐东海. 山东济南市回民小区回汉关系调查研究 [D]. 宁夏大学, 2013.

[3] http://www.muslem.net.cn/bbs/thread-28053-1-1.html.

[4] 李晓玲. 宁夏沿黄城市带回族新型住区空间布局适宜性研究 [M]. 北京：中国建筑工业出版社, 2014.

[5] 陈艳美. 都市民族社区建设研究——以武汉市四道社区为例 [D]. 中南民族大学, 2005.

[6] 郁颖姝. 基于历史城区和风貌区理论的济南商埠区保护更新研究 [D]. 清华大学, 2015.

[7] 林吉玲, 董建霞. 胶济铁路与济南商埠的兴起（1904～1937）[J]. 东岳论丛, 2010, 31（3）: 105-110.

[8] 王静文. 传统聚落环境句法视域的人文透析 [J]. 建筑学报, 2010, 1.

[9] http://www.muslem.net.cn/bbs/thread-28053-1-1.html.

传统村落人居环境营建的生态智慧探讨

曾 卫 朱雯雯

（重庆大学建筑城规学院）

摘 要：传统村落是乡村在历史演进与发展中形成的地域特色鲜明的人居环境典范，其营建涉及村落选址与形态、总体布局、建筑营建以及村民生产生活、安全防灾等方面，充分体现了古人尊重自然、利用自然及改造自然的生态智慧。笔者从"天人合一"的生态和谐智慧、"因利而为"的生态发展智慧以及"避险防灾"的生态安全智慧三个视角对传统村落人居环境建设进行探讨，并以汉源县九襄镇为例进行阐释，为我国传统村落的保护及延续、新农村人居环境的生态可持续建设提供了借鉴意义。

关键词：传统村落，人居环境营建，生态智慧

1 引言

在城乡一体化热潮中，乡村建设得到了空前发展；与此同时也产生了诸如环境恶化、资源枯竭等问题，乡村人居环境遭受了前所未有的破坏。[6]传统村落人居环境具备美学与生态双重特征，其营建充分体现了尊重自然、尊重人本的生态观，凝聚了古人的营建经验与智慧。因此，借鉴传统村落人居环境营建思想和方法对改善当今乡村人居环境，解决城市化进程中乡村被侵蚀等问题具有重要意义。

武启祥等人在2010年提出传统村落的生态系统具有时空复杂性、演化过程缓慢渐变的特点；王邦虎在2008年从古村落民居建筑和人居空间着手，提出古村落的人居环境具有自然的人格化、人居空间的自然化、"人自关系"的伦理化等特点；范霄鹏在2010年提出传统村落的选址方式促使民居、村落和自然环境要素的组合是农耕社会的理想栖居形式；王树声在2008年提出古村落营建中将人工环境与自然环境相统一的整体规划理念。通过整理国内相关学者的研究发现，其多集中于村落人居环境的系统特征、营建理念等视角，涉及了村落人工和自然环境两大层面；但对于村落人居环境与村民的生产生活之间的关联性研究较缺乏，忽略了人居环境营建过程中"人的主观能动性和主动选择权"。因此，本文在前人研究基础上，以传统村落与"自然"以及与"人"的密切关联性为切入点，就传统村落人居环境营建的生态智慧进行思考，以期为我国传统村落的保护及新农村建设提供借鉴。

2 传统村落人居环境的研究概述

2.1 传统村落人居环境的内涵

吴良镛院士在其《人居环境科学导论》一书中对人居环境进行释义：人居环境，顾名思义，是人类聚居生活的地方，是与人类生存活动密切相关的地表空间，它是人类在大自然中赖以生存的基地，

是人类利用、改造自然的主要场所。乡村人居环境是人居环境的重要组成部分。[1] 传统村落是乡村在历史演化与发展中形成的"人-自然-空间相互和谐"的人居环境典范；各个领域对传统村落人居环境的理解不一：从建筑学角度，认为传统村落人居环境是村落建筑与环境有机结合的地域空间；从风水学角度，认为理想的传统村落人居环境要以尊重自然规律为原则；从形态学角度，认为传统村落是人与自然和谐，生产与生活结合的人类栖息地；从生态学角度，认为传统村落人居环境是以人地和谐为目的的复合生态系统。总结得知，传统村落人居环境的核心主体是"人"与"自然"，其营建是一项以满足人类生产生活需要为目的，以"人与自然和谐统一"为诉求的环境营造活动。

2.2 传统村落人居环境的特征

2.2.1 传统村落人居环境的稳定性与发展缓慢性

传统村落是我国农耕社会的产物，且对自然环境有着很强的共生性和依赖性，《阳宅十书》有"人之居处宜以大地山河为主"。[2] 古时，自然环境是营造人居环境的基础，农耕活动是村落发展的经济基础，自然环境与农耕经济的双重属性决定了村落的形成与发展具有稳定性和缓慢性两大特征。一方面，人类生产力低下，对自然的改造能力有限，土壤沙化、泥石流、地震等一系列由人类过分活动引起的自然环境问题在当时发生的可能性较低，因此保证了自然环境的稳定性和安全性[4]；另一方面，农耕社会下经济发展缓慢，人类聚居的区位与规模不易发生较大变化，村落功能也较为简单，决定了村落内部结构的封闭性和稳定性，村落常常会在几十年甚至几百年内保持一种相对静止而封闭的状态（图1）。

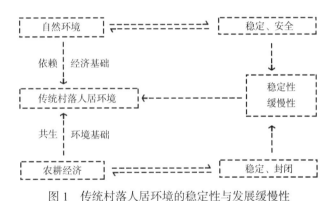

图1 传统村落人居环境的稳定性与发展缓慢性

2.2.2 传统村落人居环境与自然和谐统一

"道法自然"、"天人合一"、"知足知止"等自然哲学观强调对自然的崇拜与尊重。古人认为自然与人是一个有机整体，村落是在自然环境中形成生长的。《管子全译》："凡立国都，非于大山之下，必于广川之上，高毋近旱而水用足，下毋近水而沟防省。因天才，就地利，故城郭不必中规矩，道路不必中准绳。"[3] 这些思想无不反映着自然环境对村落人居环境的巨大影响。人们借自然之利进行村落人居环境的营建，在形成静谧秀丽的村落景观的同时也形成了深厚的文化底蕴，营造了"自然"与"人文"和谐统一的理想聚落风貌。

2.2.3 传统村落人居环境关注"人"的基本需求

古时人类活动相对单一，在此基础上村落功能也较为简单，主要形成生产、生活两大基本生存功能。[7] 村落人居环境建设所考虑的主要因素是人的生产、生活需要，即考虑是否为村民提供充足的生产生活资源,是否利于村民农业生产、生存安全、身体健康等生理、心理需求,体现在村落选址布局、建筑营建、文化景观营造等方面。另外,传统村落人居环境建设还非常注重人的精神及信仰追求等方面。以"人"的基本需求为村落人居环境的建设依据,肯定人在村落环境中的主体地位,提升对人的关怀是传统村落人居环境营建中最为重要的一点。

2.3 传统村落人居环境的营建

传统村落人居环境的营建是一项人类与自然在漫长博弈中进行适应性选择的行为活动,并逐渐形成为人类生产、生活服务的"自然-村落-人"的复合聚落景观和人居环境模式。[4] 其中,自然环境与不同时期不同地域的社会生产等经济活动方式是影响传统村落人居环境特色的直接因子。"天人合一"、"因利而为"以及"避险防灾"三大人居环境营建的生态智慧饱含了古人对人与自然协调方面的整体认知和建设智慧,对促进我国乡村聚落的生态建设与发展有举足轻重的意义(图2)。

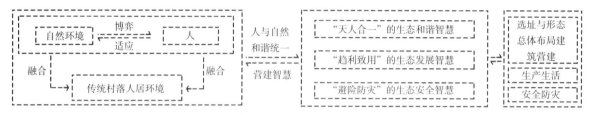

图2 传统村落人居环境的营建模式

3 传统村落人居环境营建的生态智慧

3.1 "天人合一"的生态和谐智慧

"天人合一"思想源于道家,也是自然生态学的起源,强调"物化自然";"天"指自然环境,"人"则指人类;认为人与自然应和谐相处。"天人合一"体现在村落营建上就是要做到村落与自然环境相互融合,强调人居环境建设必须遵循自然发展规律,并在此基础上积极发挥人的主观能动性,最终实现人与自然的和谐统一及村落可持续发展。[8] 主要表现为村落选址及形态、总体布局、建筑营建等需考虑地形、气候、水文等地理环境要素。

传统村落的选址在于协调村落与地形、气候、水文、日照、风向等自然地理要素之间的相互关系,达到人与自然和谐的双赢局面,即所谓的"天人合一"。[5] 总体来讲,村落选址以"枕山、环水、面屏"的理想风水环境模式为指导,在形成"背山面水、左右围护"的生态聚落的同时满足村民对宗族兴盛、村落繁荣的希冀。另外,传统村落在对自然的适应过程中逐渐形成了与环境相得益彰的形象图案,村落以一种具有生命力的仿生形态居于自然肌理之中,隐喻"效法自然,天人合一"的自然生态主义思想。同时,也代表了村民的某种美好的精神寄托,如黟县宏村牛型、渔梁村"鱼"型等。

村落总体布局的"天人合一"思想主要体现在村落建筑、街巷、农田要素的布局上。首先,建筑布局以尊重和利用地形为原则,因此便形成了不同的村落格局(表1)。村落街巷布局与地形地貌以及建筑布局形态密切相关;农田布局主要考虑区域地质地貌、水源、气候等与生产活动紧密相关的因素。

村落总体布局与自然环境的关系　　　　　　　　　　　表 1

自然环境	特征	布局
平原型	水源充足，适宜农耕，交通便利	趋于均匀。适宜生产生活
山地丘陵型	地形相对复杂，土地资源不足	因势就利集聚于山谷、山脚、山麓边缘等宜建区立体景观丰富
水乡型	水域丰富，景观灵动，气候滋润	因水而隔呈分散布局。形态灵活丰富

村落在建筑布局、形式等营建方面也充分体现了与自然和谐的思想。（1）不同地形地貌、气候区域形成了独特且丰富的建筑类型（表2）;（2）建筑朝向、结构、材料等充分考虑与自然环境的生态适应性，主要体现在改善室内外物理环境舒适度、建筑选材多以地域性材料为主等方面，如浙江诸葛八卦村。

建筑类型与自然环境的关系　　　　　　　　　　　表 2

区域	环境特征	建筑类型	营造特征
西藏高原	辐射强烈，日照多，寒冷，干燥，降水稀少，多大风	碉房	防寒、防风、防震；设置天井、天窗等达到通风、采暖效果。
福建地区	山区密林，建筑材料缺乏。豺狼虎豹，盗贼猖狂	环楼	依山就势，生土建筑。适合群居、节约、坚固、防御性强
西南地区	气候潮湿闷热，蚁重较多	干栏式建筑	以竹，木，茅草为材料，分上下两层，上层住人，下层养畜。防潮、通风、御蛇、虫和野兽侵害
陕北地区	山大沟深，万壑纵横	窑洞	热惰性好，冬暖夏凉，日照充足，通风差

3.2 "因利而为"的生态发展智慧

"因利而为"是村民在长期生产、生活中形成的智慧结晶；强调在尊重与利用自然的基础上，适当改造自然以达到人与自然和谐，保证子孙后代可持续发展。体现在村落营建上就是指在人与自然和谐的前提下发挥主观能动性，主要指对耕地、水、气候等与人类生产、生活紧密相关的自然资源的综合、充分利用，为人类自身生存与发展提供条件。

在我国农耕社会的漫长历史中，人们改造自然的能力有限，耕地作为最基础的生存资本，是村落可持续发展的决定性因素。[7] 因此，区域土地面积、土壤肥沃度、地势平坦度、水源充足度等是村落建设的首要考虑因素。由于对耕地资源的重视，一般将地势平坦、土壤肥沃的土地作为耕地，而山地丘陵等薄地上多用来聚居；这样既可预留足够的耕地面积，又可避免因地势过低而受到山洪灾害影响；另外，在一些耕地紧缺的区域，村落选址布局不仅充分利用周边耕地、林地，还尽可能利用地形高差预留出土地耕作，这种在较为严酷条件下尽最大可能获得更多耕地面积的村落数不胜数，如浙江乌岩古村。

传统村落的生存与发展除了与耕地资源有密切关系之外，更离不开水资源。一方面，水作为生产资源，主要用于村落农田灌溉等；作为生活资源，主要用于村民日常饮水、洗涤等。另一方面，水系也能给村落带来适宜微气候、良好的生态环境及人文景观。传统村落长期以来形成了一整套理水、用水的方法，体现出安全、便捷、生态、可持续的自然智慧。首先，水源常会成为村民聚居及村落布局形态的依据，村落依水而建提高了村民用水的快速、便捷性。再者，村民常进行筑坝蓄水、分流灌溉等，保障了村落地下水水位、井水的可持续补水，为村民日常生产生活提供足够水源；反映出古人在应对自然气候变化时保障水资源安全、可持续的伟大智慧。[3]

气候资源不仅与村民居住生活的物理舒适度紧密相关，同时也是古村落农业发展不可或缺的自然资源。古人非常注重对日照和风力两大自然资源的利用。（1）日照资源：村落择址讲究"负阴抱阳"，建筑布局以南、西南、东、东南等方位居多以获得更多日照；尤其在山地丘陵区，村落选址及建筑布局以顺应日照走势强调向阳性。（2）风力资源：适宜的风速具有促使空气流动，减小湿度的作用，从而保障村落物理环境舒适度以及人畜的身体健康，因此，村落布局非常注重风道、风廊的形成，以营造良好的通风条件；尤其在山地丘陵区域，常将山体作为屏障以抵御西北风、北风的寒流侵袭，同时常常利用河流水系的流动带动作用形成自然风，用以调节村落小气候。[5]

3.3 "避险防灾"的生态安全智慧

"避险防灾"最先是在战乱年代产生的一种防范思想和心理；后来在人类遭受山体塌方、水流冲沟、山洪侵袭、旱涝等自然地质灾害之后更加以强调和重视。避险防灾是一种"防患于未然"的先验智慧，主要指人类通过各种方法和措施以规避或减弱各种灾害，体现在村落营建上就是要充分利用环境的优势，并以各种方法规避环境的劣势，以保障村民生存及生产生活的安全。

古时，战乱不断，人们为了生存便聚集到地势险峻、易守难攻的区域，形成并逐渐发展为村落；另外，为了防止乱兵侵入、盗匪横行、民族入侵等，村民在村落建设时也非常注重安全防御的考虑；安全防御体系是村落生存与发展的基础。[4]古村落的防御体系建设主要通过选址布局、筑建城墙、院落组织、重要节点防御等方式来保障与强化。我国黄檀硐村、河南寨堡、苗寨等在安全防御方面极具代表性。

历史上由于未能抵御自然地质灾害冲击而衰落或消失的古村落数不胜数，如楼兰古城、庞贝城、新奥尔良等；对自然地质灾害的承受力成为决定一个村落安全生存与可持续发展的重要条件。村落营建须考虑地形地貌、气候水文、工程地质等对村落安全性、适宜性的影响，以避免山体塌方、地震等地质灾害和水流冲沟、山洪侵袭、旱涝等自然灾害。[9]灾害防御涉及村落选址、总体布局、建筑营建、植被种植、基础设施建设等方面。首先，村落选址前须调查研究区域自然地质环境，避免于灾害易发区或潜发区进行建设；另外，可以通过建筑布局及建筑结构、建筑组合形式等方法强化村落防御功能；再者，可以通过保护植被加强土壤涵养力、抗沙化力等，使区域地质结构保持稳定，减小自然地质灾害发生的可能性。除以上防御手段外，村落还形成了一整套治水防洪和理水排涝、蓄水防旱和储水消防等避水患的技术。（1）治水防洪和理水排涝：在选址布局上，将村落靠近山体且居高位，顺应山势和坡向，以避免山洪侵袭和突发强降雨的冲击；同时，通过水闸、河道疏浚等防洪排涝的技术方法保证村落安全。（2）蓄水防旱和储水消防：一般通过水塘、水渠、水井等的布局来储水防旱；而一些地形复杂的山地丘陵中的传统村落，难以建造人工水渠、水塘等进行蓄水救灾；先民便通过大水缸进行储水蓄水，以预防规避旱灾；此外，还可通过收集天然雨水进行蓄水，以发扬节俭、质朴的节水传统。[6-8]

4 乡村人居环境生态营建策略——以汉源县九襄镇为例

4.1 九襄镇自然资源概况

九襄镇位于四川省雅安市汉源县北部，四川西南大渡河流域，属河谷堆积地貌；夏季闷热、冬季湿冷，年降水量较大，常年主导风向为南风和东南风。[10]河流众多，主要有流沙河、木槿水、干沟三大水系；植被种类繁多，包括山林、果树、农田等，被称为"花果之乡"。全镇所辖村落有满堰、大木、堰坪、梨花、大庄、刘家、民主、周家、梨坪等，镇域面积83.2km^2。九襄镇各村落的发展与其优渥的自然资源条件以及村民人居环境营建的生态智慧紧密相关。

4.2 村落人居环境的营建原则

4.2.1 尊重自然

传统村落人居环境的营建与自然环境紧密相关，处理好乡村人居环境建设与"自然"的关系是其生态建设的本质需求。当今传统村落的空间、景观、功能与古时相比产生了很大变化，不再具备封闭性、静止性、渐进性等特征，反而呈现一种开放、活跃、快速的特征，但其与自然的互生互利关系却丝毫没有减弱；建构人与自然和谐、适应性强、自我调节性强的乡村人居环境是乡村可持续发展的基础。

4.2.2 以人为本

传统村落的发展与人的生产生活紧密相关，协调好村落人居环境建设与"人"的关系是新时期传统村落保护与发展的重要内容。当今"人"的需求与古时相比已不再局限于基本的生产、生活需要；随着经济快速发展和生活水平的提高，人们不仅关注物质生活，同时更加关注精神需求。人居环境建设应在满足人类生产生活、安全防御需求的基础上为人类提供一个可以放松身心、缓解压力的世外桃源，创造一个以人为本的人居环境。

4.2.3 生态-经济可持续

纵观人类发展历史，村落总是在与自然适应与平衡中发展起来，但也不乏出现一味追求经济发展而无节制索取和破坏生态环境的行为，人类因此受到来自自然的惩罚。近年来的乡村旅游热将乡村视为一种商品，对乡村自然及人文生态环境无节制牺牲破坏的现象数不胜数。乡村土地、林地、山体、水体、农田等自然资源都具有不可再生性，也决定了乡村生态系统具有脆弱性和不可恢复性。村落营建要在保护自然资源前提下寻求生态与经济可持续发展之道，为后代留有足够的发展资源。

4.3 村落人居环境的营建策略

九襄镇各村落人居环境的营建是以尊重自然、以人为本为原则寻求生态-经济可持续发展的典范；其选址布局、建筑营建、生产生活景观营造等策略渗透着古人"天人合一"的生态和谐智慧、"因利而为"的生态发展智慧以及"避险防灾"的生态安全智慧；充分体现了村民的生态营建智慧；为我国乡村人居环境的营建提供了参考（图3）。

图 3　传统村落人居环境的营建模式

村落选址注重对地形、水文、植被等自然资源的尊重与利用。九襄镇位于流沙河河谷台地，四周群山环抱，南临流沙河，西临木槿水，呈山环水绕格局。其择址首先以"避险防灾"为主要考虑因素，综合分析区域地形地貌、地质构造等多项建设条件，以避免村落于灾害易发或潜发区落址，选址于地势相对平坦、土质结构稳定、近水位置，既有效减免山体塌方、滑坡、山洪等地质灾害的发生，又利于村民生产生活。其次，择址依托周边山水环境，呈现"青龙、白虎、朱雀、玄武"的传统风水宝地模式（图4）。

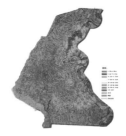

图4 村落选址

村落建筑、街巷、农田等布局在充分利用地形、日照、风向等有利资源的同时，避免不利环境的影响，达到人与自然和谐统一（图5）。首先，建筑依山势呈阶梯状布局，层层跌落，呈现丰富的立体景观；其布局模式充分利用区域主导风以及流沙河、木槿水、周边山体所形成的水陆风和地形风，同时也通过河水蒸腾作用营造良好的通风环境。其次，街巷顺应地形和建筑，其走向平行于当地夏季主导风向，由两侧密布的民居围合而成，较为狭窄；不仅能够增强导风效果，有效改善区域风环境和空气质量，而且还可以通过错落布局来获得良好日照，营造舒适小气候。再者，农田、果园布局充分利用地形、水源、气候等自然资源，紧邻流沙河、木槿水，密布于村落、山林台地间，顺应地势层层跌落，形成立体农田生态景观。

图5 村落建筑、街巷、农田布局

村落建筑的营建充分展现了古人适应、利用、改造自然的生态智慧；主要体现在建筑形式、结构、材料等对日照、风力等资源的利用以及对洪涝、火灾等自然灾害的应对策略等方面。首先，传统建筑兼容北方的封闭及南方的开敞特征，平面多以天井为中心，以廊围合四面房屋呈合院形制（图6a）。一方面，天井有助于通风采光，改善潮湿环境；庭院与廊结合有利于形成穿堂风，增加日照；甚至有居民在庭院加盖凉棚，兼具通风、采光、防雨、防晒等功能。另一方面，下沉式庭院结合阴沟利于收集及疏导雨水，某些大宅甚至建有月池、堪湾等，用以汇集雨水，防止雨水过多而倒灌院内；其次，还通过抬高居室地平、铺设木地板等方法来防潮。此外，建筑屋顶为呈微升起曲线的双坡屋顶，且采用穿斗式构架，结合出挑深远的檐部以及檐下气窗（图6b）。一方面既利于排水，也可排除室内不断上升的热空气，防暑降温；另一方面也可作为村民晾晒粮食的天然晒场，适合川西潮湿多雨的气候（图6c）。再者，建筑采用石、砖、木、竹、土等多种地域性材料，既具有很好的气候调节作用，又节能环保；由于木结构建筑易引发火灾，因此加以不开窗的马头墙来防范火灾。

村落生产生活景观的营造兼具生态、安全、可持续智慧，享有"花果之乡""梨城三月雪"等盛誉。首先，九襄镇受到来自川西南高原气候的影响，日照充足，独特的光热资源适合多种水果、蔬菜和粮食的生长。另外，九襄地形丰富，山、林、水、田密布，村民充分利用土地资源，依地形种植农作物，

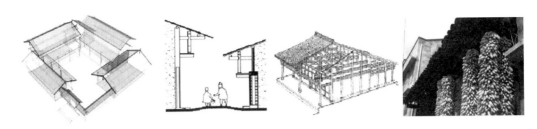

图6 村落建筑营建

(a) 合院建筑形式　　(b) 建筑结构　　(c) 建筑细部

在田里种粮、种菜，在田坎上种植果树，形成典型的立体生态农业典范。再者，九襄镇位于河谷堆积区，土壤肥沃，水源充足，有流沙河、木槿水及干沟等水系，为农业发展提供了有力保障。镇区水系集景观营造、小气候调节、生产、生活用水等功能于一体，成为村内不可或缺的珍贵资源；其中，流沙河是村内主要农业灌溉水源，人工修筑水渠、水池等，将水系引入农田果园；干子河穿流于村内，成为蓝色廊道，在调节微气候的同时成为村落活水景观；木槿水结合农田、林地，最大限度发挥生态效益。村民为方便生产生活，通过加强道路建设、水利建设，营建蓄水池、水窖等，方便居民用水的同时保证用水安全；除此之外，村民还通过建设沼气池、屋顶种植及雨水收集等现代方式充分利用自然资源，达到生态可持续发展（图7）。

图7 村落生产生活景观

5 结语

在一定地域内，特定的人居环境模式是多种因素相互作用的结果，不同的自然环境和社会生产方式对人居环境的建设有不同的影响。传统村落人居环境营建最重要的特征是与自然和谐统一以及关注人的基本需求，其"天人合一"的生态和谐智慧、"因利而为"的生态发展智慧以及"避险防灾"的生态安全智慧等营建思想与自然生态环境和人类社会生产生活模式紧密相关。因此，处理好村落人居环境建设与自然、与人的关系，达到"人与自然和谐互融"，是新时期传统村落保护与发展的工作重点，也是新农村生态可持续建设的重要准则。我国传统村落的保护与建设、村落人居环境的营建需要向系统化、自然化、经济化、人性化转型。

附

基金名称：重庆市科研创新项目，项目名称：山地城市高密度建成环境热舒适度模拟研究，编号：CYS16004。

The Ecological Wisdom on the Construction of the Human Settlements for the Traditional Village

Zeng Wei, Zhu Wenwen

(Faculty of Architecture and Urban Planning, Chongqing University)

Abstract: The traditional village is a typical example of the rural area in the process of the historical development. It's construction involves the location and shape of the village, overall layout, construction and the production of the villagers, safety and disaster prevention, etc. It is a process for adapting to nature, using nature and remodeling nature. The author discusses the ecological wisdom on the construction of the human settlements for the traditional village from the harmony between man and nature, the using with the nature and the disaster prevention. It not only provides the way for the protection and continuation of the traditional villages, but also has a beneficial influence on the ecological, sustainable construction for human settlements of the new countryside.

Keywords: Traditional village, The construction of the human settlements, Ecological wisdom

参考文献

[1] 吴良镛. 人居环境科学导论 [M].

[2] 王惠犬先生. 阳宅十书 [M].

[3] 谢浩范, 朱迎平. 管子全译（下册）[M]. 贵州人民出版社, 2009.

[4] 杨贵庆, 蔡一凡. 传统村落总体布局的自然智慧和社会语义 [J]. 上海城市规划, 2016, 4: 9-16.

[5] 杨贵庆. 我国传统聚落空间整体性特征及其社会学意义 [J]. 同济大学学报：社会科学版, 2014, 3.

[6] 王薇, 温泉. 多维角度下传统聚落的人居环境阐释——以赣北地区传统聚落为例 [J]. 西部人居环境学刊, 2016, 31（6）: 97-100.

[7] 郭妍. 传统村落人居环境营造思想及其当代启示研究 [D]. 西安建筑科技大学, 2011.

[8] 肖路遥, 周国华, 唐承丽等. 改革开放以来我国乡村聚落研究述评 [J]. 西部人居环境学刊, 2016, 31（6）: 79-85.

[9] 曾卫, 袁芬. 从生物气候学的角度解读川东山地传统民居的设计语汇 [J]. 南方建筑, 2014, 2: 96-103.

[10] 吴越. 地质生态视角下小气候对山地城镇设计的影响研究——以四川省汉源县九襄镇为例 [D]. 重庆大学, 2015.

中美城市居住区步行友好性比较研究——武汉与奥斯汀的六个居住区实证研究

彭 雷

（华中科技大学建筑与城市规划学院）

摘 要：源于美国的以小汽车为导向、忽视步行的居住区规划对中国产生了全面的影响。本文分别研究了中国武汉市的三个典型居住区和美国奥斯汀的三个典型居住区的步行友好性现状，从三个影响步行友好性的因素进行分析比较，首先比较两个城市居住区步行友好性在100多年来的发展变化，再比较两个城市居住区步行友好性的异同。最后，论文试图总结中国居住区步行友好性建设需要从美国吸取的教训，并提出建设中国可持续发展理念下步行友好的居住区设计策略。

关键词：居住区步行友好性，比较研究，武汉市，奥斯汀市

1 全球城市步行友好的发展趋势

美国从20世纪30年代就拉开了居住郊区化序幕，这种完全依赖小汽车的发展模式对社会各方面利益的损害极为严重。近年一系列的研究提供了越来越多的证据（Ewing, 2003; Handy, 2002; Sallis, 2004），证明步行友好的住区不仅能提高房产价值，还能减少住区犯罪、促进健康、鼓励住区公民的参与意识。美国社会开始意识到步行已不再是虚无的可持续发展理念，而是切实保持社会前进的动力。

然而，源于美国的居住区规划理念对中国城市交通与居住区规划都产生了全面影响，尤其在20世纪90年代之后，这种影响的负面效应越发凸显。本文拟对20世纪以来的中国城市居住区典型发展阶段的步行友好性的现状与同时期美国居住区的发展现状做一横向比较，总结美国城市居住区步行友好的特点，及其对中国居住区的影响。

2 研究内容与数据来源

2.1 研究重点

要建设步行友好的住区，对步行友好性的衡量成了相关研究的重要基础。虽然学界对其定义还未完全统一，但西方国家已开展了部分理论研究和实践工作。TERRI J.PIKORA（2006）等人的研究得出，与步行交通出行强烈相关的是道路连通性、服务设施的直达性；相比之下，与道路安全性、街道美学等因素的相关性稍弱一些。Eva Leslie（2007）等人的研究显示，步行出行与住区的土地混合利用程度显著相关。陈泳（2012）有关上海轨道交通站点周围街区的宜步行性研究得出：不同性能步行环境的满意度与步行便捷性（道路绕行率低）最相关；其次是微观步行环境。

综合多方面研究结论,对居住区步行友好性产生决定作用的首先是城市形态方面的因素,其次是微观步行环境。本文拟重点研究与城市形态有关的三个要素来讨论中美两国城市居住区的步行友好性现状。①道路连通性,本文重点讨论道路密度、交叉口密度和街区平均长度等反映道路连通性的指标。②公共设施直达性,本文选择与居民每天必要出行的相关公交站点计算公共设施覆盖半径和绕行情况,其中到达公共设施的绕行情况采取计算路线直接性比率PRD(Pedestrian Route Directness)来衡量。PRD是出发点到目的地的实际距离与出发点至目地直线距离之间的比值,PRD越大则绕路越多(图1)。③居住区的土地混合利用程度。

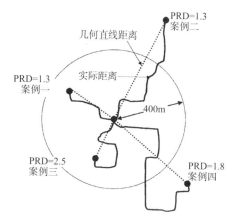

图1 FRD示意图

资料来源:Todd A. Randall, Brian W. Baetz. Evaluating pedestrian connectivity for suburban sustainability[J]. Journal of Urban Planning And Development. March 2001: 2-15.

2.2 研究对象

本文分别选择湖北省武汉市和得克萨斯州奥斯汀市两个城市作为比较研究对象,主要基于两点原因,首先,两个城市分别具有两国现代城市居住发展的典型特征;第二,从数据的获取方面,笔者可获得两个城市较为详细的GIS和CAD数据,便于开展研究工作。

中国现代城市居住建筑发展经历了6个阶段,其中有三个大发展阶段,分别为:①19世纪末20世纪初的现代城市住宅建设起始阶段,以城市低层里弄和多层公寓为主;②20世纪50年代,中国"一五"时期全面向苏联学习阶段,以大型工厂的工人新村建设为主;③20世纪90年代至今,社会主义市场经济阶段,全面推进试点小区示范工作以及住宅商品化。本文分别选择三个典型

图2 武汉市三个居住区分布图

居住区作为这三个大发展时期的代表。其中,汉口原租界区的2.24km²范围作为第一阶段的代表,简称A片区;其特点是以老式里分住宅为主。武汉钢铁公司生活区钢花新村作为第二阶段的代表,面积15.5km²,简称B片区;其特点是道路主次分明,由方格路网围合成的街区一般在8hm²左右,称为"街坊"。武汉南湖新城作为第三阶段的代表,面积12.5km²,简称C片区;呈现大街区宽马路、配套不足就业与居住分离等"卧城"特征(图2)。

在此需要指出的是,由于中国城市居住区内的居住单元多以封闭围合的住宅小区或居住街坊形式呈现,而不是像美国居住区多为开放式住区,为了更深入地比较研究两国居住区步行环境的差异,本文在A、B、C三个居住区中各选取三个完整独立的居住单元进行研究,其中A片区分别为坤厚里(A1)、三德里(A2)、汉润里(A3);B片区分别为8街坊(B1)、110街坊(B2)、115街坊(B3);C片区分别为宝安花园(C1)、中央花园(C2)、松涛苑(C3)(图3~图5)。

美国早期多数城市的道路建设都可追溯到1683年的费城方格网城市规划。20世纪30年代开始,为了应对城市中心区域人口密集、卫生堪忧的状况,联邦住宅管理局FHA(Federal Housing Administration)鼓励居民迁往郊区住宅。联邦住宅管理局通过政策导向、贷款优惠、制定规范等一系列措施对居住区规划推荐等级路网、曲线型、尽端路(Cul De Sac)。这种道路形式被认为可以活跃住宅区形态结构,减少穿越交通,进而减少事故并提供安静安全的郊区居住形态。在郊区化发展80多年间,

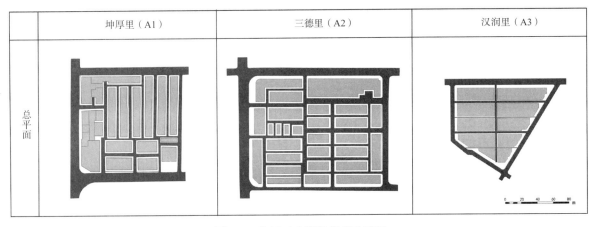

图 3　A 片区三个研究案例总平面

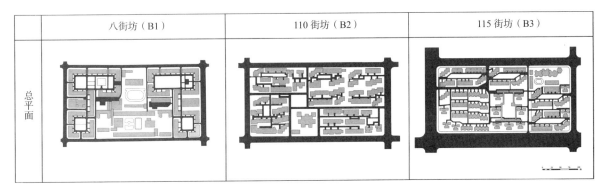

图 4　B 片区三个研究案例总平面

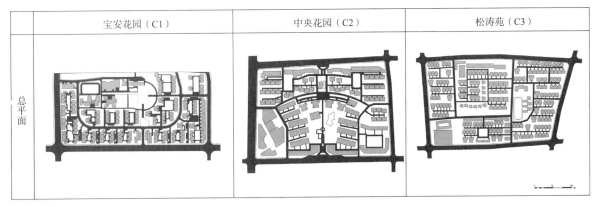

图 5　C 片区三个研究案例总平面

各地呈现出曲线形尽端式的毫无地方特征的高度相似的居住区形态。本文选择奥斯汀分别建于 20 世纪初期、中期的三个典型居住进行对比研究。

Hyde park 是奥斯汀最早经过规划的居住区（简称 HP），典型的小尺度方格路网体系，以独户住宅为主，零星分布一些日杂商店和餐馆，面积 2.24km^2。Hancock 住区（简称 HA），面积 1.77km^2，建于 20 世纪初期，经过 60 年代的规划改造，建设了占据一个街区的大型销品茂（shopping mall），成为混合了小尺度方格网街区和大尺度购物街区的居住区。Northwest Hills 住区建于 20 世纪 50 年代后期（简称 NH），面积 15km^2，是典型的郊区居住区大街区、曲线型尽端路和集中在一个大街区的购物广场（图 6）。

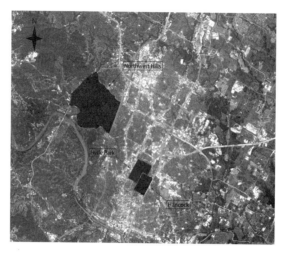

图6 奥斯汀三个居住区分布图

3 调查结果与分析

3.1 道路连通性比较

3.1.1 道路密度

两个城市六个居住区道路密度比较　　　　表1

	A	B	C	HP	HA	NH
总面积	2.24	15.5	12.5	2.24	1.77	15
道路密度	14.5	8.9	5.6	15.6	17.5	9.5

两个城市在20世纪初期的住区，都采用小街区方格路网形式，道路密度比较接近，连通性比较好（表1）。50年代开始分化，武汉的B片区较之A片区道路密度下降了59%，C片区继续了下降的趋势。按照中国《城市道路交通规划设计规范》GB 50220—95规定，大城市支路以上级道路总密度为 5.4~7.1km/km^2。B、C两个片区的道路密度都已达到规范规定的下限要求。众所周知，美国郊区化居住区是以小汽车为导向而设计的低密度路网形态，而武汉50年代以后的居住区道路密度甚至低于奥斯汀郊区化居住区NH，这说明中国的道路交通规范受到美国的影响，是在以小汽车为导向的规划思想影响下设定，并深刻影响了20世纪后半叶以后的城市道路规划（图7、图8）。

根据《城市居住区规划设计规范》GB 50180—93 第2.0.8和第8.0.1.2规定，居住区级道路相当于城市支路，小区内道路不算入城市路网。这就造成了中国住宅小区内的道路系统与居住区的道路系统相互隔离，自成一体。事实上，中国城市住宅小区内大量道路仅被小区内居民使用甚至有些被作为停车场，浪费了大量的道路资源。

以下将武汉市三个片区内所有街区内部路网计算进去，比较两者的差异（图9）。可以看出，加入街区内部路网后，三个片区的道路密度相差并不大。这说明，B、C片区实际可利用的道路路网总长并不少，但由于被封闭在各个不同的住宅区内，无法对增加城市道路密度作出贡献。90年代建设的C片区问题更加严重，小区内部的道路利用率不高，这就导致90年代后的居住区道路密度低于美国郊区化居住区的道路密度。

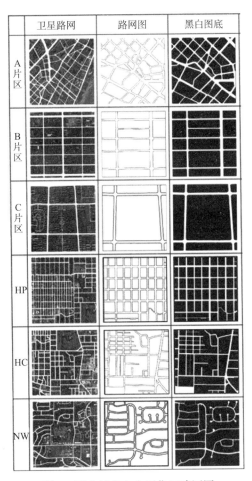

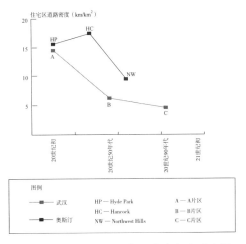

图 8 两个城市六个居住区道路密度对比图

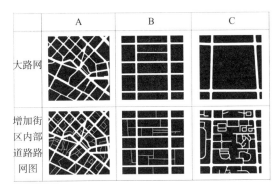

图 7 两个城市六个居住区路网图

图 9 武汉市三个居住区增加了街区内道路的路网图

3.1.2 交叉口密度

道路交叉口密度指标可以很好地衡量道路的连通性，交叉口密度越大则道路连通性越好（图10、图11）。

通过测算，中美两个城市 20 世纪初的居住区道路交叉口密度高于 50 年代后的居住区。

从十字交叉口百分比来看，奥斯汀 20 世纪初的居住区 HY、HA 为方格路网形态，但丁字路较多；居住区 NH 则为曲线形尽端路网形态，道路连通性较差。武汉的三个居住区都呈现以方格路网为主的路网形态，B，C 两个片区更是整齐划一的方格路网形态，道路连通性较好。

由于中国住宅小区内的道路系统与居住区的道路系统相互隔离，自成一体，以下比较一下武汉市三个居住区内的九个住宅小区的道路形态。

从图中（图 12~图 14）可以看出，90 年代后建设的 C 片区的住宅小区，总体呈现出环形路和尽端路增多的趋势，零碎杂乱，连通性差，且与小区外城市路网形态无明显衔接关系，形成了内部自我封闭、自成一体的道路格局。这是由于 90 年代住建部推荐试点小区的道路规划规划应遵循"顺而不穿、通而不畅"的原则，曲曲折折的主路迫使驶入小区的车辆减速，达到安全与安静的目的。后经由 1993 年发布的《城市居住区规划设计规范》GB 50180—93 通过法律条文的形式固化下来。可以看出，中国住宅小区内部的道路系统受到了美国郊区化居住区的影响。但美国郊区这种曲线尽端式路网是居住区级道路，相当于城市支路。美国所谓的"减少穿越交通"，是指避免笔直的城市快速路或高速路穿越居住区。中国实际上是将美国郊区居住区的道路系统搬进了住宅小区内部，道路等级与居住规模尺度都相去甚

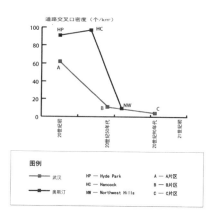
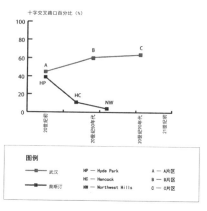

图10 两个城市居住区交叉口与十字交叉口比较图

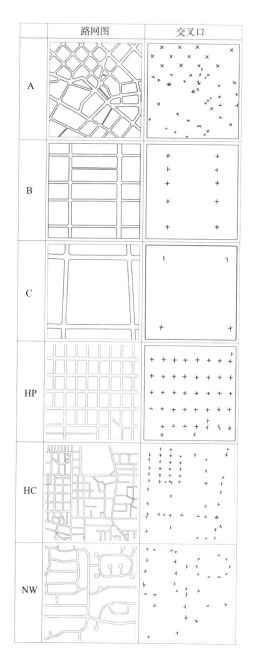

图11 两个城市六个居住区道路交叉口对比

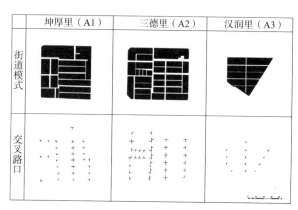

图12 A片区三个研究案例街道模式图

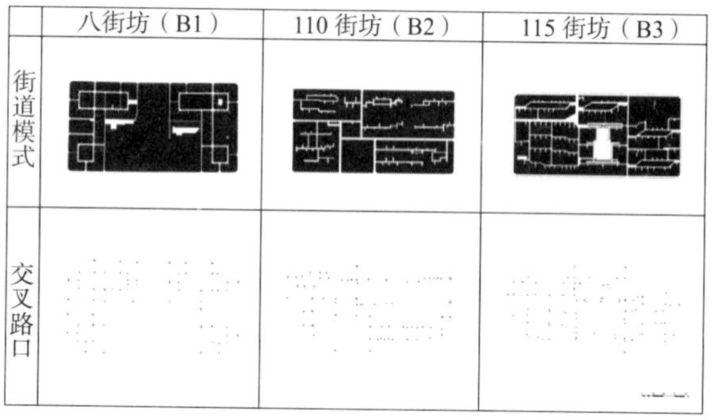

图13 B片区三个研究案例街道模式图

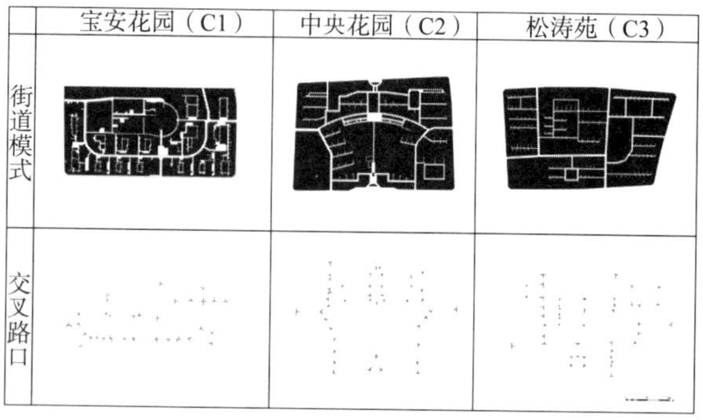

图14 C片区三个研究案例街道模式图

远,其直接的后果就是中国城市居住区中支路的缺失和住宅小区内大量道路的闲置浪费。最后呈现出大的方格路网+小区内曲线形尽端路网的混合模式、路网形态相互割裂的局面。

3.1.3 街区平均长度

两个城市六个居住区街区平均长度对比　　　表2

	A	B	C	HP	HA	NH
总面积（hm²）	2.24	15.5	12.5	2.24	1.77	15
街区平均长度（m）	151	318	415	116	129	-

从表2街区平均长度来看,两个城市20世纪初的居住区都是小尺度街区,街区平均长度都在100~150m之间。武汉的居住区街区平均长度在50年代后逐渐加大,90年代的居住区街区平均长度甚至超过400m。由于中国居住区规范倾向于将住宅小区划分为有完整边界的独立个体,并规定城市支路不得穿越小区内部,那么一个住宅小区就是一个街区,由此我们就可以将居住小区的规模与街区平均长度联系起来。以下讨论居住区规范对小区用地规模的规定。

《城市居住区规划设计规范》GB 50180—93表3.0.3明确规定了人均居住区用地控制指标,条文2.0.2规定居住小区人口规模在10000~15000人之间。综合以上条款,笔者将武汉所属Ⅲ类气候区的人均用地面积,按照居住小区人口数的下限10000人,计算出相应的居住小区用地规模,得到表3。

根据《城市居住区规划设计规范》GB 50180—93计算得出的居住小区用地规模　　　表3

层数	人均用地面积（m²）	居住小区规模（hm²）
低层	28~40	28~40
多层	19~26	19~26
中高层	15~22	15~22
高层	10~15	10~15

资料来源：根据《城市居住区规划设计规范》相关条例计算自绘。

从表中数据可以看到,居住小区的用地规模最小也达到10hm²,最大的竟达到40hm²。相应的,武汉90年代以后的住宅小区规模受到居住区规范的影响,出现了20hm²、40hm²,甚至50hm²的大型住宅小区。20 hm²的住宅小区对应的街区平均长度就是440m。由此可见,中国的居住区规范和道路交通规范对90年代以后形成的大街区、稀路网的城市形态起到了决定性作用。

3.2 公共服务设施直达性

本文对公交站点的可达性测量,采用赫斯（Hess,1997）的方法,计算公交站点400~800m范围内的可达性PRD值,步骤为:a.以居住区的主要公交站点为圆心,分别以400m和800m为半径划定圆圈;b.将圆圈均分为8个象限,在每个象限内随机选取一条与圆圈相交的道路,设交点为终点;c.从圆心出发,取最短的路线到达终点,得到最短路径的长度(L1,L2,L3…L8);d.计算上述路线的平均长度L=(L1+L2+…L8)/8,以L分别除以400和800,即可得到400~800m范围内的可达性PRD值。

PRD的结果显示,奥斯汀建于20世纪初期的两个居住区绕行率都不高,在1.2左右;郊区化居住区绕行率较高,达到1.55。这一结果与赫斯（Hess,1997）和兰德尔（Randall,2001）的研究结果相似。赫斯对美国西雅图住宅区的对比研究中,测得老城中心区以小地块划分的方格路网住区PRD值为

1.2，在城市郊区以曲线型尽端路网为特点的住区 PRD 值达 1.7 以上。同样，兰德尔对加拿大汉密尔顿住宅区的对比研究中，测得两个以小地块划分的传统住区的 PRD 为 1.3 左右，两个郊区蔓延式住区的 PRD 为 1.8 左右（图 15）。

武汉的三个居住区 PRD 值都不高，在 1.2 左右。这说明方格路网形态的绕路情况都不严重，即使是大尺度街区，PRD 值都不高。但武汉市居住区内的居住小区情况又如何呢。笔者分别测量了三个居住区的 9 个居住单元，结果显示，以鱼骨状街道为骨架的 A 片区居住单元和以围合式大院为骨架的 B 片区居住单元，其 PRD 值在 1.2 左右，绕路情况不严重。而以曲线形尽端路为骨架的 C 片区居住单元，其 PRD 值在 1.5 以上，与奥斯汀的郊区居住区相似。因此可以得出，武汉市居住区的绕路情况主要体现在住宅小区内部。近年来住宅小区规模不断扩大，其内部的步行距离加大，更加重了绕路情况。

3.3 土地混合利用程度

本文使用以下的数学公式来进行量化评估。

$$MUI = -\frac{\sum_k (P_k ln P_k)}{lnN}$$

MUI——土地混合利用程度指标
N——土地利用种类的数量
K——土地利用的种类
P——各土地利用种类所占比重

此指标结果为 0 ~ 1，数值越接近 0，则表明土地混合利用程度越低；数值越接近 1，则土地混合利用程度越高。取对数的意义在于：某一项土地种类所占比例越大，则其对土地混合利用多样性的贡献越小，数值也越小；如某一项土地所占比例超过 50%，则对多样性的影响更大。本文选取四种土地利用类型进行比较：居住用地、商业用地、教育用地和办公用地，则 MUI 不会超过 0.25，即指标结果均在 0 ~ 0.25 之间。

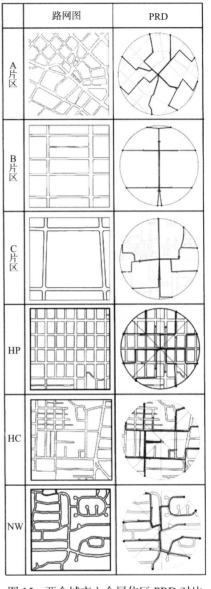

图 15 两个城市六个居住区 PRD 对比图（作者绘制）

结果显示，奥斯汀的 HA 土地混合利用程度最高，达到 0.22。这是因为 Hancock 内商业设施和办公设施较为完备。HP 由于只有分散的小卖部，商业设施用地的比例少于 HA，而居住用地比例较大，导致其土地混合利用程度偏低，为 0.19。郊区居住区 NH 土地混合利用程度最低，只有 0.17，土地混合利用程度最低（图 16）。

武汉市三个历史时期的居住区其土地混合利用程度逐渐降低，分别为 0.23，0.19，0.17。20 世纪 90 年代新城与奥斯汀的郊区住宅区一样，单一功能的居住用地所占比重过大。同时也说明武汉市在 50 年代以后的城市建设中都是遵循的现代主义功能分区规划思想，不重视土地混合利用。这一思想反映于中国的居住区规范可以看出，将居住区作为一个独立的单位大院，以居住为主，并配套少量的服务设施。《城市居住区规划设计规范》GB 50180—93 第 3.0.2.2 条规定的居住区用地指标中，居住用地比例超过 50%，这直接影响了居住区的步行友好性，并有向美国这类"车轮上国家"看齐的趋势，这将对可持续性的城市建设构成严重挑战。

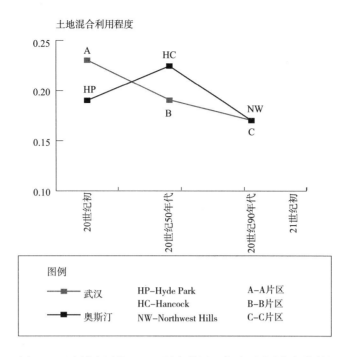

图16 两个城市居住区土地混合利用程度对比图（作者绘制）

4 结论与建议

本文采取量化评估的方法，对武汉市和奥斯汀市有代表性的居住区进行了步行友好性的比较研究，大致可以得到以下几点认识。

4.1 道路的连通性

第二次世界大战前中美两国城市居住区道路都是适宜步行的。美国在第二次世界大战后转变为以小汽车为导向的交通体系，郊区居住区的道路连通性急剧降低。在中国，新中国成立后经历了两次变化，第一次，20世纪50年代受到现代主义城市规划的影响以及"邻里单元"的居住模型的影响，道路密度开始降低，街区尺度增加了一倍，达到300m。第二次，90年代以后迎来社会主义市场经济发展时期，道路密度继续下降，街区平均长度放大到400m左右。从增强道路连通性的角度，中国的城市居住区须尽早摆脱封闭的"独立王国"的现状，从修改居住区规范入手，改变住宅小区过于封闭和规模过大的现状，使住宅小区内的道路与城市路网有机衔接，并统筹计算入城市路网之中以增加城市道路密度。

4.2 公共设施的直达性

美国郊区化居住区的路网形态导致绕路情况严重，增加了实际步行距离。中国90年代以后的城市居住区主要呈现大的方格路网+小区内曲线形尽端路网的混合模式，居民的绕路情况主要集中在住宅小区内部。由于居住区规范规定的住宅小区的规模偏大，对近年来的大型住宅小区建设起到了直接的引导作用，各地都出现了很多30hm^{2}甚至40hm^{2}的住宅小区，加剧了小区内的绕路情况。因此，中国居住区规范须及时调整住宅小区规模过大引起的步行不友好状况。

4.3 土地的混合利用

美国的郊区化居住区土地混合利用程度较低，主要是受到"邻避症候群"的思潮影响，导致居住区的功能过于单一纯化。中国现行规范标准仍然延续着现代主义城市规划理论的影响，将居住区作为一个独立的单位大院，以居住为主，致使用地性质过于单一；居住区配套公建并未与城市的公共服务与商业服务用地统筹安排，导致土地混合利用程度较低，与美国郊区化居住区接近。因此，中国须适度降低居住区中居住用地的用地比例，根据国情鼓励公交导向型的混合用地模式；调整居住区用地分类中的配套服务设施用地，使之与城市用地中的公共管理与公共服务用地、商业服务设施用地统筹安排。

综上所述，美国当代居住区是在现代主义城市规划思想下发展而来，强调功能分区和以小汽车为导向的发展方向，形成了低密度蔓延的郊区化居住模式。这些错误做法延续 80 多年，使得美国城市居住区不再适于步行。中国当代城市居住区不仅受到现代主义城市规划思想影响，亦受到美国郊区化居住区规划影响，美国这种低密度郊区化发展模式被中国运用到高密度城市形态中，造成中国城市近 30 年间新建居住区步行友好性急剧下降。如今美国社会上下已充分认识到回归步行友好居住区的紧迫性并已行动起来，中国城市更须及时认识到近 30 年所走弯路，尽快向步行友好的居住区方向转变。

Comparative Study on Neighborhood Walkability between Chinese and American Cities——Empirical Study on Six Neighborhoods in Wuhan and Austin

Peng Lei

(School of Architecture and Urban Planning, Huazhong University of Science and Technology)

Abstract: The car-oriented with ignoring walking neighborhood mode from America affected contemporary Chinese residential district deeply. In order to learn the lessons from the American car-oriented neighborhood, the paper tries to compare three typical neighborhoods in Wuhan, China, and three neighborhoods in Austin, USA, to analyze three important factors of walkability, that are street connectivity, accessibility and mixed land use. The paper first evaluates the neighborhood walkability separately, and then compares their similarity and difference between Wuhan city and Austin city. As a conclusion, the Paper attempts to highlight what lessons shall be learnt from America to benefit China's neighborhood walkability and proposes such design strategies of living quarters that can promote the neighborhood walkability in the atmosphere of China's sustainable development.

Keywords: Neighborhood walkability, Comparative study, Wuhan city, Austin city

参考文献

[1]　Far D. Sustainable Urbanism[M]. John Wiley & Sons, Inc, 2008.

[2] Leslie E, Neil C, Lawrence F et al. Walkability of local communities: Using geographic information systems to objectively assess relevant environmental attributes[J]. Health & Place. 2007, 13: 111 ~ 122.

[3] Ewing R, Schmid T. L, Killingsworth. R, et al. Relationship between urban sprawl and physical activity, Obesity, and Morbidity[J]. American Journal of Health Promotion.2003, 18（1）.47-57.

[4] Gallin N. Pedestrian Friendliness: Guidelines for Assessing Pedestrian Level of Service[R/OL]. 2001.

[5] Handy S L, Boarnet M G, Ewing R, et al. How the Built Environment Affects Physical Activity: Views from urban planning[J]. Am J Prev Med. 2002, 23（2）: 64-73.

[6] Hess P M. Measures of Connectivity [Streets: Old Paradigm, New Investment]. Places, 1997.

[7] Isaacs, R. The urban picturesque: An aesthetic experience of urban pedestrian places[J]. Journal of Urban Design. 2000, 2: 145-180.

[8] James F Sallis a, Lawrence D Frank b, Brian E Saelens. Active transportation and physical activity: opportunities for collaboration on transportation and public health research[J]. Transportation Research Part A. 2004, 38: 249–268.

[9] Jeffery C. Springer. A qualitative study of the connection between the built environment and public health. Morgan state university, 2006.

[10] Levine J, Lawrence D Frank. Transportation and land-use preferences and residents' neighborhood choices: the sufficiency of compact development in the Atlanta region[J]. Transpotation. 2007, 34: 255-274.

[11] Lamont J. Where do people walk? The impacts of urban form on travel behavior and neighborhood livability. D. University of California at Berkeley, 2001.

[12] Southworth M. Designing the Walkable City[J]. Jurnal of urban planning and development. 2005, 12: 246-256.

[13] Pikora T, et al. Devloping a reliable audit instrument to measure the physical environment for physical activity[J]. American Journal of Preventive Medicine. 2002, 23: 187-194.

[14] Powell K E. Land Use, the Built Environment, and Physical Activity[J]. American Journal OF Preventive Medicine, 2005.

[15] 陈泳,何宁. 轨道交通站地区宜步行环境及影响因素分析——上海市12个生活住区的实证研究 [J]. 城市规划学刊. 2012，6: 96-104.

[16] 邓浩,宋峰,蔡海英. 城市肌理与可步行性——城市步行空间基本特征的形态学解读 [J]. 建筑学报. 2013，6: 8-13.

隔热涂料在建筑中应用的节能评价方法探讨

范宏武

（上海市建筑科学研究院）

摘　要：南方地区建筑节能的重点是降低夏季空调能耗，而太阳辐射是造成建筑夏季空调负荷的主要影响因素，隔热涂料被认为是有效控制太阳辐射的主要技术措施之一。为评价隔热涂料的节能效果，国家和行业相关标准提出了传热系数修正法或等效热阻评价法。但研究结果显示，该方法无法反映客观隔热涂料的作用机理，也无法有效解释隔热涂料的实际节能贡献，反而给人们对建筑节能技术路线产生认识误区。本文从隔热涂料的实际作用机理出发，通过实验测试与理论分析方法对隔热涂料在空调状态下的节能贡献进行了系统分析。结果显示，（1）采用隔热涂料后建筑墙体热阻或传热系数变化不明显；（2）隔热涂料主要通过降低建筑外墙内外表面的温度差来实现节能目的。而基于研究结果，本文提出了评价隔热涂料节能贡献应采用温差修正法的概念。

关键词：隔热涂料，节能指标，评价方法

1　引言

在我国南方地区，降低夏季空调能耗是建筑节能的重点任务。以上海为例，建筑夏季制冷能耗约为冬季采暖能耗的两倍，因此夏季隔热措施对于降低南方地区建筑能耗起到至关重要的作用。

隔热涂料是一种近年来发展的新型功能型涂料，其在可见光和近远红外区对太阳辐射有较高的发射率，将其用于建筑物的表面可达到降低建筑物内部温度，减少空调等能源消耗的目的，因此是建筑节能的重点发展领域之一。

为了促进建筑外墙隔热涂料的应用，我国陆续出版的相关国家和行业标准提出采用传热系数修正法或附加热阻法评价隔热涂料的节能贡献，为隔热涂料的市场应用起到了积极促进作用。但理论研究和试验测试结果显示，传热系数修正法或附加热阻法无法客观反映隔热涂料的节能作用机理，不能有效解释隔热涂料的实际节能贡献，反而使人们对建筑节能技术路线的理解产生认识误区。

本文从隔热涂料的实际作用机理出发，通过实验测试和理论分析方法对隔热涂料在空调状态下的节能贡献进行了系统分析。结果发现，采用隔热涂料后建筑墙体的传热系数或热阻变化并不明显，而其外表面温度则得到明显降低，引起室内外表面温度差减少，建筑能耗随之降低。因此，本文从传热理论角度出发，提出了隔热涂料节能贡献评价方法——温差修正法。

2　现有隔热涂料节能贡献标准评价方法介绍

根据国家标准《建筑用反射隔热涂料》GB/T 25261—2010[1]，采用反射隔热涂料后，建筑围护结构的热阻可按式（1）进行计算，

$$R_e = \left(\frac{1}{\varepsilon} - 1\right) \times (R+0.15) \tag{1}$$

式中：R_e——反射隔热涂料等效涂料热阻，$(m^2 \cdot ℃)/W$；

R——涂料基层墙体热阻，$(m^2 \cdot ℃)/W$；

ε——反射隔热涂料年传热修正值。

反射隔热涂料年传热修正值按式（2）计算，

$$\varepsilon = \frac{\varepsilon_s \sum h_s \Delta t_s + \varepsilon_w \sum h_w \Delta t_w}{\sum h_s \Delta t_s + \sum h_w \Delta t_w} \tag{2}$$

式中：$h_s(h_w)$——夏（冬）季空调（采暖）时间，h；

$\Delta t_s(\Delta t_w)$——夏（冬）季空调（采暖）温差，℃；

$\varepsilon_s(\varepsilon_w)$——夏（冬）季传热系数修正值，具体计算方法见参考文献[1]。

标准中指出，当太阳反射率和半球发射率为0.80时，南京地区等效涂料热阻可达（0.16～0.20）$(m^2 \cdot ℃)/W$，广州地区等效热阻为（0.15～0.28）$(m^2 \cdot ℃)/W$。

行业标准《建筑反射隔热涂料应用技术规程》JGJ 359—2015[2]中明确，当采用规定性指标进行节能设计时，外墙或屋面的传热系数应采用等效热阻，并按式（3）计算，

$$K' = \left(\frac{1}{R_{eq} + \frac{1}{K}}\right) \tag{3}$$

式中：K'——外墙或屋面使用建筑反射隔热涂料的传热系数，$W/(m^2 \cdot ℃)$；

K——外墙或屋面未使用建筑反射隔热涂料的传热系数，$W/(m^2 \cdot ℃)$；

R_{eq}——外墙或屋面使用建筑反射隔热涂料的等效热阻，$(m^2 \cdot ℃)/W$。

根据标准附录表C.0.1中的数据，当太阳反射率为0.7以上时，南京地区（夏热冬冷地区）等效热阻值为（0.19～0.40）$(m^2 \cdot ℃)/W$，广州地区（夏热冬暖地区南区）等效热阻可达（0.27～0.95）$(m^2 \cdot ℃)/W$。

但文献[3]中的测试结果却显示，隔热涂料本身导热系仅为0.0838 W/（W/(m·℃)），热阻附加并不明显。而文献[4]中对190砌块+35保温砂浆墙体传热系数的测试结果也显示，涂反射隔热涂料前后的传热系数分别为1.043 W/$(m^2 \cdot ℃)$和1.038 W/$(m^2 \cdot ℃)$，即采用隔热涂料后围护结构热阻没有发生明显变化。因此采用热阻附加或传热系数修正方法评价隔热涂料的节能贡献这种做法值得商榷。

3 隔热涂料节能贡献测试分析

为客观了解隔热涂料的实际作用机理，科学反映隔热涂料的节能贡献，课题组对隔热涂料的隔热性能进行了冬季、过渡季和夏季的性能测试。

测试过程中采用的隔热涂料与普通涂料光谱曲线如图1所示，测试平台如图2所示。图3～图6为冬季（2月）、过渡季（4月、6月）和夏季（8月）的隔热涂料使用时对建筑墙体表面温度和传热量的影响测试结果。

图3为冬季墙体温度和热流测试结果。从温度测试结果可知，与普通涂料相比，采用隔热涂料后墙体晴天时外表面温度有所降低，而阴天或晚上则变化不大。热流测试结果则显示，采用隔热涂料后进入室内热流减少。这有两种可能，一是隔热涂料引起墙体热阻增加，二是隔热涂料引起室内外传热温差降低。而晚上测试结果显示，无论是否采用隔热涂料，两者内外表面温差和热流都基本相同，说

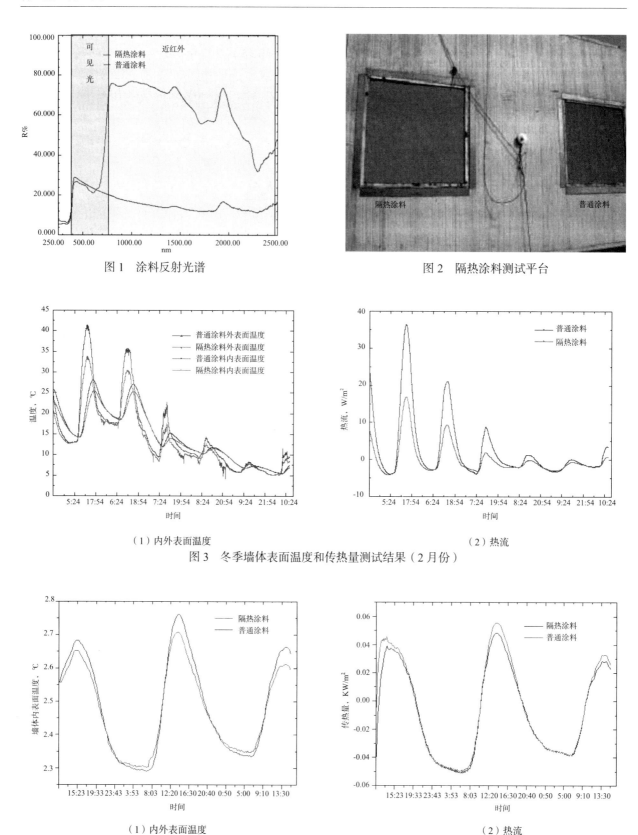

图1 涂料反射光谱

图2 隔热涂料测试平台

（1）内外表面温度 （2）热流

图3 冬季墙体表面温度和传热量测试结果（2月份）

（1）内外表面温度 （2）热流

图4 过渡季墙体表面温度和传热量测试结果（4月份）

明采用隔热涂料后墙体热阻并没有发生明显变化，因此造成进入室内热量的减少只能是使用隔热涂料后墙体内外表面温差变小引起的。

图4和图5为过渡季建筑墙体温度和热流测试结果。测试结果显示，过渡季隔热涂料对于外墙内

外表面温度差及热流几乎没有明显影响。

图6为夏季建筑墙体温度和热流测试结果。根据温度测试结果,夏季白天隔热涂料对建筑外墙外表面温度产生明显影响,因此墙体内外表面温度差明显降低,进入室内的热流也明显减少。而夜间温差和热流测试结果也再次证明隔热涂料并未引起墙体热阻的明显变化。

这说明,目前采用的隔热涂料节能贡献评价方法——传热系数修正或附加热阻法不符合隔热涂料的实际作用机理,也无法有效解释隔热涂料的实际贡献。

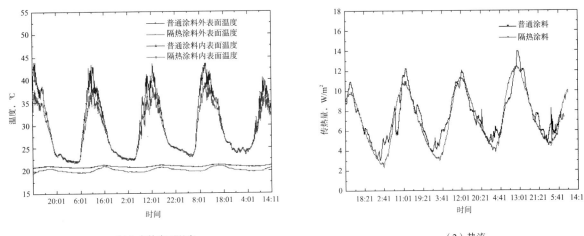

(1)内外表面温度　　　　　　　　　　　(2)热流

图5　过渡季墙体表面温度和传热量测试结果(6月份)

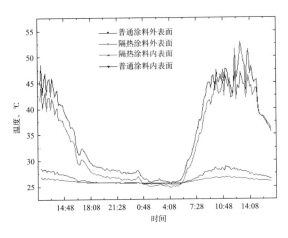 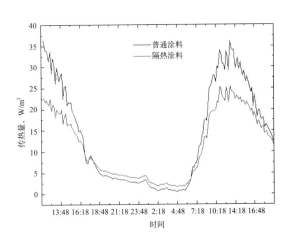

(1)内外表面温度　　　　　　　　　　　(2)热流

图6　夏季墙体表面温度和传热量测试结果(8月份)(作者自绘)

4　隔热涂料节能贡献评价方法研究

4.1　温度修正法的提出

为了弄清楚隔热涂料的作用机理,课题组通过分解外围护结构的传热过程进行了相应的理论分析。根据能量平衡原理,通过建筑墙体传入室内的热量可用式(4)计算,

$$Q = K\left(T_o + \frac{\rho I}{\alpha} - \frac{\varepsilon\sigma(T_w^4 - T_s^4)}{\alpha} - T_i\right) \tag{4}$$

式中：Q ——从室外通过墙体传入室内的热量，W/m²；
　　　K ——墙体传热系数，W/(m²·℃)；
　　　T_o ——室外空气温度，K；
　　　ρ ——墙体外表面太阳辐射吸收系数；
　　　I ——太阳辐射量，W/m²；
　　　α ——墙体外表面对流换热系数，W/(m²·℃)；
　　　ε ——墙体外表面发射率；
　　　σ ——玻尔兹曼常数；
　　　T_w ——墙体外表面温度，K；
　　　T_s ——天空温度，K；
　　　T_i ——室内空气温度，K。

根据上式，采用隔热涂料后墙体外表面的太阳辐射吸收系数和发射率将发生变化，造成括号内的数值即引起传热的势能——温差发生了变化，而非传热系数K。因此，如果引入温差修正系数[见式(5)]，则可有效解释隔热涂料的作用机理。

$$\Delta T = \frac{\rho I}{\alpha} - \frac{\varepsilon\sigma(T_w^4 - T_s^4)}{\alpha} \tag{5}$$

对于平屋面，

$$\Delta T = \frac{\rho I}{\alpha} - \frac{\varepsilon\sigma}{\alpha}\left(\frac{T_w}{100}\right)^4 (0.49 - 0.208\sqrt{e}) \tag{6}$$

对于外墙，

$$\Delta T = \frac{\rho I}{\alpha} - \frac{\varepsilon\sigma}{\alpha}\left(\frac{T_w}{100}\right)^4 (0.295 - 0.104\sqrt{e}) \tag{7}$$

式中：e ——室外空气水蒸气分压力，kPa。

4.2 温度修正法与附加热阻法的对比

为了更清楚地认识这两种处理方式存在的差异，课题组对三种情况下的温度场和传热量进行了数值模拟对比分析，即普通工况（吸收率为0.70，发射率为0.80）、隔热涂料工况（吸收率为0.20，发射率为0.80）和附加热阻处理工况（吸收率为0.70，发射率为0.80），附加热阻根据相关标准取值0.15（m²·K）/W，计算结果如图7~图8所示。

图7为三种工况下墙体冬季典型日失热量逐时情况。根据统计，普通工况下墙体热损失为727.15W/m²，隔热涂料工况下热损失为818.15W/m²，附加热阻法热损失为545.4W/m²。与普通工况相比，采用隔热涂料后墙体实际热损失增加12.5%，而采用附加热阻法则降低了25%，偏差明显。

图8为三种工况下墙体夏季典型日得热量逐时情况。根据统计，普通工况下墙体得热为410.47W/m²，隔热涂料工况下得热为211.58W/m²，附加热阻法的得热为211.58W/m²。与普通工况相比，采用隔热涂料后墙体实际得热减少51%，而采用附加热阻法则降低了25%，偏差同样明显。

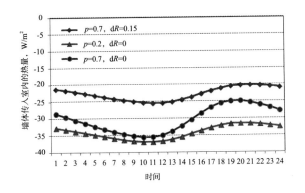

图7 不同处理方式冬季得热对比（作者自绘）

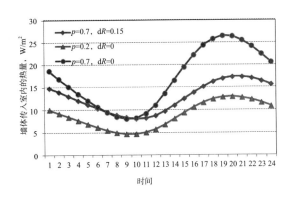

图8 不同处理方式夏季得热对比（作者自绘）

5 结论

本文通过对隔热涂料对建筑墙体全年影响的测试分析和理论研究，得出如下结论：

隔热涂料可明显降低建筑夏季空调能耗的原因在于其有效降低了建筑墙体内外表面温差，而墙体的传热系数或热阻并没有明显变化，因此认为采用传热系数修正法或附件热阻法并不能有效反映隔热涂料的节能贡献，而采用温差修正法则相对合理。

致谢

该研究受到上海市优秀技术带头人计划"近零能耗居住建筑节能理论体系研究（16XD1422500）"的资助，在此表示感谢。

Discussion on the Energy Saving Evaluation Method of Heat Insulating Coatings Used in the Buildings

Fan Hongwu

(Shanghai Research Institute of Building Sciences)

Abstract: To control the solar radiation is the key measurement to reduce the energy consumption of the air conditioning in Hot Summer Zone of China, and using Thermal Insulation Coating is considered as one of the effective method. In order to evaluate the energy saving result of Thermal Insulation Coatings, the Heat Transfer Coefficient Correction Method or Equivalent Thermal Resistance Evaluation Method is proposed by the national relative standards. However, the studies show that the above method cannot explain the heat transfer mechanism and the actual saving contribution very well when using the Thermal Insulation Coating, but make people have a misunderstanding about the energy-efficient concept. In this paper, the energy saving contribution of Thermal Insulation Coatings is analyzed under the air conditioning conditions. The results show that: (1) UsingThermal Insulation Coatings does not change the heat transfer coefficient of building envelop significantly, and (2) The energy saving of Thermal Insulation Coatings achieved mainly by reducing the temperature difference between the outer surface and the inner one of building exterior walls, and increasing the solar radiation absorption coefficient can get more energy saving than that of the emissivity. At last, the Temperature Difference Correction Method is proposed as a reasonable approach to evaluate the energy saving by using the Thermal Insulation Coatings in this paper.

Keywords: Thermal insulation coatings, Energy saving index, Evaluation method

参考文献

[1] GB/T 25261—2010 建筑用反射隔热涂料 [S]. 中华人民共和国国家质量监督检验检疫总局，中国国家标准化管理委员会，2010.

[2] JGJ/T359—2015 热反射涂料应用技术规程 [S]. 中华人民共和国住房和城乡建设部，2015.

[3] 蔡玉斌，吴国坚，金骏. 薄层隔热涂料导热系数测定方法的研究 [J]. 新型建筑材料，2011，4: 89-91.

[4] 徐峰，蒋宇平. 建筑反射隔热涂料隔热保温性能研究 [J]. 上海涂料，2011，49（6）: 42-46.

Building E-pathy City[①] from an Age-friendly Unit

Chang Ping Hung Wallace
(Faculty of Architecture, University of Hong Kong)

Abstract: The discourse of localizing age-friendly city of Hong Kong is challenging the policy-makers' institutional mindset in addressing the pressing issue of ageing population. Starting from designing a single unit in public housing for the elderly use, the initiative generates a holistic approach to involve an interdisciplinary collaboration as well as the engagement of the elderly. As an evolving process, this social innovation practice is building a grounded foundation for the construct of E-pathy City.

Keywords: E-pathy city, Age-friendly single unit, Social innovation

1 Introduction

Under the prevalence of the Western "scientific" mindset, like many developed countries in the West, Hong Kong SAR, China, as well as Mainland China and some other neighboring countries in Asia share a similar institutional response to the challenges of the aging society. The current institutional response is dominated by pragmatic, quantifying and hence de-humanizing approaches, which are assumed antidotes to the aging problems. Under this framework, elderly people are objectified, and they fall into a dualistic and opposite relationship with the society. This dualism has a far-reaching and negative effect on the making of policies, including the retirement protection, healthcare and welfare services, housing development and urban planning. In view of it, medical humanities, history, sociology and other disciplines in social sciences could certainly contribute to proposing refreshing perspectives and insights to the public policy discourse on aging society.

A renewed interest in and re-search for a holistic worldview, which could definitely benefit the understanding of aging issues and the corresponding social practices, becomes a new trend in various research fields, including philosophy, anthropology, architecture, history, social innovation, medicine, sociology and so on. In this perspective, researches on the making of places from a humanistic perspective become one of the key topics in sociological and architectural studies. They reinstate the importance of the relational aspect of space and the corresponding valuable everyday experiences, contributing to the creation of an empathic society, in which elderly are not isolated objects, but indispensable subjects of the whole. This paper is to illustrate this humanistic perspective through an interdisciplinary collaboration from the practice of designing an age-friendly unit towards the theoretical construct of the E-pathy City.

[①] E-pathy City is a concept developed by the author to integrate the faculties of Green, Art and Elderly within a holistic framework to build up a human landscape whereby empathy is the cohesive synergy to resolve social conflicts and to share community resources.

2 Localizing Ageing Society in Hong Kong

The ageing population of Hong Kong is growing rapidly in the last decade and will become an imminent issue in the upcoming future. Before the closure of the demographic window by 2019, the government of Hong Kong has initiated researches and directives to ensure the society is well prepared to tackle this foreseeable challenge. Started from a crisis management perspective, these initiatives meant to collect data, probably with certain inclinations, for policy-makers to formulate corresponding policies to address the ageing society, are necessary but insufficient to bring along new thinking framework.

The inevitable fact, however, is that our city has been building without a long-term vision for people to age in place with comfort and convenience. While high density in the urban areas is efficient for communication, the spatial limitation, however, restricts the actualization of ageing-in-place. That probably explains why the ratio of elderly home residency is abnormally high in Hong Kong when the ordinary apartments are not spacious enough to allow intergenerational cohabitation[①]. It is even worse for Hong Kong is situating on hilly terrains where the disabled pedestrian movements are through an array of mechanical means. As these physical conditions are setting hurdles to realize the ideal age-friendly city that the Western countries are promoting, what, then, should we do to respond to this call for age-friendliness within our given constraints? Would the construct of E-pathy City contribute to design both physical and social environments to address the ageing-in-place issue?

3 Nestling Elderly Concerns at 4 Levels

Should we rethink the general conditions of our built environment where the verticality of workplaces, residences and even entertainment venues is common and widely accepted as the way we work, live and play, it may be a hint for us to ponder on a possibility of program stacking and spatial interconnectivity. This said architecture of urban nestling is the conceptual framework that allows people to move and rest at ease in the city. The nestling idea is where the elderly find places to accommodate their needs of living, socializing and commuting within an affordable range and reachable distance. To anchor these places in the city, in the conditions of Hong Kong, is not an easy task, but should request a concerted effort from all walks of the society, namely, at levels of individual households, community neighborhoods, urban enclaves and social constructs.

If we perceive ageing spaces are inseparable from the overall social and urban networks, it may be reasonable to integrate these spaces as essential spatial components in the planning and design processes. The overall conceptual correlation of these spaces at different levels should carry a common theme that the universal design should treat the elderly respectfully with specificity. Seemingly contradictory, these qualities are not apparent but should be attained together with the end users, i.e. the elderly. The approach to understand the end users' need is essential for any architectural designs. However, when we are tackling the ageing population in Hong Kong, the target group may not be so obvious where a hard-lined differentiation may be

---

① According to Social Welfare Department, there are 73,235 nos. subsidized and non-subsidized Residential Care Homes for the Elderly (2014-2015).

inappropriate. Therefore, we are trying to think proactively about who and what should be provided with specificity. In defining the needs, it may not be easy to set design criteria for a layperson who is not familiar with any spatial or architectural conventions, but when the elderly are invited to the real-to-life setting, it is much easier for them to respond and suggest any alternative improvements.

Under this directive, the design approach towards an empathetic understanding, the keystone to support the E-pathy City, is through an action-and-reaction process. That helps to pre-empt any set standards or given conventions but simply through proposed designs and feedbacks to resolve and refine age-friendly designs and provisions. This seemingly direct and obvious approach, however, is not taken systematically among institutional settings in Hong Kong. In response to this situation, an initiative to form a collaborative effort between Department of Architecture HKU, I-Care CUHK, Longevity House and Hong Kong Silver Park Association, each contributing their respective expertise on spatial design, academic research, interior renovation and social innovation is to address the ageing society with a concerted holistic approach. As a dynamic process to re-investigate the validity of current housing provisions, the collaboration follows 5-stage steps within a one-year cycle as follows:

- Profile research to niche the most beneficial group of single unit in public housing.
- Proposals for the identified unit as testing model.
- Questionnaires on the proposed provisions within the unit.
- Evolution of the proposal with suggestive improvements.
- Engagements of stakeholders to advocate design principles towards policy changes.

4 Single Unit as Living Space

From the statistics, we try to configure the most needed group of elderly who can be directly benefited from the improvement of the design. In the analysis of the housing profile, we understand that single units in public housing provided by the Housing Authority in the past are designed without specific concerns for the elderly use. These units, however, are accommodating the majority of the grass-root class "self-cared elderly" who are living by themselves with minimal nursing assistance[1]. Because this elderly group does not own their residences, there are no incentives for any home improvement beyond tolerable standards unless being recommended by social welfare officers. According to the Housing Authority's current practice, these households will only be provided with minimal age-friendly facilities, like handrails, non-slippery tiles, upon official referrals. In other situation, they will be swapped to double-units to enable wheelchair accessibility. For both cases, the solutions are not optimal because the renovation nuisance will occur during the former situation and in the latter excessive spatial resources are consumed. So, within the existing confinement of the unit shell envelop, by rethinking the behavioral modes of the elderly, particularly those accessed on wheelchairs to every corners of their living spaces, it is meaningful to challenge what can be remodeled to make the single unit more age-friendly.

At the beginning the single unit is not solely designed for elderly household, the flexibility in furniture

---

[1] About 578,500 people aged 60 or above live public housing, equals to 37% of Hong Kong elderly population (2016) :Housing Authority allocates 36,500 small flats to eligible single persons in genuine need:over 70% of these allocated to the elderly.

Figure 1 Design panel of single unit to arouse discussion among exhibition visitors

arrangement is necessary to accommodate different end-user groups' preferences. However, when we are targeting at the ageing population, particular attentions to spatial design and details are critical to enable the ageing inhabitants to manage their daily life. Based on the typical single unit of a Harmony Block at Cheung On Estate on Tsing Yi Island built during the 1980s, a 10-square-metre unit is chosen as a testing model (Figure 1). The unit's layout is with an external end arranged with wet zones including a fire-rated kitchen and an elongated bathroom plus toilet. For a young and normal person, the layout may not incur any hindrance to cook, to bath or to wash, but for a crippled elderly who has to rely on walking stick or even wheelchair over 50% of the area may not be directly accessible. Thus, the question is whether the framework of consideration should be 'universal' to allow sufficient flexibility or it should be specific enough to enhance the livelihood space for the elderly use.

To answer this question may not be a simple "yes" or "no", but that may take into account a testified verification of who and how the unit is designed for. Whether it is addressing 'anonymous general person' or 'real specific person' is the key to respond to this question. When there are 70% of the current inhabitants living in the single units of the public housing estate are aged population that accounts for 22.5% of the overall single living aged population[①], to revisit the 'basic and flexible' design becomes necessary. Together with the upcoming ageing trend of the population in the overall society, there should be an urgency to transform a large extent of the existing units into 'age-friendly units'. The second question, thus, is "how to design these units?"

5 Unit Design as Research Process

To design a 10-square-meter single unit as a testing model is enabling the involvement of different stakeholders to contribute. It may serve as a starting point to arouse discussions, as well as modifications

---

① About 25,500 single units for aged households in public housing, out of 113,000 single living aged population in Hong Kong.

of the current design that are rigidly framed by the considerations of efficiency and fire safety regulations. The intention is to provide a two-way street that allows the end-users, in this case both 'anonymous general person' and 'real specific person' to respond to the testing design, as well as both researcher and designer to understand the actual needs of the elderly through the feedback process. Positioning the elderly at the central role with a focus of empathetic understanding of the limited space in the single unit, the scenario becomes revealing of whether designed environment is conducive to better use and enjoyment of living. Even within the tight constraints of Hong Kong typical living conditions, if there are relatively satisfactory solutions respectfully treated with specificity for the grass-root elderly, it will then prove the feasibility of localizing age-friendly city within the vertical and dense urban conditions of Hong Kong.

To extend the learning from the single unit design process, the project will follow a cyclical feedback system. From a real-to-life mockup of the testing model at the convention "Golden Age Expo & Summit" in Jan 2017, we are using this opportunity to invite feedbacks from exhibition visitors. By collecting data systematically together with their specific scores (see Table 1) regarding spatial features of sufficient storage space, connected spatial layout, safe friendly furniture, combined kitchen/living space, approachable kitchen cabinet, and age-friendly bathroom, we can understand their preferences as well as responses for further improvements.

From the survey, the interviewees are satisfied in general with the design, but at the same time, we can identify certain shortfalls in storage space (score 4.28) and kitchen cabinet arrangement (score4.77). In the interviews, to our surprise there are aspiring suggestions on the design and considerations beyond. Thus, the reactions on how to articulate the elderly domestic space can be further elaborated not by the designer but by the multitude of commentary. In the same manner, we are learning how their concerns deviate from our presumptions and we can envisage a bigger picture that can spin off from digesting their suggestions towards a further end.

List of the spatial features with corresponding scores for usefulness	Table 1
Degree of Design Usefulness (1=completely useless to 6=extremely useful)	Average Score
Sufficient Storage Space	4.28
Connected Spatial Layout	5.04
Safe Friendly Furniture	5.08
Combined Kitchen/ Living Space	5.08
Approachable Kitchen Cabinet	4.77
Age-friendly Bathroom	5.01

6　Interactive Evolution as Community Design

As the 'action and reaction' cycle is completed in the above exercise, we are trying to evolve the model further as an acquiring tool for the construct of E-pathy City at different levels. When the design ideas applied in the single unit including the breaking of compartments, the continuity of central space, and the functional compactness are becoming strategies to enhance mobility and accessibility of the elderly. These qualities are equally valid to apply in architecture and in the community design at urban level.

The methodology of this *"design proposal → questionnaire → evolution → engagement"* flow is enhancing an open dialogue among stakeholders who are relevant but not communicated in the institutionalized setting. Throughout this process, it is possible to reinstate the significance of 'people-oriented' approach in shaping our environment from domestic scale up to urban scale for the ageing society. When we are investigating the design of the single unit for the elderly as the starting point, there are concerns and themes common for community design. By consolidating these findings as commonalities, we discover that the following principles are relevant in application:

- *Barrier-free accessibility*

By prioritizing wheelchair accessibility within the unit, unnecessary barrier/ compartment in terms of level and separation between kitchen and washroom is removed or modified. The challenge is how to interpret the technical performance of the barrier, i.e. fire engineering, through innovative means instead of strictly following conventions. The same idea in architectural and urban situations applies to reconsider unnecessary boundaries due to management demarcation, e.g. visual barrier to replace physical blockage.

- *Spatial connectivity*

Upon the accessibility issue, connectivity of dedicated spaces is to allow easy maneuverings and minimal circulations. The lesson is articulating multi-directional interconnections to create useable spaces instead of long passages and dead corners. In architecture and community design, widened hallway and pedestrian nodes in connecting different spaces are to enhance visibility and movement for the elderly.

- *Functional flexibility*

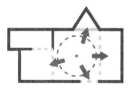

The limited spatial provision within the single unit is questing for an optimal usage of different functions including living, sleeping, cooking, bathing, etc. within the 10-square footage for one elderly person. Given that privacy is not a major concern for single inhabitant, physical separation of functions may not be necessary. Thus, the spatial configuration of a non-specific central space shared among other functions is essential to allow sufficient flexibility for spatial conversions. At architectural and urban scale, communal spaces and public squares at central locations may conduce to spatial extensions for elderly activities at various times.

- *Utility compactness*

As a result of the above arrangements, functional spaces overlap with optimal locations where irreplaceable utility is located along peripheral edges. By reconsidering reachability of these utilities including operation and storage, the elderly may access all functional needs with convenience and ease. The lesson of compacting utilities in shelf-containments within reach is to organize daily life effectively and safely. When applying this concept at architectural and urban levels, the necessary nuisance of elderly services should be reachable adjacent to communal spaces as nodes or service stations.

7   People-Oriented Design for Ageing Society

When the above lessons from the single unit design are appreciated as "universal" applications towards extended scales in architectural and urban design, we find the spatial concepts helpful to address the current challenges of the ageing society of Hong Kong. The centrality of the debate focused at "people-oriented" design calls for a thorough understanding of how people act and react to our physical environments. In this process, the spinning effect on relating people to their immediate living setting is essential because spatial appreciation is abstract but intuitive. The intention to connect *body→unit→architecture→urban* at progressive scales is to testify how far the axial understanding of empathy can nestle the elderly users as responsive subjects instead of passive objects to be served.

The implication of whether the E-pathy City construct can converge into consents all depends on the users' understanding of these principles, namely *barrier-free accessibility, spatial connectivity, functional flexibility, and utility compactness.* These principles should apply in the design of ageing places where multiple stakeholders may have diverse views, but more importantly is whether these diversified opinions can constitute a forward-looking approach to create or modify places that the elderly users can accustom themselves as natural nestling without any further instrumental learnings. Under this directive, the next step forward will be a testing design of communal spaces that take into account of elderly users as part of the public instead of individuals. With similar research strategy, the team is investigating the possibility of extending our findings from the single unit design into a public realm where the entry and use is beyond personal control. As the parameters are conditioned in different manner, the team is open to set up consultative dialogues with elderly users for them to input through sketches and physical settings.

Although the evolving process in terms of degree of publicness and scale of influence is pointing towards an elevated complexity, the basic idea is still singular, i.e. putting the elderly at the center of concerns. In the end whether the configured designs can only apply locally or limited to specific conditions in Hong Kong is subject to a continuous refinement and evaluation cycle. However, the experimental attempt of this exercise is achieving two ends in one go, i.e. arousing the awareness of engaging elderly as subjects, and collating relevant disciplines into a self-propelling process of elderly-focus development; hopefully with the official effort, the approach will be adopted to construct the E-pathy City by localizing the age-friendly spatial practice in Hong Kong.

8　Conclusion——Spatial Practice as E-pathy Construct

The "E-pathy City" as the author's advocacy since 2014 towards a better intergenerational understanding of our city in which we live and share, is providing a construct to address the ageing society as well as to accommodate the pressing needs of elderly spaces. The spatial practice of designing the single unit can attract the elderly to participate proactively in a dual role of end-user and designer. The alliance of collaborative efforts together with the engagement of the elderly allows a propelling evolution of the spatial design in terms of social innovation, i.e. both product of the living unit and ongoing process of communal education (Figure 2).

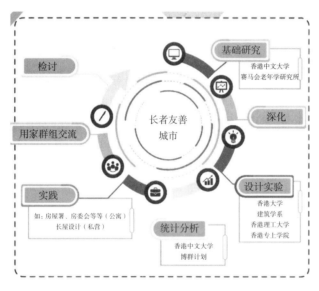

Figure 2　Interactive evolution cycle diagram

In this manner, what we are initiating is a dialogue among stakeholders from housing provider, in this case the Housing Authority, to social services receiver, the Single Elderly. However, this demonstrates how the evolving construct of E-pathy City may display an empathetic position for both provider and user to localize our elderly environment. The experience is empowering the elderly in shaping their own living space with a trajectory to influence policy-makers in setting "elderly-centric" policies.

Through the remodeling of the public housing in Hong Kong it pushes forward the attention in spatial design of age-friendly environment, particularly within an affordable framework of the grass-root communities. Without support from the government, but through a self-propelled initiative among a group of social enterprises and academic research units, the author tries to testify the validity of an "age-friendly" habitat by transforming an existing "standardized" single-unit within a public housing estate. By engaging expertise from sociological enquiry, interior renovation, design performance, and financial viability, the team attempts to develop an approach to build up the E-pathy City via a bottom-up social innovation process.

As an evolving process, the initiative takes a cyclical feedback system via sequential steps of basic research, design experiment, statistic analysis, on-site remodeling, and user-group exchange, in order to establish a platform to arouse the authority's attention and consent to reconsider the current housing design and environmental agenda. Although it is a small step ahead, it will be a solid impact to revamp our current policy to address the ageing issue through a holistic and humanistic perspective. The findings of the initiative will provide a backbone of knowledge for an alternative approach whereby a concerted coordination among research bodies, architectural professionals, and social enterprises is essential to form a solid foundation in responding to the pressing need of the ageing society.

从长者友善单元建立同理城市

郑炳鸿

(香港大学建筑学院)

摘 要：长者友善城市在香港本土化的难题正挑战着政策制定者处理人口老化的固有思维。若从设计公共房屋的长者友善单元开始，此推动可衍生一套由跨界协作与长者共同建构的全面模式。作为一个演进过程，这次社会创新实践正为建立同理城市奠下扎实的基础。

关键词：同理城市，长者友善单元，社会创新

References

[1] Dale J J. Shared Housing for the Elderly:Gerontological Society of America[M]. New York: Greenwood Press, 1989.

[2] Pastalan A L. Optimizing Housing for the Elderly: Homes Not Houses[M]. New York: Routledge, Taylor & Francis Group, 1990.

[3] http://www.lcsd.gov.hk/CE/Museum/APO/en_US/web/apo/oyip_e-pathy_city.html.

Travel in Tin Shui Wai as A Housewife

Wang Danning

(Gender Research Center, The Chinese University of Hong Kong)

Abstract: The paper takes the gender perspective to analyze residents' experience and understanding of the urban space in the welfare housing neighborhood. Inspired by New Zealand case study on women's memories of travel, the author interviewed women of different age groups to understand their utilization of the neighborhood facilities, perception of the urban space, and formation of self-identity. This research can improve our understanding of the formation of the alienation feeling that the middle-aged housewives have towards their neighborhood of Tin Shui Wai, the largest welfare housing in Hong Kong. It can also explain their understanding of "home".

Keywords: Gender, Urban space, Welfare housing

1 Introduction

Tin Shui Wai New Town is the largest welfare housing neighborhood in Hong Kong. The neighborhood was developed in the 1980s by two large real estate companies and was able to provide welfare housing for total 292, 000 people in Hong Kong in 2014. The Town locates in Yuen Long District, New Territory and it is one of the neighborhoods in the city with the highest population density——67, 906 per square kilometer. For years, Tin Shui Wai New Town suffered from a disturbing social label, "the city of misery", and the dubious social stereotypes caused by the increasing family and social issues such as suicides, mental illness, and domestic violence, etc. General explanations include remote location, lack of job opportunities, and high population density. There are also reports targeting the local housewives to understand their under-employment status. What happened within the neighborhood, however, we need more systematic studies.

In June 2016, after the annual workshop on Gender and Space at Chinese University of Hong Kong, a team of college students, professors and researchers visited Tin Shui Wai for a field site trip. During the trip, local NGO members brought us to super markets, schools, theatre, town office, playgrounds, and green gardens to show the sites of daily activity. In particular, the NGO members demonstrated us, from the local housewives' perspective, how difficult it would be to travel to schools and grocery markets with stroller or shopping cart in hands. Due to the trolley line running through the neighborhood and the lack of crossovers and escalators, food shopping and sending children to schools turned to be the major daily travel challenges.

This paper will focus on the socio-cultural perspectives on daily travel, a topic enriched by Law (2002) in the case study of Dunedin, New Zealand. It analyzes how gender as a pattern of social relations, a cultural system of meaning and a component of personal identity can improve our understanding of transport studies. My on-going work is based on the collection of life histories from fifteen to twenty housewives in the neighborhood and the participating observation information collected from following their daily travel routines. With the focus on individual and subjective meanings, perceptions and experiences, the paper shows how practice of daily mobility constitutes gender. In other words, by understanding how women travel in Tin Shui Wai on the daily basis, we can find what it means by being a woman and a housewife in Tin Shui Wai.

In addition, the paper will also apply Cresswell's study of "place" (1994), Seamon's idea of "time-space routines" and "place-ballets" (1980), and Massey's idea of "sense of place" in a global era (1997) to understand the housewives' sense of home and how they look at the daily travel in terms of everyday meanings, routines, experiences, negotiations and norms set in everyday life. High percentage of the Tin Shui Wai housewives came from the mainland and moved to the neighborhood with their Hong Kong husbands and families. How the sense of home in a welfare housing project was articulated and constructed is the key for the researcher to understand the meaning of the facilities and the housing project to them. Cresswell, Seamon, and Massey's works provide the analytical tools to understand their articulation and life histories. From these articulations we can not only find which part of the facilities are more important in their daily routine, we can also learn how to improve these to make their quality of life increased.

From the preliminary field site visit, we also found the number of the retail business in the neighborhood is extremely limited. Nearly no vending machine, wet market, food cart, food stand, nor eateries could be found in the area. There are also limited food markets. Residents normally travel long distance for food shopping. Monopolized and collective management of stores prohibited a lively neighborhood life. When the housewives organized their own NGOs to produce some small products for their own market in the neighborhood, surprisingly none of them is related to food. Further research needs to find out for what reason these women could not run their own food-related business when their daily life is so inconvenient and challenged by the neighborhood management. Harvey's idea of social justice (2009) will be applied to analyze the management of urban space. By adding the gender perspective, the article will argue that the difficulties faced by Tin Shui Wai housewives was caused by the urban designer's gender senseless. In order to create a healthy, lively, livable, convenient, and affordable neighborhood live, more inclusive management plans and accessible facilities need to be added to the neighborhood.

2 Gender, Travel, and Life Stages

2.1 Gender As A Pattern Social Relation

Gender has been the effective analytical lens for scholars to study the division of labor, the capitalist operation of labor market, and the structure and function of modern family. Human geography also adopted the gender tool to understand men and women's practices in the public space. With Butler's idea of gender as performance, we now can see how men and women approach the public space with different gender patterns, constructing the symbolic meaning, and finally, form the subjective identity. Men and women's utilization of public transportation, modern technologies, as well as their travel patterns and psychological reactions to topic such as safety all became research topics in the realm. Different travel behaviors and gender patterns were also studied. With these studies, we found consistent gender variations caused by the socially constructed gender difference and its impact to the way we travel. In general, women would travel shorter distance, have constraints in accessing public transportation, limit their daily mobility because of children accompanies, fear of darkness, and worries of personal security (Beuret 1991 and Little 1994). Using the New Zealand's historical data, Law showed these feminist studies of women's travel patterns was actually caused by the rising of private vehicles and the change of the capitalist division of labor in the labor market and at home. Before all of these social factors were available, crowded streets in New Zealand was full of surveillance and women traveled with less fear and more vigorously. Perception of safety can shift throughout time. Household income and allowance also determined who had the right to travel farther. Age, job, marital status all determined who can travel farther. In order to save money, men and women can choose to walk. When public transportation was universal, gender difference was not obvious compared to the rise of private ownership of bicycles, motorcycles, and cars. Working away from home made the significant gender difference in daily mobility. For women, marital status made the significance of the travel pattern, too (Law2002).

In Tin Shui Wai case, we found that women at different life stages traveled differently. Oral history data collected among the different age groups showed unique patterns of traveling experiences. Different from the previous studies and general impressions, we found first, senior women enjoyed traveling in Tin Shui Wai more than the middle aged housewives. Second, when senior women recollected their traveling experience in the middle age, instead of emphasizing the physical strength, vigorous moves, and long distant traveling, they focused on the household burdens, economic difficulties, and changes of class status that caused confinement and hardship in traveling. Finally, social workers and middle-aged housewives in Tin Shui Wai all complained the urban design of the neighborhood. These finding not only contribute to our better understanding of the gendered travel studies, but also reconfirm our understanding of how the unequal social structure affects women's life in different life stages. After all, in Chinese culture, Women's domestic status improved in their senior years.

From the housewives' perspective, Tin Shui Wai was the worst and failed urban design with the trolley line divided the neighborhood into unconnected pieces. Residents from different sides of the trolley could hardly meet each other in the social activities and impossible to form a united sense of neighborhood.

" *new immigrants and new comers can easily get lot in Tin Shui Wai. All of the buildings look similar and the trolley is everywhere. There is no sense of direction and people can walk round and round in the neighborhood with going nowhere.*"

" *when I went to Shenzhen and my hometown in Guangdong, I never got such feelings. I know where I am going and I can easily go there. But here, I got lost easily and I thought I am stupid and confused.*"

There were also complaints about the design of the shopping centers which conveniently located and distributed in the neighborhood with easy access. However, because of monopoly, these shopping centers had the bad reputation of "luring" the residents to "dump" their limited income into endless and useless high-price shopping.

" *the shopping centers were designed with no windows, just stores after stores. When you get in, you can spend hours and hours in the center and spend all of your money to buy stuff. There are escalators everywhere directing you to stores of fashion, accessories, and useless stuff. There is no natural light in the centers so people can easily spend hours in the centers till late in night.*"

" *I think they design the shopping centers on purpose. Look, when you get in, you can easily see escalators but no elevators. All of the elevators are hiding somewhere inside and it is hard to find. This is the design for the young people, not for the handicaps and people who have to push strollers. Mothers with little babies can hardly come and enjoy here, only people with money.*"

Even though most overpasses have the slop-design for the wheel chairs, strollers, and bicycles, most trolley stations lacked such easy access. Pedestrians also need to take big U-turns to walk around for such access.

The other major complaint is about the road blocks for the bicycle riders and the lack of shadows for the pedestrians in the sunny and rainy days. In order to allow the pedestrians walking across the trolley trails, the city build road blocks for the bicycle road and it was difficult to ride a bike in the neighborhood.

" I had to walk everywhere. It is such a bad design. The whole neighborhood looks like a construction site for me. With trolley lines and pedestrian paths, there is no way to ride a bike here. I walked everywhere. Only if the destination is further than three trolley stops, otherwise, I would just walk."

" after working here for years, I know where the short-cuts are and I know where I can walk without umbrella in the sunny and rainy days. There is no trees next to the road, if you call those roads. I would call them blocks. Everything here is cut into pieces and you have to be careful everywhere you go. You need to be alert and cautious. We need to have the road back and we need to have the trees back."

Tan Popo was the first senior granny who told me how much she actually enjoyed Tin Shui Wai and traveling in Tin Shui Wai. At age 77, she has lived here for ten years alone. Her husband passed away about twenty years ago because of cancer. Her son is settled in the USA and her daughter's family lived in the same neighborhood. Tan Popo enjoyed the neighborhood and her life here.

"If I told you that Tin Shui Wai is the heaven for the single seniors like me, I am exaggerating. But I have to say it is big garden for me and my senior years."

She is active in the local senior choir and also teaches singing in a senior choir in Tun Men. Regularly, her friends from these choirs would come to her home to party. She invited me to here colorful home for the afternoon tea. In the 50 square meters single-bed room apartment, she filled it with paintings, piano, plants, fruits, and food. Everywhere is clean and well managed and she had no complains of her daily life at all. When I raised the questions of traveling and the difficulties, her answers are totally different from the middle-aged women.

"I had no need to rush to anywhere and I have no worries when I am walking. There are traffic lights everywhere and I walk everywhere safely. I like the design of the neighborhood, very convenient and thoughtful."

" but I was not like this when I was young. My husband stuck in bed for eleven years before he passed away. I was the only one taking care of him every day. It was so tough for me. No one could help me. I was exhausted, lonely, and depressed. Finally I got severe depression and I suffered for about ten years. Those were the days I had hard time traveling. My memories were short, and I could not remember roads, directions, nor my shopping list. I could lose in the streets or go into the market but forget where I need to buy. I moved slowly those days and could not see hope. My husband is stubborn and fear of losing faces. He did not want me to search for help and I also did not want to bother my children for their own lives. I faced everything by myself till he passed away. Those were the hardest time in my life."

Tan Popo recovered from her depression after she moved to the US to live with her son's family for ten years. During those ten years, she emerged herself to the church life and found the active local community life. She became a Christian and an active local church members even after she came back to Hong Kong. She said it was the faith of God and her church members rescued her so that she could enjoy life now.

2.2 Gendered Space: Gender As A System of Meaning

The concept of gender is also used to classify environment and things. The gendering process of technology, space, and settings for mobility, such as streets, the interior space of tram, was universal. How did objects, spaces and settings come to carry social norms of gender-appropriate behavior and cultural notions of the "natural" gender associations? How to regulate public space according to gender norms?

Tianxiu Market

After I introduced my project, local social workers immediately introduced me to Tianxiu Market, which they thought would be the perfect site for my research because it was organized by housewives to serve the housewives. They were so sure that I can collect different perspectives from the store owners and the customs, and I can simply collect my data by siting there for days. I was surprised to see such intensified gendered labeling and wanted to pursue the reason. Things were never like what the social workers predicted. Many stores were owned and managed by men and school kids are the most frequent customers of the market. Handicapped and seniors with wheel chairs came here more often than the local housewives.

Tianxiu Market was established by Dong Hua San Yuan, a famous charity NGO in Hong Kong with the intension to create local jobs for residents in the neighborhood. Gendered concern was among the original design. With the location within the neighborhood, housewives could save travel time and spend more time to take care of their children and domestic chores. However, it has never practiced that way. One of the requirements for those who can rent the stalls asks the store keeper to open the store eight hours a day. The inflexible schedule could be hardly met by the housewives who need to pick up the school kids in early afternoon and running for chores during the day.

Also, few housewives would come to the market to do shopping. The most famous local site for them to get together is the fast food chain store Café Decora in the shopping center where they would sit together after sending their children to schools and have breakfast. With early working hours, same price of food, air conditioning, no wonder the housewives preferred to stay in the food chain stores.

High price and opened shopping environment remained to be the shortcoming of Tianxiu Market. The size of each rented stall is two by two square meters and they were all painted white. There was no tree shadows, hoods, or facilities to prevent the sunshine and rain. In mid-April, when the day temperature was already around 25 degrees and the raining season is coming, sitting outside to have lunch or afternoon tea was impossible. Additionally, the market was crowded and shabby. Few owners would want to rent two stalls to make sure they have larger space. As the result, each store was more like a storage. There is no banking facilities. The alley is narrow. With the hoods and umbrellas installed by the store owners, the area looks more crowded, unplanned, and shabby. Not far from here, the shopping centers are all air-conditioned, with escalators, bright lights, shining advertisements, labels, ATMS, cafes, chairs, and indoor/outdoor gardens for the customers. To the locals, they represent professionals, modern, glamorous, foreign, and trendy.

Few south Asian women opened stores in Tianxiu Market to sell decorations and spices. They could speak enough Cantonese to do business with the customers but they were treated as outsiders and the communications between the locals and them were limited. Further, Tianxiu Market was also victimized by its feminine reputation. Customers do not think it is a real shopping area. Office ladies would never come here to have lunch, and it was not glamorous enough for the ones who want to enjoy shopping.

Street Vendors

If Tianxiu Market has been labeled as the "housewife market", the street vending business is preoccupied by housewives. They sell all kinds of goods, such as fruits, wallets, umbrellas, hats, and clothes illegally in the public space. With no rent, more business, and higher profits, these women took all of the risk of being caught and penalized by the government. They are connected by phones and watched out for each other. All of the products are loaded into a moving cart and can be pushed away anytime.

Ah Ping came from Zhanjiang and married a construction worker in Hong Kong. At age 40, she is beautiful and cautious. She has two daughters with her husband. Her husband's work is by contract and could not be reliable on the monthly basis. With her income from street vending, her family income can guarantee to have HK$5, 000 to HK$6, 000. Her two daughters are all in schools and their rent is HK$1, 000. With her "stable" income from street vending, she felt more control over her Hong Kong life.

" our minimum monthly expense is about this amount. I need to pay rent, gas, water and electricity. I also need to purchase food and groceries. The girls also need to go to school. Every month, this is the minimum amount that I need. Without this number, there is no way I can run the household. Without this amount, I would feel insecure."

To the anthropologist, Ah Ping's household division of labor fits into the hunter and gatherer pattern when men went out to hunt and women stayed nearby to gather and statistics showed women's limited by continuous supply of veggies, fruits and nuts provided the stable daily nutritious necessities to help human survived. However, in Ah Ping's case, her street vending job required her frequent long and short distance travel with demanding labors. First, her vending carts is full of goods and every day she needs to push it around from home to different locations. In order to avoid the city's surveillances, she needs to frequently change spots and she also need to rely on her friends to call and to inform her for potential dangers. Second, she purchased all of the products from the mainland and she need to travel to Shenzhen and her hometown for the purchase. To her, it is very easy to cross the border and to deal with the whole sealers.

" the price is much cheaper in the mainland and I know where to find the whole sealers."

Her husband could hardly helped her because of their different working schedules and also he would treat it as losing face. His construction work requires him travel far outside of Tin Shui Wai and his much higher hourly payment maintained his higher status at home. To Ah Ping, travel in Tin Shui Wai as a street vender is dangerous, illegal, and full of cautious. Only by working with a group of female street venders that she felt secured and legitimized. They protected each other's privacy and they relied on each other for connections and information. To Ah Ping, the streets of Tin Shui Wai are their business sites. There is no way for her to go to Tin Siu Market and her responsibility of household gave her courage and legitimacy to justify her daily conducts.

2.3 Embodied Identity: Gender As A Component of Place/Personal Identity

Sense of Belonging and the Attachment to a Place

Human geographers' studies of individuals' sense of belonging to a place focused on the embodied process, i.e. how individuals internalized and embodied rules by practicing to demonstrate their strong attaching emotions to a place. Cresswell's study shows when individuals adapt the rules by repeating practices, the sense of belonging would easily emerge. Otherwise, people would hardly fit in (Cresswell, p. 47). Seamon, on the other hand, developed this idea with the concept of "place-ballets" to describe how the time-space routines in a particular place regulate individual's body movements. Like the ballet dancers, each of their moves are regulated, coded, and labeled with physical standards and posture rules. When they dance with music on the stage, the rhythm sets up the pace and the stage regulates the positions. By following such regulated body-subject rules, dancers embodied the roles and belonged to the drama. In reality, by practicing the body-subject rules of certain time-space routines in certain places, the sense of belonging could be found (Seamon, p. 58). From here, it is easy to recognize who belongs to the "circle", the "place", and the "position", and who are the "others" that could never fit in. Further, we can also tell that even among the rule-followers, with awkward practices, limited capability to master the embodied moves, and incompetence to control the pace or the actions, the sense of belonging can hardly form.

For people who live in Tin Shui Wai, whether they identify with the place or not is the key. For this largest welfare housing project with about 300,000 residents that the city government started to plan and build back in 1972, a sense of belonging is the critical key for the residents to settle in. For years, we heard the neighborhood with all kinds of social problems and the label of "misery city" was wide spread. Public stereotypes and teasing reinforced the negative images of the neighborhood. During the interviews, we found such negative impact in nearly every middle-aged housewives.

"I never felt easy after I moved to the neighborhood until I joined the church. I found calm and peace in the church. Even when I slept in the church, I had no nightmares."

Ah Yan is a part-time social worker in the neighborhood and a single mother of two daughters. Originally, she was from Henan Province and lived in Beijing and Shanghai with her parents when she was young. She met her husband in Zhengzhou, the provincial capital of Henan, when she just graduated from the local college. Ambitious and romantic, she felt in love with him because he could understand her. Grown up in an intellectual family, Ah Yan was spoiled by her parents. Traveling experience in mainland China also gave her a knowledgeable childhood that she found hard to share with her local Henan peers. When they met each other, her husband was part of a Hong Kong Youth Exchange program to visit the mainland and they kept exchange letters afterwards. Soon, he convinced her to move to Shenzhen where they both can start business together and work for a brighter future. Ah Yan followed his suggestion and married him later in Shenzhen. In the following years, they had two daughters and the business was bumpy and finally failed. In order to pay off the debt, Ah Yan moved to Hong Kong with two daughters to work on jobs with better payment and her husband kept on trying in Shenzhen. Their marriage started to have problems when Ah Yan found out that he had another woman in Shenzhen. She just could not bear with it and they filed divorce. With the series of hard attacks in her life, Ah Yan moved to the neighborhood and decided to work as a part-timer so that she could have more time to stay with her daughters. To her, Tin Shui Wai was only a suitable but temporary place for her daughters to live and she wants them to move out ultimately. Her memories of Beijing, Shanghai, and Zhengzhou was more pleasant and her friends there mattered more to her. Joining the church helped her to settle down and she can have peaceful life now. However, she never wants her daughters moved back after their college education. To her, education was the only way for them to get out of the neighborhood.

If Ah Yan's cultural capital can helped her children to move out of the neighborhood, not every other housewives has such capability. For those who married into the neighborhood either felt stuck here, or believed in fate for such move.

"The business here is never good. No one would come here to eat. With the same amount of money, they could go somewhere else. My working hour is long and we won't close the store till seven in the evening. It is still a business and I would continue it no matter what."

Ah Fen came from Meixian in Guangdong Province and she moved to Hong Kong with her husband. In the neighborhood, she found her business partner to open a rice noodle shop in Tianxiu Market, but mainly she is the one sustaining the business on the daily basis. Her partner is an older local man who barely showed up. But with his connections and his name, they rent two stalls to open the rice noodle shop. Ah Fen missed her hometown in

Guangdong where her life was much more relaxed and free. Moving to Hong Kong from her home village was supposed to be celebrated, but her busy and stressful life never really convinced her it was a right move.

Even social workers disliked their working experience in Tin Shui Wai. Ah Yin came from village in Tai Pu, the other side of the New Territory. After graduating from Chinese University of Hong Kong with a bachelor and a master degree, she was ambitious to work in the cities for the government. After she joined the social work team in Tin Shui Wai, she found the reality was never as bright as she predicted in college. Her position was not a government position and her payment relied on the funds that her team could apply from the government. In order to cut the cost of social work, the government contracted this part of work and the fund was never easy to apply. After several years working here, Ah Yin was stressed and worried. She never treated herself as an office lady, the ones she admired as a college girl. All of the hopes that her studies in the good university gave her are disappearing. To her, traveling three hours on the road to work in the neighborhood is becoming aimless and gradually, she echoed the local housewives and became their loudest supporter.

All of the alienated feelings towards Tin Shui Wai were articulated while women talked about their life and work in the neighborhood. In particular, they mentioned this in their narratives of life histories and traveling experiences. The message was clear that they would rather to be somewhere else and not here in Tin Shui Wai. The harsh and bitterness-loaded articulations were further constituted a sense of identity for the informants as gendered beings. Living and working in Tin Shui Wai as a woman was never easy. How the gendered experience of embodiment was constituted through mobility and what emotions were attached to it remain further question. As individuals, what was the ideal embodiment in terms of daily moving and how that was gendered can be further studied.

Gendered Individuals and Daily Mobility

Studies of the embodied subjectivity in the realm of gender and travel focused on how men and women experienced the embodied skills, such as driving, riding bicycles and motorcycles, and so on. Experiences of mastering these skills showed who they were and how they did it. Within Tin Shui Wai, we found that walking experience itself already demonstrates a lived experience of inhabiting a sexed body and self-identity, understood as both deeply personal and situational. For the middle-aged housewives, when they articulate the way they travel and walk, we did not find the pride of their prowess at walking long distances with physical vigor, nor the sense of being control and in charge to challenge the traditional femininity. Instead of being healthy, active, resourceful, and risk-taking, we found their narrations of the daily moves with sense of frail and ailing from inside.

Once a month, Ah Yan needs to deposit rent that she collected from Tianxiu Market into the local Bank of China branch, where two trolley stops away from her office is. With load of cash in her handbag, she is cautious and alert. The trolley was crowded and she would rather walk to the bank. While we walked together, she kept on reminding me it is long and far away from her office. The ten-minute walk was not long but she made me pay attention to all of the turns and potential dangers.

"There are only two bank branches in the neighborhood, very inconvenient. There is no traffic lights throughout these shortcuts and you have to look around. There is no way to ride a bike here. Look at these blocks and turns, and the overpasses. The buses can also come from different directions."

Ah Yin was more direct while we walked together in the neighborhood.

"Three is no straight road here at all. Look at all of these ups and downs, and block bars. If you are a runner, how can you ever run here?"

"The mainland businessmen invested in these luxury hotels and stores, but who would come here to dine and to do shopping? They thought by opening brand-name stores, they could create more job opportunities for the locals to serve the mainland buyers, but it would never work out that way. All of the brand-names are chain stores and they allocate employees internally to different branches. For those Tin Shui Wai employees, once a while they would need to be sent away to the other locations and the cost of travel would be much higher because we are in the middle of nowhere. Married women here can hardly work on those positions because they need to take care of babies and chores. Later on, these women all ended in Tianxiu Market."

"After a while, everyone recognized the problems and even brand-name stores stopped coming. Now the building is filled with restaurants and only office ladies would come here to dine because it is expensive and glamourous."

"Every day, it takes me nearly three hours to commute from home. It is exhausting and I need to change buses several times. I do not know what I am going to do if I got married. That is too far for me to think about."

To the street venders, traveling in the neighborhood is really hard. Each cart is filled with loads of commodities and they need to be ready to move whenever they heard the police is coming. They refused to show up in my pictures and want to remain nameless in my interview record. Even when I promised to do so, they would disappeared in the second day when I returned to continue my interviews.

Surprisingly, all of our informants at different age groups are experienced travelers and their migration histories spread out to Guangdong Province, other parts of China, and even the USA and Canada. Different from their traveling experience in the neighborhood, their lives in the other regions demonstrated more physical fitness and courage. They could undertake long distance travel without a second thought even when the hardship could be unusually demanding by Tin Shui Wai standards. These seniors could nostalgically remember their traveling experience in a foreign country when they could not understand the language or be able to drive. Moving to a new region would be motivated by curiosity and risk-taking could be fun. They celebrated their reunion with overseas family members with the pride of their spirited courage and physical fitness. With family connections, social networks, and reliable cultural capitals, they were resourceful modern women outside of Tin Shui Wai. The narrative was more often deployed to describe experiences and memories of their daily mobility in Tin Shui Wai.

Tan Popo could not speak English, but she lived in the USA for ten years after her husband passed way. She joined the local Chinese church there and found her faith. She was active among her church friends and quickly adjusted the American life. Compared to her troubled middle-age life, she enjoyed foreign traveling and claimed the church life healed her depression. Originally she moved to Hong Kong with her husband and two children in 1975. She met her overseas Chinese husband in Harerbin where he left Singapore in the chaotic 1960s to search for better education and settlement in his motherland. During the Culture Revolution, they two suffered because of his "untrustworthy" overseas background and decided to migrant to Hong Kong for the sake of their children's development. There were no office jobs waiting for them here and the only employment they could find was working in the factories. The down-graded class status was unbearable to them and the husband started his own Chinese medicine practices so that they could have higher income to send the son studying in the USA. Those middle-aged years were filled with harsh work and non-stopping labors. When her husband was diagnosed cancer, she started to have depression.

To Tan Popo, she worked her whole life as wife and mother for her family. Even when she suffered from depression, there was no way for her to stop working. At the point when she lost her sense of direction because of depression, she blamed herself for not being able to take care of her family. Her senior years were the first time that she could live for herself and she totally enjoy it.

Ren Popo suffered from arthritis at age 78. She said she stopped seeing the doctors because going to the hospital is too troublesome. Every day, she forced herself to walk with an umbrella in the neighborhood but she never complained about the neighborhood. To her, moving here ten years ago was a wonderful decision. Living by herself, she enjoys the good air quality here and all of the trees and plants. She compared the neighborhood with the other old neighborhoods in Mong Kok and Tun Men. With too much commercial lives and neon lights there, she prefers the tranquility here. Walking is becoming a daily exercise for her because of the arthritis. When she talked about her middle age and the forty years living in Hong Kong, she showed pride of being in charge. With college education in the mainland, she moved to Hong Kong while working for a state-owned company. She needed to travel around and negotiated businesses with men in different places. Her professional status sustained her and in her own words, "I was able to keep a heart of girl's with pure fun and curiosity."

3   Conclusion: Experience and Memories of Travel Are Age-Relative and Gendered

Streetscape and social positions shaped the city dwellers' daily mobility. Transport technologies are never socially neutral. In a world of gender structured societies, they were introduced to "enable the social practices that maintained that structure, but they also sometimes provided opportunities for new practices and meanings that would transform that world" (Law, p. 426). The mutually constitutive relationship between urban daily mobility and gender deserves more research. With the framework provided by the earlier academic effort, more scholarly work can enable us to understand the city dwellers' experience better with an effective renovation and change to implement.

With the early academic researches, we know gendered subject position shaped city residents' daily mobility. Also city residents' practice of daily mobility constitute the system of gender relations, the cultural meaning of gender differences and gendered notion of self. Gender is constructed by attention to everyday trip-making and presence on the street. On top of the gender division of labor in the home, the structure of the labor market and so on. The symbolic and subjective aspects of gender have been largely neglected in transport geography. Mutual constitution of place and gender might be studied. Place and space play a crucial active and constitutive role in the ways in which femininities are (re) formulated. We need to beware of fixating on bounded places and forgetting about the networks that link them. Daily mobility linked home, shopping mall, the workplace, or more specific settings is analytically useful. Travelling between sites are a fundamental part of social life. Gender is performed in public spaces and is constituted and challenged through social practices and cultural meanings.

To the cultural meanings of transport practices and places, gender is the key axis of social difference for feminist geography to understand the meaning of places and impact to the residents. Oral histories are used to explore how gender and mobility are interrelated in one particular time and place.

师奶的天水围之旅

王丹凝

(香港中文大学性别研究中心)

摘 要：本文从社会性别视角入手，分析城市福利住房居民对于城市空间的理解和经历。研究者受惠于有关新西兰城市中女性的旅行记忆研究，从性别研究的三个层面分析不同年龄段的女性对于城市空间的使用、理解、赋予的含义，以及在旅行过程中自我认同的产生。该研究有助于理解香港最大的福利住房区域天水围中的中年女性对该社区的疏离感的产生以及她们对于"家"的概念理解。

关键词：社会性别，城市空间，福利住房

References

[1] Cresswell Tim. Putting Women in Their Place: The Carnival at Greenham Common[J]. *Antipode*, 1994, 26(I): 35-58.

[2] Harvey David. *Social Justice and the City*[M]. Athens: University of Georgia Press, 2009.

[3] Law R. Gender and Daily Mobility in a New Zealand City, 1920-1960[J]. *Social and Cultural Geography*, 2002, 3(4).

[4] Massey D. A Global Sense of Place in Barnes. T and Gregory D (eds.). *Reading Human Geography*. Arnold, London. 1997: 315-23.

[5] Seamon D. Body-Subject, Time-Space Routines, and Place-Ballets in Buttimer.A. and Seamon, D (eds.). *The Human Experience of Space and Place.* London: Croom Helm, 1980: 148-65.

基于 BIM 的主动式防灾通知系统之即时通信架构设计

郭韦良　李秋明　吴轩竹　谢尚贤

（台湾大学土木工程学系）

摘　要：一般建筑室内的群众聚集地方，若突然发生如火灾、地震等灾害，常因未能实时通知所有人正确的信息，而造成群众错失最佳逃生时间，加上事先的疏散动线规划难以周全，疏散指示也不易明确，无法有效保障建筑物内人员的生命安全，因此即时信息通知、疏散路径的动态规划及指引成为重要的安全课题。本研究提出一个适用于建筑物室内群聚场所的紧急防灾通知系统的初步构想，并先探讨利用 DDS（Data Distribution Service）通信协议，IoT 物联网感测设备，与个人手持设备及 Apps 软件，并搭配 Beacon 定位做到即时消息传递的方式。同时也导入 BIM（Building Information Modeling）技术作为系统的数据库与展示建筑信息与图形可视化的基础，让使用者或管理者能简易地操作系统。当灾害发生时，可实时将正确的信息通知相关人员进行避难或让救灾人员能清楚现场人员的逃生状况，以利紧急逃生与救难。

关键词：建筑信息模型，数据分发服务（DDS），通信协议，物联网（IoT），紧急逃生

1　研究背景

一般建筑物若发生火灾或重大灾难事件，现场人员常因恐慌、对逃生或疏散动线不了解，或逃生指示不明确，而无法顺利平安地逃离。因此第一时间如何自动将警报信息传送给建筑物范围内的人员，并依所发生的事件状况进行实时判断，配合建筑信息系统通知及指引现场人员进行疏散，是重要的安全课题。然而，现代建筑物内的空间趋向复杂化，人们在发生灾害（例如火灾）时对于建筑内的信息掌握度常不足，无法在第一时间做出正确的判断与反应，导致一时恐慌甚至延迟了逃生的最佳时间点。目前，已有不少学者投入人群避难导引相关研究。[1, 2]Okada[3] 等人的研究亦指出，过去许多重大灾难（例如地震、火灾等）造成人员死伤惨重，最关键的原因就是无法于灾害发生时让现场人员知道确定的事发地点，以及立即为现场人员规划安全逃生路线并提供导引，这也是主动式防灾系统能于建筑物及公共空间里扮演重要角色的地方，而其中物联网技术是最适合用于防灾疏散系统的。因此，如何架构合适的通信机制是本研究发展主动式防灾通知系统的第一要务。

目前的防灾疏散研究大多以 2D 及 3D 的模拟分析环境为主，黄志翔[4] 则以 3D 环境加入时间轴方式，开发 4D 灾害疏散路径分析系统，并考虑各种灾害环境影响因子来规划与仿真灾害疏散路径。此外，已有研究以物联网（Internet of Things，IoT）技术完成紧急事件状况侦测回报的各种感测对象相连接，形成普及运算（Ubiquitous Computing）的环境并快速将信息回传中央控制系统。[5] 然而，在灾难发生期间，即时消息通知系统可能因供电系统或网络系统服务中断，如何在此种状况之下，将发生事件的位置及楼层空间等相关信息传递给现场的所有人员，包含受困者、导引人员甚至后续赶来的救难人员，尤其是针对大型建筑物、演唱会或巨量群众聚集的地方，是非常重要的。BIM 是目前建筑与营建业利用数字空间进行事前仿真与知识管理的热门技术，建筑物的 BIM 模型不仅具有立体化呈现建筑空间配置之功能，而且模型内亦可挂载防救灾相关之模型组件与信息，因此，本研究的实时防灾信息通知系统以建筑信息模型（BIM）作为可视化及室内位置定位信息的来源依据，在系统接收到灾害事件信息后，会利用模型中的空间与防灾信息主动规划避难路线，除可减少群众惊恐及逃生判断错误外，亦可提供

救难人员规划救难计划与掌握救难现场状况,达成防灾规划、防灾训练及灾害救援作业之整合。[6]当紧急事件发生时,信息的立即性与正确性是相当重要的一个环节,如何将现场实际状况反应至BIM模型上,使监控人员或是防灾救难人员第一时间掌握现场状况,进而导引或救难,是防灾信息系统的重点。

以往当灾难事件发生时,人们通常都处于被动地等待通知状态,因为通知信息传达的实时性与有效性会影响疏散的时间长短。若建筑物防灾信息系统能主动地透过手持或穿戴装置,将防灾信息通知建筑物里的群众,以利主动避开灾难,将可大幅提升疏散效率。因此,本文探讨如何利用建筑物现有的BIM信息将建筑物的空间与防灾信息建置于数据库系统中,结合DDS网络通信平台与物联网(IoT)的信息收集回传设备,并结合Beacon无线低功耗蓝牙(Bluetooth low energy,BLE)与在该现场人员手机定位,达成信息传递,以通知及警示灾害点,并结合逃生规划的相关设计,以利逃生疏散。而当现场环境断电时,需要一个特制路由器(Router)在停电时可以持续提供一段时间的电力,保持网络透通。如此一来,就算主机断讯,本研究所提出的实时通信架构也能自成网络沟通。有这样的防灾通知系统,于发生灾害的第一时间,救援人员也可以知道哪些人员仍深陷在灾害事件现场中,有利救援行动之安排。

2　研究方法与目的

本文探讨利用DDS网络通信架构结合物联网(IoT)设备,以及Beacon的联结应用在群众聚集的室内场所,例如演唱会场、校园教室、演说厅或发表会,现场的所有人可以通过所在的网络利用手持装置APP软件与中央控制面板做联机互动,并将所在室内的位置回传到中控台数据库,甚至利用交互式的手机APP发送活动信息就近互联与分享。因此,根据图1所示本研究整体系统蓝图将以BIM建筑物特性数据库作为中央管控中心,搭配DDS架构构筑物联网传感器设备,兼具收集各点的环境状况,例如温度、湿度、火警侦测与一氧化碳等基本感测环境信息。建构主动式手机APPs软件,用户一旦进入该建筑地区,中控中心将促使使用者手机下载特定DDS架构APPs,并将自己宣告为参与者(subscriber),在该特定室内地区也已建置相对应的Beacon,建置时候已经完整构筑连通网络,随时监控内部状况。借由MariaDB数据库系统收集物联网设备硬件环境感测信息,并同时使用Beacon技术,建置室内定位并联结个人手持式设备软件Apps,借由图形化的信息2D或3D信息功能,规划出用户接口易懂的防灾紧急通知系统与逃生路线。通过本研究初期设计紧急信息通知系统的网络传输平台之架构。当紧急事件状况发生时,事件发生地点就近的传感器(Publisher)将透过DDS数据传输架构回报现状到其他参与者与中央控制台,并将事件状况透过紧急事件与逃生QoS(Quality of Service)优先通道机制发送出给其他参与者,实时告知事件发生点的实际状态并联结相关的逃生规划。针对来救援的人员也可以透过相同机制达成救援计划。最终目的就是通过点对点的即时消息传递以减少伤亡人员,尤其在当现场网络或电力断讯时,实时通知的机制仍然可以正常运行。

2.1　建筑信息模型(BIM)

BIM是近年来在工程界中所兴起的一项技术,目前越来越多的工程导入BIM技术在建筑全生命周期中各阶段使用,也因为BIM技术可将建筑生命周期中从规划、设计、施工、营运维护至拆除的所有信息,包含几何信息、地理位置、周遭环境等,根据使用者需求透过统计、分析及模拟等方法,将其结果利用多维度,如1D(文字)、2D(图形)、3D(模型),甚至加上时间或成本等相关数据来展示信息。而BIM模型提供3D的环境以符合现实中的真实情况,亦可以可视化的方式将建筑信息予以呈现,也因过去系统仅局限在2D模式,若防灾系统与BIM的3D环境结合开发,将能提供更详细的防灾信息。

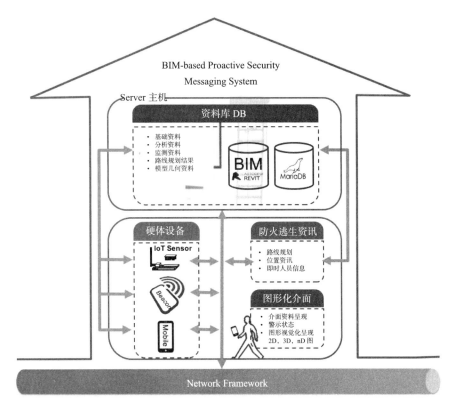

图 1　主动式防灾通知系统蓝图

资料来源：由本研究绘制。

然而，为了将模型更贴近真实情况以收集实时信息，目前有研究将 BIM 与物联网技术结合做许多应用的趋势，其应用领域可包含绿色建筑、物业管理、空间舒适度评估等，如刘其昌[7]等人开发的 PMV 环境评估系统，是于既有的空间环境中布置好所需的传感器，再于 Revit 环境中做 PMV 热舒适度实时可视化的呈现，其中也提到 BIM 数据可视化的特性对于用户来说是相对直觉，不需通过复杂的表格或数据表方式呈现。在 Wu[8] 等人的研究中，也将 BIM 与地理信息系统（Geographical Information System，GIS）技术结合至云端架构上，整合开发一套设施能源评估工具（Virtual Facility Energy Assessment，VFEA），使用者可通过这套工具了解建物基础信息，并透过 BIM 动态仿真的优点，透过传感器将实时的能源性能呈现于模型上，并针对其做检测分析，甚至辅助决策以提升优化。

综合上述，本研究系统架构以 BIM 技术为基础，将建筑物内感测装置与 BIM 模型中已建置好的对象做映对链接，作为人员室内定位方式，通过前述优点，借由传感器将实时的环境监测信息与状态呈现于模型上，利用此状态变化链接紧急信息状况，将实时通知送至现场群众的手持设备。并以 BIM 技术为基础，利用其仿真可视化将数据回馈于模型上作为系统接口的呈现，以提升整体系统的一致效能与操作性，让使用者容易理解所读取的信息。

2.2　常见通信协议比较

目前，一般物联网通信协议常见的有 MQTT（Message Queue Telemetry Transport）[9]，XMPP（Extensible Messaging and Presence Protocol）[11]，AMQP（Advanced Message Queuing Protocol）[12] 和 DDS（Data Distribution Service）[10] 等，由这几种传输机制达到物联网信息收集与传递的功能，以下将比较这几种通信协议的特点。

（1）MQTT 为主从式（Client Server）架构，由一个顶端的服务器作为统整者，数据会从传感器传送至顶端的服务器（Device to Server，D2S），若是有信息要发布的时候，服务器会把信息发送给已经注册过的使用者（Server to Device，S2D）。但若发生线路阻断时，信息传递则可能发生异常。

（2）DDS（Data Distribution Services）：DDS 属于参与者点对点（Peer-to-Peer）架构，每个客户端都可以同时是服务器端，信息会在参与者之间互相传递（Device to Device，D2D）。有信息的时候，DDS 架构会将信息分散给各个客户端，若两参与者中间有线路阻断时，仍然可以通过其他参与者相互传递。

（3）XMPP（Extensible Messaging and Presence Protocol）：XMPP 是以 XML 作为信息传递的基底，属于主从式架构，类似 SMTP（Simple Mail Transfer Protocol）。信息要先传递给 A 伺服（D2S），再由 A 服务器交给 B 服务器（Server to Server，S2S），最后才会由 B 服务器将信息交付给收件者（S2D）。且信息以 XML 传递，造成其头文件（纪录传递过程所需信息）容易过大，效率较低。

（4）AMQP（Advanced Message Queuing Protocol）：与 MQTT 类似，属于主从式架构。服务器收到信息之后（D2S），服务器间会先进行交换，若接收端尚未联机，则数据会储存在一个等待容器中，当接收端联机时便会将信息传递过去（S2D）。AMQP 最主要的目标就是可靠且异步的信息传递，但一如以上主从式架构，一旦服务器无法联机时，数据便无法传递。当建筑物中有如火灾等灾难发生时，会希望信息可以迅速地传递，并且不会受限于单一的数据源。

在以上介绍的几个通信协议之中，根据表 1 中的比较，DDS 所能提供的效果应最能符合本研究所期待的信息传输方式。本文采用 OMG DDS（Object Management Group，OMG）于 2015 年 4 月 10 日修正的 1.4 版本规范，其应用领域相当广，像航空、军方、工业自动化等需要实时信息发送或处理多个领域等。

IoT 常见通信协议比较表　　　　　　　　　　　　　　　　　　　　　　　表 1

协议名称	MQTT	DDS	XMPP	AMQP
可靠度	高	高	低	高
数据传递架构	Client-Server	Pear-to-Pear	Client-Server	Client-Server
服务器受损对通信影响	高	低	高	高
IoT 通信关系	D2S & S2D	D2D	D2S & S2S & S2D	D2S

资料来源：本研究整理。[9-12]

DDS 通信协议是建置以 D2D（Device to Device），跳脱与以往星状网络架构不同的方式（图 2），其优点就是可在短时间内将数据散布给其他的装置，不需要将数据先传回服务器后再发送于接收端，信息依然可在各装置间传递。

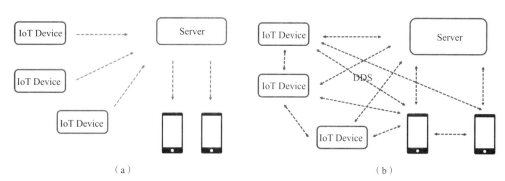

图 2　传统网络架构与 DDS 网络架构示意图
（a）传统星状网络架构；（b）DDS 网络架构
资料来源：由本研究绘制。

2.3 DDS 通信协议与防灾通知系统

本文利用物联网（IoT）感测设备作为环境状况的数据收集，例如温度、湿度、火警信息及一氧化碳等。一旦所处的环境信息有异常，可以通过这些设备发出警讯并传递通知给所有在同一建筑物的群众，以利主动采取防灾行动。虽然目前的物联网技术及设备成熟度高，但因现在的环境条件日趋复杂，传输上容易碰上一些瓶颈[11]，其中最主要的原因是每个物联网传感器皆来自不同的厂商，一般设备商为求降低成本及节省电源，处理器已经被换成更简单的架构，省掉许多功能。而为了避免电源耗电的浪费，设备端也无法随时开启。如此一来便将传递信息的负担转到网络传输上，容易造成网络塞车问题。同时还需要调节网络封包大小用以适应网络有限的链接，也是信息传递的弱点。为了解决以上的弱点，可利用如 REST 技术（Representation State Transfer）方案来改进，其中以 DDS 架构利用网络仿真器各项评比，包括窄带宽、系统效能延迟及封包遗失等的结果优于其他如 MQTT，客制化 UDP 及 CoAP（Constrained Application Protocol）等的协定。[14] 从 DDS 架构来看[15]，此规范标准化了分布式系统针对数据信息发布、传递与接收的使用端和接收端的发布-订阅机制（Publisher-Subscriber）行为，根据图 3 所示，在所有参与者中，一旦事件信息（例如"火灾"）启动，发布端将会根据所指定的 QoS 优先级将此事件信息利用 DataWriter 传送给所有参与者，而订阅端将利用 DataReader 机制处理此信息的传递确认或变更，达到点对点的通信连接。

如此事件信息定义为 Topic，并带有数据及 QoS 优先传送顺序与唯一的名称，不会跟其他参与的数据信息冲突。为了快速传达事件信息到参与者，DDS 重新定义了传输平台，包含了 OSI 网络上的传输层（Transport Layer）、会议层（Session Layer）、表达层（Presentation Layer）等（如图 4 所示），透过此种通信协议架构方式，更突显 DDS 的紧急信息点对点快速传输方式的应用优势。

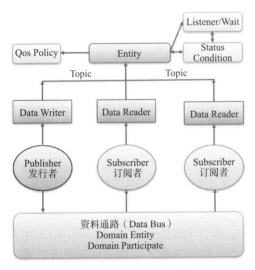

图 3　DDS 网络架构图[15]

资料来源：由本研究绘制。

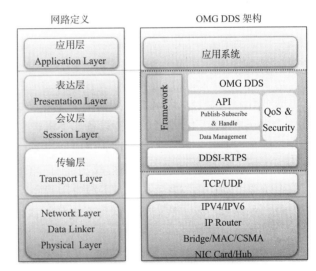

图 4　DDS 架构上下层关联图[13]

资料来源：由本研究绘制。

3　系统架构及流程展示

本研究将 BIM 模型信息建置于中控数据库主机中，包含建筑空间信息及 IoT 传感器检测值、位置，同时将建筑内的 Beacon 位置建置起来。所有进入此建筑物的移动式设备必须下载附有 DDS 引擎的应用程序，以利建置整个系统的传输架构机制。利用 DDS 点对点传输的能力，一旦有紧急事件发生时，传感器会以发行者（Publisher）身份将事件的状况及疏散规划（Topics）通过 Data Writer 机制发送到已建置的参与者网络，QoS 也会根据所定义的高优先级传送；其他移动式装置及远程订阅者（Subscriber）将根据订阅方式通过 Data Reader 机制读取实时信息进行反应，而不至于让使用者产生惊恐而延误疏散最佳时机。详细信息传送架构及流程请参考图 5，当系统在没有事件发生时，各个传感器会将数据传回至主机，以利信息收集统计分析使用。

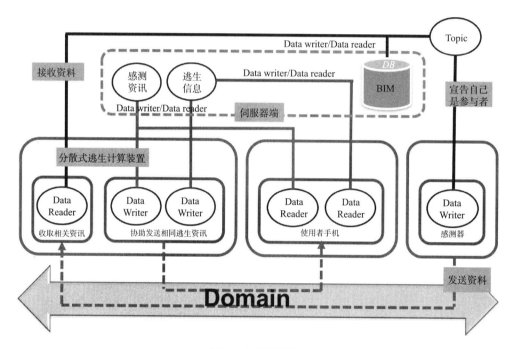

图 5　系统架构图

资料来源：由本研究绘制。

本研究针对大型公众建筑物，如演唱会、体育场，或者聚众集会场所等作为目标。这些场所大多已设有无线网络系统，参与者的手持设备如手机、平板与场地预先设置的 Beacon 等可以串连成一个信息传递系统，方便所有参与者及管理者可以通过参与者网络快速传递信息。本研究建置一个 BIM 建筑信息管理主机，与具有 DDS 的网络协议功能的 IoT 设备持续连接，一旦使用者进入建筑物并链接至网络后，系统会主动让参与者手持设备下载应用程序以及预先准备的逃生避难信息，并利用 Beacon 技术进行定位。如图 6 所示，我们将分两种系统状态：（1）未发生灾难（闲置状态）；（2）发生灾难。在闲置状态时，环境监测值将持续收集环境资料（例如温湿度、二氧化碳浓度、热源感应等）传至中央控制主机端数据库中，进行环境状态分析。发生灾难时，传感器将直接判断灾难发生的情况并传递警示信号给中央主机及所参与的网络中，同时通知各装置启动对应的逃难策略，以达到快速主动通知并链接导引逃生的功能。

4　结论

顺应智慧城市的发展，许多大型建筑物采用 BIM 技术进行维运管理将渐趋成熟，对建筑物内，尤

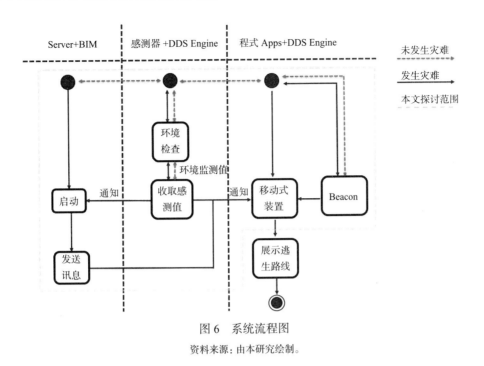

图 6　系统流程图

资料来源：由本研究绘制。

其是众人群聚的场所，主动提供实时防灾信息通知给建筑物中的所有人，以利灾难突发时进行相关的避难引导，并将灾难降到最低，应会是智能建筑的重要服务之一。因此，本研究提出以建筑物 BIM 模型信息为基础，结合物联网（IoT）设备，通过 DDS 点对点的网络协议，利用当今人手普遍使用的手持式装备，结合 Beacon 的定位功能，链接成为一个紧急事件信息传递网络的架构，不受现场环境因为电力设备及网络设备服务中断的影响，仍能提供紧急防灾信息通知的服务，以利群众避灾。本文将讨论重点放在实现此主动式防灾通知系统的实时通信架构设计上，希望提供给未来智慧城市中的智能建筑作参考。

致谢

特别感谢李孟阳先生提供相关 DDS 的信息，以利探讨本研究的可行性完整度。

Communication Framework Design for a BIM-based Proactive Security Messaging System

Kuo Wei-Liang, Lee Chiu-Ming, Wu Hsuan-Chu, Hsieh Shang-Hsien

(Department of Civil Engineering, Taiwan University)

Abstract: During a disaster, such as fire, earthquake, etc., in an indoor environment, it is important to inform the crowd in the building correct and timely disaster-related information, especially guidance for evacuation if needed. This paper proposes a BIM-based proactive security messaging system to provide disaster-related notification services in a building for people to have better understanding of what is happening and what actions they are suggested to take in response to the situation. The system takes advantage of BIM (Building Information Modeling) technology to manage spatial information and disaster-related attributes of the building, and integrates IoT (Internet of Things) sensing devices, personal hand-held devices with Apps, and an advanced communication protocol to form a reliable communication framework for messaging services. The focus of this paper is placed on the design of the communication framework in which DDS (Data Distribution Service) protocol is proposed in this work.

Keywords: BIM (Building information modeling), DDS (Data distribution service), Communications protocol, IoT (Internet of things), Evacuation

参考文献

[1] 张书维. 体育馆空间避难路径之视觉仿真研究——以文化大学新建体育馆为例 [D]. 台北中国文化大学建筑与都市计划研究所，2004.

[2] Gunnar G L. Models of Wayfinding in Emergency Evacuations[J]. Europe Journal of Operational Research, 1994, 105（3）: 371-389.

[3] Okada C, Miyamoto R, Yamane A, Wada T, Ohtsuki K, Okada H. A Novel Urgent Communications Technologies for Sharing Evacuation Support Information in Panic-type Disasters. Proceedings of the 2010 Sixth International Conference on Networking and Services（ICNS）, IEEE, Cancun, Mexico, March 7-13, 2010.

[4] Huang C H, Wu I C. Applying 4D Simulation in Disaster Evacuation Route Planning. Proceedings of the 11th International Conference on Construction Applications of Virtual Reality. Weimar, Germany, November 3-4, 2011.

[5] 王淑卿，王顺生，陈庆维，王信杰. 建构以服务为导向的防灾监测物联网 [J]. 信息科技国际期刊，2013，7（2）: 51-62.

[6] 石世佑. 以 BIM 模型为基础之防灾管理案例探讨 [D]. 新竹交通大学土木工程系所，2013.

[7] Liu C C, Kuo W L, Shiu R S, Wu I C. Estimating and Visualizing Thermal Comfort Level via a Predicted Mean Vote in a BIM System. Proceedings of the 16th International Conference on Computing in Civil

and Building Engineering. Osaka, Japan, July 6-8, 2016.

[8] Wu W, Yang X, Fan Q. GIS-BIM based Virtual Facility Energy Assessment（VFEA）—— Framework Development and Use Case of California State University, Fresno. Proceedings of 2014 International Conference on Computing in Civil and Building Engineering（2014）. Orlando, Florida, June 23-25, 2014.

[9] Locke D. MQ Telemetry Transport（MQTT）V3.1 Protocol Specification. Technical Report, International Business Machines Corporation（IBM）and Eurotech. https: //www.ibm.com/developerworks/library/ws-mqtt/, 2010.

[10] DDS Portal——Data Distribution Services. 1997 [2017-4-29]. http: //portals.omg.org/dds/.

[11] XMPP. https: //xmpp.org/. [2017-4-29].

[12] AMQP. https: //www.amqp.org/. [2017-4-29].

[13] Wentao S, Yingdi Y, Droms R, et al. Challenges in IoT networking via TCP/IP architecture. NDN Project, Tech. Rep. NDN-0038, 2016.

[14] Yuang C, Thomas K. Performance evaluation of IoT protocols under a constrained wireless access network. Selected Topics in Mobile & Wireless Networking（MoWNeT）. 2016 International Conference on. IEEE, April 11-13, 2016.

[15] Gerardo P. Omg data-distribution service: Architectural overview: Proceedings. 23rd International Conference on. IEEE. Distributed Computing Systems Workshops, May 19-22, 2003.

SENS project: A User Experience Approach for Smart Energy Environment

Chang Teng-Wen [1], Huang Hsin-Yi [1], Sambit Datta [2]

(1. Yunlin University of Science and Technology, Taiwan; 2. Curtin University of Technology)

Abstract: In recent years, Internet of Things (IoT) applications have been proposed for energy informatics in smart homes and cities. Taiwan has the technology, research and development and manufacturing capabilities and a solid foundation of abundant talent, to take advantage of these new developments. One aspect of the convergence of Internet of things with Smart home applications is the user experience. There is a need for a more dynamic energy infrastructure to provide feasible services for the users. We believe through the user experience of the system through human computer interfaces. A system called "Sensible ENergy System" (SENS) is developed through the user experience design methods with sensor network technology. Through SENS, we combine smart meter informatics to achieve IoT function to understand user behavior and electricity consumption. The interaction between users and the devices through SENS can also optimize and reduce the power consumption. Furthermore, SENS will, through the smart grid address the combination of power services, and use the solar PV power storage and discharge characteristics. SENS enables users to immediately understand their electricity situation. Finally, through the user process it might change the user behaviors.

Keywords: Smart energy, Smart home, Smart grid, User experience, User interface

1 Background

Recently green energy is an important topic especially when It's an nounced that Taiwan is seeking for a nuclear-free proposal for energy.The Energy Bureau issued the latest power reform policy in July 2016 to open up a new development in green energy in the future[1], there will be more green power industry open in different levels such as supply chains, the maintenance of energy generators and other associated supporting companies. Creating your own energy plan will be easier and have better supports than ever. Expect that, it will encourage individual families to set up their own solar photovoltaic facilities and generate energy either to the power grid or just for their own uses.

Even with all the developed technologies, the key person: the user is missing. Without studying the user behaviors and their consequence for contribution to the green energy process, the ultimate optimization that can meet both users and energy generators is not achievable. Consequently, the research question in this paper is what kind of user experience for a knowable green energy users

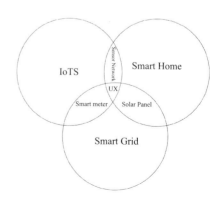

Figure 1 Three layers

should be.

User layers, built-environment layers and energy layers are adapted to study the interaction between users and the energy generated or consumed. User layers provide the interface for users to interact with the devices in the environment. Built-environment layers connect the networked objects with built-environment such as solar panel and network services. Energy layer will be the infrastructure for connecting to the grid. Each layer is described in the following section.

1.1 Users Layer: User Behaviors and IoTs

This layer studies user behaviors and how they can interact with the environment that is full of connected objects, *a.l.a.* Internet of Things (IoT). Through the modular connected components, IoTs can allow users to appraise the current situation and interact with them immediately. Through the Smart energy and smart grid connected to the smart home, the user can switch from different locations and different energy supply (such as solar, wind, etc.), and can provide a stable power to the user. The interaction between users and the devices can also generate and reduce the power consumption of the location. Additionally, via the device users can connect to built-environment layer below to access the power generation information such as solar panel storage status.

1.2 Built Environment Layer: Smart Home and Solar Panels

With user layer, the surrounding environment form the built-environment layer. This layer emphasizes the smart environment between users and the energy system. Built-environment with smartness provide the base to allow user layer to interact with components in this layer to access the information from energy layer underneath. Understandiny the actual device used in the working condition and change status can help to more accurately understand the dynamic variable type of boby cortex which produced in the actual application. This can be used as a model of adjustment functions. The smart home allows user to control the external situation by which the function through the IoTs can also achieve the effectiveness of energy conservation. By connecting IoTs in user layer and solar panels, this layer can further build up the energy storage and saving effect. However, the roof type solar powers every 3 Ping and can store up to 1 kilowatts power. With this kind of power storage of 1 kilowatts, different regions can achieve different wattage power. In the case of Yunlin county, averagely 3.52 kilowatts of electricity can be generated every day, and 1,284 kilowatts the relative power can be produced (as shown in Figure 2).

1.3 Energy Layer: Smart Grids and Smart Energy

With Built-environment layer, there is a need for a more dynamic energy infrastructure to provide feasible services for the users. While all components in smart living environment have been IoT-ized, all the energy flow needs the support of dynamic energy generators. A model to understand and design such distributed interaction is needed [2]. Smart grid technology recently developed provides some insights. Smart grid incorporating with more efficient solar panels and batteries can keep energy as information that can be stored and re-distributing among built-environments. Apparently, smart grid development status has three key points: (1) Communication integration; (2) The popularity of measurement equipment; (3) Development of

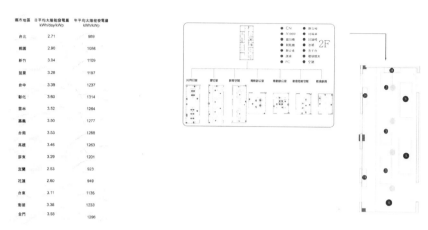

Figure 2　Solar power proportion　　　Figure 3　device installation

applications[3].

Among these advanced technologies, smart grid is an integrated cross network communication technology, with the advanced control system, sensor, measurement and meter reading, and electric power equipment and power grid components as collocation combination, this technology can improve the short-term Taiwan power network on distributed load, and in the long term it can be used for the electric equipment asset management transformer, load management and prevention of electric larceny[4]. With smart grid infrastructure, smart meters can improve the consciousness and awareness of the people, to understand the power consumption of various appliances in the home situation, and further regulate the user's electricity consumption and electricity. Through the smart meter communications and cloud features, it can instantly let users understand the use of the situation, and can save unnecessary energy consumption. Therefore, under the smart grid infrastructure, and the effect of green energy such as solar panels, and thus we can achieve the power transmission, distribution and power generation needs, then electricity will no longer be one-way transmission and profitability.

2　Literature Reviews

2.1　Two Smart Grid Systems

For the average family usages, two smart grid systems are reviewed: Off-Grid Connected PV system and Grid Connected PV system[5, 6].

Off-Grid Connected PV system (as shown in Figure 4) requires batteries installed. The solar barrier array output needs to be suited with a barrier diode to avoid power backflow to burn the solar module. When the sunlight intensity is high, the generated electricity not only provides the use of the current load but also allow the excess power to be stored in the battery pack via discharge controllers for night or rainy days. In addition, independent system design must pay special consideration for the capacity of the battery, which battery capacity of about 10 times the system power generation, to be required for nighttime electricity in the off-grid situation.

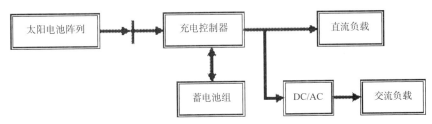

Figure 4　Off-grid connected PV system[6]

Grid Connected PV system power (as shown in Figure 5) increases with the increase in sunlight intensity, but the system design load is often about the solar cell array power generation. If the load is small or no load case, even the summer noon, the solar array generates electricity without any proper load consumption, electricity is wasted. If the system can produce 10 Kilowatts electricity at noon, the load power consumption is 7 Kilowatts, then the power generation system remaining three kW powers are wasted. The optimized solar photovoltaic system is in parallel with the mains as shown in Figure 5. The installed converter has the counter-current power generation function, that is, when the solar cell power generation is larger than the power consumption of the power load, the system will automatically send the excess power back to the main grid; otherwise, if the load is greater than the load power consumption of solar cells, or solar power on the night when the solar power, the main grid will supply the power apparently.

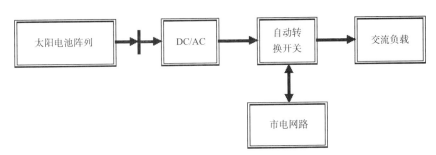

Figure 5　Grid connected PV system[6]

2.2　Sensor Networked Smart Home

Most of smart home cases are built with sensor networks either point to point connection or the hierarchical view of layers. With the realization of point to point communication and determination of network topology, sensors nodes are often connected, and the effect nodes are to control multiple home appliances. Sensors nodes in the built-environment are responsible for perceived data's which users care. Central node is the controlling center of the whole network. In most of cases, central node can connect to the PC or gateway device to construct a small wireless sensor network and communicate with Internet and GSM network. This will be convenient for users to get real-time and reliable data by ways they are used to and good at, like by web services or SMS[7].

Such smart home network provides the users with a real-time feedback mechanism about energy consumption needed for this research. It makes the smart home automation be energy-saving as well smart. On behalf of user experience, the smart home should also provide different ways to meet users' demands. Web sites, smartphone terminals and interface of virtual reality can be used to improve the user experience of smart home automation[8]. In the terminal sub-systems, smartphones and the PC will behave as terminal devices in this system. They make it easy and convenient for users to access home appliances' real time energy consumption information.

2.3 User Experience Design

To connect users with green energy or energy consumption, awareness plays an important role as demand for huge amount of energy generation is growing daily. This research gives a solution to encourage people to know their energy footprint and take required action to reduce it[9]. Here the proposed model is comprised of hardware setup that includes smart meters and embedded hardware establishing a smart grid network using smart meter are measured by embedded controller that collects data from smart meters and then sends all data to an internet based server.

User experience design methods that are often explored in finding contextual information and its analysis towards user-centered design prototype are used in refining and analyzing the information unbalance between habitants (end users) and the energy usages surrounding them. Persona, contextual inquiry and user journey maps that towards scenario design are used as design methods.

End user not only can access his consumption statistics but also can remotely control power supply to his household using Android App on his mobile device[10]. This approach will be the base for our system implementation.

3 The System

In order to find the contextual scenario that is suitable for this research, an experimental field and construction of sonar panel as an experimental system are conducted for evaluating and finding the possible interaction that are desirable for our users.

3.1 The Field: Idea Factory

Idea Factory is a platform for the people-oriented creators from either engineering or design domain to learn, think and make by providing the inter-disciplinary workshops in both physical space and virtual space. Thinking part, Idea Factory contains many distributed thinking corners that allow makers to relax and think. For Learning, all of the innovators of learning space and the flipped classroom are connected either virtually or physically to provide dynamic and feasible learning spaces for makers. For Making, the facility and management of design workshop, digital workshop and craft workshop are integrated together to offer a seamless working pipeline (shown in Figure 6).

3.2 The Steps

In this research, following the user experience design paradigm, four steps are conducted. First, users and contextual studies have done in the field we in an existing in the field (as shown in Figure 7). Persona of energy consumption and preservation (as shown in Figure 8) are researched and classified in order to plan the

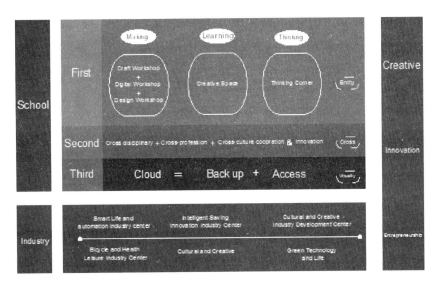

Figure 6   Idea factory system

user journey and the journey map is made.

Several interactive processes for several personas are decided with the architecture of the IoT in parallel. With environmental support, the solar panels and smart meters are built-in to form a test case for a sensor networked smart home environment for reifying the user experience. Through the smart meter data updated to the cloud and the collected data shown in SENS, the system can control and record the user's electricity situation. Through the existing solar panel with smart grid energy storage, it can achieve two-way power, when the storage consumption reached can be self-sufficient, will reduce the invisible waste of energy, and achieve energy utility recycle.

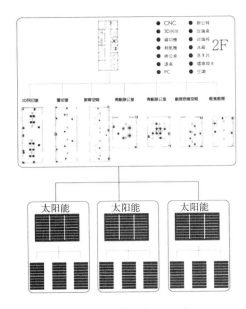

		人物A	人物B	人物C	人物D	人物E	人物F
雷切室	雷切机使用	√		√		√	√
	模型制作					√	√
	割纸机使用	√		√		√	√
	专案讨论	√	√			√	√
	电脑使用	√				√	√
	雷切机课程使用	√				√	√
	工坊导览	√		√			
3D列印室	3D列印课程	√				√	√
	3D列印	√				√	√
	CNC使用	√					
	工坊导览	√		√			
青创办公室	行政管理	√	√				
教育空间	课堂演讲				√		√
	会议	√	√		√		
	主管开会				√	√	
	助教辅导课程	√	√				
创意发想空间	专案讨论					√	
	创意发想活动	√	√		√		
轻食厨房	饮食制作	√			√		√

Figure 7   Idea factory plan   Figure 8   persona analysis

3.3   A Scenario

In order to evaluate and understand the scenario of our end-users in the energy consumption situation, we develop a system called "Sensible ENergy System" (SENS) with smart grid embedded in the Idea Factory. The basic scenario of SENS is to display the necessary information while users approach that location or situation and response when condition changes. The interaction sequence of SENS from entering the space to explore the energy consumption is analyzed and derived from user journey map and shown from Figure 9 to Figure 12.

Starting with entering the space, users enter each space of Idea Factory with an app on the QR code on the screen on the door as shown in Figure 9. After scanning QR code, the energy consumption/generation of that location is displayed in the SENS with basic location information such as room number and function as shown in Figure 10.

(a) Enter the place　　(b) View

Figure 9　Everyone enters the room in idea factory is via an app with QR code

(a) Location Information　　(b) View

Figure 10　The energy usages of a particular location is shown associated with related information

(a) Plan the energy usages　　(b) Response from SENS

Figure 11　The energy usages of each machine is shown in SENS with notification

(a) Unplug the devices　　(b) SENS responses with lower consumption

Figure 12　When user unplugs the device, the lower energy consumption is immediately shown in SENS

When user is near these electronic devices located in the room, SENS will display the energy consumption and their information such as devices names as shown in Figure 11. User can make a choice if they want to know how much can they save. If user unplugs the device, SENS will display how much the energy usages or monthly payment are saved as shown in Figure 12.

4 Conclusion

The system design proposed in this paper aims to help users to understand the energy patterns in their built environment and identify potential sources of energy saving. Through SENS energy information that might normally be missed is transparently provided to enable the user to make energy consumption decisions. Therefore, the SENS infrastructure, through the equipment on the QR code device, smart meter, and user experience analysis as described in this paper will enable a more suitable user scenario for green energy development, awareness and consumption. With the SENS system, users can understand the immediate power consumption data, and assess their energy decisions and to control the energy consumption, and changing their interactive behaviors accordingly. In order to access the user experiences, the field is a controllable factor that might affect the contextual study for a normal family context. Therefore, future studies will focus on the feasible structure and components of energy sensor networks for testifying different scenarios and possible usages with different persona.

SENS：以使用者经验探讨智慧电能环境之互动体验模式

张登文[1]　黄馨仪[1]　Sambit Datta[2]

（1. 台湾云林科技大学；2. 科廷科技大学）

摘　要：近年来，有很多互联网的物联网智能家居案例。台湾具有优良的技术研发和制造能力，具有各行各业，坚实的人才基础，这些优势在相关行业的发展中容易向前发展。而与智慧家居连接的物联网是模组化的，缺乏用户体验。我们相信通过使用者经验可以轻松匹配使用者需求。本研究通过使用者经验生成新的 SENS 系统。通过设备结合智能电表实现 IoT 功能，更简单地了解使用者使用电力情况。且数据会即时的传志介面。此外，我们将通过智慧电网作为电力整合服务，并采用太阳能电池板的蓄电放电特性。可以让使用者立即了解他们的电力状况。最后，通过使用者之使用过程可能会改变用户行为。

关键词：智能电源，智能家居，智能电表，使用者经验，使用者介面

参考文献

[1] 能源局. 电业法修正草案. 2016. Available from：http：//xn--zbv96gu45cwma.tw/2016/10/20/%E8%A1%8C%E6%94%BF%E9%99%A2%E6%9C%83%E9%80%9A%E9%81%8E%E3%80%8C%E9%9B%BB%E6%A5%AD%E6%B3%95%E3%80%8D%E4%BF%AE%E6%AD%A3%E8%8D%89%E6%A1%88/.

[2] Chang T-W，S Datta，I.-C Lai. Modelling Distributed Interaction with Dynamic Agent Role Interplay

System[J]. International Journal of Digital Media Design, 2016. 8（2）: 1-14.

[3] 高铭志等. 美国地方政府推动智慧型电网规范对台湾之启示 [J]. 台湾科技法律与政策论丛, 2013. 10（1）: 1-48.

[4] 陈崇宪, 苏桓娴. 浅谈"再生能源发展条例"立法内容. 能源报导, 2010. 能源局. Available from: http: //energymonthly.tier.org.tw/outdatecontent.asp?ReportIssue=201006&Page=5.

[5] Padiyar H U, P N Sreedhar, G P Kini. Grid Connected PV System. in National Renewable energy Convention of Solar Energy Society of India & International conference On New Millennium——Alternative Energy Solutions for Sustainable Development. 2003: Coimbatore, Tamil Nadu.

[6] Lin T. Economic Analysis for On-Grid c-Si PV System with Auxiliary Software Developing, 应用工程科学研究所, 高雄应用科技大学, 2009: 145.

[7] Yuan X, S Peng. A research on secure smart home based on the Internet of Things. in 2012 IEEE International Conference on Information Science and Technology, 2012.

[8] Pedrasa, M A A, T D Spooner, I F MacGill. Coordinated Scheduling of Residential Distributed Energy Resources to Optimize Smart Home Energy Services. IEEE Transactions on Smart Grid, 2010. 1（2）: 134-143.

[9] Mckay, E N, UI is communication. How to design intuitive, user-centered interface by foucing on effective communication. 2013.

[10] Patttanayak, A S, B S Pattnaik, B N Panda. Implementation of a smart grid system to remotely monitor, control and schedule energy sources using Android based mobile devices. in 2014 9th International Conference on Industrial and Information Systems（ICIIS）. 2014.

建筑屋顶绿化对于顶楼空间降温效益的评估研究：以高雄市建筑为例

程达隆[1] 李彦颐[2] 张七斗[3] 林嘉雄[3]

（1.台湾树德科技大学计算机与通信系；2.台湾树德科技大学建筑与室内设计研究所；3.台湾树德科技大学室内设计系）

摘　要：高雄市因为过度城市化造成市区内绿地过小，且大楼林立造成城市的过度开发，且城市规划多属于高建筑密度和容积率，低绿地覆盖率，加上又有交通繁杂与空调废热的负面因素，造成了热岛效应以及地球暖化的问题。且间接造成冷气空调系统的负荷变高，日常生活的能耗也会慢慢增加，对于当下以节能减碳为发展目标的构想，是首要处理的问题。鉴于城市发展用地有限，高雄市政府因此开始推动建筑物立体绿化及屋顶绿化的系列计划以推广高雄市区建筑绿化活动，希望借由建筑物的绿化提高城市内绿化植栽面积，建筑物屋顶与外墙的垂直立体绿化方式随着使用者与建筑形态之间的讨论与研究逐渐朝向以建筑立面与绿色屋顶的设置为主流，期许高雄市建筑物透过立体绿化带动一波新节能减碳举措与生活方式。高雄市近年积极推广屋顶绿化与阳光屋顶计划，此两项政策正面意义除了应对都市气候变迁以及奠定生态城乡发展基础外，还为朝向低碳住宅发展做好准备。本研究希望通过监测高雄市既有进行相关绿化工程的建筑，借由搜集屋顶绿化以及顶楼的温度差异，经由汇整分析后作为未来市政府推动屋顶绿化倡导的基础科学研究参考。

关键词：隔热，屋顶绿化，温热环境，节能减碳

1　缘起

高雄市因为过度城市化造成市区内绿地过小，且大楼林立造成城市的过度开发，城市规划多属于高建筑密度和容积率，低绿地覆盖率，加上又有交通繁杂与空调废热的负面因素，造成了热岛效应以及地球暖化的问题。且高雄市外部气候属于亚热带气候，加上高度城市化间接造成市民在日常生活中过度依赖冷气空调系统，造成能源负荷高，整体城市能耗量也会慢慢增加。这对于当下以节能减碳为发展目标的构想，是首要处理的问题。

1.1　计划缘起

鉴于城市发展用地有限，高雄市政府因此开始推动建筑物立体绿化及屋顶绿化的系列计划，以推广高雄市区建筑绿化活动（图1）。希望借由建筑物的绿化提高城市内绿化植栽面积，建筑物屋顶与外墙的垂直立体绿化方式随着使用者与建筑形态之间的讨论与研究，逐渐以建筑立面与绿色屋顶的设置为主流，期许高雄市建筑物通过立体绿化带动新一波节能减碳举措与生活方式。

本研究希望通过监测高雄市既有进行相关绿化工程的建筑，借由搜集屋顶绿化以及顶楼的温度差异，经由汇整分析作为未来市政府推动屋顶绿化宣传倡导的基础科学研究参考。

图 1　高雄屋顶绿化计划——高雄美术馆屋顶绿化航拍

1.2　计划目标

高雄市近年积极推广屋顶绿化与阳光屋顶计划，此两项政策正面意义除了应对都市气候变迁以及奠定生态城乡发展基础外，还向低碳住宅发展做好准备，降低室内温度与减少冷气空调用电量。

在高雄市政府推动发展健康低碳城市，因此推动绿光屋顶计划（包括太阳能光伏以及屋顶绿化），透过相关计划执行过程中传导市政府积极推动此两项政策的用意，不管是架构太阳光伏系统或者屋顶绿化工程，都是为降低使用能源的需求。但因为不是每栋建筑物或市民的条件均适合装设太阳能光伏系统，届时可以建议进行屋顶绿化以降低受热，甚至将绿化的方式从常见草地置换成顶楼农场进行绿化，一方面能灵活使用空间，另外一方面可以达成建筑物降温的目标。

为了有效降低热岛效应以及达成城市节能减碳两项目标，高雄市政府推广建筑绿化系列政策，以改善城市环境。设置绿色屋顶可有效降低建筑物辐射热，调整气候，创造生物栖息地，减少二氧化碳排放等，进而改善城市热岛效应，提升生活品质。于建筑外部设置自然遮阳隔热系统，例如通过屋顶绿化或立面绿化等方式降低建筑物的直接日射，可降低建筑物获得的热辐射。但均以减少建筑物使用空调系统为目标，继而在居住使用时符合室内环境的舒适度。

综上所述，本研究计划目标约略分列如下：

（1）检视屋顶有无设置绿化时室内外的温度差异；

（2）针对不同建筑案例的朝向以及绿化面积进行比较；

（3）分析比较绿色屋顶的降温效益；

（4）借由本研究推估绿化面积对于减少室内使用空调降温的时数。

2　研究内容计划说明

2.1　选定检测案例

- 案例 A——小港区透天厝建筑

以高雄市区内透天厝建筑且已完成屋顶绿化工程者为优先量测对象，同时寻找周边邻近建筑物屋顶未做任何遮阳工程的案例，进行比较监测分析（图2）。对实际建构完成屋顶绿化的透天厝案例，进行量测室外屋顶与室内温度，同时运用热显像仪器进行辐射热的对比。

- 案例B——河堤圆舞曲大楼

高雄市之示范社区"河堤社区"，具有高度生态廊道意象区，配合高楼住户既有建筑屋顶绿化的示范，强化河堤社区评估得到的意象，转化为屋顶立体绿化的高雄市示范点。本计划在屋顶上进行规划，包含兼具屋顶突出物遮阴区的"中低日照植栽区"、"全日照景观植栽区"以及"屋顶农园社区共享区"三部分。

- 案例C——国邦企业商办大楼

国邦企业大楼位于高雄市青年路与中山路交叉口，为一栋住办混合综合大楼，现阶段有高雄市金融、设计、国贸、商业等属性企业进驻于此，其中由许家彰建筑师事务所针对顶楼空间进行规划设计。许建筑师长年来极力推动高雄建筑的生态化转型，并身体力行改造自家事务所顶楼空间，期望未来可将其经验应用于相关透天厝设计方案中，为改善高雄热岛效应尽一份心力。

- 案例D——苓雅区洪家透天厝

本案例为位于苓雅区河北路的透天厝，屋顶现已有大量盆式植栽，但因无法有效降低顶楼室内温度，且透过室内温度监测分析得知室内温度偏高，所以期望未来进行绿化工程后能有效扩大农场面积，以及利用薄层绿化保留部分雨水以减少浇水的用水量。

图2　本研究进行改造前后之四案例位置

2.2 现场实测操作仪器

仪器名称	仪器规格
CDR06 无纸记录器	取样速率:5 次(秒)储存容量:内部 Flash 储存器容量 8MB，另附 CF Card 256 MB
可监测物质	通讯协定:Modbus TCP/IP 10Base T(RS-232 / RS-422 / RS-485 选配)
温度（Temperature） 多点温度表示 最高最低温度位置显示 自动温度追踪	工作环境: 温度:5 ~ 50 ℃, 湿度:20% ~ 80% RH 电源:90 ~ 264V AC，47 ~ 63Hz 尺寸:W166 × H144 × D174mm

仪器名称	仪器规格
热电偶温度测线	检测温度范围:-50 ~ 200℃。 可测量空气或表面温度
可监测物质	
温度（Temperature）	

仪器名称	仪器规格
FLIR A325sc 红外线热显影系统（图3）	机身尺寸:W70 × H70 × D170mm 机身重量:0.7 kg 通信协定:以太网路电缆 CAT-6，2m 工作环境温度:-15 ~ 50 ℃， 电源:90 ~ 220V AC，12V 输出
可监测物质	
温度 热影像分布 温度精度 ± 2%	

图 3　热显像仪摄像成果示范

2.3 微环境检测

基础要求实测日期必须为夏季晴天，且温度须高于 30℃。长时间进行现场监测，并进行现场监测与室内外温度比对，以探讨温度偏高且较明显炎热气候之下可能造成温度过高的问题（图4）。

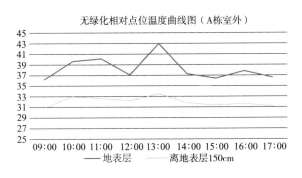
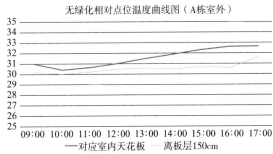

图 4 初步量测实测成果（无绿化室外）

期望于日间日照最充足的时段进行数值采样，以解析一天当中不同时段的夏至微气候差异。因此从 9：00 ~ 17：00 时段，针对上述量测项目进行微气候环境因子采样。各时段采样时间必须依序进行两个案例的检测（图4）。

量测时需选定气候条件为低风速及低云量的晴朗天气（若遇雨天则停止测量）。为比较区域高温与低温状态的差异，分别于日间及夜间两个时段进行量测。量测温度、湿度、风速及风向时，因采用直读式仪器，敏感度较高，各采样点须等待仪器数值呈现稳定状态时方可记录，并同时纪录天空状态及周边环境照片。

在记录数值同时进行现状条件与采样项目数值的交叉验证、误差校正等步骤，将误差值降至最低，并详细记录现状环境特征，取得完整资料后再绘制成微气候地图进行解析。

量测点位以单点方式进行，择定基地顶楼与屋顶，并配合区域尺度范围，选择能有效代表该区域之温度场的适宜位置（不适合有遮阳位置或有恐有积水位置）。

室内采样点：利用固定式仪器，实测过程与屋顶空间同步进行，以在降低替换测点时减少误差值，并在室内空间比较贴近顶棚位置与下方150cm位置的测量数据，如图5所示。

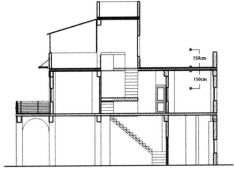

图 5 实测气候及位置示意图

3 历史资料汇整与实地监测数据

3.1 历史资料汇整

参考高雄市政府在市区中设置之气象站作为基础数据进行分析，同时针对高湿高温区段进行对策研拟，依照不同面向之气候数据进行交叉比对，以高雄市气候特征进行评估与解析（图6）。

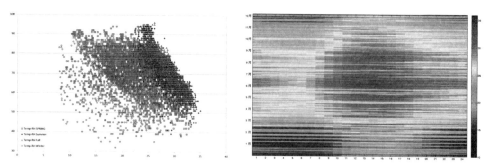

图 6 左图高雄市年平均温度与湿度交叉比对，右图高雄全年温度分布图

3.2 实施步骤与流程

挑选已完成屋顶绿化与未实施屋顶绿化建筑案例作为分析基础，且透过高雄市推动屋顶绿化政策的契机，进行初步分析有无屋顶绿化时室内外空间的热辐射与室内外温度差，进而分析屋顶绿化达到多少百分比时能有效遮断太阳日照的热能传导。

未来期许透过数个代表性屋顶绿化或立体绿化案例的有效降低热能水平监测，以其初期研究的降温数据支持未来市政府进行计划宣导与节能减碳的效益提倡，以增加计划推动的可信度与前瞻性（图7）。

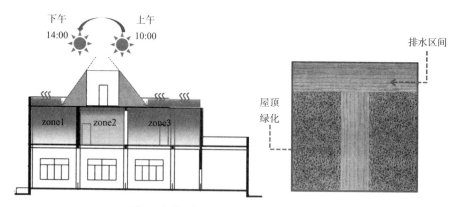

图 7 高雄厝屋顶绿化与阴影屏蔽之效益

4 计划执行成果

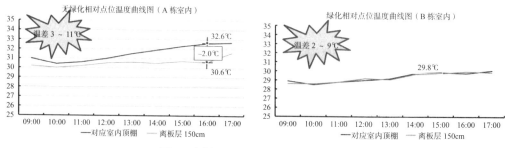

图 8 案例 A 改造前后顶楼室内温度

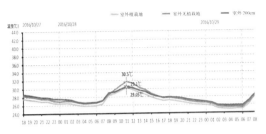
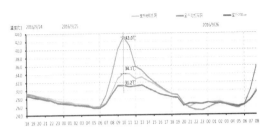

图9　案例B　改造后屋顶层温度

图10　屋顶层热显像分析

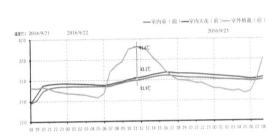
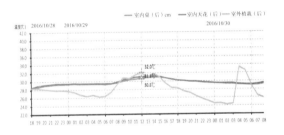

图11　案例C　改造前室内外层温度

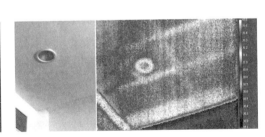

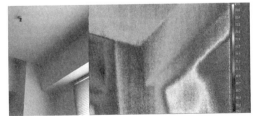

图12　顶楼室内热显像分析

97

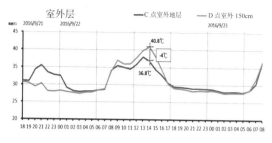
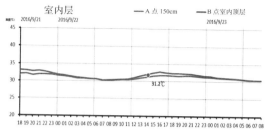

图 13　案例 D　改造前室外层温度

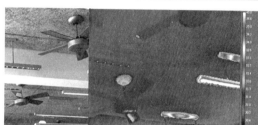

图 14　屋顶热显像分析

5　年度计划研究成果

本研究预计将对高雄市政府调查热岛效应较明显或配合建筑立体绿化计划进行工程改善的案例(表1、表2),检验标准案例并检测实质降温成效与初步推估减碳贡献。

- 运用热显像仪器能快速进行检测
- 人员现场实测搭配周边条件分析提出改善建议
- 针对屋顶绿化的高雄厝降温效益进行资料收集与分析
- 检验实测环境数据以了解高雄厝屋顶绿化以及室内温湿度变化差异
- 提供研究成果作为市政府与相关从业人员进行实作运用的依据

高雄厝屋顶绿化对于顶楼室内温度变化的影响　　　　表1

案例	屋顶面积	绿化面积	绿化比例	原始温度	改造后温度	降温
A. 小港区透天厝建筑	220.2m²	187.8m²	85.2%	38.8℃	29.8℃	9.0℃
B. 河堤圆舞曲大楼	80.9m²	60.4m²	74.6%	34.1℃	29.1℃	5.0℃
C. 国邦企业大楼	108.7m²	90.8m²	83.6%	33.2℃	30.9℃	2.3℃
D. 苓雅区洪家透天厝	18.2m²	13.2m²	72.5%	36.8	31.2℃	5.6℃

表2 高雄厝屋顶绿化对于顶楼室内温度变化

案例	冷气耗能（小坪数）（w）	每年使用时间估计	年耗电量（度）	高雄大楼数量（6层以上）	发电排碳量（kg/度）	总排碳量（吨）
屋顶无绿化案例	1200	5小时×30日×6月=900	1080	306313	0.873	288804
	2400		2160			577608
屋顶绿化案例	1200	2.5小时×30日×6月=450	540	306313	0.873	144402
	2400		1080			288804

The Evaluation of the Roof Greening Benefits for the Roof Space Floor Cooling: A Case Study of the Building in Kaohsiung City

Cheng Da-Long[1], Li Yenyi[2], Chang Chi-Tou[3], Lin Chia-Hsiung[3]

(1.Shu-Te University Department of Computer and Communication; 2.Shu-Te University Graduate School of Architecture and Interior Design Dept; 3.Shu-Te University Department of Interior Design)

Abstract: Kaohsiung City due to excessive urbanization caused by urban green space is too small, and the building caused by excessive urban development, and urban planning and more belong to the high building capacity, low green rate, coupled with traffic and air conditioning waste heat negative factors, Resulting in heat island effect and the problem of global warming. Indirectly causing air-conditioning system load higher, the daily life of energy consumption will gradually increase for the current energy-saving carbon for the development of the concept of the idea which is the primary problem. In view of the limited land for urban development, Kaohsiung Municipal Government has started to promote the three-dimensional greening of buildings and roof greening series of projects to promote the greening activities of urban buildings in Kaohsiung, hoping to increase the greening of the urban greening plant, the roof of the building Vertical and green with the external walls of the way with the user and the architectural form of the discussion and research gradually towards the building facade and green roof set for the mainstream, promising Kaohsiung City buildings through the three-dimensional green after a wave of new energy savings Carbon and lifestyle. Kaohsiung City in recent years to actively promote the roof greening and sunshine roof plan, the two positive significance of the policy in addition to the face of urban climate change and lay the foundation for the development of eco-urban and rural areas, to prepare for low-carbon residential. The study hopes to monitor the construction of the relevant greening project in Kaohsiung City. Through the collection of roof greening and the temperature difference of the top floor, it can be used as a reference for the future scientific research of the promotion of roof greening.

Keywords: Insulation, Green roof, Warm environment, Energy saving and carbon reduction

参考文献

[1] 江哲铭. 建筑物理 [M]. 三民书局，1993.

[2] 赖荣平，林宪德，周家鹏. 建筑物理环境 [M]. 台湾：六合出版社，1991.

[3] 田中俊六，武田仁，足立哲夫，土屋乔雄. 最新建筑环境工学 [M]. 台湾：六合出版社，2004.

[4] 李有田，张淑贞，博以文. 屋顶绿化技术手册 [M]. 台北建筑研究所，2015.

[5] 徐森雄. 不同土壤之地温、水分与热流之变化 [J]. 作物、环境与生物资讯，2005，2：201-210。

[6] 林姵均. 不同屋顶绿化形式对屋顶隔热效果影响之研究——以草种、灌木及棚架为例 [D]. 朝阳科技大学硕士论文，2011.

[7] 张育森. 绿屋顶适用栽培介质的选择与应用 [G]. 绿屋顶推广交流讨论会资料，台北市锡琉环境绿化基金会，2008.

[8] 许瑞铭. 屋顶绿化热效益之研究 [D]. 朝阳科技大学建筑及都市设计研究所硕士论文，2006.

[9] 张简宏裕. 屋顶覆土植栽之热收支研究——以鹅掌藤植栽为例 [D]. 台湾科技大学营建工程系硕士论文，2012.

[10] 谢维芳. 不同植栽对建筑物隔热效果影响之研究 [D]. 中兴大学园艺学系硕士论文，2005.

[11] 苏荣宗. 屋顶植草覆土层热效应之研究 [D]. 高雄大学都市发展与建筑研究所硕士论文，2009.

[12] 许荣辉. 绿屋顶的规划建置与管理 [G]. 绿屋顶推广交流讨论会资料. 台北市锡琉环境绿化基金会，2008.

[13] 郭伯岩. 都市公园微气候观测解析——以台南市公园为例 [D]. 成功大学建筑系硕士论文，2000.

[14] 郭岩. 种植屋顶建筑技术的研究 [J]. 太原理工大学学报，2008，39（6）：616-619.

[15] Ryan Martens, Brad Bass, Susana Saiz Alcazar. Roof–envelope ratio impact on green roof energy performance[J]. Urban Ecosystems，2008,11（4）：399-408.

[16] Liu K, Baskaran, B. Thermal Performance Of Green Roofs Through Field Evaluation. National Research Council, Ottawa, Canada, 2003.

[17] Wong N H, Tan P Y, Chen Y. Study of thermal performance of extensive rooftop greenery systems in the tropical climate[J]. Building and Environment，2007，42：25-54.

住区规划、设计与住宅类型研究

Residential Planning, Design and Housing Typology Research

上海围合式住宅理想模型设计研究

卢 斌

(同济大学建筑与城市规划学院)

摘 要：本文首先通过对上海中心城区182个既有围合式住宅的调研和统计获取一系列与上海围合式住宅相关的数据，然后以此为依据建立起上海围合式住宅理想模型的原型，接着对初成模型进行变形（包括转向、开口和高低三种方法），再对变形模型进行多点日照时长分析和通风方向速度分析的双重检验，最后根据检验结果的反馈信息进一步完善模型（包括开洞、混合和补缺三种方法），以求获得综合评价下表现最佳的上海围合式住宅理想模型，为今后的住宅规划及建筑设计提供一定的参考和借鉴。

关键词：围合式，住宅，理想模型，上海，设计

1 引言：三届会议，一个主题

包括本届研讨会在内，本文作者已经连续三次参加中国城市住宅研讨会（China Urban Housing Conference），2013年在上海举行的第十届研讨会上发表和宣读了论文《上海保障性住房设计类型创新探索——以围合式为例》，2015年在青岛大学举行的第十一届研讨会上又发表和宣读了论文《上海中心城区既有围合式住宅调研及启示》，而2017年在广州中山大学举行的第十二届研讨会，本人将第三次发表和宣读论文《上海围合式住宅理想模型设计研究》。三届会议全部关于同一个主题"围合式住宅"，从围合式类型创新举例到上海既有182个案例调研，再到上海围合式住宅理想模型设计研究，可以看作一份博士论文课题研究的大致框架及部分内容。

2 上海围合式住宅理想模型设计研究

2.1 依据

作者从2013年10月起，前后历时两年时间，通过Google地球卫星航拍图在上海中心城区及其附近的约700km²范围内，地毯式搜索出182个（此数据更新截止到2015年10月底）现存的上海围合式住宅实例，并分批分区地前往实地亲自进行勘察调研、拍照记录和收集资料。在这两年时间里，作者几乎走遍了整个上海外环线以内及其邻近周边的所有区域，往东到过浦东金桥，往西到过长宁虹桥，往南到过闵行莘庄，往北到过宝山顾村。关于调研的详细情况和得出的初步启示已经在上一届研讨会上发表和宣读过，之后又对所有182个实例进行了关键参数考证、三维尺寸测量和体块模型复原等几个重要工作，进而从定性和定量两个层面的多个考量角度对所有实例进行了系统性的梳理，做出了相应的归纳和总结。这些考量角度包含9个基本分类（如住宅类型、围合类型等）、建成年代、住宅朝向、住宅层数、围合宽度与围合宽度的关系以及自然层数与围合面积的关系等，统计分析结果列表如下：

住区规划、设计与住宅类型研究

上海市围合式住宅 182 个实例现状调研统计分析结果　　　　　　　　　表 1

序号	分类	结论
1	基本属性	街道型围合式住宅数量多于小区型
2	住宅类型	老公房围合式住宅数量最多
3	高度类型	多层（4～6 层）围合式住宅数量最多
4	围合类型	U 形围合即三边式围合的案例最多
5	开口朝向	朝东开口最多，朝西开口次之
6	有无底商	围合式住宅大多数案例有底层商业
7	有无庭院	围合式住宅大多数案例有围合庭院
8	建成年代	1985～2002 年之间的围合式住宅相对较多，共有 117 个，平均每年建成 7 个案例
9	住宅朝向	共有 142 个样本的朝向位于正南朝向与东南朝向之间的 45°范围内
10	住宅层数	上海围合式住宅的平均住宅层数为 6～7 层 建筑高度约合为 18～21m
11	围合宽度、围合深度、围合庭院三者之间的关系	上海围合式住宅的平均围合宽度约为 37.55m 上海围合式住宅的平均围合深度约为 24.18m 上海围合式住宅的平均围合庭院面积约为 907.959m²
12	自然层数与围合面积的关系	自然层数的平均值为 7.7 层，而围合面积的平均值为 664.44m²，两者之间呈现二次平方增长的函数关系

从定量这个层面出发，以上表格里的调研统计分析结果和相关数据将成为建立上海围合式住宅理想模型的最初依据，并为能够进一步深入研究工作打下扎实的基础。同时，关于定性层面的有关调研结果亦能在对上海围合式住宅理想模型进行变形和完善这两个重要过程中起到辅助参考的作用。

2.2 初成

参考住宅层数（6～7 层）、围合宽度（37.55m）、围合深度（24.18m）以及围合庭院面积（907.959m²）这四个重要参数的统计平均值，可以先建立起一个外围尺寸为 60m×50m 的平面轮廓，并将围合住宅部分暂定 10m 进深，所以其内部围合庭院尺寸即为 40m×30m，由此可以获得一个最初的总平面轮廓，它的朝向暂定为长边朝正南北，短边朝正东西。换一个角度讲，这个总平面其实是由 18 个 10m×10m 的正方形单元组成的。接着，再给予这个轮廓以 7 层（约合 21M）的高度，进而可以获得上海围合式住宅理想模型的最初形态。它占地面积 3000m²，每层建筑面积 1800m²，建筑覆盖率达到 60%，容积率 4.2（图 1）。

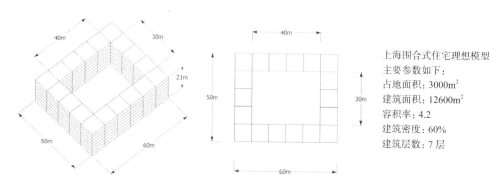

图 1　上海围合式住宅理想模型初成（作者自绘）

同时，它也是由 126 个 10m×10m×3m 的立方体盒子组合而成的，所以，每一个盒子都能被看作是一户人家。

2.3 变形

在获得初步形成的理想模型之后，参考围合类型（三边围合）、开口朝向（朝东最多）、住宅朝向（45°范围内）这三个重要参数的统计结果，对模型进行以下三个步骤的变形处理（图2）：

（1）变形一：转向。将原本的正南北朝向转动45°，将全部单元变为东南和西南两种朝向。这一步至关重要，与其说是改善，不如说是在平衡围合式住宅的朝向更为妥当。原本最好的南北朝向单元转向之后全部变成了西南朝向，而原本最差的东西朝向单元转向之后全部变成了东南朝向。换一个角度说，比较上海市地方设计规范《住宅设计标准》前后两个版本（2007年版和2014年版）中关于住宅朝向规定的变化[①]，可以发现从"应"到"宜"的一字之变已经充分表明了规划管理部门对于住宅朝向的规定从严格走向了宽松，那么上海的住宅建筑设计自此也将抛开陈旧的束缚，或许未来能够以更加多样的形式呈现在这座城市之中。有必要补充一句，在博士论文课题研究中会深入讨论转向不同角度（比如15°、30°和45°）所带来的不同结果，而本次会议论文篇幅有限，所以仅以45°为例进行讨论，为其他部分留有空间，以求阐明设计和研究的全过程。

（2）变形二：开口。对完全闭合的围合式住宅进行开口处理是提升其适用性的最为关键的一步，根据调研结果显示上海围合式住宅开口朝向东面的实例数量最多，这可能与其夏季主导东南风有关，因为开口有利于将风引入围合庭院内部，从而改善庭院和面向庭院的每家每户的居住舒适度。在决定开口的位置和大小时，分为三种不同的情况：对边各开一口、单边开满和角部打开。第一种开法等同于将原来的口字形封闭围合变为一对双L成组形围合，第二种开法是变形为U字形的三边围合，第三种开法是"牺牲"一个完整的角部。应该说三种方法各有优劣，需要等下一步检验之后再进行判断和调整。

（3）变形三：高低。由于前一步的开口处理，三种开法都会损失一部分容积率（共计21个盒子，即2100m²），在变形的第三步高低处理中，将试图通过"该高的高起来，该低的低下去"的逻辑对这三个模型进行修正，同时把之前损失的容积率弥补回来。从下图中可以看到，经过高低处理后的三个

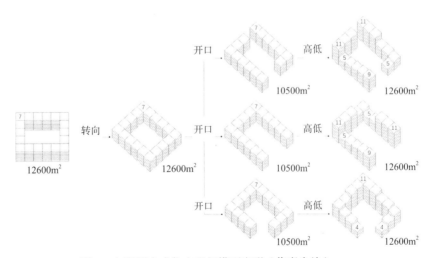

图 2 上海围合式住宅理想模型变形（作者自绘）

---

① 《住宅设计标准》DGJ 08—20—2007/J10090—2007 中 4.1.4 条：小套、中套至少应有一个，大套至少应有两个居住空间向南或南偏东35°至南偏西35°。在特殊情况下，其朝向可南偏东45°至南偏西45°；而在《住宅设计标准》DGJ 08—20—2013/J10090—2014 中 4.1.4 条：小套、中套至少宜有一个，大套至少宜有两个居住空间向南或南偏东30°至南偏西30°。

模型，其最高的地方被拉到了 11 层，而这个层数依照目前实行的设计规范还是比较经济划算的，同时最低的地方被压低到了 4 ~ 5 层，也就是 12 ~ 15m 的高度，尺度较为亲切宜人。总而言之，经过这一步的变形处理，上海围合式住宅理想模型在其形态上变得更加丰富，在功能上变得更加合理。

从定性上来说，上海围合式住宅理想模型从初成状态经过转向、开口和高低三次变形之后，在适用性上的进步是显而易见的。但从定量而言，还需要通过具体的模拟检验加以证明。

2.4 检验

使用天正建筑[①]和 Ecotect Analysis[②]这两组软件对已得出的三组理想模型进行日照和通风模拟测试和分析，得出的数据汇总成图如下（图 3）。（1）从日照层面来讲，三组模型的表现比较一致，由于打开了一边或一角，大部分围合庭院内部底层单元的日照时长至少都保持在了 2 ~ 3 小时（绿色）及以上，共同的问题则发生在了西角附近面向围合庭院的一个单元，其在两个朝向上的采光面日照时长都仅有 1 ~ 2 小时（黄色），因而还需要得到进一步的完善。另外，在变形 1 中东角附近面向围合庭院的一个单元，它朝西南的采光面日照时长仅有 0 ~ 1 小时（红色）。（2）从通风层面来讲，变形 1 由于在其东北肢上打开一块，从而形成了通过风，而变形 2 和变形 3 中围合庭院内的风由于找不到出口，只能原路返回，从而形成不利的涡流。另外，从开口位置与风速的关系来看，变形 3 略好于变形 1 和 2，风速达到 2.00m/s（7.2km/h）以上，属于轻风程度，而后两者的风速平均在 1.00 ~ 1.50m/s 之间。

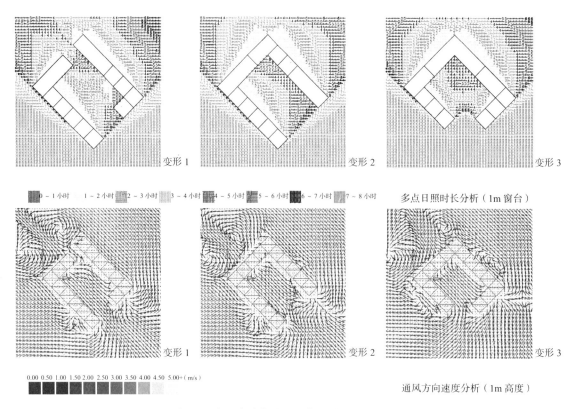

图 3　上海围合式住宅理想模型检验（作者自绘）

---

① 天正建筑多点日照时长分析主要参数：地点上海，大寒日（1 月 22 日），有效日照时间 8：00 ~ 16：00，累计而非连续日照时长，计算精度 10 分钟，计算网格 2m，窗台高度 1m。
② Ecotect Analysis 通风方向速度分析主要参数：假设为夏季通风，取风向为东南向（-45°），Weather Data 气候数据选取上海 Shanghai. CSWD，测试高度为距离地面 1m。测试的结果以 Flow Vector 形式显示，它的箭头代表的是风向，不同颜色代表的是不同风速，其中蓝色表示静止无风或者较低速风 0 ~ 0.50m/s，红色表示中速风 2.00 ~ 3.00m/s，黄色表示较高速风 4.50 ~ 5.00m/s。

2.5 完善

相比之前调整模型幅度较大的变形，在完善这一步里，对三组模型进行的主要是局部微调。根据检验得出的部分结论，分别对三组模型进行如下三种完善方法：（1）完善1：开洞。三个模型均在原有基础之上挖走一列单元，以增设一处通风口，这样做的目的主要是为了使庭院内的通风有进有出，从而更加顺畅，有助于改善围合庭院和朝向围合庭院单元的居住舒适度；（2）完善2：混合。根据检验的反馈，把日照时长表现不佳的西南肢和西北肢底层统一设置为商业服务功能，如图中灰色体块所示，既避免了此处设置住宅无法满足日照时长要求，又能与住宅功能互补、各取所需；（3）完善3：补缺。把由于本次完善中损失的容积率再次补足，如图中灰色体块所示，以求在容积率上保持与前次接受检验的模型相一致。

最后，对完善后的理想模型进行第二次多点日照时长和通风方向速度测试，以复核历经完善之后的整体效果（图4）。检验和完善的过程既是互为因果的，同时也是相互促进的，经历了检验—完善—二次检验的三组模型可以认定为综合角度评价下表现最佳的三组上海围合式住宅的理想模型。

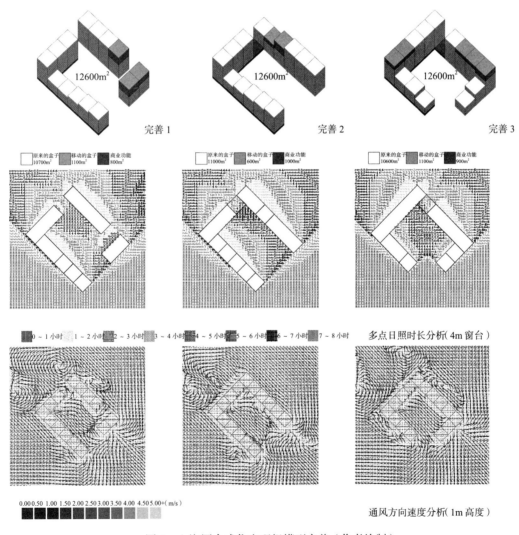

图4 上海围合式住宅理想模型完善（作者绘制）

3 结论

从对既存182例上海围合式住宅实例调研所获统计数据到初成模型,再历经变形—检验—完善(再检验),最终得到三组关于上海围合式住宅的理想模型。它们的特征可以概括为"围而不绝、形态不拘、天际不平、功能不一",也就是说围合不再是封闭的而是网开多面的,形态不再是拘束的而是变化多端的,建筑不再是齐平的而是高低多重的,功能不再是单一的而是混合多元的。但是,本文毕竟篇幅有限,所能涉及的论述仅占整个课题研究的一小部分,还有很多可能性尚未展示和探索(比如:理想模型的整体尺度、转动方向、开口位置与数量、高度差异等各种可能性)。无论如何,本篇论文还只是一个简要的纵览,它把研究思路和过程浓缩在了一起,就其本身而言是完整的,需要完善的地方还有很多。

致谢

本篇论文的写作受到国家自然科学基金项目《长三角地区"城中厂"的社区化更新技术体系研究》的资助(编号:51678412),在此谨向基金及基金项目负责人同济大学李振宇教授表示由衷的感谢和敬意!

Research on the Ideal Model of Shanghai Enclosed Housing

Lu Bin

(College of Architecture and Urban Planning, Tongji University)

Abstract: Through researching on the 182 existing enclosed housings in the center city of Shanghai, some important datas about them are obtained. These datas play an essential role in setting up the prototype of the ideal model of Shanghai enclosed housing. Three transformations are made to the prototype which are turning the orientation, breaking and making higher or lower. Then, virtual experiments of sunshine and ventilation are done to the transformed models. According to the experiment results, some improvements are done to the models which are making holes, mixing the function and making compensation. Therefore, the best performing ideal models of Shanghai enclosed housing can be obtained and they are supposed to be good examples for future planning and architectural design of housing.

Keywords: Enclosed, Housing, Ideal model, Shanghai, Design

参考文献

[1] Li Zhenyu, Lu Bin. 4 Suitable Design Strategies on Enclosed Housing in China——Case of Shanghai[C]. UIA World Congress of Architecture, 2014: 117-123.

[2] Lu Bin. Form Follows Ventilation——One Design Strategy on the Current Shanghai Enclosed Housing[C]. International Seminar of Urban Form, 2016.

[3] 卢斌. 浅析1949年以来上海围合式住区设计策略的演化及趋势[J]. 城市建筑, 2016, 6: 67-69.

[4] 卢斌. 上海中心城区既有围合式住宅调研及启示[C]. 第十一届中国城市住宅研讨会论文集——绿色低碳：新型城镇化下的可持续人居环境建设: 548-553. 北京：中国建筑工业出版社, 2015.

[5] 卢斌. 围合式公寓设计策略研究[J]. 时代建筑, 2016, 3: 176-178.

[6] 卢斌, 李振宇. 上海保障性住房设计类型创新探索—以围合式为例[C]. 第十届中国城市住宅研讨会论文集——可持续城市发展与保障性住房建设: 259-265. 北京：中国建筑工业出版社, 2013.

[7] 卢斌, 李振宇. 以上海临港新城WNW-C1限价房项目6A地块规划及建筑设计为例谈中国保障性住房类型创新设计[J]. 城市建筑, 2013, 1: 34-37.

北方家属楼的特征性演变：以哈尔滨职工住宅为例

顾 闻 李振宇

（同济大学建筑与城市规划学院）

摘 要：本文以哈尔滨几处典型职工住宅为例重点分析，力求从研究职工住宅的空间形态和人群居住行为同时入手，从形成原因、发展历程、布局形态、建筑风格、建筑单体5个方面一一进行分析，探讨并总结人群居住需求的变化趋势和特点，为探索更好的集合职工住宅设计方法和理念提供基础。

关键词：职工住宅，东北老工业区，中东铁路，哈尔滨，住宅演变

1 引言

随着城市发展，各单位为方便员工设立的职工住宅，从无产权保障房逐步发展成福利房、商品房等多种形式。针对北方家属楼的特征性演变，对哈尔滨历史遗留和现有职工住宅的历史、环境及建筑进行调研，并与居住人群进行沟通，以了解他们的居住状况和感受，同时通过对居委会的咨询，了解整个住区的发展历史和住宅使用情况，对职工住宅的进一步发展具有一定的意义。

2 哈尔滨职工住宅的现状与演变

调研的开展遵循职工住宅建成或使用时间的顺序，循序渐进：从19世纪末的中东铁路职工住宅开始，到20世纪50~80年代因东北老工业基地产生的大量工业区职工住宅，再到20世纪末现有的哈尔滨铁路局家属楼。

2.1 中东铁路职工住宅

哈尔滨中东铁路职工住宅可以说是近代哈尔滨建筑特色的缩影，其有着多重风格的建筑样式：俄罗斯传统风格的单层独立式、联户式住宅；折中主义独立式别墅；"新艺术"风格独立式别墅和多层公寓式住宅等。

2.1.1 历史保护价值

哈尔滨建城伊始，沙俄把其当作革命后移居的首选栖身之地来规划建设，而中东铁路的修建更是重中之重，大批铁路建设者汇集于此成为中东铁路局的职工，并为其统一规划和设计了相应的职工住宅，包括供中东铁路管理局高级职员使用的独立式别墅（花园街、公司街、民益街、松花江街、马家沟沿岸及太阳岛部分地区）和供普通员工居住的俄式民居以及多户型公寓式住宅。这些住宅不仅具有俄罗斯民居的传统韵味，还有当时西方流行的"新艺术"风格和折中主义风格等。

2.1.2 "百年黄房子"花园街历史文化街区

花园街的"黄房子"始建于1898年,由大直街、木介街、海关街、红军街、耀景街等围合形成的四个街区,当时被称为"新城子",也就是后来人们俗称的"黄房子"铁路员工住宅区,这里曾是哈尔滨最繁华的俄罗斯社区(图1)。

图1 花园街"黄房子"现状(作者自摄)

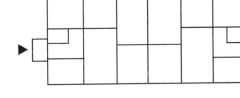

图2 二户型平面简图(作者自制)

花园街周边的中东铁路职工住宅主要为单层联户花园式的住宅,一般等级较高的为两户一栋,有6种不同面积标准,以30平方俄丈(136.6m² 左右)为高级标准,除起居室、卧室、儿童室外还有工作室和仆人室共五室,还带有室内卫生间(图2),如同街区名字一样,该住宅一般都各自配有冬季花园。

2.2 老工业区职工住宅

东北老工业区职工住宅则是在20世纪50～80年代的历史和时代背景中形成的,为老工业基地的蓬勃发展做出了很大的贡献。大多数坐落于东北老工业区附近的居住建筑都借鉴了苏联的建筑设计模式,具有极其明显的工业时代特征。

2.2.1 20世纪五六十年代职工住宅

此时工业区发展势头强劲,大量的职工住宅也作为厂区配套建筑同时兴建起来,建筑形式在最初有很多苏联建筑的痕迹。这一时期的住宅室内层高偏高,普遍都在3000mm以上,结构为砖混结构墙体承重,外墙尺寸615mm,即俗称的"62墙"(图3)。

图3 香坊区电碳厂职工宿舍现状(作者自摄)

3~5 层的低层住宅为主要模式，外墙以"清水砖墙"铺贴，红砖是早期老工业区住宅的一种标志性符号，与同样材质的路面相呼应，更加厚重，也很符合老工业区住区的气质与文化。屋顶形式则以两坡或四坡为主，为进行无组织排水，极少为平屋顶，老房子的韵味很浓。

2.2.2　20 世纪七八十年代职工住宅

经过了十几年的发展，职工住宅发生了很大的变化，尝试摆脱单调的红砖灰瓦模式，以简洁的方盒形为主，建筑体量和层数都有所增加，但在建筑构造和细部上更多地延续了早期建筑的形态，仍然可以很容易地发现俄式建筑的早期痕迹。

除了早期的基本平面形式，还出现了很多连廊式的住宅形式（图 4，图 5），这种连廊式的住宅主要为了遮阳和通风，相对于东北严寒地区更适用于纬度较低的南方，而通过与哈尔滨现有的几处这样的连廊式住宅居民的沟通，也已经得到了验证。

图 4　连廊式职工住宅　　　　　　　　　图 5　走廊内部（作者自摄）

资料来源：见本文参考文献 [3]。

2.3　哈尔滨铁路局家属楼（20 世纪 90 年代后）

随着计划经济向市场经济转变的大趋势，1999 年左右建成的哈铁路局家属（图 6）楼紧邻哈尔滨铁路局东北侧，职工住宅逐渐由公司企业无偿分配转为单位同个人各自负担一部分费用的保障房，未来进一步的发展趋势可能是全部转变成商品房。

此时期哈尔滨的职工住宅具有现有居民楼典型的特征，以 7 层为主，外形统一中富有变化，住宅外墙主要使用乳白、浅黄、浅粉等颜色的涂料，几种颜色交错搭接，简洁中不失活泼。

为了在有限的地段上尽可能多的建设住宅，简单的一字形在这一时期的哈尔滨已经很少见了，小区内多为 L 形、U 形的围合式住宅。随着形式和功能不断调整，各项配套设施也逐渐出现在现代化的职工住宅区里，居民可以就近办理与休闲，方便社区生活（图 7）。

2.4　哈尔滨职工住宅演变的五个方面

（1）形成原因

哈尔滨早期的高级职工住宅主要集中在城市的新城区（大直街附近，如公司街、花园街历史文化街区等），这是因为这里的地势居于城市中较高的地带，削弱松花江洪水侵袭的危害。城区的位置相对整座城市较为居中，紧邻职工工作的地点，环境优美，同时配有相应的行政和商业区，具有良好的自然和

图6 哈铁路局家属楼现状（作者自摄）

图7 家属楼住区环境（作者自摄）

社会环境。这些住区占据了城市建设伊始最繁华的路段，作为较早期的单位家属区，与现在住区规划中重视的邻近公共服务设施和交通便利等有着相同的原则，可以说是整体布局考量的综合性居住社区。

工厂职工住宅住区的形成，则是从放任自流到集中统一管理的过程，周边环境也多是从无到有。建设初期主要形式是密布的棚户，道路窄小，随后组建的社区单位对其进行了分别管理，从而逐渐改善了住区环境，并加大了住区建设力度，改善道路和居住环境，增设更多的公共设施，从而初步形成了适宜居住的和谐环境。

（2）发展历程

建设时期的不同，职工住宅的外在形式和内部格局自然有所不同，但其发展历程并非无迹可寻。

以始建于20世纪50年代，位于太平区的哈尔滨第一兵工机械厂职工住宅区为例，南起大有坊街，北至宏图街，东起宏伟路，西至南直路，整个住区都在二环以内。根据2006年工厂统计资料，有居民18147人，本厂职工占比90%以上，儿童占比25%，老人占比6.7%。

经调研，本社区共分为8个区进行管理，平房9栋，楼房84栋，约5500户。从20世纪50年代初建设，向西增设了3个小区，初期楼房仅有十几栋，60年代开始不断发展扩张，70年代有部分住宅在原有的3层基础上加建改建到5层，外部形式则有一部分在80年代与其他住宅进行了统一修缮。由此出现了浅色方形点缀在红砖灰瓦住宅群中的独特形式。到90年代，住宅形式已经全部都是楼房了。

这些职工住宅突出一个"老"字，住宅使用年限老，居住者年龄偏老化，邻里关系都是老同事、老朋友，生活习惯老样子，对于住区环境和室内环境的舒适要求也是老感觉。然而，从居住人群的角度出发，随着家庭结构更多地从三代人转向两代人，邻里关系由于单位房屋产权的放开也不再是纯粹的同事关系，加入了租住或是转手的商人、学生、流动人群等，使得原本因为住宅使用年限较老而形成的邻里老朋友关系从密切到疏离，形成了不同层次的需求。

（3）布局形态

总体布局上属于"组团式"的组合方式，住宅单元的排布形态上则作"周边式"布置。

以组团为单位形成小区，使道路的通达性增强，同时利于设置公共服务设施。如铁路局后身的哈铁路局家属楼所处的居住街区组团，由于广场节点和街道的放射性交叉，就形成了比较特殊的组团形态，多为矩形和三角形（图8）。

花园街住宅则是典型的周边式布置，住宅排列大多沿着组团的边缘行进，形成较强的向心性，使沿街面形成统一的立面景观，并使这些单层住宅具有良好的通风采光环境和私密性（图9）。

（4）建筑风格

早期由于受到中东铁路的文化辐射影响，"新艺术"、折中主义、俄罗斯传统风格等多种建筑风格在哈尔滨汇集，风格各异的职工住宅建筑将哈尔滨文化的开放性和兼容性体现得淋漓尽致。随着工业

图8 组团式布局（作者自制）

图9 周边式布置
资料来源：见本文参考文献 [8]。

厂区的大步向前发展，其配套的住区也变得极具当时工业时代特征：整体布局统一集中，建筑形式简洁清晰，整体感觉敦厚沉稳，内部空间则相对局促。来自外界的建筑风格在与当地文化的相互渗透中，形成一个独具特色的城市住宅多元体。

（5）建筑单体

在上述提到的中东铁路职工住宅的调研中，其独栋别墅将不同人群使用的房间进行分层布置，在保证个人使用私密性的同时，又兼顾家庭成员间的相互联系。联户式住宅则更多地侧重于满足居民生活的各种需求，力图在较小的房间面积中适当合理布置，兼备良好的交通组织与独立性空间。

对于那些老工业区的职工住宅，多为一居室或二居室的小户型，建筑面积在30~50m²之间，少数三居室则为60~80m²。一楼几乎全部被改造为商户，其中部分小商户为户主外搭出店面，自己在一楼居住；其他大商户的经营者租用一楼住房，并将其全部改造为商铺。

这些职工住宅因为面积紧张，套型多是穿套式或是两侧式，流线混杂，因而突出于墙体的阳台空间被住户以不同方式加以利用，根据调研（表1）可知绝大部分居民将阳台扩充改做厨房，以挪出入户门厅的空间（图10）。

户内阳台改造统计表（作者自制） 表1

阳台	厨房	储物晾衣	养花	其他
11	59	23	9	5

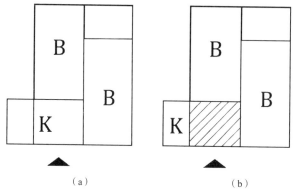

K—厨房；B—卧室
图10 户型平面简图（作者自制）
（a）穿套式户型；（b）阳台改造后户型

3 职工住宅的更新与发展策略展望

（1）城市布局：以如花园街这样历史性的职工住宅街区为重点，依照建筑遗产中的整体性保护原则，进行集中保护。

（2）建筑单体：对具有历史价值的职工住宅进行保护更新，对现有或新建的职工住宅进行合理的结构或立面修缮，进一步梳理空间形式与功能间的特征关系，采用合理方式进行探索职工住宅新的类型，以适应城市更新的脚步和使用人群改变的可能性。

（3）管理使用：对既有职工住宅进行统一管理，制定相关的规范或保护条例，而对于新建的职工住宅则需要在建筑设计中进一步考虑职工及其家属的需求变化。

致谢

本篇论文的写作得到国家自然科学基金项目《长三角地区"城中厂"的社区化更新技术体系研究》的资助（编号：51678412）！

Characteristic Evolution of Northern Family Building: Cases of Harbin Staff Housing

Gu Wen, Li Zhenyu

（College of Architecture and Urban Planning, Tongji University）

Abstract: The paper takes several typical residential buildings in Harbin as significant examples, and trying to start from the study of both the spatial form and the residential behavior of the staff housing. It is shown in five aspects: forming reasons, development course, layout form, architectural style, and monomer building, to explore and summarize the changing trends and characteristics of the population living demand, in order to provide a basis for exploring the methods and concepts of the better collection of residential buildings.

Keywords: Staff housing, Northeast old industrial area, Middle East Railway, Harbin, Housing evolution

参考文献

[1] 李振宇，张玲玲，姚栋. 关于保障性住房设计的思考——以上海地区为例 [J]. 建筑学报，2011，8: 60-64.

[2] 刘松茯. 哈尔滨城市建筑的现代转型与模式探析 [M]. 北京：中国建筑工业出版社，2004.
[3] 宋菲. 东北老工业区职工住宅人居环境的生态化改造研究 [D]. 哈尔滨工业大学，2006.
[4] 赵天宇，程文. 历史文化街区复兴规划设计中的新元素——哈尔滨中东铁路花园住宅街区复兴规划 [J]. 华中建筑. 2006，11.
[5] 刘松茯. 近代哈尔滨城市建筑的文化结构与内涵 [J]. 新建筑，2002，1: 13-15.
[6] 林学伟，邓亚娟，吴阳. 哈尔滨中东铁路职工住宅建筑风格的保护研究 [J]. 黑龙江科技信息，2011，27: 304.
[7] 曲扬. 东北老工业基地原大型企业职工住区环境活力重构 [D]. 哈尔滨工业大学，2014.
[8] 张毅. 哈尔滨中东铁路职工住宅研究 [D]. 东北林业大学，2009.
[9] D Ponzini，U Rossi. Becoming a Creative City: The Entrepreneurial Mayor，Network Politics and the Promise of an Urban Renaissance[J]. Urban Studies. 2010.

住宅通用化设计之课题与实践
——以台北市兴隆公共住宅为例

高文婷[1]　郑人豪[2]　陈雅芳[3]

（1. 中国文化大学；2. 台湾大学；3. 淡江大学）

摘　要：为保障身心障碍者参与社会之权利并改善公共环境可及性，台湾于1988年正式将无障碍设计规定纳入法规，并自1990年起于残障福利法明文规范公共建筑物未考虑无障碍设计不得核发使用执照。而联合国更于2006年12月13日通过"保护身心障碍者人权的国际公约（CRPD）"，由此可知建构无障碍环境已为当前世界重要趋势与迫切需要因应之课题。另一方面，至2014年年底在台湾65岁以上的老年人口已达2808690人，占总人口11.99%。预计将于2018年正式迈入联合国定义之高龄化社会。这样的人口发展趋势，凸显友善高龄者居住环境的重要性。在这样的发展下，台北市政府都市发展局首次将完整的居住空间通用设计理念，纳入台北市兴隆公共住宅之规划设计需求。透过实际的案例操作发现，通用设计不仅止于单一空间形式的调整或设备的配合，而需要在设计之初即进行通盘考虑，以制订通用之建筑计划。无障碍与通用设计推动所面对的课题，亦借由此公共住宅的操作获得验证并找出解决方案，这些经验的归纳将可作为后续政策推动与规划设计之参考。

关键词：无障碍，通用设计，公共住宅，高龄化社会

1　引言

台湾因土地空间发展持续城市化，导致人口高度集中于大都市地区，以2013年度人口分布资料，近60%人口居住在五都，而有28%人口居住在台北市及新北市，但该两市土地面积仅占全省6.4%；又从同年度人口迁出迁入信息观察，偏乡地区迁出趋势依然存在。依当局委托调查的岛内各行政区房价所得比信息显示，就时间轴观察，大约自2008年底起全省房价所得比开始快速攀升，由5.87增至8.37，另台北、新北市也在当时与全省平均大幅拉开。就区域观察，该指数之变化主要发生在双北市，台北市从8.79短短两年内攀升至12.89再至2013年的15.01；新北市则从7.40攀升至目前12.67。其他地区与上开两市相比，趋势明显缓和，显现房价问题集中在大台北都市区。爰此，公共住宅为协助财务基础尚未稳定之民众以租屋方式取得适宜之居住空间策略之一。

20世纪前半叶，学者专家们忧心人口爆炸将带来世界大灾难，甚至预测地球将进入"剩下供人站立空间、野生环境被破坏、自然资源消耗殆尽"的恐怖时代。世事难料，才多久时间，人口生育率、人口结构产生巨大转变，多数国家担忧的不再是人满为患的问题，而是少子化、高龄化所带来的新冲击。值得注意的是，台湾少子化情势比其他地区更为严峻。1951年时，平均每位15～49岁妇女还生育了7名以上的子女，到了1984年，已经降为2.05名子女，跌破2.1个人口替换的水平。依当局人口统计资料，台北市之人口数占全台湾人口数之11.5%，以台北市12个行政区人口成长趋势进行比对内湖和文山区的人口成长曲线高于全省趋势，居住的需求尤显重要。因此，如何兼顾居住单元及不同年龄层使用需求已是当前极为重要之课题。

为保障身心障碍者参与社会之权利并改善公共环境可及性，台湾于1988年正式将无障碍设计规定

纳入建筑技术规则，并自1990年起于残障福利法明文规范公共建筑物未考虑无障碍设计不得核发使用执照。经过多年努力，已大幅减少公共空间中对于身心障碍者之阻碍。而联合国更于2006年12月13日通过"保护身心障碍者人权的国际公约（CRPD）"，由此可知建构无障碍环境已为当前世界重要趋势与迫切需要因应之课题。另一方面，至2014年底在台湾65岁以上的老年人口已达2808690人，占总人口11.99%。预计将于2018年超过14%的老年人口，进入高龄社会之列，2025年则可能超过20%，正式迈入联合国定义之高龄化社会。这样的人口发展趋势，凸显友善高龄者居住环境的重要性。

2　建筑物无障碍规定与通用设计理念

按身心障碍者权益保障法第57条规定，新建公共建筑物及活动场所，应规划设置便于各类身心障碍者行动与使用之设施及设备。未符合规定者，不得核发建筑执照或对外开放使用。公共建筑物及活动场所之无障碍设备及设施不符合前项规定者，各级目的事业主管机关应令其所有权人或管理机关负责人改善。为推动建筑物无障碍环境，当局已自1988年起陆续订有建筑技术规则建筑设计施工编无障碍建筑专章、建筑物无障碍设施设计规范、既有公共建筑物无障碍设施替代改善计划作业程序及认定原则、公共建筑物建造执照无障碍设施工程图样种类及说明书应标示事项表、公共建筑物无障碍设施勘检作业原则等规定，据以推动建筑基地与建筑物之无障碍设施设置事宜，由规划设计起至使用执照核发的各个阶段逐步落实无障碍规划设计，并持续配合推动成果办理相关修正。属建筑法之适用者，自应依上开规定办理建筑物无障碍环境设计与相关设施之设置。

而通用设计与无障碍环境设计的差别，在于通用设计进一步探讨更广泛的设计内涵，不再局限于身心障碍者，而将设计的重心着眼在广大的用户身上，拓展产品使用性与适用范围。通用设计是积极主动的，并适合多数人的使用需求，并不是消极的仅是为了满足特定人士需求的设计技术。世界的趋势，系以正常化、排除（软硬件）障碍排除、普及正常化理念并实现"完全参加和机会均等"进行推动；而美国，则由无障碍设计理念推广到无障碍政策落实，并进行通用设计转换；至于日本，系以身心障碍者"点状福祉小区营造"到高龄者"全面性福祉小区营造"朝向建构通用性生活环境进行。目前通用设计最常被采用的定义与原则，是1998年美国北卡罗来纳州立大学通用设计中心主任 Ronald L. Mace 提出的定义："通用设计是一种设计途径，它集合了能在最大限度上适合每一个人使用的产品及建筑元素。"最常见7大原则：平等使用、灵活运用、简单易用、简明信息、容许错误、省力操作、尺度合宜。

根据统计资料，身心障碍者人数于1997年为500138人，至2015年则为1159740人，而身心障碍者占总人口比率：于1997年为2.3%至2015年则为年4.93%。其中台北市领有身心障碍手册或身心障碍证明人士亦有11万人，占全市人口比例约4.44%。台北市考虑辖内65岁以上老人人口已达37万多人，占全市人口比例近14%，已显见台北市迈入高龄化社会；为打造更人本宜居的环境，以及设计出满足大多数人需求之住宅，因此应先带头推动通用设计住宅，过程可分为导入期、试办期、改造期、推广期等四个阶段。

第一为导入期，在2008年进行项目研究并出版《台北市居住空间通用设计规范》专书，2009年编印《台北市居住空间通用设计指南》手册，借由轻松活泼的方式引导市民了解通用设计。第二为试办期，2010年率全省之先将通用设计想法及理念落实于文山区万乐出租国宅，完成第一户住宅通用设计改造，作为后续出租国宅改造及推广全市住宅通用设计之参考。第三为改造期，自2011年起分阶段办理实质改造计划，于出租国宅退租整修时，挑选适宜户进行通用设计改造，目前已完成出租国宅通用设计改造86户。2013年更以"安心"、"安全"且"安乐"的三安居家环境为主轴推动之"出租国宅通用设计改造"，辅以出租国宅实际改造施工前后照片及图解，向市民推广通用设计理念。第四为推广期，本府于后续推动新建之公营住宅，将通用住宅纳为规划设计之基本要求，以通用设计重点原则进行设计，提供无障碍的居住空间，以服务身心障碍者或高龄者之市民使用。

3 台北市兴隆公共住宅通用设计之实践

3.1 基本设计目标

全球正面临气候变迁及能源枯竭等环境议题，亟须导入智慧策略、永续环保等相关产业技术，且近年台北市出现房地价格飙涨、购屋痛苦指数大增、青年市民无力购屋之近忧，致有人口外移、竞争力减弱之远虑。为确保提供更佳之性能与环境质量，使居民在安全、健康、舒适、便利等方面能接受到更实时与全面性的照护，于是以实践居住正义，落实城市美学，成为智慧城市实验场域，创造新的居住营模式等四大目标进行规划公共住宅，并导入绿色建筑、智能建筑、能源管理等相关策略，运用BIM 从规划、设计、施工、管理，透过可视化与信息化，协助各阶段管理作业，提前发现工程问题并迅速解决，达到优良的规划流程，促使建筑物生命周期各阶段效能提升，实质回馈建筑使用的质量管理。

基于"推动公共住宅政策，增加公共住宅数量"及"安康平宅更新改建"两股社会趋势的激荡下，台北市政府政策决定优先推动"安康公共住宅旗舰计划"。本研究系以兴隆公共住宅 1 区为研究对象，本案基地位于台北市文山区华兴段一小段 318 地号（台北市文山区木栅路 2 段 2 巷）。邻近文山区木栅路二段及兴隆路四段交叉口（再兴中小学），基地面积 3595m^2，已兴建地下 3 层、地上 18 层（2 栋），计 272 户住宅，其中公共住宅户数比例占 67%，平价住宅户为 33%。于 2013 年 9 月 17 日核发建造执照，已于 2015 年 5 月全数完工，并 2016 年初开放入住。为提供安全且住得安心之公共住宅，该案已取得耐震标章、智能建筑标章、绿色建筑标章，及无障碍住宅单元标章合格，是全省首座同时取得前述标章之公共住宅。

3.2 通用设计规划策略

兴隆公共住宅系属台北市政府通用设计住宅推动计划中第四阶阶段的重点工作，于推动新建之公营住宅，将通用住宅纳为规划设计之基本要求，并依有关部门订颁《建筑物无障碍设施设计规范》及住宅法《无障碍住宅设计基准》之相关规定进行设计及施工，且设置至少 5% 比例住宅自用空间以"下肢障轮椅用户"为设想使用对象，其余则均以通用设计重点原则进行设计，提供无障碍的居住空间，以服务身心障碍者或高龄者之市民使用，期待带给更多使用者舒适友善的居住空间。公共住宅之通用设计环境以下将分从供共同使用之共享空间及具有使用上之独立性空间之自用部分两部分进行说明。

3.2.1 共享部分

WHO 高龄友善城市指南提到，户外开放性空间与公共建筑对高龄人口的行动力、独立性与生活质量有决定性的影响。其中包含关于愉悦与干净的环境、绿色空间的重要性、休憩环境、友善和健康的步道空间、人行安全空间、可及性、安全的环境、行走步道、友善的建筑空间等层面。对于行动不便者而言，通行不便的困扰尤为显著，若不能提供适当之通行空间，将使其不是走入社会，自主生活，不论是身体或是心理，皆会造成甚大影响，同时，也会增加社会福利与医疗保险等之社会支出。因此，良好的居住空间，首要，即应达通用设计之平等使用原则，让所有的使用者都能平等使用，排除差别感，提供选择及消除不安等，进出便利。共享部分空间可以由基地内环境与建筑内环境两部分，基地内环境包括：室外通路、坡道、停车空间、骑楼与人行道等由道路进到建筑基地的部分，而建筑内环境，则包含大楼出入口、共享楼梯、共享走廊、升降设备等建筑物内共享通行的部分。谨说明如下：

（1）骑楼、人行道、室外通路与坡道

骑楼为位处亚热带且多雨的我省都市常见景象。骑楼除可提供行人遮风避雨外，亦具有让商业活动不因下雨而中断的功能；然而，由于早年管理骑楼的相关法令未臻完备，加上产权私有，致使骑楼高低不平造成行人通行不便、影响都市景观的景象，亦屡见有因天雨路滑而发生滑倒之意外，多年来无法获得改善，让原本温馨的骑楼反成都市不友善空间。因此，台北市政府基于都市设计应从"以人为本"的理念出发，自2002年起率先推动的"骑楼整平"工作，期望提供友善的步行环境。而有关部门所订定之《市区道路及附属工程设计规范》已于2015年7月22日完成编修并函颁发布，将因应高龄者之行动需求及融入通用设计概念编修，如人行道及无障碍坡道净宽度宜达2.5m以上，以增加并行之舒适性及安全性，路缘斜坡应配合无障碍通路之动线与行人穿越道对齐并平缓顺接，以确保安全及可及性。

在兴隆公共住宅的规划设计中，将基地内骑楼与人行道维持平坦无高差，且铺面材料为防滑材质，在人行道末端衔接道路时，设有1：8的下斜路缘石，长度至少120cm，宽度至少130cm，且表面为防滑材质。在骑楼或人行道衔接建筑物出入口处平坦无高差，但因兴隆公共住宅基地地形本即为有坡度，因此，设有宽度90cm以上之斜坡道衔接。另外，现行使用电动轮椅作为辅具之行动不便者已日益增加，考虑充电需要，在公共住宅一楼之骑楼部分也设有充电所需之设插座，并依下肢障轮椅使用者操作可及范围，将设置高度规定应足地板面70～100cm，以方便使用。

（2）停车空间

自2013年1月1日起，台湾已全面推行新建增建建筑物设置无障碍环境，如建筑物依法规检讨需设置停车位者，即应依比例设置无障碍停车位。但建筑物之设计、施工、构造及设备所依循之建筑技术规则仅有汽车位之设置，但台北市土地使用分区管制自治条例为因应使用需求，亦规定要求设置机车停车位与无障碍机车停车位。兴隆公共住宅无障碍停车空间，系设置于地下一楼，并邻近建筑物升降设备，并在车道入口及转弯处设有明显的指引标志，以引导无障碍延出位的方位与位置。

（3）建筑物公共出入口

建筑物公共出入口为所有使用者共同使用，须兼顾所有使用者不同之需求，如使用轮椅之下肢障碍者、高龄者或是推婴儿车之使用者；而对于日常使用时，若是公共出入口过于狭窄，将不便于家具物品搬运。因此，在兴隆公共住宅规划时，将建筑物出入口宽度设置为150cm，出入口外衔接建筑物之骑楼空间，便利使用与进出。

3.2.2 自用部分

依台湾现行之无障碍法规规定，建筑物使用用途如为住宅，其专有部分与经约定提供区分所有权人使用之约定专用空间得不受应设置无障碍空间之限制，其主要系将专有部分之空间规划设计依所有权人之使用需求进行规划。然而公共住宅系以只租不卖之方式营运，且为保障公民居住权益，健全住宅市场，提升居住质量，使用户居住于适宜之住宅且享有尊严之居住环境，于规划之初已将且设置至少5%比例住宅自用空间以"下肢障轮椅用户"为设想使用对象，因此，对于专有部分之空间，依通用设计之理念进行设计。谨说明如下：

（1）整体隔间与布局

住宅的隔间与布局的调整，影响家人的生活质量与气氛，运用通用设计的原则，可以将有限的生活空间，变成宽敞没有阻碍且可弹性运用的空间。在兴隆公共住宅规划中，全栋采用通用设计，其中的六户并设计为无障碍住宅，分别为一房型（约53m²）4户及二房型（约83m²）2户，因空间有限，于是将厨房客厅及餐厅整合为一体，扩大浴厕的使用面积。就下肢障轮椅使用者、高龄者须使用行进辅助器或是使用婴幼儿推车者，若未设置适当之走道及足够的移动回转空间不利进出。为利行动不便者进出，使用空间，于公共住宅中，对于非属法规规范之自用部分空间，亦设有宽度90cm以上室内通路。

（2）门槛与门扇

于建筑空间中，常见因门框或为达防水溢流等目的设有高低差的门槛，然对于下肢障轮椅使用者、高龄者或是年幼之幼儿等使用者，易发生绊倒或不利行进之危险，据研究统计，跌倒为居家意外事件发生频率最高。因此，为提高居家安全，于公共住宅规划时，即设定地面平坦无门槛，以便利使用。至于浴厕空间、阳台与室内空间之界面，则辅以截水沟方式进行设计。至地板面使用止滑材质，避免因地面油渍、潮湿衍生意外。

现行建筑法规中，除须具备防火性能之防火门或无障碍通路上之出入口应达法规规定之门宽外，并未对于门宽加以规定。但就下肢障轮椅使用者、高龄者须使用行进辅助器或是使用婴幼儿推车者，若未设置适当之门宽、走道及足够的移动回转空间不利进出。为利行动不便者进出，使用空间，于公共住宅中，对于非属法规规范之自用部分空间，而区隔空间的门，以不需要太费力较容易开启与关闭之推拉门为主，以符合简单易用、省力操作之通用设计准则，门宽则为扣除门框间之距离至少90cm，以便于行动不便者进出，同时也可以让居住单元中的家具物品移动较为容易。而经常使用的门扇，也不须容易开启与开关，并且不需要太费力就可以达成，因此，在兴隆公共住宅的自用空间中，多使用容易开关又不妨碍动线的推拉门，得以容易的进出，门锁并采用拨杆式门把（锁），方便使用。

（3）厨房与厨具

民以食为天，厨房与厨具是生活中不可缺乏之要件，以厨房与厨具常见不便使用之情形有：厨房、家事空间面积过小、通道狭窄，无法容纳轮椅进出或是两个人同时使用，料理台高度过低、台面下缺乏可容纳膝盖空间、橱柜高度不便使用或无法使用、抽屉无轨道及U形把手、开关需要用力、给水器具不易抓握或不易清洁等，以致影响自主生活之质量。

为能让使用者住的便利、舒适、安心，台北市依据先前推动出租国宅通用设计改造之实际案例经验，在兴隆公共住宅中，配合整体隔间布局将厨房餐厅与起居空间合并，留设宽度120cm之通道，以容纳两个人进出或轮椅通行。料理台台面距地面高度应介于75～80cm，且下方橱柜深度应介于50～60cm之间，上方橱柜深度不要超过30cm，尽量让轮椅使用者或坐着的人伸手就能开启或使用，下方可利用供收纳餐桌，移出时即可提供足够之容纳膝盖空间，以利接近及使用料理台空间。为达省力操作、尺度合宜之原则，设置容易拉出的抽屉，让各种使用对象不用蹲下亦可轻松取物，而上方的橱柜抽屉则设有下拉式滑轨设计，方便轮椅使用者或高龄者坐着也能拿到东西，兼顾手部不便使用者之使用需求。

（4）浴厕友善得回转

据世界厕所组织（WTO）统计，每人每天上厕所约6～8次，一年约2500次，厕所及浴室是家中最常使用的空间，干爽、舒适、明亮又好用的浴厕空间，不仅让家中的孕妇、高龄者及儿童更加安全与便利，也让行动不便者更有尊严。以高龄者或是下肢障轮椅使用者而言，因身体机能条件因素，需要有更多的辅助性设施以确保使用过程的安全。于兴隆公共住宅中，扩大浴厕的门宽（门框间之净宽）至80cm，除去门槛，使用推拉门，增加门后活动空间，以利进出。马桶周边设有设置直径至少150cm之回转空间，两侧并设有L形扶手及活动扶手，作为体弱者及老年人使用时移位之辅助。其次，考虑下肢障轮椅使用者盥洗时须于洗面盆下方需留设膝盖容纳空间以利靠近，将洗面盆台面高度设置于距离地面以上85cm且下方应留设膝盖容纳空间65cm。浴厕亦为居家环境中易发生危险之处所，据此，设有两处紧急求助铃，一处在距离坐便器前缘往后15cm、坐便器座位上60cm，另在距地板面高35cm范围内设置一处可供跌倒后使用之求助铃，以强化浴厕使用的安全性。

（5）洗衣晒衣空间

通风宽敞没有门槛可以顺畅进出的阳台或露台以及可以调整高度的晒衣设施，对于高龄者、孕妇、行动不便者或是儿童而言，都是重要的通用设计考虑。就台湾通常之家事操作形态，多将洗衣机置放于阳台或露台，为防止清洗时水漫入室内空间，均设有门坎，但却无法容纳轮椅进出或是灵活的使用，另外阳台宽度较窄晒衣架又较高，须使用撑竿等较费力，对于高龄者或行动不便者皆不便于使用；若遇雨天，可能因为积水或地面材料防滑性不足而衍生滑倒之危机。因此，在兴隆公共住宅中，设置家事工作的阳台宽度为150cm，以方便轮椅使用者移动及操作，同时为了让晒衣过程更加省力与便利，设有升降式的晒衣杆。为了使用者安全，阳台地砖加设有防滑设施，并考虑防坠意外发生，阳台栏杆与防护墙高度亦符合建筑技术规则的规定，以强化居家安全。

4 结论

居住正义的美好境界是"住者适其屋"的概念，也就是不管收入高低，每个人都要有适当居住的房子，让每个人能自由选择买屋或租屋。公共住宅的规划与兴建，亦是为了达到此一政策目标。以往所规划与兴建之公民住宅或社会住宅多以一般使用者需求为考虑，但随着人权议题日受重视与高龄化之趋势，台北市所提供之公共住宅已开始纳入通用设计之理念，先达"安居"才能"乐业"。

无障碍环境之推动，目前已为身心障碍者保障法所明文规范保障，且已订有相关设计规定，并有初步之成果；然而通用设计系为观念，没有准则，而是能否考虑到更多不同使用者的需求，其与强调保留特定使用需求之无障碍有所不同，却仍须逐步进行推动，亦因如此，更需要关注以及进行与跨领域之科技整合相关的研究去探究各种不同年龄、身体状况、性别在环境、空间上使用之需求，进而落实到空间-建筑-环境之规划设计，以最大限度适合每一个人。

The Subject and Practice of Universal Design in Residential Projects: Taking Taipei Xinglong Public Housing Project as An Example

Kao Wen-Ting[1], Cheng Jen-Hao[2], Chen Ya-Fang[3]

(1. Chinese Culture University; 2. Taiwan University; 3. Tamkang university)

Abstract: In order to protect the rights of the physically and mentally disabled persons and improve the accessibility of the public environment, Taiwan formally incorporated the barrier-free design regulations into the regulations in 1988 and has since been standardized in the case of the Disabled Welfare Law since 1990. The license will not be issued to public buildings with no barrior-free design consideration. And the United Nations has adopted the International Convention on the Protection of the Human Rights of Persons with Disabilities（CRPD） on December 13th, 2006, and it has been found that the construction of an accessible environment has been an important international trend and an urgent need to follow. On the other hand, by the end of 2014, the number of elderly people aged 65 and above in Taiwan reached 2808690, accounting for 11.99% of the total population.

It is expected to officially enter the United Nations-defined aging society in 2018. This trend of population development highlights the importance of friendly elderly people living environment. In this development, Taipei Municipal Government Urban Development Bureau for the first time will be a complete residential space design concept, into Taipei City Xinglong public housing planning and design needs. Through the actual case operation, it is found that the universal design not only deals with the adjustment of a single space form or the cooperation of the equipment, but needs to be considered at the beginning of the design to develop a general building plan. Accessibility and general design to promote the subject, but also by the operation of this public housing to verify and find a solution, the induction of these experiences will be used as a follow-up policy to promote the planning and design reference.

keywords: Barrier-free, Universal design, Public housing, Aging society

参考文献

[1] 建筑技术规则 .2011.

[2] 建筑物无障碍设施设计规范 . 2011.

[3] 台北市出租国宅通用设计改造大作战手册 . 2014.

[4] 身心障碍者权益保障法 . 2015.

[5] 台北市居住空间通用设计指南 . 2016.

[6] 张金鹗 . 打房与居住正义有什么差别？ [J], 天下杂志，2016，9.

[7] 世界厕所组织 . http：//worldtoilet.org/.

[8] 信息网 https：//www.stat.gov.tw/np.asp?ctNode=3606.

从开放社区到三维都市：中国当代社会住宅建筑设计趋势与方法研究

孙二奇

（同济大学建筑与城市规划学院）

摘　要：居住问题在任何一个国家、任何一个时期，都是相当重要的社会问题。其中，中低收入者的住房问题，更是一个重大的民生问题。自改革开放以来，我国城市化进程发展迅速，大量人口涌入城市，住房数量需求越来越大。中低收入者在城市中的居住空间短缺、居住质量较差等问题更是日益凸显。为了使城乡广大非富裕居民拥有自己的住所，政府开始兴建大量的社会住宅。社会住宅的建设迎来较好时机，但是在这样的大背景下，国内却鲜有高质量的社会住宅项目，其设计中存在诸多不足。同时，新建的住宅建筑如何向城市敞开，与城市形成良好的互动关系，营造良好的城市空间，是需要考虑的重要问题。作者借由在国外学习的机会，实地走访了西班牙诸多优秀的社会住宅案例，通过现场调研，进行归纳和分析。在预研究的基础上，本论文重点探索城市空间、居住密度、公共空间、内部空间的问题。本论文试图寻求一些社会住宅的设计策略和手法，为国内的社会住宅设计提供一些参考，促进国内社会住宅设计的发展，改善中低收入者的居住环境。

关键词：社会住宅，开放社区，居住密度，公共空间

1　国外社会住宅发展的现状

1.1　社会住宅的含义

社会住宅（Social Housing），是城市保障性住房的一种。在欧洲称之为"社会出租住宅"（Social Rented Housing）或者"廉价出租住宅"（Affordable Housing），是指政府直接兴建、补助兴建或民间拥有的适合居住的房屋。在国外，社会住宅一般采取"只租不卖"模式，以低于市场租金或免费出租给所得较低的家庭或特殊的弱势对象。但社会住宅这一概念只是一个意指，并没有准确的定义。在国内，其含义和模式相当于我国的公共租赁住房，例如广东的土楼公舍，上海的龙南佳苑公租房，嘉定的福临佳苑公租房等。

1.2　国外社会住宅的发展

从社会住宅在欧洲大陆出现起，迄今已有超过百年的历史。社会住宅的出现是源于城市化进程中住房短缺，导致中低收入者买不起住宅，引起社会矛盾与政治冲突，或造成诸如个人健康、家庭离散、就业、教育、环境卫生、治安等社会问题，经过诸多社会改革倡议后，最后由政府扮演起住宅市场外的补救角色，以提供"只租不售"的社会住宅，来解决弱势群体的居住问题。第二次世界大战之后，欧洲各国更是大力发展社会住宅以解决住房短缺问题。

时至今日，在欧美发达国家，社会住宅已成为国家住宅政策的重要一环。在荷兰，社会住宅占住

宅总量的比例高达35%（2008年），在整个欧洲乃至全世界名列前茅。以MVRDV为代表的一些荷兰事务所设计了数座优秀的社会住宅建筑，为其建筑空间的理论研究提供了丰富的实践素材。在西班牙，伴随着佛朗哥的独裁政治在20世纪70年代末的解体，社会住宅的开发在20世纪90年代末的社会经济发展大潮下也迎来了自己新的高峰，社会住宅的研究、设计和建成作品层出不穷。这些新作品大多由年轻的当地建筑师和国际知名建筑师的合作完成。建成的作品风格杂糅，时代性和都市风格的考虑大于地域性和历史态度，代表了当代集合式宜居住宅国际较高水准。数据统计，欧洲一些发达国家公有社会住宅占住宅总量比例：英国20%、丹麦19%、芬兰18%、瑞典18%、欧盟平均14%，这反映出各个国家对于社会住宅建设的重视以及社会住宅在国民居住体系中的重要地位。

2 二维到三维，密度到高度

1961年，简·雅各布斯的专著《美国大城市的死与生》出版，在书中，她极力推崇城市的多样性，并且犀利地批判了现代城市规划理论，认为它们在推崇区划（Zoning）的同时，贬低了高密度、小尺度街坊和开放空间的混合使用，破坏了城市的多样性。她提出人口应高密度聚集，因为密度意味着安全。以现在的观点与情况来看，密度也是解决城市巨大住房需求的一个重要方法。

1973年，George B.Dantzig和Thomas Isaaty出版了专著《紧凑城市——适于居住的城市环境计划》。书中提供了有关高密度的城市生活的最新思考，认为紧凑城市的主要特征为城市高密度、功能混用和紧凑以及密集化。城市高密度即为人口和建筑的高密度，功能混用即为城市功能的紧凑和复合，而密集化即为城市各项活动的密集化。从我国当代大城市的发展来看，城市核心区域建筑密度越来越高的趋势显而易见。紧凑城市提出要最大限度实现对土地的利用，但如果只是单纯增加建筑高度，则会在水平方向上遏制人的活动范围，忽略城市居民的社交需求。所以，真正的高密度城市应该是指在垂直方向同样创造能够让人自由活动的领域。扬·盖尔在其《人性化的城市》指出，现代主义的城市规划方法分离城市功能且强调独立的单体建筑，将城市空间与城市生活置于不顾，从而导致了缺乏人气的无活力城市。他认为要增加城市空间的社会职能，即聚会场所功能，并提出人性化的城市的四个重要目标是充满活力的、安全的、可持续的、健康的。

2005年，MVRDV出版专著《KM3》，主要研究城市的密集度问题。他们认为，密集度问题的迫切性是由城市空间短缺所造成的，他们的三维城市理论KM3认为，城市不仅仅需要在两维平面上扩展，还要增加竖向维度，高空也将成为城市发展的方向——建立一个可拥有更多公共层次的城市，以扩展城市的容量，并且在三维度量上，创造出更加丰富多样的公共空间。在这个理论指导下，MVRDV先后设计了马德里"瞭望塔"社会住宅、"塞洛西大楼"社会住宅。

3 国外社会住宅设计的案例与经验

在欧洲发达国家，社会住宅的发展起步早，制度完善，有诸多社会住宅设计的优秀作品，这对于我国社会住宅设计具有重要的借鉴意义。一方面，随着我国城市化的加速，城市问题也越来越多，而欧洲发达国家在城市化的进程中也曾面临相同或相似的问题。另一方面，我国幅员辽阔，气候、环境种类多样，欧洲各个地区的社会住宅设计策略各异，这对于我国诸多不同的地区有不同的参考价值。

3.1 低层高密：Carabanchel 11 社会住宅

Carabanchel 11 社会住宅由美国建筑师汤姆·梅恩和西班牙建筑师合作完成。

建筑位于马德里南部的新兴住宅区 Carabanchel。这里汇聚着众多优秀的社会住宅作品，其中大部分采用围合式、大体量、整体性的体量处理方式。但是，汤姆·梅恩采用了在社会住宅设计中比较少见的低层高密度的设计方式。除了场地边缘的两座 6～7 层塔楼以外，整个项目的中心区域采用的是低层联排住宅的方式。在低层高密的区域，建筑师借鉴了村落的特征，诸多的"孔隙"被置入到低层的住宅群之中，形成多层次的公共空间。这个项目打破了传统认知，使通常为富人服务的低层住宅类型，大规模出现在以中低收入者为主要服务对象的社会住宅中，代表着建筑师对于传统社会住宅的反思。

整个设计以白色为主，由于建设时间较短，花架目前仅仅表现为一种另类的装饰元素。然而我们可以想象，随着时间的推移，当植物爬满屋顶和墙壁，这个有白色和绿色构成的社会住宅，将成为一个真正的乐园。

图 1　Carabanchel 11 社会住宅（作者自摄）

3.2 垂直社区：马德里米拉多尔（Mirador）大楼

Mirador 在西班牙语中指西班牙式房屋上可眺望优美景色的塔楼或眺台。这一建筑由 MVRDV 和西班牙建筑师布兰卡·列奥合作完成，坐落于马德里桑齐纳罗区，是马德里新的都市发展计划中的一个新住宅区（图 2）。

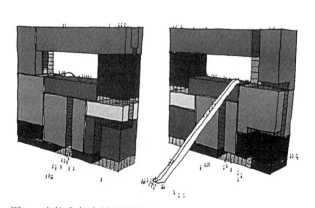

图 2　米拉多尔大楼及其分析

资料来源：作者自摄及布兰卡·列奥. 当代社会住宅的可持续性与交往空间 [J]. 时代建筑，2011.

这幢建筑内共有165套住房,为了适应不同的家庭类型和多样的需求,设计师设计了15种户型类型,既有直套间,又有双跃层公寓、三跃层公寓、转角公寓等。大楼内整合多种社会群体和生活方式,既有单身青年,又有一家三口等其他家庭类型。从大楼外部来看,整个大楼宛若一座立体城市,由9个社区堆叠而成,公共空间穿插其中。9组住宅通过外立面材料和开创方式加以区分。大楼内最独特的空间就是被"举起"高达40m,面积达500m^{2}的空中庭院。这一庭院成为这个城市中凌空而立的大型取景框——马德里市郊和远处瓜达拉马山脉的景色尽收其中。通过建筑内的直达电梯,可以到达这个半公共的空中广场,这里成为社区生活的中心的标志。大楼内住宅组团、走廊、垂直街道和广场,像城市功能的变异和延伸,形成垂直立体的邻里关系。

3.3 空中花园:马德里塞洛西(Celosia)大楼

塞洛西大楼(图3)同样坐落于马德里桑齐纳罗区,与米拉多尔大楼相距不过数百米。在这座建筑中,建筑师更加注重作为一个整体的社区之间的交流与空间的共享,打破建筑传统住宅封闭的形式,以空置的过渡空间,形成内与外的相互联系。

在平面上,塞洛西大楼采用四方形围合式,对外形成一个完整的界面,对内围合出一个大的公共花园,成为居民活动交流的中心。底层虚体块形成的架空区域,形成连接街区的通道,又将底层体院开放向城市;在竖直方向上,塞洛西大楼由分布均等、虚实相间的小体量组合堆叠而成,住宅空间的"实体块"和公共空间的"虚体块"紧密结合,互相交错。"虚体块"形成的公共空间成为居民邻里交往、公共生活的平台,也成为整座大楼和外部城市环境沟通的场所,避免了社区与外界环境的隔绝。不仅如此,这些空白体块成为介于城市公共空间和家庭空间之间的交往空间,成为公共生活的"灰空间"。大楼内的社区和居民,通过地面的庭院、空中的平台,变得开放和外向,形成由开放到私密的多个层次的交往空间。

图3　塞洛西大楼及其底层庭院开口(作者自摄)

4 国内社会住宅的发展

4.1 国内社会住宅发展的现状

由于国内的社会住宅发展相比欧美国家起步要晚,所以国内目前对于社会住宅的研究还主要集中在政策、经济、选址等方面,对于建筑空间的研究还相对薄弱。但是随着最近几年的住房问题越来越严峻,国家对社会住宅的投入也越来越大,国内也出现了个别高品质的社会住宅实践项目。

土楼公舍：都市实践将中国福建传统的土楼居住形式，运用到当代社会住宅设计中。将土楼作为当前解决低收入住宅问题的方法，不只是形式上的承袭。土楼和现代宿舍建筑类似，但又具有现代走廊式宿舍所缺少的亲和力，有助于保持低收入社区中的邻里感。将传统客家土楼的居住文化与低收入住宅结合在一起，更标志着低收入人群的居住状况开始进入大众的视野。

龙南佳苑公租房：由高目建筑事务所设计，采取了集约化的设计方法，根据人体尺度设计各个空间的需求，有些空间尺度甚至超过了原有的《上海市住宅设计标准》，为此，上海市经过研究谈论，专门修订了《上海住宅设计标准》。这也反映出，在我国当下，对于社会住宅的设计越来越重视，也越来越根据实际情况，考虑中低收入者的住房条件问题。

4.2 国内社会住宅发展的问题

虽然国内也出现了一些优秀的社会住宅设计项目，但就整体而言，还存在许多问题。首先在政策层面，国内社会住宅的发展还处于起步阶段，以高目事务所设计的龙南佳苑为例，上海市的原有《上海市住宅设计标准》落后于实际的需要，还需要根据新的情况，调整修订新的住宅设计标准。其次，在设计师层面上，国内建筑师对于社会住宅的关注还相对较少，许多优秀的建筑师，较少从事社会住宅的设计工作。从设计层面来说，国内社会住宅的设计也存在一些问题。一是社区空间缺少对城市的呼应。由于之前我国一直采取的是封闭小区的政策，所以在住宅设计领域，对于社区空间和城市空间的互动、交流方面，一直缺少关注和设计，建筑和城市缺少对话。二是社会住宅建筑的形式缺少创新，单调雷同，采用"样板"设计的方式。三是建筑空间设计单调乏味，缺少对空间品质的营造，尤其是缺少公共空间，致使社区居民之间缺少交流，难以形成良好的邻里关系。

5 结论

对于刚刚起步的中国社会住宅设计来说，欧洲一些优秀的社会住宅设计具有重要的参考意义。首先在城市层面上，建筑和城市应该相互交融，建筑向城市敞开，形成开放的城市-建筑关系。其次，在土地资源有限的条件下，应该采取高密度的设计办法，提高场地上的"人积率"，最大限度解决需求问题。最后，在高度密集的空间中，应该注重空间品质的营造，创造丰富的公共空间，供邻里之家，供社区居民，甚至为城市居民，提供优质的共享区域。在建筑材料方面，多采用轻质结构和低价材料；传统的钢筋混凝土框架结构是主要的结构类型。素混凝土、GRC板等廉价材料作为表皮材料。以经济实用为主要原则。

欧洲的社会住宅的成功，对于社会住宅刚刚起步的中国，无疑是有很好的借鉴作用的。建筑师的组织，对于适用人群的定位等特点，都有着一定的普遍性和适用性。然而整个系统的全面建立和完善，却非一日之功，需要一个相对漫长的循序渐进的过程。

致谢

本篇论文的写作受到国家自然科学基金项目《长三角地区"城中厂"的社区化更新技术体系研究》的资助（编号：51678412）。

From Open Community to Three-dimensional City: Research on the Tendency and Methods of Social Housing Design in China

Sun Erqi

(College of Architecture and Urban Planning, Tongji University)

Abstract: Housing problem is a very important social problem at any time in any country. The problem for the low-income earners is a major livelihood issue above all. Since the Reform and Opening, the urbanization process in China has been accelerating, so that the population of city has increased rapidly and caused growing demand for housing. The houses for the low-income are of critical shortage and poor living quality, which have been prominent problems today. In order to provide the non-wealthy residents with houses, the government have started up a large number of social housing construction. However, high-quality social housing projects hardly appear, and their designs expose many deficiencies. Meanwhile, there are three important issues to be considered: how to open the new residential building to the city, how to form a good interactive relationship between them and how to create a good urban space. When studying abroad, the author visited many outstanding social housing cases in Spain, Holland, Austria, Germany, Italy and other European countries. Through the in-depth investigation, this paper is trying to analyze these cases from four aspects of urban space, dwelling density, public space and internal space. By summarizing some design strategies and practices of social housing, it attempts to provide reference for the domestic social housing design and improving the living environment of the low-income.

Keywords: Social housing, Open community, Density, Public space

参考文献

[1] 克里斯蒂安·德·包赞巴克. 开放街区——以欧路风格住宅和马塞纳新区为例 [J]. 城市环境设计, 2015, 7.

[2] 李振宇. 在历史与未来之间的妥协——关于包赞巴克开放街区的断想 [J]. 城市环境设计 2015, 7.

[3] 布兰卡·列奥. 当代社会住宅的可持续性与交往空间 [J]. 时代建筑, 2011, 4: 62-69

[4] 雨果·普利莫斯. 荷兰社会住宅: 明确的传统与未知的将来 [J]. 国际城市规划, 2009, 2: 58-64.

[5] Ray Forrest. 社会住宅: 过去现在和未来 [J]. 住宅学报, 2012, 2: 91-99.

[6] 李振宇, 张玲玲, 姚栋. 关于保障性住房设计的思考——以上海地区为例 [J]. 建筑学报, 2011, 8: 60-64.

[7] 余子碧. 新世纪马德里社会住宅现象与形成原因 [J]. 中外建筑, 2016, 7: 60-62.

[8] 马岩松, 齐子樱, 何晓康. 社会住宅的社会性 [J]. 建筑创作, 2015, 8: 295-299.

[9] 马奕鸣. 紧凑城市理论的产生与发展 [J]. 现代城市研究, 2007, 4: 10-16.

[10] 寒梅, 邹颖. 高密集度理想——MVRDV 的三维城市理论 KM3 [J]. 青岛理工大学学报, 2007, 5: 32-35.

[11] 宋玮. 马德里社会住宅. http://www.treemode.com/theory/type/230.html [2017-04-20].

以 Upside-down 体系为核心的住宅适应性设计研究

欧阳文　甘振坤　张　超　陈婉蓉　倪晨辉　陈　旭
（北京建筑大学）

摘　要：当前中国正进行世界上最大规模的城镇化建设，在这一过程中大量的建筑未达到使用年限而被拆毁重建，从而造成资源浪费、环境污染等一系列社会问题。造成这种现象的原因是：建筑的使用功能和内部空间随着社会需求处于持续的变化之中，设计者在建造之初并未考虑建筑全生命周期的使用，导致已建成建筑无法适应未来时代的变化。开放建筑作为一种建筑设计理论方法，着眼于建筑全生命周期的使用，为未来建筑的建造提供一种全新的导向思维。"开放建筑"的核心在于用"开放"的思维和眼光来看待、设计并建造建筑。开放建筑学理论不单局限于建筑空间上的转变，更是时间、功能和与人的关系上的转变。本文以 Upside-down（倒梁体系）为核心，通过多个方案分析，分别探讨了其在低层高密度与高层高密度的两种居住建筑类型的适应性设计，为开放建筑在中国现存住宅改造设计中的应用提供了借鉴与思考。

关键词：开放建筑，住宅，倒梁体系，适应性，可持续

1　引言

在历史发展的很长一段时间里，传统建筑设计是基于功能性的，不同的空间因为不同的使用需要被设置在一个永恒固定的位置或状态，直到建筑整体因为种种原因而被拆除。在大拆大建、迅速发展的中国，该现象尤其明显而且常见。但是换一种视角来看，正如 N. J. Habraken 教授所说的"住就是建"，建筑应该是一种行为，一个平台，而不单单是一种形式。开放建筑设计理念是一种着眼于人与时间和建筑的设计新思路，空间与功能随着人和时间的"互动"与需求而在不同的层级上具有了不同于以往的灵活性，由小动作入手，节约资源与成本，同时满足其新的需求，以此更好地保证建筑全生命周期的使用。

2　时代语境下的开放建筑理念

2.1　开放建筑的理念与特征

开放建筑最早由荷兰建筑师 N. J. Habraken 提出，强调以适应性为着眼点，完善建筑的全生命周期中不同环境与不用使用者所导致的不同需求。具有以下特征：（1）层次性：建筑个体内部应该分为不同的层级，各层级相对独立且具有不同的时效；（2）参与性：非专业的住户或者房屋的使用者应该与专业的设计师和施工者一样具有决策权，从而更多地参与到建筑的实践活动中，增强人与建筑的互动性；（3）关联性：建筑中的各个体系之间要具有一定的关联性，以便相互衔接、拼合；（4）灵活性：建筑与环境是不断变换的，所以设计是一个随时间循序渐进不断变化的过程。

2.2 开放建筑的发展及在中国的实践

开放建筑主要经历了三大历史阶段：20世纪20~30年代，现代建筑大师们对小面积住宅空间灵活性的尝试；第二次世界大战后，由工业化大规模生产所引发的对建筑构件和设计施工方法的探讨；近30年来，由于人们对于人–时间–建筑之间关系的理解与认识的加深，高舒适、低能耗的理念被广泛认可。

中国的开放建筑体系与理论开始要比欧洲国家、日本等晚一些，其第一个实践案例是由南京大学的鲍家声教授于1984年在无锡郊外建造的支撑体住宅。由此，中国的开放建筑研究与实践沿着构成组件的开发与建筑设计策略的研究两个方向普及发展起来，本文下面提到的Upside-down（倒梁体系）在当代中国住宅改造中的应用探索，来自于Steven Kendall教授主持的北京建筑大学与中国建筑标准设计研究院开放建筑联合工作营的教学实践。

3 Upside-down 构成及特征

3.1 Open Building 特征

我们将Open Building（开放建筑）中不同的墙体分为三个层级，分别为永不更改墙体（Black Wall）、开发商可更改墙体（Grey Wall），以及使用者自行更改墙体（Red Wall）即内部填充墙体（图1）。通过所属权的不同，对开放建筑的可变性进行合理的控制。使用者可以根据自身使用需求，改变内部填充墙体的分隔空间，以适应不同时期的居住需求，实现百年住宅的愿景。而Open Building中的核心技术Upside-down实现了基础结构（Skeleton）与填充结构（Infill）的分离。

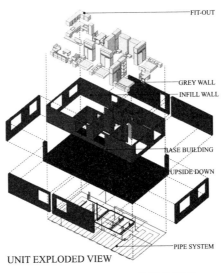

图1 Open Building 体系分解图

资料来源：开放建筑国际工作营团队绘制。

3.2 一种开放性适应体系——Upside-down

Upside-down（图2）是一种倒置梁的体系，其操作方法是将梁翻转位于地板层，并将传统住宅中吊顶层、墙面，以及楼板层中的管线系统全部收集于倒置梁系统中，使空间中墙体和吊顶的移动与变化不再涉及到管线问题，也使墙体的可变性得到实现。卫生间采用装配式，在确定了基础结构的管道井之后，卫生间可以在一定范围内根据住户需要放置在不同区域。

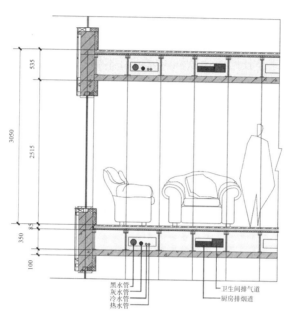

图 2　Upside-down 结构示意图

资料来源：开放建筑国际工作营团队绘制。

3.3　Upside-down 与住宅建筑设计结合的可行性

20 世纪 60 年代，荷兰 SAR 建筑研究学会 N. J. Habraken 教授提出了开放建筑的理论，并应用了 Upside-down。近年来，我国也以开放建筑为依托发展出了适合我国国情的 CSI 体系。SI 体系是指住宅的承重结构作为长久不变的基础体系（Skeleton），其特征需要有较强的耐久性，可百年不变。但是住宅内部的分隔构建则是灵活可变的，可以根据不同的需求进行适应性设计，同一住户也可根据其人口的变化进行及时的空间调整。这一适应性的内部空间（Infill）使得百年建筑的构想更易于实现。同时，也正是由于 Upside-down，使内部填充墙脱离管线束缚，获得灵活性，更加适合住宅的多向需求。

4　Upside-down 在住宅建筑适应性设计中的试验性研究

4.1　低层高密度住宅类型

4.1.1　低层高密度住宅特点

低层高密度住宅有着低层、贴近地面的天然优势，它会更便利地为住户提供独立的活动场地，使得人们更容易贴近自然，尤其适合于老年人和儿童。如今，越来越多的城市居民开始向往低层住宅的生活。然而早期的低层高密度住宅内部管道系统错综复杂，严重影响室内的使用空间，使得室内空间的更改变得困难，不能很好地适应住户的需求。

4.1.2 原型选取与研究

笔者调研了多个高校宿舍楼，并以此为原型进行了本次设计研究。出于对建筑的产权归属、实际改造的可实施性考虑，我们最终将设计定位为高校的学生宿舍楼。高校宿舍产权属于学校，且由于时代的发展、政策的变动等因素，其最初的功能将被替换。对于没有应用开放建筑设计理念的建筑而言，如此大的功能变动造成了大量的资源浪费、环境污染和高额费用。由此我们以北京外国语大学的某宿舍楼作为原型，提炼其建筑结构特点，引入开放建筑理念及Upside-down，适应新时期高校宿舍楼的使用需求。

4.1.3 低层高密度住宅适应性设计——以北京某大学公寓为例

根据开放建筑的设计原则以及Upside-down的结构特征，可将建筑分成主体结构体系（框架结构与交通盒）、灰墙体系（外立面及分户墙）、填充体系（户内隔墙与整体厨、卫）以及家具四个层次，并根据其使用者的不同拟定不同的需求，研究出可能的户型套型以及套型内的可变内装体系方案（表1）。

适应性户型设计研究（部分） 表1

面积	34.81m²	67.38～73.19m²	99.94m²	132.44m²	147.11m²
人群	学生、青年单身教师	留学生、中青年教师	中青年教师	中青年教师	中青年教师
人数	1～4人	1～2人	2～4人	2～6人	4～8人
部分套型					

4.2 高层高密度住宅类型

4.2.1 高层高密度住宅特点

高层高密建筑是当今城市主要的建筑类型，被广泛用于居住、办公、商业等。以高层高密度住宅为设计研究对象，探讨如何适应人口结构的变化、家庭需求的变化，为未来住宅产业的发展提供一套合理的策略。设计中采用了开放建筑Upside-down，打破传统住宅内部各种管道布置的束缚，发挥内部空间的灵活性与开放性，满足不同人群对住宅空间的不同需求。这种理论体系并不是在建筑技术上的革新，而是依托当今时代特征和经济技术，对住宅的观念和设计的改变，即适应社会各种需求的"开放"建筑。

4.2.2 原型选取与研究

当前中国城市面临的主要问题是由无限蔓延引起的系列城市病，开放建筑以建筑的全生命周期为突破点，能够解决其中众多城市问题。本节以高层高密度住宅为研究对象，以 Upside-down 体系为依托，研究不同人群对住宅空间差异需求的问题，选取的建筑原型是北京市某高层塔式住宅。

4.2.3 高层高密度住宅适应性设计——以某高层住宅为例

中国人口结构的变化对住宅空间类型的需求有很大差异，例如单身或是刚组成家庭的年轻人与有小孩的家庭或是有老人居住的家庭对住宅空间的需求存在很大差异，因此，研究以家庭人口结构的变化为主线，讨论一个普通家庭在不同时期对住宅空间的需求特点（表2）。

"人口结构"影响下的适应性研究（部分） 表2

家庭人口结构变化	新人阶段	新生儿独居阶段	二孩独居阶段	父母照料阶段	养老阶段
阶段特点	对住房单元面积的需求不大	对住房单元面积的需求加大	对住房单元面积的需求进一步加大	需要的住房面积更大，空间的变化更加灵活	空间布局不那么紧凑，更多地考虑老人居住空间的舒适性
平面形式 — 卫生间、厨房靠近管道					
平面形式 — 卫生间、厨房靠近外立面					

5 结语

中国城市住宅在快速建设发展的过程中对住宅的适应性和灵活性要求越来越高。而以 Upside-down 体系为核心的开放建筑的设计理念着眼于未来，更大程度上地将人－时间的元素加入建筑中，增强人与建筑之间的互动，有利于在不同时期满足人的不同诉求，为我国住宅的适应性研究提供了一种新的思路，对推动住宅产业的健康发展有着重要作用。经过工作营半个月的试验性研究，我们发现将开放建筑理念运用到住宅设计之后，空间的适应性得到很大程度的提高，空间划分更灵活，为住户后期根据自身的生活需求进行改造提供了更多的可能性。

致谢

感谢北京建筑大学与中国建筑标准设计研究院举办的开放建筑联合工作营为本次研究创造了宝贵契机，尤其感谢 Steven Kendall 教授、欧阳文教授、刘东卫教授、伍止超博士、李珊珊博士在整个工作营期间对每一位团队成员的耐心指导。还要感谢刘若凡、闫晶晶以及刘赫同学在工作营期间的共同努力，使得这一份扎实的设计研究得以呈现。

Research on the Adaptability Design of Residential Buildings Based on the Upside-down System

Ouyang Wen, Gan Zhenkun, Zhang Chao, Chen Wanrong, Ni Chenhui, Chen Xu

(Beijing University of Civil Engineering and Architecture)

Abstract: Currently, in the urbanization construction of world's largest scale, China has been a test field for domestic and foreign architects to achieve self-ideal. However, many buildings within age limit have been demolished and reconstructed in this process, which results in waste of resources, environmental pollution and a series of social problems. The reason for this phenomenon is: the usable function of the buildings and the internal space are in continuous change with the social needs, and at the beginning of the construction, instructors did not take the whole life cycle of buildings into account, which has caused buildings that had been built could not adapt to changes of future. Open building, as a method of architectural design theory, focuses on the use of the whole life cycle of the building, to provide a new guiding thinking for the future construction of buildings. Theory of open building is not only limited to the transformation of architectural space, but also the change of relationship among time, function and people. This paper takes the upside-down system as the core, and probes respectively two adaptive designs of residential building types in low-rise high density and high-rise high density through a number of program analysis, to provide references and thoughts for designs of the existing residential building transformation in China.

Keywords: Open building, Dwelling, Upside-down, Adaptability, Sustainable

参考文献

[1] Skendall. Open Building: An Approach to Sustainable Architecture[J].Joumal of Urban Technology.1999，12.

[2] S. kendall. Residential Open Building[M]. Spon Press.2000：200-210.

[3] N John Habraken. The structure of ordinary: Form and Control in the Built Environment[M]. MIT

Press,2000.

[4] 刘东卫. SI住宅与住房建设模式 理论·方法·案例[M]. 北京：中国建筑工业出版社，2015.

[5] 贾倍思，江盈盈."开放建筑"历史回顾及其对中国当代住宅设计的启示[J]. 建筑学报，2013，1：20-26.

[6] （日）深尾精一. 日本走向开放式建筑的发展史[J]. 新建筑，2011，6：14-17.

外廊式集合住宅中外廊空间邻里交往研究——广州深圳6个典型案例的比较分析

郭　萌[1]　杜宏武[2]

（1.广州市岭南建筑研究中心；2.华南理工大学）

摘　要：以广州、深圳6个典型外廊式集合住宅为研究案例，对外廊空间与邻里交往活动的影响，进行调查与分析，得出了影响邻里交往的外廊空间要素。研究发现，外廊空间对邻里交往产生较大影响的因素为：外廊长度与每层邻里规模范围；在外廊空间中设置静态交往空间时，相比于交往空间面积，交往空间的设置位置更为重要；交往行为多伴随其他行为发生，因此在设计中应注意赋予廊空间更多意义。

关键词：外廊式住宅，集合住宅，外廊空间，邻里交往

1　引言

我国当前城市化进程加快，助推了住宅成片开发、标准化复制设计的状况，使宅形趋向单一化。只注重户型与居住面积及以绿化率作为商业噱头的住区开发模式，使建筑师和开发商都将注意放在对套内面积和大型公共空间的开发中。造成居住形态单一枯燥，邻里关系淡漠的现状。而住宅设计中，邻里交往对居住品质的作用至关重要。外廊式住宅作为一种住宅类型，曾广泛活跃于世界各地的住宅设计领域，而近年来这一住宅类型却鲜少出现在我国的住宅设计中，与此形成对比的是，外廊住宅在欧洲及日本作为一种集合住宅类型，仍得到重视，对于居民日常邻里交往，外廊空间有何影响？

扬·盖尔（2002）在《交往与空间》中发现空间的边界是人们愿意停留的区域，同时指出交往行为通常伴随其他行为一同发生。[1]木村文雄和秋本敬子对日本积水住宅公司实验住宅进行研究，发现"外廊"作为建筑与外界空间之间的暧昧空间，同时具有多义性。[2]张天洁、李泽（2015）在对新加坡高层公共住宅社区营造研究中，较之以往的电梯紧邻家门，居民需沿着隐蔽的"空中街道"才能入户，创造与邻居相遇相识的机会。[3]

本研究试图在文献基础上，深入分析外廊空间对邻里交往活动的影响，即实证研究外廊空间变量与邻里交往活动的关系，对比总结出不同外廊空间形态是否对邻里交往有促进作用，以此作为今后宅形选择的设计参考。

2　研究设计

2.1　研究变量

在文献研究是基础上，笔者将影响交往活动的空间和界面变量分为5类：（1）外廊的空间尺度变量，

包括外廊的长度和宽度；（2）外廊长度与邻里规模之间的关系；（3）邻里交往空间的设置位置；（4）邻里交往空间设置尺寸；（5）外廊界面。以上这些变量在有些定量研究中曾被研究过，但针对外廊式集合住宅的案例很少。有的变量通常都是定性描述而很少被考证，譬如外廊长度与邻里规模和界面对邻里交往的影响。本研究就外廊空间尺度变量、外廊界面变量及外廊中构筑物对邻里交往行为的影响进行研究对比。

2.2 案例选取

通过对广州和深圳比较有代表性的外廊式集合住宅各3个案例——广州万科金色城品、广州万科土楼、广州芳和花园和深圳龙跃居2期、深圳光明锦鸿、深圳同创·新作为调研对象（表1）。对居民在不同形态的外廊空间中的交往行为进行数据统计，总结出邻里交往活动与外廊空间形态的关系。

实地观察居民对外廊空间的使用状况，并进行邻里交往行为的问卷测试，完成空间综合品质评价。考虑到天气因素对户外活动的影响行为调研选择在冬夏两季分两次进行。为了全面把握不同宅型对于居民交往程度的影响，对物业及部分居民进行了访谈。

研究案例概况　　　　　表1

案例	万科土楼	龙悦居2期	芳和花园
平面图			
外廊空间环境描述	内庭边长：22.00m 外环廊道周长：380.00m 外廊宽：2.00m	水平方向长度：65.00m 垂直方向长度：35.00m 外廊宽：1.80m	水平方向长度：20.00m 垂直方向长度：10.00m 外廊宽：1.50m
案例	光明锦鸿	万科金色城品	同创·新作
平面图			
外廊空间环境描述	外廊长：36.00m 外廊宽：1.50m	长边长度：60.00m 短边长度：60.00m 外廊宽：1.80m	水平方向长度：33.00m 垂直方向长度：10.00m 外廊宽：2.40m

3 交往与空间的测量与分析

3.1 外廊长度分析

芦原义信对外部空间的尺度的分析中指出，空间的高度（H）与进深（D）是空间尺度的重要度量，但根据我国住宅设计规范中的要求，走廊宽度不得少于1.2 m，且由于层高限制。空间D/H比极少能有较大不同，因此，对空间感受有较大影响的因素为外廊空间长度。

统计不同外廊形态的居民对外廊空间的空间满意度平均值（图1）。可以看出万科金色城品的外廊空间的居民满意度最高，芳和花园居民舒适度最低，排除其他因素的干扰，就空间尺寸的比值而言，在空间D/H比相似的情况下，居民的舒适度在一定范围内与外廊长度呈正相关。但在这类长匀质外廊中，当走道长度较长且无节点变化时，容易变成冗长而单调的过道空间。使人们不会愿意在其中停留，仅仅成为简单的过道空间。

3.2 外廊长度与邻里规模

为满足对容积率的诉求，一般会尽可能多地沿廊道布置套型，随着廊长度的增加是否每层邻里规模越大，邻里交往就越密切。针对"是否每层户数越多，居民认识的邻里数就越多"这一问题进行分析。

对居民认识的同层邻里人数进行统计（图2），并进行均值计算，可知短外廊式认识邻里人数相似，都维持在3户左右；而长外廊式，当每层户数在8~12户之间时，认识的邻里人数是最多的，当出超过这个范围时，居民间的相识度不但没有增高，甚至随着户数增长而下降。可见每层邻里户数并非越多越好。美国社会学家也指出："一定范围内的邻里（如同一楼层）作为集体，住户愈多，集体感及亲切感愈差，其典型的社会活动方式是居民的消极回避。"由此可见，当认识人数超过个人结识能力范围时，邻里间就会出现相互回避的现象。

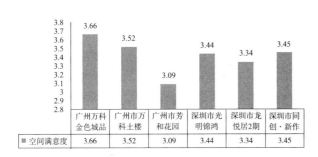

图1 外廊空间满意度

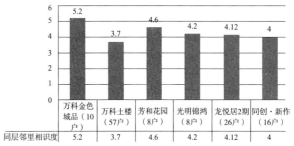

图2 邻里规模与同层邻里相识度关系

3.3 邻里规模与交往深度分析

从交往深度而言，每层邻里户数有何作用，根据邻里交往深度将邻里交往分为四个层级：知道但不认识、点头之交、寒暄之交、相互熟识。再将四个层级分为三个人数层级进行统计，分别为：（1）相识人数在1~3人之间；（2）相识人数在4~6人之间；（3）相识人数在5~7人之间。对3个层级进行均值统计。

根据图表（图3）可知：无论长短外廊及每层邻里规模如何，在"点头之交"这一交往层级的均值相似，而在"知道并不认识"这一交往层级中，均值与邻里规模成正比。而在"相互熟识"这一交往层级中，均值随邻里规模有显著提高。也就是说，虽然邻里交往广度始终与邻里交往规模呈正比，但在"知道并不认识"及"相互熟识"这两个交往深度，邻里规模有较大影响。在对居民的访谈中得知，当邻里规模扩大时，由于每层串联户数较多，在日常生活中，会经常在交通空间及廊道中碰到彼此，虽然并不是每一个人都能够相识，但经常碰面为邻里相识创在条件。且对自身居住环境人员的熟识，在一定程度上起到了邻里间视线监督的作用，保证了安全性。并由于平层串联户数较多，日常相互熟识的邻里较多。

	万科金色城品（10户）	万科土楼（57户）	芳和花园（8户）	光明锦鸿（8户）	龙悦居2期（26户）	同创·新作（16户）
知道但不认识	1.65	2.08	1.67	1.6	1.67	1.64
点头之交	1.32	1.42	1.42	1.5	1.47	1.27
相互熟识	2.85	2	2.11	2.5	2.33	2.09

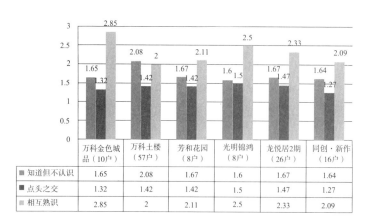

图 3　邻里规模与交往深度研究

3.4　交往空间位置及空间尺度进行分析

在外廊空间中设置点状交往空间，改善外廊空间环境，现有点线空间组合形式可分为两种：沿住户入口设置点状入户花园和另一种较为常见的交往休憩空间设置方式，是结合楼电梯间等交通系统，布置公共休憩空间。

金色城品案例中，沿外廊边界设置入户花园，每户居民都有用一个空间归属明确的小院子，前院的存在为居民提供了更多的选择。（图 4）由于沿边界设置，前院靠着自己家的墙，居民很容易形成安全感，整个入户花园向外廊开敞，形成了由外廊向住户过渡的柔性边界。居民愿意在这种半私密半公共空间中停留，为邻里交往创造条件。玄关形成阴角空间，具有极强的入口暗示且入口位于侧边，不破坏整体外廊空间形态。因此，入户花园空间成为使用率较高且为邻里碰面提供机会的场所。

入户花园长 6m，宽 8.5m，面积约 20m^2 左右的（图 5）。调研得知居民大多愿意在入户花园中停留。在听觉范围内入户花园与外廊经过居民可进行正常交谈，入户花园与外廊之间设置高差近 1m 高差，有效避免视线干扰，且有植物、家具等物件布置。

在土楼公社中在交通楼梯旁设置平台（图 6）。一方面为减少实体体量对外圈住户的空间压迫感，另一方面想要为居民提供交往活动的平台空间。在调研中，我们发现，虽然设计之初是为居民交往考虑，但实际生活中极少有居民使用这个空间。物业人员表示，曾有一段时间内，居民会聚在此处打麻将，但由于声音过大，对其他居民日常生活造成较大影响，最终，该空间闲置无人使用。

而土楼公社中，结合交通空间设置活动平台长 12m，宽 8.5m，面积达 100m^2 左右（图 7）。却很少有人使用。据此可推断：在活动空间私密性较强，空间较小时，人们更愿意停留。这是由于空间的中心往往是暧昧的，当空间越小，空间的边界就越突出。根据前文分析可知，相较万科土楼公社，金色城品中的居民更愿意在入户空间停留，对两者尺度进行分析。

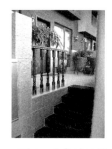

图 4　金色城品外廊交往空间

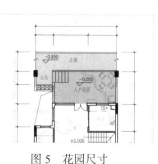

图 5　花园尺寸

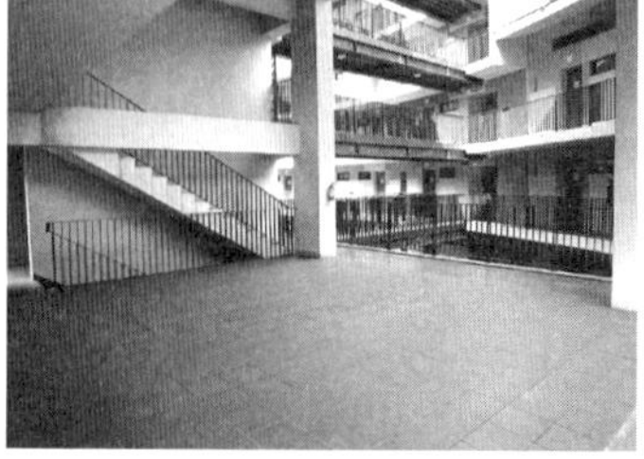

图 6　土楼公社外廊交往空间

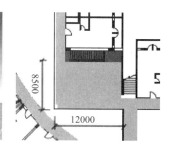

图 7　交往平台尺寸

3.5 边界性

外廊空间自身就具有一定的边界性，在设计中如果能使居民回家的过程中，有从半公共空间—半私密空间—私密空间的空间体验，这样层层划分的空间，有助于形成邻里互助守望。而生硬的边界的空间将难以作为邻里交往的空间被使用。在调研中，观察到住户直接与走道相连接，没有其他过渡的情况下，居民自发使用物品占用走道空间。可以观察到居民将自行车、鞋柜放到走廊。由于外廊空间主要担负的责任还是水平交通，当空间被占用时，人们会本能地避开被占用的空间（图8、图9）。

对将外廊划分出入户花园的万科金色城品进行调研（图10），受访者表示由于夏季外廊通风良好，温度较室内低，会将餐桌搬到入户花园，一家人在入户花园吃晚餐。几乎所有住户入户花园都有植物的种植，修剪花草、美化自家入户花园环境的行为，使得人们在入户花园的停留变得有意义。扬·盖尔也指出"如果人们想在宅前待上一会，总有许多有意思的杂事可做，如扫地、浇花等，既是有意义的活动，也是在户外待较长时间的解释和托词。"由此可见，人们并不是为了认识更多邻居而在入户花园停留的，相反，是在做自己的事情时，认识了更多的邻居。此时，入户花园就不再是单纯的交通空间，人们在使用过程中赋予该空间更多的使用价值。

图8 龙悦居外廊晒晾衣物　　图9 龙悦居自行车占用走道　　图10 金色城品外廊空间层级分明

4 总结和讨论：

4.1 外廊空间长度是影响空间满意度的因素之一

受规范限制，一般外廊宽度都在1.2～2.4m之间，对空间感受影响较大的因素一般为外廊空间的长度，由调研可知在外廊宽度相似的情况下，外廊长度在一定范围内越长，邻里交往有效性越高，居民对外廊的使用度越高，同时对外廊空间的满意度也越高。但外廊长度不能够无限增长，根据现有案例调研可知一般外廊长度在30～50m之间时，空间满意度较高。

4.2 同层邻里规模是影响邻里交往的一个重要因素

《美国大城市的死与生》曾指出小街段的意义："10～20户围绕街道或院落组构的住区，可以在保证人与人之间必要的距离和自我状态下，形成持久的邻里集体。"[4]可见无论居住模式如何改变，小而美的景象都是人们所憧憬追寻的。具有较一定交往深度的邻里规模一般控制在8～12户为宜，《建筑模式语言》中指出"8～12户正好可以维持和谐的邻里关系，当户数超过12户时，和谐的邻里关系就难以维持了。"[5]调研得出超过15户时，认识的邻里人数就开始呈明显下降趋势。因此要保证邻里间的接触及更深层次的交往，将邻里范围控制在这个范围内，有利于营造富有温情的空间。此次研究可知：外廊长度与每层邻里规模范围在同层邻里规模范围在8～15户时，最利于形成交往。

4.3 静态交往空间的设置位置是影响邻里交往的一个重要因素

在对聚落的研究中发现，聚落有将空间都建造得稍小一点的倾向，因为将空间调小一点，是产生人情味的主要原因。例如在热带雨林中用地和材料都取之不尽，但住宅却很狭小，安第斯山脉中，住宅也保持了精小的尺寸。原广司认为"这种追求小尺度是刻意的"。[6]人们在外廊空间的交往行动都是静态行为，对于空间面积的需求并不是很大，相反，一定尺度内，空间越小，归属感越强，也就越受人们喜爱。由此相比于交往空间面积，交往空间的设置位置更为重要。而一般沿外廊空间设置的宅前柔性边界，更受居民欢迎，在这样的空间中居民往往赋予外廊空间更多意义。

4.4 丰富的空间边界对邻里交往行为存在积极影响

在外廊住宅的设计中，由于仅把外廊看作通道型空间，而不是日常居处对待，忽略了外廊空间的空间价值。萧默先生在《敦煌建筑研究》中提到，壁画中廊庑有床榻之设，即廊庑有常规栖止之用。[7]可见外廊空间中绿化、座椅、遮阳等设施对于丰富空间边界有重要作用，空间支持物为外廊空间带来生气。这对促进邻里交往有重要作用，人们更愿意在富有情感的空间逗留。

由此可见，外廊空间由于具有传统街巷空间的特征，能实现良好的视线监视，有利于空间活力的激发。外廊式住宅对促进邻里交往和塑造社区感具有独特价值,而外廊式住宅适合珠三角地区气候特点，只要设计得当，就能丰富住宅类型，满足多样化居住需求。随着人们对邻里交往重视度的日益重视及对外廊空间认识的不断加深，住宅中外廊空间的发展存在有着较明朗的发展前景。

致谢

本文由国家自然科学基金面上项目"住区休憩空间价值的量化研究——基于珠三角住区规划控制与设计视角资助"，项目批准号：51378209。

Residential Neighborhood Communication Space in the Veranda Style House——A Case Study of Six Typical Gallery House in Guangzhou and Shenzhen

Guo Meng [1], Du Hongwu [2]

(1.Guangzhou Lingnan Architecture Research Center; 2.South China University of Technology)

Abstract: Based on the case study of six typical corridors——type residential buildings in Guangzhou and Shenzhen, the impact of the communication between the corridors and the activities of neighborhood has been investigated and analyzed. The result is elements of the corridors would influence the communication of neighborhood. Specially speaking, the main reasons followed will influence this communication. The length of the corridors and the scale of the neighborhood of each floor. When the static communication space is set in the corridors' space, the setting space of the communication is more important, as interactive behavior always occurring with other acts. Therefore, more meaning should be given and more attention should be paid to the gallery space in the design.

Keywords: Corridors - type residential building, Apartment, Space of verandas, Neighborhood communication

参考文献

[1] （丹麦）扬·盖尔. 交往与空间 [M]. 何人可译. 北京：建筑工业出版社，2002.

[2] 木村文雄，秋本敬子，王琋慧. 可持续发展实验住宅——日本积水住宅公司实验住宅案例介绍 [J]. 建筑学报，2010，8.

[3] 张天洁，李泽. 新加坡高层公共住宅的社区营造 [J]. 建筑学报，2015，6：52-57.

[4] （美）简·雅各布斯. 美国大城市的死与生 [M]. 金衡山译. 江苏：译林出版社，2005.

[5] （美）克里斯多弗·亚历山大. 建筑模式语言 [M]. 常青译. 北京：中国建筑工业出版社，1977.

[6] （日）原广司. 世界聚落的教示 100[M]. 于天祎等译. 北京：中国建筑工业出版社，2003.

[7] 宋鸣，王鲁民. 廊院式住宅使用探讨 [J]. 新建筑，2012，4：148-151.

中外文化的交融在近代闽南侨乡民居中的体现

卢汀滢　边如晨

（中国科学院大学）

摘　要：建筑是一种文化的标志，包含建造主体的情感寄托。从传统大厝到洋楼民居，侨民和侨眷用建筑表达自己对生活的美好愿景，逐步创造了从空间结构、功能布局、局部装饰都独一无二的侨居文化。本文通过文献阅读、案例调研、归纳总结等研究方法，从建造主体的建筑审美和情感表达出发，深入地理解和发掘侨乡建筑的艺术和文化价值，以期为侨乡民居的保护发展提供可靠的依据，对于今天的社会现实有特殊的启示意义。

关键词：闽南侨乡，民居建筑，中外文化，情感心理，建筑表征

1　引言

闽南侨乡民居建筑是近代华侨文化的物质化表达，也是近代中外文化交流与融合的见证。作为建筑创作的主体，闽南华侨在侨乡民居中寄托了他们的复杂情感和审美追求，这也是侨居建筑文化独特性的起源。研究侨居建筑文化，需要深入华侨的生活背景，了解他们的心理特征，从而更深刻地解读侨乡民居的建筑表征。更重要的是，通过研究华侨群体在面对外来文化冲击与中国传统建筑的矛盾时，他们所采取的积极态度，可以在如今我们遭受着更广泛的文化冲击时，引发我们对文化本源的思考。

现有近代闽南侨乡建筑文化的相关研究大致包括地域性研究、史论研究、类型学研究和美学研究几大类（李岳川，p153）。[1] 基于建筑学角度的研究大多围绕建筑本身的特征展开，而较少谈及历史因素和主体意识的影响。本文主要从历史背景出发，探讨建造主体在侨居建筑文化形成过程中的主观能动性，从情感和心理角度解读近代闽南侨居建筑中的文化交融现象。

2　侨乡民居中的建筑审美与情感表达

华侨在我国历史上是一个命途坎坷的群体。自 1860 年签订《北京条约》开始，大批失去土地的中国农民和破产的小手工业者就以"契约劳工"的身份出国，这是我国近代史上第一批华侨。此后，中国政府曾设侨务机构、立侨务法规，极力保障华侨的切身利益。辛亥革命后，侨汇经济逐渐发展起来，身居海外的华侨通过邮寄外汇支持国内亲眷的生活，帮助建造当地侨居、兴办学校和公益性建筑等。[2] 其中，以侨居的建筑数量最为可观。华侨的命运几度起落，在外饱受苦难，屡受他国排挤。在这种极其特殊的历史背景下，侨民在侨居文化中流露出他们矛盾的心理活动。

1910 年之前，闽南侨乡建筑以传统大厝为主。因其常用红砖砌筑，故又被称为红砖厝（图 1）。传统大厝的基本单元为一个"回"字形合院，由一进门的"下落"、端头的"顶落"、左右两边的"榉头"，以及由其围合而成的"深井"组成。随着土地的扩张，房屋扩建，又逐渐发展出三落双护厝、五落大厝、单边双护厝、双边双护厝等多种灵活的布局形式（图 2）。在建筑装饰上，以轻盈的燕尾脊为典型形象。

随着辛亥革命后侨汇经济的迅猛发展，华侨渴望用西方文化实现自我的情感表达，认为西方建筑所象征的财富、地位和阅历可以为自己带来身份认同。正如程建军所述，华侨"崇尚西方的建筑风格，爱好浮华的装饰，以显耀财富，张扬个性，对过去穷困生活的伤痛得以淋漓尽致地宣泄。"[3] 这种苦尽甘来的情感宣泄成为他们学习外来建筑文化的动因之一，也是侨乡民居建筑发生后续变化的关键起因。

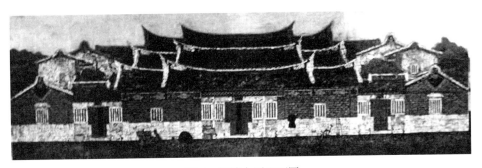

图1 红砖大厝立面图
图片来源：http://bbs.artron.net。

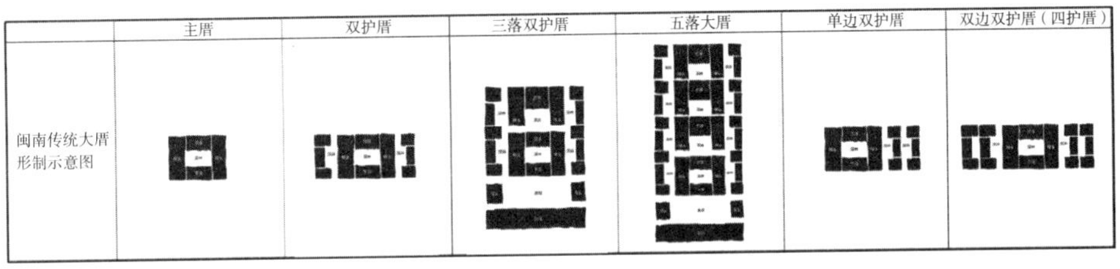

图2 闽南传统大厝布局示意图（作者自绘）

3 闽南侨乡民居中的文化交融现象

3.1 从模仿到创造

华侨对异国建筑的惊羡和向往，促使他们开始凭借模糊的印象和不完整的技术资料，对西洋建筑进行被动式学习。这种学习从最核心的建造技术、结构、材料，到最表层的柱式、山花、栏杆，基本只是一种"模仿"行为。在具体建造过程中，华侨一般不会亲自设计房屋，而是由国内的亲属委托当地工匠设计和建造。但华侨根据他们的海外阅历所提出的设计要求，对建筑物的艺术特征产生了决定性作用。相关资料显示，起源于地中海、后经欧洲殖民统治传入印度和南洋的商住骑楼是闽南地区最早借用的建筑形式之一。之后随着洋楼民居的传入，闽南地区的工匠们开始学习外来建筑的空间布局和建造方式。

然而，根深蒂固的传统观念使华侨无法舍弃祖先传承下来的生活方式，再加上转述和记忆得来的西洋建筑技艺始终有限，这种被动的模仿逐渐发展为群体的"再创造"活动。正是他们的再创造，才造就了不同文化之间的多元融合与共同发展，留下了今天我们所见到的形态各异、土洋结合的侨乡民居。侨居建筑与西洋文化联系密切，一方面保留着中国传统建筑文化，另一方面也吸收了西方建筑特征，逐渐形成了集合中西美学的创新、开放、自然、活泼的独特风格。

根据外来文化引入之后，侨乡民居所受影响和发展的先后时间顺序，可将其分为三个主要类型：一是几乎完全照搬西式洋楼建筑形制的单栋洋楼；二是建造工艺有所创新和融合之后，结合古厝布局发展而成的传统大厝局部洋楼；三是只在大厝外立面体现西洋元素而未进行竖向楼化的番仔厝（陈志宏，曾坚，p73）。[4]

3.2 空间结构立体化——单栋洋楼

中国传统民居因受文化、材料、技术等影响，多表现为平面展开的单层建筑。而殖民文化对华侨的心理冲击，使闽南地区开始引入西式洋楼的建造技术和建筑形制。

单栋式洋楼是将单层的传统民居进行楼化（俗称"叠楼"），并以殖民地外廊样式及装饰语汇作为建筑门面的建筑形制，又称"番仔楼"。这类建筑在外观上几乎完全模仿西式洋楼，最典型的平面布局类似于传统大厝的"顶落"部分，被称为"四房一厅"。根据建造技术和材料不同，番仔楼基本可以分为两类，一类是按照传统的闽南民居木结构营造技艺所建，另一类是采用钢筋混凝土所建。番仔楼最早可以追溯到清朝时期，闽南地区现存大部分番仔楼是在清末到新中国成立前后所建（图3）。

从整体来看，单栋洋楼内部的传统生活伦理空间与外部的南洋殖民地外廊布局存在着并置关系。从功能使用来看，由于合院建筑直接楼化时，原本作为室外活动空间的天井部分变得采光通风较差，因而西式建筑的外廊取代了传统民居合院的天井成为主要的休闲场所，内向围合的生活空间逐渐被外向开敞的外廊所取代。最后，在某些单栋洋楼中，发生了祖厅位置的转移，将传统位于一层核心大厅的祖厅转移至二层，增加底层起居空间的开窗面积，改善其采光通风效果。

图3 鼓浪屿租界的单栋洋楼（作者自摄）

3.3 功能布局多元化——传统大厝局部洋楼

在传统大厝所代表的传统伦理生活之中，华侨渴望寻求一种西化的生活空间，故而发展出了传统大厝局部洋楼的形制，这是工匠们熟悉西式建造技术后的大胆创新。洋楼从早期后落花园中较松散的布局，逐渐融入后落、护厝、榉头等位置，成为传统合院空间序列的组成部分。相对而言，护厝、榉头、回向等位置的洋楼是大厝的附属空间，而后落洋楼大多是独立于主厝的居住单元，功能使用合理性较强（图4）。

此类民居主要有三大特点：首先，在空间布局上，严格遵守传统大厝的空间形制与风水禁忌，只将局部房屋置换为西式洋楼；其次，被置换的局部洋楼建筑往往隐藏在内部的合院中，含蓄地表达西式建筑的象征意义；最后，在装饰层面形成传统燕尾脊与西式山花并存的独特文化景观（图5）。总体来说，传统大厝局部洋楼的建筑形制代表了传统文化的回归，建筑的西化变得更为隐晦低调。此时，进入了用民居建筑表达情感诉求的一个新阶段，形成了以本土文化为主，异域文化为辅的侨居文化。

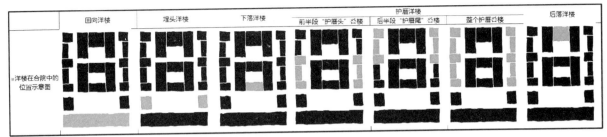

图 4　洋楼在合院中的位置及相应名称示意图（作者自绘）

图 5　鼓浪屿租界的西式山花和燕尾脊（作者自摄）

3.4　局部装饰精致化——番仔厝

番仔厝是平面布局遵循传统大厝的形制，未进行竖向楼化，只在外观装饰和建筑局部加入西洋元素的一种侨乡建筑形制（图 6）。[5] 在这类民居中，建筑空间更加回归传统，没有大量堆砌西式装饰。华侨对于西式建筑元素有更为明确的选择，主要通过建筑符号的联想表达对西洋文化的追求。

开敞的外廊、精美的山花、成列的花瓶栏杆都是西洋建筑文化的抽象符号，也许在今天看来它们与传统民居仍显得格格不入，但它却是群体性艺术审美的高度提炼和自我表达。相较于中国近代的官式建筑营造严谨、追求永恒、纯粹的建筑精神，华侨没有受过专业的建筑训练，因此不会被程式化的制度束缚，在建筑营造过程中追求时尚和流行，代表了平民的审美趣味。[6] 然而正是这种集体性的主观选择，让西洋建筑文化没有吞噬掉传统大厝的文化核心，中式的格局和西式的装饰在同一座建筑中清晰可辨，主次分明。

图 6　厦门市西珩村番仔厝（作者自摄）

4 总结

近代侨乡民居是特殊的历史背景、矛盾的文化心理、充足的经济支持和发展中的建造技术共同作用的结果，侨乡民居不同于其他民居的核心价值在于其文化性。建造主体在侨居文化形成和发展过程中起到了至关重要的作用，从最初的单纯模仿，到局部拼贴的再创造和去繁就简的自主选择，这体现的不是个人爱好，而是一个特殊群体的集体意识。

基于建筑审美和情感需要，闽南华侨选择性地学习西洋的建筑风格，并对其进行本土化的再创作。自1912年起，侨汇经济的涌入促进侨乡建筑产业迅猛发展，这是侨乡民居建筑不断创新的经济基础。在经历了苦难的移民生涯之后，华侨急于表达他们的阅历和财富，洋楼形制和西式装饰是这种情感的外在表现。但是，中华民族传统的家族伦理，使坚守民族文化的闽南华侨提取了中西建筑中最核心的设计要素，并做出大胆融合，逐渐出现了中西融合的建筑形制。

近代闽南华侨民居建筑中，中外文化的交融主要体现在空间结构、功能布局和建筑装饰三个层面，其真正传达的是对待外来文化冲击时，华侨这一特殊群体的态度。实际上，外来文化对本土文化的冲击从未停止过，如今千城一面的现状正是外来文化冲击的负面结果。文化的碰撞能为各个领域带来新的思想，激发新的灵感，能产生许多积极的效应。但是，如果对外来文化全盘接受，而将本民族文化完全舍弃或置于附属地位，那么我们看到的侨乡民居建筑绝不是今天呈现的面貌。因此，华侨在文化交融中采取的态度和方式，是除了华侨民居生动华丽的建筑表征之外，更值得我们不断思考和回味的内容。

致谢

感谢导师张路峰老师对本研究的悉心指导，以及合作者边如晨同学的倾力帮助。

The Blending of Chinese and Foreign Culture in the Houses of Overseas Chinese in South Fujian

Lu Tingying, Bian Ruchen

(University of Chinese Academy of Sciences)

Abstract: Architecture is a cultural sign. As the most typical kind of the overseas Chinese architecture, the traditional house is an epitome of culture blend during the history of their struggling. From the traditional Da Cuo to the foreign houses, the overseas Chines and their relatives express their eager of a better life. In different historical stages, they create their unique culture of residence from the spatial structure, functional layout as well as local decoration. However, with the increasing expansion of modern cities, houses of overseas Chinese have been gradually eroded, facing the dual challenges of protection and development. How to better understand and explore the art and cultural value of the hometown architecture in order to provide a more reliable basis for the protection and development of the hometown houses, which is of great significance to the social reality of today.

Keywords: Overseas Chinese in south Fujian, Residential buildings, Chinese and foreign culture, Emotion and psychology, Architectural characteristics

参考文献

[1] 李岳川.近代粤闽华侨建筑审美心理描述 [J].华中建筑，2013，4：152-155.

[2] 中国华侨历史博物馆.

[3] 程建军.开平碉楼：中西合璧的八百乡文化景观 [M].北京：中国建筑工业出版社，2007.

[4] 陈志宏，曾坚.闽南侨乡近代地域性建筑文化的比较研究 [J].建筑师，2007，1：72-76.

[5] 陈志宏.闽南侨乡近代地域性建筑研究 [D].天津大学，2005.

[6] 唐孝祥，吴思慧.试析闽南侨乡建筑的文化地域性格 [J].南方建筑，2012，1：48-53.

共享园林"园中园"创意与营造实践

吴永发[1] 张 玲[2]

（1.苏州大学金螳螂建筑学院；2.苏州苏大建筑规划设计有限责任公司）

摘 要：共享园林"园中园"是在当今高密度居住环境下一种新的居住模式的探索。依据现代人的生活方式和习惯，将自然山水融入居住空间中，有机结合建筑和园林的营造，融合传统"园""院"的开放性和集聚性布局特点，利用传统地方材料，因地制宜，提高居住品质，营造"结庐在人境，而无车马喧"的高品质人居环境。

关键词：园中园，人居，环境

1 中国古代理想的人居环境与现代"园中园"的创意

1.1 以环境为先导

我国传统的儒家"仁者乐山，智者乐水"，道家的"山林静修，清静无为"的思想，阐释了人对自然的向往。在这种传统哲学思想影响下，建筑多是和庭院空间一同考虑。中国传统园林住宅以环境为先导，通过自然山水修风景园林，是人类聚居山水环境观和文化观的体现，是自然空间向人类生活蔓延的过渡。同时，古代园林住宅的独特意趣，园林与建筑的和谐共存使其成为可居可游的理想环境，是一种较为理想的聚居模式。明代江南才子仇英在《园居图》、《独乐园图》等中描绘了幽深静逸的居住空间，再现了古代人文理想的传统宅园居住环境（图1）。

图1 仇英的《独乐园》

注：共描绘了七幅场景，依次是：见山台、浇花亭、采药圃、种竹斋、钓鱼庵、读书堂、弄水轩。

但是传统人居追求的"宇宙同构",对于现代城市居住条件模式有很大的局限性。如何结合社会形态与生活方式发生的改变,适应高密度居住的现代生活,又能回归到向往的桃源生活,是当今构建适宜人居所需要寻找的答案。

1.2 共享园林的理念

在倡导人性回归的今天,人们越来越渴望回归自然、回归乡土、回归生态。将自然山水融入居住空间中,寻求人与自然之间真正和谐的精神共鸣,是人类延续千年的人居梦想。共享园林是基于当今用地紧张的现实条件,以及人对高品质人居环境的情感需求,结合对当代地域居住模式的理解,以世界文化遗产苏州园林和徽州民居为研究对象,针对江南地区居住模式的多年研究。徽园受程朱理学影响,聚簇而居,建筑布局紧凑规整,空间阴阳反转,以天井和庭院为特色;苏州园林则空间自由扩散且渗透感强,常以独户独院形式存在。二者同为吴越文化在人居环境上的典型,又分别是城市与乡村居住的代表,契合当代城市人居的研究。

2 "园中园"——共享园林的设计模式

笔者通过近10年对特定地区适宜人居居住模式的实践探索,提出"园中园"的概念。"园中园"是以文化为背景、以环境为主题、山水为素材、以园林思想为立意,以建筑语言为载体,有机结合建筑和园林的营造。将自然山水景观引入城市居住环境,汲取徽园和苏园的布局营造特点,将独立小园和组团大园并存,既有共享空间,亦保障了较高建筑密度(表1)。

"园中园"设计理念的生成[1]　　　　　　　　　　　　表1

	徽州园林	苏州园林		"园中园"
外部环境空间	边界开放性,围合空间私密性强,曲折的街巷空间	边界封闭性,围合空间渗透感强	⇨	内敛外放的庭院空间,私密性和渗透感并存,曲折的街巷空间
建筑布局	众户居住,空间限定,边界围合,高密度	一户独院,空间自由,扩散丰富,低密度	⇨	"独户独院+组团大园",公共空间可共享,较高密度

2.1 环境体系协调适应

梁思成先生曾说:"建筑之始,产生于实际需要,受制于自然物理,非着意创制形式,更无所谓派别。"园中园作为地域性的园林建筑,是在历史沉淀中挖掘,所以既要有历史的连续性,又要适应新时代的要求,形成对地域建筑文化的延续。

园中园的营造因地制宜,考虑到地形、气候,区位和四周的自然环境。利用当地的青石、黏土、石灰、山木等基本材料,汲取传统徽州建筑"天井""地孔"采光和排水的手法方式,实现空间的流通与循环、净化和清洁,节省能源,改善室内小气候环境;同时园林所营造的视觉和感觉对快节奏的生活平衡与调节。即体现对地域自然环境的尊重,又建立人、建筑与环境的连续性,创造出一个自由的统一的整体(图2)。

2.2 建筑空间同质异构

形意并存是同质异构的基本特征。在建筑体系中,"形"包括建筑的空间模式与象征性语言的设计,"意"是指需要遵循的地域特征与传达的建筑特质。园中园的设计,是从地域文化中借鉴旧有模式,包括天井、院落、园林等;从形式、空间层面上具象承传。同时,又要汲取现代建筑设计理念,结合新的生活方式,创造出满足现代功能需求的新的地域建筑。

"园中园"是结合地形有机围合成公共园林组团的空间模式。首先,园与园通过高墙之间的边界围合和引导,形成了一条条蜿蜒曲折的巷弄,呼应徽州传统街巷空间。其次,园内建筑三五成组,每一组团有独立的停车,以及公共活动空间,如堂、榭、亭等。建筑与建筑之间通过自由丰富的廊道联系,以及外墙的漏窗洞门产生了视线的渗透和空间的进深感。最后,建筑以独户形式存在,每一户住宅均有自己独立的庭院和绿化景观,保证均好性。

图 2　园中园意象模式

2.3 建筑技术选择适宜

从技术上来看,园中园的营造是从地域文化中有选择地借鉴与汲取各种经验与技术,吸取传统建筑中的生态处理方式,充分利用地形、水面、植被、自然光、风等自然环境来调节建筑内微气候。同时积极利用先进科技,尽量利用高效清洁的能源,如地热、太阳能、风能、光能等。不排斥"低技术"或"高技术",通过将新技术与传统技术相结合,选择适宜技术,使建筑结构适合于环境,同时将被动应对自然环境和主动维护生态环境相结合。

3 "园中园"——共享园林的营造方法实践

"园中园"是在现代城市居住层面上,形成了沟通传统与现代的内在意识桥梁。笔者通过多个实践项目,总结出"园中园"的营造方法,即符合现代城市生活的居住需求,又满足人对园居生活的向往的心理需求。

3.1 方法一:"意象"与"意致"

3.1.1 场所意象

建筑即处在它特定的"氛围"中,同时他又向周围发散自己的气场。在黄山丹白露项目中,基地位于潜口镇,是陶潜故居,素有隐居文化。"园中园"正是基于这种地域文化与环境,以徽居的意匠,从入口开始进行氛围的营造,满眼的树林,湖中的岛屿,尽头一汪绿水,环绕着"栖丘"、"饮谷"两座山丘,走过渔桥,进入了桃源意外之境,唤起了人们对桃源文化的初始感知。

3.1.2 生活意致

"致"乃情趣也。建筑通过对场所氛围的塑造,但更需要传达出人们所向往桃源生活的意趣,所谓"大象无形，大美无言，大音希声"。丹白露项目中的"园中园"以三五人家，一院而聚的模式，形成院墙内，坊门里，书香人家比邻而居，青石板，荷花池，可品茗饮的生活方式，追求"达理通情，情景合一"的审美情趣。园内一共14组小园，有桃蹊柳陌的"定初园"、清淄修竹的"乐道园"、浮香绕曲岸的"也是园"、圆影覆华池的"悉归园"等，每组园子虽然取义不同，但意同象异，得"意尽林泉之癖，景余园圃之间"，各见其趣（图3）。

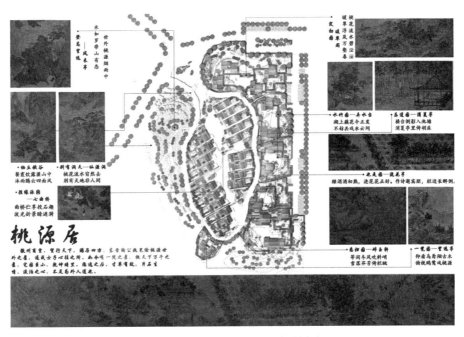

图3 黄山"丹白露"项目场所意象

3.2 方法二："语义"与"语境"

3.2.1 建筑元素阐释语义

建筑元素的表现其实是一种图像符号的表达，凝聚了地方文化的具象特征。园中园的设计，除了考虑自然、人文环境，还要对传统建筑语言运用与变异，从建筑与园林各部分独立的元素表层结构移情于对整体园居空间环境的内涵探究上。

在黄山的多个实践项目中，都基于项目所在的徽州文化，以徽学为源，结合地域特征，运用现代建筑语言简化"马头墙"、"粉墙黛瓦"、"四水归堂"等建筑符号，整合建筑元素，片墙纵横，拾级上下。同时融入苏州园林的亭台轩榭廊的布局，漏窗透景、步移景异，配以假山池沼，花草树木的映衬，构建园林的整体空间。徽廊苏景，贯通南北，以复廊相隔，廊壁花窗，曲廊环绕庭院，缀以花木石峰，池水居中，环以假山、花木与建筑相映（图4）。

3.2.2 环境语言再现语境

海德格尔强调处于栖居状态的人要"拯救大地而不是要征服大地"。"大地之上，苍穹之下"的人，最先面对的就是自然场所。"园中园"作为徽派园林建筑，除了需要继承和传扬徽派建筑形式，更需要营造一种园林环境的空间氛围。项目用地范围内有山有水，所以依此为线索，沿用中国山水园的特点，修山理水，将山与水这两大要素联系起来创造景观，形成了"山因水而动，水因山而活"的景象。东边地势平坦，临水而居，背山面池，自得其乐；西边西处地势渐高，以山林为胜，利用山体高低起伏、俯仰有致的自然形态,建筑随山就势,层层叠落,与环境虚实相兼、形势相衡,正所谓"无画处皆成妙境"。同时沿等高线形成路网,建筑与地形和谐有机,自然山水与徽州文化融为一体,自成天然之趣(图5)。

图4　黄山"徽州文化园"项目——街巷空间

图5　黄山"徽州文化园"项目——环境空间

3.3 方法三："形式"与"法度"

建筑的形式是一种自主的逻辑操作，建筑法度可以理解为建筑的内在性。从历史上看，徽州建筑是不断演化而成，结构上自成体系，形制上互补互融，表现出建筑的"法"古今流变，融汇出新。沿袭这一传统，园中园对"形"与"法"，依据现代生活方式和习惯，对传统空间进行新的诠释。

传统空间中的"井"、"院"、"园"，是这种千年延续下来的美，是一种自明性的东西。通过对传统形式的继承以及演变转译，三个层次的空间形式不同，但都体现了相同特质的一种空间秩序与法度：以"园"来吸引容纳人的进入，与场地发生第一级的关系；以"院"来形成相对独立的内部中心；以"井"围合而成绝对中心，形成由内而外的秩序感染。完成空间在序列及组织关系上的秩序之法（图7）。

（1）"井"

"井"即是生活之源，也是文化之源。天井是传统向心式文化的结晶。第一层次以"天井"的形式来组织布局室内空间，同时结合现代建筑设计手法演变、异化成围合、半围合等多种形式，于建筑物内部形成小环境，同时也作为室内空间与室外空间的过渡。

（2）"院"

《辞源》里对"院"的解释为"周垣也"，四周围墙以内的空地可谓"院"。第二层次的院落空间，院子作为进入的第一个门厅，然后才是室内，是即是室内环境的过渡，又是对室外环境的回应。既能以其特有的穿透性，与入口形成渗景关系，又能形成相对独立的内部中心，满足独门独户的需要。是园林居住同构的空间组合方式（图6）。

（3）"园"

"园"是由合院空间组合而成的不同空间组群。以院造园，院在园中，园院相融，院园相通。第三层次是整体园林的布局，形成"大园"与"小园"两种空间形态。首先，"小园"是借鉴中国传统园林以庭院为中心，建筑包围庭院的造园手法，三五一组的建筑组团共享庭空间。组团与组团之间形成曲折萦回不规则的折线形道路体系。其次，园与园之间围合边界，形成曲折及街巷空间与公共空间，彰显徽质空间。

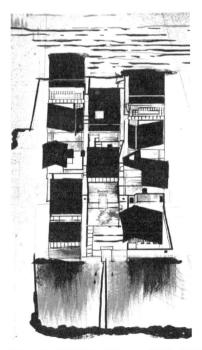

图6 黄山"鱼亭书院"项目——"井""院"空间

"井""院"合而成"小园"

"小园"组合成"大园"

图7 黄山"丹白露"项目

4 总结

"园中园"是基于在现代城市的发展，与契合现代人居住的空间的现实矛盾中，对地域性文化和人居环境营造的思考与实践，是一种以环境为主体，人、建筑、环境和谐共存的新的理想居住空间模式。这种以庭院空间为图底、以环境为主的模式，不仅拥有高品质人居环境，而且建筑密度相对较高，在保证居住环境的同时也满足了现代居住的需求。

Creative Concept and Practice of Shared Garden Space

Wu Yongfa [1], Zhang Ling [2]

(1.Gold Mantis School of Architecture, Soochow University; 2.Soochow University Architecture & Urban Planning Design Institute Co., LTD)

Abstract: The shared garden is the exploration of a new living pattern in the high-density living environment currently. According to the modern lifestyle and habits, the natural landscape is blended with the living space to improve the high quality of living environment, with the organic combination between architecture and landscape, the fusion of traditional "garden" and "courtyard", and by using the traditional local materials to adjust measures to local conditions.

Keywords: Shared gardens, Habitat, Environment

参考文献

[1] 吴永发，江晓辰. 山外山，园中园——徽州文化园二期设计 [J]. 建筑知识，2013.
[2] 吴永发. 地区性建筑创作的技术思想与实践 [D]. 上海：同济大学建筑与城规学院，2005.
[3] 吴永发，徐震. 徽州文化园规划与建筑设计 [J]. 建筑学报，2004.
[4] 张永岳等. 诗意的栖居——现代居住文化思考 [M]. 北京：中国出版集团东方出版中心，2003.
[5] （美）阿摩斯·拉普卜特. 建成环境的意义——非语言表达方式 [M]. 黄兰谷等译. 北京：中国建筑工业出版社，2003.
[6] 刘敦桢. 苏州古典园林 [M]. 北京：中国建筑工业出版社，1979.

基于空间布局形态的住栋环境要素分类研究

张明科 范 悦 高 莹 赵 涛

（大连理工大学建筑与艺术学院）

摘 要：对于住区户外环境而言，物理环境的实体要素具有特殊的意义，它是空间存在的前提和空间特征的根源。本文从住区物理环境出发，以大连市 20 世纪八九十年代既有住区为例，通过实地调研、拍照、访谈以及图示法，图表统计法、分析归纳法等方法，结合居住环境的问题，选择与居住生活联系最为密切最具吸引力的住栋空间作为研究对象，分别以几种布局形态为研究主体，进行环境要素的分类研究。在选取的典型住区中挑选各类住栋布局形态，将住区街道剖面以及宅间空间进行三维标注，尽可能详细地表达出环境要素。将街道空间定义为由街道两侧的建筑、植物等围合起来的空间（XY 轴），将宅间空间定义为相邻两栋建筑物之间的绿地与场所等围合起来的空间（XZ 轴）。依据具体分类进行统计、对比、分析，总结环境现状，探讨了其对住区居民活动的影响。为后续试图寻求新的解决方法，提升既有住区住栋环境的整体品质，增进居民与外部环境的动态交往提供基础条件。

关键词：空间布局形态，住栋，既有住区，环境要素，分类

1 引言

我国的城市更新从 20 世纪八九十年代开始，为了解决住房有无的问题，住宅建设量较大，建设速度较快，大拆大改。快速建造所导致的既有住区功能与人性化的缺失，忽略了对住区居民中特殊需求的考虑。全面发展的 21 世纪，落后的居住区规划与户外环境已经难以满足人们对居住品质的追求，肆意地搭建、占用，绿地废弃，各类设施的劣化，出现大量的废弃堆积地，严重影响了原有的空间利用率。城市规模、城市形态，城市发展不同，更新的标准、方法不是单一的，城市更新首先是环境的改善，空间狭窄道路拥堵，光照通风较差，基础设施的改造。对于住区户外环境而言，物理环境的实体要素具有特殊的意义，它是空间存在的前提和空间特征的根源。具体而实际的环境要素影响居民本身的生活质量，掌握其环境的特征、规律，能够使人们更能舒适随意地在环境中享受美好生活。

2 国内住区环境发展概况

我国对住区外环境的研究要从 20 世纪 80 年代开始，根据新中国成立以来住区规划的设计与实践，建设部与国家技术监督局于 1993 年联合发布了《城市居住区规划设计规范》，成为住区规划设计的强制性国家标准。大连市 2002 年颁布的《大连市规划建筑设计有关规定》2005 年、2014 年先后进行补充与修订，在各类指标方面对用地与建筑、住宅、绿地等方面进行更为详尽的规定。

2015 年 8 月，根据住房城乡建设部 2000 年前老旧住区统计表，全国共有老旧小区约 159412 个，老旧小区总建筑面积约为 $4 \times 10^9 m^2$，近年来，已经进行不同程度改造的 $1.069 \times 10^9 m^2$。仅大连市 2006 年末住据统计，就存在既有住宅 80 万套，由于发展过快，既有住区及建筑的外部环境、技术水平及

标准要求经历了复杂的演变过程，明显出现功能退化的问题，体现为住区环境恶化，设施不健全，围护结构破损，住户加建等。住区的建设条件与今日需求的矛盾日益显著，对功能提升的需求日益迫切（表1）。[1]

住区的建设与现状　　　　　　　　　　　　　　　　　表1

建造年代	功能衰退程度	改造实践涉及程度	存量
20世纪70年代	严重	部分城市涉及	不足15%
20世纪八九十年代	严重	涉及较多	65%~70%
2000年以后	轻微	局部涉及	
2005年以后	轻微	基本不涉及	15%~20%

3 研究方法

本文从住区物理环境出发，以大连市20世纪八九十年代既有住区为例，选取台山小区、后山社区、西沟小区作为实例，通过实地调研、访谈以及图示法、图表统计法、分析归纳法等方法，结合现状的问题，以住区规划空间布局形态为落脚点，并选择与居住生活联系最为密切最具吸引力的住栋空间作为研究对象，进行环境要素的分类。在选取的住区中，从街道剖面和宅间住栋空间两个方面分析其空间环境要素，将环境要素以图示语言进行统一标注，依据具体现状分类进行问题汇总，探讨了规划环境要素与自发的环境要素对住区居民活动的影响，为提升既有住区住栋环境的整体品质，增进居民与外部环境的动态交往的后续研究提供基础条件。

4 研究内容

4.1 住区概况

4.1.1 后山社区

后山社区建成于20世纪80年代7层砖混住宅，位于大连市沙河口区南沙街管辖处，占地面积0.65km^2，总户数5362户，总人口数14102人，2011年进行住区改造（含户外环境）。

4.1.2 台山小区

台山小区建于1985~1990年的6层砖混住宅，周边主要以散楼为主，位于大连市沙河口区南沙街管辖处，由城建和沙区房产开发建。主要户型30~70m^2，多以老人及一对夫妻生活居。2016年进行住区改造。

4.2 规划空间特征

居住建筑群体的不同组合方式会直接影响居住外环境空间的组合方式以及相应的公共空间的设

置，而外环境空间的分布位置及空间形状也会对服务对象及服务半径产生影响。[3] 本文将从后山社区、台山小区两个小区提取老旧住区的规划空间现状，分析规划空间布局形态对居民的使用率的影响。后山社区处于坡地，住栋排列模式为庭院式的半围合形式，以围合的形式获取较高的容积率，增加室内使用空间，创造了室外空间的丰富层次，牺牲了少量居住单元的生活品质；台山小区处于缓坡地，住栋排列模式为点群式考虑到日照、通风、地形及场地形状等问题，外环境空间的布局相对松散的同时也较为自由活泼。由于建设时间较早等问题导致，点群式的空间布局会出现布置不均匀，场地设置不合理等问题；西沟小区处于平地，住栋排列模式为行列式，外环境空间过于均质化的问题，造成空间的分割和可识别性差的问题，缺少相对完整的大面积公共空间，布局相对单调呆板，失去趣味性（表2）。

调研小区规划空间特征图			表2
小区名称	规划总平面		提取原型/现场现状
后山社区			
台山社区			

4.3 住栋空间要素

本文将住栋空间以三维模型的理念应用在单位空间的划分上，将住区街道剖面以及宅间空间进行三维标注，尽可能详细地表达出环境要素。[4] 将街道空间定义为由街道两侧的建筑、植物等围合起来的空间（XY轴），将宅间空间定义为相邻两栋建筑物之间的绿地与场所等围合起来的空间（XZ轴）（图1）。

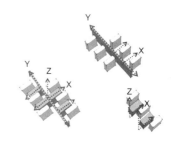

图1 住栋空间的三维模型的原型

4.3.1 街道剖面 XY 轴

《图解街道设计要素》[5] 一书中将街道断面定义为街道中车道、人行道、绿化带等设施的布局、比例和宽度。本文参考该分类方法进行空间分析研究，划分住区外环境进行三维空间的不同维度分析，将住区内部街道两侧主动形成的空间关系简称为街道剖面（图示XY轴），通过对街道平面，横剖面，纵剖面的要素划分，就交通、绿地、场地、废弃/占用等空间进行简单剖析（表3）。

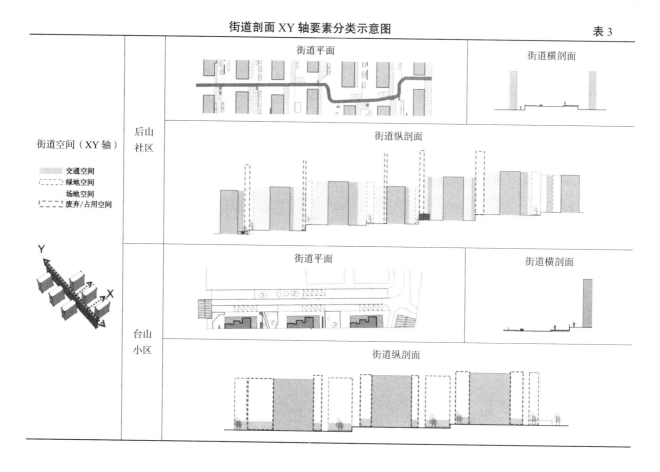

4.3.2 宅间空间 XZ 轴

《图解街道设计要素》一书中将街道线型称为街道两侧建筑围合起来的空间，简单定义为定义为空间可被利用的程度，其中包含空间可达性与连续性、户外活动场所、铺装地面的破损度与整洁度、楼梯与坡道利用的安全性与完整性等。本文参考该分类方法进行空间分析研究，将住宅与住宅之间围合的空间简称为宅间空间（图示 XZ 轴）。将宅间空间内部规划与自发空间进行汇总分类，依据《城市居住区规划设计规范》[6]、《居住区环境景观设计导则》[7]将规划空间分为场地、绿地、道路、住宅单元出入口、盲道、休闲点；将自发空间分为晾晒空间、搭建空间（表4）。

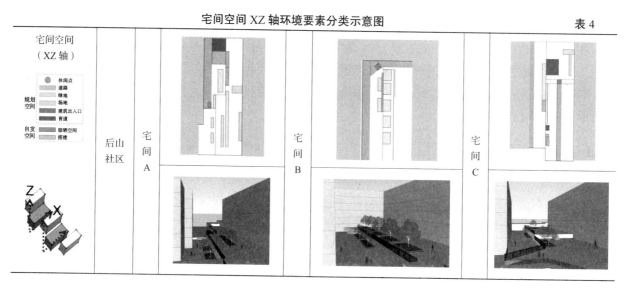

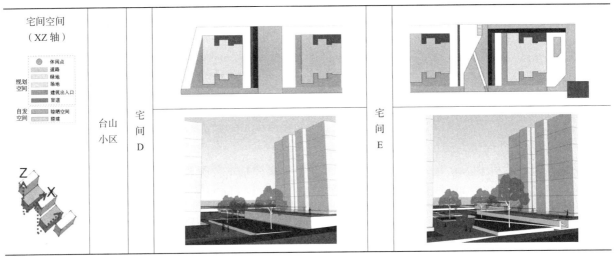

4.4 现状总结

小区整体物质环境老化严重，部分住栋庭院进行过外环境整治，改造内容仅仅是对裸露破损的内部道路和场地进行硬质铺装。后山社区研究范围内外环境可使用公共空间为48%，空间占用率达约30%，现存绿化空间达约22%，其中废弃率达绿化面积的约45%。台山小区内外环境可使用公共空间为57%，空间占用率达约25%，现存绿化空间达约18%，其中废弃率达绿化面积的约55%（图2）。

由于资金缺乏等问题，并没有缓解住区中的居住矛盾，居住环境依旧面临许多问题（表4）：老化现象严重：墙面劣化较为严重，部分出现墙皮脱落的情况，影响了美观，同时也带来了一定的安全隐患；私搭乱建：底层空间私搭乱建现象严重，部分住户将私人空间延伸到公共空间中，影响住栋间的交通组织，也占用了大量的庭院空间；植被凌乱：部分树木由于疏于管理，存在不良长势，占用公共空间的同时并没有给人带来美观的感受，由于空间有限，且没有凉亭座椅等设施，因而一定程度上影响了邻里交往；肆意停车：道路宽度有限，以及未划线停车，因而大部分机动车辆停放随意，秩序混乱的同时也给路过的行人带来一定的安全隐患（表5）。

图2 现状空间统计表

现状问题示意图 表5

| 老化严重 | 私搭乱建 | 植被凌乱 | 肆意停车 |

5 结语

限于实际条件，本研究还有不少欠缺，调查样本不够大，可能导致普遍适用性偏差。比如，对于不同位置与尺度的绿地、场地，存在不同的空间感受与使用适宜度，这需要在今后的研究中进一步细化，希望可以从大范围调查样本中，从外环境空间要素入手进行了空间的梳理和重置，能对住区外环境空间的改善提出一定的策略。

致谢

感谢国家自然科学基金重点项目（51638003），中央高校基本科研业务费资助（DUT16RW105）国家自然科学基金（51608090），大连市社科联年度课题：2016dlskyb024 对本论文写作过程中的基金支持。

Research on the Classification of Environmental Factors Based on the Layout Pattern between Buildings

Zhang Mingke, Fan Yue, Gao Ying, Zhao Tao

(School of Architecture & Fine Art, Dalian University of Technology)

Abstract: Physical environment of the entity elements which is the precondition of space, has special significance for the residential outdoor environment. Start from the physical environment, taking existing residential area in Dalian in 1980s and 1990s as an example. According to the problems of residential environment, the most attractive residential space is chosen as the research object, by the ways of the spot investigation, taking pictures, interviews and diagrams, charts and statistics, analysis and induction, etc.Taking several layout patterns as the main body of the study, the article will study on the classification of environmental factors.The street section of the residential area and space between houses are divided into 3D dimensioning. The street space is defined by buildings, plants and other enclosed spaces. On both sides of the street (XY axis), the space of between residential will be defined as the space between the two adjacent buildings and green places enclosed space (XZ axis). According to the specific classification of statistics, comparison, analysis, the article will summarize the present situation of the environment, and probe into its influence on the residents' activities. In order to find a new solution to improve the overall quality of the living environment, and to provide the basic conditions for the dynamic interaction between the residents and the external environment.

Keywords: Spatial distribution pattern, The space of between building, Residential buildings, Environmental elements, Classification

参考文献

[1] 曹嘉明. 国内城市更新主要政策汇编 [G]. 北京：[出版者不详]，2017.

[2] （日）MIKAN. 住区再生设计手册 [M]. 范悦，周博译. 辽宁：大连理工大学出版社，2009.

[3] 董丽，范悦，苏媛，冯碧岳. 既有住区活力评价研究 [J]. 建筑学报，2015（S1）：186-191.
[4] 王翔. 既有住区外环境空间类型化及品质提升策略研究 [D]. 大连理工大学，2016.
[5] 上海市城市规划设计研究院城市设计研究中心. 设计点亮城市：城市街道的十个名词解释 [EB/OL]. [2014-12-28]. http://m.thepaper.cn/news Detail_forward_1289408#rd.
[6] 中华人民共和国建设部. 城市居住区规划设计规范 [S]. 北京：中国建筑工业出版社，2016.
[7] 建设部住宅产业化促进中心. 居住区环境景观设计导则 [S]. 北京：中国建筑工业出版社，2006.

北京四合院建筑形制和气候适应性中阴阳关系的解读

郭 聪 王惜春 戴 俭

（北京工业大学建筑与城市规划学院）

摘 要：北京四合院建筑作为中国传统民居建筑的典范，自元代开始出现雏形，距今已有 800 多年的历史。其既是我国古代劳动人民的智慧结晶，也是传统文化的代表，特别是建筑中蕴含着丰富的阴阳关系处处遵从了传统文化中的重要组成部分。本论文以四合院在构成和空间组合体现的阴阳思想为出发点，着重探讨房舍围合的阴阳关系、"门堂制度"的阴阳关系、建筑布局与"后天八卦"对应的阴阳关系、建筑布局的轴线体现出的纵主横次的阴阳关系，以期能对我国四合院中的传统文化的研究和传承起到促进作用，引起人们对于传统民居中所蕴含的传统文化进行更多的关注和思考。

关键词：四合院建筑，房舍围合，门堂制度，后天八卦，纵主横次

　　北京四合院最初的产生可追溯到商周时期，而且中国传统文化的深刻影响着四合院的发展，比如中国传统的哲学观念、政治制度、家庭伦理、审美标准以及人们的生活方式等都在四合院的形制中有相当的体现。在影响四合院发展的众多因素中，传统的哲学观念起到了最为重要的作用，由于在《易经》中我们可以探寻到中国传统哲学观念的起源，因此，本文即以《易经》中的阴阳学说为出发点，简要解读四合院在建筑形制上和气候适应性中所蕴含的阴阳关系，以期促进和补充四合院的研究，同时引起人们对于传统民居中所蕴含的传统文化进行更多的关注和思考。

1 阴阳学说

　　《易经》是我国重要传统哲学思想的重要著作，关于《易经》的"易"已有很多的解释，此处查询了古今易学家大多认同的观点。"易"可以解释为日月之意，表达着一种阴阳变化的关系。将"易"拆开来解释，上半部为"日"，下半部为"月"，因此日月合为易，相互变化，表达阴阳交变的关系。阴阳是中国古代哲学中最基本的两种属性，《周易·系辞上》曰："易有太极，是生两仪，两仪生四象，四象生八卦"，其中两仪即指阴阳。关于阴阳，主要的观点是其对立的关系，表达的是世间万物都有相互对立的关系；其次还有相互消长，相互变通的含义。阴阳学说是《易经》的灵魂，《易经》是我国古人的宇宙观和方法论的精髓，是人们通过对各种自然现象的长期总结得出的具有朴素唯物论和辩证法思想的学说。

2 外"实"内"虚"的四合院空间布局

　　据老北京人的记忆，他们多数会将四合院称为"四合房"，即以房子围合起来的院落，这种以房子围合起来的院落有多种形式，北京四合院是其中最典型的一种，由正房、厢房、倒座房、后罩房、耳

房等房屋围合。如图1所示，从大门开始，最南侧的房屋是倒座房，过垂花门之后的庭院空间两侧是东西厢房，庭院北侧是正房，三开间，正房两侧是耳房，绕过正房往后处于整个院落最北侧的是后罩房，整个的院落是由四周的房屋所围合，从四合院的外部看，我们只能看到从四合院探出的树梢以及高出围墙的屋顶，而看不见四合院内部的其他细节。四合院外部围合的房舍和围墙在阴阳关系中可以理解为"实"的部分。在绕过大门前的影壁进入到四合院的内部空间后又是另外一番景象，合理的结构，精致的门窗，参天的古树，连通的走廊，宽大的庭院，局部小天井等一一呈现在人们面前，四合院内部的这些情景可以理解为阴阳关系中"虚"的部分。

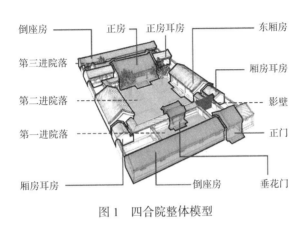

图1 四合院整体模型

北京四合院的这种外"实"内"虚"的形态即是《周易》中一种阴阳关系的体现，外"阳"内"阴"看似虚幻，实则体现着对于气候的适应性。北京春季多风，风沙大，为了适应当地的气候，北京四合院的房屋都朝中心庭院开窗，这样是为了防止春季的风沙；另外四合院朝北不开窗和后墙较高的处理方式有利于更好地阻挡冬季寒冷的西北风（图2）；封闭的外墙还具有很好的防卫性，为院落内部环境的稳定提供了一个可靠的保证，此为"实"。连通的连廊既为流连于庭院景色中的人们提供了一个休憩场所，同时也能在雨雪大风天气为行走在院落中的人们提供一个遮蔽的空间；露天通透的庭院空间为整个四合院营造了一个微环境，在自然风压的作用下，庭院中形成了上下对流的空气，既形成了流畅的通风，又能给院落不断提供新鲜的空气，保证了空气的质量（图3）；"四水归堂"的布局既有风水上的讲究，同时也是一种功能性的体现，庭院能更好地收集雨水和有组织地排放雨水；四合院的庭院空间中经常会绿植，以此来营造一个舒适的人居环境，以提高生活质量；建筑中的大木作和小木作的合理分工也具有很强的科学性，大木作是建筑最重要的部分，建筑因大木作而屹立不倒，小木作也是建

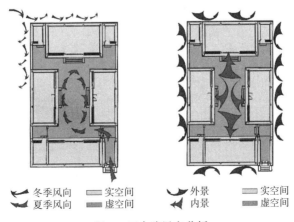

图2 四合院风向分析

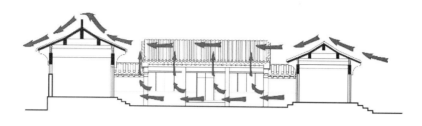

图 3　四合院通风分析

筑的重要组成部分，建筑因小木作而精美，此为"虚"。可以看出，空间布局体现了《周易》中的虚实的阴阳关系，此阴阳关系既存在科学价值，为四合院营造出了一个丰富的内部空间和稳定的舒适的生活环境，体现了四合院存在的价值。

3　主轴线引导下的"门堂制度"

中国传统文化注重的是礼制，以尊卑有序，中央为尊，两侧为卑，秩序井然为先。因此在北京四合院的布局中，整个院落最重要的房屋必然是处于中轴线线上的房屋。重要房屋的数量与院落的进数有关，一进院落为一处重要房屋，两进院落则有两处，以此类推。四合院建筑中讲求中轴为尊的同时，又讲究中轴对称或中轴均衡（图 4）。重要建筑房屋沿中轴线布置，其他附属房屋则建在中轴线的两侧，并注重左右对称均衡。这种尊卑有序的格局亦是《周易》中阴阳关系的体现，主为"阳"，次为"阴"，相互对立，但同时又相互统一，也体现了阴阳关系中"阴阳对立"的重要特点。北京四合院主轴线上布置正房、垂花门，主轴线的两侧布置厢房、耳房、厢耳房。正房是四合院最主要的建筑，供家中最年长或者最权威的人居住，另外二进院落或更多进院落中，主轴线上也布置有供家中会议、请安、团拜之用的主房；主轴线两侧的厢房或其他的附属用房供家中的子女、儿孙分别居住；后罩房供未出阁的香闺女子居住；其他附属的耳房作厨房厕所之用。以上为四合院中的房屋在用途上的"阴阳对立"关系。正房处在全院最重要的位置上，坐北朝南，拥有最充足的阳光，而且正房的地基较高，不仅显示出了地位，

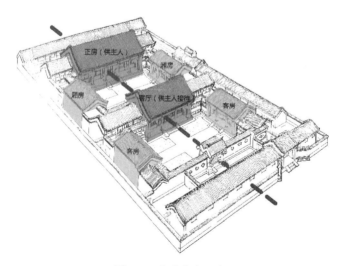

图 4　四合院尊卑有序

同时也是能够充分获得阳光的一个重要条件；厢房位于主轴线的东西两侧，各朝东西，采光条件不如正房，且地基低于正房，无论是朝向还是所处位置较正房而言都是出于次要的位置，此为四合院中的房屋在位置朝向上的"阴阳对立"关系。正房在体量上是四合院内最大的建筑，是四合院建筑的核心；厢房的体量要比正房小，并且厢房的前檐要尽量躲闪到正房的山墙线之外，还要保证正房的前脸不被厢房所挡住；正房的耳房平面进深在正房的基础上要往后退很多；厢耳房的体量也要比正房的耳房小，厢耳房的屋顶大多数时候只能采用平顶的形式；垂花门与抄手游廊的关系中，垂花门的开间进深要比抄手游廊大；宅门与倒座房的关系中，由于宅门是门户的象征，外形显要，因此宅门的进深开间尺寸也要大于倒座房，此为四合院中房屋在体量上的"阴阳对立"关系。以上几点可以看出，正房在位置、朝向、体量等方面均要优于其他房屋，在四合院的阴阳关系中处于"阳"的位置，居于首要地位，其他房屋处于"阴"的位置，居于次要地位，但是正房和厢房、耳房等构成了整个的四合院，阴阳关系相互统一，整个四合院的建筑之间处于一种"阴阳对立"的关系之中，体现了朴素的辩证法思想，这也是四合院中传统文化智慧的重要体现（图5）。

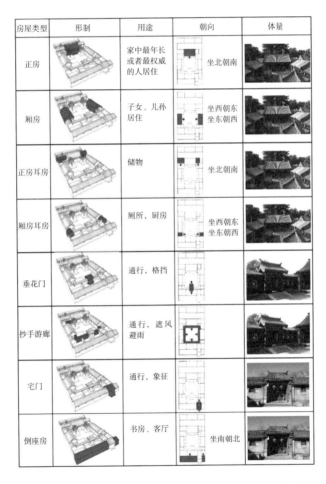

图5　四合院中房屋用途、朝向、体量上的阴阳关系比较四合院尊卑有序

4 "后天八卦图"下的建筑布局

人类始祖伏羲奠定了《周易》哲学的内核：阴阳概念与八卦象征。他在阴阳象征的基础上，通过

图6 后天八卦图

非凡的洞察力，以阴阳符号三画重叠的方式构成八种线型卦象，来象征大自然最基本的八种物质形态，形成了"先天八卦"。"后天八卦"是由"先天八卦"演变而来，相对于"先天八卦"而言，其位置变化很大。在"先天八卦"中，各八卦的位置是：南乾、北坤、东离、西坎、东南为兑、西南为巽、东北为震、西北为艮，在"后天八卦"中，各八卦的位置是：南离、北坎、东震、西兑、东南为巽、西南为坤、东北为艮、西北为乾。"先天八卦"主要是表明宇宙形成的大现象，"后天八卦"是说明宇宙以内的变化和运用的法则（图6）。

北京四合院的方位多为坐北朝南，即为一种"坐坎朝离"的空间格局。将宅位以九宫格的方式划分，按后天八卦标出每个方位，根据九星临宫的情况，按星的吉凶以及阴阳五行相克的关系判定宅中各宫位的吉凶，依吉凶程度确定宅舍的形势、各房高卑大小及层数等。一般吉位应建高大的房屋，凶位宜建低小的房屋，或依吉凶确定房屋的功能。吉地宜做主房、厅堂、宅门等，灶也应处吉位，仓库、厕所应放凶位。处于"坐坎朝离"的北京四合院，其北房、南房、东南和东房均处于吉位，应建高大的房屋。四合院中高大的正房即处于北房的位置，与"后天八卦"中的吉位正好对应，除了风水上的讲究，其也具有一定的科学道理。

北京的建筑气候分区处于寒冷地区，因此冬季采暖是建筑设计的主要考虑因素。处在北房位置的正房具有最佳的采暖条件，这种房屋在冬季的时候由于太阳高度角偏低，这样阳光就可以更多地进入室内，有利于提高室内的温度，夏季的时候太阳高度角偏高，由于屋檐的遮挡，阳光很难直射进屋内，再加上庭院内的通风效果，室内会很凉爽，这样坐北朝南的房屋就有冬暖夏凉的功效，其也迎合了现代建筑中被动式的理念（图7）；坐北朝南的四合院其大门都开在东南角，在"后天八卦"中东南角的位置是巽位，巽位属风，大门开在东南角有利通天地之元气，以科学的角度来解释就是北京夏季盛行东南风，冬季盛行西北风，大门开在东南角有利于夏季的院内通风和冬季的保暖；通常情况下，四合院的厕所被安放在西南角，因为在"后天八卦"中西南角是煞位，根据其理论煞位是有可能带来凶祸的地方，此处设置厕所就以恶治恶了，晦气相冲，在建筑布局的科学道理上来说，因为西南角，人流很少，且处于不利风向，此处安排厕所很合适；在四合院的建筑布局中，厨房应体现"坐煞向生"的方位，因此厨房的位置经常被安排在东房南面的一个房间，或者被安排在东北角，体现了"东厨司命"的说法，也是"坐煞向生"的一种表达方式。四合院的建筑布局依据"后天八卦"的理念，既是我国传统文化智慧和民居中蕴含气候适应性的体现，同时将传统文化与生态智慧有机融合的实践是四合院文化价值和科学价值的最好体现。

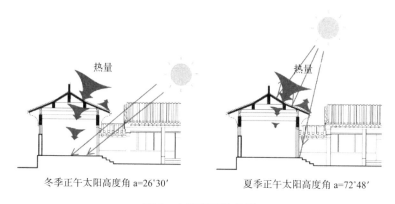

冬季正午太阳高度角 a=26°30′　　　夏季正午太阳高度角 a=72°48′

图7 太阳高度角分析

5 轴线中的纵主横次

北京四合院的基本格局分为一进院落、二进院落、三进院落、四进及四进以上院落、一主一次并列式院落、两组或多组并列式院落、主院带花园院落等。无论是什么类型的院落，在纵向和横向上都有轴线关系，纵轴和横轴亦可与阴阳对应上。以纵为"阳"，以横为"阴"，纵主横次。另外在轴线关系上，纵向表达出了种族的延续，横轴象征了种族的兴旺，二者相互依托，体现了阴阳关系中阴阳交感，阴阳互通，表达了家族兴旺的美好期待。四合院中存在的这种阴阳关系也是生活在四合院中的人情感的流露，四合院的存在也是这种传统文化的见证，具有很重要的情感价值（图8）。

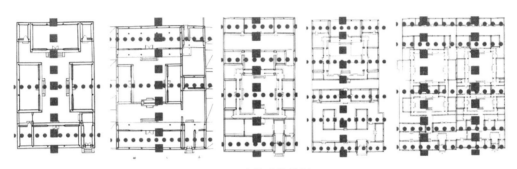

图8 院落进数分析

6 结论

四合院是中国具有代表性的传统民居之一，其中富含的阴阳关系和气候适应性不仅仅是中国传统文化和当地自然生态条件的重要体现。如今随着现代化的建设，越来越多的四合院已逐渐消失在我们的视野中。虽然四合院的保护工作已取得一定的成效，但是仅仅通过保存四合院的建筑是远远不够的。保护四合院的核心就是发掘和保护其文化价值，本文通过四合院阴阳关系的解读，希望能挖掘出四合院所富含的文化和生态价值，以此来引起人们对四合院的关注。

The Interpretation of Yin Yang of the Forms and Climatic Adaptation in Beijing Courtyard House

Guo Cong, Wang Xichun, Dai Jian

(College of Architecture and Urban Planning, Beijing University of Technology)

Abstract: Beijing courtyard house is a typical type of traditional Chinese buildings, dating back to Yuan Dynasty, with a history over 800 years. It shows the wisdom of ancient Chinese people, a representation of traditional culture, and especially expresses the Yin Yang——key components of traditional Chinese architecture. This paper investigates the Yin Yang relationship in the formation and spatial combination of Beijing courtyard house, the closeness and openness, "door-hall system", the architectural layouts, "Postnatal eight trigrams", axis. It aims to encourage the research and inherence of traditional wisdom and have more researchers participate in the contemplation and concerns in this area.

Keywords: Courtyard house, Closeness and openness, Door-hall system, Postnatal eight trigrams, Vertical and horizontal

参考文献

[1] 马炳坚. 北京四合院建筑 [M]. 天津：天津大学出版社，1999，6.
[2] 贾珺. 北京四合院（第1版）[M]. 北京：清华大学出版社，2009，5.
[3] 刘甦. 第十八届中国民居学术会议论文集 [G]. 北京：中国水利水电出版社，2010，9.
[4] 高巍. 四合院 [M]. 北京：学苑出版社，2003，7.
[5] 王其钧. 图解中国民居 [M]. 北京：中国电力出版社，2008.
[6] 王其明. 北京四合院 [M]. 北京：中国书店，1999，3.
[7] 褚良才. 易经·风水·建筑 [M]. 上海：学林出版社，2003.12.
[8] 张丽丽. 传统阴阳五行视角下的敦煌壁画研究 [D]. 燕山大学硕士论文，2014.
[9] 刘巍巍. 关于阴阳五行之基本概念-理论体系结构及动态变化联系之假说 [D]. 天津中医学院，2000.
[10] 林洁. 论阴阳五行学说与中国传统艺术的关系 [D]. 重庆师范大学硕士论文，2005.
[11] 肖生萍. 阴阳五行学说在居住区绿地景观中的应用研究 [D]. 中南林业科技大学，2016.

维也纳社会住宅的可持续整合性设计策略：以 Mautner-Markhof 为例

胡裕庆　李振宇

（同济大学建筑与城市规划学院）

摘　要：中国快速的城镇化进程加剧了一二线城市的人口聚集，在带来人口红利的同时也使城市居住空间面临着巨大挑战。居住成本高昂，住区环境单调，职住分离等现象日益严峻，探索如何在大型城市建设对城市、居民和环境都能可持续发展的住区是极具社会意义的命题。作为对这一命题的现实回应，素有世界最宜居城市美誉的维也纳通过"四支柱模式"设计导则对社会住宅建设提出了经济、社会、建筑和生态多方面的可持续设计要求。本文以 Mautner-Markhof 地块为例，通过项目信息收集与实地考察，并结合"四支柱模式"，对案例进行分析论证，提出在不同空间尺度的可持续整合性设计策略，为中国城市的可持续住区建设提供借鉴。本论文写作受到国家自然科学基金项目（编号51678412）资助。

关键词：维也纳，社会住宅，可持续，整合性设计策略

1　引言

维也纳被公认为全球居住建筑和住房政策建设的典范，约 60% 的维也纳人居住在社会住宅里。维也纳市政府一直致力于推动低价高质的社会住宅，历史长达百年，两次世界大战期间的"红色维也纳"时期在世界范围内产生了广泛影响。到今天维也纳依旧保持着稳定的社会住宅建设量，每年新建约 14000 套，完工 7000 套，翻新 10000 套老旧住房。[①] 同时与时俱进探索创新更加高质低耗可持续的居住模式，从 1995 年以来维也纳推行开发商设计竞赛（Bauträgerwettbewerbe）的运作模式，结合"四支柱模式"（Vier Säulen Modell）作为考核准则。"四支柱模式"从经济、社会、建筑和生态四个方面提出分项指标指导住宅的可持续设计。[②] 该举措极大地提升新建社会住宅的公寓户型和公共空间的创新设计，促进社会居住融合，降低建筑能耗（最高标准 $50\text{kwh/m}^2/\text{a}$），节约建造成本 20% 等，在探索可持续住区建设领域走在国际前沿。本文将立足"四支柱模式"的核心理念，通过个案精析，研究其住区建设的可持续整合性设计策略，尝试探讨对中国保障房建设的借鉴意义。

Wolfgang, F. 和 William, M.（2015）编辑的《Das Wiener Model》介绍了以开发商设计竞赛和"四支柱模式"为核心的维也纳的社会住宅模式和理念，以及当前社会住宅建设的关注点，如延续与创新、社会混合、市民参与、气候与环境保护、公共空间的设计与使用、更新既有住宅等。本文在此基础上，采用文献研究，实地调查和资料分析等方法展开研究。首先研读翻译"四支柱模式"以及相关政策文件，利用网络资源收集整理案例资料；其次利用作者在维也纳学习期间实地调研案例，收集第一手资料图像；最后通过数据列举、实例举证、建模图表分析等方法推进研究，得出结论。

新建住宅地块设计需要处理两个基本关系：一是新建地块与既有城市环境的关系；二是地块内部各单体项目之间的关系。因此可持续整合性设计策略研究从空间尺度入手，通过居室尺度，单体项目尺度，

[①] 维也纳住宅年报 2015。

[②] 维也纳住宅基金会 wohnfonds_wien。

地块组团尺度和城市尺度的分析，指出在各个尺度层面展开设计时需要处理的核心问题和具体实现手法。

2 Mautner-Markhof 地块项目概况

Mautner-Markhof 地块（表 1）是维也纳对城市工业棕地进行业态转型和居住化更新的典型项目，位于维也纳工业重区 11 区 Simmering 的中心位置。地块前身是 Mautner-Markhof 食品工厂，其成立于 1841 年，是奥地利重要的"老字号"企业（享有国家品牌徽章授权）。厂房在 2005 年末被政府收购后紧接着开始了两轮开发商设计竞赛，建设周期从 2012 年起年历时三年。8hm² 的厂区旧址更新为以居住为主，包含商业、办公、酒店等多业态的混合社区。总建设面积近 $14 \times 10^4 m^2$，其中住宅总共有 1100 多户住宅，其中包括约 950 户补贴性社会住宅，和一个 150 间客房的 JUFA 酒店。公共设施有超市、幼儿园、商店、诊所和医疗福利设施等。整个地块划分为 8 个建筑项目和两个开放空间项目，由多家开发商和建筑师团队设计合作完成。项目总开支约 1.123 亿欧元，其中约 0.37 亿欧元来自于维也纳住房基金会补贴。该地块交通便利，门口即是 U3 地铁站，附近还有四路电车和公车以及两路轻轨。附近配套设施齐全，临近 Simmeringer 主商业大街，各类设施齐全。场地自身绿化较好，原有公园古树大部分得以保留。这块 Simmering 区昔日最大的工业地块之一现在已经更新成为该区的核心。

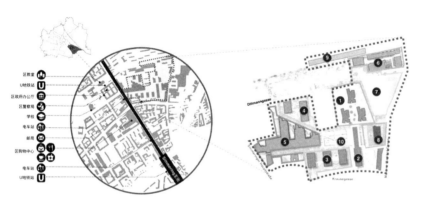

图 1 MauterMarkhof 地块区位，周边设施及地块内项目分布（作者自绘）　　图 2 各建筑项目照片

资料来源：①⑤⑥⑦⑧各建筑师网站，其余作者自摄。

Mauter Markhof 地块各建筑项目信息列表　　表 1

地块名称	完工时间	住房数量及性质	建筑面积	公共设施（对外/社区内）	开发商	建筑设计	景观设计
11 号地块 MM11	2014 年 12 月	51 户补贴式可售租赁房/47 户补贴式出售房/48 户普通商品房	14467	社区活动室、社区会馆、社区花园等	Wiener Heim/Gebös	Rüdiger Lainer+Partner	Doris Haidvogel
2 号地块 Simmering City	2015 年 6 月	132 户补贴式可售租赁房/19 户普通商品房	6886	幼儿园、社区诊所、餐饮/游泳池、桑拿、社区活动室、楼宇管理员、邻里中心	Wien Süd	Harry Glück/Atelier 4 architects	Anna Detzlhofer
3 号地块 Global Park	2014 年 6 月	38 户"特级"补贴租赁房/77 户补贴式可售租赁房	15650	幼儿园/会议室、社区活动室、儿童活动区等	Neues Leben	Geiswinkler & Geiswinkler	Auböck+Karasz
4 号地块 Join In	2014 年 6 月	18 户"特级"补贴租赁房/56 户补贴式可售租赁房	18974	儿童日托、咨询中心/社区活动室、社区花园、楼宇管理员等	Familienwohnbau/ÖSW	Tillner & Willinger	Jakob Fina

续表

地块名称	完工时间	住房数量及性质	建筑面积	公共设施（对外/社区内）	开发商	建筑设计	景观设计
5号地块 Simmering City	2015年6月	64户补贴式宿舍公寓（MIGRA）/190户补贴式可售租赁房/33户普通商品房	35600	办公、大型超市、商业店铺、医药康复中心、亲子中心等/游泳池、桑拿、社区活动室、儿童室内游玩场、楼宇管理员、邻里中心。其中办公7800m^2/商业5200m^2/住宅20300m^2/宿舍2300m^2	Wien Süd	Hermann & Valentiny/Peter Podsedensek	Jakob Fina
6号地块 Wohnoase Simmering	2015年1月	145户补贴式可售租赁房其中49户隶属女性住区 Frauenwohnprojeke ro:sa	11490	幼儿园/社区活动室等	Building Development Network/GSG	s & s Architekten	Carla Lo
7号地块 Bauprojekt in Vorbereitung	2016年	46户补贴式智慧租赁房/91户补贴式可售租赁房/53户普通商品房	17595	办公、商铺/社区活动室等	Wien Süd	Hermann-Valentiny/Peter Podsedensek	Jakob Fina
8号地块 JUFA Wien City	2012年12月	157间酒店客房	11000	会议室、咖啡屋、餐厅	JUFA Hotel	Peter Podsedensek	/

3 可持续整合性设计策略

3.1 居室设计重在"弹性自由"

公寓及居室品质是保障性住房的核心，其品质主要体现在硬性和软性层面。硬性层面不做赘述，本文侧重介绍其软性层面的品质体现，即"选择的权利与自由"，给予用户在经济上、生活模式上以及空间品质上能自主选择的余地。

（1）补贴种类的弹性自由。维也纳的一个社会住宅项目往往混合了多种补贴模式。例如Join In（图3）项目为住户提供了56户补贴式租赁公寓和18户"特级"补贴租赁公寓，还有一个老年人居住社区。"普通"的补贴式租赁公寓的首付款平均为242欧元/m^2，月租金（包括经营费用和营业税）平均约7.62欧元/m^2。"特级"补贴租赁房可以申请额外的国家贷款，月租金平均在7.9欧元/m^2，首付款则低至59欧元/m^2，有些还可以申请月租减免，帮助低收入人群减小首付压力，实现入住高品质公寓的梦想。

（2）居室户型的弹性自由。Join In项目通过前期调研确定住户的喜好需求，设计了两居室、三居室和四居室之间可以相互转换的房型，如图3所示，B1小户型两居室有多种平面布置，从常规布局到空白模式完全交由用户DIY。而B1户型加一个房间就成为三居室的C4户型，与B2户型组合就成了四居室的D5户型。相邻户型之间设计有非承重墙构件，去掉构件即可合为一户。最特别的是他们还设计了一套网上自由选房的系统，用户完全可以自主操作，直观地看到房间的楼层、位置、平面布置、室内外面积等相关参数，确定后即可生成一份报告。

（3）私人开放空间的弹性自由。维也纳的社会住宅不会将有限的资金用于非必要的立面装饰，但是却"奢侈"地花在每家每户的"私人花园"上。"四支柱模式"规定社会住宅的每户住房都必须有"私人开放空间"（图4），也就是户外阳台（Balkon，无覆盖无围合）或凉廊（Loggia，有覆盖无围合）。私人户外空间能"升级"居室品质，提高住户满意度，有效降低住户的搬迁流动性。在维也纳的社会住区中所见之处都是生机盎然的"小花园"，自有一番天地。Join In项目的所有公寓都配置阳台和凉廊（图5），阳台凉廊组合部分进深可达2.3m，适用于室外就餐、休憩、家务等需求；单凉廊部分进深约1.3m，可做绿植盆栽、苗圃培育以及储物等功用。

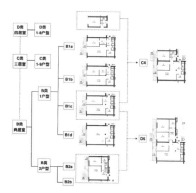

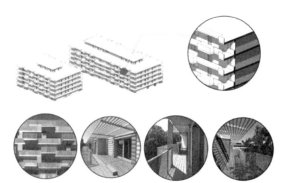

图3　Join In 项目的户型组合（作者自绘）　　图4　维也纳社会住宅的私人开放空间　　图5　JoinIn 项目的阳台凉廊（作者自绘）

资料来源：Seestern 和 JAspern 社区网站。

3.2　单体设计重在"场所归属"

单体项目是最基础的邻里社区，营造"社区"最核心的是建构"场所归属"，一个有着高度"归属感"的社区也意味着和谐可持续的邻里关系。"场所归属"需要物质条件与社会关系的双重建构。

（1）决策参与和自组织管理。Join In 项目的口号是"多样化的共同生活"（Vielfalt Gemeinsam Leben），旨在为不同年龄层次和多元文化背景的群体打造和谐的邻里社区。建筑师与社会学家合作对申请用户展开了文化背景与生活方式的调研，根据反馈设计了居民可以自主选择组合的灵活平面户型。等住户确定后通过多次见面会（图6），住户们协商讨论室内外公共空间的具体功能和设施配置，最后经过建筑师协调确定设计方案。住户在项目前期策划阶段的深入参与并且大部分意愿得以实现，有助于提高住户的居住满意度并培养其"主人翁"意识。在正式交付入住以后，住户们自发成立管理小组，对住区内的公共设施的使用、维护、管理以及社区活动的策划筹办等进行协商管理。

（2）公共生活丰富多样。Join In 项目布置了丰富的公共设施（图7），除了常规的社区活动房、儿童活动房、自行车儿童车停放室、社区厨房之外，还有一些对外服务的公共机构，如健康咨询中心、儿童托管所、便利商店以及隶属于维也纳援助工会（Wienerhilfswerk）的邻里中心。Join In 的公共设施布局是典型的"三明治"模式，建筑地面层全部为公共及后勤设施，屋顶层是屋顶花园，地面户外开放空间还布置了沙池、秋千、廊架、座椅等各样活动设施，为住户尤其是孩子们提供了活动场所。

（3）空间特征与可识别性。富有个性的室内外空间和建筑形象能有效塑造场所特征与可识别性，对强化"场所归属"也有辅助作用。Join In 项目由一长一短两栋建筑组成，以适应其三角场地（图8）。

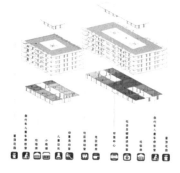

图6　MM11 项目的住户自组织会议　　图7　JoinIn 项目的公共设施布置（作者自绘）　　图8　JoinIn 项目的特征空间（作者自绘）

资料来源：MM11 社区网站。

建筑立面以温馨的原色木材为背景，连续的凉廊和阳台将整个建筑包裹起来，强化了一种"开放展廊"的性格特征，与其"多样化的共同生活"理念相呼应。此外屋顶花园的苗圃花田和楼梯井内壁艺术家Herbert Pasiecznyk的现代涂鸦等特色元素都为社区增添了鲜明的个性。

3.3 组团设计重在"多样统一"

大中型开发项目易对城市风貌带来巨大影响，因此需要避免过于单调或纷乱，充分协调统一性和多样性的平衡。维也纳的社会住宅地块常常被划分成多个项目分别招标，鼓励多家设计团队共同参与，联合开发，促进地块组团的建筑与空间多样性。当然社会结构多样性亦同样重要，包容不同文化背景和收入阶层的人群，促进居住融合，对于实现社会可持续具有重要意义。

（1）立面形态多样。通过灵活巧用立面构件元素，大胆选取色彩与材料等方法来丰富立面形态（图11）。比如Join In项目的木质墙板搭配凹凸连续的灰色金属阳台连廊显得沉稳朴实；MM11项目的亮橙色金属折板阳台在白墙映衬下格外抢眼；JUFA Hotel酒店的外立面通过欢快明亮的彩色百叶遮阳板装饰了立面，也巧妙地传达了青年家庭旅馆的形象定位。Global Park项目的银色金属穿孔卷板塑型的波浪形阳台与立面垂直绿化结合起来，既丰富了每户的私人开放空间，穿孔板在阳光下又能创造漂亮的光影效果，也有助于视线遮挡保护隐私，成为维也纳保障性住房的示范项目。

（2）功能设施多样。整个组团内的公共设施配置涵盖了办公、商业、酒店、医疗、儿童、咨询等多种设施业态，相互依托，互为补充。其中位于主入口的5号项目是一个十足的居住综合体，总建筑量达35600m²，其中办公7800m²，商业5200m²，住宅20300m²，宿舍2300m²。项目底层入驻大型超市Merkur，以及医药康复中心、社区诊所、健康咨询中心等医疗设施，亲子中心、幼儿园、儿童日托中心等教育托管机构。组团中心的公共开放空间Franz-Haas广场提供了多样化设施。

（3）居住人群多样。Mautner-Markhof地块1100多户住宅，涵盖了多种补贴模式，其中补贴式可售租赁房共742户占比67%，其他特别优惠的特殊类补贴租赁房（特级补贴类，智能住房类，宿舍类）共166户，占比15%；补贴式出售房47户，占比4%；普通商品房153户，占比14%。不同类型住房的混合促进不同收入阶层的人群的居住融合，从一定程度上缓解了居住分化现象。Join In项目的130名申请者中有1/4的人其母语为非德语，有土耳其语、匈牙利语、克罗地亚语、阿尔巴语、波兰语、罗曼语、法语、西班牙语、塞尔维亚语、汉语、俄语、斯洛伐克语、捷克语、沃洛夫语等14种之多[①]，是一个真正的"国际社区"。

（4）建筑体量统一。受总体规划控制，Mautner-Markhof地块的单体项目高度都为6~7层（图9），

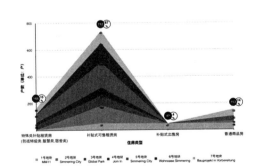

图9 Mauter Markhof地块住房类型及数量分布（作者自绘）

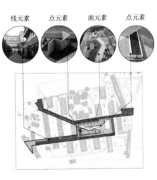

图10 地块空间系统（作者自绘）

图11 JoinIn，MM11，JUFA酒店和Global Park项目的立面局部（作者自摄）

---

① 资料来源：JoinIn社区网站 www.joinin.at.

虽各建筑风格迥异，但相似的建筑体量确保了空间尺度和空间秩序的一致性，从而在视觉效果的多样性中建立内在的统一感。

（5）空间系统统一。通过点线面元素和多样的空间限定手法，以核心空间整合其余，统领全局，建立丰富而统一的空间系统（图10）。Mautner-Markhof地块以核心空间Franz-Haas广场（面元素）组织各空间，先通过主入口直向道路和次入口斜向道路（线元素）将人流汇聚于广场，再通过黄色步道以及2号住宅大楼的底层架空引导至大楼背后的JUFA酒店。广场上的座椅、攀岩墙、水池等丰富的设施（点元素）促使人们驻足停留聚集。广场中央还通过下沉区域（高差）来定义攀岩墙场所，增强场域感。住宅项目都围绕在广场周边（围合），限定了广场边界，烘托强化其"枢纽"作用。

3.4 城市设计重在"融合共生"

由于受到城市规划的严格控制，要求住区边界须清晰定义道路界面，维也纳的新建住区常常是"守边式"布局，维护完整的街道立面，同时结合场地以适宜的方式延续场地文脉，形成意象层面的融合共生。但另一方面新建住区又被赋予激活老旧城区的职能，改善老旧城区缺乏开放空间与活力的现状（尤其是高密度居住片区）。所以新建住区一般都会采取公共设施"城市化"措施，在场地中央布置开敞公共空间，并新增混合业态，同时服务于自身住区和外部城市，起到改善城市空间，激发社会交往，并协助城市业态结构升级的作用。而住区也需要依赖周边既有城市公共服务和交通设施，以此相辅相成，形成与城市生活的"融合共生"。

（1）意象的融合共生。①城市界面延续。Mautner-Markhof地块主入口（图12）的5号项目的主体部分延续了比邻的老建筑尺度，保持檐口高度的一致，然后通过过街楼退进让出入口广场，顶上的三角钢架结构隐喻着入口"雨篷"形象，暗示片区主入口，起到空间引导作用。立面主要采用高反射玻璃和蓝灰色条纹板材，既彰显现代高技质感，形成新旧对话，又努力消解自身体量感，低调融入城市。②场地文脉延续。场地北侧在工厂年代就是个郁郁葱葱的小公园，栽有不少古树，边上还有栋老别墅（图13）。古树和别墅在地块更新时均得以保留。8号地块JUFA酒店前身是一栋带有17世纪的庭院"玫瑰园"（Rosenhof）的老建筑，被列入文物保护单位。建筑师在庭院西边新建一栋楼作为酒店客房主体，在新老建筑之间加建透明玻璃屋顶将历史庭院保护起来，成为酒店大堂，中央布置有咖啡屋（图14）。而老建筑则用作餐饮服务类功能，充分利用其保存数百年的砖拱酒窖和优雅经典的维也纳传统餐厅，如此新旧结合也使JUFA酒店独具特色。

（2）生活的融合共生。Mautner-Markhof地块就将中央的Franz-Haas广场（图15）用作城市级开放空间，在主入口一眼便可看到边侧的商铺和远处的广场，良好的视觉和路径可达性使得内部的广场乃至最深处的JUFA酒店都始终不缺人气。道路两侧的绿化及座椅，广场的攀岩墙、戏水池、座椅等丰富的设施可以满足孩童嬉戏，少年轮滑攀岩，妇女结伴聊天，老人看报晒太阳等各类活动需求，还时不时开展大型活动等吸引大批周边市民参与，是不少市民日常休憩的好去处。

图12　地块主入口界面（作者自绘）

图13　保留的古树和别墅（作者自绘）

图14　JUFA酒店大堂
资料来源：Architekt Podsedensek.

图15　Franz-Haas广场
资料来源：Jokob Fina.

4 总结

维也纳社会住宅的可持续整合性设计策略可以从四个空间尺度展开："弹性自由"的居室设计充分给予用户选择住房类型、居室户型和私人开放空间的自由，提升居住品质；注重"场所归属"的单体项目设计，鼓励用户参与前期决策及后期的自组织管理，同时合理布局的公共空间可以支持丰富多样的公共生活并促进住户融入社区，此外富有特色的建筑形态和场地设计可以强化住区空间特征和可识别性；"多样统一"的组团设计可以通过形态、设施及人群的多样性和体量与空间系统的统一性来实现；"融合共生"的城市设计通过延续城市界面和场地文脉等方式来达到城市意象的融合共生，也可将住区的部分公共设施"城市化"来改善或升级城市空间，促成城市生活的融合共生。以上四个层面的设计策略都对中国的保障房可持续社区建设具有相当参考借鉴意义。

Sustainable Integrated Design Strategies of Social Housing in Vienna

Hu Yuqing, Li Zhenyu

(College of Architecture and Urban Planning, Tongji University)

Abstract: Rapid urbanization process exacerbates the population gathering in big cities in China, while bringing demographic dividends also challenging urban living space. It is of great social significance to explore how to build sustainable community for the city, residents and environment. As the world's most livable city, Vienna puts forward sustainable requirements for social housing in four aspects of economy, sociability, architecture and ecology through the design guideline "four pillar model". Taking Mautner-Markhof as an example, through information collection and field investigation, this paper brings out sustainable integrated design strategies in different spacial scales, in the hope of providing reference for sustainable community construction in China. This paper is subsidized by No.51678412 NSFC Project.

Keywords: Vienna, Social housing, Sustainability, Integrated design strategy

参考文献

[1] Wolfgang F, William M (eds.). Das Wiener Modell, Wohnbau für die Stadt des 21.Jahrhunderts. Berlin: Jovis, 2016.

[2] 维也纳住宅基金会 Wohnfonds Wien. Vier- Säulen Modell. Vienna, 2015.

[3] 维也纳住宅研究部门 Wohnbauforschung Wien. Vienna Housing Annual Report 2015. Vienna, 2016.

[4] Join In 项目网站，www.joinin.at. [2017- 4 -16].

既有住区底层开放空间的功能构成及布局研究

王轶鸥 范 悦 赵 涛 李汀蕾

（大连理工大学建筑与艺术学院）

摘 要：20世纪八九十年代的既有住区多为开放社区，底层空间的利用率较高，其利用情况与住区的活力度和舒适度有着直接的联系，故对其研究具有重大意义。本文以大连市台山三小区为例，对其底层开放空间的使用现状进行总结归纳，探讨其功能构成及布局规律，以期为之后的相关研究提供一定的研究基础。

关键词：既有住区建筑，底层开放空间，功能构成，布局规律，开放化

1 引言

既有住区底层是与城市关系最密切的位置，是住区空间与城市活动空间的过渡区域。它的利用情况直接关系着住区的活力度与舒适度。本文选取大连市台山三小区进行研究，该小区是开放型、集中型的住区，具有一定的代表性。本文提出了底层开放空间的概念，尝试从功能构成和布局规律的层面研究其使用现状。

2 既有住区底层开放化的功能构成

我国城市住区的规划设计主要参照《城市居住区规划设计规范》GB 50180—93（以下简称《规范》），其中，配套公建设施共分为教育、医疗卫生、文化体育、商业服务、金融邮电、社区服务、市政公用和行政管理及其他8类设施。[1]概括而言，住区底层的功能构成主要包括具有居住功能的住宅和为居民生活服务的配套设施等。

"开放"的意思是指"张开、释放、解除限制"。底层功能的开放化是指功能的重置、空间的重新利用。根据《规范》中的住区商业服务设施主要包含以零售业、餐饮业和其他便民的服务性产业为主的商业设施，以及《规范》中对配套公建设施的分类，研究将底层功能分为住户个人半开放式花园、商业服务类以及生活配套类（图1）。其中，生活配套类的底层功能包括以下几类：教育类、医疗卫生类、文化类、社区服务类、金融邮电类[2]。

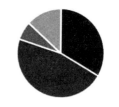

图1 功能构成配比

住户半开放式的功能构成有自建花园、加建储物、加建门窗（表1），其中，自建花园大部分为首层室外，少部分为屋顶楼台花园。除了住户半开放式、商业服务类以及生活配套类，住区中有部分底层空间正在进行功能重置，文中统称为未知类。

底层开放空间功能构成	表1
底层开放空间功能构成	
住户半开放式	自建花园、加建储物、加建门窗
商业服务类	超市、饭店、粮店、食杂店、早点店、小百货、汽修、理发店、浴室、照相馆、综合修理部、服装店、中西药房、蛋糕房
生活配套类	银行、棋牌室、门诊所、社区服务中心、教育培训

3 底层开放空间布局研究

3.1 功能布局及规律

由图1可以看出，住区底层开放的功能构成以商业服务类与住户个人半开放式居多，而生活配套类相对较少。

住区中个别位置出现底层商业、生活配套与住户半开放式的垂直功能复合化（图2），二层的住户利用一层加建的区域自建活动空间、露天花园。

图2 垂直功能复合化形式（作者拍摄）

住户半开放式总体布局主要集中在小区内部，以组团形式出现，且呈现一定的布局相似性。大多数分布在首层地面，以单独功能的形式出现，少数分布在建筑转角处的首层屋面，和其他开放功能以复合化的形式出现。影响这类开放性功能布局的因素有很多：（1）从组团形式的角度来看。由上文可知，这类开放功能大致有自建花园、加建储物、加建门窗三种形式。住区内集中绿化较完善、住栋之间的场地环境较丰富的区域，这类开放性功能出现较少，以极少的加建门窗形式出现，建筑底层开放性活力较低；而在场地条件不完善，集中绿化较少的区域，建筑底层的开放形式较丰富，开放活力较高，三种开放形式交替出现。由此可知，住区环境的完善程度直接影响到这类底层开放性功能的出现。（2）从个体角度来看。组团内部的开放性功能布局呈现一定的相似性，究其原因，同一组团内，住栋的平面形式相似，首层住户对于自家开放化的做法，在某种程度上，会为同一住栋的相邻住户提供一个方法参考和取向，以致这类开放性功能的布局往往出现极大的相似性（图3）。（3）从建筑形式的角度来看。在首层加建或建筑外界面有凹凸变化的住栋中，会出现二层露天花园、花池的开放形式。

商业服务类总体布局呈带形分布，主要集中在住区主干道及次干道两侧，即建筑的沿街面。除了受道路层级的影响外，地形高差情况也会对商业类的开放程度有着一定的影响。在高差较大的道路两侧，此类功能的开放性表现出较大差异，与道路标高接近、与行人水平视线接近的一侧，建筑底层开放性较强（图4）。坡地为大连市较为典型的地形特征，对底层的开放活力有着一定程度的影响。

生活配套类总体布局呈现点状不均匀分布，也呈现沿主要道路分布的趋势。其中，教育类底层开放性功能的布局会受周边基础设施的影响，这里的基础设施特指住区内学校。分布在面向学校大门一侧的建筑底层沿街面，并在学校视线可达的范围内（图5）。

未知类是指在底层结构上已做改动，但功能未知的一种开放形式。在某种程度上可以表示住区底层开放的一种未来布局走向。它的布局主要集中在开放情况较好的住栋及区域内，无明显的总体性规律。由此看来，底层开放是有连续性和紧凑性布局趋势的（图6）。

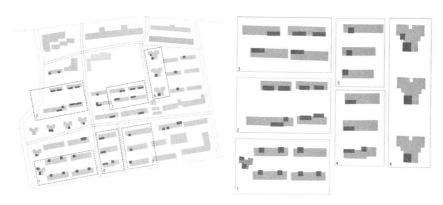

图3　布局相似性（作者自绘）

图4　高差对开放性的影响（作者自绘）

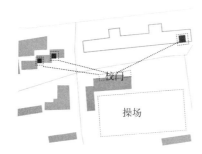

图5　视线可达性（作者自绘）

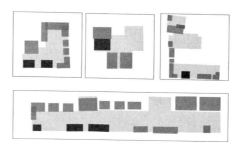

图6　布局连续性和紧凑性（作者自绘）

3.2　形态布局及规律

根据上述研究发现，住区底层开放程度分为完全开放和半开放两种。商业类的开放功能以完全开放式为主，即对户内进行整体开放化改造，少数服务性商业采用半开放式，即只将沿街房间对外打开。住户个人类以半开放式为主，即只将户内的局部空间或界面对外打开。选取几种典型的平面形态，进一步研究底层不同的开放形式在住栋中的具体位置。

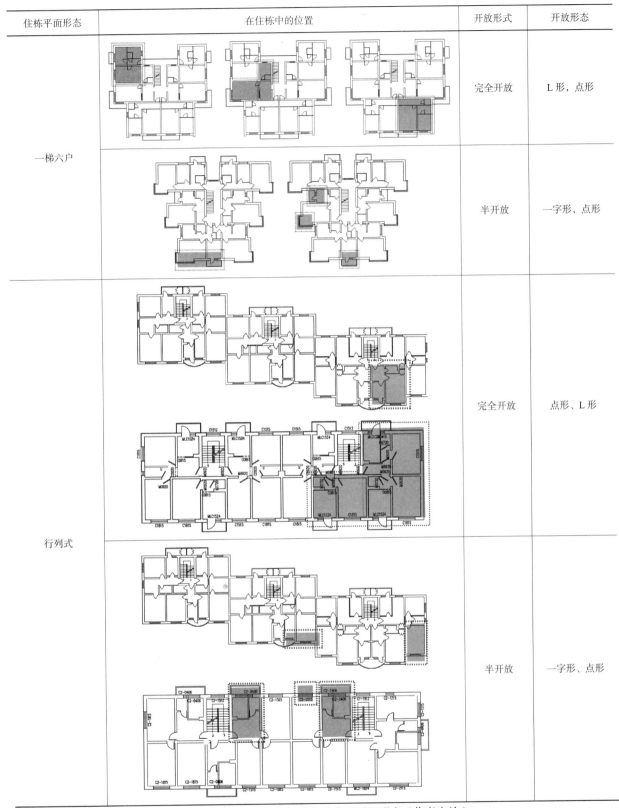

图7 住区低层开放空间的几种典型平面形态（作者自绘）

可以看出，开放形态与住栋平面形态、户型、开放形式有一定的关联。（1）与住栋平面形态的关系。点式住宅中，底层开放多以独立户点式存在，在行列式住栋中，存在多户集中改造的情况。（2）与户型的关系。户型主要对完全开放式有着直接的影响，对半开放式影响甚微。（3）与开放形式的关联。

可以看出，半开放式主要有界面开放和独间开放两种类型，以一字形和点形为主。

4 结语

本文以台山小区为例，研究住区底层开放空间的利用情况，总结其功能构成、功能布局规律及开放形态布局规律，试图探讨底层开放化布局的影响因素，为住区底层开放的类型化及相关研究打基础。

致谢

感谢国家自然科学重点基金资助（51638003）及中央高校基本科研业务费资助（DUT16RW105）。

Research on the Function Composition and Layout of the Bottom Open Space in the Existing Residential Area

Wang Yiou, Fan Yue, Zhao Tao, Li Tinglei

（School of Architecture & Fine Art, Dalian University of Technology）

Abstract: The existing residential areas in 1980s、1990s are mostly open communities, the utilization rate of the bottom space is high, and its utilization is directly related to the vitality and comfort of the residential area. Taking Taishan three District of Dalian as an example, this paper summarizes the current situation of the use of the open space, and discusses the function and layout of the open space, in order to provide a basis for further research.

Keywords: Existing residential buildings, Bottom open space, Function composition, Layput pattern, Opening

参考文献

[1] （日）松村秀一. 住区再生——重获新生的欧美集合住宅 [M]. 范悦，刘彤彤译. 北京：机械工业出版社，2008.
[2] 周扬，钱才云. 利于居民低碳出行的住区功能构成及布局 [J]. 规划师，2014，9：82-87.
[3] 权虹. 城市住区公共设施的研究 [D]. 清华大学，2004.
[4] 刘惠惠. 重庆公租房住区商业设施调查研究 [D]. 重庆大学，2013.
[5] 王翔. 既有住区外环境空间类型化及品质提升策略研究 [D]. 大连理工大学，2016.
[6] 刘萍. 山地城市住区外部空间特色景观营造初探 [D]. 重庆大学，2014.

密度视角下城市住区公共空间环境特征研究初探

鲍 莉 湛 洋 詹佳佳

（东南大学建筑学院）

摘 要：本研究剖析与住区公共空间相关联的一系列密度指标，立足南京城区三个开放住区公共空间的实证调研，通过对调研数据进行多向对比及数理分析，从公共空间供应量和物理特性等方面揭示不同密度住区的公共空间环境差异以及差异产生的内在原因，进而探讨住区密度与其公共空间环境特征之间动态的关联关系。

关键词：密度，住区公共空间，环境特征，公共空间供应量

1 引言

  面广量大的居住类建筑构成了城市的基本形态，也是承载市民日常生活与公共交往活动的主要场所。住区公共空间作为城市居民公共活动的重要载体，其品质高低更是决定了城市生活的质量乃至社会的和谐安定。随着物质生活水平的提升，城市居民对居住空间的追求已不再限于居住面积的大小，而开始注重住区公共空间的品质水平。在居住套型日趋产品化与模式化的同时，公共空间的"量"与"质"已经成为衡量住区宜居水平的重要标准。

  随着政治经济和社会文化的变迁，居住建筑的密度与空间形态也会不断演变，并直接导致城市整体风貌和形态的嬗变。城市新区不断蔓延的同时，原有城区内的住区也被大量拆迁重建以获得更高的容积率。不同建设年代且密度不同的住区间杂共存，这些住区不仅在平面肌理和建筑形态上有显著区分，在公共空间形态、类型和品质上也有着相当的差异。

  密度是一个包括多个指标的概念群，能够客观地反映出城市既有住区土地利用率和建设量的大小，因而可以成为揭示城市住区现状特征与发展演变过程的客观切入点。本研究将选取南京城区范围内的三个开放住区并展开实证调研，然后把密度指标与表征住区公共空间环境特征的相关参数进行比对研究，探讨二者之间的关联性。以期为住区设计提供理论参考依据，促进城市空间活力与居民生活水平的提升。

2 调研取样

  本研究选取了南京城区范围内三个边界明确、面积大小相似且入住情况良好的开放住区作为调研对象：小西湖片区、公教一村、东升沿一小区。由于它们建设年代不同，在密度指标、物质空间形态以及空间品质上均具有一定的时代差异性，因此具有历史可比性。这三个小区的基本情况见表1。

  小西湖片区是始建于清末民国时期的传统居住街区，位于老城区南部，处于夫子庙和老门东之间，北临小油坊巷、小西湖小学，东至箍桶巷，南抵马道街，约有低层民居544间，占地面积约$0.0486 \times 10^6 m^2$。

  公教一村是计划经济时期典型的住区类型，位于老城区北部，南京市市政府大院东侧，北靠明城

墙和玄武湖，南邻北京东路。该小区共有居民住宅53幢，占地面积约$0.0612 \times 10^6 m^2$，建成于1975年。

东升沿一小区位于老城区的城墙之外，集庆门大街与南湖路交叉口，属于南湖新村一期工程的一部分。南湖新村是我国改革开放后较早的回迁户小区，为解决回城下放户的问题而建设。该小区共有居民住宅61幢，占地面积约$0.0605 \times 10^6 m^2$，1985年年底竣工。

住区样本基本情况（作者自绘） 表1

住区名称	小西湖片区	公教一村	东升沿一小区
平面肌理			
所在区域	秦淮区	玄武区	建邺区
建成年代	始建于清末民国时期	1975年	1985年
占地面积	$0.0486 \times 10^6 m^2$	$0.0612 \times 10^6 m^2$	$0.0605 \times 10^6 m^2$

3 样本住区的密度表征

密度（density）是源于物理学的词汇，通常指每一空间单位中量的分布。在建筑学与城市规划领域，密度是一种反映使用土地利用强度、紧凑度和压力的综合指标，与城市肌理、空间形态相互关联。密度不仅包括表征建设强度的物质空间环境相关指标，例如建筑容积率、建筑覆盖率、建筑立面密度、居住单元密度等，也包含与人及活动相关联的人口密度、年龄结构、公共功能配比、底层空间开放率等。因此，与住区相关的密度概念不是单一指标，而是具有更多内涵、含多个具有相关性和一定值域的指标概念群。

本研究择选出建筑容积率、建筑覆盖率、平均建筑层数、居住单元密度、楼栋密度和建筑立面密度这6个与公共空间环境特征具有紧密关联的密度指标，并通过实证测绘测算了三个住区的现状数据（表2）。

住区密度调研数据 表2

住区名称	小西湖片区	公教一村	东升沿一小区
建筑容积率	0.93	1.24	1.84
建筑覆盖率（%）	56.2	29.3	42.1
平均建筑层数	1.7	4.2	4.4
居住单元密度（户/hm²）	340	175	280
楼栋密度（栋/hm²）	112.1	8.7	10.1
建筑立面密度	0.99	0.73	0.75

建筑容积率是指总建筑面积与建筑所在用地面积的比率。从调研结果来看，小西湖片区、公教一村和东升沿一小区的容积率逐渐升高，分别为 0.93、1.24 和 1.84。

建筑覆盖率表示建筑基底面积与建筑所在用地面积的比率，小西湖片区的数值最高，达到 56.2%，其次为东升沿一小区的 42.1% 和公教一村的 29.3%。

平均建筑层数可以用于衡量场地中建筑物的平均高度，其计算方式为：平均建筑层数 = 总建筑面积/建筑基底面积。如表 2 所示，公教一村和东升沿一小区的平均建筑层数均达到小西湖片区的 2 倍以上。小西湖片区的建筑单体以 1~2 层为主，公教一村以 4~5 层为主，东升沿一小区以 6 层为主。

居住单元密度是指住区内居住单元数量与用地面积的比率，其变化趋势是小西湖片区、东升沿一小区和公教一村的数值逐渐降低，这一指标会影响住区所能承载的人口密度的高低。

为了更加全面客观地表征住区密度特征，我们对楼栋密度和建筑立面密度这两个非典型指标也做了测算（表 2）。楼栋密度是场地内的楼栋数量与建筑所在用地面积的比率，能够表征住区建筑体量的分散程度，计算方式为：楼栋密度 = 楼栋数量/用地面积。小西湖片区的楼栋密度要远高于公教一村和东升沿一小区。

建筑立面密度是有关建筑的立面总面积与总建筑面积的比率，计算方式为：建筑立面密度 = 建筑立面总面积/总建筑面积。这一数值越大，说明该住区内的公共空间越零散，与公共空间的接触面越大。同时，室内外发生联系的可能性也会增大，公共空间的围合性愈佳。结果显示，建筑公共立面密度最大的是小西湖片区，最小的是公教一村，东升沿一小区居中。

4 住区公共空间环境特征

住区公共空间指的是住区中住宅单元之外的开放空间（包括道路、绿化、景观、小品及公用服务设施等），强调基于这些物质空间所发生的人的活动和场所氛围。根据哈布瑞肯教授的开放建筑层级理论，住区内公共空间可以分为对城市开放的公共空间、社区共有的公共空间及楼栋邻里间的共享空间三个层级。本文重点探讨对城市开放和社区共有两个层次的公共空间。

高品质的住区公共空间可以激发住区活力，创造更多的自发性停留活动，为居民带来生理、心理层面的益处。既有研究中出现了很多被广泛应用的公共空间品质评价模型，主要涵盖物质环境特征、社会环境、微观品质、文化内涵等多个角度。住区公共空间首先是客观存在的物质空间，因而空间环境特征是公共空间品质评价的基础。住区公共空间环境特征指的是公共空间所提供的物质基础以及空间的物理环境质量，前者主要指公共空间的供应量，后者强调物理特性。在众多指标中，我们选取公共空间密度、公共空间配比和有效公共空间比例三个指标去衡量公共空间供应量，选取公共空间日照强度作为物理环境质量的衡量指标（表 3）。

住区公共空间物质环境调研数据　　　　表 3

住区名称	小西湖片区	公教一村	东升沿一小区
公共空间密度（%）	21.0	61.1	53.9
公共空间配比（%）	22.7	49.3	29.3
有效公共空间比例（%）	94.1	79.6	86.3
公共空间日照强度（h/m²）	4.6	4.3	3.7

公共空间密度是衡量空间供应量的硬性标准，其计算方式为：公共空间密度 = 公共空间总面积 / 用地面积。如表 3 所示，东升沿一小区、公教一村和小西湖片区的公共空间密度分别为 53.9%、61.1%、21.0%。这说明东升沿一小区和公教一村这两个以板式多层为主的住区所提供的公共空间要多于以传统低层住宅为主的小西湖片区。小西湖片区供给的公共空间量非常少，且表现为巷道、院落的形式，呈现均布零散的特征，缺乏可供集中活动的大面积空地。

公共空间密度所表示的是公共空间在场地中的分布强度，而公共空间配比则能够将总建筑面积纳入考量范畴，其计算方式为：公共空间配比 = 公共空间总面积 / 总建筑面积。东升沿一小区、公教一村和小西湖片区的公共空间配比依次为 29.3%、49.3%、22.7%。结果表明，三个住区这一指标数值的高低顺序虽与公共空间密度相同，但东升沿一小区和公教一村的差距在变大。

住区内的水面、不可践踏的草地等空间虽可以提升环境品质，创造更宜人的空间氛围，但并非容纳居民活动之处。因此，我们将广场、道路、可进入的草坪和运动场地等可以满足使用者基本停留性活动的空间定义为有效公共空间，并将有效公共空间比例也纳入公共空间供应量的指标中去，其计算方式为：有效公共空间比例 = 有效公共空间面积 / 公共空间总面积。三个住区的有效公共空间比例数值的变化趋势恰恰和公共空间密度相反，小西湖的数值最高，这是因为小西湖公共空间类型过于单一、公共绿化严重匮乏。公教一村由于小区内不可跨越的绿地较多，因此有效公共空间比例较低，同时这也反映出该小区绿化情况更佳。从公共空间密度、公共空间配比以及有效公共空间比例来评价，公教一村的公共空间供应最大，小西湖最小，东升沿一小区处于中间。

住区公共空间日照强度能够对公共空间品质和居民生活质量产生显著影响，充足的日照时长意味着居民在进行公共活动时能够享受更多的"阳光"。我们将这一指标定义为大寒日每平方米公共空间在 8：00 ~ 16：00 之间所能享受到的平均日照时数，其计算方式为：公共空间日照强度 = ∑公共空间有效日照时数 / 公共空间总面积。经测算，小西湖片区的公共空间日照强度为 $4.6h/m^2$，公教一村为 $4.3h/m^2$，东升沿一小区为 $3.7h/m^2$。根据此结果，小西湖片区公共空间的日照水平最优，其次为公教一村和东升沿一小区。

5 住区密度与公共空间物质环境比对分析

将住区密度相关指标与其公共空间品质相关评价结果绘制出折线图进行比对分析，我们发现：对于所调研的三个住区而言，住区密度和公共空间物质环境的部分指标之间具有一定的非线性对应关系（图 1、图 2）。

结果显示，建筑覆盖率、居住单元密度、楼栋密度和建筑立面密度这四个密度指标的变化趋势较为相似。数值从高到低依次为小西湖片区、东升沿一小区和公教一村。且在建筑覆盖率和居住单元密度上，相较于东升沿一小区和公教一村之间的数值差异，小西湖片区与二者的数值差异较大。四个指标的变化趋势与用于表征公共空间供应量的公共空间密度和公共空间配比两个参数的变化趋势恰恰相反。这说明对于三个住区来说，随着建筑覆盖率、居住单元密度、楼栋密度和建筑立面密度数值的增加，住区公共空间的供应量逐渐降低。

针对这三个住区而言，建筑容积率与平均建筑高度的变化趋势较为接近，随着平均层数的升高，建筑的容积率的数值也在升高，只不过其数值的波动幅度会受到覆盖率等指标的共同影响。同时，公共空间日照强度的数值会逐渐降低。这两个指标的分析结果与公共空间日照强度相似，似乎说明公共空间日照强度与容积率的关系是负相关。至少在所调研的三个住区样本中，建筑容积率和平均建筑高度越高，公共空间日照强度越低。

而住区公共空间供应和容积率之间则没有必然的对应关系，这说明高强度的住区开发并不一定会

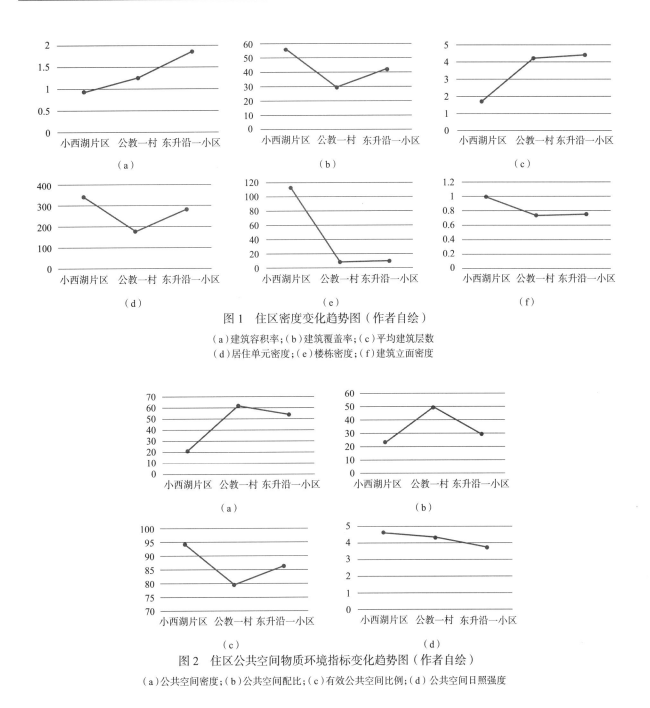

图 1 住区密度变化趋势图（作者自绘）
(a) 建筑容积率; (b) 建筑覆盖率; (c) 平均建筑层数
(d) 居住单元密度; (e) 楼栋密度; (f) 建筑立面密度

图 2 住区公共空间物质环境指标变化趋势图（作者自绘）
(a) 公共空间密度; (b) 公共空间配比; (c) 有效公共空间比例; (d) 公共空间日照强度

导致公共空间供应量的丧失。一个住区公共空间物质空间形态和品质氛围的塑造受到多个指标的共同影响，如果能够建立这些指标之间的合理动态关联机制，那就可以为适当提高建筑密度提供理论依据。

6 总结与启示

目前在中国的城市建设中，开发地块地密度指标多由宏观抽象的上位规划所确定，指标值主要依靠较为主观的经验判断。但住区形态和公共空间物质环境特征不仅仅由容积率等少数指标所决定，只有多个指标的合理组合才能使技术管控更加理性且具有弹性。本文以密度概念群作为对住区密度及其公共空间环境特征展开定量分析的切入视角,通过对三个不同时期的典型开放住区的实证调研,得出不同密度的住区在环境特征上的差异性及其成因,尝试更为准确精细地建立指标与建成空间反馈之间的关联性。

此外,在研究过程中,我们发现所调研的住区公共空间不仅在物质环境特征上有所区别,在社会环境、心理感受和空间活力上均体现出一定的差异性。这些差异与密度的差异是不是也有一定的关联性?住区密度在对公共空间物质环境产生影响之后,是否也会继而影响空间品质?这些问题将会在后续的研究中继续探讨。

Research on the Public Space's Environmental Features of Urban Residential Area Based on Density Perspective

Bao Li, Zhan Yang, Zhan Jiajia

(School of Architecture, Southeast University)

Abstract: This study analyzes a series of density indicators associated with residential public space. Based on the empirical research on the public space of three open residential areas in Nanjing and a multi-directional comparison and mathematical analysis of the survey data, the study reveals the otherness among three residential areas with different densities from the perspective of public space supply and physical environment, and the inherent causes of it. Then it explores the dynamic relationship between the density of settlements and the environment features of their public spaces.

Keywords: Density, Public space of residential area, Environment feature, Public space supply

参考文献

[1] Sacha Menz. Public space Evolution in High-density Living in Singapore——Ground and Elevated Public Spaces in Public Housing precincts. Singapore: Future Cities Laboratory, ETH Singapore SEC Ltd, 2014.

[2] Dietmar Eberle, Eberhard Troger. Density & Atmosphere: On Factors relating to Building Density in the European City[M]. Switzerland: Birkhauser, 2015.

[3] 董春方. 高密度建筑学(第1版)[M]. 北京:中国建筑工业出版社,2012.

[4] (丹麦)扬·盖尔. 交往与空间(第四版)[M]. 何人可译. 北京:中国建筑工业出版社,2002.

[5] 徐磊青,刘念,卢济威. 公共空间密度、系数与微观品质对城市活力的影响——上海轨交站域的显微观察[J]. 新建筑,2015,4:21-26.

[6] 董丽,范悦,苏媛,冯碧岳. 既有住区活力评价研究[J]. 建筑学报,2015,s1:186-191.

[7] 翟宇佳,徐磊青. 城市设计品质量化模型综述[J]. 时代建筑,2016,2:133-139.

[8] 龙瀛,周垠. 街道活力的量化评价及影响因素分析——以成都为例[J]. 新建筑,2016,1:52-57.

[9] 蒋竞,丁沃沃. 从居住密度的角度研究城市的居住质量[J]. 现代城市研究,2004,7:44-47.

[10] 黄一如,朱培栋. 城市高密度住区控制密度与感知密度关联性研究[J]. 时代建筑,2016,6:50-59.

[11] 周静,黄建中. 城市公共空间品质评价指标体系的探讨[J]. 建筑师,2003,3:52-56.

碎片整理：针对未来租赁住房的开放建筑新模式

姚严奇　李振宇

（同济大学建筑与城市规划学院）

摘　要：本文以上海市创智坊青年社区设计为契机，提出一种开放建筑的新模式——碎片整理：作为针对未来租赁住房的设计策略。对传统开放建筑作为租赁住房的优势和问题进行了分析，指出传统开放建筑模式中普遍存在低效利用的"碎片空间"的现象。基于计算机领域的磁盘碎片整理，提出开放建筑领域的"碎片整理"新模式，并分别从城市层级、住栋层级和户内层级阐述了因时因地、共享共赢和一户一型的碎片整理策略。

关键词：碎片整理，租赁住房，开放建筑

1　引言

现阶段，我国住房租赁比例仍然较低，到 2010 年租赁比例仅 21%，住房自有率常年维持在 70% 以上，远高于西方发达国家水平。[1] 参照海外经验，住房供给体系立体化是大势所趋，租赁住房建设仍然存在大量空间。因此，建立一套适合租赁住房的建筑体系具有重大的现实意义。开放建筑（Open Building）支撑体与内装体分离的体系为满足租赁住房高流动性和多样性的需求提供了可能，具有作为未来租赁住房设计策略的潜力。

2　传统开放建筑与租赁住房

2.1　开放建筑理论

开放建筑理论起源于工业革命带来的建筑产业革新[2]，1914 年勒·柯布西耶在"多米诺体系"中将建筑的承重结构和内部隔断区分开来。1961 年，荷兰学者哈布瑞肯教授最早提出将建筑分为支撑体和可分体两部分，进而成立 SAR 建筑研究基金会，真正形成所谓开放建筑理论。[3] 20 世纪 90 年代，日本研发出 SI 住宅体系，形成支撑体和填充体完全分离的新型住宅供给与建造模式、体系和方法。[4] 开放建筑理论提倡"层级控制"和"用户参与"，将整个体系划分为城市肌理（Urban Tissue）、建筑主体（Base Building Level）和可分体（Infill Level）三个层级。长期以来，开放建筑理论主要应用于自有住房的设计和建造，但是也不乏应用于租赁住房的案例，其中以公共租赁住房为主，如瑞士罗溪住宅和北京光合原筑项目等。一方面，开放建筑理论在解决租赁住房问题上具有明显优势和巨大潜力，另一方面传统的开放建筑在面对租赁住房的特定需求时依然存在问题。

2.2　传统开放建筑作为租赁住房的优势

相对于普通住宅，开放建筑作为租赁住房具有多适性的优势。租赁住房具有住户多变、流动性高

的特点，在建筑使用寿命内，同样的空间需要满足不同家庭结构和生活习惯的需求，这对建筑的多适性提出了更高的要求。开放建筑中，建筑构件部品化、整体卫浴、轻质隔墙等特点方便了住户对建筑的快速改造，从而适应多样化需求。日本NEXT21实验住宅以探索21世纪集合住宅模式为目标，于1993年由大阪煤气株式会社建造。1994年开始，该项目一直持续根据居住者需求的变化进行空间改造实验。1996年及1999年，实施了住户改装实验，验证了其建筑体系的多适性。[5]

同时，开放建筑的分层设计降低了租赁住房生命周期内的更新成本。开放建筑将具有公共属性的主体部分和具有私密性属性的住户内装部分分离建设，进而实现户内布局、设备设计的高自由度和更新性，不但可以使建筑物得到长期使用，而且使降低租赁住房高频率更新的造价成为可能。

2.3 传统开放建筑作为租赁住房的问题

虽然开放建筑具有作为租赁住房建造体系的种种优势，但是在应对租住人群的特定需求时，依然存在一些问题。

在城市肌理层级上，开放建筑理论对层级寿命的判断是理想化的。传统开放建筑理论从欧洲实践经验出发，认为城市的空间形态相对稳定，该层级被作为最永久的层级（100～300年），而建筑主体结构的寿命则被预判为上百年。但是，实际使用寿命与耐久年限（physical life）是不同的概念。耐久年限很大程度上由构建自身设计和生产情况决定，容易计算；而使用寿命可能由于外界原因大大缩短，不容易预测。[6]从中国实践来看，城市空间形态变化迅速，在高流动性的租赁住房中，建筑与环境的关系更加不稳定，一些最初设计良好、充满活力的城市空间在数年后即可能出现闲置，但建筑结构难以作出回应调整，闲置空间往往成为"城市死角"。

在建筑主体层级上，开放建筑在面对租住人群对空间规模的需求变化时是消极被动的。当租户有增加空间的需求时，他需要相邻住户贡献出自己的空间，才能扩大空间；当租户有减小租住面积的需求时，他退租的空间可能因为过于细小零碎而无人租住。类似的空间规模变化，只有在各方需求恰巧吻合的情况下才能被动发生，例如NEXT21中"三代同堂之家"的住户改建为两个住户的设计，然而这样的巧合情况远不能满足租户变化空间的大量需求，以至于大多数情况下空间无法扩大，或是空间被退租闲置，又或是租户使用着超出自己需求大小的空间，造成空间利用效率低下。

在可分体层级上，开放建筑在满足租住人群对空间布局的需求变化时是缓慢不便的。大多数情况下室内改造依然低效，例如，尽管卫生间的管道是允许卫生间的位置在一定范围内变化，但是由于工程量巨大，在经济和时间上的花费太多，很多时候卫生间都会尽量保持不变。[7]由于工业化程度不足，一些改造施工依然使用湿式作业，实验项目NEXT21中的一处外墙改造也无奈使用湿式施工法。这些改造施工的障碍导致租户放弃对空间布局的合理改变，在一定程度上也造成空间浪费。

城市肌理层级的空间闲置、建筑主体层级的空间利用效率低下和可分体层级的空间浪费，都反映了传统开放建筑作为租赁住房时普遍存在的空间低效利用现象，这与开放建筑本身的灵活多适形成了矛盾，我们将这些利用率不高的空间定义为"碎片空间"，并试图寻找解决这一问题的方法。

3 碎片整理：开放建筑新模式

3.1 概念来源

以同济大学研究生设计课程"创智坊青年社区设计"为契机，我们针对租赁住房提出了"碎片整理"

的开放建筑新模式。这一概念来自计算机领域的磁盘碎片整理：电脑磁盘由于长期读写文件产生了碎片和凌乱的文件，通过整理，可以使得磁盘空间重新连续可用，提高电脑的整体性能。类比到建筑空间中，作为租赁住房的开放建筑由于租户高流动性的进出更替，产生了利用率不高的碎片空间，通过对这些碎片空间的整合再利用，可以提高整个建筑的空间利用效率（图1）。针对传统开放建筑理论中三个层级的碎片空间问题，开放建筑新模式从城市层级、住栋层级和户内层级分别进行碎片整理（图2）。

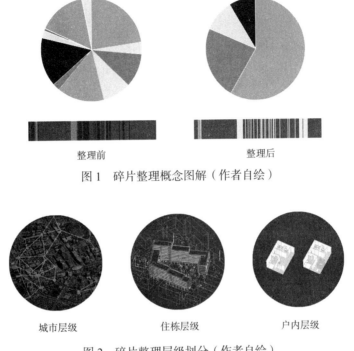

图1 碎片整理概念图解（作者自绘）

城市层级　　　　　住栋层级　　　　　户内层级

图2 碎片整理层级划分（作者自绘）

3.2 因时因地：城市层级碎片整理

城市层级的碎片空间指的是租赁住房周围闲置的城市公共空间，常见类型包括低利用率的中心花园、二层平台、城市广场等。碎片空间产生的原因分为两种，一种是因为租户生活习惯导致的具有时段性的空间闲置，另一种是由于地理位置不利导致的空间闲置。另外，租住人群对公共空间有较高需求。以我们在租住人群集中的上海市创智坊地段的问卷调查为例，101份有效调查问卷中，有41人目前租房生活，其中35人对交往和活动的空间有需求。因此，如何整合闲置公共空间以满足租住人群的空间需求成为城市层级碎片整理需要解决的问题。

针对时段性的空间闲置，需要因时进行碎片整理。赋予建筑生命力是开放建筑的最初目标：将时间的维度引入建筑设计中，让稳定的元素具有更强的适应性，从而让易变的元素更易变以适应不同的需求。[8] 在建筑与城市空间连接的部分可以通过灵活隔断的设置分时段营造具有公共活动氛围的场所，例如在建筑的一层设计可伸缩的顶棚或格栅，白天租户出入较多时收起保证交通空间，晚上打开形成夜间集市供租户使用。

针对地段性的空间闲置，需要因地进行碎片整理。开放建筑主体结构的使用寿命预设为上百年，但是并不意味着所有结构的恒定不变。传统开放建筑的主体结构稳定不变，缺乏对城市环境中出现的闲置空间进行及时调整回应的机制。对于城市层级的碎片空间，适当改造次要结构甚至主体结构是必要的也是可行的。针对不同时期租户的公共空间需求和空间实际使用情况，可以进行例如串联组团、架设平台、引入人流等碎片空间整理改造。

3.3 共享共赢：住栋层级碎片整理

住栋层级的碎片空间主要由租户空间规模需求的变化产生，进一步定义该层级的碎片空间，可能存在以下几种情况：

（1）租户空间需求减小，退租少量空间，例如半个开间，由于空间过小无人租住而闲置；

（2）租户空间需求增大，相邻租户均不愿意贡献本户空间；

（3）本身闲置的几个空间，其面积总和符合租住条件，但由于零散分布无法整合而闲置。

分析以上几种碎片空间的产生原因，我们发现其根本原因在于传统开放建筑体系分配空间的原则的局限性。传统开放建筑体系中，一处空间只能分配给空间相邻的住户。一旦出现不宜出租的碎片空间，只能寄希望于相邻两户消化吸收，如果相邻住户均不需要，就会出现空间浪费。为了打破这种空间分配原则的局限性，有必要将空间拥有者的可能性扩大，在整个住栋范围内基于共享原则整合碎片空间。所谓共享原则，即是注重空间的使用属性、可获得属性，而不限定空间的所有权。

为了实现住栋范围内的碎片空间共享整合，就需要在传统开放建筑设计和建造过程后加入碎片整理的过程。传统开放建筑强调设计阶段的用户参与，但是缺乏投入使用后的评估和调整机制。开放建筑在建成后空间分配格局不再发生明显改变，在空间整合层面上与普通住宅几乎无异，碎片整理新模式即是在建造完成后持续跟踪住栋空间使用情况，收集碎片空间信息，完成碎片整理（图3），从而实现住栋内空间利用最大化。开放建筑体系中支撑体与内装体分离的特点为碎片整理创造了条件，内装体存在灵活移动的可能性。例如西班牙ACORDE项目中，设计方应用开放体系，在住宅建成后依然可以根据家庭人口结构变化调整住栋空间分配，形成整个住栋的住户对空间的共享（图4）。

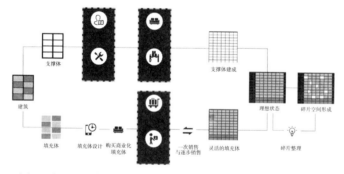

图3　加入碎片整理机制的开放建筑全生命周期（作者自绘）

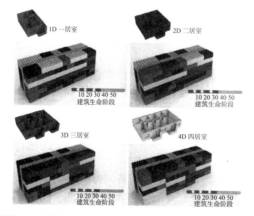

图4　西班牙ACORDE项目中加入空间整理机制

资料来源：Branchi，Pablo，Emilio等.可适性居住建筑——基于用户需求的空间高效利用[J].建筑学报，2013，1：36-39.

基于共享原则的空间再整理，可以形成碎片空间租户、承租户和出租方的三方共赢。首先碎片整理满足了各方的空间需求，租户通过退租闲置空间，减少了租金支出，承租方则通过空间整合得到了合适的租住空间，同时出租方通过提高空间出租率实现了收益的最大化；其次碎片整理还提供了形成大型商办空间以及形成交往圈子的可能性。通过多户空间的整合，可以形成连续的大型空间供商业或办公使用；通过内装体的移动也可以形成相同交往圈子的集聚，满足租户的交往需求。

3.4 一户一型：户内层级碎片整理

户内层级的碎片空间主要由租户多样的户内空间布局需求产生。相同的空间，由于租户不同的家庭结构和生活习惯，可能会产生截然不同的空间布局需求。如果户内存在一处空间，却不为租户所需要，即形成了户内层级的碎片空间（图5）。

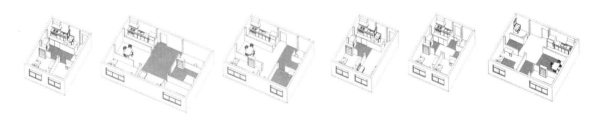

图5　户内层级碎片空间（作者自绘）

租户的需求多样且不断变化，针对租户需求个性化定制户内空间布局才能实现空间利用率的最大化，即采用"一户一型"的策略。传统开放建筑在理论上已经能够实现"一户一型"的个性化定制，但是由于租住人群高流动性的特点，户内空间划分的灵活性要求大大提高，传统开放建筑中的复杂施工难以满足租赁住房快速改造的需求。因此，碎片整理新模式提出一套适合多样需求并且方便改造的内墙隔断系统。

内墙隔断系统通过计算确定为四种生产模数：10cm、30cm、90cm和110cm（图6），以满足任意长度内隔墙的组合。在结构上，内隔墙结构由外壳、填充、竖向支撑、横向支撑、密封橡胶以及竖向

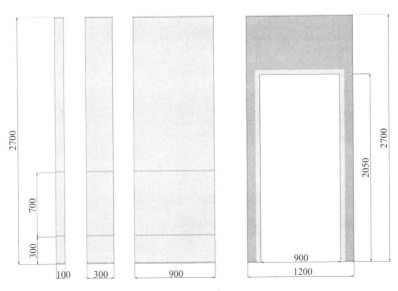

图6　内墙隔断系统（作者自绘）

调节装置组成。竖向调节装置的结构又是通过紧固螺丝连接紧固滑块以及竖向支撑滑竿和竖向支撑底座组成。安装内墙，只需要用内六角扳手旋紧竖向调节螺丝，使墙体略微伸长，上下分别顶住内装体的顶棚和地板即可固定。墙体与墙体之间的连接可以通过密封胶条完成。户内的电线网线也可以结合内隔墙体系实现灵活布线，在墙体离地面分别 30cm 和 100cm 处设置暗槽，电线在槽内放置并加盖封条以方便在房间内灵活布置插座。传统墙体改造需要专业施工人员施工，而此种内墙体只需单人就可拆卸和安装，施工工具也只需一个内六角扳手，真正实现内墙体的快速改造。

4　小结

"碎片整理"的开放建筑新模式最初仅仅是为了解决传统开放建筑模式中的"碎片空间"问题，旨在高密度的城市背景下提高未来租赁住房的空间利用效率。然而，长远看来，"碎片整理"的开放建筑新模式还可以带来以下几方面的启示：

（1）住宅设计应该关注建筑的全生命周期，同时也应该关注人的全生命周期。综合考虑建筑空间、时间和人的关系是住宅设计与建造的一个重要课题；

（2）针对高流动性租赁住房提出的"碎片整理"的开放建筑新模式对建筑的工业化程度提出了更高要求，尤其是住宅产业的加速工业化值得期待；

（3）建筑空间的共享符合当代城市的生活性、共享性、社群性特征，具有较强的现实意义。碎片整理模式对空间共享的讨论仍然表浅，有待进一步研究。

（4）哈布瑞肯认为建筑及环境都是不断变化的，"碎片整理"模式不是开放建筑的最初模式，也不会是开放建筑的最终模式。

致谢

本篇论文的写作受到国家自然科学基金项目《长三角地区"城中厂"的社区化更新技术体系研究》的资助（编号：51678412）。

Defragmentation: Open Building as A Strategy for Future Rental Housing

Yao Yanqi, Li Zhenyu

(College of Architecture and Urban Planning, Tongji University)

Abstract: This paper puts forward a new model of open architecture: defragmentation, as a strategy for future rental housing. First, the advantages and problems of the traditional open building used as rental housing are analyzed, and the phenomenon of "fragment space" which is common in the traditional open architecture model is pointed out. Based on disk defragmentation in the computer field, the paper creates a new open architecture model called "defragmentation", and respectively explains defragmentation on three levels, which are urban level, building level and inner level.

Keywords: Defragmentation, Rental housing, Open building

参考文献

[1] 崔裴, 张永岳, 谢福泉. 关于发展、完善上海住房租赁市场的建议 [J]. 科学发展, 2011, 11: 68-74.

[2] 黄杰, 周静敏. 基于开放建筑理论的建筑灵活性表达 [J]. 城市住宅, 2016, 23（6）.

[3] 郝飞, 范悦, 秦培亮等. 日本 SI 住宅的绿色建筑理念 [J]. 住宅产业, 2008（z1）: 87-90.

[4] 刘东卫, 刘若凡, 顾芳. 国际开放建筑的工业化建造理论与装配式住宅建设发展模式研究 [J]. 建筑技艺, 2016, 10: 60-67.

[5] 加茂, 胡惠琴. NEXT21 实验住宅建筑体系和住户改装的实验 [J]. 建筑学报, 2012, 4: 72-75.

[6] 任智劼. 开放建筑理论的反思.

[7] 贾倍思, 江盈盈. "开放建筑"历史回顾及其对中国当代住宅设计的启示 [J]. 建筑学报, 2013, 1: 20-26.

[8] 葛文俊. 感知建筑设计中的时间维度——记迪特玛·埃伯勒教授 2015 年秋港大教学 [J]. 新建筑, 2017, 1: 116-119.

寒地城市住区室外公共空间居民使用受限情况改善
——以沈阳浑南新区新建居住片区为例

张东潇[1]　高智慧[1]　刘玥彤[1]　胡　帅[2]

（1.沈阳建筑大学建筑与规划学院；2.大连市城市规划设计研究院）

摘　要：城市住区居民的生活质量与幸福指数是整个社会关注的焦点问题。在北方寒地城市，冬季漫长的室内生活会对居民的心理情绪和生理健康产生不利影响，导致生活舒适度下降，归属感缺失等现象的出现。本文尝试改善寒地城市住区户外公共空间设置，来满足居民交往与户外活动需求。使用测风仪、日照分析软件等工具，问卷调查与访谈等方法，对沈阳市浑南新区6个居住小区进行连续12个月的观察统计，分析季节变化对新城居民户外活动的影响，总结不同居民类型的心理感受，深入探索破解"猫冬"困境的方法。研究表明：老者与儿童户外活动受寒冷天气影响最为显著，大尺度草坪、广场、儿童游乐设施在冬季利用率低。建议寒地新城居住区利用风光定位技术，尝试规划大尺度口袋空间，合理提供小尺度的"口袋广场"、巧设"戏雪区"等策略，共同提升居民对住区公共空间使用的舒适度。

关键词：城市住区，寒地，户外公共空间，活动受限，口袋空间

引言

随着全面深化改革的不断推进，城市化进程加快，城市居民在物质生活得到满足后，越来越追求精神层面上的愉悦，例如进行户外活动来缓解压力、锻炼身体、满足交往需求等。但在我国北方寒冷地区，寒季期较长，住区居民长时间因天气寒冷而无法下楼活动，逗留在室内过着特有的"猫冬"生活。因此，分析研究在寒地住区规划中可采用的有效设计方法，改善居民户外活动受限情况，是一种以人为本，满足居民需求的有益尝试。

1 研究区域概况与方法

1.1 研究区域界定

近年来，随着浑南新区成为沈阳市重点建设发展的区域，沈阳市南扩进程加快，其用地和人口规模不断增长，其中新建住区占有相当大的比重。随着"新移民"的大量涌入，寒冷天气、人际关系疏远、公共空间有限成为居们经历的生活困扰，特别是在寒季，仍然过着特有的"猫冬"生活。

1.2 研究对象与方法

调研以浑南新区的6个居住小区为对象（图1），分别位于浑南大道两侧（图2）。这六个小区随着

图 1 调研对象区位图

浑南新城的形成先后建设，设施完备，入住率较高，建筑高度高低结合，具有一定的代表性。调研使用测风仪、温湿度计、照度计、日照分析软件等工具，通过连续 12 个月的观察统计，记录居民户外活动的变化规律，重点分析冬季居民户外活动情况，包括居民户外活动方式、空间分布、时间分布，不同年龄居民活动人数和阴影内外活动人数等。同时采用问卷调查与访谈法了解住区居民的真实感受，并查阅国外同类问题的研究成果和研究方法，对比国外成熟案例，评价样本小区的优缺点（图 3）。

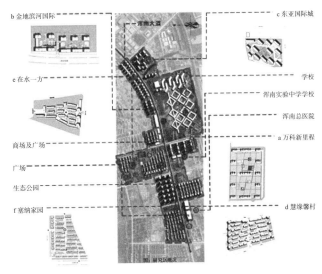

图 2 研究对象分布平面图

1.3 研究思路

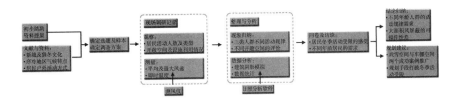

图 3 研究思路框架图

2 引起寒地住区居民室外活动受限的缘由

2.1 城市新"猫冬"

与传统东北农村的"猫冬"生活相比,新猫冬生活的问题更加突出(图4)。主要体现为:(1)人际网络疏远,人们互相串门的活动减少。(2)现代人随天气变化适应性变差,"猫冬"时间更长。(3)中老年人大多有慢性病,"猫冬"易损害身体健康。在沈阳冬季,人们室外活动的时间普遍低于世界卫生组织的要求,我们分析其原因:(1)邻里之间不熟悉;(2)天气寒冷,冬风凛冽,人们在室外待不住。

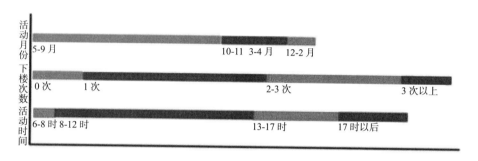

图4 冬季居民活动频率调查结果

2.2 温度限制

沈阳市的冬季寒冷漫长,冬季、春季伴有明显季风。调查数据表明:温度是影响一年中户外活动总人数变化(图5)的主导因素。受限月份可分为两个时期:绝对寒冷期、冷暖过渡期。

(1)绝对寒冷期:时间为每年的12月、1月、2月,冬季温度最低的3个月,尽管日照和风速两个因素较好,但户外活动人数极少,活动空间及设施利用率几乎为零,我们把这个时段称为"绝对寒冷期"。这个时期和严格意义上的猫冬期是一致的。

(2)冷暖过渡期:绝对寒冷期与适宜活动期之间存在温度过渡段,每年出现两次,一共有3个月,有一些居民进行户外活动。时间为每年10月、11月、3月。特点是在日照和风速两个因素较好的情况下存在着大量户外活动需求,但是居民户外活动方式受到一定限制,设施利用率很低。

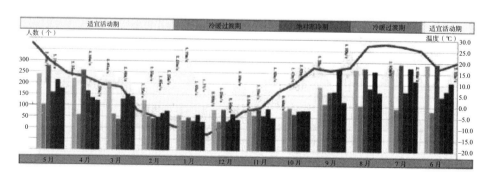

图5 全年小区活动总人数变化

2.3 居民类型受限

在一年的观察中,我们把居住小区居民按年龄分为三种类型:老人(55周岁以上)、中青年(18～55周岁)、儿童(18周岁以下)。这三类人群的活动规律存在显著差异(图6)。老人们:闲不住,不远走、不花钱。中青年:不得闲、不受限、主观强。儿童:喜动不喜静,环境影响大,时刻需陪伴。

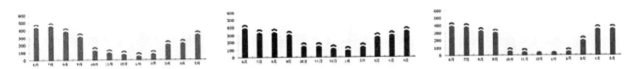

图6 老人、中青年、孩童户外活动人数变化

小区满足了老人诸多需求,包括出行距离、消费水平等使他们的性格得以释放,老人成为冬季居住小区里活动人群的主体。中青年人们活动频率最低,是由于工作忙有较强的主观选择,行动能力好等原因,儿童是最渴望和喜欢进行户外活动的群体(图7)。老年人的出行不会因为气温降低而明显减少。但是,老人抵抗凛冽寒风的能力较差即在低温大风的情况下,出门的概率大大降低。中青年的活动人数始终很少,但是,进入夏季有明显的增多,而且随着儿童人数的变化而变化。很多女性家长会陪伴儿童在园区内进行活动。由于儿童抵抗能力较弱,所以受到温度、风速、光照等自然因素影响较大,加之家长的主观因素,因此他们的活动也是最受限制的。在一年中,儿童的整体人数波动很大,夏季和冬季呈现两个极端。

人群	活动频率	人数波动	制约因素
老人(55周岁以上)	持续很大	小	风
中青年(18-55周岁)	持续很小	很小	时间、儿童
儿童(18周岁以下)	冬季大、夏季小	很大	温度、光照、风

图7 三类人群户外活动变化

2.4 寒季住区室外设施利用受限

根据调研数据,设施利用率极低的时段为10月至第二年3月,共约6个月的时间。即绝对寒冷期和冷暖过渡期。如图8所示:a,b,c类设施利用较不好d,e,f类空间利用较好。

73%的家长表示寒季孩子大多在客厅活动,偶尔会进行户外活动,只作短暂玩耍(图9)。20%的家长选择每周带孩子去专业的儿童活动场所(图10)。

冬季,气温较低,缺乏活力,但人们对光照的渴望强烈,集聚活动更加明显。居民集聚活动便于居民互动交流,增进邻里关系。但50%的居民表示,温度低、设施都在建筑阴影里、没有可以适合闲坐的空间成为冬季小区不适合进行户外活动的主要原因。大部分居民冬季利用的设施为健身器材和木质的座椅,43%的居民认为设施不充足,分布不合理。所以,设施完备且集中、维护及时,阳光充足,不受其他人为因素影响的大开敞空间是最受冬季居民青睐的。

图 8　各类设施现状

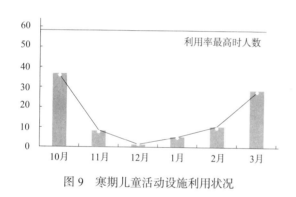

图 9　寒期儿童活动设施利用状况

图 10　儿童室内活动场所

3　改善住区居民户外运动受限

3.1　大尺度口袋空间营造：

掩蔽物、建筑物能在相当于其高度 4～10 倍距离范围降低 30% 的风速。因此，在寒冷地区北侧

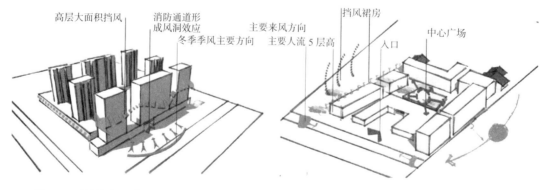

图 11　万科消防通道形成风洞效应　　　　　图 12　魁北克分析图

较长风屏蔽建筑可以营造能避风且有阳光的区域，一年中可以使用很久。在所调研的万科小区的入口广场的冬季，北侧的楼在一楼部分架空，有大的开口，冬季产生很大的风速（图11），使此地不宜长时间停留和聚集。而在一个加拿大魁北克市的住区，一栋5层楼长度的多功能风屏蔽建筑，为居民区阻挡了来自北、东北及西北的寒风，通过试验，多数该镇的居民住宅都能从风屏蔽中受益（图12）。寒地的住宅区可以尝试类似的设计手法，营造大尺度的口袋空间，但是需要注意的是，在我国民用建筑设计规范中，明确规定要设置消防通道，这也导致风屏蔽的措施操作性较差。

3.2 小尺度口袋广场设置

由于大面积风屏蔽的可操作性很差，我们试图去解决点状的小围合空间。口袋广场是一个很好的选择，其规模不大，可容纳十几人至数十人。在6个小区里，闲坐的空间普遍是"四柱一棚"型的座廊或座亭。在冬季，这种类型的闲坐空间由于不能有效遮挡寒风利用率并不高。在东亚小区，一个地下停车库的人行入口人气超高，每天上午都有老人在这里打牌而且观看的人也很多（图13）。通过观察和对比发现4个可以利用在寒地住区小尺度口袋空间布置方面的优点：(1)布置在可以被太阳光长时间照射的地方，保持温度。(2)材质可以选择透明材料，完全透光。(3)东、西、北三面围合，有效屏蔽北风。(4)开口处保持2m以上见方，可以容纳一桌四椅。

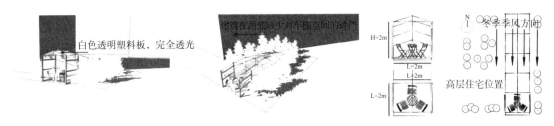

图13　东北亚车棚优点分析

3.3 合理规划"戏雪区"

北方人对于"雪"有着独特的喜爱，而戏雪文化更是由来已久。在冬季冰雪运动最受年轻人和儿童的欢迎。万科新里程是我们调研的几个小区中戏雪文化体现最充分的小区（图14），小区内的水系在冬季被改造为戏雪空间，雪后保留了水系内松散的积雪供居民嬉戏。这种处理方法使得水系空间在冬夏两季都能够得到充分利用。在对家长的访谈中40%家长表示会经常带孩子戏雪。其中16%的家长表示等孩子大些也会开展冰雪运动。因此在寒地住区户外空间规划中，应该有意识地设置"戏雪区"。

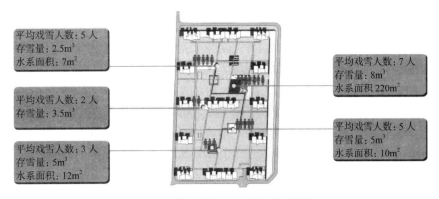

图14　万科戏雪场地分布及利用情况

4 总结

对于改善寒地住区居民寒季户外活动受限的情况,进行数据化的分析、合理化的研究是现实的需要,也是寒地住区未来发展的需求。本文通过对实际案例的调查分析,针对户外活动老者与儿童户外活动受寒冷天气影响最为显著,大尺度草坪、广场、儿童游乐设施在冬季利用率低等问题,提出了寒地新城居住区利用风光定位技术,尝试规划大尺度口袋空间,合理提供小尺度的"口袋广场"、巧设"戏雪区"等改善策略。关注寒地城市寒冷气候的影响,提出适应气候的城市住区规划建设方法具有突出地域特征的应用价值;依靠科学的实验设备将主观感受进行客观数据量化,为设计与评价提供准确的科学依据对今后其他同类设计提供指导与参考。

The Improvement of the Situation that the Use of Outdoor Public Places Restricted by Residents in Cold Urban Residential District ——A Case Study of A New Residential District in Shenyang Hunnan New District

Zhang Dongxiao [1], Gao Zhihui [1], Liu Yuetong [1], Hu Shuai [2]

(1.School of Architecture and Urban Planning, Shenyang Jianzhu University; 2.Dalian Urban Planning & Design Institute)

Abstract: Living quality and happiness index of Urban residents is the focus of attention of the whole society. In the northern cold city, a long indoor life in winter will have a negative impact on the psychological and physical health of residents, resulting in the living's comfort decreased, loss of belonging and so on. This paper attempts to improve the urban public space setup in the cold urban residential area to meet the needs of residents and outdoor activities. The observation and statistics of six residential areas in Hunnan New District of Shenyang were conducted by means of tools such as wind measuring instrument and sunshine analysis software, questionnaire survey and interview. The influence of seasonal changes on the outdoor activities of residents was analyzed, Summed up the psychological feelings of different types of residents, in-depth exploration of the "Maodong" predicament approach. Studies have shown that the elderly and Children's outdoor activities are mostly affected by the cold weather. Utilization rate of large-scale lawn, square and children's recreational facilities in the winter is low. It is recommended to use the scenery positioning technology in the new residential area of the cold area to try to plan the large-scale pocket space and provide the small-scale "pocket square" with the strategy of "playing the snow area" to enhance the comfort of the residential public space .

Keywords: Urban residential, Cold area, Outdoor public space, Activities limited, Pocket space

参考文献

[1] 柯鑫. 寒地城市口袋公园人性化设计研究 [D]. 东北林业大学硕士论文，2011.

[2] 毛开宇. 适应气候变化的寒地城市设计思考 [J]. 湘潭大学自然科学学报，2005.

[3] 董智慧. 严寒地区城市居住区景观设计及开发的研究 [D]. 长春工业大学硕士论文，2012.

[4] 范慧婷. 北方寒地城市居住区外环境景观设计研究 [D]. 东北师范大学硕士论文，2008.

[5] 孙虎. 新疆严寒地区城市住宅外环境规划设计研究——以昌吉市为例 [D]. 西安建筑科技大学硕士论文，2013.

城市交界空间激活策略初探

袁成龙　鲍　莉

（东南大学建筑学院）

摘　要：在现代城市空间设计中，人们往往关注的是城市地块的主体功能空间和剩余边缘空间，以至于不同的功能地块或者功能地块与城市空间环境之间的相互关联性无法得到充分的考虑，从而造成二者在其交界处空间的失落。这种失落在城市化快速发展、城市人口压力不断增大的背景下，既扮演了加剧城市人居环境不断恶化的角色，同时又为城市高密度、紧凑式发展提供了巨大潜力。本文提出城市交界空间的概念，并对城市交界空间存在的问题以及研究的价值进行阐述，最后对提高城市人居环境质量，营造城市交界空间的活力的策略进行初步探究。

关键词：城市，人居环境，交界空间，策略

引言

20世纪90年代后，我国经济和社会进入新一轮的转型期，最主要的变化是向过剩经济的转型，使得生产型的空间结构向生产 – 消费的空间结构的转化。与此同时，要求代表着计划经济时期的均衡、封闭的空间结构，向开放的、流动的和多样化的空间结构发展。城市建设和发展方向逐渐由新城、新区建设逐渐转向对城市储量的开发挖潜。优化既有城市结构，提高城市居民日常生活的质量，寻找城市发展的新起点。[1]

1　城市交界空间现状及问题研究

1.1　城市交界空间概念

城市交界空间（图1）是指在城市中，一种功能区块与另一种功能区块或者一种功能区块与城市大环境受制于各自性质、形态、结构的不同以及权属范围等因素影响而形成的由二者相交的边界处向各自功能有效控制和使用的空间范围过渡的空间区域。如图1所示，为东南大学与成贤街和学府路交叉路口形成的城市交界空间。一侧为城市人行道路，另一侧为东南大学的停车场。

目前，城市交界空间作为对城市日常生活具有重要影响作用的一类空间，一方面，其重要性还未得到重视，以至于在城市设计和环境治理过程中，处于被忽视的状态；另一方面，城市交界空间作为城市中还未被开发的空间资源，具有很大潜力影响城市功能和空间结构的优化与发展。

1.2　城市交界空间的"失落"

源于《雅典宪章》的功能分区思想的现代城市设计，使得城市功能和空间结构失去联系性，城市

图 1　城市交界空间

界面连续性断裂。功能分区思想"事实上，这是一种对城市的分析方式——一个一个用途的分析——已经成为通用的规划策略。最后，把按类别对用途研究的结果集中到一块，'拼成一大块完整的图画'"。[2] 这种设计方法在简·雅各布斯看来等同于瞎子摸象，然后其把各自想象中的内容拼凑到一起，无法得出一幅大象的"完整图画"。对城市缺乏综合性的考虑，以"功能分区来取代空间秩序，缺乏对空间秩序的社会功能认识"，破坏了城市的历史环境和城市日常生活秩序，割裂了城市各种因素之间的有机联系，使得城市的连续性丧失。

功能理性主义城市设计造成的城市的割裂，使功能区块各自为政，缺乏相互支撑性，迫使其各自具有能够使各自功能正常运行的一套完整的配套系统。城市交界空间成为各个功能区块追求空间资源最大化的边界标志和保证各自业主利益最大化而具有排他性的工具。

与此同时，我国目前每个城市区块内的建设都普遍需要遵守退红线的规定，往往使得城市建筑边界脱离城市功能区块的边界。一方面，建筑失去了直接参与城市空间组织的机会。另一方面，城市区块中建筑功能单一，往往无法对区块充足利用而产生剩余的"无用"空间。斯坦福·安德森（Stanford Anderson）指出"到了 19 世纪，当建筑物在其系统中变得更实用，对功能的理解逐渐由外部移至合理组织内部空间，建筑从其环境中分离出来，向着自成一体的方向发展"，使得城市空间越来越成为建筑占据后的"缝隙"，而这些"缝隙"空间往往成为难以利用和缺乏设计的边角料空间，难以为人们提供具有良好感知质量的活动空间。

由于城市交界空间被利用的积极价值缺失，逐渐沦为城市中的"失落"空间。罗杰·特兰西克在《寻找失落空间》中指出，失落空间是令人不愉快，需要被设计师重新设计的反传统的空间，它对于城市空间环境以及使用者而言都没有益处，它没有可以界定的边界，而且不能以连贯的方式去连接城市各个景观要素。[3]

1.3　城市交界空间"失落"产生的问题

城市交界空间的"失落"，首先造成了城市具有封闭性的"孤岛"的现象。城市交界空间往往使得功能区块脱离城市整体环境结构，形成具有相对封闭性的独立区域。相对封闭的独立区域成为阻碍城市发展的"死疙瘩"，其内部功能单一而僵化，结构秩序自治造成城市肌理的混乱和城市空间的碎片化；与此同时，封闭性的结构也造成了城市空间、人力等资源的巨大浪费。

其次，城市交界空间往往使得城市空间结构巨大化，缺乏对人性化尺度的考虑。目前，城市交界空间的尺度往往等同于城市功能区块的尺度，是一种基于汽车和汽车交通的，脱离适应人类感官和潜能的非人性化的尺度。城市中巨大的建筑尺度，或者巨大的开敞空间都不利于高质量的城市人居环境要求。

最后，城市交界空间往往被当成是城市功能区块之间的区分的边界空间而成为不被重视的空间，所以在该区域的场所环境往往被简单化处理，不仅无法为城市居民营造良好的感知，反而成为城市空间环境中质量较差的区域。

2　基于城市日常生活的激活

诺伯格·舒尔茨在《场所精神：走向建筑现象学》中认为建筑和城市设计应当首先关注日常的"生活世界"。[4]胡塞尔指出生活世界是人们进行日常生活的世界。随着胡塞尔"生活世界"的提出，从20世纪，人类理性开始转向日常生活的世界，日常生活世界逐渐从背景世界中回归到人们的视野中。

对城市交界空间的营建旨在为城市居民的日常生活提供高质量的空间环境。德国哲学家马丁·海德格尔曾经说过："边界不是某种东西的停止，而是如同希腊人的认识，是某种东西在此出现。"美国著名的城市规划师凯文·林奇在《城市意象》中也将这种具有边界意义的空间列为构成城市活力的五要素之一。[5]一方面，在对城市交界空间的营建过程，完善和优化城市功能和空间结构，构建结构紧凑，整体感强的城市空间，保证城市居民生活活动的有序完整的展开。另一方面，通过对城市交界空间的营建，提高城市空间环境的质量，提供良好感知的空间细节，增强人们对城市的认同感和归属感。

3　策略一：丰富城市多样性，提高城市交界空间利用价值

3.1　构建城市半网络化结构

丰富城市功能地块的功能结构，有助于形成城市的"半网络化结构"。"半网络化结构"是有C·亚历山大在《城市并非树形》中提出的观点。亚历山大通过对比"自然城市"和"人造城市"得出城市结构可以分为"树形结构"和"半网络结构"的结论。"树形结构"的微单元需要通过上一层级的大单元才能与其他的微单元进行联系，这样的城市结构单一，缺乏可变性和灵活性。与"树形结构"不同的是，"半网络结构"则没有明确的单元性，其结构呈现为开放性的特点，从而使得微单元之间产生比较多的和相互交叉的可变性，是一种复杂而灵活的结构。

3.2　丰富城市多样性，促进对城市交界空间利用

城市是人们生活的聚居地，成千上万的人每时每刻都有着不同的需求，因此城市需要尽可能错综复杂并且可以相互支撑的多样性来满足人们多样化的需求。雅各布斯认为"多样性是城市的天性"。丰富城市多样性的功能需求，一方面，可以将大量的城市交界空间转化成城市中新增的建设量，满足多样化功能所需的物质空间。另一方面，改变交界空间自身功能性质，如社区公园，或者成为服务于各种功能的相关的附属空间，如街道、广场空间等。[6]打破城市交界空间的隔离性，使之在组织城市居民日常生活中发挥积极的作用。

3.3 增强多样混合性，均衡对交界空间的利用

城市多样性是城市多样混合的前提，多样性并不一定会带来城市空间的活力，还要对多样性在时间和空间上的合理组织，才对城市的活力营造具有重要作用。英国政府在1995年城市环境报告中指出："城市功能的混合有利于提高城市的紧凑度和多样性；降低城市交通的需要，特别是对于小汽车的依赖性；能够促进更为安全舒适和具有吸引力的城市中心区的形成；这些优势的综合将进一步带来城市的经济发展与社会进步，改善城市环境质量。"[7]

在时间意义上，通过合理组织功能与需求，使得城市中的每个时间段都有足够高的人群密度，这样才能促使城市产生足够多的活动。雅各布斯指出，在一些成功的城市街道中，人流必须是在不同的时间段里出现的。一种功能和另一种功能混合在一起的时候，如果只是在同一时间中把人群引向一些地方，对城市多样性也是无效的。在空间意义上，城市中的每种功能与城市中人的活动的关系也有很大不同，麦克马克根据这一现象建立了一种有关公共领域活跃度的"功能层级体系"[8]。根据这一理论，城市主要公共活动的区域或者街道界面上，应当混合与城市公共活动具有紧密关系的功能。

4 策略二：重组空间结构，系统性整合城市交界空间

4.1 大城市区块中的小街区塑造

小尺度街区是简·雅各布斯所认为构成城市多样性必需的四个条件之一，"大多数的街段必须要短，也就是说，人在街道上能够很容易拐弯"。对目前既有的大尺度城市功能区块向人性化空间尺度的小街区的再设计，一方面能够将城市交界空间的大尺度化小；另一方面，又可以增强其开放性，有效改变城市交界空间的隔离性问题。

4.2 融合城市交界空间的空间序列

在重组城市功能区块的人性化结构过程中，整合城市交界空间，使之成为城市中关键的空间形态要素参与到城市空间结构系统的组织中。凯文·林奇在其著作《城市意象》中，认为城市中的关键的空间形态要素分为五种类型：路径、边界、区域、节点和标志物。五种城市形态要素彼此相互联系，空间中的节点构成区域，区域被边界限定，并且被路径所渗透，而标志物则有规律地散布其间。城市交界空间只有转化为关键的空间形态要素，并且与其他要素共同构成城市空间形态时，才能产生一个令人满意的城市空间"意象"。

4.3 密度再开发，构建人性化空间形态

对既有城市功能区块进行适宜的密度再开发，以完善和构建人性化的城市空间形态。密度的再开发一方面包括通过增加建设量，缓解整个城市人口增加的压力，同时增加特定的空间的区域性人口密度。雅各布斯在研究城市活力的时候，认为具有较高的人群密度是必需条件之一。另一方面，通过城市密度的再开发，增大建筑面积的覆盖率，加强建筑结构的紧密度，缩小建筑横向间距，构建具有人性化尺度的空间形态。[9]正如西蒙兹（J. O. Simonds）阐述："现代城市规划中有一种错误的认识，认为建

筑物之间的空间愈大、后退红线愈多愈好，但在事实上，人们并不太喜欢太多的空地，而是希望有与他们的尺度相宜，可以产生共鸣的空间"（图2）。[10]

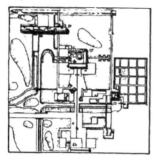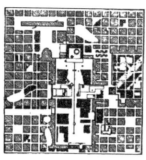

图2　昌迪加尔城市中心区"再都市化"改造方案

5　策略三：营造场所品质，改善城市交界空间质量

5.1　综合多种感知体验，建设高质量物质空间

城市居民在日常生活中无时无刻不在通过自身的感知系统，感知周边物质性元素组成的城市空间环境，然后上升到对空间品质的好与坏的认知判断。凯文·林奇提出"营造区域感"，认为人们在城市空间中的感觉质量是评定一个场所品质的重要指标。[11]感知质量是包括视觉、听觉、嗅觉-味觉、触觉和方位感的综合的良好感受。良好的感知质量能够给予人即时的快乐和生动的直觉的愉悦感，是营造良好城市人居环境的重要目标。[12]

5.2　延续历史痕迹，塑造城市交界空间时间层次

尊重并结合既有城市功能区块内的历史印记，塑造城市交界空间的时间层次，是能够赋予城市空间多样性的有效手段，并且在历史基础上延续而来的城市更新设计总是能够强化城市的地域感和场所感。营造城市交界空间的场所的时间层次，首先，结合可能的历史遗迹的保护措施，设计和组织城市的公共空间，如图3所示；其次，通过延续或者对比的方式，展现既有的城市建筑和空间的时间性信息，可以是代表某一个时代风格的建筑，也可以是某一个时代的空间尺度等。[13]最后，城市空间环境中的临时性元素有效维护城市既有面貌的同时，赋予空间新的感知机会和活力，增加城市空间环境的时间层次的厚度。[14]

5.3　激发人行为与空间互动，营造人文性空间

城市人文性的居住环境营造，除了历史、文化等信息的保留与传达，更重要的是激发人们在城市空间中的各种日常性的活动行为。通过对城市交界空间的营建，创造不同的并且复杂的城市生活，使得人们娱乐休闲行为与必要的社交活动与步行交通空间相融合，并且为人们提供感知其他人活动，以及随时参与到城市活动中的可能性。[15]

首先，通过对城市交界空间的柔性化处理，形成建筑室内空间与室外空间、私密空间与公共空间

的过渡，增加人们可以感知城市居民活动的机会[16]；其次，创造城市交界空间处的"边界效应"，为人们在城市空间中的停留提供机会；最后，利用城市交界空间营建，形成适合和鼓励人们自我表现的广场空间。E·瑞尔夫认为，场所是从城市日常生活经验中提炼出来的意义的本质中心。通过意义的渗透，个体、群体或者社会把"空间"变成"场所"（图4）。

图3　爱丁堡玻璃屋改造方案　　　　　　　　图4　城市中人与空间的互动

6　结语

通过对城市交界空间的研究表明，首先，人们对城市交界空间概念还缺乏必要的认识和足够的重视，使之成为城市中的"失落"空间；其次，重视对城市交界空间的设计，能有效塑造高品质的城市日常生活空间，激发城市的活力；最后，城市交界空间对城市功能和结构的优化和再设计具有重要作用，为城市的再次发展提供重要的空间资源。

Study on the Activating Strategy of Interface Space between Urban Quarters

Yuan Chenglong, Bao Li

（School of Architecture, Southeast University）

Abstract: In modern urban space design, people always focus on the main function of the city site and the residual space, so that the connection between different functions or the connection between the site and the city environment is not fully considered, causing a gap between them. With the acceleration of urbanization and the growth of population pressure, this gap, on one hand, deteriorates living environment, while on the other hand, provides huge potential for a high density development. This issue raises the concept of border space, elaborates the problem of it and the value in its research, and does some preliminary study of the strategy to improve living environment and create active city border space.

Keywords: Urban quarter, Human habitat, Interface space between urban quarters, Strategy

参考文献

[1] 陈修颖. 区域空间结构重组——理论与实证研究 [M]. 江苏：东南大学出版社，2005.
[2] （美）简·雅各布斯. 美国大城市的死与生 [M]. 金衡山译. 江苏：译林出版社，2005.
[3] （美）罗杰·特兰西克. 寻找失落空间——城市设计的理论 [M]. 朱子瑜等译. 北京：中国建筑工业出版社，2008.
[4] （挪）诺伯格·舒尔茨. 场所精神：走向建筑现象学 [M]. 施植明译. 湖北：华中科技大学出版社，2010.
[5] （美）凯文·林奇. 城市意象 [M]. 方益萍等译. 北京：华夏出版社，2001.
[6] 黄晶，贾新锋. 重塑街道——中心城区街道边缘的碎片化整合 [M]. 北京：中国建筑工业出版社，2014.
[7] 陈晓虹. 日常生活视角下旧城复兴设计策略研究 [D]. 华南理工大学博士学位论文，2014.
[8] 袁野. 城市住区的边界问题研究——以北京为例 [D]. 清华大学博士学位论文，2010.
[9] Allan B Jacobs. Looking at Cities[M]. Cambridge：Harvard University Press，1985.
[10] 方知果. 基于近人空间尺度适宜性的城市设计研究 [D]. 天津大学博士学位论文，2013.
[11] 董禹. 凯文·林奇人文主义城市设计思想研究 [D]. 哈尔滨工业大学博士学位论文，2008.
[12] （日）大野隆造，小林美纪. 人的城市——安全与舒适的环境设计 [M]. 余漾，尹庆译. 北京：中国建筑工业出版社，2015，3.
[13] 何依. 四维城市——城市历史环境研究理论、方法和实践 [M]. 北京：中国建筑工业出版社，2016.
[14] 韩西丽，斯约斯特洛姆. 城市感知 城市场所中隐藏的维度 [M]. 北京：中国建筑工业出版社，2015.
[15] （丹麦）扬·盖尔. 交往与空间 [M]. 何人可译. 北京：中国建筑工业出版社，2002.
[16] （丹麦）扬·盖尔. 人性化的城市 [M]. 欧阳文，徐哲文译. 北京：中国建筑工业出版社，2010.

城乡规划与人居空间设计
Urban-Rural Planning and Human Habitat Design

洮南市城市收缩的表现特征及精明成长策略研究

何邕健　杨琳

（天津大学建筑学院）

摘　要：笔者基于吉林省洮南市城乡总体规划实践的基础上，利用洮南市 2000～2015 年的人口、经济、空间等方面统计数据，首先确定洮南市为收缩城市，其次运用趋势分析法对洮南城市收缩的时间和空间表现特征进行总结：时间上来看，2000～2015 年间人口萎缩程度较小；空间上来看，中心城区的萎缩程度大于市域；人口密度最大的两个地区是人口流失最严重的地区，同时也是老龄化最严重的地区。进一步通过研究逐年的人口变动趋势，发现在市域范围内，收缩和增长的区域存在交替的过程；15 年来人口收缩的乡镇数量不断增多且强度逐渐增大；市域北部有 5 个乡镇一直处于人口流失状态。全球经济萎靡、区域非均衡发展等外部影响因素和地方工业化刚起步、有增长但动力不足等内部影响因素共同构成了洮南市收缩的驱动力。通过研究美国和德国两种不同的应对收缩方式，提出"滴入式规划"的行动模式，即从大规划到小规划的蜕变，技术层面要变加法规划为减法规划，实施与管理方面要转硬性控制为软性引导等策略，期望对新常态下中国收缩城市的发展和规划有所启示。

关键词：收缩城市，洮南市，表现特征，规划策略

1　引言

国内的多数关于收缩城市的论文已指出中国 180 个城市的人口密度呈现下降趋势[1]，但收缩特征与西方国家有所不同：(1) 存在收缩现象，但收缩程度远没有西方国家大；(2) 这些收缩城市还未经历结构性的经济危机。但中国确实面对着人口流失与城市扩张并存的城市发展悖论[2]，且不同城市由于不同的发展历程和背景其收缩的动因机制不尽相同，往往都是多因素综合作用的结果，而收缩所表现出的特征与结果又很有可能引发二次收缩。因此，有必要对收缩城市个案进行量化分析研究，在总结共性与个性收缩表现的基础上，提出应对城市收缩的规划策略。

国外学者在收缩城市理论和实践案例方面的研究已经相对成熟；国内目前对城市收缩的研究文献非常有限，以案例分析和对国外相关研究的介绍为主[3-5]；在收缩城市的量化分析研究方面，以龙瀛为代表的北京城市实验室选取乡镇和街道办事处两个尺度的人口数据分析中国 654 个县级及以上的城市人口变化[6]；杨东峰等利用我国五普、六普人口资料和收缩悖论进行现象观察和类型学描述，并就我国城市收缩悖论现象给出初步理论解释[7]；刘合林将量化描述收缩城市的指标归纳为社会经济类指标，地理空间类指标及地理景观类指标，并对各类指标提出的理论逻辑及具体计算方法作了详细阐述。[8]但极少关于收缩城市个案的量化分析研究，基于此笔者尝试以洮南市为例选取该市的人口、产业等社会经济类指标，分析总结其收缩表现特征，进而提出适应性的规划策略。

2　收缩的表现特征

研究对象洮南市隶属于吉林省白城市，位于吉林省西北端，白城市西南部，东邻大安市，南接通

榆县，西与内蒙古自治区突泉县为邻，北与内蒙古自治区科尔沁右翼前旗相连，东北和白城市洮北区接壤。研究范围为洮南市域，包括 8 个街道办事处，6 个镇和 10 个乡，总面积 5102.8km²，2015 年末总人口为 421393 人，其中中心城区人口为 143318 人。研究数据来源于 2000～2015 年的人口和社会经济统计指标、《洮南统计年鉴》和《吉林省统计年鉴》及有关部门提供的社会经济数据。研究发现，洮南市 2000～2015 年 15 年间人口总量呈现波动下降趋势，且市域总人口减少了 2.4%，中心城区总人口减少了 7.1%，其萎缩程度大于市域。因此，确定洮南市为收缩城市。

2.1 人口收缩的时间表现

2.1.1 人口增长率变化

2.1.1.1 人口出生率、死亡率和自然增长率

洮南市 2002～2015 年出生率都在 0.6%～1% 之间，2015 年更达到了 15 年来的最低值 0.63%，仅为中国 2015 年平均人口出生率 1.27% 的一半。从人口的自然增长率来看，洮南市的人口自然增长呈现波动下降的趋势。在 2001～2015 年期间，几乎每一二年人口自然增长就表现出不断的"增长 - 下降 - 再增长 - 再下降"的规律。如果用曲线拟合，可以发现总体上自然增长率呈现出下降的趋势。极低的人口出生率使洮南市面临人口红利提前结束的困境，亦成为经济活力下降与城市收缩的原因之一。

2.1.1.2 人口机械增长率

根据公安局统计年报，2007 年以来，洮南市的人口机械增长一直是负值且稳定在 -1‰～0‰ 之间。因此，洮南市在区域中实际上属于人口流出区。在人口的流向上，通过比对 2007 年以来的数据可以发现（图 1），每年总流出人口介于 6000～8000 人之间，其中，以县（市）内流动人口比重最高，其次为省外流动。人口的流失实际上反映了洮南市经济增长乏力，而其又会加速人口尤其是青壮年、高素质人才的流失，从而很可能引发城市的二次收缩。

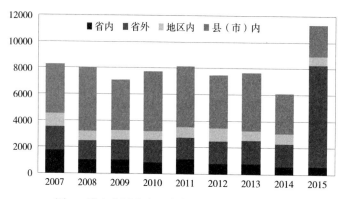

图 1　洮南市迁出人口去向（2007～2015 年）

资料来源：洮南市公安局统计数据（2007～2015 年）。

2.1.2 人口结构变化

2014 年全市共有 432415 人，各年龄段人口如表 1 所示。确定一个社会的人口是否进入老年型人口类型，通常有四个指标可供参考：(1) 0～14 岁人口占总人口比例小于 30%；(2) 65 岁及以上人口占总人口比例大 7%；(3) 老少比大于 30%；(4) 年龄中位数在 30 岁以上。根据中国的人口老龄标准（60 岁），洮南市已经全面进入人口老龄化阶段。人口老龄化亦意味着洮南市人口红利的逐渐消失，适龄劳动力供给的减少，将制约着洮南的经济增长，引发经济活力和城市活力的下降。

洮南市人口年龄结构（2014年）				表1
年龄段	18岁以下	18～35岁	35～60岁	60岁以上
人数（人）	64438	97896	199360	71811
比例（%）	14.90	22.64	46.10	16.61

资料来源：洮南市公安局统计数据（2014年）。

2.2 人口萎缩的空间分布

从图2和图3对比可以看出，洮南市人口收缩呈现较为明显的空间分布特征，即全市两个人口集聚区中心城区和万宝镇也是人口流失最显著的地区；市域北部是人口主要流失地。在人口老龄化的空间分布上来看（图4），市域已全面步入老龄化。且全市人口密度最高的城区和万宝镇，也是老龄化最严重的区域。也就是说随着中心城区和万宝镇青壮年人口的外流，居留在原居住地的老龄人口比重也越来越高。

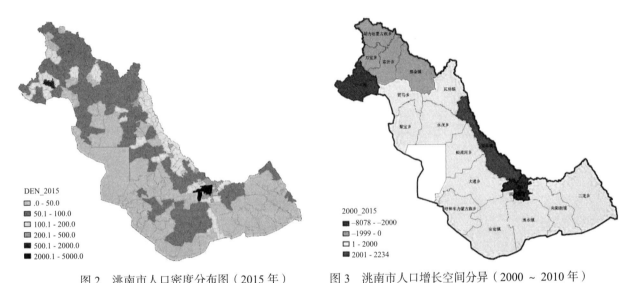

图2 洮南市人口密度分布图（2015年）　　图3 洮南市人口增长空间分异（2000～2010年）

资料来源：作者根据洮南市统计年鉴（2000～2015年）绘制

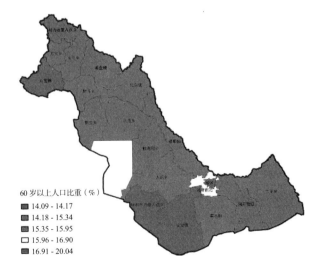

图4 洮南市60岁以上人口分布（2015年）

资料来源：作者根据洮南市公安局统计数据（2014～2015年）绘制。

2.3 建设用地和设施的过度供给

2.3.1 建设用地

根据国家下发的洮南市 2014 年土地调查成果，计算得到人均城市建设用地面积为 164.9m²，人均镇建设用地为 438.5m²，人均村庄建设用地面积达 553m²，均大大超出国家相关标准。同时从图 2 和图 5 对比可以看出，人口密度相对越低的区域，其人均村庄建设用地越大，土地资源相对更浪费。

2015 年洮南市中心城区现状人口 13.4 万，城市建设用地 26.55km²，人均城市建设用地 198.13m²/人，远远超过国家标准 115m²/ 人（城市用地分类与规划建设用地标准 2012 版）。其中，人均居住用地面积达到 111.89m²/ 人，远远高于国家标准。进一步调研发现，位于中心城区的洮南工业园区就业密度为 13 人 /hm²，远远低于发展成熟的工业园区就业密度（如无锡工业园区为 82 人 /hm²）。这表明中心城区的土地利用效率较低，空间资源有待进一步挖掘。

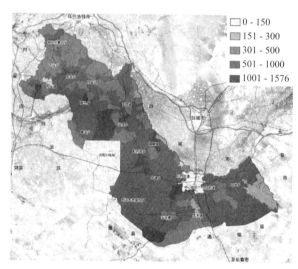

图 5　洮南市人均村庄建设用地空间差异（2014 年）
资料来源：作者根据洮南市公安局统计数据（2014～2015 年）绘制。

2.3.2 设施

在公共管理与公共服务设施方面，洮南市教育设施呈现较为严重的过度供给现象，因此着重分析教育设施的过度供给程度。以国家规定的中小学教师配比（资料来源：国务院办公厅关于制定中小学教职工编制标准的意见 2001-10-11）作为参照，可以发现，除安定镇由于小初并校原因导致教师资源紧张外，其他所有乡镇皆表现出较为严重的教师资源浪费现象。中心城区在职业教育方面缺乏生源，表现出比较浪费的现象。

3　动因与机制

通过对洮南市收缩表现特征的分析，总结出洮南市还远未达到西方国家收缩城市的标准，但确实存在收缩现象。经济增长乏力往往是城市人口收缩和活力下降的本源动力，因此以下着重对洮南市的经济与产业进行分析，总结归纳洮南市城市收缩的驱动因素。

3.1　外部原因

全球经济复苏动力的匮乏，国际国内需求的低迷，既抑制了中国乃至全球的出口，又对大宗商品价格形成压力。降低的供给需求对洮南的对外贸易产生了打击，进而制约着洮南的经济增长和产业振兴，从而引发人口的流出和城市的收缩。

3.2 内部原因

3.2.1 第一产业效率不高

虽然 2000~2014 年以来，洮南市越来越多的劳动力从第一产业转移至第二、三产业，但第一产业就业占比仍较高（2014 年为 60%）。但农民的可支配收入不高。全市人均耕地面积 11.8 亩，是吉林省平均水平的 3 倍多，而农民人均收入 9800 元（2014 年末），低于全省平均水平（10780 元）近 10 个百分点，农业生产效率明显不高。

3.2.2 第二产业体系有待完善

工业生产总值占 GDP 比重由 2008 年的 30.2% 增长到 2014 年的 43.2%，工业发展对经济增长的贡献率逐步增强，工业经济不断壮大。但由于农业占经济比重仍较高，而服务业比重相对较低，洮南市工业化发展处于初期向中期转型阶段。且现有产业主要发展产业链的核心环节，上下游产业配套不足，产业间的关联度仍十分薄弱，循环产业链发展待完善。且形成的五大产业辐射带动能力不强，占工业产值比重较大的产业主要分布在位于中心城区的洮南市工业园区，城乡二元化发展格局较为显著。因此经济增长的全域性动力不足，难以吸纳就业人口，从而造成人口的流出。

3.2.3 第三产业发展缓慢

从第三产业占 GDP 比重的贡献程度看，从 2005 年 32.4% 至 2014 年的 35.8% 仅增长 3.4%，说明第三产业发展较缓慢，对经济增加的带动作用略显不足。且占第三产业比重较大的多为交通仓储、批发零售等基础性物流产业，而新兴服务产业如软件和信息技术服务业、金融业则见效甚微，对高端技术人才的吸引力有限，从而引发青壮年人口的流出。

4 精明收缩策略初探

在应对收缩方面，首先我们应该认识到城市发展不是线性的，是螺旋形上升，动态变化的，我们要接受和适应收缩。其次，在收缩的规划策略方面，李翔等总结以美国为代表的大部分发达国家延续利用传统的增长主义价值范式应对收缩，却导致收缩效应的强化；而德国率先转变收缩价值观——采用关注城市存量空间的精简主义价值取向,应对收缩取得良好效果。[9] 因此，以德国的精简主义为范本，对于洮南的城市收缩提出"滴入式规划"的行动模式,主要分为大规划到小规划、加法规划到减法规划、从硬性控制到软性引导三个方面。

4.1 从大规划到小规划

在总体规划层面，可以总体规划的专题研究为基础，延伸为多方面多层次的横向规划，如经济与产业、道路与交通、公共管理与公共服务、综合管廊、生态保护等。规划专业人员作为统筹梳理者，应起到中介人作用，密切同专题相关部门管理人员协同配合，制订更深入、精准的发展规划。同时在控制性详细规划层面，可以扩展为城市-社区-建筑的纵向规划体系，延伸控规的引导和控制深度，由大及小的改善城市环境，引导城市活力重塑。

4.2 从加法规划到减法规划

空间方面，建立各类用地和设施集约度评价体系，划分可收缩合并类、维持现状类和可扩张增质类等几个方面，使产业、公共设施、基础设施发挥最大的集聚效应，如使公共设施适度向中心城区和重点镇集中，一般镇和乡采取置换为城市绿地、绿楔的收缩策略。政策方面，减少棕地和废弃地置换流程及手续，给予更多的优惠福利政策，推动空间资源的高效率利用。

4.3 从硬性控制到软性引导

建立规划师-政府-民间组织-民众的循环反馈机制，减少自上而下的决策效应，增加自下而上的反馈效应。通过互联网交互平台等新技术手段的运用，了解居民对于城市生活、宜居生态的需求（如票选出市民觉得最好的和最差的城市空间，市民觉得最需要提升的服务和设施），真正做到精准规划，精明增长，在提高土地利用效率的基础上控制城市扩张，保护生态环境，促进城乡协调发展，提高人们生活质量，探索出一条适合我国国情的收缩城市发展之路。

Research on Performance Characteristics and Smart Development Strategy of Shrinking Cities
——Taonan City as An example

He Yongjian, Yang Lin

(School of Architecture, Tianjin University)

Abstract: Based on the practice of overall planning of Taonan City in Jilin Province, with statistics data from 2000 to 2015 on population, economy, space and so on, the article first identified Taonan City as a shrinking city.Then using trend analysis method for Taonan City shrinkage research from time and space aspects, it is concluded that first, on time aspect, there exists a small decline between 2000 and 2015 population.Second, on space aspect, relative to the centre urban part, the rural and suburban contraction are more intense.The two regions with biggest population density are just the most serious areas of both population loss and aging growth. Through further research of population change trend year by year, it is found that process of contraction and growth both exist in the whole city; In the past 15 years the number of shrinking villages and towns has been growing gradually, among which five on the northern areas have always been a loss state. Based on the summary of characteristics research, shrinkage of Taonan City is driven by external influence such as global economic malaise and regional imbalance development and internal factors such as low industrialization and underpower of growth. By studying two different ways for coping with shrinkage in the United States and Germany, "trickle-down planning" mode is put forward, that is, a transformation from big to small planning. On technology aspect, it is necessary to change addition planning to subtraction one.

Moreover, on implementation and management way, authorities should turn rigid control to soft guiding strategy. The article expects to give some enlightenment to development and planning of Chinese shrinking cities.

Keywords: Shrinking cities, Taonan city, Performance characteristics, Planning strategy

参考文献

[1] 毛其智，龙瀛，吴康．中国人口密度时空演变与城镇化空间格局初探——从2000年到2010年[J]．城市规划，2015，2：38-43．

[2] 杨东峰．人口流失与空间扩张-——中国快速城市化进程的城市收缩悖论[J]．现代城市研究，2015，9：22-24．

[3] 杨东峰，殷成志．如何拯救收缩的城市：英国老工业城市转型经验及启示[J]．国际城市规划，2013，6：50-56．

[4] 龙瀛，吴康，王江浩．中国收缩城市及其研究框架[J]．现代城市研究，2015，9：14-19．

[5] 周恺，钱芳芳．收缩城市：逆增长情景下的城市发展路径研究进展[J]．现代城市研究，2015，9：2-13．

[6] 吴康，龙瀛．京津冀与长江三角洲的局部收缩格局类型与影响因素识别[J]．现代城市研究，2015，9：26-35

[7] 杨东峰．人口流失与空间扩张——中国快速城市化进程的城市收缩悖论[J]．现代城市研究，2015，9：20-22．

[8] 刘合林．收缩城市量化计算方法进展[J]．现代城市研究，2016，2：17-22．

[9] 李翔，陈可石，郭新．增长主义价值观转变背景下的收缩城市复兴策略比较——以美国与德国为例[J]．国际城市规划，2015，2：81-86．

[10] Wiechmann T. Errors Expected ——Aligning Urban Strategy with Demographic Uncertainty in Shrinking Cities[J]. International Planning Studies, 2008, 13（4）: 431-446.

[11] Oswalt P. Shrinking Cities. Vol. 1: International Research[M]. Ostfildern: Hatje Crantz, 2005.

城乡关系重构背景下村落人居环境提升策略研究：
以柳州环江村为例

张恺 李乘 沈杰

（浙江大学建筑工程学院）

摘　要：随着中国城镇化建设的推进，广泛的城乡社会演变与空间重构进程对变迁中的村落人居环境产生了剧烈的影响与挑战。本文以柳州市城乡重构进程中的环江村村落改造建设为主要研究对象，从柳州市域、城中区环江村村落群、雷村屯微观案例三个环境层次的空间演变脉络入手，在人居环境学和城乡空间规划的视角下对环江村自然环境、建筑空间、产业经济和乡土文化的变迁进行调查研究，通过环江村雷村屯片区风貌改造案例的实践总结提出生态为本、内部激活、平衡调控的人居环境更新理念。然后依托宏观层面上动态反馈的策略体系，尝试以自然和乡土特质的修复激活与网络化支撑系统的构建等更新营造方法来推动村落人居环境的造血提质，为存在城乡差距扩大现象的众多西部发展不平衡地区针对性地提供城乡统筹发展体系的理论补充及策略创新。

关键词：城乡重构，乡村人居环境，空间重构，更新理念，动态反馈策略

1　引言

城市发展是一个由平衡到不平衡，再从不平衡到平衡的连续不断的过程，人类生活的发展使得各自由局部之间始终处于不完全均衡状态。在中国城镇化高速发展时期中，投资和产业的集中使城市已成为社会快速发展的空间载体，同时伴随的是城市空间的大幅扩张现象。另外，当今社会信息流动速度加快，城乡交流变得愈加容易，城市经济社会的巨大影响力和虹吸效应正在促使乡村特征发生着转变。政府、社会资本及村民的建造活动混杂，推动着乡村人居环境的变迁与重构，乡镇形态也在城市趋同化进程中抗争矛盾着。[1, 2]

从社会经济学的角度分析，中国城镇化的突出特征有政府主导、大范围规划、整体推动、空间上有明显的跳跃性、民间社会尚不具备完善的自发推进城镇化的条件等。[3] 这种源于中国特殊条件的城镇化模式特征在新一轮的乡村开发建设中获得了延续，其中政府主导的整体、大范围推动模式在乡村发展进程中表现出了明显的跳跃性。这种自上而下开发模式的跳跃性常常伴随着在人文、景观、建筑风貌及一系列人居环境支撑系统上的发展滞后现象，引发对乡村空间和社会的冲击与断层。因此，深入研究在这种广泛的城乡关系重构现象下的乡村演变，探索适宜、高效、可持续的人居环境更新开发策略，对城镇化新阶段中村落的健康发展有着重要的促进作用和指导意义。

2　柳州城乡空间重构脉络与问题分析

2.1　柳州市域空间发展分析

柳州市城镇化率由 2010 年的 55.1% 提升到 2015 年的 62.11%，市区建成区面积由 135.06km² 里扩

增至 183.92km², 增长率高达 36.2%。2015 年末全柳州市常住人口为 392.27 万人, 与 2010 年同期相比增长 4.36%, 年均增长 0.86%[4], 可以看到 2010～2015 年间柳州城市建成区面积增长速度远快于同期城市人口增长速度。这些数据显示出柳州城区空间的大幅扩张和对外来人口的巨大引力, 使众多边缘村落被纳入中心城区空间体系。

"从整个城市大的形态结构的合理性来看, 向东北官塘方向发展, 中间的莲花山景区, 作为城市的'绿肺', 综合环境条件相对占优。"[5] 在柳州"十三五"规划及近期公布的柳州市近期建设规划（2016～2020）提出了"一江两岸、一主三新、多点支撑"的城市发展格局, 其中"一主"代表了市中心城区（主城区）, "三新"分别为柳东新区、柳江新区和北部生态新区。[6] 如图1所示, 综合比较两组城市规划范围呈现出的柳州市域空间发展脉络, 可看到柳州中心城区向东北方向柳东汽车工业新城的空间发展轴线在新时期得到了进一步的强化和发展。

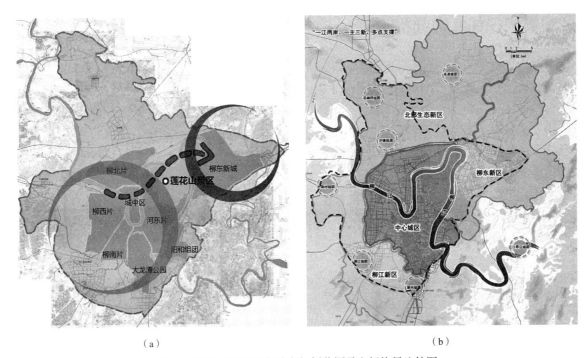

图1 柳州市不同时期城市规划范围及空间格局比较图
(a) 2010 年总体规划的柳州市空间结构；(b) 2016 年柳州近期建设规划空间发展格局
资料来源：(a) 柳州市城市规划局．柳州市城市总体规划（2010～2020）, 2010；(b) 柳州市城市规划局．柳州市近期建设规划（2016～2020）, 2016。

2.2 莲花山片区环江村落群的空间重构与普遍问题

莲花山片区作为柳州"十三五"规划中的休闲旅游服务的示范样板, 与柳东汽车城、主城区组建柳州的"一心两城", "一心"即莲花山片区规划定位为柳州未来的"都市绿心"部分, 与柳江共同组成柳州的生态基础。隶属于城中区静兰街道办的环江村落群由沿江 17 个大小村屯组成, 共 670 户, 3368 余人。2016 年初, 长 20km 的连接柳州市城中区与静兰街道办环江村的环江滨水大道建成通车, 使往返市区的通勤时间大幅缩短, 改变了过去村民不走旱路而选水路进出村的情况。并以此成为该片区融入城市发展的重要节点, 各村屯由相对孤立的边缘区位真正意义上并入了柳州城区体系, 演变为夹在主城区与柳东新城间的"城中村"部分

综合多层级的空间分析和现场实地调研, 环江村在城乡重构过程中主要面临着以下四个方面的问题：(1) 生态破坏的威胁。一方面城市建设活动不可避免地对脆弱的柳江滨水生态和内部山林生态产生了影响, 另一方面村民对生态保护缺乏概念, 许多回乡人员的无序建设活动在近一段时间内失控,

对山林、河岸植被及村落内部水塘等生态环境产生了负面作用。（2）内部通达性差与基础设施缺失。环江滨水大道的建成提升了村屯的可达性，但村屯内部道路多是水泥及砂石路面，总体质量较差。出入村的渡船交通被道路交通替代后，现状渡口缺乏维护或被弃置，同时村屯内部未形成完善的公共交通系统，致使风景可观不可游。（3）村屯建设无序化和乡土特质碎片化。由于欠缺完善的乡村治理，建筑风格混乱，且整体质量较差。原生乡土记忆与村庄特质不断碎片化，众多传统建筑未能留存，公共空间被弃置和撕裂，除个别重要活动场所很难再看到传统习俗和乡土生活方式。（4）经济产业单一化低端化。虽然城乡距离的缩短带来了一定的外出务工村民的回流，因建设征地而失去田地的村民开始转向农家乐等低端服务产业，但经济模式仍以耕作菜地、果林等小范围且未产业化的小农经济为主，同时村落风貌的破坏在一定程度上阻碍了生态旅游产业的发展，村民收入增长缓慢。从环境品质到产业经济的多重挑战构成了环江村在城乡重构进程中的尴尬境地。

2.3 雷村屯空间重构分析

雷村屯为环江村村委所在地，坐落于莲花山片区环江滨水大道中间点和环江村落体系的核心位置。村庄布局颇有特色，池塘、广场及渡口码头、环江小学等特色元素与182户村民农宅以一种自发生长的原始形态散落于茂密的百年龙眼林中。随着环江滨水大道建成通车，由于缺乏整体规划及治理，雷村屯村落发生了剧烈的变化重构，如图2所示表现在以下几个方面：一是村屯建筑的大幅增长。根据环江滨水大道建成前后一段时间的资料对比，雷村屯村民自建房新增近1/3，村宅密度上升，组团扩张联结，无序的新建筑则蚕食了原有茂密的树木植被和公共院落；二是村屯内部交通的淤塞。村屯内部原有道路空间虽然大致延续了原有的带状分布，但现有道路空间缺乏梳理，建筑交通节点变得无法满足现代通行需求；三是乡土特色空间存在不同程度的破坏。原有的渡口、道路两侧农田、水塘等特色空间不同程度地萎缩或碎片化，公共交往空间如村民广场和院落的开放性降低。

 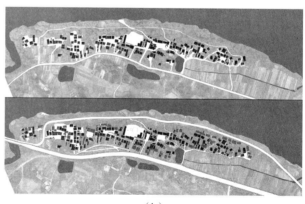

(a)   (b)

图2 环江滨水道建设前后雷村屯空间肌理变化示意图
(a) 环江滨水道建设前雷村屯卫星图；(b) 建设前后空间肌理对比
资料来源：(a) 天地图卫星；(b) 笔者自绘。

3 环江村更新理念的重构

城乡重构背景下的村落更新改造必然与已经成熟的城市旧城区更新活动在建设强度、土地使用、人口组成和产业结构上有诸多不同，这些因素将对具体的改造方式产生较大影响。[7] 村屯更新营造的难度和特殊性十分明显，故而有必要根据重构中的乡村特征来推动更新理念重构。

3.1 生态为本：以"绿心"的生态服务愿景为出发点

根据"一心两城"的城市空间发展格局，以莲花山片区的"都市绿心"愿景为出发点，着重治理和提升莲花山景区、环江村落群及柳江沿线自然环境的生态质量，集中展示柳江沿线的自然生态之美与"山水生活"为核心的人居环境特质，打造良好的生态服务功能，为发展生态旅游打下基础，对完善柳州城中区城乡的良性重构和促进城乡功能互补意义重大。

3.2 内部激活：以促进村屯内部现代功能的植入融合为着力点

针对雷村屯的村落人居环境的营造提升要在恢复和打造村屯特质建筑风貌、景观风貌和场地组织的工作外着重促进人与信息在乡村空间环境下流动的便捷性，健全相应的公共服务支撑系统，使村落更新营造进程与现代村落功能需求相适应。同时注重公共服务、基础设施、家庭生活设施等现代功能与传统村落人居特质的融合，使村民充分享有与城市匹配的现代便捷服务，又可为城市居民和资本的来往驻留提供完善的环境条件。

3.3 平衡调控：刚性控制与弹性调适相结合

把握城乡重构后的区位优势，扎根于村屯特色风貌与产业基础条件进行特色化的人居环境提升改造，有所为而有所不为是影响改造提质成效的重要因素。具体而言，刚性控制体现在下列几个方面：一是生态功能、自然景观的刚性保护与维护，严格保护或修复原生的村落生态环境和空间格局；二是刚性控制以农宅为主体的建筑群体形制和肌理，对违建现象实行有效的控制；有助于缓解和改善风貌紊乱和空间环境恶化的问题。而弹性调适主要体现在：在宏观上合理调整各类用地结构布局，在微观层面上融合本土建筑元素和传统建筑风貌，根据复杂的需求差异动态化地进行相应风格干预或改造调适，以实现统一风貌特质下微观形式的再平衡。

4 营造策略措施的总结归纳

"重构"寓意重新组合、重新构筑，通过调整相关因素以达到系统的体架趋于合理性，是一个去异同化的过程。同时空间的变化少不了时间对其的作用积累，因此空间重构的内涵强调的是不间断情况，而非作用过后的固定结果。[8]基于对空间重构的分析与理念重构的指导，我们在充分考虑城乡重构的动态性和不确定性的前提下，提出以生态环境保护为根基，依托人文民俗底蕴与村落风貌脉络的再激活为村落人居环境造血提质，动态化系统化地构建村落更新体系：

4.1 动态化反馈的策略体系构建

在现今日新月异的城乡关系重构进程中，乡村空间、社会文化、产业发展等方面均无时无刻不在演变，重构进程中不断显露的挑战与问题也要求乡村人居环境的改造提升必须在不同阶段进行动态调整，故而需要一套动态化的反馈机制和系统化弹性设计策略来应对从调研、设计到营造施工不同阶段中的各种挑战。如图 3 所示在雷村屯风貌改造进程中我们尝试构建这样一套动态化的设计反馈机制来对设计中出现的问题进行灵活变动，逐步实现多样化的微观设计调整和系统性的风貌掌控。

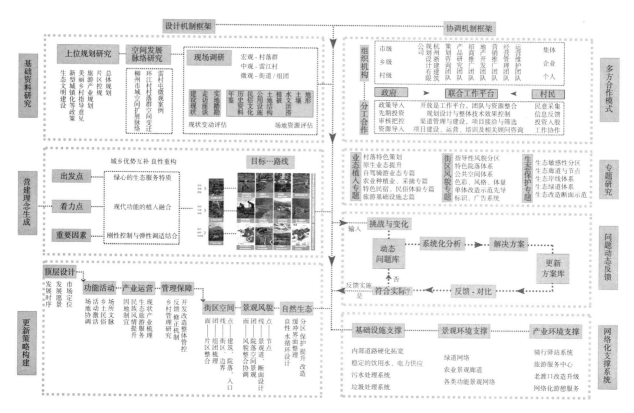

图 3　环江村落群风貌改造动态系统流程图（笔者自绘）

4.2　以生态环境保护为根基修补生态特质，恢复自然景观

自然环境是构成城镇特色的最重要的因素。构成城镇空间的人工元素，如建筑是可以抄袭的，但一定地域的自然景观则是难以模仿，它具有永恒的魅力。[9] 要以柳江沿岸及村屯的生态安全作为建设基础，营造连接城乡空间的生态景观廊道和富有地域特质的田园游憩节点与网络：一是要完善生态基础设施，如保护完善河岸植被缓冲带，建立起滨水及山林保护区，严格规范内部开发活动。二是要修复生态及生产性景观，如农田、菜地、果林及滨水植被，重建乡土化的大地植被景观。

4.3　村落乡土人文风貌的再激活，为乡村人居环境造血提质

对于村落风貌要修复和发展当地传统乡土元素，应注重交往空间的保留与塑造，强化空间形态的人文性。[10] 通过全面认识乡村地域性与资源条件，分类指导空间环境和人文环境的修复激活，主要分为：一是乡土空间的改造激活。要尊重原有形态，将人性需求、文化、历史和自然因素[11] 列入空间营造维度，将传统乡土材料通过现代更新手法融合在村落空间中，引导村民对村域范围、街巷空间和宅前屋后三个空间层级的认同感和归属感。二是乡土空间内部人文活动的恢复激活。注重村屯内部空间民俗活动的组织恢复，加强公共空间活力，延续发展新时期的特色村落记忆。三是基于空间特质与城乡需求进行产业的培育优化。

在雷村屯风貌更新改造中，我们认识到环江滨水大道建设后，当地风景区的吸引力提升不能只依

赖沿途风光，可被参与的本土生活和乡土风情是特色吸引力的源泉。以特色农业的规模化现代化提升为先导，积极融合柳州城市发展对当地生态服务功能的新要求，推动传统乡土产业转型升级，保存雷村屯龙眼果林为代表的特色生产生活方式和优质的滨江风景特征。通过梳理公共场所开展民俗节庆活动并鼓励游客参与其中，重唤乡土民俗文化，使体验式旅游与乡村传统人居环境相结合，促进优化后的现代乡土产业结构成为当地村落人居环境可持续发展的重要维度和长久支撑。

4.4 网络化支撑系统的营造

当前城乡统筹的核心目标是促进乡村现代化发展，构建以城乡空间一体化、基础设施和公共服务均等化为内涵的新型城乡关系。面对当前城乡重构进程中空间及资源引力的不平衡，人居环境的改造提质同样必须以公共资源的均等化为目标构建网络化的村落人居环境支撑系统，主要包括以下几个方面：（1）基础设施支撑系统：要实现村屯内部道路的硬化和拓宽，保证稳定的饮用水供应系统和电力供应系统，同时注重污水处理系统和垃圾处理系统等市政基础设施的植入与完善。（2）景观环境支撑系统：将景观功能节点、绿道网络、农业景观廊道等环境支撑系统的培育营造有机串联在村落的生态、生产、生活空间中，防止乡村空间要素的碎片化趋势，加强乡建环境与自然环境的融合性与整体性。（3）产业环境支撑系统：针对雷村屯发展龙眼果林主题的观光农业、滨水骑行游憩产业及民宿体验经济的产业发展方向，风貌更新改造中通过设计打造一系列相对应的公共服务设施来构建产业环境支撑系统，使村屯改造与产业培育工作相结合，强化村屯产业发展的包容性和吸引力。如设立富有环江村特色的骑行驿站和旅游服务中心，提供自行车停靠点和休憩场地，满足城市日益高涨的骑行需求，打造骑行主题民宿；针对长久以来承载着村民出行交通功能的老渡口进行风貌及功能升级，打造百里柳江水上游线在环江村区段的延伸游憩景观段；另外还注重加强百年龙眼果林林下休憩空间的梳理打造，与滨水骑行设施、游憩接驳码头共同打造网络化的游憩服务支撑系统。

5 讨论与结语

面对城乡间发展的不平衡和村落自身固有的发展掣肘，剧烈的城乡重构进程不断地为村落人居环境提出新的挑战和不确定性因素。在这一剧烈变化的城镇化发展新时期中，需要以更综合、动态的视角看待乡村发展的机遇与掣肘，以生态环境和乡建环境的保护出发，以积极的态度融合历史与现代元素，促进村落人居环境的再激活。此次论文的成文时间比较局促，很多部分还不够精练和细致，希望能够通过研究的进一步展开和深入来实现更完善的理论体系和文章内容。

The Integrated Strategies Research for Improving the Rural Human Settlements Environment under the Reconfiguration of Urban-Rural Relation: A Case Study in Huanjiang Village of Liuzhou City

Zhang Kai, Li Cheng, Shen Jie

(College of Civil Engineering and Architecture, Zhejiang University)

Abstract: With the development of national level urbanization process in China, a wide range of the reconfiguration of urban-rural society and space has a severe impact on the traditional rural human settlement. Starting from the analysis of spatial reconstruction on the three level of Liuzhou City, village group of Huanjiang and the micro case of Leicun, this article chooses the renovation design project of Huanjiang village as the research target. With the perspective of human settlements and urban-rural spatial planning, we make a comprehensive investigation on the changes of spatial features, industrial economy and regional culture. Then through the practice of Huanjiang village case, the article aims to put forward the rural renewal concept system including ecology-oriented restoration, internal activation and balance regulation. Then based on the dynamic feedback strategy on the marco level, try to promote the restoration of local characteristics and the construction of supporting network towards exploring an adaptable approach to improve the regeneration of rural human settlement. This article will be effective to provide the targeted supplement and strategic innovation for the theoretical system of urban-rural integration in the unbalanced development of western China.

Keywords: The reconfiguration of urban-rural relation, Rural human settlement, Spatial reconstruction, Renewal concept, Dynamic feedback strategy

参考文献

[1] 张鸿雁. 循环型城市社会发展模式: 城市可持续创新战略 [M]. 江苏: 东南大学出版社, 2007.
[2] 刘捷. 城市形态的整合 [M]. 江苏: 东南大学出版社, 2004.
[3] 李强, 陈宇琳, 刘精明. 中国城镇化"推进模式"研究 [J]. 中国社会科学, 2012, 7: 82-100.
[4] 广西壮族自治区统计局, 柳州市统计局. 柳州市 2015 年城市发展报告, 2016.
[5] 中国城市规划设计研究院, 柳州市城市规划局. 柳州市城市总体规划 (2010 ~ 2020) [Z]. 2010.
[6] 中国城市规划设计研究院, 柳州市城市规划局. 柳州市近期建设规划 (2016 ~ 2020) [Z]. 2016.
[7] 马航, 何宁宁. 边缘效应下的深圳市城市边缘村更新改造研究——以龙岗区年丰社区为例 [J]. 华中建筑, 2014, 3: 122-127.
[8] 郁枫. 空间重构与社会转型 [D]. 清华大学, 2006.
[9] 陈秉钊. 当代城市规划导论 [M]. 北京: 中国建筑工业出版社, 2003.
[10] 邓春凤, 冯兵, 龚克等. 桂北城镇聚落空间形态及景观 [J]. 城市问题, 2007, 9: 62-68.
[11] 杨东峰. 周边整合·形态调适·场所再造的空间重构策略——以天津市开发区为例 [J]. 城市规划学刊, 2007, 3: 76-80.

Village Planning Adapted to China Planning System and Urban Rural Integration

Zheng Shujian

(Guangzhou Geowise Planners & GISers Co., Ltd)

Abstract: The amendment of China Planning legal system in 2008 introduced Village Planning as a new kind statutory planning. While in the hierarchy of China Planning, "System Planning-Master Planning-Detail Planning", Village Planning becomes the only one which is defined by the object of planning, other than by the purpose of the planning. The confusions has been caused by this is the adaptability of Village Planning in China Planning System and even the adaptability of China Planning Methodology in the background of Urban Rural Integration. Perspectives of shifting these adaptabilities are to be discussed in this paper.

Keywords: Village planning, Planning system, Urban rural integration, Methodology

Legal system of China Planning can be summarized into "System Planning, Master Planning and Detailed Planning" from the perspective of methodology (hereinafter referred to as "SMD Structure"), which has been formulated in Urban Planning Act since 1990, and kept in Urban-Rural Planning Act in 2008, when Village Planning was first introduced into the legal system, without a very clear definition of its relationship with the origin SMD Structure. Which tier does Village Planning belong to, a certain one or the all? Meanwhile, Village Planning is the only one in the system which is defined by the object of planning, other than by the purpose of the planning. These confusions lead to the issues to be discussed in this paper: the adaptability of Village Planning in China Planning System and Urban Rural Integration, and new perspectives to look into.

1 Village Planning on the System Planning Tier

System planning is to provide logical thinking and technical guideline for policy making, especially in terms of public finance and resources allocation. Three perspectives are proposed here firstly, for a more rational and equal Urban-Rural System Planning, which influence the development resources distribution for the villages from the top.

1.1 Village Evolution by Feet-Voting

Chinese nationals are now relocating actively or passively under rapid urbanization, which results in the decrease of village both in ratio and quantity. A large number of villages are to disappear eventually, while the remaining will play more important roles in the human settlement system and cannot be replaced by other urban communities, in terms of serving the farmers with ecological living environment in remote rural areas, providing low cost residence in the sub-urban areas and so on. It is a feet-voting process. Thus, we need to find out which villages will still be selected as suitable places by more nationals and which are not. This can be concluded into a concept **Village Economic Capacity** (VEC), which can be seen as basis for Urban-Rural System Planning, and here proposed to be evaluated quantitatively by **Nominal Residential Electricity Consumption per Capital**.

VEC= Annual Residential Electricity Consumption (kWh) /*hukou Population*

Electricity consumption is an objective index showing the vitality and modernity of village. *Hukou* Population, the Nominal Registered Inhabitants are also precisely recorded in the public security. So-called "nominal" indicates the differences between real population and *hukou* population in a village. In urban villages, real population will be much higher for more migrants moving in and less original residence moving out, versus in most remote villages. As the table showed below, the VEC index of Guangzhou, the third largest city of China and accommodating approximate 7 million migrants, is about 20 times of the national level, 7 times of the provincial level and 7 times of another nearby city Jiangmen. Obviously, it is a showing of popularity of Guangzhou to migrants compared with other cities, not the living standard of rural area of Guangzhou.

VEC Index in different areas of China (KWh/p.a)[①]   Table 1

Area \ Year	2007	2008	2009	2010	2011	2012
China	770.66	811.54	885.50	988.24	1087.43	1169.14
Guangdong Province	2406.90	2407.67	2493.92	2575.64	2760.21	2903.38
Jiangmen City	2962.09	3044.18	2945.37	2939.51	2993.34	3132.93
Guangzhou City	19390.56	20444.02	19337.51	19511.87	20381.22	23152.55

Thus, based on similar living standard, villages with higher VEC value, are those places where nationals, no matter whether they are originals or migrants, would like to live. Public finances and resources should incline to such villages, and stop follow to those villages abandoned by nationals. In China, same population can be accommodated on the same amount of land in many different settlement patterns (LeGates, 2014). This approach attempts to stop this situation on Urban Rural System Planning Tier, as response to the calling of CPC, "letting the market playing the decisive role in resources allocation".

1.2 Village Conservation on Triple Bottom Line

VEC provides a basic index of understanding village's economic value. However, more issues besides economy are in need of concerning from a perspective of sustainable development, which often explained in the way of "Triple Bottom Line", that is the "Profit", "People" and "Planet". with similar expression in Chinese, *San Sheng*, that is, *Shengchan* (production), *Shenghuo* (living) and *Shengtai* (ecology). This

---

[①] Data resources: the yearbook of statistics of China, Guangdong, Jiangmen and Guangzhou from 2008-2013, from the indicator of "Electricity Consumed in Rural Areas", and "Agricultural Population". China: http://www.stats.gov.cn/tjsj/ndsj/ , Guangdong: http://www.gdstats.gov.cn/tjsj/gdtjnj/, Guangzhou: http://data.gzstats.gov.cn/gzStat1/chaxun/njsj.jsp, Jiangmen: http://tjj.jiangmen.gov.cn/NewsListPage.aspx?SiteId=1&fcolumn=统计数据&scolumn=统计年鉴&ItemId=168.

framework especially highlights those villages without strong economic features, and helps strengthening their value of conservation on the System Planning Tier.

(1) **Agriculture Conservation:** Even though agriculture is also a kind of economic activities, it is not that profitable compared with industry and commerce, but the foundation of national economy. It is necessary that public finance and resources should incline to those nationals living in remote areas, based on their contribution to the agriculture production. System Planning should try to provide enough living space and facilities to ensure acceptable living standard for farmers. While currently our planning policies do not have too much ways of supporting those villages with higher agricultural importance.

(2) **Culture Conservation:** Rapid urbanization did not happen in the history of China until 1990s, when Reform and Open policy came in force in the field of urbanization. Thus, people believe that the traditional Chinese culture is mainly rooted in the rural villages, but now vanishing with the demolishing of villages. System Planning should also need to protect historical sites and non-physical historical heritages in villages legally.

(3) **Ecology Conservation:** For most of the villages, more than eighty or even ninety percent of its territories are occupied by land not for construction by ecological conservation. So it should not be ignored in any tier of planning. While the policy for ecology conservation often carry out on a large scale on county level or municipal level, and requiring compensation policy for conservation areas which have to give up their rights to develop. These should be clarified by System Planning with coordinating between urban rural areas.

1.3 Village Integration with Urban Areas

Urban-Rural Integration is advocated widely in China currently, more than its practice. The most practical possibilities of Urban-Rural Integration from the perspectives of planning lies in the enlargement of the externality of urban public services to **Village-By-City**, in terms of public transportation, infrastructure, etc. Obviously, this is not available for remote villages. However, the separation of Village Planning and the Urban SMD Structure by legal system as I mentioned above, has caused that villages, no matter villages-by-city or remote villages, are always excluded out of the urban planning system, without mentioning be incorporated into the planning for urban public services.

Can we treat village-by-city equally as urban communities? Besides institutional innovations, it is in need of technically support as well. Currently we do not have feasible technical standards to define what kind of villages can be taken into the system of urban planning. This may mainly depend on the proximity of the villages with the cities and towns, especially the sites of urban public services, for example, water supply plant, sewage water plant, bus terminal or stops and so on. However, quantitatively solutions to this question still remain a large amount of researches.

2 Village Planning on the Master Planning Tier

"Ordinance for Village and Market Town Planning and Construction Management" (issued by the State Council in 1993), required that Village Planning should be conducted by two phases, Master Planning and Construction Planning, even though it was not clearly admitted by the Urban-Rural Planning Act in 2008.

Villages in China looks tiny and small, compared with those new urban communities. While the Master Planning of villages may be more difficult to be implemented than urban communities' development. This can be understudied from institutional and technical perspectives.

2.1 Institutionally: Master Planning on Village Autonomy

Master Planning, no matter for Metropolitan or tiny village, is a result of a certain level autonomous right, which is separately bore by Residence Committee (*juweihui*) for urban community and Village Committee (*cunweihui*) rural village. Rapid urbanization of China means that most of the urban communities and their Residence Committees are just formed in a very short time, which may be less than a decade. Neighbors may even not know each other that live in the same communities, without mentioning forming close related organizations to intervene in the community affairs.

While the inhabitants in rural villages are in the same clan in-law and have settled down for hundreds of years. Clearly administrative hierarchy has been established long before the Village Committee, generally with elderly people in power. Village Regulation and Civil Agreement (*cungui minyue*), plays a constitutional role in the village administration, parts of which will regulate the use of land, the layout of house and other things about village development literally, like a Master Plan, which seems simple and general but effective. Two examples from two ancient villages are listed as below (Dong, 2008):

"十五、乡内田园屋址，各凭契据管业。如涉他地，不得蒙混欺占。至于风水山场、通衢古迹地方，尤不许影射侵占，违者呈究。"——《长乐梅花里乡约》

"Article 15: Fields, gardens, and houses in the village should be occupied and managed with one's certificate or contract. It is forbidden to occupy other land by fraudulence. Mountains and courtyard for fengshui, arterial roads, historical sites, are not allowed to be occupied by any means. Offenders will be prosecuted."

From "*Changle Meihuali Civil Agreement*"

"十八、本里宅墓，来龙、朝山、水口，皆祖宗血脉，山川形胜所关。各家宜戒谕长养林木，以卫形胜，毋得泥为己业，掘损盗砍。犯者，公同重罚理论。"——《文堂陈氏乡约》

"Article 18: House, tombs, dragon-style mountains, worship mountains and water gates, are all the blood linkages of the ancestors, formed in this morphology. Every household should be instructed to insist in afforestation, to protect the spirit of its morphology, and must not occupy them as own property, must not excavate, broken, steal or cut the forest. Offenders will be prosecuted and heavily punished."

From "*Wentang Chen Clan Civil Agreement*"

It can be learned from the evidences above that most of the principles of Village Planning have passed via centuries, in terms of the layout of houses, the protection of natural resources, and the respect of fengshui are still popular in villages now. It also proves the necessity of conducting Master Planning for village base on village autonomy. Planning villages is totally different from creating new urban communities in towns and cities from a white paper, in which the negotiating is only between the planners and designers with the government officers and property developers, while never having the end-users enrolled in. While in the villages, "urban" planners and designers, who are the out-comers and committed by the government from the top, are now facing a group of people who have lived here for a very long time and knowing everything about here (as Figure 1 shows below). Negotiation with this autonomous organization is a new course for most of the planners and designers. However, we can still believe that a combination of the village autonomy and the modern planning and design technologies will help in creating our new and beautiful villages, where "the homesickness can be remembered".

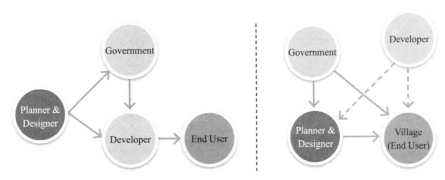

Figure 1 The mechanism of urban community and village developing

2.2 Technically: Master Planning for Village Modernization

The shortages of current Village Planning not only lie in the respect of village autonomy, but also the understanding of rural village life by the urban planners and designs, most of whom may not have much experience of village living. Actually, this so-called "elite planning" is also controversial in the urban planning. To avoid this, three aspects are in need of further investigation and research by urban planners and designers: housing, rural infrastructure and non-agricultural industries.

(1) **Housing:** China has laid down the strictest policy for cultivate land protection on rural areas. For most of the villages, it will be quite difficult to obtain new quota of development land converted from the agricultural land. Government may wish the villages to make full use of those abandoned development land in the villages, in terms of the old houses, the "hollowed villages", etc., or even to construct higher dense apartments to accommodate more people, which is called "go upstairs". No fixed solutions are available for the housing modernization of each village, and planners are required to be devoted into the negotiation among the villagers, Village Committee and the government, to find out balanced programs, by clearly understanding the current situation of housing, the willingness of the villagers, the potential of land recycle, the policies of government in different villages and so on. It can be recognized as the most important part in the Master Planning of a village.

(2) **Rural Infrastructure**: Unlike the urban communities which are developed integrally, it is quite common that houses in the villages are constructed independently by the farmers themselves, lack of infrastructure, but not that kind of urban infrastructure. For example, human waste can be collected for agricultural fertilization other than by flush toilet, with less black sewage water need to be treated, and less plastic products can be used in the villages by adopting more vernacular and recyclable materials. Anyway, the modernization of rural infrastructure is not a simple duplication of urban practice. Basically, the core principal is "distributed", for rural area provides boarder bases for energy and materials cycling. Wind, solar, hydro energy can all meet the scale of energy demand of villages, while wetland, fish ponds, biogas plants can all be served for waste recycling. No need of long distance sewage water pipe or refuse transferring, but requiring more flexible solutions for each village.

(3) **Non-Agricultural Industries:** Compared with the Residence Committee in the urban communities, the duties which a Village Committee affords may be far more complex, for a village is more than a place for

people living, but also producing. In the past, "producing" can be simply understood as agricultural production. But now, more possibilities are emerged, in terms of agro-tourism, small scale industry, warehouse and so on. Management of the resources of the village, especially the land resources is a challenging task, which the Residence Committee will never face. Village Committee may look forward to more professional suggestions on the land use for non-agricultural industries, which mainly targets on the service for urban people.

3 Village Planning on the Detailed Planning Tier

Detail planning is composed of Regulatory Planning and Site Planning for different purpose in the legal system of China Planning. Many people may consider the legal Village planning to be Village Detailed Planning, or even a Site Planning, not that sophisticated as what I have illustrated above. But a village can be more complex than an urban community indeed.

3.1 Village Regulatory Planning

Regulatory Planning is not for immediately implementation, but setting precondition for unknown or uncertain intervention, and can be divided into market oriented and self-regeneration oriented.

(1) **Market Oriented Village Regulatory Planning:** Main function of Regulatory Planning is to set precondition for land and property develop, before its use right transferred, while is not required for village collective land, and not forbidden neither, as a kind of method or tool for management. As a trend, more village collective land would be able to be exchanged in the land market. New challenges lie in fixing the indicators for the redevelopment of village collective land, which means the interveners are not only the government, but also the developers caring about the compensation for villagers and finally the profit of development. Thus, the intensity of development for every case will be different from one to another, targeting balance model for the profit, the living environment of residence and the rural landscape and morphology.

(2) **Self-Regeneration Oriented Village Regulatory Planning:** Main constrain of current Regulatory Planning widely conducted in urban areas of China now, is that they are more suitable for the newly to develop areas with few built constructions on site. While for a built community, it is meaningless to calculate the indexes, such as FAR, density, green coverage, no matter whether it is an urban community or rural village. Everything built is more concrete than indicators for residence, and space available for regeneration is often clear and limited. How to find out the need of the residence, feasible technical solutions and method of implementation are where the challenge lies. It can be recognized as a kind of Self-Regeneration Oriented Village Regulatory Planning, for no profitable purpose will be included in and funding may be supported from various channels, in terms of self-funding, donations, government finance and so on. From a long term perspective, village should get well prepared for every opportunity which may introduce in investment.

3.2 Village Site Planning

Site Planning in urban planning system is designated as technical document in applying planning permit of construction. Rural Construction Planning Permit is specially introduced for villages in 2008. However, as N. Smith argues, cookie-cutter villages are now increasingly prevalence because the villagers are now integrated into the existing "top-down" process of planning and regulation (Smith, 2014). This may not be easy to be avoided, for currently it is difficult for most of the villages to organize the planning themselves. Thus, Village Site Planning organized by government will be normalized inevitably, for efficiency and budget saving purpose. With the developing of village economy, especially the collective economy, villages should be encouraged to organize the Village Site Planning independently.

However, to most of the non-professional residence, Village Site Planning is the easiest technical document to understand. So a wide consultation about villagers' need is fundamental step before planning and design. Various ways of public participatory can be adopted to make consensus in villagers, for example, planning workshop, posters and villagers' conference and so on. Moreover, planners can organize villagers to visit the built cases and other good practices to understand how we can make our living environment better. However, it really takes a long time to help villagers to build the vision of the village. For most of the villagers, not many of them have ever taken much consideration about their villagers. So it is the planners' responsibility to find out the characters of each village. However, this is not only a question about science and technology, but business.

适应中国规划体系和城乡统筹的村庄规划

郑书剑

（广州格域信息化规划有限公司）

摘　要：2008年中国规划法的修改引入了村庄规划这种新的法定规划类型，但是在中国传统的规划层级体系中，即"体系规划—总体规划—详细规划"结构中，村庄规划是唯一一种以对象定义而不是以目的定义的类型。这就引发了关于村庄规划在规划体系中的适应性问题以及中国规划方法论在城乡统筹背景下的适应性问题。本文所要讨论的即是提升这种适应性的一些观点看法。

关键词：村庄规划，规划体系，城乡统筹，方法论

References

[1] Dong J H. The Theoretical and Practical Development of Community Covenants in Ming and Qing Dynasties[M]. Xiamen: Xiamen University Press, 2008: 204-206

[2] LeGates R T. Visions, scale, tempo, and form in China's emerging city-regions. J. Cities, 2014.

[3] LU Chen, WU Yuzhe, SHEN Qiping, WANG Hao. Driving force of urban growth and regional planning: A case study of China's Guangdong Province[J]. *Habitat International,* 2013, 40: 35-41.

[4] Sanyal B. Comparative planning cultures[M]. London and New York: Routledge, 2005.Smith N R. Beyond top-down/bottom-up: Village transformation on China's urban edge[J]. *Cities* 2014.

From Gentrification to Studentification: A Case Study of HEMC in Guangzhou, China

Liu Yongshen

(Department of Public Policy, City University of Hong Kong)

Abstract: Existing literature on gentrification in China mainly emphasizes the dominant role of the state (especially local governments). Compared with the cases in the Western counterparts, gentrification in China tends to be pushed forward according to the blueprints designed by the local governments, which has also shown its profound impacts on all aspects within the process, such as the urban landscapes, urban growth, demographic changes, housing patterns and neighborhood characteristics, etc. Nonetheless, little effort in the literature has been attended to the long-term socioeconomic impacts of gentrification in contrast with the governmental blueprints. This research, therefore, aims at filling the research gap with a case study on the Higher Education Mega Center (HEMC) in Guangzhou, China. In the inception stage, the municipal government intended to gentrify the rural area with the HEMC project, aspiring to make the HEMC a high-end community through clustering of prestigious universities. Though the local government has devoted to leading and facilitating the gentrification process, some unexpected socioeconomic impacts arose over the decade, frustrating the state-led gentrification of the area. Based on the case study, this research aims to reexamine the position of the local government in the process of gentrification under the trend of neoliberal urbanism. Policy implications will then follow.

Keywords: state-led gentrification, local state, governmental blueprint, studentification, neoliberalism

1 Introduction

Under the threefold driving forces of market-oriented economic reforms, land and housing reforms as well as fiscal decentralization over the decades, neoliberalism as a new approach to urban redevelopment has been extensively practised[1], and thus has significantly boosted the trend of gentrification in urban China[2]. Until now, gentrification has developed into diverse forms determined by different locations, resources and approaches, such as commercial gentrification[3], tourism gentrification[4] and rural gentrification[5]. No matter which type of gentrification, in most cases under the Chinese contexts, local governments tend to play a crucial role for their monopolies on land ownership and urban planning. Stimulated by the fiscal system reforms, local governments are taken as entrepreneurs[6] or industrial firms[7] striving to maximize their financial revenues[8]. Especially, the implementation of tax-sharing system since 1994 has motivated the local governments to increase their revenues through land leasing and real estate development[9]. Therefore, a large number of urban redevelopment projects have emerged over the last two decades. These urban redevelopment projects, different from those in the Western counterparts, normally start from the grand blueprints proposed by the local governments which also keep directly intervening in the whole process from planning to implementation. To be more precise, local governments initiate and facilitate the redevelopment process through legitimizing the market-oriented operation, accommodating the demands of gentrifiers, making supportive and preferential policies, constructing infrastructure, organizing land acquisition and so forth [1,3,10].

Certainly, state-led gentrification has significantly influenced the urban landscapes. Local governments devote themselves to beautification and improvement of urban areas, seeking to accelerate the economic growth and reimage the cities for moving towards the 'world-class' ranks[11]. In fact, there are more successful cases in Shanghai, Guangzhou and other metropolitan cities. Yet, the local governments have to face the downsides of gentrification like large-scale resident displacement[10, 11]. In addition, the gentrification process has led to some other social impacts. As for demographic changes, low-income residents have been gradually replaced by the enlarging middle class in the cities while the displaced residents are prone to marginalization and impoverishment[10, 12]. Besides, to extract huge profits in the urban redevelopment projects, real-estate developers called for more real estate developments. This consequently led to the booming of commodity housings. The abrupt shift of housing patterns has also changed the characteristics of neighborhoods. The originally thriving and closely connected urban neighborhoods have been destructed and replaced by gated communities[2, 13].

By placing the Chinese-style gentrification back into the theoretical battlefield about the formation of gentrification, which has been divided into two opposite sides of view, i.e. production-side and consumption-side forces, it appears that the gentrification progress in China is always pushed forward according to the scripts written by local governments. Local governments as the production-side forces own the hegemonic power over spatial production[8], which is reflected by their profoundly influential control of land use, capital flows, distribution of public goods and other productive factors. Nonetheless, little effort in the literature has attended to the long-term socioeconomic impacts of gentrification compared to the governmental blueprints, in order to examine the influence of the state on gentrification in the long run. Have the governmental blueprints been fully realized? Or, is the gentrification progress always on the path paved by the local governments? Are there any unexpected outcomes of the process? This research, therefore, aims at filling the research gap with a longitudinal case study.

2 Case Study on HEMC in Guangzhou: The State-led Gentrification Progress

The case of Higher Education Mega Center (HEMC), which is located in Guangzhou, will be introduced in this research. By observing the long-term socioeconomic changes caused by the gentrification process, this research attempts to reexamine the position and influence of the local governments in the Chinese gentrification trend. Secondary data from the governmental sources, media and literature and primary data from in-depth interviews as well as participatory observations were employed for the empirical inquiry.

2.1 The Governmental Planning and Its Implementation of the HEMC Project

The HEMC is located on the *Xiaoguwei* Island with the total area of 20.15 square kilometers. It originally contained six administrative villages (including *Nanting* Village, *Beiting* Village, *Suishi* Village, *Beigang* Village, *Guolang* Village and *Lianxi* Village) with a total population of 12,899 people. The HEMC project began with its siting implemented by the municipal government in August 2000. Taking factors like the proximity to the city's center and topography into account, *Xiaoguwei* Island was finally chosen as the site for the HEMC project in March 2001. The planning scheme of the project was proposed in 2001, subsequently followed by the construction in 2003. Eventually, the first-stage project was completed in 2004, and the HEMC was officially put into operation from then on. Since the construction of the project, the rural island has been gradually transformed into an urbanized university town with the following parts:

(1) **University Clusters:** As the most crucial part of the first-stage project, ten prestigious universities have been introduced into the HEMC. The spatial layout of the university clusters has been designed into the threefold concentric-circle frame. The outermost circle consists of the teaching areas of all the ten universities. The middle circle has been divided into five residential clusters (see Table 1). The idea of residential-area clustering has been implemented for the sharing of public facilities within each cluster, as well as for the community building across the adjacent universities. Besides, the innermost circle has also been used for the construction of shared public facilities such as the sports center and the HEMC hospital.

(2) **Partial Preservation of Villages:** As per the state's planning scheme, two administrative villages (*Guolang* Village and *Lianxi* Village) and one-third of the area in *Beiting* Village were totally demolished. The remaining two-third of the area in *Beiting* Village and other three villages (*Nanting* Village, *Suishi* Village and *Beigang* Village) were preserved. The total area of the four preserved spots took up 1.127 km^2, accommodating 1,802 households and 5,954 villagers. This arrangement had several features. First, the large-scale land acquisition on *Xiaoguwei* Island would greatly aggravate the financial difficulty of the municipal government, and thus the government decided to divide the land acquisition exercises phase by phase. Second, the preservation of some villages with modest proportions of villagers could create various supporting service sites and provide related labor forces. This helped to relieve the operating pressure of the HEMC in terms of the supporting service provision in the early stages. In fact, over these years, various types of small business (e.g. restaurants, retail stores, hostels etc.) emerged in the four villages, effectively satisfying most of the daily-life demands of the students and other residents in the HEMC. Third, a large number of cultural built heritages which warranted conservation were concentrated inside or near the four preserved villages. In the governmental discourses, the preserved villages would prospectively be transformed into the housing clusters specifically for the academics in the future.

Distribution of the universities and the clusters in HEMC   Table 1

University	Area of the teaching area (ha.)	Residential cluster	Area of the residential cluster (ha.)
Sun Yat-sen University	88	Residential Cluster 1	39
Guangdong University of Foreign Studies	52		
Guangdong Pharmaceutical University	30	Residential Cluster 2	57
GuangDong University of Chinese Medicine	45		
South China University of Technology	83		
Guangdong University of Technology	110	Residential Cluster 3	50
Guangzhou Academy of Fine Arts	29		
Guangzhou University	80	Residential Cluster 4	23
Xinghai Conservatory of Music	18	Residential Cluster 5	27
South China Normal University	61		

Source: "The Planning Scheme of the HEMC", from Guangzhou Planning Bureau (2001).

(3) **Additional Functions of the HEMC:** The HEMC adjoins city landmarks such as Pazhou International Exhibition Center and Guangzhou Science City and is surrounded by tourist attractions like Xiaozhou Artist Village, Changzhou Island, Guangzhou International Bio-island and Yingzhou Ecological Park. In addition to sustaining and extending the innovative technology industry clusters with the support of the university resources, the HEMC was also planned to become a tourism spot which combined natural and cultural sights on the island and form a tourism cluster with the attractions in the surrounding. In order words, the HEMC has been designed for versatile functions (i.e. educational, scientific research, cultural, tourist, recreational and residential functions).

(4) **Development of Commodity Housing:** As for housing development, the planning scheme of the HEMC project stipulated that only 22 pieces of land would be used for the construction of commodity housing. Moreover, the maximum height for all the buildings erected on the island was 50 m. Therefore, in light of the limited supply, commodity housing in the HEMC has become a scarce resource. Taking the advantages of the favorable environmental conditions, good reputation of the prestigious university cluster, and development priorities on higher education, innovative technology and tourism, the municipal government was ambitious to turn the HEMC into a high-end community. So far, eight commodity housing projects have been completed. Most of the residential units have been configured into large-size flats with 150-300 m^2. Seemingly, these commodity housing units are tailored for the affluent groups.

2.2 The Municipal Government Facilitating the Gentrification Progress of HEMC

In fact, apart from the project planning on the outlines of the gentrification outcomes, the municipal government has also played an important facilitating role in pushing the gentrification progress along the way of the construction and operation of the HEMC. To be more specific, the municipal government has at least made great efforts in the following aspects:

(1) **Organizing land acquisition and demolition:** Following the accomplishment of siting and planning, the municipal government began to organize the land acquisition and demolition on the island in 2002. It formulated a compensation scheme, providing the villagers and the displaced residents with low levels of compensation (e.g.: 450-850 RMB/m^2 for the demolished dwellings, and 49,382 RMB for each villager in *Beigang* Village as the land acquisition compensation); meanwhile built the alternative dwellings in *Xinzao* Town for the displaced residents, with the selling price between 1,200 and 1,450 RMB/m^2. To avoid being examined by the central government on the large-scale land acquisition, the local government even divided the 1402.64 hectares of land on the island into 39 pieces, which had greatly accelerated the acquisition progress. Furthermore, confronted with the fierce resistance by the villagers and displaced residents, the municipal government made use of the coercive measures, calling out the police to implement the demolition plans compulsorily.

(2) **Justifying the economic value of the HEMC through the urban blueprints:** In 2000, the municipal government proposed a set of urban development strategies, one of which was the 'southward expansion' strategy prioritizing the development of *Panyu* District in the ten-year urban blueprint (2001-2010). The HEMC was prospectively within the jurisdiction of *Panyu* District. In 2010, the municipal government formulated another ten-year urban blueprint (2010-2020), further elaborating and updating the implications of the 'southward expansion' strategy which repeatedly emphasized the key role of the HEMC on higher

education and innovative technology industry. In 2012, the municipal government came up with the idea of 'a third central axis' in Guangzhou City which contained a set of technological, commercial and tourist landmarks including the HEMC. With the urban blueprints and visions proposed, the economic value of the HEMC has been justified, leading to the rapid inflation of the house prices in the HEMC.

(3) **Investment on the public facilities:** To facilitate the operation of this new town with its mulitple functions, the municipal government has devoted itself into the large-scale infrastructure construction, while channeling the inflows of capital from the developers[10] to the investment of commercial development and public facilities. For instance, the annual fixed-asset investment on the HEMC project amounted to 1.9, 19.3, 5.7 billion RMB in 2003, 2004 and 2005 respectively. Over the decade, more than 20 bus lines, metro stations, five commercial areas, and other facilities (for education, health, sports, scientific exhibition or research, cultural exhibition or performance, outbound traffic etc.) have been built.

(4) **Operational management and social governance:** At the beginning of the operation of the HEMC, the local government specially established an institution named 'the Construction Headquarter of the HEMC' which was responsible for the social governance and other aspects of management like afforestation and beautification. Since 2008, in order to widen the management scope and decentralize the power on the HEMC governance, the Management Committee of the HEMC has been set up to replace the original Construction Headquarter. The management committee is in charge of all aspects of operational and social affairs, including infrastructure construction, public security, and cooperative programs on scientific research or higher education.

3 Frustrated Gentrification: Long-term Socioeconomic Impacts of HEMC Project

Even though the local government has been committed to the redevelopment and gentrification progress with specific goals, clear plans, large-scale financial investment, forcible implementation and remarkable justification, the gentrification of the HEMC has suffered from some setbacks. These downsides were reflected by some unexpected socioeconomic outcomes:

(1) **Vacant commodity housings with absent gentrifiers:** The compounding forces of the long-term urban development blueprints, advantaged environmental conditions and limited housing supply in the vicinity have supported the price of the commodity housing in HEMC to stay high over the years. The average price has increased from 18,000 RMB/m^2 in 2010 to 30,000 RMB/m^2 in 2013, then to more than 40,000 RMB/m^2 in 2017. Moreover, the predominance of large-size housing units in the HEMC has resulted in misplaced development of the housing market within the HEMC. On one hand, only the affluent can afford to buy the housing in the HEMC and their purchase intentions are normally driven by the investment demands rather than their owner-occupation demands. On the other hand, the working class who work in the HEMC show stronger desire to buy a property in the HEMC. Yet, the house price is too high to be affordable to them. Therefore, the commodity housing in the HEMC has a high level of vacancy rate. In other words, the gentrifiers contributing to the gentrification progress as the consumption-side forces are absent.

(2) **Differential development of business sectors:** There have been five commercial areas in the HEMC, including the Guangzhou Univ. Commercial Center (GUCC), GOGO New World, Northern Commercial Area,

Southern Commercial Area, and *Beiting* Commercial Square. In fact, only the former two still survive and the other three have closed down. Take *Beiting* Commercial Square as an example. It opened in 2007 as the first commercial area in the HEMC. In the very beginning, there were 250 shops and recreational sites running their business. However, for various reasons like long distance from the student residential areas, overestimated market orientation, insufficient support of public transportation (with only one bus line) and few consumers from outside of the HEMC, most of the retail tenants, cinema and video-game center went bankrupt one after another. Only few shops like the McDonald's survived.

(3) **Negative Externality of the Reserved Village Spots:** The reserved village spots have succeeded in turning into the supportive service sites for the daily-life demands of the HEMC. However, distinct from the redeveloped landscapes on other parts of the island, the preserved villages kept their original forms without much beautification or regeneration. The living conditions of the villages remained dirty, dense and chaotic. The boom of rental flats provided in the villages has attracted a large amount of low-incomers moving into the HEMC for the low-level rental prices compared with the central part of Guangzhou. Consequently, the preserved villages have degenerated into low-income and disordered neighborhoods with poor living environment and complex floating population. The environmental degradation and increased concentration of the disadvantaged group have also had some negative externalities around the HEMC, such as increasing crimes (e.g. thefts, frauds, and even murders), and formation of gangs. One of the gangs, mainly organized among the villagers, manipulate the motorcycle passenger service. On account of the inadequacy in public transportation in the HEMC, this gang is able to monopolize the industry and set the fare at an unreasonably high level.

4 Studentification: An Unexpected but Reasonable Social Outcome in the HEMC

As more and more universities were put into operation within the HEMC from 2004 onwards, tens of thousands of university students kept moving in, and gradually became the main resident and customer cluster. Unexpectedly but reasonably, the HEMC has been studentified instead of gentrified. As the main resident cluster, students from the universities in the HEMC have become one of the strong forces shaping the socio-spatial landscape within the HEMC. For instance, the innermost circle of the HEMC, surrounded by the student residential clusters, has been changed into a track for running by the students. In each evening, a large group of university students came and did exercise there. Besides, cycling has been the main way of commuting within the HEMC. During the school hours, a large number of bicycles keep flooding across the campuses. The roads around the campuses have even become the parking lots for bicycles, blocking the vehicular traffic sometimes. Furthermore, many public spaces around the student residential clusters have been used for the student activities (e.g. road shows). On the other hand, as the main customer cluster, the commercial sector and villagers run various businesses specifically targeting the students (e.g. restaurants, retail stores, rental rooms, recreational sites and training institutions). Most of the businesses are featured by small size, low price, fashion and diversity, which greatly meet the consumption demands of the students. The businesses of two commercial areas (GUCC and GOGO New World) and the villages thrive due to their proximity to the student residential clusters. In addition, the studentification of the HEMC is also distinguished by the seasonality. During the summer and winter vacations in each year, the HEMC tends to become an empty town with most of the businesses and public sites temporarily closed or sluggish because most of the students return to their hometowns.

5　Policy Implications and Conclusion

The case study on the HEMC reveals that the local government may not be able to the goals of the gentrification process even though the process is state-led. Many other forces such as contextual, institutional and social factors also shape the gentrification process and determine the outcomes. Given that local governments are still playing a crucial role in planning and facilitating the gentrification progress, the findings of this research have some policy implications. First, in the planning stage of a redevelopment project, local governments should have more realistic expectations about the social changes in the neighborhood. Second, in the operation stage of the project, the governments should enable collaborative governance among different social groups in the redeveloped area, letting them to air their concerns and grievances about the project. Instead of blindly sticking to the governmental blueprints, the local governments should respond to the unexpected outcomes. Last, in light of possible studentification, the state needs to rethink if the development of higher education hub is a good way to gentrify an area.

从绅士化到学生化的演变——基于中国广州大学城的案例研究

刘永深
（香港城市大学公共政策系）

摘　要：关于中国绅士化的已有文献强调了国家（尤指地方政府）的主导角色。与西方国家相比，中国的绅士化往往根据政府所设计的规划蓝图来推进，并且政府在绅士化过程中对城市景观、城市增长、人口变化、居住形态以及邻里特征等方面都产生了深远影响。然而，已有研究鲜有以政府规划作为对照，来分析中国绅士化在较长时期内产生的经济社会结果。因此，本研究通过广州大学城的案例研究，旨在填补这一理论空白。在起始阶段，市政府试图借助大学城项目将小谷围岛从一个乡村地区打造成一个高端的绅士化社区。尽管政府一直致力于扶持广州大学城的绅士化，但经过10多年的发展，广州大学城还是产生了某些负面的经济社会结果，使其绅士化遭遇挫折。基于对这一案例的分析，本研究试图在新自由主义城市化的潮流下，进一步讨论地方政府在绅士化过程中的角色扮演，并在最后提出某些政策启示。

关键词：国家主导的绅士化，地方政府，政府规划蓝图，学生化，新自由主义

References

[1]　He S, Wu F. China's emerging neoliberal urbanism: perspectives from urban redevelopment[J]. Antipode, 2009, 41(2): 282-304.

[2] He S, Wu F. Socio-spatial impacts of property-led redevelopment on China's urban neighbourhoods[J]. Cities, 2007, 24(3): 194-208.

[3] Wang S W H. Commercial gentrification and entrepreneurial governance in Shanghai: A case study of Taikang Road Creative Cluster[J]. Urban Policy and Research, 2011, 29(4): 363-380.

[4] Du Cros H, Bauer T, Lo C, Rui S. Cultural heritage assets in China as sustainable tourism products: Case studies of the Hutongs and the Huanghua section of the Great Wall[J]. Journal of Sustainable Tourism, 2005, 13(2): 171-194.

[5] Qian J, He S, Liu L. Aestheticisation, rent-seeking, and rural gentrification amidst China's rapid urbanisation: The case of Xiaozhou village, Guangzhou[J]. Journal of Rural Studies, 2013, 32: 331-345.

[6] Duckett J. Bureaucrats in business, Chinese-style: The lessons of market reform and state entrepreneurialism in the People's Republic of China[J]. World Development, 2001, 29(1): 23-37.

[7] Walder A G. Local governments as industrial firms: an organizational analysis of China's transitional economy[J]. American Journal of sociology, 1995, 101(2): 263-301.

[8] Wu F. State dominance in urban redevelopment: Beyond gentrification in urban China[J]. Urban Affairs Review, 2016, 52(5): 631-658.

[9] Zhou F. A Decade of Tax-Sharing : the System and its Evolution[J]. Social Sciences in China, 2006, (6): 100-115. (in Chinese) 周飞舟. 分税制十年：制度及其影响 [J]. 中国社会科学, 2006, (6): 100-115.

[10] He S. State-sponsored gentrification under market transition the case of Shanghai[J]. Urban Affairs Review, 2007, 43(2): 171-198.

[11] He S. Two waves of gentrification and emerging rights issues in Guangzhou, China[J]. Environment and Planning A, 2012, 44(12): 2817-2833.

[12] He S. New-build gentrification in Central Shanghai: demographic changes and socioeconomic implications[J]. Population, Space and Place, 2010, 16(5): 345-361.

[13] Song W, Zhu X. Gentrification in urban China under market transformation[J]. International Journal of Urban Sciences, 2010, 14(2): 152-163.

EPC-PPP 模式下建构小城镇全域旅游体系的探索与实践：以开化县域的整体营造为例

李 乘 沈 杰 唐玉田

（浙江大学建筑工程学院）

摘 要：随着全国城镇化进程的不断发展，小城镇环境、社会、产业的融合提升的需求越来越强烈。粗放型的小城镇产业开发模式的失衡现状有目共睹，近年来出现的全域旅游概念则可一定程度通过全方位系统化的开发策略，对区域内的经济社会资源尤其是旅游开发资源及相关产业进行优化提升，解决小城镇常见的混乱开发模式带来的问题，实现资源、产品和需求的动态平衡。EPC-PPP 模式融合了两种模式的优点，能够有效整合公共资源与社会力量高度集成性地推进项目。本文以开化县综合整治改造项目实践出发，探索 EPC-PPP 模式在全域旅游概念上参与小城镇建设更新改造的定位与推行体系，追求充分发挥 EPC-PPP 机制的优势，结合开化实际，探究总结出从项目包装、政策争取、融资贷款、规划设计、统一采购的全方位周期建设的体系方案，为今后阶段的小城镇建设机制体制探索提供积极的理论基础。

关键词：全域旅游，EPC-PPP 模式，更新理念，集成设计策略

1 引言

在近年来全国城镇化进程不断发展的过程中，浙江注重从根源上、区域上解决城乡环境问题，联动推进区域性路网、管网、林网、河网、垃圾处理网和污水处理网等一体化建设，全面开展高速公路、国道沿线、名胜景区、城镇周边的整治建设和整乡整镇的环境整治。积极开展生活垃圾资源化、减量化处理，注重抓好日常维护和管理。从村庄建设、产业定位、社会管理等方面着手，通过完善基础设施，提升村庄环境。《计划》的出台，让物和人的相互依存更为和谐。接下来，浙江将进一步全面改善农村生态环境、人居环境和发展环境，不断提升农村的美丽度和广大农民群众的幸福感。美丽乡村建设从"一处美"向"一片美"转型，突出"以点带面"，注重把盆景变成风景并要加强农村垃圾、生活污水、村庄环境综合治理，发展旅游经济、电商经济，积极推进扶贫开发。

以中共十八届三中全会提出"允许社会资本通过特许经营等方式参与城市基础设施投资和运营"政策为背景，能够有效融合公共资源与社会力量的 PPP 模式承载着经济转型和国家治理多方面使命。而 EPC 模式则强调和充分发挥设计在整个工程建设过程中的主导作用。对设计在整个工程建设过程中的主导作用的强调和发挥，有利于工程项目建设整体方案的不断优化。在这样的背景和模式下，全域旅游的规划理念正好适应了当前小城镇的发展需求，通过集成性的规划设计策略，系统性地高效利用社会经济旅游资源，利用项目投资模式的优势推行新的开发整治模式。本文以开化县综合整治改造项目实践出发，重点从四个镇入手，探索 EPC-PPP 模式在全域旅游概念上参与小城镇建设更新改造的定位与推行体系，追求充分发挥 EPC-PPP 机制的优势，结合开化实际，探究总结出从项目包装、政策争取、融资贷款、规划设计、统一采购的全方位周期建设的体系方案，探索新的小城镇综合建设体系。

2 开化县域调研情况概览及分析

2.1 开化县调研概况

浙江省衢州市开化县，地处长三角经济圈、海峡西岸经济区内，连接浙皖赣三省六县（浙江淳安县、常山县，安徽休宁县，江西省婺源县、德兴市和玉山县），是浙江省母亲河——钱塘江的源头。初次调研片区位于以村为基本单位进行考察研究。将自然环境风貌、交通条件、人居条件、经济发展状况、文化艺术氛围、土地性质及项目对接渠道纳入考察范围，并结合当地规划发展设想及实际项目发展建设需求进行综合性客观分析，形成了完整、客观的技术性研究报告，为将来的项目发展提供客观参考和依据（图1）。

在开化县的整体调研中采用一系列村落选点标准，以点带面进行开发优化，促进开化县域整体人居环境和经济环境的提升。村落选点标准：（1）具有美丽乡村建设的典型性示范性和带动性，目标是建成后能够成为当地的村落建设的区域性标杆，起到引领作用。（2）依山傍水、风景优美、动静相宜的区域，有利于民宿休憩疗养等功能业态的布置。（3）交通便捷，到开化县主城区十几分钟范围较合适，也要考虑到距离高速公路下口距离，方便杭州上海方向车流。（4）产权相对明晰，成分单一，避免过分拆迁、租赁和运行过程中产生不必要的纠纷和问题。（5）符合浙江省美丽乡村建设的一系列原则和补助标准，尽量争取相应政策的有利条件和支持。

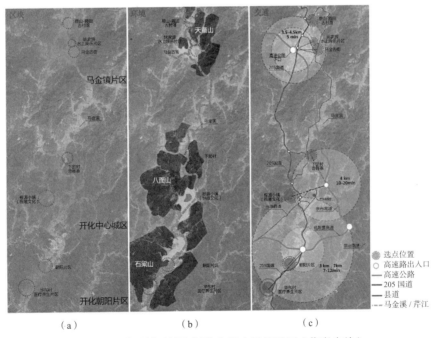

图1 开化县域地域资源分布及空间格局图（作者自绘）
（a）开化县主要片区分布图；（b）开化县重要旅游资源分布图；（c）开化县路网空间格局图

2.2 小城镇综合整治行动背景下的全域旅游体系规划策略

现阶段大力推行的小城镇综合整治行动（图2）在优化城乡人居环境过程中起到重要的推动作用，在小城镇的旅游环境资源的开发整治中系统性地介入，可以和全域旅游规划策略有机集成，在提升优化小城镇旅游环境的过程中互相支持。全域旅游体系在多维度、多尺度下的小城镇综合整治行动中可以产生重要的优化效应，自然资源、城乡环境、城乡空间结构及整体风貌有计划地进行优化调配。

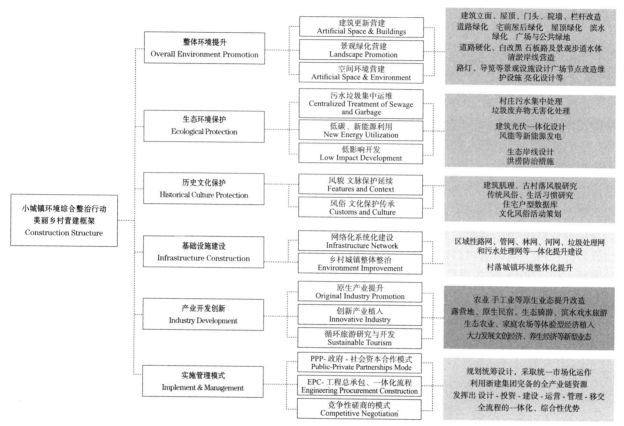

图 2　环境综合整治行动及美丽乡村营建框架（作者自绘）

2.3　PPP 模式 +EPC 设计为龙头的工程总承包模式

2.3.1　PPP 模式（公私合作关系：Public-Private Partnerships）

PPP（图 3）是政府与社会资本为提供公共产品或服务而建立的全过程合作关系，以授予特许经营权为基础，以利益共享和风险共担为特征；通过引入市场竞争和激励约束机制，发挥双方优势，提高公共产品或服务的质量和供给效率。

模式名称	英文含义	中文含义	说明	合同期限
DBTO	Design-Build-Transfer-Operate	设计-建造-转移-经营	社会企业投资建设基础设施，完工后以约定好的价格移交给公共部门，公共部门再将该设施以一定的费用回租给社会企业，由企业经营该设施（预计反租费率6%）	2~8模式
PUOT	Purchase-Upgrade-Operate-Transfer	购买-更新-经营-转让	社会企业购买已有的公共基础设施，经过一定程度的更新、扩建后经营该设施。在经营期间企业拥有该设施的所有权，合同结束后将该设施的使用权和所有权移交给公共部门	8~15年
BT	Design-Build-Transfer	设计-建造-移交	社会企业按照公共部门规定的性能指标，以事先约定好的固定价格设计并建造基础设施，建成后移交公共部门	经商定

图 3　PPP 模式详解分析图（作者自绘）

2.3.2 EPC模式（Engineering Procurement Construction）

EPC是指公司受业主委托，按照合同约定对工程建设项目的设计、采购、施工、试运行等实行全过程或若干阶段的承包。在EPC模式中，Engineering不仅包括具体的设计工作，而且可能包括整个建设工程内容的总体策划以及整个建设工程实施组织管理的策划和具体工作。

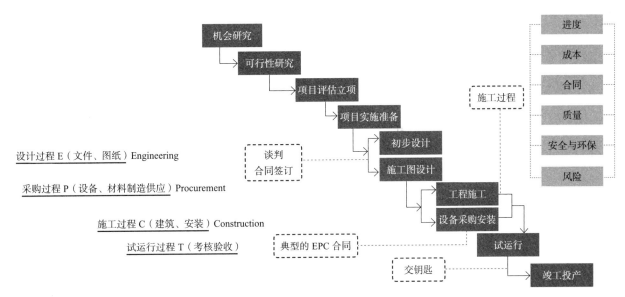

图4 EPC总承包建设流程图（作者自绘）

PPP融资模式为社会资本进入公共产品或服务领域提供了平台，EPC工程总承包模式为投资人获得了更高的投资收益率，两者结合的投资运作方式可以使投资企业的利润达到最大化，有效控制工程成本，缩短建设周期，降低投资风险，更重要的是可以整合利用社会资源高效地把控项目进度，系统性地推进项目，在这种模式下和全域旅游的规划理念结合可以更好地进行小城镇开发建设。

3 开化县四个试点小城镇环境综合整治规划

3.1 开化县马金镇小城镇环境综合整治规划

在马金镇的旅游开发规划中，结合大区块自然山水条件、村庄布局与建设情况及现状历史、人文、自然等方面资料优势，规划提出"一核引领，一带拉动，功能互补，产业共建"的布局结构。形成以马金-霞山片区的古村、古道、古树等为核心的"文化净谷、漫游马金"特色旅游核，引爆马金区块。整体规划设计中运用全域旅游规划理念，结合EPC-PPP模式的优势对马金镇进行多维度多尺度下的综合开发整治。

3.2 开化县齐溪镇小城镇环境综合整治规划

本规划延续上位规划及先期城镇总体规划，与马金镇历史、文化与各场地的总体功能格调相结合，强化城镇景观节点与特色风貌区，引导城镇形成特色化集镇风貌结构。总体形成"一核一带，一环联三区"的风貌格局。全域旅游规划策略从规划开始就介入，系统性地设计开发当地旅游资源，形成和

  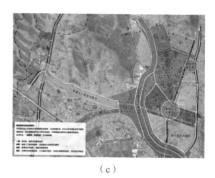

（a） （b） （c）

图 5　马金镇空间结构及旅游资源分布图（作者自绘）

（a）马金镇整体空间布局图；（b）马金镇用地属性图；（c）马金镇旅游区规划分布图

谐的生态旅游圈，最大化旅游资源利用率，高效带动整体地域经济发展。EPC-PPP 模式加快了施工进度，使规划更具有控制力，形成更集成的设计施工体系。

 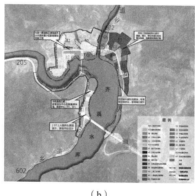 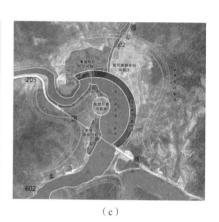

（a） （b） （c）

图 6　齐溪镇空间结构及旅游资源分布图（作者自绘）

（a）齐溪镇整体空间布局图；（b）齐溪镇用地属性图；（c）齐溪镇旅游区规划分布图

3.3　开化县华埠镇小城镇环境综合整治规划

在整体规划中，承接上位城镇规划，以及老城镇空间的特点结合华埠的历史文化强化华埠城镇景

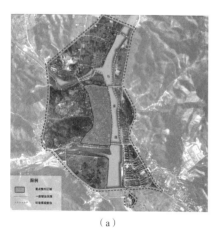  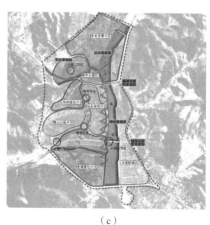

（a） （b） （c）

图 7　华埠镇空间结构及旅游资源分布图（作者自绘）

（a）华埠镇整体空间布局图；（b）华埠镇用地属性图；（c）华埠镇旅游区规划分布图

观特点和建筑风貌，总体形成"一带、四轴、五点、多片区"的风貌格局，也作为全域旅游的空间格局，系统性地调配旅游资源及相关产业资源。EPC-PPP 模式则解决了项目资金及施工问题，极大地推进了华埠镇旅游开发的进度。

4 结语与讨论

面对目前小城镇混乱开发的现状，小规模的设计力量显得束手无策，多作者的设计模式虽然运作灵活，但也带来很大弊端。本文提出的在 EPC-PPP 项目模式下的全域旅游开发模式很好地适应了当前的小城镇综合开发整治行动和美丽乡村建设的背景，也契合了当前新型社会资源调配方式。通过高度集成型的设计系统，多维度、多尺度地进行规划设计，开发和优化乡村旅游资源，带动新型小城镇的建设。但 EPC-PPP 模式也有一定的局限性，全域旅游的规划理念推行起来也有一定困难，希望能够通过进一步的研究来完善、优化目前的设计体系和规划策略。

Exploration and Practices through Reconfiguration of Region-based Tourism System in Small Towns under the EPC-PPP Model: A Case Study of Comprehensive Construction in Kaihua County of Zhejiang Province

Li Cheng, Shen Jie, Tang Yutian

(College of Civil Engineering and Architecture, Zhejiang University)

Abstract: With the development of national level urbanization process in China, the tendency of integrated optimization of environment, society and industry is becoming more important. The concurrent chaotic development pattern of urbanization has caused lots of problems and the new conception comes into being: region-based tourism, which is able to take advantage of public resources systematically and create dynamic balanced relationships among industry, products and demands. The EPC-PPP model integrate multiple advantages and will systematically and efficiently boost the development of projects. In this paper, we start by a case study with region-based tourism of comprehensive construction in Kaihua County of Zhejiang Province exploring new design system and orientation for the construction in small towns under EPC-PPP model. We try to create new design and construction system integrating with project packing, policy reorientation, financing credit, planning and design and unified purchase subsystems, which will provide positive theoretical basis for development in small towns in the future.

Keywords: Region-based tourism, EPC-PPP model, Renewal theory, Integrated design strategy

参考文献

[1] 菅梓君. 基于 PMO 的国际工程 EPC 总承包项目组织管理研究 [M]. 北京：北京交通大学出版社，2016.

[2] 刘捷. 城市形态的整合 [M]. 江苏：东南大学出版社，2004.

[3] 李强，陈宇琳，刘精明. 中国城镇化"推进模式"研究 [J]. 中国社会科学，2012，7：82-100.

[4] 陈沛. "BOT+EPC"模式下项目组织特征及其对项目绩效影响研究 [M]. 重庆：重庆交通大学出版社，2016.

[5] 游勍. 不同承包模式下建筑供应链中利益相关方行为研究 [Z]. 天津：天津大学出版社，2011.

[6] 曾祥辉. 全域旅游视角下永定县旅游发展探讨 [J]. 福建农林大学报，2016.

[7] 马航，何宁宁. 边缘效应下的深圳市城市边缘村更新改造研究——以龙岗区年丰社区为例 [J]. 华中建筑，2014，3：122-127.

[8] 郁枫. 空间重构与社会转型 [D]. 清华大学，2006.

[9] 刘玉春，贾璐璐. 全域旅游助推县域经济发展——以安徽省旌德县为例 [J]. 经济研究参考报，2015.

[10] 邓春凤，冯兵，龚克等. 桂北城镇聚落空间形态及景观 [J]. 城市问题，2007，9：62-68.

[11] 杨甜，胡永红. 全域旅游导向下许昌市旅游业发展策略研究 [J]. 华中建筑学报，2016.

Pro-growth Coalition of the Local Political Economy and the Contemporary Upsurge of Sustainable Urbanism in China: Three Cases in Shenzhen

Fu Yang, Zhang Xiaoling

(Department of Public Policy, City University of Hong Kong)

Abstract: With the assistance of an integrated theoretical framework, the paper aims to explore the possibility to reshape our built environment into a more sustainable urban form with the upsurge of green urbanism. Since the very beginning of the reform and opening-up policy, China has implemented marlcet economy throughout the country, and Chinese cities have been rendered competitive entrepreneurs for economic development, joining the global development enthusiastically and attracting capitals from worldwide. From then on, powerful local pro-growth coalitions have been encouraged and established by the local entrepreneurial governments, which have been constantly fueling the economic boom and staggering urbanization process in this country. The coalitions, often with the core of a powerful local government under Chinese institutional arrangements, turn the cities into growth machines serving the established local interest in a self-reinforcing manner. It is in such a context that a new initiative of green/sustainable urbanism is promoted and comes as the priorities of the national agenda. This trend is led by large-scale policy mobility of management & governing institutions and knowledge transfer of green & smart technology. Under such circumstances, multiple flagship new town development projects with various focuses on sustainability have been implemented. This study concentrates on three parallel new town development projects [Guangming Eco New Town, (Pingdi) International Low-carbon City and Pingshan New District]that are almost simultaneously initiated in Shenzhen. The pro-growth coalition, although put sustainable principles at the core of its development agenda, still creates some social and ecological problems while proffering stimuli for the city economy. However, the prospect of these projects is not as bleak as indicated by some researchers and with properly arranged institutions and policies, sustainability in these projects can be promoted substantially.

Keywords: Urban experiment, Sustainable urbanism, Entrepreneurial governance, Pro-growth coalition, Low-carbon city

1 Introduction

The 20th century has been recognized as the urban Anthropocene as the majority of the population started moving in the built environment in the urban areas [1]. The rising inclusive urbanism, aiming to improve the overall living quality in the urban areas in the first leaf of the century gradually turned in the welfarism after World War II [2]. Finally, represented by Regan and Thatcher, the globe made the neo-liberal turn, commoditizing people, space, resources and everything for capitalist accumulation and production worldwide [3]. Enthusiastically jumped onto the global development bandwagon, China has adopted multiple measures, including tax and devolution reforms to stimulate the local economy growth. Therefore, the local governments were rendered active competitors for global capital, resources and intelligence [4]. They take the lead in the local pro-growth coalitions and initiates different kinds of urban development or mega projects to maintain the growth of the economy. This process has been facilitated by the knowledge/policy transfer mechanisms [5]. It has mutually reinforced each other with the rapid urban development in China.

The neo-liberal turn has, on the one hand, created the economic success and on the other, made great pressures on the environment and society. The most recent decades witnessed the rising of multiple urbanisms, including the urban metabolism, low-carbon and eco discourses as well as the smart city discourse which resorts to technological solutions to the urban problems [6, 7]. Since implementing market economy, China has made many urban experiments, as responses to the ups and downs of the sustainable urban discourse. The local entrepreneurial governments are equally enthusiastic to be engaged in such experiments as they may be a potential boost for the local economy and these projects will receive endorsements from the national level. To investigate such sustainable urban trend in contemporary China, this study chooses 3 cases in Shenzhen, each representing a different approach to sustainable urbanization. The study will reveal what are the characteristics of each approach of sustainable urbanism and what will the potential risks be. The following section 2 is a summary of the previous literature on entrepreneurial governance mode, pro-growth coalition and different kinds of urban experiments in recent decades. While section 3 introduces the methods of the study and section 4 and 5 are discussions and the conclusion respectively.

2 Literature Review

A basic governance taxonomy has been contrived by DiGaetano and Strom, which includes five fundamental models, namely, the "clientelistic, pluralistic, corporatist, popular democratic and managerial" [8]. It is almost impossible to find the above mentioned five models existing in pure forms. The reality is more like a mixture of more than one of them [9]. It has been argued by many that China has gradually transformed from managerial governance to entrepreneurial governance [10]. It is depicted as a result of the market economy turn in China's policy. New urban space has been created as "spatial fix" for global capitals and the prosperity of such new space will guarantee an advantageous position in the global competition for the local players [11, 12]. Therefore, the local pro-growth coalitions, led by the government in Chinese context, and the capitalist production mutually reinforced each other [13, 14]. For instance, Wu Fulong has argued the market and state are not contradictory but complementary to each other in China [15]. Such trend continues in the era of sustainable urbanisms and more urban experiments projects are implemented to promote local growth [16]. The established coalition in China is a "regime with high authority" [10, 17]. The free discretion and financial capacity generated from the public land in cities has made the local governments powerful players in the local coalitions [10, 18-20].

Although pro-growth coalition is a western concept, it is widely applied in other political and economic contexts. The majority of local interests all supposed to benefit from such a coalition [21]. Many scholars have analyzed the mechanism of such coalitions in China. This is particularly true in the urban renewal projects or new town development cases [22, 23]. As mentioned in the introduction part, the policy mobility/transfer process, in which Chinese partners have forged networks with overseas ones, have boosted such a process [24]. Nevertheless, the neo-liberal competition and the economic gains are not without consequences, especially after the economic crisis in 2007 when the global community started to reconsider the balance between economic development and eco-social capacity [25]. And as a result, many countries began to revisit their urbanization process by promoting a myriad of sustainable urban experiments [26]. They believe the experiments will sustain the urban growth without depleting the environmental and social resources[27].

The urban experiments in China have been thriving in recent decades, with "ecological civilization" highlighted in the successive 12th and 13th five-year guidelines [28]. Green/sustainable urbanism has been promoted as a national agenda. For example, the Ministry of Housing and Urban-rural Development (MHURD) started a low-carbon pilot scheme nationwide in 2012 while in parallel, the Ministry of Environmental Protection (MEP) launched an eco-city counterpart. These schemes, together with other smart, green and resilient city etc. initiatives have been drawing the attentions from both the academics and policy makers.

3 Comparative Case Studies in Shenzhen

We choose Shenzhen as the target for our case studies due to the following reasons. Firstly, Shenzhen municipality, as a model and experiment field for Chinese government, enjoys a greater degree of discretion and therefore are more actively engaged in various sustainable urban experiments. For instance, both pilot projects of eco-city and low-carbon city can be found here. Besides, Shenzhen is the city that has experienced the most rapid urbanization process in China, the environmental pressures, as well as the economic achievement, are equally outstanding here, indicating a stronger impetus for sustainable urban experiments. It is a snapshot and epitome of the broader picture in China. In addition, the three new town projects (Figure 1) are comparable on many different scales. They were initiated around the same period of time, cover the similar size of land and hold a large amount of population. During 2015 and 2016, constant site visiting was made to the above-mentioned sites. Interviews with local officials, businesses, planners and other actors are the major source for the study. On top of this, we also retrieved data from government documents, reports and yearbooks. Figure 1 shows the location of the three cases.

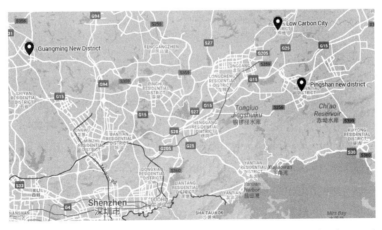

Figure 1 Location of Guangming (eco) new district, Pingshan new district and Shenzhen international low-carbon city

4 Three Urban Experiments in Shenzhen

Shenzhen has experienced a boom in its size of population and economy since the opening up reforms.

As suggested by a high-ranking local official (deputy mayor level) in an interview, "although the officially reported residents in Shenzhen is just over 11 million, the actual number has surpassed 20 million already. In effect, 2 million people flooded in last year (2015)". The great momentum pushes the local government to find new models for urbanization. As a result, Guangming (eco) new district, International low-carbon city and the Pingshan new district are launched as experiments for more sustainable forms of urban development. However, the three cases are on different tracks for sustainable urbanization.

Shenzhen international low-carbon city is a typical case resulted from the cooperation between the local pro-growth coalition and foreign partners. The following Figure 2 reveals how such coalition is formed to promote urban growth. "We have intensive networks with our European partners. This is particularly the case at the beginning stage of our project. We constantly invited urban scholars, planners, engineers and import management skills and urban policies. But they are not directly involved in the operation of our project." The communication with the international partners makes this project a high-profile showcase, illustrating all most up-to-date green technologies. However, during our visit there, the site is so peculiar, with a well-equipped exhibition center surrounded by sprawling village houses. For instance, they have designed a green facade for the exhibition center, which is expensive and requires delicate maintenance. Such technologies are rarely seen in the surrounding companies and factories, let alone the villagers' houses.

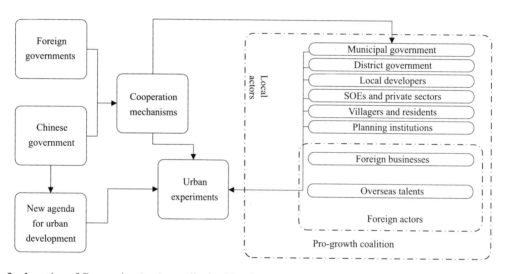

Figure 2　Location of Guangming (eco) new district, Pingshan new district and Shenzhen international low-carbon city

On the other hand, Guangming (eco) new district and Pingshan new district adopted a totally different development strategy. These two projects started only 3 years before the International low-carbon city. However, they have made much better progress in terms of population and infrastructure, which seems to indicate a potentially more prosperous prospect for these two cases. *"Since I moved here in 2012, the housing price here has been tripled"*, a residence in Guangming new district said. Statistics echoes such comments, the investment in both Guangming and Pingshan district increased over 5 times in the past four years and their floor area also increased over 4 times. It proves that at least the real estate market is growing quickly and people keep moving in. Nevertheless, the energy consumption per unit of GDP in these two districts performed no better, if not worse, than the overall Shenzhen municipality, implying the growth model in these two districts is not really sustainable.

With new metro lines under construction and a constantly growing population, it is for sure these two new towns will grow at a staggering rate. They took a more grounded track of development by investing heavily in the real estate and infrastructure. However, the green technologies in the low-carbon city exhibition center are rarely seen in these two districts. These two are more practical projects implemented solely by the local government and businesses without much foreign involvement. Therefore, they are more low-profile. Yet it should be noted that, although they are more prosperous as new towns, they are less so as eco towns. It is likely that they are just "sustainability fix" created for a new round capitalist production while the ecological performance has not been paid enough attention to. Figure 3 demonstrates the two models of sustainable urban experiments. Although the two tracks bear distinctive characteristics, it is still too early to give a final judge, as all of the three cases are still in the construction stage.

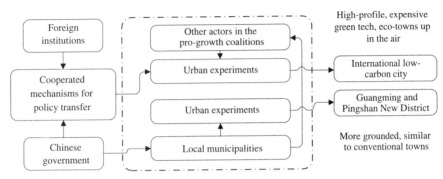

Figure 3 Two modes of sustainable urban experiments: characteristics and potential risks

5 Conclusion

The entrepreneurial local governments in China responded proactively to the trend of sustainable urbanism by promoting various kinds of sustainable urban experiments. These experiments may engage with policy mobility mechanisms with foreign partners to different extents. Their implementation strategies also vary significantly with some aiming high while others taking a more grounded approach. These approaches bear their own characteristics and potential risks. For instance, the experiments with a higher level of foreign involvement tend to be more high-profile. They are often equipped with all kinds of expensive green technologies and design that require delicate maintenance, rendering them an eco-paragon that is difficult to be replicated in other places. The stark contrast between the exhibition center in the low-carbon city and the surrounding environment is a case in point. At least at the current stage, they look more like ecotopia up in the air. On the other hand, the projects with a lower level of policy/knowledge transfer from foreign partners are not as outstanding as the former ones. Although they fare quite well in terms of new town development, it is less the case regarding their ecological performance. The local government tends to depend on the conventional track of urban expansion whose ecological and social performance may not necessarily be better than conventional new towns. This more grounded strategy may easily render the new towns as "sustainability fix" for a new round of capitalist accumulation and reproduction. Due to the limitation of length, this paper only investigates two types of urban experiments. More future research is called for to probe into other types of urban experiments in China and even in the world as well.

城市增长联盟与可持续城市化策略：
以深圳三个新城建设为例的研究

符 阳 张晓玲

（香港城市大学公共政策学系）

摘 要：20个世纪以来，多种城市化潮流相继涌现。早在20世纪70年代改革开放之初，中国就开始推行市场经济，不断拓展城市空间，培育城市人口，改善城市基础设施与服务，经历了前所未有的快速城市化过程。在此期间，通过行政放权和财税改革，地方政府的创业潜能得到了激发。以各个地方政府牵头形成的地方增长联盟在全球范围内竞逐人才、资本与技术。然而以资本积累和再生产为核心的发展模式给生态环境系统和社会体系带来了巨大压力，这种发展模式是不可持续的。为了应对这些生态与社会问题，可持续城市化应运而生。中国也通过各种知识、技术、人才、管理制度的转移机制，引进先进的可持续城市化经验。希望通过试点，继而在全国推广可持续城市化模式，解决传统城市发展模式的弊端。创业型的地方政府与增长联盟积极响应这一浪潮，推进了各类城市实验，低碳城市、生态城市等应运而生。深圳市的光明（生态）新城、国际低碳城和坪地新城就是典型代表，这些城市实验工程采取了迥异的可持续发展策略。本文着重讨论了不同发展策略的特点、优势以及未来可能面临的风险。

关键词：城市实验，可持续城市化，创业型治理，城市增长联盟，低碳城市

References

[1] Swilling M, Annecke E. Rethinking urbanism. Just Transitions: Explorations of Sustainability in an Unfair World. 2012: 107-36.

[2] Mayer M. First world urban activism: Beyond austerity urbanism and creative city politics[J]. City, 2013, 17: 5-19.

[3] Graham S, Marvin S. Splintering urbanism: networked infrastructures, technological mobilities and the urban condition[M]. Psychology Press, 2001.

[4] Zhou L-A. The Incentive and Cooperation of Government Officials in the Political Tournaments: An Interpretation of the Prolonged Local Protectionism and Duplicative Investments in China [J]. Economic Research Journal, 2004, 6: 33-40.

[5] Dolowitz D, Marsh D. Who learns what from whom: a review of the policy transfer literature[J]. Political studies, 1996, 44: 343-57.

[6] Voytenko Y, McCormick K, Evans J, Schliwa G. Urban living labs for sustainability and low carbon cities in Europe: towards a research agenda[J]. Journal of Cleaner Production, 2016, 123: 45-54.

[7] Fu Y, Zhang X. Trajectory of urban sustainability concepts: A 35-year bibliometric analysis[J]. Cities, 2017, 60: 113-23.

[8] DiGaetano A, Strom E. Comparative urban governance: An integrated approach[J]. Urban Affairs Review, 2003, 38: 356-95.

[9] Howlett M. Governance modes, policy regimes and operational plans: A multi-level nested model of policy instrument choice and policy design[J]. Policy Sciences, 2009, 42: 73-89.

[10] Zhang L, Chen J, Tochen RM. Shifts in governance modes in urban redevelopment: A case study of Beijing's Jiuxianqiao Area[J]. Cities, 2016, 53: 61-9.

[11] Young A. The razor's edge: Distortions and incremental reform in the People's Republic of China[J]. The Quarterly Journal of Economics, 2000, 115: 1091-135.

[12] Rodríguez-Pose A, Gill N. The global trend towards devolution and its implications[J]. Environment and planning C: Government and Policy, 2003, 21: 333-51.

[13] Wu F, Xu J, Yeh AG-O. Urban development in post-reform China: State, market, and space[M]. Routledge, 2006.

[14] Yu XJ, Ng CN. Spatial and temporal dynamics of urban sprawl along two urban–rural transects: A case study of Guangzhou, China[J]. Landscape and Urban Planning, 2007, 79: 96-109.

[15] Wu F. China's changing urban governance in the transition towards a more market-oriented economy[J]. Urban Studies, 2002, 39: 1071-93.

[16] Mazzucato M. The entrepreneurial state[J]. Soundings, 2011, 49: 131-42.

[17] He S. State-sponsored gentrification under market transition the case of Shanghai[J]. Urban Affairs Review, 2007, 43: 171-98.

[18] Han SS. Urban expansion in contemporary China: What can we learn from a small town? [J].Land Use Policy, 2010, 27: 780-7.

[19] Wu QY, Zhang XL, Li HB, Chen H, Li ZJ, Shang ZY. Pro-growth giant business, lock in, sustainable urban development and effect on local political economy: the case of petrochemical industry at Nanjing[J]. Journal of Cleaner Production, 2015, 107: 324-32.

[20] Zhu J. Local growth coalition: the context and implications of China's gradualist urban land reforms[J]. International Journal of Urban and Regional Research, 1999, 23: 534-48.

[21] Jonas AEG, Wilson D. The city as a growth machine: Critical reflections two decades later1999.

[22] Xu J, Yeh AG. City repositioning and competitiveness building in regional development: New development strategies in Guangzhou, China[J]. International Journal of Urban and Regional Research, 2005, 29: 283-308.

[23] Wei YHD. Restructuring for growth in urban China: Transitional institutions, urban development, and spatial transformation[J]. Habitat International, 2012, 36: 396-405.

[24] Filatotchev I, Liu X, Lu J, Wright M. Knowledge spillovers through human mobility across national borders: Evidence from Zhongguancun Science Park in China[J]. Research Policy, 2011, 40: 453-62.

[25] Knox PL, McCarthy L. Urbanization: an introduction to urban geography: Pearson Boston, MA, 2012.

[26] Li L-H, Li X. Land readjustment: an innovative urban experiment in China[J]. Urban Studies, 2007, 44: 81-98.

[27] Zhang SM. Land-centered urban politics in transitional China——Can they be explained by Growth Machine Theory?[J]. Cities, 2014, 41: 179-86.

[28] Tiejun W, Kinchi L, Cunwang C, Huili H, Jiansheng Q. Ecological civilization, indigenous culture, and rural reconstruction in China[J]. Monthly Review, 2012, 63:29.

Communities Inside the Ruins: A study of the Nature of Communities in Abandoned Buildings in Manila as An Alternative Housing Solution for Urban Areas

Mar Lorence G. Ticao

(Far Eastern University)

Abstract: Urban growth and development is unstoppable. In the age of globalization, cities and urban areas are expanding continually. This upward movement is central to development and growth of cities and of nations. Economic opportunities and services available in cities serve to magnet the population movement from rural areas. With the onslaught of population in these urban environments, the demand for housing increases and housing backlog has become an ongoing concern to both the public and private sectors. Slums have organically provided the solution for low-cost housing for these rural migrants. Idle lands, spaces under bridges, open public spaces serve as their places of residence as more high-end developments have pushed them out and the increased value of land in cities. In the organic development of informal housing, settlements and communities have developed in abandoned and unused buildings in Manila City, which is also the city with the highest density in the Philippines. Generations of families have occupied and lived inside these structures for decades; Sometimes with the consent of the building owners while others illegally living inside the abandoned walls. These families have made a home out of these abandoned buildings such as former theater buildings, office structures, and commercial shopping spaces. This paper explores the various layers of these communities to give a better perspective into their nature, to serve as a guide for future integration into urban policies development.

Keywords: Alternative housing, Informal settlements, Communities inside the ruins, Slums, Abandoned buildings

1 Introduction

Urban growth is a natural occurring phenomenon that has been brought about by rapid industrialization, modernization and the trend to look for a better life in the developing cities. Globalization, quick and easy forms of communication, and easier travel options have played a big role in the growth of cities over the last decade. This has brought in more business opportunities and easier access to services that makes living in these growing and highly urbanized areas more appealing to a vast population especially in countries where rural growth is sacrificed to prioritize what governments and majority stakeholders see as better suited areas for urban growth. Though these centers are essential to the growth of nations and the upliftment of its citizens as a whole, positive change comes negative factors, high development rate has brought about an exponential increase in populations choosing to live in the cities rather than in rural towns in the hopes of a better life and easier access to services. Migration from rural towns which offer slower and limited growth potential, especially in developing countries, is one of the biggest causes of the population booms in the cities or the better developed and more urbanized areas. The onslaught of population, demand for housing increases and housing backlog in urban areas become an ongoing concern that both public and private sectors need to address. The high demand for housing results to an accelerating growth of informal settlements, overcrowding of rental accommodations, and exploitation of new arrivals by landlords charging exuberant rental fees.

The low income families in urban areas become the marginalized population as a result of the economic imbalance. They are the least who have access to affordable housing. Most of them resort to living in informal settlements. Public spaces become their abode. In urban areas where money is the bottom line, low income families or those who have recently moved to the cities to look for job opportunities, end up in situations that perhaps are worse than that of their situation living in a rural town. Developing countries, most especially, "are struggling to provide adequate housing, physical infrastructures, and economic, social, and environmental services" to these people, while conventional planning approaches have failed to address challenges of rapid urbanization. [1,4]

2 Slums as a Way of Life

Shelter is a basic human right, as basic as the rights to food and clothing. However, the lower 30 percent of the urban population in the Philippines have difficulty accessing affordable housing. This leads them to engage in informal and self-help types of housing, while in constant danger of eviction and demolition. Informal settlements are normally found in previously unoccupied or idle public lands, but in some cases, more organic forms of settlement have formed inside abandoned buildings and complexes around Manila City in the Philippines.

RA 7279 or the Lina Law became a light for the poor when it was approved in 1992. The law provided the families in slums the right to a due process from eviction and demolition of their dwellings.

3 Inclusive Development

3.1 Inclusive Development Makes Cities More Sustainable

The UN-HABITAT defines a slum household as a group of individuals living under the same roof who lack one or more of the following conditions: security of tenure, structural quality and durability of dwellings, access to safe water, access to sanitation facilities, or sufficient living area. [2]

According to Steinberg, the continuing marginalization of the poor in city planning and development, together with the growing environmental and social problems call for a more inclusive development framework, rooted in the changing context of urbanization and sensitive to new opportunities for and challenges to slum rehabilitation. Such includes the following: defining greater roles for the corporate sector, nongovernmental organizations (NGOs), community-based organizations (CBOs), and citizens; public authorities and local governments as facilitator of urban processes; identifying opportunities for new partnerships between public and private sector organizations; addressing on-site upgrading and rehabilitation challenges; addressing adverse impacts of climate change and episodic events; meeting the challenge of strategically managing slum rehabilitation.

According to ADB's Managing Asian Cities, "Cities should be places where people want to live and where they can have safe and secure, affordable houses and neighborhoods that are appropriately serviced and have adequate access to services and supporting equity in asset distribution, maximizing the use of national programs like social funds. This means designing and implementing systems that allow local communities to make decisions on key facilities they will use, especially for health and education. Cities must prepare and implement housing and urban renewal strategies to provide affordable shelter and basic needs. This includes the upgrading of slums. With the help of concerned communities, cities should more rigorously enforce laws against land occupation and illegal construction to prevent the reappearance of illegal settlements in the future." [3]

3.2 Integration into Development Policies

A proposed framework made by Solaun and Kronus assessed the existing official planning framework in Colombia and afterwards emphasized the integration the squatter communities to their framework for development policy-making. [4] These are inclusion of settlements within the future urban planning context (legal), coordination of policies for improvement, granting of loans, and leases, collection of taxes, etc (administrative), provision of services such as water, sanitation, health services, electricity, street lighting, and paving. Technical and material assistance for house improvement (physical), provision of employment, and / or training opportunities (economic), inclusion of squatter and other unauthorized settlement households on voting registers on an equal basis to the remainder of the urban population and freedom to establish local political pressure groups (political), and provision of opportunities for the community to develop their own cultural patterns and to have right of access (and where necessary assisted access) to schools and community facilities (cultural / social).

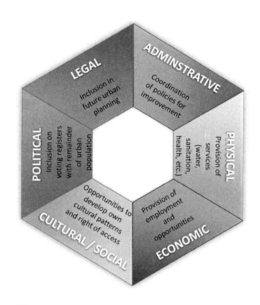

Figure 1　Integration of squatter settlement into the officially approved planning

Source: Solaun, Flynn and Kronus, 1971.

It is necessary for planners, architects and policymakers "to learn from the poor… work with them rather than to make arbitrary assumptions and plan for people…" in order to reduce inequality [5].

4　Homes Inside Abandoned Buildings as An Alternative Housing Solution

The need for new concepts and adapting inclusive frameworks to address the social and economic problems of people living in the urban slums should be focused on. As starting point, this study looks into the thriving organic communities formed inside old, abandoned buildings or ruins[①] along Rizal Avenida in Manila

---

① 　The term "ruins" is used for this study denoting structures that have now either been abandoned or in major disrepair.

City, the historic high-street of Manila. Generations of families have occupied and lived inside these structures for decades.

Members of the communities inside old buildings were interviewed regarding their perception of territorial ownership, space utilization, and community organization. This constituted the aspects that were studied for the integration into the frameworks mentioned above.

Figure 2　Façade of an old movie theatre

4.1　Organic Communities Versus Planned Ones

Studies on homegrown communities[①] all over the world have been conducted showing how informal settlements have established slums as a more viable and sustainable solution to the growing population in urban areas.

Figure 3　Abandoned theatre's facade

Historically, different aspects of cities——economic, social, and cultural "occupied different spaces and operate under different rules" to maximize control and minimize conflict today, these worlds "have come to share the same space, they understand and use it differently" development plans. These "formal or static city" —— built of more permanent materials such as concrete, steel, and bricks and is understood as a "two-dimensional entity on conventional city maps." They have become cities in motion, three-dimensional

---

① The Colombian architect Andres Arias has an ongoing project on the study of community structures of informal settlers.

construct of incremental development, temporary in nature, built with recycled materials: plastic sheets, scrap metals, canvas, waste wood. [6] The residents of these informal communities have established a home for their families inside these buildings. They recreate what is familiar to them from their rural hometowns and even defining territories for each family: making use of the old structure's toilet cubicles to define personal spaces, even converting lobbies into public spaces, providing the ubiquitous basketball court present in most Filipino communities.

5 "Places Retain Their Importance Because the Human Body Is Always Local, Living A Particular Life in A Particular Place, with Others, for Better or Worse" [7]

The main reason why people are naturally attracted to cities is due to the phenomenon of urbanization. People always get attracted to where opportunities are. Housing is essential, but based on the hierarchy of needs, immediate need or survival comes beforehand. Living in places near places of opportunities comes first even if this means living informally, illegally, or at the detriment of one's safety. Despite government efforts to provide socialized housing for the low income population, many of the poor families in Metro Manila who have been previously relocated return to the cities after a while. Housing inside abandoned buildings can prove to be an alternative solution to the housing backlog in the Philippines. The government would always be for the welfare of its people. If conditions inside the old buildings prove to provide a safe, sustainable, and viable, these could be an addition to the solution needed by the growing urban population of Metro Manila to address homelessness.

废墟内的社区：作为城市地区替代住房解决方案的马尼拉废弃建筑物性质研究

Mar Lorence G. Ticao

（菲律宾远东大学）

摘　要：城市增长和发展是不可阻挡的。在全球化时代，城市和城市地区不断扩大。这种向上运动是城市和国家发展和增长的核心。城市的经济机会和服务可以吸引农村人口流动。随着这些城市环境中的人口爆炸式增长，住房需求增加，住房积压已成为公共和私营部门持续关注的问题。贫民窟为这些农村移民提供低成本住房解决方案。空旷的土地，桥梁下的空间，开放的公共空间作为他们的居住地，因为更多的高端发展推动了他们，以及城市土地价值的增加。在非正规住房的有机发展中，定居点和社区已经在马尼拉市的废弃和未利用的建筑物中发展，马尼拉市也是菲律宾密度最高的城市。几代家庭已经在这些结构中居住了几十年；有的得到业主的同意，而其他人则非法居住在被遗弃的墙壁内。这些家庭已经从这些被遗弃的建筑物，如前剧院大厦，办公楼和商业购物场所中做了一个家。本文探讨了这些定居点的性质，作为这些社区融入未来城市政策发展的指南。

关键词：替代住房，非正式定居点，废墟中的社区，贫民窟，废弃建筑物

References

[1] Steinberg F, Lindfield M, eds. Inclusive cities. Urban Development Series. Mandaluyong: Asian Development Bank, 2011.

[2] United Nations Economic and Social Commission for Asia and the Pacific (ESCAP). Statistical year book for Asia and the Pacific, 2008.

[3] ADB. Managing Asian cities——sustainable and inclusive urban solutions. Manila, 2008.

[4] Solaun M, Flynn W, Kronus S. Diagnosis and solutions for squatter settlements——the case of Los Colinas. Mid-West Universities Consortium for International Activities and the Graduate Research Board, University of Illinois, 1971.

[5] Payne G. Urban housing in the third world[M]. London: Leonard Hill, 1977.

[6] Mehrotra R, Huyssen A, ed. Negotiating the static and kinetic cities: the emergent urbanism of Mumbai. Urban imaginaries in a globalizing age[M]. London: Duke University Press, 2008.

[7] Kogl A. Strange places: The political potentials and perils of everyday spaces[M]. New York: Lexington Books, 2008.

绿色建筑与可持续环境设计

Green Building and Sustainable Environment Design

A Study of the Energy Conservation Potentials of Earth Sheltered Housing for Purposes of Urban Scale Developments

Jideofor Akubue[1], Liu Suya[2]

(1.Architecture Department, Baze University Abuja; 2.Beijing University of Civil Engineering and Architecture)

Abstract: Earth sheltered houses have evolved over time into prospective green construction options with significant energy saving values. With the potential thermal conservation qualities and physical characteristics of earth as building mass, earth shelters depend on the earth placed against walls as its external thermal mass, which reduces heat loss and maintains a steady indoor air temperature throughout the seasons. Research shows that building underground provides energy savings by reducing the yearly heating and cooling loads when compared with conventional structures. This paper presents some of the valuable analysis and results in earth-sheltered building evaluations as premise for assessing the potentials of passively heated subterranean houses for urban scale development. Through this review, thermal integrity factors (TIF) of existing earth-sheltered homes are obtained which can easily be compared with other housing types.

Keywords: Earth shelters, Building with earth, Earth homes, Underground building, Energy conservation.

1 Introduction

The use of earth in building construction is an age long traditional practice which has evolved into an energy conservation option for home designs in modern times. Studies show that building underground provides energy savings by reducing the yearly heating and cooling loads when compared with known conventional structures. This is achieved firstly, via the reduction of heat loss due to conduction through the building envelope by the high density of the earth cover and secondly because the building is also protected from the direct solar radiation. The ground temperatures in an earth-sheltered building at very shallow depths and within normal environmental conditions, seldom reach the outdoor air temperatures in the heat of a normal summer day[1]. This condition allows the conducting of less heat into the house due to the reduced temperature differential. However, in the case of colder climates, the rate of heat loss in the earth supported structure (bermed type) during winters is less in comparison to that in above grade structures. Kumar R (et al), indicates that the floor surface temperature increased by 3℃ for a 2.0m deep bermed structure due to lower heat transfer from the building components to the ground, thus suggesting the presence of passive heat supply from the ground even at the extreme cold temperatures of winter[2]. These findings provide the front for research that will drive the improvement of subterranean designs in terms of thermal performance, structural integrity and general outlook in the modern city sprawl.

2 Related Reviews

2.1 Background of the Study

Energy conservation in earth shelters is dependent on certain principles which form the ground rules for the design and construction of these dwellings since prehistoric periods. These buildings in the past were erected by locals without the knowledge of formal architectural design or identifiable building techniques rather they depended on the cover the structure of the earth could provide them for purposes of shelter, warmth and security. In China, modern earth shelters habitats were discovered with histories that dated back to 2000 B.C. In the North-west of China, variety of these structures evolved, which ranged from cave dwelling units to the more advanced subterranean housing types. These traditional subterranean homes ('yao dong') in China were constructed of rooms dug into loose, loess soil to primarily combat the hot summers and cold winters. In the early 20th century the provinces of Shanxi, Jiangsu and Henan still had traditional dwellers that preserved agricultural land and housing by digging up entire cities beneath their lands as seen in Figure 1.

Figure 1 Earth shelter homes in Sanmenxia, Henan, central China

In 2006, estimated 40 million people in northern China still lived in *yao dongs*[3]. The earth shelters in Henan were buried at depths of up to 10 meters with homes built around courtyards as shown in Figure 2.

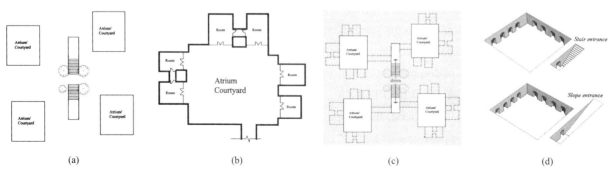

Figure 2 Schematic features of the Sanmenxia earth shelters

(a) Typical layout of combined earth shelter units; (b) Typical earth-shelter home plan; (c) Detail of underground rooms; (d) Illustration of entrance types

2.2 Analysis of Design Typologies

Investigation of the most efficient application of earth shelter principles reveals classifications of the major typologies. The typologies identified are the Bermed and the Sunken or True underground types.

2.2.1 Bermed Typology

Bermed earth shelter construction uses earth piled up against exterior walls and heaped to incline downwards away from the house. The roof may, or may not be, fully earth covered, and windows/openings may occur on one or more sides of the shelter. This type of construction also includes the hillside and the elevated designs. Since the building is mostly above ground, fewer moisture problems are encountered. To maximize its energy efficiency in colder climates, all the living spaces are arranged on the side of the house facing the equator. This provides maximum solar radiation to the most frequently used spaces like bedrooms and living rooms. The compact configuration of this construction provides it with a greater ratio of earth cover to exposed wall thereby improving its energy performance benefits through earth-contact. Proper orientation with respect to solar path and wind is significant for maximized energy performance. Figure 3 (a) and (b) below illustrates the bermed earth shelter design typology.

2.2.2 Sunken or True-Underground Typology

In the true underground construction, the house is built completely below ground on a flat site, with the major living spaces surrounding an outdoor courtyard or atrium as shown in Figure 3 (c). The windows and glass doors that are on the exposed walls facing the atrium provide light, solar heat, outside views, and access via a stairway from the ground level. The atrium effect offers the potential for natural ventilation.

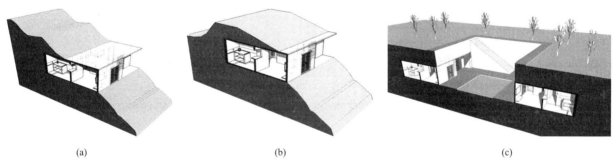

(a) (b) (c)

Figure 3 Earth shelter typologies

(a) Bermed hillside type; (b) Bermed elevated type; (c) sunken or true underground type

Comparative studies of existing typologies in[4] reveals conditions which are dependent on climate and physical challenges indigenous to each typology which can be summarized as shown in table 1.

Comparing the efficiency of the earth shelter building typologies   Table 1

FEATURES	TYPOLOGIES	
	Bermed Earth shelter design	Sunken/true underground design
Passive solar	Excellent	Less effective
Thermal stability	Less effective	Excellent

Continued

FEATURES	TYPOLOGIES	
	Bermed Earth shelter design	Sunken/true underground design
Winter impacts	Excellent	Less effective
Summer impacts	Excellent	Excellent
Natural lighting	Effective	Less effective
Natural ventilation	Assisted	Assisted
Noise protection	Less effective	Excellent
Visual convenience	Excellent (allows single direction view)	Poor (allows open sky view)

2.3 Review of the Structural Integrity of Earth Shelters

The soil-walls of the earth shelter trench are regarded as the most valuable structural member in the traditional building system. Study in[5] revealed certain traditional considerations for deciding the depth, thickness of mass and curvature of the support ceilings (vault) of the earth homes found in the northern regions of China which can also be applied in modern day construction of earth shelters. Figure 4 shows the structural consideration for room space excavation. The Dotted/shaded area (h) indicates possible fault lines due to the pressure from the overlaying earth mass.

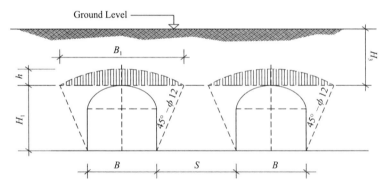

Figure 4 Structural consideration for typical room space excavation in traditional earth shelter construction

$$1/2\ B_1 = 1/2\ B + H_1\ tg\ (45° - \phi/2) \quad (1)$$

$$(h = 1\text{–}2,\ \phi = 18°)$$

$$1/2\ B_1 = 3.5/2 + 3\ tg\ (45° - 18°/2)$$

$$1/2\ B_1 = 1.75 + 2.19 = 3.94 \text{m}$$

H_1 = Extent of depth clearance

H_3 = Extent of depth clearance

Assuming B (room span) = 3.5m and H_1 (room height) = 3m

H_3 = Depth from ground surface to ceiling. This should be greater than h

Then S = Thickness of Earth thermal mass wall

3 Defining Thermal Efficiency Factors in Earth Shelter Design

Apart from the reduction of infiltration, studies identified that the application of thermal coupling of the earth-soil to the building wall places significant values to the thermal conditions of the earth shelter environment. This process allows for improved thermal storage through the soil into the building walls. Thus, the most significant factors that influence thermal efficiency are presented as the earth's soil energy balance and the passive annual heat storage (PAHS).

3.1 Soil Energy Balance

External factors like weather conditions acting on thermal balance on the earth's surface have the greatest influence on temperature fields in the ground. In colder seasons, the building absorbs excess energy from the soil; this absorbed heat is naturally released back into the building whenever indoor air temperature is below that of the thermal mass. This thermal absorption and releasing process (energy balance) provides essential heat energy required in the house for days without mechanical heating. Hence, the soil's thermal diffusivity coefficient influences the energy balance of earth-sheltered buildings. Accordingly, a mathematical method for predicting long-term annual pattern of soil temperature variations as a function of depth and time for different soils is presented (with the unit of cosine expressed in rad). This method is sufficiently accurate in the case certain thermal and physical characteristics are accurately estimated [6].

$$T_{(x,t)} = T_m - A_s e^{-x} \sqrt{\pi/365\alpha} \cos\{2\pi/365[t - t_0 - (x/2)(\sqrt{365/\pi\alpha})]\} \tag{2}$$

Where $T_{(x,t)}$ ——Subsurface temperature at depth x (m) on day t of the year (°C);

T_m——Mean annual ground temperature (equal to steady state) (°C), as the annual temperature amplitude at the surface ($x = 0$) (°C);

x——Subsurface depth (m);

t——The time of the year (days) where January 1 = 1 (numbers);

t_0——Constant, corresponding to the day of minimum surface temperature (days);

α——The thermal diffusivity of the soil (m²/day).

Through this equation, the resulting temperature profile at different depths can be graphed and compared with the annual average air temperatures. Following the evaluation of subsurface climate, calculated soil temperatures can then be used to calculate the heat flux through building surfaces.

3.2 Passive Annual Heat Storage (PAHS)

Globally, the earth receives electromagnetic radiation from the sun as short-wave radiation and emits it at longer wavelengths (long-wave radiation). When averaged annually, about 49% of solar radiation is absorbed at the surface (the atmosphere absorbs 20% of incoming radiation and the remaining 31% is reflected back to space). This absorbed 49% of solar radiation presents a foundation for energy efficiency. The absorption and re-emission of radiation at the earth's surface level yields the idea for PAHS. Energy efficiency in earth shelter developments focuses fundamentally on utilization of this absorbed and retained heat from annual absorption and re-emission of radiation for the indoor thermal environment control.

4 Thermal integrity analysis

Evaluations of earth sheltered buildings against conventional (above-ground) buildings are mostly in the area of thermal integrity and energy conservation. Thermal integrity factor (TIF) is utilized for comparing energy performance of different building types. It is expressed in units which allow for a direct comparison of such criterion as heating, ventilating, air conditioning as well as the effect of various climatic conditions. The standard unit for measuring thermal integrity values is Btu/ft^2 per degree day of the provided space conditions. A typical TIF of 7.5 Btu/ft^2 per heating degree day is considered as a baseline-factor for moderately insulated houses[7], while values in the ranges of 0.6 to 1.1 Btu/ft^2 are predicted for super-insulated houses[8]. Measurements conducted on existing earth sheltered houses in South Dakota[4], shows that earth shelter consumed about 28,000 Btu/ft^2 for 8144 heating degree days, which yields a TIF of 3.5 Btu/ft^2, while the typical above-ground homes in the same location required about 10 to 12 Btu/ft^2 (Figure 5). This displays a 70% difference in the TIF of these two homes in the same location.

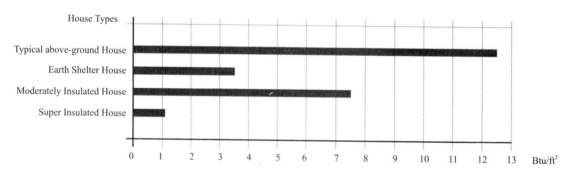

Figure 5 Thermal integrity values of different housing types

5 Optimizing Earth Shelter Developments

To achieve maximum benefits of thermal efficiency as discussed in this paper, application of earth shelter concepts at urban scale with optimized conditions is essential. Rather than individual homes or small cluster of houses which will absolutely be affected by the surrounding conventional structures, design of earth shelter districts that will take advantage of the energy balance the earth microenvironment provides is ideal for modernized urban development of earth shelters. Optimization in terms of structural integrity, construction materials, interior finishes and planning of external environment will produce improved living environment for occupants. The Aloni house (Figure 6) which won the Greek Piranesi award in 2009, displays a modernized environment of a combined sunken/elevated (bermed) earth shelter [9].

(a)   (b)   (c)   (d)

Figure 6   Views of the Aloni house by Deca Architecture
(a) Approach view; (b) Atrium view; (c) View from the top; (c) Interior view of the living room.

6   Soil suitability Analysis

Soil suitability for earth shelter construction is dependent on the ratio of macro to micro-pores of the soils. The more macro-pores a soil has the easier it is for water to soak into it and drain away. Soils with coarse particles like sand or gravel have high proportion of macro-pores and as a result have high infiltration rates. Soils such as clays have a high proportion of micro-pores and therefore have low infiltration rates. Determining the thermal performance of the soil for earth shelter construction involves assessing the long-term subsurface environment and above-ground temperature. Consequently, this requires accurate environmental information on boundary conditions, like the temperature of the surrounding soil. Most of the earth shelters (*yao dongs*) discovered in China was found around the Loess Plateau. The loess soil type which is silty in nature has high infiltration rate and was suitable for traditional builders in the past. However, challenges of flooding and erosion resulted in damages of these structures over time. Modern concepts apply optimized structural supporting members and compacted backfills in which case strength and composition determine the ability to withstand overhead loads of moisture, dead and live loads.

7   Conclusion

This study presents some of the valuable analysis in earth shelter building evaluations as premise for assessing the potentials of earth sheltered houses. The analysis of energy conservation elements, thermal integrity values and general optimization ideas present significant values for further investigations and applications of earth shelter designs in future urban housing schemes.

覆土建筑的节能潜力在城市开发尺度的研究

安 赛[1]　刘素雅[2]

（1. Baze 大学建筑学院；2. 北京建筑大学）

摘　要：从绿色建筑的视角，覆土建筑已经演化成为具有显著节能价值的建筑形式的选择。由于土壤被视为具有潜在热保温性能和物理特性的建筑材料，覆土建筑把置于建筑墙体的土壤当作外部保温材料，以此减少不同季节热量损失并保持室内温度的稳定。通过研究发现，与常规建筑相比，地下建筑可以通过减少每年供暖和制冷的负荷来节约能耗。针对城市尺度的开发，本文以覆土建筑的评估作为前提评价被动式加热的地下建筑，展示相关具有价值的分析和结果。通过文献研究获取已有覆土建筑的热性能因素 (TIF)，宜于与其他形式的建筑做比较。

关键词：覆土建筑，以生土建造，生土住宅，地下建筑，节能

References

[1] Carmody J, Sterling R. Design considerations for underground buildings[J]. Underground Space, 1984, 8: 352-362.

[2] Kumar R, Sachdevab S, Kaushik S C. Dynamic earth-contact building: A sustainable low-energy technology[J]. Building and Environment, 2007, 42: 2450-2460.

[3] Lloyd J, Mitchinson J. The Book of General Ignorance. Faber & Faber, 2006: 157.

[4] Wendt R L, Earth-Sheltered Housing: An Evaluation of Energy Conservation Potential. U.S. Department Of Energy Oak Ridge Operations, 1982: 8-18.

[5] Golany S. Earth Sheltered Habitats. New York: Van Nostrand Reinhold Company Inc, 1983.

[6] Labs K. Underground building climate[J]. Solar Age, 1979, 4: 10 44-50.

[7] Lewis D, Fuller W. Restraint in sizing direct gain systems[J]. Solar Age, 1979, 1: 28-32.

[8] Shurcliff W A. Super insulated houses and Double envelope houses: A Preliminary Survey of Principles and Practice[M]. Massachusetts: Brick house publishing Inc, 1980.

[9] Beautiful Underground Aloni house blends in with the earth. Inhabitat. 2010 [08/03/2017]. http://inhabitat.com/beautiful-underground-aloni-house-blends-in-with-the-earth/aloni.

应对雾霾——人口结构变迁下的城市旧有住宅的弹性转型与有机更新

田 昊 周 博

(大连理工大学)

摘 要：高密度、紧凑模式的住宅建设已经成为大多数城市发展的主要趋势。这种趋势不仅带来了城市高层建筑的密集建设，降低了人民的生活品质，而且使建筑工地和道路交通产生了大量的扬尘，造成空气不流动，因此也加剧了如今备受关注的全球雾霾现象。2016年，"二胎政策"全面开放，现下适应家庭人口结构、生命周期以及生活方式等未来变化的低碳住宅空间势在必行。本篇论文主要从旧有住区住宅居住结构模式的弹性转型和绿色低碳改造的角度出发，选取大连市区内20世纪八九十年代的住宅为具体的研究对象，根据其不适应人口结构变迁下的制约因素，结合住宅空间改造与室内设计，从住宅的居住模式、住宅的弹性空间设计和能源消耗三个方面提出具有针对性的改造策略。

关键词：人口结构，旧有住宅，弹性转型，低碳改造

1 引言

现如今，从"计划生育"到"二胎政策"的全面开放，中国家庭的人口结构正在发生变化，家庭人口数增长，代际关系正在发生调整。但是日前，国家卫生计生委确认，"单独二胎"政策开放以来，大约有1100万户家庭符合条件，但是平均申请率只有6%。另外国家统计局统计，2016年全国人口出生率为12.95%，而北京和上海等一线城市的出生率仅为0.7，因此未来30年中国新生人口不会有很大的发展。但是从长远来看，必定会影响家庭的未来的住房需求结构变化，新生婴儿或将成为家庭购买新房和改善性住房的主要因素。再加上30~45岁的青年人的工作发展需求，老年人也可能加入家庭结构中，"两房"显然不再是刚需，更大的居住空间如"三房"、"四房"将会成为主流需求。本论文主要根据住宅的结构特点，户型特点，灵活地对住宅内各功能区域之间重新组合，各房室之间合理地再切割和巧妙布局，增加开敞、弹性、动态以及与户外联结伸展的区域。使住宅可以随着家庭的全生命周期的"成长"而"进化"，使其承载每一位家庭成员的生活所需。从绿色低碳的理念出发，通过成本较低的有机更新完善，挖掘既有住区较大的潜力和居住价值，创造适宜人口结构变迁下的理想的弹性生活环境。

2 研究背景和方法

2.1 国内外的研究

从整体来看，欧美和日本的旧有住宅转型的实践比较成熟，法国甚至出台了对整个大巴黎的既有住区（包括废弃的厂房、老旧的住宅以及闲置的商场等）的改造策略。日本由于国土面积较小，人口

密度过大，所以早在 20 世纪七八十年代就出现了关于既有住宅更新改造的研究，并且还提出了"团地再生"的理论，重视居民决策和鼓励自发性的改造。在 20 世纪 80 年代初，我国很多城市经历过类似国外棚户区的再生设计等住宅区的更新活动，但是大多停留在建筑立面和小区的整体规划尤其是外部环境设计上，实践的经验还不算成熟且大多改造集中在北京、上海等一线城市。

2.2 研究方法

论文主要从住宅的现状和应对人口结构变化的出发，以大连市 20 世纪八九十年代既有住宅为对象，通过文献调研、实地调查和数据分析等方法，探索大连旧有住宅的弹性转型方法。

首先阅读整理了国内外旧有住宅改造与更新的相关文献，结合国内的政策要求和住宅的实际情况，尤其是针对大连市既有住宅改造的论文研究，进一步明确论文的研究对象。其次结合对大连市南石道街小区（获得 1989 年建设部优秀设计奖）和星海一街小区进行实地调研、拍照、访谈，深入了解当地居住的生活现状以及对住宅的需求，辅以从新闻和网络上采集各种数据等方式，为论文提供准确有力的支撑点，探讨旧有住宅弹性转型的可行性和有效性。

3 20 世纪八九十年代大连市城市旧有住宅的弹性转型与更新

3.1 20 世纪八九十年代大连市旧有住宅居住的一般模式

1980 年以后，大连市住宅建设进入新一轮的大潮，至 1990 年，大连市新建住宅面积达到 $3 \times 10^6 m^2$。该时期住宅建设标准低，且长期缺乏维护和管理，在技术、经济、社会等多重因素的作用下产生品貌陈旧、功能落后等问题。

八九十年代建造的住宅大多为 6 ~ 7 层（图 1、图 2）的多层住宅（一梯两户或三户），也有 8 层以上的点式住宅（一梯四户或六户）。住宅面积较小，大多在 50 ~ 80m² 之间，户型为两室一厅或三室一厅。住宅为砖混结构承重体系，因此住宅的进深较窄并且强调三道纵墙对齐。20 世纪 80 年代的住宅，在建造时并不注重"厅"的功能，因此一般为走廊串联两侧房间，再加上面积较小，因此起居室、客厅或者起居与卧室或者餐厅并用一间。20 世纪 90 年代的房屋，在户型设计上开始出现"厅"的概念，讲究"大客厅、一梯两户"。

图 1 大连市星海一街小区（作者调研拍摄）

图 2 大连市南石道街小区（作者调研拍摄）

从 80 年代的单元房到 90 年代的商品房，总体来说住宅功能相对较为完善，设施相对完备，形成自成体系的独立房子，设有独立卫生间、阳台等，平面布局较为合理。虽然在结构、空间以及总面积等方面都不适应未来家庭结构的需要,但是由于使用年限相对较短,大拆大建的更新模式显然不适合可持续发展的主题。因此在当下人口结构逐渐转型的时期,住宅空间的转型也显得尤为必要。

3.2 20世纪八九十年代大连市旧有住宅的现状问题分析

20世纪八九十年,受经济、技术、观念等方面的影响,大连市乃至全国的多层集合住宅设计均处于初级阶段,随着人口结构的调整和生活观念的改变,人们对居住空间的质量要求提高,旧有住宅不适应人们生活的各个方面也日益凸显。从适应人口结构的角度出发,通过对大连市典型的旧有住宅进行调研,发现主要存在以下几个难点和问题。

3.2.1 结构落后,空间的可塑性差

砖混结构由于造价便宜,施工难度低,因此大量应用于早期的住宅建设。为了满足抗震性和稳定性,住宅的开间、进深受限制且一般不能拆除或者改动,因此住宅空间格局的灵活性差。而且墙体较厚,占用了室内的空间,纯多层砖混结构不能实现较大空间,建筑功能布局上也受限。但是砖混结构具有良好耐久性和保温隔热性,甚至要优于混凝土和其墙体材料。

3.2.2 套型面积小,功能缺失,分区不明确,流线交叉

1981年原国家建委颁布了《关于职工住宅设计标准的几项补充规定》,《规定》将住宅按面积标准分为四类,每套平均建筑面积最小为42m^2,最大为90m^2。八九十年代的住宅多数按照前两类标准,每套平均建筑面积最大为50m^2,人均住房面积不到15m^2,远远不符合现代住宅的标准。功能交叉,起居室和卧室共用,书房和主卧串套,厨房和餐厅无分隔且就餐空间是在压缩厨厕空间的基础上形成的,这造成了动线和静线的混乱。套型必要功能缺失,入口门厅较为混乱,且住宅的洁污分区不明确,对室内的生活环境产生了一定影响。

3.2.3 开放性、灵活性差,缺少公共交流和娱乐等弹性空间

整体套型过于封闭、呆板,由走廊串联两侧房间,缺乏弹性空间,活力元素。且没有独立的起居室,即使是套型面积较大的住宅,其室内空间划分也较为独立,家庭成员的交流不够灵活。

表1是针对八九十年代大连市既有住宅的典型住宅所存在的不适应人口结构变化的问题进行分析,进而提出针对性的转型改造的建议。

3.3 对20世纪八九十年代大连市旧有住宅的弹性转型的建议

所谓弹性转型与有机更新,就是结合绿色、节能、可持续发展的理念,避免资源浪费,在尽量不大拆大建、大改大动的基础上,通过空间的变化、功能的转化,室内的改动,使住宅可以随着家庭的全生命周期的"成长"而"进化",承载每一位家庭成员的生活所需。

我国的家庭生命周期从形成期到衰退期持续的时间大约为50年,按照住房的家庭生命周期来说,不同家庭对住宅的类型有不同的要求,即使是同一个家庭,在不同的发展阶段也有不同的需求。例如在家庭形成期,这个时期一般考虑1~2个居室空间,满足夫妇的基本居住需要即可。但是到了家庭成熟期,伴随着一个或两个孩子的出生,甚至老年人的加入,各代需要各自的空间。因此在当下人口

表1 20世纪八九十年代典型的住宅分析（作者自绘）

	典型住宅1	典型住宅2
标准平面	（见图）	（见图）
转型分析	存在问题： 1. 一梯三户，面积较小，没有独立的门厅或者可以作为门厅的弹性走廊空间。 2. 起居室和卧室共用一间，流线交叉。 3. 餐厨面积过小，厨房过于开敞，洁污分区不明确。 4. 卫生间面积较小，洁具设置不合理，采光通风效果差	存在问题： 1. 一梯两户或者三户，但是建筑功能并不完善分区不明确。 2. 房间串套，造成的空间利用率低。 3. 厨房面积相对较大，餐厅位置不合理。 4. 卫生间没有采光，通风效果差。 5. 住宅空间没有因为面积的增加而更具开放性，过于封闭，没有公共交流、娱乐空间

结构逐渐转型的时期，住宅空间的转型也显得尤为必要。

另外，虽然在1987年的《住宅建筑设计规范》规定了7层（含7层）以上应设电梯，但是由于规范力度不够，大量住宅没有设置电梯，这严重影响了老年人的出行和生活的便利。中国在1999年就已经步入老龄化国家，因此对旧有住宅进行适老性改造也势在必行。考虑到住宅的结构、面积等问题，可以在紧邻楼梯间的位置设置外挂电梯，解决老年人的通行问题。

表2、表3分别针对典型住宅中阻碍其发展的因素，主要是住宅的面积和整体空间格局，居室的功能、采光、位置，室内家具的排列、分布等方面。按照住宅的现状和家庭周期的转化规律，保证相邻两个时期过渡的顺延性，并考虑每个时期为后期转型所需要准备的可行性条件。主要从建筑设计和室内设计的角度提出转型的建议，因此对旧有住宅的设备、管线、采暖、保温层等建筑物理性能方面的改造不再赘述。

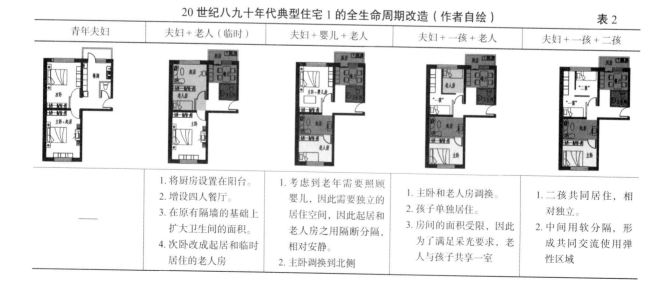

表2 20世纪八九十年代典型住宅1的全生命周期改造（作者自绘）

青年夫妇	夫妇+老人（临时）	夫妇+婴儿+老人	夫妇+一孩+老人	夫妇+一孩+二孩
—	1. 将厨房设置在阳台。 2. 增设四人餐厅。 3. 在原有隔墙的基础上扩大卫生间的面积。 4. 次卧改成起居和临时居住的老人房	1. 考虑到老年需要照顾婴儿，因此需要独立的居住空间，因此起居和老人房之用隔断分隔，相对安静。 2. 主卧调换到北侧	1. 主卧和老人房调换。 2. 孩子单独居住。 3. 房间的面积受限，因此为了满足采光要求，老人与孩子共享一室	1. 二孩共同居住，相对独立。 2. 中间用软分隔，形成共同交流使用弹性区域

续表

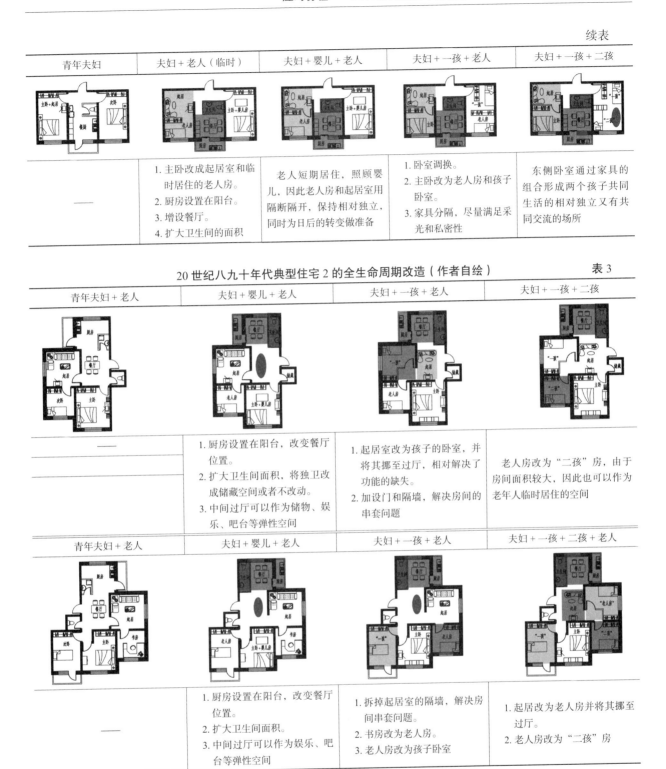

青年夫妇	夫妇+老人（临时）	夫妇+婴儿+老人	夫妇+一孩+老人	夫妇+一孩+二孩
—	1. 主卧改成起居室和临时居住的老人房。2. 厨房设置在阳台。3. 增设餐厅。4. 扩大卫生间的面积	老人短期居住，照顾婴儿，因此老人房和起居室用隔断隔开，保持相对独立，同时为日后的转变做准备	1. 卧室调换。2. 主卧改为老人房和孩子卧室。3. 家具分隔，尽量满足采光和私密性	东侧卧室通过家具的组合形成两个孩子共同生活的相对独立又有共同交流的场所

20世纪八九十年代典型住宅2的全生命周期改造（作者自绘） 表3

青年夫妇+老人	夫妇+婴儿+老人	夫妇+一孩+老人	夫妇+一孩+二孩
—	1. 厨房设置在阳台，改变餐厅位置。2. 扩大卫生间面积，将独卫改成储藏空间或者不改动。3. 中间过厅可以作为储物、娱乐、吧台等弹性空间	1. 起居室改为孩子的卧室，并将其挪至过厅，相对解决了功能的缺失。2. 加设门和隔墙，解决房间的串套问题	老人房改为"二孩"房，由于房间面积较大，因此也可以作为老年人临时居住的空间

青年夫妇+老人	夫妇+婴儿+老人	夫妇+一孩+老人	夫妇+一孩+二孩+老人
—	1. 厨房设置在阳台，改变餐厅位置。2. 扩大卫生间面积。3. 中间过厅可以作为娱乐、吧台等弹性空间	1. 拆掉起居室的隔墙，解决房间串套问题。2. 书房改为老人房。3. 老人房改为孩子卧室	1. 起居改为老人房并将其挪至过厅。2. 老人房改为"二孩"房

4 总结

1980～1984年，计划生育政策全面推行，国家普遍提倡一对夫妇只生育一个孩子。1982年更是把计划生育作为基本国策，因此20世纪八九十年代的家庭人口结构相对简单，住宅的面积也相对较小，基本能满足家庭周期的变化。到了2016年，从"计划生育"到"全面二孩"的转变，家庭人口数量和家庭中的代际关系发生明显的变化，人们需要更大的面积，更灵活的空间划分，家庭成员需要更多的交流。因此旧有的、独立的、封闭的居住模式显然远远落后人们的需求。

考虑到目前高房价以及亟待解决的雾霾等一系列环境问题，如何在尽可能不大兴城市建设，如何在尽可能不重新购置新房或者搬迁租房下转变房型，如何在尽可能不多增加面积的前提下增强多功能户型，创造适应人口结构以及未来家庭人口流动的住宅模式，增强住宅内部空间的活力和变化的灵活性，实现住宅绿色低碳发展，将是新一轮的城市住宅建设中需要思考的问题。

"城市旧有住宅模式的弹性转型"是基于人口结构变迁下的针对我国城市已建成住宅改造更新的迫切性需要，在改善人们的居住质量，放缓因高密度城市带来的城镇化速度，实现绿色有机可持续发展等方面大有裨益。

Responding to the Fog —— The Elastic Transformation and Organic Renewal of the Old Residential Buildings under the Changing Population Structure

Tian Hao, Zhou Bo

(Dalian University of Technology)

Abstract: High density, compact mode of residential construction has become the main trend of most urban development. This trend not only brings the intensive construction of urban high-rise buildings, reduces the quality of life of the people, but also makes the construction site and road traffic produce a lot of dust, causing the air unflowed, and therefore also exacerbates today's concern global fog Haze phenomenon. In 2016, the "two-child policy" is fully opened, nowadays to adapt to the family population structure, life cycle and lifestyle changes in the future of low-carbon residential space is imperative. This paper mainly starts from the elastic transformation of residential structure model and the green low-carbon transformation, and selects the existing houses in the urban area of Dalian in the 1980s and 1990s as the specific research object. According to its non-population structure under the constraints of the change, combined with the residential space reform and interior design, from the residential mode, residential elastic space design and energy consumption in three aspects of targeted transformation strategy.

Keywords: High density urban, New and old residential, Elastic transformation, Low carbon transformation

参考文献

[1] 周燕珉，秦岭. 老龄化背景下城市新旧住宅的适老化转型 [J]. 时代建筑，2016，6: 22-28.
[2] 王翔. 既有住区外环境空间类型化及品质提升策略研究 [D]. 大连理工大学，2016.
[3] 周奕龙. 基于可持续理念的城市既有住宅更新改造手法研究 [D]. 燕山大学，2015.
[4] 张祥智. "有机·互融"：城市集聚混合型既有住区更新研究 [D]. 天津大学，2014.
[5] 咸光军. 大连市既有住宅（区）更新改造的方法研究 [D]. 大连理工大学，2009.
[6] 杨仲华. 城市旧住宅可持续性更新改造研究 [D]. 浙江大学，2006.

基于家庭尺度的混合形态社区居民碳排放影响因素研究：以天津为例

亢梦荻 杨 琳 陈 天

（天津大学建筑学院）

摘　要：在居民碳排放将逐渐成为我国大城市碳排放重要组成的背景下，识别居民碳排放的构成特征及影响机制，对建设低碳城市，实现低碳发展至关重要。研究通过实地调查采集数据，从家庭社会属性和居住区空间形态两个角度研究影响居民碳排放的关系。家庭收入、家庭构成影响居民生活习惯，对生活碳排放均有显著的影响；住宅面积、住宅层数和居住区建筑密度对建筑碳排放有显著影响；土地功能多样性和道路交通可达性对交通碳排放有较大影响。低碳社区应当适当增加建筑密度，控制住宅建筑面积；完善居住区周边商业设施和公共服务设施，提升公共交通设施的可达性。

关键词：家庭碳排放，社区空间形态，家庭社会属性，可达性

1 引言

中国目前是世界上碳排放量最大的国家。2012年，中国的碳排放量达 8.5×10^9 t 二氧化碳，占全球总量的25%。[1] 由于碳排放的快速增长，中国成为全球碳减排和低碳发展的热点地区。城市是能源和资源的集中消费地，也是温室气体的集中排放地。城市的绿色低碳化成为中国城市应对气候变化，实现可持续发展的重要支柱之一。低碳城市强调以低碳理念为指导，在一定的规划、政策和制度建设的推动下，通过经济发展模式、消费理念和生活方式的转变，在保证生活质量不断提高的前提下，实现有助于减少碳排放的城市建设模式和社会发展方式。[2] 社区作为城市的基本生活单元，是居民生活消费的主要场所，居民消费多以家庭消费方式展开，家庭碳排放是社会总碳排放的主要来源之一。构建以"低碳"为目标导向的社区是实现"低碳城市"的基础。[3]

国内外学者对于家庭碳排放的影响因素开展了几个方面的研究。一是从宏观尺度上，对碳排放的空间分布差异的研究。研究发现，城市规划对土地利用管制越严格，城市建设密度越高，城市气候适宜程度越高，家庭碳排放量越小。居住在郊区的家庭碳排放量显著高于居住在城市的家庭。[4,5] 二是从微观尺度上，研究家庭基本特征和居民生活方式对碳排放的影响。研究发现，家庭碳排放受到经济收入、家庭规模、文化程度等因素的影响。[6] 通过改变居民的生活方式，可以显著降低家庭直接碳排放和间接碳排放。[7] 三是从微观尺度上，研究社区空间形态对家庭碳排放的影响。普遍的观点认为，居住密度和土地功能多样性与碳排放存在负相关关系。紧凑型的城市发展模式，有利于减少生活碳排放。总体来看，对碳排放的研究正在从宏观和中观层面逐渐转向微观层面，国内研究的地域主要集中于北京、上海，对于其他特定地区的研究较少。本文以天津为例，主要研究2000年后建成的建筑结构较为相似的混合型形态居住区，居民的社会属性与家庭碳排放的关系，以及居住区空间形态与交通碳排放的关系。

2 研究对象与分析方法

研究对象选取新园村一期、二期及邮电公寓的低层区、高层区为研究对象。这些居住小区均兴建于 2000 年左右。其中新园村一期和邮电公寓低层区为 6 层的行列式住宅，新园村二期主要由四幢 29 层和两幢 26 层塔式高层住宅构成，邮电公寓高层区由 8 幢 25 层的塔式高层为主。由于处于城市中心区，经过多年的发展，小区的居住人群从单一的学校及邮政职工逐渐成为成熟、混合、多样化的城市住宅小区。

研究以空间分层随机抽样的方式发放，共发放问卷 120 份，回收有效问卷 113 份。结合居民能源消费习惯和日常出行习惯的调查，分别从社会经济属性和居住区空间形态两个角度研究影响居民碳排放的因素。社会经济属性角度，选取家庭年收入、家庭人员构成及针对家庭个体的年龄、受教育程度、职业等指标，与家庭人均碳排放进行相关性分析。居住区空间形态角度，选取密度、多样性和可达性的等因素，经过量化为指标，与家庭碳排放进行对比分析。

3 居民碳排放估算

家庭生活碳排放主要分为两部分，家庭交通能耗碳排放和家庭建筑能耗碳排放。通过问卷的方式得出每个分项的用量，再分别进行汇总统计。家庭交通碳排放主要源于出行过程中，交通工具消耗能源产生的二氧化碳。建筑能耗主要指居民在建筑内消耗的电、天然气、热力等能源。考虑到调查中人们更容易准确描述日常行为，因此采用基于人的出行活动及能源消耗量调查进行计算。碳排放系数上，采用适用于天津的系数[8, 9]，因此计算居民能耗的碳排放量公式如下：

$$C=\sum_{j=1}^{m}\sum_{i=1}^{n}E_i \cdot e_i$$

式中 C——碳排放总量，g

E_i——使用能源 i 的消费量，kg；

e_i——能源 i 的碳排放强度，g/kg；

i——家庭能耗类别，种类为 n；

j——调查的有效样本类型，数量为 m。

为便于统计和研究，本文选取家庭每月人均碳排放值作为研究对象。通过估算生活碳排放得出以下结果：

家庭每月人均碳排放量统计值　　表1

分项名称		家庭每月人均碳排放量统计值（单位：g/人）			
		均值	标准差	最大值	最小值
建筑	生活用电	38032	19571	78020	9102
	生活燃气	7298	5383	24640	0
	总计	45329	20390	82538	14290
日常交通	通勤交通	10643	9310	24750	0
	购物娱乐	2340	3685	16200	0
	总计	12983	11342	36450	0
生活总量		56456	26574	103668	17542

混合形式居住区中，居民人均每月碳排放 56456g。从家庭碳排放构成来看居民建筑碳排放占生活碳排放的 78%，日常交通碳排放占生活碳排放总量的 22%。在建筑碳排放中，燃气和用电分别占 16% 和 84%，交通碳排放中，购物娱乐和通勤分别占 18% 和 82%。

4 家庭社会属性与碳排放的关系

不同家庭社会属性通过影响居民的生活习惯导致了家庭人均碳排放的不同。其主要因素为家庭年收入和人员构成，家庭个体的教育背景和职业习惯也有影响（图1）。

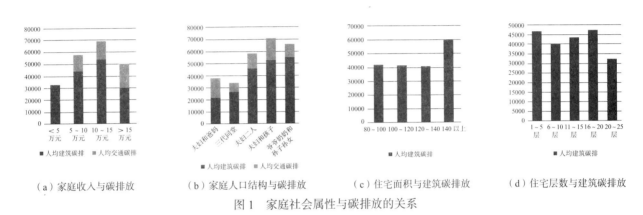

（a）家庭收入与碳排放　（b）家庭人口结构与碳排放　（c）住宅面积与建筑碳排放　（d）住宅层数与建筑碳排放

图1　家庭社会属性与碳排放的关系

4.1 家庭收入与碳排放

从人均家庭碳排放总量来看，年收入小于 15 万元的家庭碳排放与收入呈现正相关性，大于 15 万元的收入群体则出现碳排放量下降的趋势。从人均建筑碳排放看，与家庭碳排放总量的趋势保持一致。而人均交通碳排放则显示出与家庭年收入的高度相关性。通过对居民家庭作息和交通工具使用频率的调查，可以看出，随着收入的增加，家庭"全天有人"的概率在减小，因此在收入大于 15 万元家庭的人均每月建筑碳排放比 10 万~15 万元的家庭要少。家庭收入一定程度上影响家庭作息，从而影响到家庭建筑碳排放。在"家庭年收入与交通工具使用频率"的调查中，收入越高，小汽车使用频率越高，零碳出行（步行和自行车）以及公共交通出行的频率减少，因此家庭每月人均交通碳排放相应增多。

4.2 家庭人口结构与碳排放

调研访谈发现，居民人均碳排放与家庭人口数并没有直接相关性，而与家庭构成存在较大相关性。譬如家庭会由于家中有婴儿而延长空调的使用时间。图 1b 中的数据间接证明了这一点，家庭中有孩子的存在，人均家庭碳排放会相应增加。而夫妇和爸妈、三代同堂这样的家庭人口较多，共同使用空调、燃气等能源，受到平均的影响，因此显示出建筑碳排放较低，交通碳排放较高的特点。夫妇日常工作出行是家庭交通碳排放的主要贡献者。

4.3 家庭住宅条件与碳排放

住宅尺度的影响因素，主要有两个，建筑面积和建筑层数。这两种因素，都是通过影响家庭通风、日照情况，影响家庭用电情况，引起碳排放情况的不同。因此，以下仅从住宅建筑面积和建筑层数对建筑碳排放的影响角度进行讨论。

从图1c可以看出，在100m^{2}以上的范围内，住宅面积越大，人均碳排放量越大。从建筑碳排放来看，80～140m^{2}的住宅人均建筑碳排放均没有明显差异，而140m^{2}以上的建筑碳排放显著增多，可见由于建筑面积的增大，人均对电、燃气等能源的需求显著增多。每月人均交通碳排放与居住面积则没有明显的相关性。可见，从节能的角度来看，住宅面积不宜过大。

不同层数的住宅，由于其通风、日照环境的不同，会影响家庭空调的使用，从而影响建筑碳排放。从图表来看，1～5层和16～20层的碳排放量较大，20～25层明显减少。低层的住宅风环境及日照环境较为不佳，会导致更多的空调使用。结合访谈发现，居住在较高的层数，夏季通风环境非常好，几乎不用使用空调，降低了家庭能耗。

5　社区空间形态与碳排放的关系

从社区层面的空间形态包括密度、多样性和可达性三个方面分析城市空间环境特征对居民出行碳排放的影响。其中密度主要指社区本身空间形态，包括建筑密度、人口密度、容积率等。多样性主要指社区周边一定地域范围内的土地利用混合程度、公共设施丰富度等。设计主要指道路系统设计，因多样性和可达性两方面对居民出行方式及距离的影响更为显著，因此只探讨与两个社区交通碳排放的关系。

5.1　密度与碳排放

从图2可以看出，随着建筑密度、人口密度、容积率的降低，人均总碳排放量呈波动性变化，其中的相关性变化趋势较为复杂。分项来看，人均交通碳排放与人口密度、容积率有一定相关性。人口密度越低，容积率越低，交通碳排放越小。可见，高密度并一定能减少居民的交通碳排放。人均建筑碳排放与建筑密度、人口密度存在一定的负相关的关系。通过对建筑进行夏季热环境模拟，建筑密度高的社区，热环境更为舒适，有效地减少空调的使用频率，降低建筑能耗。因此适当的高密度可减少单位建筑采暖和降温的能耗（图2）。

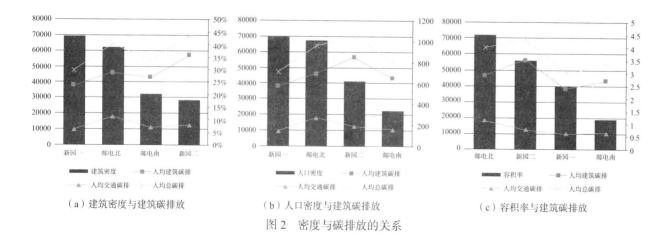

（a）建筑密度与建筑碳排放　　（b）人口密度与建筑碳排放　　（c）容积率与建筑碳排放

图2　密度与碳排放的关系

5.2 多样性与交通碳排放

多样性主要指的是土地利用混合度[10]、就业设施丰富度及公共设施丰富度等。研究以居住小区为中心，步行20分钟可以到达的2km×2km的范围为研究对象，探究多样性与碳排放的关系。初步统计两个社区通勤和购物娱乐的主要交通方式，其中通勤交通碳排放占交通碳排放量的80%以上。从交通碳排放总量看，邮电公寓交通碳排放量大。通勤交通碳排放量邮电公寓较大，而购物娱乐交通碳排放量新园村较大（表2）。

多样性指标与交通碳排放统计表　　表2

	人均交通碳排放（g）	通勤交通碳排放（g）	购物娱乐交通碳排放（g）	土地混合度熵值*	公共设施数量	公共设施平均距离（m）
邮电公寓	14658	13001	1657	0.714	28	293
新园村	11141	8149	2992	0.609	20	374

注：* 土地利用混合度可以用熵值大小表示土地混合程度的高低。计算公式如下：$S=-\sum_{i=1}^{n}P_i \cdot \log_{10}P_i$。式中：$S$—土地利用混合程度的熵值；$n$—土地利用类型的划分数目；$P_i$—第$i$类土地面积所占比例。

新园村作为单位的配建住宅，居民距离工作单位近，有效降低通勤交通碳排放。相较之下，邮电公寓居民通勤距离远，时间长，因此通勤碳排放量较大。可见建立小区域范围内的职住平衡可以有效降低交通碳排放。通过对比土地利用混合度、公共设施数量及平均距离可以看出，邮电公寓的土地混合度较高，公共设施多样性较好。步行20分钟可达范围内，丰富的公共设施可以有效减少居民在购物、娱乐的必要性的出行时选择小汽车的出行方式。因此增加商业与公共设施的丰富程度，有利于减少居民出行碳排放。

5.3 可达性与交通碳排放

公共交通可达性和道路网密度可能通过影响居民的出行行为，对居民交通碳排放产生影响。从表格可以看出，新园村购物娱乐交通碳排放较大，一方面是由于土地混合度较低，另一方面是由于居民出行对小汽车的依赖程度高。从公共交通可达性和道路网密度的统计中可以看出，邮电公寓的可达性比新园村高。因此居民更愿意选择低碳的公共交通方式出行。提高社区公共交通可达性和支路网密度有利于引导居民使用公共交通出行，降低居民交通碳排放（表3）。

可达性指标与交通碳排放统计表　　表3

	购物娱乐交通碳排放（g）	小汽车出行方式的占比（%）	公共交通可达性*	次干路网密度（km/km²）	支路网密度（km/km²）
邮电公寓	1657	26	35	2.6	10.4
新园村	2992	46	20	0.5	6.2

注：* 公交可达性可以理解为单位时间内所能接近公共交通站点的数量，计算公式如下$P_i=\sum_i k_i \cdot N_i \cdot \frac{500}{D_i}$。其中，为该站点类型的通达性系数，公交线路小于10的普通站点系数为1，公交线路大于等于10的区域性站点系数为2，地铁站点的系数为3。为i站点经过的公交线路数量，为i站点距离居住区的距离，以500m可达性为1计。

6 结论与建议

随着我国大规模城市化进程的推进，特别是大规模人口向城市的聚集，面临着更大的控制温室气体排放的压力。城市规划与空间形态优化对于降低城市碳排放有一定的积极影响，被认为建设低碳城市的重要政策手段。研究表明，家庭的经济和社会属性及城市空间形态是影响城市与社区碳排放的两个重要因素，家庭收入、家庭结构等非空间因素与居民建筑和交通直接碳排放呈现更为显著的相关性。因此建议不仅仅要从规划设计者入手，还应从对于低碳、生态理念的宣传教育入手。

从社区建设的角度来看，建议高层住宅的高度20层以上。住宅户型的设计以80～130m²为宜。适当提高建筑密度、控制房屋建筑面积、推行紧凑的空间格局。提高土地利用多样性，保证商业服务设施和公共服务设施在适宜的步行距离内可达。注重住宅、就业、商业、服务等用地功能在社区层面的混合利用。社区道路体系尽量体现步行友好原则，增加支路的建设，适当增加社区出入口，提高社区交通可达性，鼓励非机动车出行。在城市建设角度来看，城市建设应充分考虑区域范围内职住关系的平衡，避免建设规模过大的功能单一的居住区。进一步完善公共交通网络，提高地铁与公交线路的分布密度，提高换乘与接驳效率，提升公共交通设施的可达性。

致谢

本文工作得到教育部社科重大项目（基金号15JZD025）资助。

Study On Influencing Factors of Family Carbon Emissions from Mixed Form Community

Kang Mengdi, Yang Lin, Chen Tian

(School of Architecture, Tianjin University)

Abstract: The residential carbon emission is gradually becoming a crucial component of China's carbon emissions. To achieve low-carbon city, it is essential to identify the composition and influencing factors of residential carbon emission. Based on the data collection from field investigation, this paper studies the influencing factors from perspective of the family socio-economic attributes and spatial patterns of residential areas. Family income, family composition affects residents' living habits and has a significant impact on carbon emissions. Residential area, residential floors and building density have a significant impact on building carbon emissions. While diversity and accessibility affect residents' travel behavior and influence traffic carbon emissions. Higher building density and smaller housing area is beneficial to build low-carbon community. Improving business and public service facilities and enhancing accessibility of public transport facilities can also help to reduce carbon emission.

Keywords: Family carbon emission, Spatial pattern of residential area, Family socio-economic attributes, Accessibility

参考文献

[1] Zhu Liu. "China's Carbon Emissions Report 2015." Sustainability Science Program and Energy Technology Innovation Policy research group, Belfer Center Discussion Paper #2015-02. Harvard Kennedy School of Government, Cambridge, MA.

[2] 刘志林, 秦波. 城市形态与低碳城市: 研究进展与规划策略 [J]. 国际城市规划, 2013, 2: 4-11.

[3] 顾朝林, 谭纵波, 刘宛等. 气候变化、碳排放与低碳城市规划研究进展 [J]. 城市规划学刊, 2009, 3: 38-45.

[4] 郑思齐, 霍燚, 曹静. 中国城市居住碳排放的弹性估计与城市间差异性研究 [J]. 经济问题探索, 2011, 9: 124-130.

[5] Glaeser, Edward L, Matthew E Kahn. 2003. Sprawl and Urban Growth. Discussion Paper No.2004. Harvard Institute of Economic Research.

[6] 曲建升, 张志强, 曾静静等. 西北地区居民生活碳排放结构及其影响因素 [J]. 科学通报, 2013, 58(3): 260-266.

[7] Yujiro Hirano, Tomohiko Ihara, Yukiko Yoshida. Estimating residential CO_2 emissions based on daily activities and consideration of methods to reduce emissions[J]. Building and Environment, 2016, 103 (7): 1-8.

[8] 柴彦威, 肖作鹏, 刘志林. 基于空间行为约束的北京市居民家庭日常出行碳排放的比较分析 [J]. 地理科学, 2011, 7: 843-849.

[9] IPCC, 2006 年 IPCC 国家温室气体清单指南 [M]. 马耳他国际翻译有限公司译. 东京: 日本全球环境战略研究所, 2006.

[10] 林红, 李军. 出行空间分布与土地利用混合程度关系研究——以广州中心片区为例 [J]. 城市规划, 2008, 9: 53-56+74.

基于最小干预度原则的既有多层住宅节能改造模式研究

常 艺 宋 昆

（天津大学建筑学院）

摘 要：本文以天津1991~2000年既有多层住宅（"一步节能"住宅）为研究对象，从"节能性、经济性、既有风貌延续性"三位一体的视角，以"最小干预度"为原则，提出一套具有适宜性和科学性的既有多层住宅的节能改造模式，并与现行节能改造模式进行比较分析；在最小干预度节能改造模式的指导下，构建一套围护结构节能改造技术方案；最后，选取"天津大学新园村一期"对所设计的技术方案进行模拟分析，得出在最小干预度节能改造模式下既有多层住宅节能改造所能达到的目标值。

关键词：最小干预度原则，既有多层住宅，节能改造

我国现阶段既有多层住宅存量较大，且多为不节能建筑，这将造成能源极大的浪费。虽然，目前全国范围内的既有住宅节能改造工程已大规模开启，但问题也随之而来，一方面是节能改造所需成本较高，居民接受节能改造的意愿不高；另一方面，大规模的节能改造工程在一定程度上影响了居民的正常生活，同时也不利于对城市既有住宅风貌的保留。因此，提供一套可推广、可实施的节能改造模式成为当前节能改造工作的首要任务。

1 最小干预度原则下的节能改造模式分析

最小干预度原则下的节能改造模式（以下简称"最小干预度模式"）是指在既有多层住宅外围护结构系统（包括外墙、外窗、屋面、热桥等部位）中，外墙为370 mm厚实心黏土砖墙，自身具有良好的保温性能，而热桥、外窗、屋面等薄弱环节保温性能较差的基础上，提出一套在不采用外墙整体保温措施的前提下，通过对薄弱环节进行保温处理，从而形成系统匹配和综合优化的节能改造模式，建立一套"低成本、低干扰、小目标"的节能改造技术方案；并得出在最小干预度原则下节能改造所能达到的目标值。实现节能改造对住户正常生活的最低干扰，缩短施工周期，提高住户对节能改造工程的接受度，达到节能改造的目的。

1.1 最小干预度模式提出的动因

（1）既有多层住宅存量大，节能改造潜力大

根据"部科技与产业化发展中心"对天津中心城区旧楼区进行拉网式调查摸底可知，市内六区和环城四区外环以内，2000年以前建成的影响居民正常使用的小区（不包括已列入拆迁计划小区、历史风貌保护建筑、超出设计年限未经加固处理的楼房和新建商品房小区）共有2192个。通过按建筑年代划分统计可知（图1），从1976年震后到2000年间，既有住宅存量较大。

此外，天津1991年开始实施一步节能，存量较大的既有多层住宅处于节能设计的萌芽期，具有较大的节能改造潜力，因此，对这部分住宅进行节能改造成为当前的首要任务。

（2）外墙自身保温性好，热桥及外窗保温性差

1991~2000年的天津既有多层住宅多为砖混结构，外墙多为370mm厚实心黏土砖墙，保温性能好。而窗洞口过梁、阳台、檐口等热桥部位，传热系数较大，且未进行保温，热损失量较大。

外窗多为单层玻璃窗，保温性能极差。虽然居民后期自行将外窗更换为推拉式的单层塑钢玻璃窗，相对于原有外窗，其热工性能了一定的改善，但依然存在耗热量较大等不足之处（图2）。

（3）保留既有住宅风貌

红色砖墙与白色檐口、阳台、窗洞口过梁构成天津既有多层住宅的主要风貌特征，以天津市河西区旭光里为例（图3）；现行节能改造模式中外墙主要以采用整体外保温技术为主，将原有清水砖墙完全覆盖，以天津市河西区景福里为例（图4），失去原有住宅的风貌。

基于上述分析，需要对天津既有多层住宅提出一套有针对性的节能改造方案。

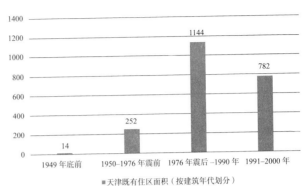

图1　天津既有住宅（含高层住宅）现状统计

资料来源：作者根据《天津调研报告》绘制。

图2　天津市河西区鹤望里外窗现状（作者拍摄）

图3　天津既有住宅风貌（作者拍摄）

图4　外墙外保温后住宅风貌（作者拍摄）

1.2　现行节能改造模式与最小干预模式比较分析

表1定性地将现行节能改造模式与最小干预模式分别从经济性、可实施性和既有风貌延续性三方面进行比较分析。

现行节能改造模式与最小干预模式比较分析

表1

	现行节能改造模式	最小干预模式
经济性	现行案例多为公产房或政府出资的示范性工程，节能改造成本高，适用范围小	外墙仅对热桥保温，节能改造成本低，适用范围广
可实施性	施工现场需要搭建大量脚手架，影响住户的正常生活；外墙整体外保温，施工周期较长	施工现场机械设备较少，对住户干扰低；外墙局部保温，施工速度快
既有风貌延续性	外墙整体外加保温板，改变既有住宅风貌	热桥部位加保温，更新并延续既有风貌

由表1可知，最小干预模式进行节能改造的主要优势为三点——"成本低，适用广"、"扰民少，速度快"、"街貌新，风貌留"。

以最小干预模式为指导的技术方案设计

（1）热桥及公共走道内墙保温技术

本文采用FLIR红外热像仪对既有住宅中热桥存在位置进行判断，通过其生成的热像图和温度值来判断住宅中的热桥部位（图5）。

热桥及公共走道内墙保温技术构造做法与传统的外墙外保温做法相同，对窗洞口过梁、阳台、檐口等热桥部位、公共走道内墙涂抹保温浆料，此种做法不受地区气候类型的限制，可推广使用。此外，公共走道内涂保温浆料，缓解了楼梯间北向外窗在冬季所造成的冷风渗透，施工简易，操作方便，缩短了施工周期，对提高住户对节能改造工程的积极性起到了促进作用。

因住宅在使用功能上的需要，空调室外机位及厨房排风口等管件需要在外墙预留的孔洞也会造成空气渗透。在施工过程中，通常忽略对穿墙孔洞的封堵或仅在预埋管件与墙体之间涂抹一道密封膏封堵，而密封膏经常年使用性能减弱，会导致穿墙孔洞处出现透风和渗水等现象。因此，需要加强对外墙孔洞的气密性处理。对外墙孔洞的密封性处理可以通过外包PVC套管，套管与外墙洞口之间选用发泡聚氨酯或岩棉填充，从而提高外墙孔洞处的密封性，增强外墙整体保温性能。

图5 红外热像仪判断热桥位置

资料来源：王立雄提供。

（2）外窗节能改造技术

外窗的热量损失主要体现在：①窗框和玻璃部分的传热损失；②外窗缝隙的冷风渗透。因此，本小节将对上述两点进行有针对性节能改造（表2）。

外窗节能改造技术　　　　　　表2

改造措施	具体做法	
外窗构件更新	外窗玻璃	Low-E 玻璃
	外窗窗框	塑钢窗框
其他弥补性节能措施	外窗开启方式	平开式
	原有外窗气密性改造	加装密封条或使用密封胶
	外窗遮阳	安装遮阳设施
各位置及朝向外窗节能技术选择	南向、西向、东向	更换双玻塑钢low-E 玻璃窗；安装遮阳设施
	北向	更换三玻塑钢low-E 玻璃窗

（3）屋面节能改造技术

屋面节能改造施工相对简易，且对住户影响较小，成本较低，因此屋面改造也是住宅最小干预度节能改造中的重要部分。表3为最小干预模式下屋面节能改造所采取的主要技术措施。

屋面节能改造技术　　　　　　表3

改造措施	具体做法		
平改坡技术	坡屋面类型选择	四坡顶形式	
	屋架结构选择	轻钢屋架	
	屋面瓦选择	合成树脂瓦	
平改平技术	无保温系统屋面	修复原屋面裂缝，在其上重新做防水层；防水层上铺保温层	
	有保温系统屋面	更换原有保温层	根据原保温层现状确定是否更换新保温层
		增厚原有保温层	需对原有屋面承载力进行计算，应用较少
平改坡与平改平技术选择	平改坡	临近城市主要干道的住宅	
	平改平	住区内部的住宅	

技术方案的模拟分析——以天津大学新园村一期为例

1.3 现状调研及存在问题分析

天津大学新园村一期建于2000年（属于本文研究范围内的1991～2000年"一步节能多层住宅"），位于天津市南开区松杉路天津大学63号教工住宅。住区建筑面积5410.24m^2，主体形状基本为矩形，南北朝向，建筑层数为6层，建筑高度18.2m；建筑结构为砖混结构，抗震烈度为七度，建筑耐火等级为二级。

通过实地调研，对住宅外围护结构现状及其存在问题进行总结如下：（1）外窗密封性差，且开启方式为推拉式，能耗较大（图6）；（2）阳台、檐口出挑的混凝土构件传热系数大，造成热量损失（图7）；（3）空调和厨房排风口孔洞处气密性差，加大冬季室外冷风渗透量（图8）。

图 6 外窗现状图（作者自摄）

图 7 阳台及檐口现状图（作者自摄）

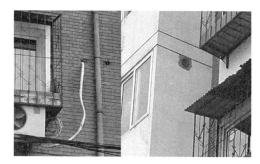

图 8 外墙孔洞现状图（作者自摄）

1.4 方案设计与模拟

针对上述存在问题，进行有针对性的节能改造方案设计，即分别选取住宅原有的方案、最小干预度模式方案和现行节能改造模式方案进行模拟与分析（表4）。

节能改造方案设计　　　　　表 4

方案			方案一（原有方案）	方案二（最小干预模式）	方案三（现行模式）
外墙	A	370 mm 厚实心黏土砖墙	√		
	B	热桥及公共走道涂 30 mm 保温浆料		√	
	C	整体外贴 50 mm 厚石墨聚苯板			√
外窗	A	单层塑钢玻璃窗	√		
	B	南向双玻塑钢 low-E 窗 北向三玻塑钢 low-E 窗		√	
	C	统一更换双玻塑钢 low-E 窗			√
屋面	A	平屋面	√		
	B	平改平		√	√
	C	平改平			

注：A 为原有方案；B 为最小干预度模式下的技术选择；C 为现行模式下的技术选择。

选用清华大学建筑科学系开发的建筑热环境模拟分析工具 DeST-h 对住宅建立模型进行能耗模拟分析，其围护结构参数见表5。

各方案围护结构参数表 [W/(m²·K)]　　　　　　　　　　表5

方案	外墙平均传热系数	外窗传热系数	屋面传热系数
方案一	4.12	6.40	0.72
方案二	1.95	2.30/1.80	0.47
方案三	0.89	2.30	0.47

1.5 结果分析

（1）节能性分析

将表5中的3组方案输入能耗模拟软件DeST-h中分别进行模拟，计算出天津大学新园村一期A单元住宅全年累计冷热负荷指标（图9）。由图19计算可得，最小干预模式下的方案二节能率为56%，达到二步节能；现行节能改造模式下的方案三节能率为68%，达到三步节能。

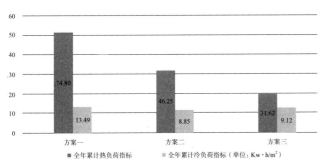

图9　各方案全年累计冷热负荷指标（作者绘制）

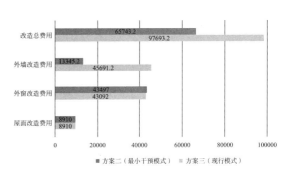

图10　各方案节能改造材料费用（作者绘制）

（2）经济性分析

节能改造所需的成本问题一直是节能改造工程中政府以及住户需要着重考虑的问题，其关系着节能改造工程的可行性与可实施性。图10将方案二和方案三外墙、外窗、屋面节能改造所需材料费用（不含施工等其他费用）分别进行统计，可知方案二的改造材料总费用比方案三节省了33%，其中外墙的材料费用可节省71%。因此，最小干预节能改造模式可极大降低节能改造所需的成本。

（3）既有风貌延续性分析

表6对方案二和方案三从既有风貌延续性展开分析，其中最小干预模式指导下的节能改造仅对热桥部位进行保温处理，不仅更新了建筑立面，还延续了既有的住宅风貌；而现行模式指导下的节能该方案，外墙整体加装保温板，改变了既有住宅的风貌。

各方案既有风貌延续性分析　　　　　　　　　　表6

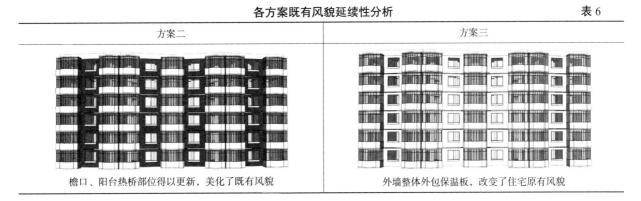

方案二	方案三
檐口、阳台热桥部位得以更新，美化了既有风貌	外墙整体外包保温板，改变了住宅原有风貌

2 结论

对于外墙为370mm厚实心黏土砖墙,自身具有良好的保温性能,选取以最小干预度为原则的节能改造模式进行节能改造,不仅提高了既有多层住宅的节能性,同时还极大降低改造过程中的人力、物力以及财力,将施工对居民正常生活的干扰最小化,最终还取得了延续既有住宅风貌的效果。另外,以最小干预模式构建"低成本、低干扰、小目标"的节能改造技术方案,提高了居民对节能改造的积极性,形成一套"居民自愿、政府推动、多渠道融资、可推广"的节能改造模式。

Energy-efficient Mode of Existing Multi-story Residential Based on the Minimum Interference

Chang Yi, Song Kun

(School of Architecture, Tianjin University)

Abstract: With the existing multi-storey residential in 1991 ~ 2000 as the research object, from the perspective of "Energy-Efficient, economy, continuity of existing style", based on the principle of minimum intervention, putting forward an Energy-Efficient mode of existing multi-storey residential, building a set of Energy-Efficient technical scheme; Finally, selecting "Tianjin University Xinyuancun" to carry on the simulation analysis, concluding the energy efficiency of the multi storey residential buildings can be achieved.

Keywords: Minimum intervention principle, Existing multi-storey residential, Energy-efficient reconstruction

参考文献

[1] 王清勤,唐曹明.既有建筑改造技术指南(第1版)[M].北京:中国建筑工业出版社,2012.
[2] 尹伯悦.天津调研报告[G].部科技与产业化发展中心,2015.
[3] 沈忱.浅谈夏热冬冷地区既有建筑屋面节能改造[J].城市建筑,2013,22:123,143.
[4] 李欣.天津市集居型多层旧住宅发展演变和改造方式研究[D].天津大学,2006.
[5] 顾放,王卉.天津地区居住建筑节能设计技术发展研究[J].建筑学报,2013,(S1):176-179.
[6] 金占勇,郝有志,刘长滨,廉苒,赵炀.北方既有居住建筑节能改造面临的障碍及对策建议[J].建设科技,2009,11:22-25.
[7] 中国建筑改造网.[2017-3-20]. http://www.chinabrn.cn/.

基于 LEED ND 绿色社区认证体系的新区慢行交通系统构建：以成都天府新区科学城为例

曾 晶[1] 郝桐平[2] 吴亚芯[3]

（1.中国中铁二院工程集团有限责任公司；2.城设（综合）建筑师事务所；3.成都天府新区规划设计研究院）

摘 要：21 世纪，面对能源危机和可持续发展这两个重要议题，传统的蔓延型城市扩张以及以私家车为导向的交通策略已逐渐被诸多国家摒弃，城市精明增长与以公交为导向的交通策略开始受到重视，慢行交通系统也逐渐发展起来。目前，我国的城市慢行交通系统规划存在不少问题，如缺乏针对道路可达性的分析方法、缺少交通节点的数据分析环节以及缺少开放空间及公共服务设施的布局研究等。新区建设如果仍沿袭"尺度过大、用途单一"的街区规划及"宽马路、大路网"的路网规划，将造成道路连接性差、社区活力丧失的消极局面。[1] LEED ND（全称为 LEED for Neighborhood Development）是全世界第一个集聪明增长、城市规划和绿色建筑原则为一体的国际评估系统，其在"社区规划和布局设计"章节的评估细则中，提倡紧凑的、步行可达的、多功能混合使用的邻里社区；该章节也要求保证人行道的连续性和行道树的栽植，严格控制建筑退距及停车区域面积，从而在邻里社区中减少机动车的使用，营造宜人的步行环境，减少交通事故的发生，避免破坏生物栖息地，保护日益消失的农地；同时在社区中开发公共空间，如公园和广场，这将促进社区的邻里交流，调控城市雨水径流，缓解热岛效应。[2, 3] 本文以天府新区成都科学城成熟街区为例，以慢行交道路网络为研究对象，以美国 LEED ND 体系为指导，旨在提升街区的可达性、舒适性及安全性。本文首先介绍 LEED ND 体系中有关慢行交通系统的条文要求，同时选取已获得 LEED ND 金级认证标识的绿色社区的实践案例进行研究，分析其如何构建与设计连接度较高的慢行交通网络；其次，分析天府新区成都科学城的慢行交通系统网络，包括各层级道路的宽度、开放空间的位置及面积、交通节点的分布和建筑功能性入口分布等；最后，利用网络分析法原理和 GIS 技术平台，将道路抽象为线，建立城市道路拓扑网络，分析并评价现行慢行交通网络的可达性，并在此基础上结合 LEED ND 关于慢行交通系统规划的经典理论和认证标准，提出改善措施和建议，从而提升科学城的便捷度与社区活力。以期本文的研究成果可以为今后新区建设中慢行交通系统的规划提供一种新思路和新技术支持。

关键词：慢行交通系统，LEED ND，新区建设

1 引言

1.1 慢行交通系统的重要性

慢行交通系统是城市综合交通系统重要的组成部分，其不仅是对绿色出行、生态城市的积极响应，更解决了公共交通工具之间以及各交通节点之间的接驳与换乘问题，是市民中短距离出行的良好选择。但是随着城市发展与人口增多，城市步行空间不足、行人环境舒适性低以及无明确自行车道等问题日渐突出，亟待城市规划师们解决。中华人民共和国住房和城乡建设部于 2013 年 12 月颁布了《城市步行和自行车交通系统规划设计导则》，呼吁全国各地意识到完善步行和自行车交通系统的重要性与紧迫性。

1.2 LEED ND 与慢行交通系统

LEED 是在竞争激烈的市场中解决环境问题的认证体系，是目前全球范围内较为领先与完善的针对建筑与社区可持续性评估的量化标准。其中，LEED ND 非常重视公众身体健康状况、自然环境与生活质量，强调精明增长与新城市主义，鼓励市民步行上班，推广节能节水的绿色建筑与公共服务设施[4]，致力于建设紧凑的、适宜步行的、混合利用的、与邻近社区有良好连接的社区。[5] 为了增加通行的效率，减少交通运输距离，帮助市民提升健康状况，减少交通事故发生，LEED ND 对步行环境与自行车道的设计进行了针对性的指引和评分，具体评分细则下文将会有详细说明。

2 研究方法

2.1 案例研究

2.1.1 迎海绿色社区

迎海（Double Cove）是香港首个获得美国 LEED-ND 金级认证、中国绿色建筑三星级设计标识认证和香港建筑环境评估 BEAM 最终铂金级认证的住宅项目。其总规划面积约 96800m^2，设有住宅楼 21 栋，包含 3500 个住宅单位，集居住、购物、会所、幼儿园和停车场等多功能于一体，并且设置了中央公园。步行和公共交通是当今低碳社会大力倡导的健康出行方式。该项目以微气候分析的角度规划步行、慢跑和自行车路线；此外，设计连廊联结公共交通枢纽，还提供可租赁的自行车，并且设置了 83 个电动汽车充电停车位设施。

2.1.2 成都远洋太古里

成都远洋太古里是以大慈寺为中心的商业街区，占地约 70000m^2，与地铁 2 号线和 3 号线交汇站直接连通，项目已获得 LEED-ND 金级认证。街区空间为全开放式，街区尺度在 15～65m 之间，建筑高度与街道宽度比值为 1∶1。建筑以 2～3 层的独栋建筑为主，通过融入川西风格的骑楼、青瓦坡屋顶、粉墙、檐梁、花窗等元素，利用露台和挑廊相连通，形成既能包容历史文化又能唤醒商业活力，同时供公众自由穿行的开放市空间。

2.2 慢行交通系统设计导则

2.2.1 LEED ND 中慢行交通系统相关评分点

LEED ND 主要包含了精明选址与连接性、社区形态与设计、绿色基础设施与建筑、创新与设计流程、地域优先等五个章节。其中在精明选址与连接性、社区形态与设计中针对性地提出了完善慢行交通系统的先决条件与得分点（表1），主要包含优良公共交通连接、自行车设施、居住和工作地点邻近、可步行街道、紧凑型开发、关联和开放的社区、邻里土地混合使用、停车位面积、城区与公共空间的连接、康乐设施可达性等。[2, 6]

选址是建设绿色社区的前提，LEED ND 鼓励充分使用城市原有的公共交通设施，加强自行车网络及相关设施的建设，居住和工作地点邻近，从而减少对机动车的依赖，也有助于身体素质的提高。社区形态与设计对建设绿色社区具有重要的指导和实践意义，LEED ND 提倡设计步行友好的街道，创建人性化、健康的社区，鼓励集约开发和土地混合使用，保障各类服务设施和公共空间的连接性和可达性，从而缩短出行距离、减少对机动车的需求，减少能源消耗和环境污染。[7]

LEED ND 中与慢行交通系统相关的内容 表1

类别	条文	具体要求
精明选址与连接性	优良公共交通衔接	至少有50%的建筑入口距公交或是电车站点400m的步行距离，或是距离快速公交站点800m的步行距离，从而实现便捷可达的高质量交通
	自行车设施	至少90%的建筑设置自行车存放空间。对于非住宅用地，临时自行车存放空间个数为高峰期人流量的2.5%，每个建筑至少设置4个；长期自行车存放空间个数为常住居民人数的5%，并且不少于4个。对于住宅用地，临时自行车存放空间个数为高峰期人流量的2.5%，每个建筑至少4个，长期自行车存放空间个数为常住居民人数的30%，每个居住单元至少一处。对于零售类用地，每465m²提供2个临时自行车停放空间，每个建筑至少设置2个；长期自行车存放空间个数为常住居民人数的5%，每个建筑至少设置2个。对于整个社区而言，至少50%的建筑功能性出入口设置在自行车道上，或者整个社区的自行车道网络大于4.8km，并且这些自行车道可以直接连接学校、工作地点等
	居住和工作地点邻近	对于有居住建筑的项目：居住建筑中30%的建筑面积步行800m可到达现有的全职工作岗位，且工作岗位的数量不小于居住单元总数
社区形态与设计	可步行街道	先决条件要求90%建筑有一个功能性入口连接到交通网络或者公共空间，如果公共空间为广场或公园，必须有15m宽；至少15%的建筑，要有大于1：1.5的建筑高度与道路宽度比；90%的社区交通网络要有连续的人行道，新建居住用地的人行道应宽于2.5m，混合用地性质的街区则至少宽1.2m；小于20%的交通网络正对停车库入口。得分项要求至少满足建筑立面和入口、地面用途和停车、人行道和自行车道设计速度和人行道障碍物等4个类别16项要求中的2项
	紧凑型开发	先决条件要求对于在步行范围以内的住宅用地，每英亩（约0.4hm²）至少要有12个居住单元；对于步行范围以外的住宅用地，每英亩至少有7个居住单元；对于步行范围内的非住宅用地，容积率大于0.8；对于步行范围外的非居住单元，容积率应大于0.5。得分项要求住宅用地每英亩至少10个以上居住单元，非住宅用地容积率至少0.75以上
	关联和开放的社区	先决条件要求面积不大于0.02km²时，距离社区边界400m的区域应该每公里有35个交通节点，社区的交通连接网络应该为公众使用，而且不应设门，除非是教育医疗军事用地；当项目面积大于0.02km²时，每平方公里至少有54个交叉口。得分项要求每平方公里交叉口达到116个以上
	邻里土地混合使用	50%的居住单元400m步行距离范围内能到达的服务设施的种类数量
	停车位面积	不建立地面停车场，或者将停车场建立在周边，避免建筑入口正对地面停车位；停车场不超过用地的20%，且单个停车场不大于0.8hm²；对于非住宅建筑，提供至少10%的停车位给共享机动车，且这些停车位须在建筑入口60m步行范围内
	城区与公共空间的连接	90%的建筑入口步行400m至少能到达一个面积不小于670m²的公共空间。如果空间小于4000m²，宽度和长度比不得小于1/4
	康乐设施可达	90%的建筑入口步行800m至少能到达一个面积不小于2325m²的室内康乐设施，或不小于4000m²的室外康乐设施

2.2.2 住建部《城市步行和自行车交通系统规划设计导则》

为了构建环保可持续的城市交通系统，共建能源节约与生态文明的美好家园，并为全国各地的步行与自行车道系统提供针对性的指导，住建部特制定《城市步行和自行车交通系统规划设计导则》[8]，本文特意对《导则》中与慢行交通系统相关的规范与标准进行了如下梳理（表2）。

步行 I 类区：步行活动聚集程度高，步行交通方式拥有最高优先权的城区，如：人口密度高的城市中心、大型公共服务设施周围、大型交通枢纽附近、城市核心商圈等。

步行 II 类区：步行活动聚集程度较高，步行优先兼顾其他交通方式的地方。如：城市副中心、中等规模的城市公共服务设施附近、一般性城市商务区。

步行 III 类区：步行活动密集程度较弱，满足步行交通的基本需求即可的区域。

自行车与步行道路平均间距与密度　　　　表2

步行分区	步行道路密度	步行道平均间距	自行车道路密度	自行车道路平均间距
Ⅰ类区	14～20（km/km²）	100～150m	12～18m	110～170m
Ⅱ类区	10～14（km/km²）	150～200m	8～12m	170～250m
Ⅲ类区	6～10（km/km²）	200～300m	5～8m	250～400m

3 天府新区科学城慢行系统分析

3.1 项目概况及基于国内《导则》的慢行系统分析

项目位于兴隆湖南岸，环湖路以南，科学城中路以北，有绿楔从项目中间穿过。街区尺度为120m～300m，范围内共10个地块，用地性质主要为商住混合及商业，研究范围周边有医院、社区中心、公交首末站、学校等公服设施。其中，商住混合用地面积为536870m²，商业面积为186998m²。本案人行道道路密度为12.27km/km²，自行车道路密度是12.82km/km²，根据我国的《导则》，自行车道符合Ⅰ类区的要求，人行道符合Ⅱ类区的标准，可适当增加人行道的密度。

3.2 基于LEED ND的慢行系统剖析

3.2.1 精明选址与连接性

优良公共交通链接：该项目范围内含地铁站1处，该项目周边共4处公交车站（含2处首末站），100%的建筑入口距离公交站在400m的范围内，距离地铁站800m以内，根据预计每个工作日班次显示也满足优良公共交通连接得分项。

自行车设施：该项目在建筑内部没有针对自行车停放空间的详细设计。笔者建议设置自行车停车位，完善相应的更衣和淋浴设施。

居住和工作地点接近：该项目所有的居住建筑均在400m的距离内可到达全职工作岗位，工作岗位数为3740个，居住单位为2685个，满足工作岗位数量不小于居住单元总数的要求。

3.2.2 社区形态与设计

可步行街道：该项目没有建筑退距小于5.4m的情况，只有3个地块的部分区域满足小于7.6m的条件，只占8%，本案在该条上达不到LEED ND的标准要求。建筑高度与街道宽度的比例上，大于1：1.5的社区连接体系占96%，满足要求。该项目中自行车道长度为5402m，步行道与机动车道交叉部分的长度为275m，交叉部分所占比例为5%，满足要求。

紧凑型开发：该项目的所有住宅用地，每英亩有37～75个居住单元的范围，符合每英亩多于12个居住单元的标准。该项目内的所有非居住用地，容积率均大于0.8，范围在0.9～3.0，均符合要求。

关联和开放的社区：该项目约0.45km²，大于5英亩，范围内含交叉口47个，每平方公里104个交叉口，满足先决条件中每平方公里大于54个的标准。

邻里土地混合使用：该项目400m步行距离可到达幼儿园2所，小学1所，中学1所，便利店54个，储蓄所8个，菜市场2个，医疗卫生中心2个，文化站2个，养老设施2个。

停车面积减量：该项目不设置地面停车场，并且避免建筑入口正对地面停车位；暂时没有提供共享汽车停车位。

城区及公共空间的连接：该项目内公共空间12处，且均大于670m²，以400m为半径作缓冲区，可根据附图14看出100%的建筑均可在400m内到达公共空间；该项目有2处公共空间大于400m²，其长宽比小于4，符合LEED ND标准要求。

康乐设施可达：该项目与3处康乐设施相邻，2处室内康乐设施，1处室外康乐设施。从服务半径来看，满足100%建筑步行800m到达的要求。但是从面积要求来看，室外康乐设施2500m²，不满足标准4000m²的要求，室内康乐设施300m²，也远不满足LEED ND标准2325m²的要求。

3.3 总结与建议

根据我国发布的《城市步行和自行车交通系统规划设计导则》，该项目人行道和自行车道路密度分别属于步行II类和I类区的要求；因此，建议适当增加人行道的密度，优化街区尺度和规模，进一步缩短出行距离，为居民选择低碳出行提供便利。

根据LEED ND，该项目的公共交通优良，距离各类公共服务设施、公共空间和康乐设施都有良好的可达性，但是也存在一些需要改善的地方。

在自行车设施方面，建议根据LEED ND的设计标准，确定不同性质的建筑所需要的自行车停放空间。

在可步行街道方面，该项目建筑退距都大于7.5m，不符合LEED ND的限制要求，但是国内住建部要求"沿城市快速路的各类建筑，后退距离至少20m；沿城市主、次干路的各类建筑，后退距离至少15m；沿城市支路的各类建筑，后退距离至少10m"，该项目中属于城市主、次干路及其他支路，建筑退距分别为15m与20m，LEED ND与国内标准有所冲突，笔者建议参照国内标准，避免机动车噪声的负面影响。LEED ND强调亲近的、连续的建筑立面，有助于提升街道的舒适度和安全性，建议控制沿街立面空白的长度不超过40%，或建筑退距不大于15m，并且沿街商业的立面至少位于地面0.9～2.5m以上的立面60%的面积有窗户；同时，建议控制项目内部机动车辆的行驶速度，保证安全的人行和自行车的交通环境，75%或以上的道路住宅地块的机动车辆的行驶速度不大于每小时30km，非住宅地块和混合地块的机动车辆的行驶速度不大于每小时40km。

在关联与开放的社区方面，路网的每平方公里交叉点只有104个，建议适当增加交通节点，缩短交通距离，加强社区关联性。

在康乐设施可达方面，该项目规划的室内外康乐设施可以满足居民步行距离的要求，可达性良好，但需要增加设施面积以满足更多居民的需求，提高其使用率，鼓励市民积极参与。

4 结论与启示

对城市综合交通系统尤其是慢行交通系统的合理评估，可以衡量城市交通的发展与城市发展的适应程度，为构建步行友好的城市交通体系和倡导低碳出行提供决策依据。本文重点关注LEED ND中可步行街区和自行车网络两大网络，通过LEED ND与住建部《导则》的学习，分析天府新区科学城现有的慢行系统，并提出改善措施，建议其在今后的慢行系统规划和设计中注意的几个方面：首先，在公共交通站点周边进行混合开发，增加交叉节点，适当提高容积率和建筑密度以进行紧凑式的开发建设，不仅有效控制街区规模和形态，也能够集约利用土地。其次，关于康乐设施和开放空间，充分考虑适宜的步行距离，使居民便捷达到，提升社区活力。最后，人是社区使用的主体，以"以人为本"为重要原则进行慢行交通系统规划和设计，从而引导人们低碳出行，是实现可持续发展的重要内容。

The Construction of Walkable Streets in New District Based on the Certification Standards of LEED ND: Take Chengdu Tianfu New Area Science City as An Example

Zeng Jing[1], Hao Tongping[2], Wu Yaxin[3]

(1. China Railway Eryuan Engineering Group Co. LTD; 2. SRT(S&P)Architects Ltd; 3. Urban Planning & Design Institute of Chengdu TIanfu New Area)

Abstract: Facing with energy crisis and sustainable development, two key issues in the 21th century, traditional type of urban sprawl and private car oriented transportation has been gradually abandoned after smart growth and TOD has been paid attention to and non-motorized transportation has well developed at the same time. However, there are several problems in our national planning of non-motorized transportation, such as lack of analysis of road accessibility, transportation intersections and the layout of public space and service. In the construction of new district, if the designers still follow the concept of "Large scale with single function" to design the community, follow the idea of "Wide road, Large network" to design the road network, it will result in the poor connection of roads and the loss of community vitality. LEED ND is an international rating system about smart growth, urban planning and green building. In the chapter of "Neighborhood Pattern and Design", advocating compact development, walkable and mixed use communities, ensuring the continuous and shaded sidewalk, strictly controlling the setback and parking area, to reduce the use of vehicles and car accidents, creating walkable environment, and thus avoid the loss of habitats and protect the farmland. In the meanwhile, develop the public space like park and square, for the neighborhood communication and the rainfall runoff controlling, relieving heat island effect. This thesis takes Chengdu Tianfu Science Park as an example to study its non-motorized system under the guidance of LEED ND, aimed at promoting accessibility and security of the communities. In the thesis, we firstly introduce the requirements in LEED ND rating system, then study two cases on its non-motorized system which already obtained LEED Gold certification to figure out the features of well-connected transport system, and then we analysis current road width, pubic space, transportation intersections and functional entrances of the project. Finally, utilizing the GIS platform we establish topology network of circulation network and thus evaluate the accessibility of road network before coming up with the improvement measures, combining requirements of LEED ND, aiming to promote vitality and convenience of the communities and expecting this thesis could provide new thinking and technologies for the non-motorized transportation system in new district planning.

Keywords: Non motorized transportation, LEED ND, New district construction

参考文献

[1] 姜洋,唐婧娴,李威,陈宇琳.住区规划推广街区制的困境与思考.规划60年：成就与挑战——2016中国城市规划年会, 2016.

[2] Zuniga-Teran A A. From neighborhoods to wellbeing and conservation: Enhancing the use of greenspace through walkability [M]. University of Arizona Press, 2015.

[3] USGBC. Reference Guide for LEED Neighborhood Development. 2014，4.

[4] 李王鸣，刘吉平. 精明、健康、绿色的可持续住区规划愿景 ——美国 LEED-ND 评估体系研究 [J]. 国际城市规划，2011，26（5）: 66-70.

[5] 李呈琛，张波，李开宇. 国外可持续街区研究、实践及其对中国的借鉴 [J]. 国际城市规划，2013，28（2）: 53-56.

[6] Adriana A Zuniga-Teran，Barron J Orr，Randy H Gimblett，Nader V Chalfoun，Scott B Going，David P Guertin，Stuart E Marsh. Designing healthy communities: A walkability analysis of LEED-ND[J]. Frontiers of Architectural Research，2016，5（4）: 433-452.

[7] DeCoursey，Jillian. LEED for Neighborhood Development and the Loring Park Neighborhood，2010.

[8] 住房城乡建设部. Editor 城市步行和自行车交通系统规划设计导则，2013.

小区型高楼住宅配置水绿规模改善热岛效应策略之仿真研究

王文安　董思伟

（淡江大学建筑系）

摘　要：都市迅速成长的情况下不但造成环境问题，也产生高房价时代的来临，都市有渐渐向外扩张的迹象，人口纷纷往城市边缘居住。热岛效应的强度也会因都市规模大小有所差异，相关文献显示即使是一个一千人人口的小城市所产生的热岛强度仍不可忽视（Gyr and Rys，1995），造成热岛效应（heat island effect）。本研究主要针对小区型高建筑群楼进行户外热环境探讨，以提高建筑材质反射率、增加水域面积与种植乔木遮阴等因素作为本次研究的设计变因，并透过计算机计算流体力学 CFD（Computational Fluid Dynamics）作为预测与分析之工具，解析在改善空间有限的基地范围内，透过设计变因改善降温的可行性与效益，依分析结果提出有利于减缓都市热岛效应的方针。

关键词：户外热环境，热岛效应，计算流体力学

1　引言

全球暖化的问题日益严重，达到减缓都市热岛效应的目的，并提出合理的改善因应措施，将是未来都市发展与规划的重要课题。本研究以设计时间的小区为研究对象，于设计规划阶段进行整体性的分析各种降低热岛效应可行方案，并提出符合地域特性及气候条件之策略及改善措施，进行实地测量及仿真，探究改变设计对都市热岛降温之帮助，创造健康、舒适及不耗能的居住空间。

1.1　研究目的

近年来，户外的环境质量越来越受到重视，尤其针对小区型住宅，国内外都有针对小区的设计规划制定了相关标准，小区型集合住宅兴建的数量快速增加，相对也造成了严重的热岛效应，使整体户外环境质量舒适度大幅降低。故本研究希望能透过分析水域与植栽的分布比例对于降低热岛之效益，并分析地理特性与气候条件，探讨本基地之退烧潜力。并探讨减缓本基地热岛效应造成影响之策略，解析其影响因子对于环境流场与温度场带来的趋势变化。

1.2　文献回顾

1.2.1　环境风场与影响因子

"风"会随着地球自转、云层的覆盖、雨水的凝结、地形的变化、地表的粗糙度及温差等因素改变，使得风场结构的变异性大且变化莫测。一般而言，地表附近的风速会随高度的增加而递增，其风速的垂向分布与地表上的地物、地况有关。都市地区高楼林立，对气流而言，阻碍空气流动的地表粗糙度较大，而边界层厚度亦较大。而平坦的沿海地区，地表粗糙度较小，边界层厚度亦较小。[1]

1.2.2 植栽相关理论

植栽的密度、高度及宽度对环境气流有不同的影响作用,选择合适植栽配置组合可以适度调节风场、温度场之舒适性。植栽对于风场作用,Guan and Zhu(2001)利用风洞实验结果对树冠的结构和风场进行分析,单株树附近风场的风速减弱区之一般特征,在树体背风面呈一纺锤形立体空间,树体背风缘减弱后的厚度较大,略厚于树高,距离增大时厚度减小,风速减低程度与透风系数或疏透度有关,透风系数或疏透度越小,风速减低越显著。[2]

1.2.3 水域对热环境的影响

水体的吸热和储热能力都强于土壤,因此水体对气候具有调节作用,形成水域微气候。另外在都市纹理部分,建构平行夏季季风方向的都市蓝带,利用水岸地区中水体的特殊优势改善户外热舒适性,透过绿化设计改善户外环境的表面吸收率降低温度对环境的冲击。因环境之不同而气温有显著差异,如湖气温27.5℃、房屋密集区34.7℃,由此可见地面温度受建筑物、道路或铺面材料及水体之影响。[3]

2 研究方法与仿真设定

2.1 研究方法

本研究以台北地区一个于规划设计时间的小区型规划设计计划为研究基地,进行气流及温度场仿真,评估当地各种地理尺度及气候条件数据,提出小区的热岛特性及其问题所在,并透过水域分布面积与植栽面积之比例调整为变因,利用计算机仿真之方式分析改善户外热环境之可行性,过程中将以气象站收集各项大气中各项物理数值,作为CFD仿真设定及验证之参考,而后,借由CFD仿真探讨变因对于小区型住宅区热环境之影响。故本研究之主要研究方法为气象数据建立与数值仿真。

2.2 数值仿真设定

2.2.1 气象数据建立及边界条件设定

基地内整体舒适度深受地方性气候因素影响,其中以气温、日照、风速尤为重要,本案位处亚热带气候区,受季风影响,属季风气候区域,故将针对气温、日照、风速之气候要素分述于下(表1),其他气候要素如:相对湿度、云量、降雨量、太阳辐射量等将一并作为整体气象数据整合而不再赘述,以作为本案仿真边界设定之依据。

台北测站气象参数表	表1
温度(℃)	31.7
风速(m/s)	2.0
湿度(%)	69
太阳直射辐射强度/(W/m^2)	487
太阳散射辐射强度/(W/m^2)	158

2.2.2 现况结果分析

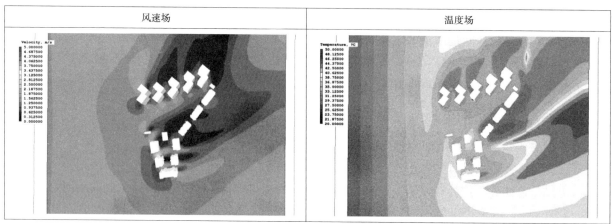

图 1　基地现况仿真图

根据黄教诚 2005 研究结论[5]，针对不同温度环境的受测者进行热接受度实验，结果显示已习惯湿热气候的台湾居民可接受较暖和的热环境，平均可接受之舒适温度最高为 29.5℃。借此，本研究将增加基地内 30℃以下之面积为主要改善重点。根据仿真分析结果显示（图 1，表 2），基地内舒适忍受温度 30℃以下之面积只占户外总面积的 0.24%。反之，基地内有 99.76% 的基地面积属于不舒适的范围，故基地内的外部空间温度过高皆属于不舒适的生活环境。

基地现况温度分布面积表					表 2
	30℃以下	31～32℃	33～34℃	35～36℃	37℃以上
现况	126.7m²	1611.14 m²	47423.43 m²	1672.15 m²	252.64m²
百分比	0.24%	3.15%	92.83%	3.27%	0.49%

2.2.3 仿真方案设定

本研究将针对基地内原设计之绿化面积与水域面积进行探讨，并计算出基地内的绿化、水域比率，将其小区内之公共空间进行绿化与水域面积比例增加或减少，分析对于整体基地内之热舒适度影响程度。仿真方案如表 3 所示。

仿真方案图		表 3
仿真方案	仿真内容	
Case1	设计现状全区 20% 绿化：10% 水域	
Case2	设计现状全区 30% 绿化：15% 水域	
Case3	设计现状全区 15% 绿化：30% 水域	

3 数值仿真与分析

3.1 设计现状全区20%绿化：10%水域

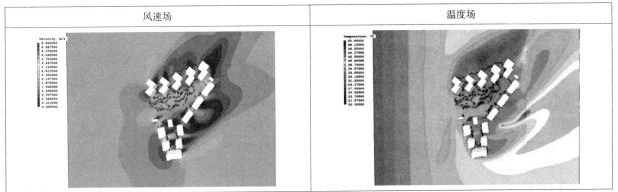

图2　20%绿化：10%水域仿真分析图

20%绿化：10%水域仿真温度分布面积表　　　　表4

	30℃以下	31~32℃	33~34℃	35~36℃	37℃以上
现况	126.7m²	1611.14 m²	47423.43 m²	1672.15 m²	252.64m²
20%绿化：10%水域	900.63m²	6345.29 m²	42340.38 m²	1428.24 m²	71.52m²
差值	-773.93	-4734.15	5083.05	243.91	181.12
比率（增加）	1.51%	9.26%	—	—	—
比率（减少）	—	—	9.95%	0.47%	0.35%

由上述分析结果显示（图2，表4），在10%水域面积与20%植栽配置下，风速介于2.0m/s的条件下，30.0℃以下相较现况面积分布比率能增加1.51%，31.0~32.0℃的温度面积分布比率增加9.26%，而在33.0~34.0℃高温以上的面积分布中，在相同的风速场域中相较现况减少了比率9.95%的面积，35~36℃以上的面积比率也减少了0.47%，37℃以上的面积比率减少0.35%的面积。总体降温效果以比率增加计算基地内约21.54%的区域面积达到改善降温之效果。

3.2 设计现状全区30%绿化：15%水域

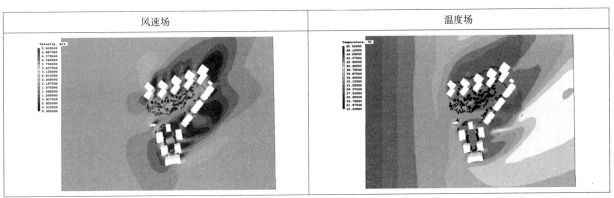

图3　30%绿化：15%水域仿真分析图

30% 绿化：15% 水域仿真温度分布面积表　　表5

	29-30℃	31-32℃	33-34℃	35-36℃	37℃以上
现况	126.7m²	1611.14 m²	47423.43 m²	1672.15 m²	252.64m²
30% 绿化：15% 水域	1032.47m²	7555.09 m²	41047.74 m²	1382.27 m²	68.49m²
差值	-905.77	-5943.95	6375.69	289.88	184.15
比率（增加）	1.77%	11.63%	—	—	—
比率（减少）	—	—	12.48%	0.56%	0.36%

将基地内水域面积增加至15%、植栽配置面积30%时，使基地内30.0℃以下相较现况面积分布比率能增加至1.77%，而在不舒适区的温度分布31.0～32.0℃的面跟分布比率增加11.63%，33.0～34.0℃高温以上的面积分布中，在相同的风速场域中相较现况减少了比率12.48%的面积，35～36℃以上的面积比率也减少了0.56%，37℃以上的面积比率减少0.36%的面积（图3，表5）。总体降温效果以比率增加计算基地内约26.8%的区域面积达到改善降温之效果。故于基地内增加15%水域与30%植栽配置面积的降温效益相较现况之降温改善效益增加了1.77%的舒适面积。

3.3　设计现状全区15% 绿化：30% 水域

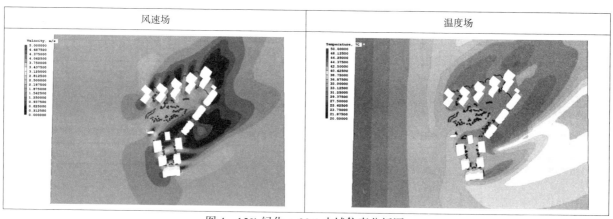

图4　15% 绿化：30% 水域仿真分析图

15% 绿化：30% 水域仿真温度分布面积表　　表6

	29～30℃	31～32℃	33～34℃	35～36℃	37℃以上
现况	126.7m²	1611.14m²	47423.43m²	1672.15m²	252.64m²
15% 绿化：30% 水域	550.54m²	4654.81m²	43955.98m²	1796.34m²	128.39m²
差值	-423.84	-3043.67	3467.45	-124.19	124.25
比率（增加）	0.82%	5.95%	—	0.24%	—
比率（减少）	—	—	6.78%	—	0.24%

当基地内水域面积增加为30%植栽配置面积15%时，30.0℃以下相较现况面积分布比率增加0.82%，而31.0～32.0℃的面跟分布比率增加5.95%，而在33.0～34.0℃高温以上的面积分布中，在相同的风速场域中相较现况减少了比率6.78%的面积，35～36℃以上的面积因植栽遮阴面积减少比率反而增加了0.24%，37℃以上的面积比率减少0.24%的面积（图4，表6）。总体降温效果以比率增加计算基地内约14.03%的区域面积达到改善降温之效果。故增加30%水域面积的降温效益相较30%植栽配置面积之降温效益减少了12.77%的舒适面积。

4 结论

本研究透过了对于小区型的建筑类别进行数值仿真实验,研究了不同的植栽与水域配置于对室外的分布关系对于热环境的影响,针对了不同的绿化与水域面积比率对于整体小区之影响及改善效益为探讨重点,本研究主要结论如下:

(1)由仿真实验可得知,植栽降温较水域降温效益佳,在本研究实验基地内增加 5% 的植栽面积,且风速 1.5～2.0m/s 的情况下可使人行高度 1.5m 处之空气温度降低 3～4℃,虽部分设置植栽的区域风速较小,但透过植栽可直接遮阴的特性,在风速较弱与静风区也能有较好的降温效果。

(2)仿真结果显示,水域面积比率与绿化面积比率之分布之降温效益并非成正比,在增加水域面积比率后,于 35℃ 以上的温度面积分布,并没有随着水域面积增加而明显减少。根据 CFD 仿真图显示,因水域面积增加反而植栽遮阴面积减少,导致日照直接曝晒,故在高温的面积分布并无明显之减少。

Simulation Study on the Strategy of Equipped with Water and Green Areas on Alleviating the Heat Island Effect of the Scale of Residential Buildings

Wang W.-A., Tung S.-W.

(Department of Architecture, Tamkang University)

Abstract: The rapid growth of the city not only causes environmental problems, but also the emergence extravagant cost of housing. The city has signs of gradually outward expansion. The population have to live in the city edge. The strength of the heat island effect will vary depending on the size of the city. The relevant study shows that the intensity of the heat island produced by a small scale city with one thousand population can not be ignored (Gyr and Rys, 1995). Our study focuses on the outdoor thermal environment of community-based high-rise buildings. Improving the reflectivity of building materials, and increasing the area of water and the shades of plants are the designed variations of our study. CFD (Computational Fluid Dynamics) is the tool for forecasting and analysis. Through improving cooling possibilities and benefitials with designed variations, to find the positive result of mitigation heat island effect in limited improvement base.

Keywords: Outdoor thermal environment, Heat island effect, CFD

参考文献

[1] Chia R Chu. 风工程概论 [M]. 台湾: 科技图书出版, 2006.
[2] Guang Dexin, Zhu Tingyao, Han Shijie. Theoretical model of drag coefficient of isolated tree, Sciental

Silvae Sinicae. 2001, 37（6）.

[3] 赖光邦, 林宪德. 台湾地区日照控制之研究〔一〕——建筑物之日影与簇群间之日照分析（D）. 台北科学委员会, 1987.

[4] Templeman A B. Civil engineering systems[M]. London: The MacMillan Press Ltd, 1982.

[5] 黄教诚. 大学教室热舒适范围之实测调查研究 [D]. 逢甲大建筑学系硕士班硕士论文, 2005.

[6] 王启. 场地与地基勘察. 见: 陈忠毅, 叶树林. 地基工程学 [M]. 北京: 中国建筑工业出版社, 1990: 51-88.

[7] 中国力学学会. 第3届全国实验流体力学学术会议论文集 [G]. 天津: [出版者不详], 1990.

[8] Martin G. Control of electronic resources in Australia. In: Pattle L W, Cox B J (ed.). Electronic resources: selection and bibliographic control[M]. New York: The Haworth Press, 1996: 85-96.

[9] 陈述彭, 陆峰. 城市人居环境的生态功能补偿. 见: 邹经宇, 许溶烈, 金德钧等（主编）. 第六届中国城市住宅研讨会论文集——永续·和谐——快速城镇化背景下的住宅与人居环境建设 [G]. 北京: 中国城市出版社, 2007: 3-6.

[10] 邹经宇. 建筑信息系统与虚拟现实系统在建筑教育科研及工程上的应用 [J]. 建筑学报, 1998, 1: 13-16.

[11] Des Marais D J, Strauss H, Summons R E, et al. Carbon isotope evidence for the stepwise oxidation of the Proterozoic environment. Nature, 1992, 359: 605-609.

低层住宅改变楼板与开口规模对通风降温舒适度效益之研究

王文安　董思伟

（淡江大学建筑系）

摘　要：全球暖化的问题日益严重，减缓都市发展所造成的热岛效应，提出合理的改善因应措施，将是未来都市发展与建筑设计的重要课题。本研究主要针对低层住宅室内热环境探讨与改善，以改变建筑外部开口规模、室内楼地板与楼梯空间等，创造垂直路径操作浮力通风改善室内环境之舒适性及降温潜力，并透过计算机计算流体力学CFD（Computational Fluid Dynamics）作为预测与分析之工具，解析在室内环境内，透过设计变因改善降温的可行性与效益，依分析结果提出有利于减缓室内热环境的方针，改善室内人员的热舒适性。部分研究结果得知，风速影响改善变因的降温效益，与无改善通风设计之条件比较，室内温度最佳能降低1~4℃。

关键词：自然通风，建筑降温，计算流体力学

1　引言

1.1　研究目的

全球暖化的问题日益严重，极端气候所带来的灾害日益严重且频繁，都市人口快速成长所造成的环境冲击甚大，其中都市热岛效应为主要影响全球温室效应的原因之一。过去相关文献对于导风或挡风设计的研究中，所讨论的位置皆以建筑之开口部居多，较少在低层建筑中探讨利用垂直浮力通风的可行性。故本研究以低层住宅为研究对象，以浮力通风与贯流通风的将住宅平面层的通风路径相结合，探讨利用热浮力通风对于实际案例应用中的改善效果。

1.2　文献回顾

1.2.1　建筑自然通风

自然通风会对室内人员的居住环境带来影响。在夏天可用于增加人体舒适度，冬天又须防寒风进入室内对人体产生负面影响，从建筑高度、立面装饰、配置的自然通风设计都需有风的设计值作依据。尽管户外通风很重要，但室内自然通风为更实用的设计实务，人一天有大半时间待在室内，室内空气环境的好坏，影响人在内部活动之舒适性与健康。一般而言，室内环境舒适度以保持0.5m/s之风速情况为最佳（陈纪融，2014）。

1.2.2　贯流通风（Cross Ventilation）

利用自然风力作用在建筑上所造成的风压差异，使得建筑物内外的空气进行交换。建筑物迎风面为正压区，背风面为负压区。若迎风面和背风面皆有开口（门窗），则迎风面的开口为进风口，而背风

面的开口为排风口。若仅迎风面有开口或仅背风面有开口亦可造成自然通风，但通风效率不及迎风面和背风面皆有开口者。若迎风面和背风面的开口正对着风向则容易造成穿堂风，其通风效果最佳（Chia R. Chu，2006）。

建筑表面所受之压力常以风速压（Velocity Pressure）V_p 表示之，其计算公示如下。V 为风速（m/s）；ρ 为空气密度〔1 大气压、温度为 20℃ 状况下其密度为 1.2（kg/m³）〕。

$$V_p = \frac{\rho V^2}{2} \text{（Pa）} \tag{1}$$

1.2.3 浮力通风

浮力通风是利用空气温度差异所形成之浮力促使空气上下对流。热压差与"进出风口之高差"及"室内外温差"有关，室内外温差与进出风口之高差越大，则热浮力作用越明显。由于室内空气通常比室外高温，因此室内通常产生如图所示的压力分布，假如墙面有上下开口，则低温的室外空气由下流入，而高温的室内空气由上流出而产生浮力通风的作用（Chia R. Chu，2006）。

热浮力通风依其进出风口之高差及室内外温差之关系而影响效果，则其浮力通风量 Q_b 之计算公式可由下列所示。α 为风量系数；A 为开口面积（m²）；g 为重力加速度（m/s²）；h 为上下开口高度差（m）；ρ_o 为室外空气密度（kg/m³）；ρ_i 为室内空气密度（kg/m³）。

$$Q_b = \alpha \cdot A \sqrt{\frac{2gh(\rho_o - \rho_i)}{\rho_i}} \text{（m}^3\text{/s）} \tag{2}$$

2 研究方法与仿真设定

2.1 研究方法

本研究主要针对低层住宅室内热环境探讨与改善，以改变建筑外部开口规模、室内楼地板与楼梯空间等变因，利用计算机仿真解析之方式分析改善室内流场及热环境之可行性，过程中将以气象站收集各项大气中各项物理数值，作为 CFD 仿真边界条件设定及验证之参考，而后，借由 CFD 仿真探讨变因对于室内流场与热环境之影响。故本研究之主要研究方法为透过理论基础分析探讨，针对研究对象进行改善策略拟定、地方气象数据建立与计算机数值仿真 CFD 预测分析。

2.2 研究对象与数值仿真设定

2.2.1 研究对象

本研究的案例位于台南市某小区的低层住宅（图1），本次研究探讨的空间为四层楼的平面，总面积约为 460m²，建筑高度为 19.2m，其空间机能包含 3 间卧房、4 间厕所，客厅、厨房及停车空间各 1 间。其各层平面图及隔间配置如下图所示（有颜色区域为本次探讨空间范围）。

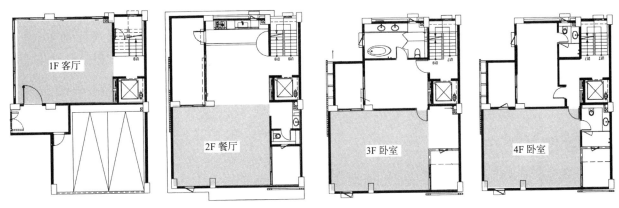

图 1　研究对象平面图

2.2.2　地方性气象数据建立

位于本研究基地周遭的共有当局提供的 3 个定点式测站，可提供长时间与实时的气象数据查询。除安南站距离本研究基地较近外，其余的两个测站应距离基地过远，不足以正确反映基地周边的气候特征，故将采用离基地较近的测点为气象数据研究依据（表 1）。

安南站夏季气象参数表　　　　　　　　　　　　　　　　　表 1

	现场实测	气象局监测数据
温度（℃）	35	27
风速（m/s）	1.5	2.2
湿度（%）	47	77.3
太阳直射辐射强度 /（W/m^2）	—	617
太阳散射辐射强度 /（W/m^2）	—	175

2.2.3　现况分析

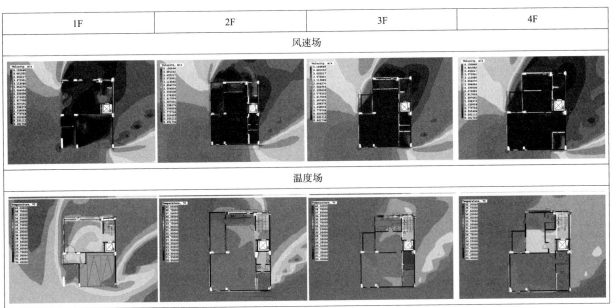

图 2　现况仿真图

仿真结果（图2）显示，在风速场分布1楼客厅测点风速为1.5m/s，2楼餐厅为0.9m/s，3楼主卧室为0.7m/s，4楼卧室0.7m/s。而室内温度分布1楼客厅测点温度为31℃、2楼餐厅31℃、3楼主卧室32℃及4楼卧室32℃，室内整体风速较低，导致热空气滞留于室内，造成整体热环境的不舒适。

3 数值仿真与分析

3.1 改变建筑外部开口规模室内降温之影响

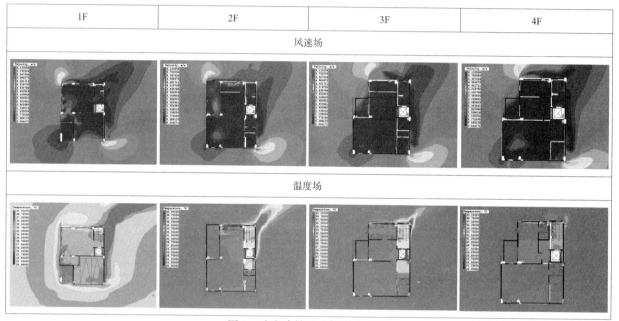

图3 改变建筑开口仿真分析图

根据改善建筑开口规模结果（图3）显示，开口规模增加40%提高了入风量及流速，在风速场分布1楼客厅测点风速提升为1.9m/s，2楼餐厅为1.3m/s，3楼主卧室为1.1m/s，4楼卧室1.5m/s。而室内温度分布1楼客厅测点温度为30℃、2楼餐厅30℃、3楼主卧室30℃及4楼卧室29℃。故增加40%的开口规模，较现况可使室内整体风速平均提升了0.4m/s，平均温度下降了1~2℃，改善较佳区域为4楼卧室。

3.2 变更室内楼地板对自然通风之影响

根据在挑空2楼楼板仿真结果（图4）显示，利用垂直与水平的流场相互影响带动整体流场，在风速场分布1楼客厅测点风速提升为1.6 m/s，2楼餐厅为1.1m/s，3楼主卧室为0.9m/s，4楼卧室0.8m/s。而室内温度分布1楼客厅测点温度为31℃、2楼餐厅30℃、3楼主卧室32℃及4楼卧室31℃，故在挑空2楼板虽风速提升较不明显，在风速场中平均风速相较现况约增加0.1m/s，效果较不佳，故整体室内温度没有较明显的改善。

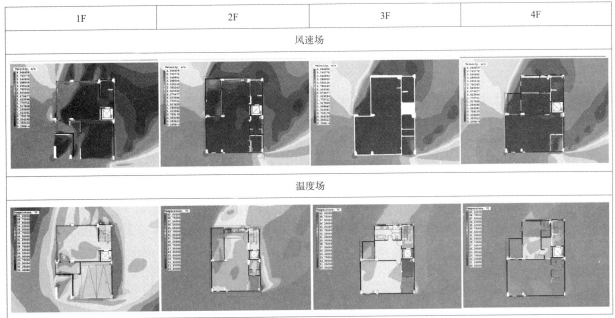

图4 变更室内楼板仿真分析图

3.3 改变楼梯空间与状态对浮力通风之影响

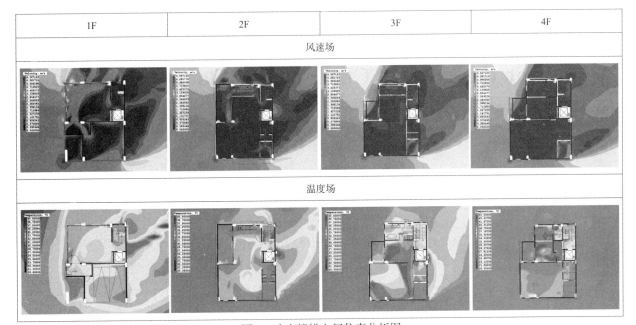

图5 改变楼梯空间仿真分析图

根据仿真结果（图5）显示，整体流场在靠近梯间附近的区域，风速有明显被带动，其余空间的流动很小。在风速场分布1楼客厅测点风速提升为1.5m/s，2楼餐厅为0.9 m/s，3楼主卧室为0.8m/s，4楼卧室0.9m/s。而室内温度分布1楼客厅测点温度为31℃、2楼餐厅31℃、3楼主卧室34℃及4楼卧室31℃，故在低层建筑室内空间中整体浮力通风效果不佳，甚至在3楼主卧室的测点处相较现况温度还升高了2℃。

4 结论

本研究透过对低层住宅建筑类别进行数值仿真实验，研究不同的开口大小与垂直浮力通风对室内热环境的影响，并分析在建筑物室内隔间所产生的不同环境风场，针对不同的风速与不同的改善策略对室内热环境的改善效益为探讨重点，本研究主要结论如下：

（1）利用增加建筑外部开口的规模，对于风速的提升有最直接的影响，随着建筑开口面积增加，除通风量增加外，室内温度也因较高的风速，使热空气容易经流气流带出室内。故不论室内的隔间配置及热源条件为何，风速越大，其室内降温的效能越佳，对于提升室内环境质量之效果显著。

（2）挑空2楼板虽对室内风速提升及降温效果较不明显，但也因在垂直与水平风场交互影响下，导致室内流场部分区域容易产生涡旋现象，造成整体室内空间容易产生较乱的环境风场，导致整体室内环境质量的不舒适性。

（3）在低层建筑利用楼梯空间制造浮力通风效益对于室内通风换气效能并无明显之变化，显示出由于浮力通风之效能与进风口、出风口之高度差及温度压力差有明显关系，因此，在建物仍有进风口的情况下会影响浮力通风的效益，开口处进入的流速会与浮力通风气流相互影响，部分热浮力上升气流受到影响可能会相互抵销，使风速下降，导致室内温度变化并不显著，甚至使热空气被往上带动时停留在楼层较高处，造成之室内温度提升。

Study on the Effect of Changing the Floor and Opening Scale on the Comfort of Ventilation and Cooling in Low-rise Residential Buildings

Wang W.-A., Tung S.-W.

(Department of Architecture, Tamkang University)

Abstract: The problem of global warming is getting serious. Slowing down the heat island effect caused by urban development, and making correct response will be an potent subject of future urban development and architectural design. This study is aimed at the discussion and improvement of the indoor thermal environment of the low-rise residential buildings. In the study we change the scale of the external openings of the building, and floor space of the building, etc., to create vertical with the effect of buoyancy ventilation to improve the comfort and cooling potential of the indoor environment. Taking CFD (Computational Fluid Dynamics) as a tool for forecasting and analysis, the study analyzes that through designed variations to improve the feasibility and effectiveness of cooling in indoor environment. According to the analysis of the results proposed to reduce indoor thermal environment, and to improve the comfort of indoor people. Part of the study results showed that the wind speed to improve the cooling effect of improved variation, compared with no improvement in ventilation designed conditions, the best indoor temperature can be reduced by 1–4℃.

Keywords: Natural ventilation, Building cooling, CFD.

参考文献

[1] Lee KP, Lin H T, Lin L J, Kuo H C, Chen T C. Experimental Analyses of Urban Heat Island Effects of the Four Metropolitan Cities in Taiwan（Ⅱ）——The Analysis of the Spatial and Temporal Features of Urban Heat Islands in Summer[J]. Journal of Architecture, 1999, 31: 75-90.

[2] Huang C C. A Field Study on Thermal Comfort in University Classrooms. Thesis（PhM）[D]. Feng Chia University, 2005.

[3] Bo Hong, Borong Lin, Bing Wang, Shuhua Li. Optimal design of vegetation in residential district combined numerical simulation and field experiment[J], Journal of Central South University of Technology, 2012, 19（3）.

[4] FENG Ning, MA Jie, LIN Bo-rong, ZHU Ying-xin, Impact of landscape on wind environment in residential areas[J]. J. Cent. South Univ. Technol, 2009, 16（s1）: 80-83.

[5] Guang Dexin, Zhu Tingyao, Han Shijie. Theoretical model of drag coefficient of isolated tree, Sciental Silvae Sinicae. 2001, 37（6）.

[6] 李亮, 林波荣, 朱颖心, 李晓峰. 用带源项 k-E 两方程湍流模型模拟树冠流 [J]. 清华大学学报, 2006, 46（6）: 753-756.

[7] 林波荣, 朱颖心, 李晓峰. 不同绿化对室外热环境影响的数值仿真研究, 绿色建筑与建筑物理——第九届全国建筑物理学术会议论文集（一）[M]. 2004: 132-135.

[8] Chia R Chu. 风工程概论 [M]. 台湾: 科技图书出版, 2006.

[9] 关德新, 单玉珍. 树冠结构参数及附近风场特征的风洞仿真研究 [D]. 北京应用生态学报, 2000: 11（2）: 202-204.

[10] 陈纪融. 连栋住宅结合导风板与通风塔之通风效益探讨 [D]. 台南成功大学建筑学系学位论文, 2014.

Comparison of the Guidelines for Heat Island Countermeasures in China and Japan

Li Qiong[1], Yoshida Shiji[2]

(1. South China University of Technology; 2. University of Fukui)

Abstract: Urban warming and heat island is the common problem for the East Asian cities. China and Japan both propose some guidelines for heat island countermeasures. This paper investigates the present situation of the existing guidelines for heat island countermeasures in China and Japan, and compares the differences of these guidelines.

Keywords: Heat island, Countermeasure, East Asia

1 Introduction

Urbanization, such as land-use alteration and increase in anthropogenic heat release, degrades the thermal environment in urban areas during the summer season. The degradation causes various environmental problems, including increased energy consumption for cooling, and increased numbers of hyperthermia patients. Recently, some countermeasure techniques have been proposed to address the problem, and introduced into practical planning and design of urban areas and buildings in China and Japan.

With the continued acceleration of China's urbanization, it is expected that by the year 2020, the urbanization rate will reach 50% to 55%, and might possibly reach 60% to 70% by 2050 [1]. In the process of urban planning and building construction, due to the lack of any design standards related to thermal environment, the outdoor environmental design has always placed an undue emphasis on things such as the luxurious artistic effects of landscape, high-intensity heat-storage ground pavement, non-ventilated building layouts, leisure venues without any shading, and impermeable hardened roads. These irrational practices can lead to the gradual decline of outdoor thermal environment quality, directly influencing the thermal safety and thermal comfort of residents when engaged in outdoor activities, and indirectly increasing the building energy consumption.

In order to improve the quality of urban thermal environments, some working groups in China have compiled Design Standard for Thermal Environment of Urban Residential Areas (JGJ 286-2013). This standard instructs designers to scientifically and rationally adopt thermal environment improvement technology in the process of urban planning and building construction.

In Japan, various guidelines have been proposed by the following central and local governments: The Ministry of Land, Infrastructure, Transport, and Tourism (MLIT), the Ministry of the Environment (MOE), and local governments, including those at the level of prefectures and cities, as well as local areas around Tokyo and Osaka. However, it is difficult to perform a comparative analysis of each guideline, because of the differences in format and availability of numerical targets.

This paper investigates the present situation of the existing guidelines for heat island countermeasures in

China and Japan, and compares the differences of these guidelines.

2 Outline of Chinese Guidelines for Countermeasures Against Heat Island

In 2006, the Evaluation Standard for Green Building (GB/T 50378-2006) [2] has been put forward in China. But the main target of this standard is to assist the green building design. Hence, the content about the urban planning and outdoor thermal environment is very little in this standard. Only the requirement on outdoor wind velocity and wind pressure are included.

In 2013, a special standard named as Design Standard for Thermal Environment of Urban Residential Areas (JGJ 286-2013) [3] is put forward. This standard applies to the thermal environment design during the detailed construction planning stage for residential areas. This standard comprises the following five key characteristics.

2.1 The Thermal Environment Design for Residential Areas Adopts Both SDM and PEM

In order to improve the thermal environment of residential areas and build a safe and comfortable living environment, whilst still taking into account such individualized needs as landscaping and planning etc, the working group put forward the SDM and PEM for the thermal environment of residential areas. Under the precondition of meeting the basic design norms of thermal environments for residential areas, the conformity to the requirements of one of the design methods is deemed to meet this standard. Refer to Figure 1 for the thermal environment design flow diagram for residential areas.

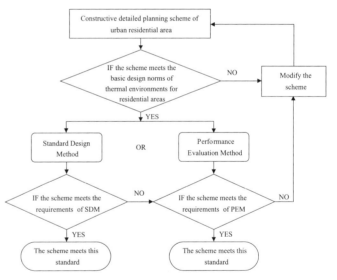

Figure 1 The thermal environment design flow diagram for residential areas

The SDM and PEM put forward by the working group enable the standard to be easily and more flexibly applied in practice. The standard will not only improve the outdoor thermal environment of residential areas, but also satisfy their landscaping and planning requirements.

2.2 SDM of the Thermal Environment of Residential Areas from the Four Aspects as Ventilation, Shading, Permeability and Evaporation, and Green spaces and Greening

During the initial research, the working group found that the four aspects of ventilation, shading, permeability and evaporation, and green spaces and greening are key design factors that influence the thermal environment of residential areas. Therefore, the working group selected these four design factors as a control when evaluating the thermal environment of residential areas, studied the correlation between design factors and thermal environment norms, and acquired the regulatory design limits for these four design factors. These design factor limits for mandatory provisions are shown as follows.

(1) The average frontal area ratio in summer of the residential areas shall comply with the provisions of Table 1, and PEM shall be carried out for the thermal environment of residential areas when failing to meet the requirements of these provisions.

Recommended value of the average frontal area ratio in summer of the residential areas　　　Table 1

Climatic regionalization	Ⅰ, Ⅱ, Ⅵ, Ⅶ	Ⅲ, Ⅴ	Ⅳ
Average frontal area ratio	≤ 0.80	≤ 0.70	≤ 0.65

(2) Within Ⅲ, Ⅳ and Ⅴ climatic regionalization, when the windward width of the buildings with upward prevailing wind exceeds 80m in summer, the ventilation area ratio at the bottom layer of the building shall be no less than 10%; and when failing to meet the requirements of the provisions, PEM shall be made for the thermal environment of such residential areas.

(3) The outdoor venues of residential areas shall have shaded areas in the summer, and the shading coverage ratio shall be no less than that provided in Table 2.

Minimum value of shading coverage ratio on the outdoor venues of residential areas　　　Table 2

	Climatic regionalization	
	Ⅰ, Ⅱ, Ⅵ, Ⅶ	Ⅲ, Ⅳ, Ⅴ
Square	15	25
Recreation area	20	40
Parking lot	25	45
Sidewalk	30	50

(4) The outdoor venues and pedestrian walkways within residential areas shall have rainfall permeability and evaporation capacity, and the permeability and evaporation indices shall not be lower than those provided in Table 3.

Permeability and evaporation indices　　　Table 3

	Climatic regionalization					
	Ⅰ, Ⅱ, Ⅵ, Ⅶ			Ⅲ, Ⅳ, Ⅴ		
Ground type	Penetration area ratio(%)	Ground permeability coefficient(mm/s)	Evaporation capacity(kg/($m^2 \cdot d$))	Penetration area ratio(%)	Ground permeability coefficient(mm/s)	Evaporation capacity(kg/($m^2 \cdot d$))
Square	40	1.0	1.6	50	1.0	1.3
Recreation area	50			60		
Parking lot	60			70		
Sidewalk	50			60		

(5) Residential areas shall be provided with green space and greening, where the green space ratio shall be no less than 30%. There shall also be no fewer than 3 trees within each 100m² of green area. This index is a basic design norm for the thermal environment of residential areas.

2.3 Heat Island Intensity and Wet Bulb Globe Temperature as PEM Norms for the Thermal Environment of Residential Areas

The working group adopted heat island intensity as the design norm for the thermal environment of residential areas, and put forward that the heat island intensity in residential areas shall be no more than 1.5℃. As a reference, they took the provisions on limit value of heat island intensity and computing methods prescribed in the Green Building Evaluation Standard GB/T 50378; the data was computed at local time between 8:00 and 18:00, where the average hourly temperature difference is obtained by comparing the design air temperature of the residential area with the typical meteorological value for that day.

Based on the extensiveness and authority of the application of WBGT indices, the preparation group adopted this index as the safety design norm for the thermal environment of residential areas. Taking into consideration the difference among buildings in different climatic regions, the working group ultimately determined to take the "median" evaluation level in Table 4 as the limit value index, and 34 ℃ as the limit value.

Quality assessment rating of the thermal environment   Table 4

Good	Median	Bad	Very bad
WBGT ≤ 33℃	WBGT ≤ 34℃	WBGT ≤ 35℃	WBGT > 35℃

2.4 Calculation of Thermal Environment in Residential Areas Under Typical Meteorological Conditions

Most areas in China have great climatic differences between winter and summer. Therefore, the concept of a typical meteorological day is adopted to describe the climatic characteristics of a specific local season. A typical meteorological day comprises multiple climatic elements, including outdoor hourly air temperatures, relative humidity, total horizontal solar radiation, diffuse horizontal solar radiation, outdoor average wind speed, and seasonal dominant wind direction.

The data related to a typical meteorological day in this standard is taken from the data of a typical meteorological year in each of China's main cities. The data for a typical meteorological year is in turn taken from the Building Climate Energy Conservation Research Center of Xi'an University of Architecture and Technology, with the data used being those originally measured for each meteorological parameter by the National Weather Service from 1971 to 2000.

2.5 Computing Hourly Air Temperature Based on Cluster Thermal Time Constant (CTTC)

Based on the CTTC model, improved CTTC model, three-dimensional CTTC model and green CTTC model, the working group put forward the hourly air temperature computing model of residential areas, and developed computing software. This software has the advantages of high speed, high accuracy and easy operability, and is suitable for use in the design of thermal environments at the detailed planning stage of construction for residential areas.

3 Outline of Japanese Guidelines for Countermeasures Against Heat Island

In Japan, The ministry of Land, Infrastructure, transport and tourism(MLIT) proposed "A building design guideline for mitigation of heat island phenomena" in 2004[4]. The aim of this guideline is to summarize the considerations for a building design that contributes to mitigation of and adaption to heat island phenomena. The comprehensive assessment system for building environmental efficiency for heat island (CASBEE-HI)[5], proposed in 2005, is a tool for evaluating both the mitigation and adaption techniques against heat island phenomena. In CASBEE-HI, the countermeasures for heat island is proposed from air path, shade, exterior building materials, and anthropogenic heat release from building equipment. And some quantitative restrict index are used for urban planning and building design. For example, the open area ratio should be greater than 40%. The frontal area ratio of a building to the prevailing wind should be less than 80%. The maximum specific energy consumption should be less than 120 W/m^2.

The Ministry of the Environment(MOE) proposed a guideline entitled "Countermeasure guidelines against heat island" in 2009 [6]. This guideline was proposed through the activity of the committee for investigating the execution of countermeasure scenarios against heat islands. This guidelines was proposed on the assumption that the staff of local governments or official agencies will refer to it in order to effectively promote the countermeasure against heat islands. Therefore, this guideline does not include any quantitative targets because of the assumption of use in a wide range of fields, including building design and redevelopment of cities. The most interesting parts of this guideline are datasheets that summarize the effects, and specific examples of each countermeasure technique.

4 Comparison and Investigation of Japanese and Chinese Heat Island Guidelines

From the comparison, we found that both in Japanese and Chinese heat island guidelines, the countermeasures for heat island are all proposed from air path, shade. In Chinese guideline, the permeability and evaporation of the road, the green space are required. But in Japanese guideline, the countermeasures are also proposed from the air path, shade, exterior building materials, and anthropogenic heat release from building equipment. Hence, in Japan, the green building design and urban heat island countermeasure are combined. It promotes to apply the guideline to practical design of buildings and their surrounding areas, along with the evaluating the performance of the BEE using the CASBEE-HI, give us quantitative standards for optimum environmental design. However, in China, the green building design and urban heat island countermeasure are separated.

5 Conclusions

Design Standard for Thermal Environment of Urban Residential Areas fills the gap within national standards related to urban climatic change in China, and provides practical and operable evaluative norms, design methods and design tools for design personnel and managers. The issuance and implementation of this standard will help improve and enhance living quality, reduce the energy consumption of residential buildings, and promote the construction of environmentally-friendly residential areas. This standard can be modified in future from building design and anthropogenic heat release. The green building design and urban heat island countermeasure should be combined effectively.

Acknowledgements

The study is supported by International Science &Technology Cooperation Program of China (Project No.2011DFA91210), National Natural Science Foundation of China (Projects No. 51178189, 51378214).

中日城市热岛应对技术标准的比较分析

李 琼[1] 吉田伸治[2]

（1. 华南理工大学；2. 日本福井大学）

摘 要：城市变暖与热岛效应是东亚城市面临的共同问题。中国和日本都提出了一些应对热岛效应的技术标准。本文分析了中国和日本现有城市热岛应对技术标准的现状，并比较了这些标准的差异。

关键词：热岛效应，应对策略，东亚

References

[1] ZHOU G Z. China's urbanization rate will reach 50%-55% at 2020 (in Chinese). 2005. http://news.xinhuanet.com/fortune/2005-.

[2] Ministry of housing and urban-rural development of the People's Republic of China. Evaluation Standard for Green Building. 2006.

[3] Ministry of housing and urban-rural development of the People's Republic of China. Design Standard for Thermal Environment of Urban Residential Area. 2013.

[4] Ministry of land, infrastructure, transport, and tourism (MLIT). A building design guideline for mitigation of heat island phenomena.2004. http://www.mlit.go.jp/kisha/kisha04/07/070716_.html (in Japanese).

[5] Japan Sustainable Building Consortium (JSBC).Evaluation Manual of CASBEE for Heat Island. 2010. http://www.ibec.or.jp/CASBEE/index.htm.

[6] Ministry of the Environment (MOE). Countermeasure guidelines against heat island.2009.

热带城市私人住宅的被动式设计方法研究：
以越南岘港市为例

鲍 莉 Duc Vien LE

（东南大学建筑学院）

摘 要： 被动式建筑设计是建筑适应气候的有效手段，可减少建筑能耗并为使用者提供一个更为舒适的使用空间。本文针对位于热带气候区的越南岘港地区面广量大、地方特征明显的私人住宅，基于气候特征分析、文献及实地调研，确定核心的建筑隔热和建筑通风问题，进而展开被动式设计方法研究。本研究旨在提出热带地区私人住宅原型设计，以期对当代的设计实践起到一定的引导作用。

关键词： 被动式设计，私人住宅，热带气候，建筑隔热，建筑通风

1 引言

地球自然环境严重污染、气候恶化、资源滥用等问题已经成为非常迫切的问题，因此世界各国的学者不断地在降低能耗污染、改善生活环境、缓解气候恶化等方面做出努力。在建筑界，被动式建筑设计是最为重要的出路之一，在国际上该方面的研究时间较早，并且涉及的领域多样，评价标准较为完善，研究成果甚为丰富。不过，还有些国家，比如越南，由于自己的经济条件、科技水平等限制，导致被动式建筑设计这一方面没有进行太多的研究。越南的战争一直延续到20世纪70年代末，从80年代开始，专业、系统的"绿色建筑"、"生态气候建筑"、"可持续建筑"等概念逐渐被引入并得到重视，多位学者针对气候特征和建筑物理的研究成果对今日绿色建筑设计，尤其是被动式设计奠定了基本的理论基础。1998年热带建筑院的成立，2007年越南绿色建筑委员会的成立，2010年LOTUS绿色工程评价体系的发布均体现了越南绿色建筑设计，被动式设计所取得的成果。但是整体上看，关于被动式设计越南的研究时间较晚，评价标准尚未完善，研究成果的开放程度较低，缺乏针对不同区域的研究和具指导性的设计方法。因此，本研究选取热带气候特点明显的越南岘港市作为研究对象，针对该地区最常见的，带有地域特征的私人住宅建筑类型展开调研以发现当地建筑适应气候的具体问题，结合对当地气候的研究进行讨论其建筑类型的被动式设计方法。

岘港市位于越南中部，大约一半是高山地形，一半是平原地形，东部沿海，基本气候特征是属于热带季风气候，冬天最低温度一般不低于10℃，不需要防冷，夏季最高温度可能超过40℃，需要防热。[1] 本研究选取从3月21日（春分）至9月23日（秋分）的最热时间段，针对岘港地区私人住宅展开研究。该地区的私人住宅是联排别墅类型居住房屋，其所有权归个人所有，建筑高度一般在5层以下，常见的建筑占地面积在100m² 上下，建筑面积一般在 100 ~ 500m² 之内，人口数量根据建筑规模和家庭规模而变化，每户一般有4 ~ 8个人。该建筑类型的一个重要特征是面宽小进深大，密集排列，其对于建筑设计带来很大的挑战（图1）。

图 1　岘港市地理特征及其住宅常见形式

2　核心问题及建筑原型

建筑隔热和建筑通风是核心问题

为了从实际中发现具体问题，本研究在岘港地区选择了 4 座不同规模、地区特征的住宅展开调研。其调研在温度最高的 7 月的晴天进行。通过 4 个案例的调研结果本研究发现岘港地区私人住宅适应气候的一些普遍问题：(1) 朝向与布局问题：朝东和朝西（尤其是朝西）的建筑受到的太阳辐射强度大，南北向的影响相对小一些。朝向也影响建筑的自然通风效果，凉风的引入可以适当降低室内温度，提高舒适度；(2) 屋面受辐射问题：简单的单层屋面构造的隔热效果不太理想，屋面被加热时热量直接传入室内，导致室内温度也变高；(3) 墙面受辐射问题：大部分建筑的遮阳措施都很简单，没有充分考虑遮阳设计。当建筑室内环境不舒适时，人们只能采用主动式的一些设备或者用一些临时的，毫无审美性的措施来解决问题；(4) 建筑通风问题：使用者和设计师不注重通风设计问题，导致建筑室内出现很多封闭和独立的房间，不利于建筑整体的通风。另外，门窗大多数情况下处于关闭状态也使通风效果不明显；(5) 建筑采光问题：一般情况下建筑的一些主要空间的采光条件达到要求。实际中，有些建筑的部分空间的采光条件不足，不过这些空间一般是不常用的空间，因此在一定程度上可以接受；(6) 材料与构造问题：单层砖砌墙面或单层钢筋混凝土屋面、金属屋面构造的隔热性能不是很好，但是目前岘港市的大部分建筑都使用这些简单的构造方式，导致建筑室内舒适度低的普遍现象。

根据调研结果结合关于当地气候特征的研究，笔者认为越南岘港市私人住宅适应气候设计要面对的主要问题有：一是建筑隔热问题，二是建筑通风问题。想要做好被动式设计就要从如何解决这两个问题入手。其他问题虽然也有影响，不过重要程度不如隔热和通风，因此可以暂不涉及。

基于传统经验的建筑原型

在人类历史中，建筑出现的最初目的就是为了减低气候环境对人的影响程度。建筑适应气候是建筑发展的推动力之一。至今，我们还是可以从传统建筑学习到很多建筑适应气候的经验。岘港及周边地区的传统住宅也是如此，这种类型的建筑有很强的历史与地方特征；建筑形态特征（规模、形式、尺度、地块形状、布局方式等）与当代岘港私人住宅的特征极为相似；传统的建筑功能布置反映传统的生活习惯和生活观念；其建筑有很多可借鉴的建筑适应气候的经验。本研究从中提取出几点特征作为今日岘港市私人住宅设计的原型：一是在长条形的建筑中布置了天井和庭院，两者共同为建筑带来更自然、更舒适的微气候环境和活动空间；二是建筑室内通风设计的经验，传统住宅的合理开口，通透的室内分隔等手段可形成较好的自然通风效果。从传统住宅推导原型并采用当代的材料和技术提升建筑气候适应性是岘港市私人住宅被动式设计的核心策略（图 2）。

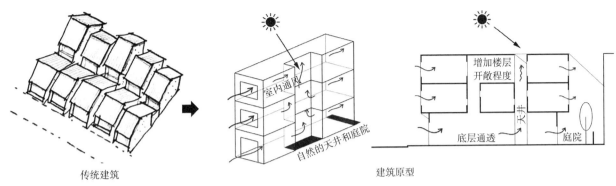

图 2　岘港及周边地区适应气候的建筑原型

3　建筑被动式隔热设计方法

据研究 [2, 3]，可以得出岘港市 7 月的舒适温度约在 28.8℃，而在实际中在早上 8 点时室内温度已经达到 29 ~ 30℃并快速增高，至中午可能达到约 34℃。可见，岘港地区的私人住宅的室内温度很高，需要建立有效的隔热方法来保证使用者的舒适度。具体表现在以下几个方面：

建筑布局与朝向

通过对岘港市太阳轨迹图、各方向的太阳直射强度以及夏季主导风向的综合研究，可得出该地区的建筑好朝向是从东向偏北 14° 往南至南向偏西 30° 的范围。如果建筑朝向在其范围之外要着重考虑立面隔热问题（尤其是在西、西北、西南三个方向）（图 3）。

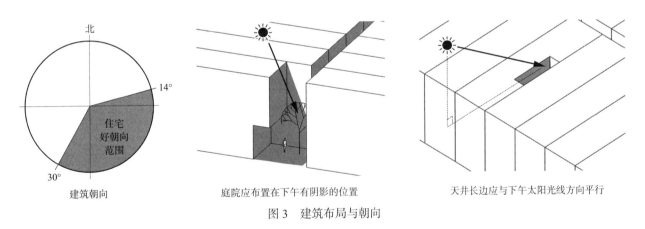

图 3　建筑布局与朝向

为了提升建筑采光通风效果，建筑设计中应设有庭院和天井：庭院要布置在下午时段有阴影的位置如建筑南、东南、东或东北边，尽量避开西晒影响强烈的位置如建筑西、西南、北或和西北边。庭院规模要以周边不同的条件而定，不过庭院宽度与建筑高度的比例不应小于 1/4 以避免其尺度造成的压抑感；建筑中的天井或中庭也要布置在建筑南、东南、东或东北边位置，同时天井或中庭的平面形状应采用长方形，长边尽量与下午太阳直射光线方向平行以减少井内墙面的得热面积。

屋面隔热

通常 20% ~ 95% 的太阳辐射会被屋面吸收 [4]，因此屋面隔热的基本目标就是减少太阳辐射产生的热量通过屋顶传到室内空间。为达到这个目标，本研究对于岘港地区私人住宅的屋面设计提出建议是：屋面构造设计要采用多层的，自身有遮阳、散热的屋面构造方法，在其构造中，外层屋面为全部或部分内层屋面起到遮阳作用，在太阳辐射的影响下，外层屋面被加热会使两层屋面之间的空气也被加热，在有风的条件下大部分热空气被散发到室外环境，只有小部分的热量能通过内层屋面传入室内，因此其屋面构造有较好的隔热效果。

以上所描述的屋面隔热方法的使用材料、空气流通层的形式与大小等有多种不同，其中较为常见、易于操作的材料和构造有：木板、钢筋混凝土板、金属瓦楞板、植物层等双层屋面（图4）。使用钢筋混凝土板或木板作为外层屋面时，空气流通层高度应在25～40cm，使用金属瓦楞板作为外层屋面时，其高度应在100cm左右以保证两层之间的通风效果和屋面的散水效果。选用种植屋面时应采用灌木植物以增加遮阳效果。

以上所提出的几种方法从原理上都可以运用于建筑平屋面或坡屋面，不过由于坡屋面的结构特征，有些方法可以运用而有些方法又不太合理。可以在坡屋面上运用的方法包括采用木板，金属瓦楞板，绿化层的双层屋面。不宜使用钢筋混凝土板，原因是钢筋混凝土板的重量大，如果零散布置在坡屋面上可能出现下滑的危险现象。

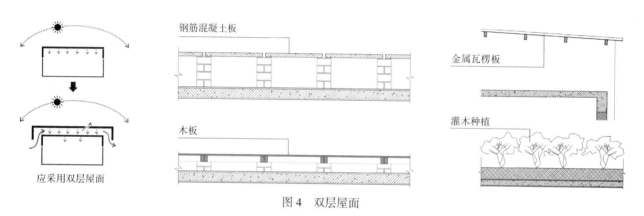

图4　双层屋面

外墙面隔热

建筑的不同立面接受不同的太阳辐射强度，因此建筑墙面隔热设计要根据本地太阳辐射特征针对不同朝向做出相应的考虑。具体策略见图5。

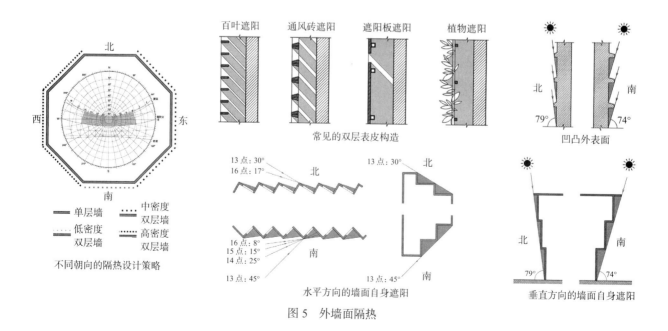

图5　外墙面隔热

岘港地区的东向和西向太阳高度角较小（约 28°）因此要加强东向和西向的墙面隔热，要采用多层的，自身有遮阳、散热的墙面构造方法。可采用百叶、通风砖、遮阳板或植物层作为外层墙面，为内层墙面起到遮阳作用，两层之间的空气层也能为墙面起到散热作用。

南向和北向的太阳高度角较大（南向约 74°，北向约 79°）因此南向和北向的墙面隔热要求相对小一些，可以通过墙面的形式或纹理来形成自身遮阳的效果。另外，在南向还可以考虑使用低密度的双层墙面构造以遮挡部分南向太阳直射。

门窗外遮阳设计

外遮阳已被证明比内遮阳的防热效果更好[5]，因此本研究仅针对外遮阳方法展开研究，根据门窗洞口的朝向选择合适的遮阳措施，从而遮挡部分或全部太阳直射以减少太阳辐射量。本研究根据岘港市一年中较热时段（约从 3 月 21 日（春分）~ 9 月 23 日（秋分），每日从 8 ~ 16 点）的太阳运动轨迹计算 8 个主要方向（南、北、东、西、东南、东北、西南、西北）的门窗洞口的遮阳构件形式和角度（图 6）。东向和西向要采用横向百叶以遮挡正面的、高度角小的太阳直射光线，西向应完全遮挡而东向可允许部分光线透过；南向可以采用横向遮阳板以遮挡正面的、高度角大的太阳直射光线；东南向可以采用过个横向遮阳板以遮挡高度角较小的东向太阳直射光线；其他 4 个方向要结合使用横向和竖向遮阳板以遮挡斜向的太阳直射光线。

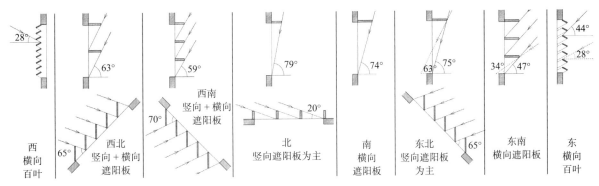

图 6　门窗遮阳构件的形式和角度

4　建筑被动式通风设计方法

从岘港地区传统住宅提取出的原型可以得出在建筑中使用天井以及加强建筑的通透程度对提升建筑通风效果有明显的作用，因此天井通风和风道通风可作为当代岘港市私人住宅被动式通风设计的基本手段。

天井通风

本研究使用软件模拟出岘港地区私人住宅的通风情况。模拟结果表示：在相同的室外风速是 2.75m/s 的条件下，当建筑无天井时，建筑底层只有局部区域有良好的风速（约 0.5m/s），二层、三层通风极差（小于 0.1m/s）；当建筑设有天井时，建筑中的各主要空间的风速约在 0.2~0.4m/s，井内风速约在 1m/s 左右。可见建筑中设有天井（或中庭）可以很好地改善室内通风效果。

天井（或中庭）还可以在无风条件下形成热压通风效果。热压通风的效果和温度差、高度差成正比，所以天井的高度和好的遮阳效果能促进热压通风。[6] 天井（或中庭）的顶部位置应设有遮阳措施以保证井内的阴凉，又能提高顶部的空气温度，底部可以考虑布置绿化、水面等景观要素，降低底部的空气温度。在高度方面，如果高度不足时，可以考虑增高井口位置。从而可以提升顶部和底部直径的温度差（图 7）。

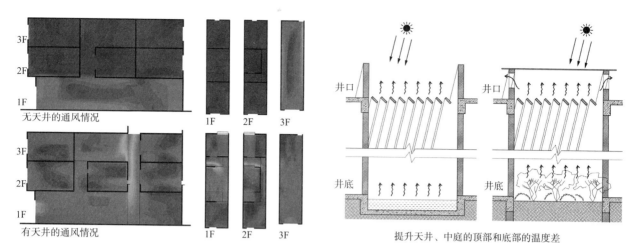

图 7 天井通风

风道通风

要形成风道通风效果就要增加开敞空间,减少不必要的封闭空间,同时还应增加室内分隔的通透性。对于风道通风来说,一个较为理想的空间是没有分隔墙面的空间,此时可以通过家具的布置,地面的高差,地面、墙面的颜色等方法来限定空间。在需要有分隔墙面时,应该使用通透的隔断而不应该使用实墙,一是能增加开敞空间之间的视线关系,二是能为通风提供一个有利条件。对于一些私密空间,可以在墙面上布置大面积的百叶窗,百叶窗既能阻挡视线干扰又能允许空气的流动。在百叶层后面可以布置另一层隔声的窗扇,在必要时,将其关闭就可以阻挡声音的干扰(图8)。

从另一个角度来看,以上的处理方法是为了形成通透空间,回归传统的空间性质,因为传统的开放空间是灵活和高效的空间,而不是封闭、独立、缺少互动的空间。

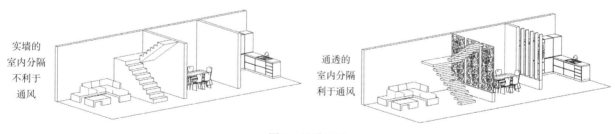

图 8 风道通风

5 小结

从对岘港地区私人住宅的被动式设计研究可以得出,湿热的热带地区被动式建筑设计应集中解决的主要问题是建筑隔热和建筑通风,其目标是减少太阳辐射对建筑产生的热量,并且提升建筑室内的通风效果,从而提升使用者的舒适度。若要实现其目标就要从当地传统建筑提取建筑适应气候经验的建筑原型,在此基础上进而结合当地气候特征以及当代被动式设计理论和实践的研究来形成合理的被动式设计方法。

Passive Design Methods of Private House in Tropical Climate: Danang City, Vietnam

Bao Li, Duc Vien LE

(School of Architecture, Southeast University)

Abstract: Passive design is an effective means to make the building to adapt to climate, to reduce building energy consumption, and to provide users with a more natural, more comfortable space. Passive methods solve different climate and building problems in different climatic zones and architectural types areas. This paper focuses on the hot tropical climate area, taking Danang City in Vietnam as an example to study the passive method in private residential buildings, which is the most common building type in this area. In this paper, lots of academic literature reading and local site study on the selected topics are carried out on the first step, and then identified more specific problems and research directions. It is found that passive design of private houses in Danang City, Vietnam should pay attention to two aspects: insulation and ventilation. Finally, a prototype of passive design private residential design in Danang, Vietnam, has been examined, which is mainly focused on the insulation and ventilation. It is believed that the results of this study can give some practical guidance to the passive design of local private residence, and can also inspire the similar study on passive design of other buildings types in similar climatic condition.

Keywords: Passive design, Private house, Tropical climate, Insulation, Ventilation

参考文献

[1] 越南社会主义共和国建设部. QCVN 02: 2009/BXD Vietnam Building Code: Natural Physical & Climatic Data for Construction. 2009.

[2] Nguyen A T. Some proposals of thermal comfort model applicable for Vietnamese in different situations and building types[J]. Journal of Science and Technology, 2012, 54 (5): 71-77.

[3] Nguyen A T, Singh M K, Reiter S. An adaptive thermal comfort model for hot humid South-East Asia[J]. Building and Environment, 2012, 56: 291-300.

[4] Suehrcke H, Peterson E L, Selby N. Effect of roof solar reflectance on the building heat gain in a hot climate[J]. Energy and Buildings, 2008, 40 (12): 2224-2235.

[5] Kim G, Lim H S, Lim T S, et al. Comparative advantage of an exterior shading device in thermal performance for residential buildings[J]. Energy and Buildings, 2012, 46: 105-111.

[6] 陈晓扬, 郑彬, 候何明等. 建筑设计与自然通风[M]. 北京: 中国电力出版社, 2011.

Thermal Profiles of A High Density City

Maing Minjung
(Dept of Architecture, University of Hong Kong)

Abstract: The high density city is compact with buildings and in-between voids that form narrow street canyons that trap heat and create microclimates within deep troughs of the city. Hong Kong is an exemplary case of tall residential and commercial towers that are situated along a dense linear strip throughout the city where 40-story public housing residential towers are being proposed and built. Trapped ventilation within the city has got much attention after the devastating effect of viral contamination in 2001, SARS epidemic, and awareness of health issues related to trapped heat, also known as urban heat island effect. Urban and thermal relief are core issues that have to be considered for sustainable development and energy efficiency in today's rapidly urbanizing cities. The paper discusses research conducted to investigate how the design of buildings affect the outdoor thermal environment of the city. Field measurements of thermal radiation and temperature were conducted at various locations throughout the city and data analysis was performed to understand the relationship of 3 key urban conditions: urban surfaces, building morphology and organization and urban canyon that describe the city living context, using short-wave, long-wave radiant fluxes, mean radiant temperature (MRT) as primary thermal comfort indices. Field data are compared to assess three urban conditions were (a) building form and layout; (b) urban geometry ; and (c) urban surfaces. The size of the urban canyon and orientation of the buildings had significant effect on whether the solar radiation radiated back into the urban open space and how well the radiated heat could escape back up to the sky. The amount of thermal mass properties of the building surface receiving direct sunlight affected the amount of heat that was radiated back down into the pedestrian open space. Glass surfaces radiated significant short-wave and long-wave radiation when under direct sunlight but under shaded conditions, was able to cool down and have almost minimal effect of radiated heat to the open space. Concrete surfaces similarly radiated significant heat when under direct sun, and continuously under shaded conditions. The orientation of the buildings and the allocation of materials on the surfaces affects the outdoor thermal environment.

Keywords: Urban public space, Thermal environment, Building envelope, High density

1 Introduction

With more than half of the world population living in urban areas (United Nations, 2014) and increasing, the living environment of growing cities are changing due to urban densification. High density cities are becoming common, especially in Asia, and in areas of hot and humid tropical climates, issues of thermal comfort, trapped thermal heat in urban areas are of concern. The urban heat island and outdoor thermal environment is of big concern in hot tropical climates where there are long periods of hot temperatures that when increased due to urban heat island can become fatal. The chosen site of investigation to study the outdoor thermal environment is Hong Kong, which is one of the highly dense city around the world with a population of 7.3 million living in total area of 1081 km^2 of land (Census Planning Section, 2017).

This paper discusses research conducted to better understand the outdoor thermal environment of a high density city where arrangement of buildings and open space can have significant impact on the urban environment. High density cities have characteristics of tall buildings and accumulation of such buildings begin to affect the urban climate which may be different under different conditions (Oke, 1987). Increase in temperatures due to urbanization compared to rural areas is described as urban heat island (UHI), and this temperature increase is further modified from mainly the impact of two parameters: urban geometry and radiation properties of urban surfaces (Oke 1991; Arnfield, 2003). Urban geometry for thermal comfort studies are described as the aspect ratio being the ratio of the average height of building (H) and the width between these buildings (W), calculated ast H/W (Johanssen, 2006). Urban surfaces are the exterior building walls, roofs and horizontal urban landscape, including trees and parks, that form the surfaces of the city that are directly affected by the climate. For this research the main focus was placed on the exterior building walls, which are primarily the vertical urban surfaces, to study how they affect the thermal environment of the pedestrians.

This study aims at investigating what are the important aspects of the building development that affect the urban outdoor thermal environment in high density cities. The descriptions of building developments that directly interface with the outdoor spaces fall primarily into two nomenclatures: urban geometry——different building orientations, scale and urban configurations and; urban surfaces——building and landscape outer or exterior materials forming the boundary conditions (Oke, 1987). The parameter of sky view factor (SVF) has been used in studying thermal comfort in numerous studies. Field testing to record thermal radiation, temperature, wind speed, view factors to determine mean radiant temperature (MRT) is commonly used by researchers and are the main data parameters collected during the field testing used in this study. Important variables to measuring human thermal comfort was most importantly solar radiation, infrared radiation and wind speed, thus the MRT is calculated using the parameters of solar radiation (short-wave) and infrared radiation (long-wave). Infrared thermal imaging was also used to study how the urban surfaces were affected due to orientation and solar radiation. The period of study was during the warm to hot summer months in 2015 to focus on the heating effects of the urban surfaces on the urban environment.

2 Field Testing and Data Processing

Sites throughout Hong Kong were selected to represent some typical conditions of housing building forms, low-rise and high-rise, orientation, building surface materials and amount of shading within the open space test areas. Sites were: Site A——On Shing Estate (TKS), Site B——One Island East (OIE), Site C——Ping Shek Estate (PSK), Site D——Wu Yee Sun of The Chinese University of Hong Kong (CUHK) campus, Site E——SHHO Hall of CUHK Campus, and Site F——Upper Ngau Tau Kok Estate (NTK). The parameter used to differentiate low-rise and high-rise developments in order to have comparable context, is the urban canyon index, also referenced as aspect ratio H/W. In the research, the sites were selected where high aspect ratio would represent taller buildings and low aspect ratio would represent lower-rise buildings (Figure 1a).

The parameters used to quantity the shading levels within the outdoor public space are SVF and the building form (shape) and organization on the ground (orientation and layout). An open layout would consist of a linear building meaning the building is on one side of the open space; semi-open layout would consist of a partially open building where the inner open space would be partially open to the landscape and; a closed layout would consist of buildings that would wrap around a middle open space (Figure 1b). A common condition required for all selected sites were that the open space where microclimatic measurements were to be taken, had to be away from main streets and areas of heavy daily traffic in order to have least disturbance from other heat sources such as vehicular traffic.

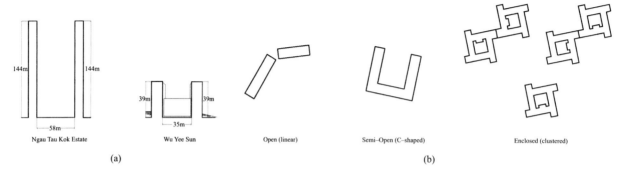

Figure 1 Testing conditions of urban geometry (a), and urban morphoglogy (b)

Mean radiant temperature (MRT) was used as the parameter to measure thermal comfort, and is defined as uniform temperature of an imaginary enclosure in which radiant heat transfer from the human body equals the radiant heat transfer in the actual non-uniform enclosure. MRT is obtained by measuring short- and long-wave radiant fluxes from six cardinal directions (namely up, down, right, left, front, back) measured with a net radiometer over a select period of time, and using the Stefan-Boltzmann equation (Sofia, T. et al, 2007). The measurements from the selected site were compared to investigate the three conditions: (1) urban geometry; (2) urban morphology (building form and organization); and (3) urban surfaces. The measured short-wave and long-wave radiant fluxes and derived MRT were the three main comparison factors.

2.1 Field Testing

The equipment apparatus setup consists of a set of net radiometers and data loggers (by Kipp & Zonen) to measure short- and long-wave radiation from six cardinal directions, temperature and humidity weather meter, wind anemometer and globe thermometer. Including the setup mentioned, a fish-eye lens camera was used to determine the view factors from the equipment setup. Data was recorded in 10-second intervals in the afternoon between 14:00 and 17:00 and only data recorded whilst there was no direct sunlight on the equipment setup, was used for analysis.

3 Results and Discussion

3.1 Urban Geometry

The measured data from two sites——(Site D) WYS and (Site F) NTK——were used to study the effects of urban geometry with an aspect ratio of 1 and 2.5 respectively (Figure 1a). Site E is a 13-story low-rise building and Site F is a new public housing 40-story tower complex.

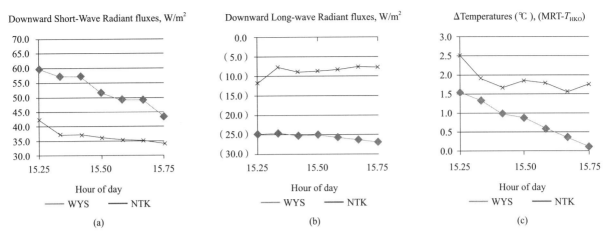

Figure 2　Comparison of measured radiation and MRT of sites representing high aspect ratio (High-rise) and low aspect ratio (low-rise)

Figure 2c shows the public spaces in tall buildings of high aspect ratio (narrow urban canyon properties) may feel hotter due to solar radiation not able to escape. However, there is less short-wave radiation (Figure 2a) due to direct sunlight not able to get deep down to the lower portions of the development and consequently, the infrared heat (long-wave radiation) is lower in the tall buildings compared to the low-rise. Long narrow urban canyons created by high aspect ratios reduces the ability for sunlight to reach down however, the heat that is reflected down tend to be difficult to escape providing a poor cooling effect than a lower aspect ratio arrangement.

3.2　Urban Morphology: Building Form and Organization

The measured data from three sites——(Site C) PSK, (Site D) WYS and (Site E) SHHO——were used to study the effects of different building morphologies and their organization on the site. Site E represents an open organization and a linear building form, Site D represents a semi-open organization with a U-shaped building form and Site C represents an enclosed organization where the buildings collectively surround the central open space (Figure 1b).

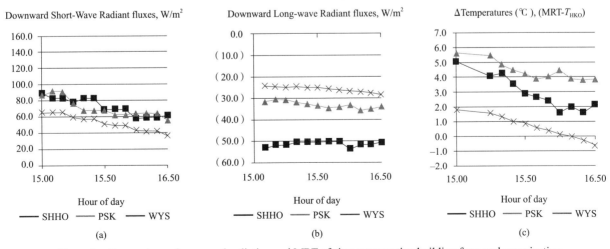

Figure 3　Comparison of measured radiation and MRT of sites representing building form and organization

The results in Figure 3 suggest that although Site C (PSK) has an enclosed layout, the closer building surfaces of Site D (WYS) provided better in blocking the direct sunlight and thus having less short-wave and long-wave radiation within the courtyard space. From Figure 3a and b, we can tell that a large SVF due to the open layout of Site E experiences higher short-wave and long-wave radiation when measured infront of the building south elevation, however the cooling effect of the open layout is better with a faster drop in temperature after the direct sunlight is gone from the tested location as can be seen in the graph of Figure 3c. Gaps in the layout Site F also helps to cool down this space faster than a configuration although semi-enclosed has closer building surfaces.

3.3 Urban Surfaces

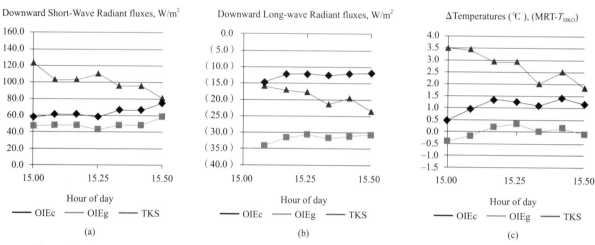

Figure 4 Comparison of measured radiation and MRT of sites representing glass and concrete building surfaces

The two main materials of the building surfaces commonly found in the test sites were glass and concrete, with the additional urban surface material of trees. In Figure 4 the all-glass building surface is represented by the data for OIEg (Site A) and concrete surfaces are represented by OIEc and TKS (Site A). During the tested time, the OIEg (glass surface) and TKS (concrete surface) was shaded from direct sun and OIEc (concrete surface) was partially shaded. From the results in Figure 4, the glass material in general, radiated less short-wave and long-wave fluxes to the outdoor space when compared with the concrete surfaces. The delta temperatures are determined from taking difference between the derived MRT from measured short-wave and long-wave radiation from the recorded temperature from the HKO weather station. For the glass building surfaces that did not receive direct sunlit, the MRT was closest to the temperature measured at the weather station. However the MRT of the shaded concrete surfaces, TKS, the difference went up to as high as 3.5 degrees meaning that even without direct sunlight, the radiant fluxes radiated from the heated concrete surfaces affected the outdoor thermal environment.

Thermal Imaging of urban elevations

As a constant time point observation of the thermal conditions of the building surfaces, thermal infrared imagery was used to study the glass and concrete surfaces in four directions (north, south, east and west) to get an overall reading of the thermal urban conditions. The thermal imaging data shown in Table 1 was taken under overcast sky with air temperature, relative humidity, wind speed and wind direction of 24.9 ℃, 96%, 2.2m/s and 90° respectively at 17:00 on April 26th, 2017, and under clear sunny sky at 28.1 ℃, 66%, 2.8 m/s and

180° respectively at 15:00 on May 3rd, 2017.

Thermal imaging comparison of urban elevations [1,2.] Table 1

Overcast (taken at 17:00, Apr 26th)				Sunny (taken at 15:00, May 3rd)				Overcast (taken at 17:00, Apr, 26th)				Sunny (taken at 15:00, May 3rd)			
NORTH ELEVATION								WEST ELEVATION							
Thermal image				Thermal image				Thermal image				Thermal image			
M1 (g)	M2 (g)	M3 (c)	M4 (c)	M1 (g)	M2 (g)	M3 (c)	M4 (c)	M1 (g)	M2 (g)	M3 (c)	M4 (c)	M1 (g)	M2 (g)	M3 (c)	M4 (c)
26.3	26.1	25.6	25.7	30.6	30.6	31.6	32.5	27.7	26.1	27.8	27.7	37.8	31.4	37.5	37.3

1. *Spot temperatures are in degrees Celsius;*
2. *(g) denotes glass exterior walls and (c) denotes concrete exterior walls.*

The thermal imaging confirms that when not under direct solar radiation, the glass building surfaces tended to be slightly cooler than concrete surfaces. For west elevation, temperatures of the building surfaces were almost 10 degrees more than the recorded ambient temperature at the HKO weather station, when under direct sun. Under overcast conditions, regardless of the orientation of the building surfaces, the surfaces were generally 2 to 3 degrees higher than the recorded ambient temperature. Under sunny conditions, the thermal conditions of the building surfaces differed based on their orientation and whether they were under direct sun or shaded with a range of 2 to 10 degrees higher than the recorded ambient temperature.

4 Conclusion

The urban geometry both in how close the building surfaces enclose a space and how deep the urban canyon affects the outdoor thermal environment in its ability to reflect heat downward to the public spaces and cooling effect within the public space. Long narrow urban canyons typical of high aspect ratio configurations and high-rise building clusters form a condition where there is little direct sunlight that can reach down to the urban ground spaces. Under this condition there may be comparatively less radiation radiating to the public spaces however has a higher tendency to trap heat and less cooling effect up to the sky, meaning reduction of MRT is later in the day. Therefore gaps between the buildings in high rise developments are helpful in increasing the cooling effect as could be seen from the comparison results of building form and organization. Glass building surfaces when under direct sunlight can have high short-wave radiation as seen through the urban surfaces results and the infrared imagery, however under shaded conditions, glass building surfaces cool much faster than concrete building surfaces, meaning that the glass surface radiates less to the environment when not exposed to direct sunlight.

How the buildings are organized on a site, the materials of the building surfaces, how tall and close the building surfaces are in relation to the public space, and gaps between the buildings can improve the outdoor urban thermal environment.

Acknowledgements

The research project was sponsored by Construction Industry Council Hong Kong under the project title "A Study of Impact of Building Envelope on Outdoor Thermal Environment". The research team would like to thank all research assistants who helped with the data collection, equipment handling and data processing.

高密度城市热剖面

孟玟廷
（香港大学建筑系）

摘　要：高密度城市紧凑，建筑物和中间的空隙形成狭窄的街道峡谷，捕获热量，并在城市深处形成微气候。香港是一个典型的高层住宅和商业大厦的案例，位于整个城市密集的线性条带，正在和已经建造了40层公寓住宅楼。2001年以来，城市内的通气受到重大影响，SARS流行病毒，以及对与被困热量相关的健康问题的认识也被称为城市热岛效应。城市和热力救济是当今快速城市化城市中必须考虑的可持续发展和能源效率的核心问题。本文研究了建筑物设计如何影响城市户外热环境。在全市各地进行了热辐射和温度的现场测量，并进行了数据分析，以了解城市生活环境的三个主要条件：城市表面、建筑形态及组织与城市峡谷的关系；波浪、长波辐射通量、平均辐射温度（MRT）为主要的热舒适指数。将测量数据进行比较，评估城市的三个条件是：(a) 建筑形式和布局；(b) 城市几何；(c) 城市表面。城市峡谷的大小和建筑物的取向对太阳辐射是否辐射回城市开放空间以及辐射热如何逃逸回天空有重大影响。接受直接阳光的建筑物表面的热质量特性影响了辐射回行人空地的热量。玻璃表面在直射阳光的阴影条件下辐射出显著的短波和长波辐射，能够冷却下来，对开放空间的辐射热几乎没有影响。混凝土表面在阳光直射的同时辐射明显的热量，并在阴影条件下持续下降。建筑物的方向和表面材料的分配会影响户外热环境。

关键词：城市公共空间，热环境，建筑围护，高密度

References

[1] United Nations. World Urbanization Prospects: The 2014 Revision, Highlights. Department of Economic and Social Affairs. Population Division, United Nations, 2014.

[2] Ahmed, K S. Comfort in urban spaces: Defining the boundaries of outdoor thermal comfort for the tropical urban environments[J]. Energy and Buildings, 2003,35(1): 103–110.

[3] Oke TR. Boundary layer climates[M]. London: Routledge, 1987.

[4] Oke TR, Johnson GT, Steyn DG, Watson ID. Simulation of surface urban heat islands under ideal conditions at night. Part 2.Diagnosis of causation. Boundary-Layer Meteorology 1991, 56:258–339.

[5] Johansson, E. Influence of urban geometry on outdoor thermal comfort in a hot dry climate: A study in Fez, Morocco[J]. Elsevier: Building and Environment 2006, 14: 1326-1338.

[6] Sofia T, Fredrik L, Ingegärd E, Björn H. Different methods for estimating the mean radiant temperature in an outdoor urban setting. Int. J. Climatol. 2007, 27: 1983-1993.

Urban Heat Island Effect (UHI) Analysis of Hangzhou Based on Remote Sensing

Wang Siqiang[1], Xiang Meng[1], He Yanan[1], Zhang Yuanzhi[2]

(1. Msc.in Advanced Environmental Planning Techaologies, Center for Housing Innovations, The Chinese University of Hong Kong; 2. The Chinese University of Hong Kong)

Abstract: Accompany with the rapid development of urbanization, the land used (land cover) has been changed a lot. It makes the phenomenon of urban heat island (UHI) become more frequent, which has brought some negative influence to human activities. This study applies the satellite images such as Landsat TM, ETM+ and OLI data to retrieve the urban land surface temperature (LST) and assess urban heat island effects in rapidly developing cities, such as Hangzhou, China. We also mapped and compared the intensity of Urban Heat Island effect in 2003, 2008 and 2013, respectively. The result shows that the intensity of Urban Heat Island in 2013 is more serious than that of 2003, and increased a lot after 10 years. In addition, this study analyzed the relationship between UHI, NDVI and NDBI and gave some helpful suggestions to mitigate the UHI effect on rapid developing cities such as Hangzhou in China using remote sensing data.

Keywords: Urban heat island (UHI), Remote sensing data, Land surface temperature (LST), NDVI

1 Introduction

Urban Heat Island (UHI), which means the temperature in urban and suburban area are higher than the surrounding rural area, has become the most significant phenomenon of climate change [1]. One important reason is that the urban land space once was moist and permeable that changed to dry and impervious surface after human activities [2]. With the continuous development and expansion of the city, this phenomenon gradually becomes more common especially in summer. The extreme temperature increases the energy consumption of city, causes respiratory diseases and other difficulties [3]. A fast and available monitoring of UHI effect has become particularly necessary. Remote sensing technology provides a continuous monitoring of Urban Heat Island in a vast scope. The land surface temperature can be easily retrieved by using the thermal infrared wave band [4].

There has been a lot of research on remote sensing temperature retrieval. I.P. Senanayake et al. used the thermal band (band 6) images of a serious Landsat satellite were analyzed to map the distribution of land surface temperature of Colombo City [5]. Huang et al. carried three different methods [one radiative transfer equation (RTE) method, two mono-window algorithm methods] to retrieve the land surface temperature and demonstrated that the accuracy of the temperature results retrieved by remote sensing data is acceptable compared with the actual temperature data [6]. Claus and Mushtaq took Toronto as an example to explore the relationship between land use and urban environment, the vector data analysis (zonal statistics) and descriptive statistics along with an analysis of variance (ANOVA) were applied [7]. Chen et al. combined the statistic of population and economic to build a model, argued the correlation between the investigation of urbanization and Urban Heat Island in Beijing [8].

Hangzhou, which is in Zhejiang province, China (30° 15′ 0″ N, 120° 10′ 0″ E), was selected as the study area in this research. The economic development in Hangzhou is very fast in recent decades, which led to urban construction activities, the rural land has now become an urban area. Besides, the weather is wet and extremely hot in summer, so it is necessary to mitigate the Urban Heat Island effect. The major city area is selected in this study, which contains eight districts as Gongshu, Shangcheng, Xiacheng, Jianggan, Xihu, Bingjiang, Yuhang and Xiaoshan.

2 Data and Methods

2.1 Data Collection

The Landsat TM, ETM+ and OLI data are used in this study. The historical meteorological data are also collected. Landsat satellite is the most widely used and most effective remote sensing source, which available on the USGS website. Figure 1 shows the Landsat images.

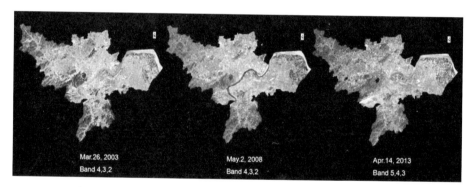

Figure 1　The landsat images of the study area

2.2 Methods

The most common ways to retrieve land surface temperature(LST) via remote sensing approaches can be basically summarized into 4 methods, which are: (1) image-based method (IBM); (2) radiative transfer equation (RTE), also called atmospheric correction method; (3) Qin et al's mono-window algorithm (MWA)[9]; (4) Jiménez-Muñoz and Sobrino single-channel algorithm (SCA).

2.2.1 General Equations of SCA

In the SCA, LST could be expressed by the general equations (1) [9]:

$$T_s = \gamma \left[\frac{1}{\varepsilon}(\psi_1 L_{sen} + \psi_2) + \psi_3 \right] + \delta \tag{1}$$

In this equation, Ts is the land surface temperature in K. and γ are parameters according to the Planck's function (2) (3) [9].

$$\gamma = \left\{ \frac{c^2 L_{sen}}{T^2 L_{sen}} \left[\frac{\lambda^4}{c_1} L_{sen} + \lambda^{-1} \right] \right\}^{-1} \quad (2)$$

$$\delta = -\gamma L_{sen} + L_{sen} \quad (3)$$

$c_1 = 1.09104 \times 10^8 W\mu m^4 m^{-2} sr^{-1}$, $c_2 = 1438.7.7 \mu mK$, λ refers to the effective wavelength in μm.

Other elements needed in the general equation are: ε (the surface emissivity); L_{sen} (the at-sensor radiance in $W/(m^2 \times sr \times \mu m)$; T_{sen} (the at-sensor brightness temperature in K) and the atmospheric parameters ψ_1, ψ_2, ψ_3).

2.2.2 Land surface emissivity

Land surface emissivity (ε) can be calculated by the value of the normalized difference vegetation index (NDVI). This index is usually used to detect the growth and coverage of vegetation. NDVI can be expressed by the equation (4) [9]:

$$NDVI = \frac{NIR - R}{NIR + R} \quad (4)$$

Based on the study of Zhang in 2006, value of NDVI can be divided into 4 ranges and each of the range corresponds to a certain value of land surface emissivity shown in Table 1 [9].

NDVI ranges and corresponding emissivity values   Table 1

NDVI ranges	Main ground covers	Corresponding emissivity
< 0.185	Water	0.99
0.185–0.157	Urban used land	0.956
0.157–0.727	Natural ground	1.0094+0.047ln(NDVI)
> 0.727	High density vegetation	0.985

2.2.3 At–Sensor Radiance

L_{sen} (at-sensor radiance in $W/(m^2 \times sr \times \mu m)$ can be achieved by applying radiometric calibration in the data processing software of remote sensing (ENVI 5.1 was used in this research). The equation used in the software is written as equation (5) [9]:

$$L_i = L_{min} + (L_{max} - L_{min}) Q_{dn}/Q_{max} \quad (5)$$

L_i stands for the at-sensor spectral radiance in $MW \cdot cm^{-2} \cdot sr^{-1} \cdot \mu m^{-1}$; L_{max} and L_{min} refer to the maximum and minimum at-sensor spectral radiance respectively; Q_{dn} and Q_{max} are the DN value and the maximum of it in pixel.

2.2.4 At–sensor Brightness temperature

T_{sen} (at-sensor brightness temperature in K) can be transformed from the radiance values of thermal band by the equation (6) [9].

$$T_{sen} = \frac{K_2}{\ln\left(\frac{K_1}{L_{sen}} + 1\right)} \quad (6)$$

K_1 and K_2 are the thermal calibration constants supplied by the Landsat in Table 2.

Thermal calibration constants　　　　　Table 2

Sensor	K_1	K_2
Landsat 5 TM band6	607.76	1260.56
Landsat 7 ETM+ band6	666.09	1282.71
Landsat 8 TIRs band10	774.89	1321.80
Landsat 8 TIRs band 11	480.89	1201.14

3 Results and Discussion

3.1 Land Surface Temperature Distribution in Hangzhou

Base on the Figure 2 and Table 3, it can be found that LST of Hangzhou has changed dramatically during the research period (in 2003, 2008 and 2013). In 2003, the mean temperature concentrated in the temperature range of 15℃ - 25℃. Higher temperature (over 20℃) appeared more in the central and west area which are Yuhang district, Xihu district, the central 3 districts (Gongshu district, Jianggan district and Shangcheng district) and the most part of south – western Xiaoshan district.

When it comes to 2008, compared to 2003, the mean temperature generally grew 5℃ in this year, which concentrated in the range of 20 ℃ - 30 ℃. The spatial distribution of higher temperature (over 25 ℃) area changed slightly towards east area and mainly appeared in Shangcheng district, Xiacheng district, Gongshu district, Jianggan district and northern part of Xiaoshan district, which are the main urban area of the city.

The LST increased severely in 2013. Area of temperature in the range of 25℃ - 30℃ expanded significantly. Higher temperature which is over 30℃ almost covered the whole Hangzhou city and extreme high temperature demonstrated in the central area aside by Qiantang River evidently. However, it should be taken note that the northwest corner of Xihu district had covered by cloud in that day, so the result of that area is inaccurate.

It is significant that the land surface temperature of Hangzhou rose up rapidly in past ten years from 2003 to 2013, and the higher temperature also presents an accelerated upward trend especially in the last five years. The expanding in spatial distribution of higher temperature also shows an increasing trend from the central urban area to the suburban area, such as Yuhang district and Xiaoshan district.

Figure 2　Land surface temperature of Hangzhou in 2003, 2008 and 2013 (℃)

Land surface temperature of Hangzhou in 2003, 2008 and 2013 (℃)   Table 3

Year	LST (Min)	LST(Max)	LST(Mean)	Stdev
2003	273.541595	309.538513	293.388575	1.683309
2008	285.579773	314.425720	297.305008	1.852384
2013	271.901184	316.897858	298.611333	3.077064

3.2 Calculation of Urban Thermal Field Variance Index

The Urban Thermal Field Variance Index (UTFVI) is commonly used to express the Urban Heat Island effect. It can be calculated by the equation (7) [8]:

$$UTFVI = \frac{T_s - T_{mean}}{T_s} \qquad (7)$$

T_s is the LST in certain point of the map. T_{mean} is the corresponding mean temperature of the whole area.

There are two extreme levels appeared in the ecological evaluation of Hangzhou in 2013: the good (<0.005) and the worse (>0.015). It reflects the fact that the difference of eco-environmental quality between urban and rural area become much bigger, the quality dropped down rapidly in central urban area and eco-environment become worse in these ten years.

3.3 Change of Urban Heat Island Intensity

Urban Heat Island intensity is defined by Iain D. Stewart as a simultaneous "urban- rural" temperature difference, with "rural" understood as the open countryside and "urban" as the built-up environment of the city, which is an index to measure the Urban Heat Island effect.

There are some calculation methods that have been used in Urban Heat Island study. One is using the difference between typical temperature of rural area and typical highest temperature of urban area, which is not easily used because it is difficult to find a meteorological station in rural area in natural situation that has not been impacted by cities. Another is to define the difference of several average temperatures between urban and rural area. This method is widely used because it is easy to calculate, however, it cannot reflect the highest rising temperature as it uses the average temperature as measure index. These methods are not easy to measure and compare because they are limited by materials and measure conditions. To avoid these disadvantages, two concepts have been introduced in this research to measure Urban Heat Island intensity. The typical rural temperature has been defined as the average temperature of random 32 positions in rural area in all 8 directions in this study (Table 4).

In terms of spatial distribution, the urban heat island intensity of Hangzhou shows a similar change trend with UTFVI. It can be easily found that the urban heat island intensity grew up in these ten years, especially the group which urban heat island intensity is between 8℃ to 12℃. Another significant point is that the area in high urban heat island intensity is along Qiantang River, which is similar to the development direction of the city. The city center which contains of Shangcheng district, Xiacheng district, Gongshu district and Jianggan district are almost in high intensity area which intensity is over 8℃.

Change of urban heat island intensity of Hangzhou from 2003 to 2013　　Table 4

	2003	2008	2013
Max temperature (℃)	11.25	21.09	22.13
Average temperature (℃)	0.5	1.24	1.33

4　Conclusion and Limitation

In this study, the land surface temperature and urban heat island intensity of Hangzhou retrieved by using Landsat TM data. Through the findings, it is significant that the area in Hangzhou which is impacted by Urban Heat Island effect is expanded annually, and another point that it should be mentioned that the highest UHI rising temperature and total amount of UHI rising temperature shows a rapid growth in past ten years from 2003-2013. In terms of the spatial distribution of urban heat island intensity, the central area (Shangcheng, Xiacheng, Gongshu, Jianggan) shows quite higher UHI value than other urban area. These changes indicate that Hangzhou, especially its central urban area, is facing a big challenge caused by climate change and Urban Heat Island effects which would have impact on people's lives and economic growth.

Based on the liner regression analysis, the NDVI is negative correlated to UHI intensity, and in contrast, NDBI has the positive correlation with UHI intensity. The liner regression models of UHI with NDVI and NDBI are Y=−0.0392x+0.5157 (R^2=0.7599, sig=0.000) and Y=0.0158x-0.2566 (R^2=0.4651, sig=0.000) respectively. As the UHI intensity has such close correlation with NDVI and NDBI index, two suggestions have been supposed to decrease the Urban Heat Island effect. The first one is greenery design which means that government should encourage developers to design green roof, green pavement, etc. Another strategy is to optimize the urban morphology; such as mix the green land with building area. These two strategies can decline the UHI intensity by spreading NDVI index or dropping down the NDBI index.

Nevertheless, we only measure three years' UHI intensity due to the limit time and resources, it is almost certain that more years' data can reflect the change clearer. Another limitation is that only NDVI and NDBI have been taken into assessment. Urban Heat Island effect is caused by a various kind of factors. Further elements can be added in future study that may reflect the response mechanism better.

Acknowledgments

The data from website of USGS and local government of Hangzhou are highly appreciated.

杭州市城市热岛效应初探

王思强[1]　向　萌[1]　何亚男[1]　张渊智[2]

（1. 香港中文大学中国城市住宅研究中心高级环境规划技术理学硕士课程；2. 香港中文大学中国城市住宅研究中心）

摘　要：本文应用卫星遥感数据初步探讨了 2003 ~ 2013 年期间杭州市的城市热岛效应及其研究意义。
关键词：城市热岛，遥感数据，地表温度，植被指数

References

[1] Adams M P, Smith P L. A systematic approach to model the influence of the type and density of vegetation cover on urban heat using remote sensing[J]. Landscape and Urban Planning, 2014, 132: 47–54.

[2] Chen W, Zhang Y, Gao W, Zhou D. (2016). The Investigation of Urbanization and Urban Heat Island in Beijing Based on Remote Sensing[J]. Procedia——Social and Behavioral Sciences, 2016，216: 141–150.

[3] Huang M, Xing X, Wang P, Wang C. Comparison between three different methods of retrieving surface temperature from Landsat TM thermal infrared band[J]. Arid Land Geography. 2006, 29(1).

[4] Iain D Stewart. Measuring the Urban Heat Island Intensity: Challenges with "Urban-Rural" Differentiation and the East Asian City. Retrieved April 10, 2016, from The Hong Kong Polytechnic University, Department of Land Surveying and Geo-Informatics. Web site: http://www.lsgi.polyu.edu.hk/RSRG/resources/News/2nd_ws/abstract/stewart.pdf.

[5] Jimenez-Munoz J C. Sobrino J A. A generalized single-channel method for retrieving land surface temperature from remote sensing data. J. Geophys. Res. 2003, 108: 4688-4694.

[6] Kumar D, Shekhar S Statistical analysis of land surface temperature——vegetation indexes relationship through thermal remote sensing[J]. Ecotoxicology and Environmental Safety, 2015, 121: 39–44.

[7] Lin Liu, Yuanzhi Zhang. Urban Heat Island Analysis Using the Landsat TM Data and ASTER Data: A Case Study in Hong Kong[J]. Remote Sens. 2011, 3: 1535-1552.

[8] Li X, Li W, Middel A, Harlan S L, Brazel A J, Turner II B L. Remote sensing of the surface Urban Heat Island and land architecture in Phoenix, Arizona: Combined effects of land composition and configuration and cadastral–demographic–economic factors[J]. Remote Sensing of Environment, 2016, 174: 233–243.

[9] Lowry W P. Empirical estimation of urban effects on climate: a problem analysis[J]. Journal of Applied Meteorology, 1977, 16 (2): 129-135.

人居环境更新、改造与历史活化
Renewal, Transformation and Activation of Human Habitat

重庆抗战时期名人旧居选址特征研究

何 嫒

(重庆房地产职业学院)

摘 要：重庆作为中国抗战时期的"战时首都"，伴随着政治经济文化中心的西迁，众多著名人物汇聚于此，留下了大量的抗战时期名人旧居。本文通过研究重庆抗战时期名人旧居的选址特征，希望从中探寻名人旧居与城市、与自然的关系。

关键词：重庆抗战时期，名人旧居，选址特征

1 名人旧居选址特征解析

抗战八年，重庆作为战时"大后方"，作为人力、物力、财力的聚集地，在日寇残酷的大轰炸之中，掀起了快速建设的高潮，至今仍保留了大量的抗战时期遗址建筑。名人旧居作为抗战时期遗址建筑中现存数量最多[1]、极具代表性的一类建筑，在近代建筑新思潮冲击和巴渝传统建筑文化共同的作用下，成为战火硝烟中的瑰丽的花朵，其历史意义和建筑特征鲜明，是重庆近代建筑史中不可忽视的篇章，具有重要的研究价值。

重庆"山在城中，城在山中"，山水纵横的地理格局造就了充满层次感的城市外部空间。重庆抗战时期名人旧居由于其主人都是当时的政要或者各界名流，享有较高的社会地位，建筑选址相比普通民居更为自由灵活，依托重庆"山城"、"江城"的地理优势，涌现出很多与周围环境完美契合的佳作。

名人旧居按照选址特征主要可分为三类，分别是：星罗棋布的城中府邸、依山傍水的城郊别墅和自由散居的乡村宅院。

1.1 星罗棋布的城中府邸

渝中半岛作为重庆的母城，无论是现在还是抗战时期，都是重庆的城市中心，重要的党政军机构云集于此，也是各界名人来渝后首选的居住地点。这些名人旧居很多都得以保存，在高楼林立的城市中，一个个星罗棋布散布其间。

尧庐（蒋介石德安里官邸）是选址于城中名人旧居的典型个案。建筑现位于中山四路重庆市委大院内（市委大院7号楼），毗邻中山四路，建筑坐南朝北，基地平坦，视野开阔。与德安里官邸仅一路之隔的桂园，是抗战时期国民党著名爱国将领张治中住所，重庆谈判期间，张将军将房屋提供给毛泽东同志，成为毛泽东于"重庆谈判"期间在市内办公、会客的地方。桂园毗邻中山四路，坐落于其西北侧一块28m×23m的长方形用地上（图1）。

---

[1] 作为国务院公布的第二批国家历史文化名城（1986年），重庆现存抗战遗址建筑348处，各类抗战遗址中，名人旧居无论从数量还是质量上都占有巨大的比重（119处）——《重庆市现存抗战遗址调查汇总表》重庆市文化广播电视局，2010年3月。

另一个城中府邸的典型案例是宋庆龄旧居，建筑位于两路口新村 5 号。建筑地处中山三路西侧一块狭长的坡地上，基地坐西朝东，进深 42m，面宽 17.8m，与道路毗邻，对外交通便利。旧居院落内绿树成荫，环境清幽，与喧闹的城市形成鲜明对比。

（a）尧庐、桂园和宋庆龄旧居在 1939 年版重庆地图中的区位

（b）尧庐和桂园现状区位图

（c）桂园

（d）尧庐

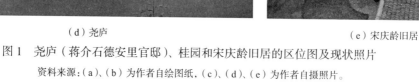

（e）宋庆龄旧居

图 1　尧庐（蒋介石德安里官邸）、桂园和宋庆龄旧居的区位图及现状照片

资料来源：（a）、（b）为作者自绘图纸，（c）、（d）、（e）为作者自摄照片。

1.2　依山傍水的城郊别墅

抗战时期，各界名人政要纷纷在渝中半岛沿嘉陵江滨江带、歌乐山、南山修建别墅官邸。这些名人旧居巧妙借助自然地貌，营造或背山面水，或众山环抱的外部空间格局，形成独特的选址布局方式。对其进行详细梳理后，发现主要可分成两类：

1.2.1　滨水高地型

以嘉陵江南岸滨江路—李子坝—嘉陵新路—鹅岭一线为例，此处直线落差巨大，俯瞰嘉陵江，仰望鹅岭，风景绝佳，沿这条纵轴线垂直分布大量名人旧居。例如位于嘉陵新路的史迪威旧居，建筑坐北朝南背山面江，独居山峦中部，与 2010 年新建的李子坝抗战遗址公园遥相呼应（图 2）。

1.2.2 山林环绕型

蒋介石、宋美龄在重庆的黄山官邸是名人旧居中择山林环绕型的典型案例。黄山位于重庆南山中，处于奇峰幽谷之间，遍山松柏簇拥，风景极佳。1938年，为躲避日机轰炸并避开夏日酷暑，蒋介石侍从室选中此地，为蒋、宋修建官邸，形成一个名人旧居建筑群。以蒋介石官邸云岫楼为中心，四周环绕宋美龄旧居松厅、宋庆龄旧居云峰楼、孔二小姐旧居孔园、马歇尔旧居草亭等，沿山脊形成"马蹄形"的分布态势。

图 2　嘉陵江滨江一带部分名人旧居现状

（a）嘉陵江滨江垂直分布名人旧居；（b）从史迪威旧居俯瞰刘湘公馆

以云岫楼为例，建筑处于"马蹄形"中心的高坡上，凭栏远眺，半岛全景尽收眼底，屋外竹木葱茏，环境秀美幽静，十分隐蔽。松厅与云岫楼"一览众山小"的布局不同，建筑建在山峰间的一块人造平地边缘，四周松树挺拔，宅前坡地上鲜花灌木点缀，营造宁静温馨的居住环境（图3）。

图 3　云岫楼、松厅与周围环境（作者自摄）

（a）云岫楼远景；（b）松厅远景

1.3 自由散居的农村宅院

抗战时期，居住于市区的名人为了躲避轰炸，迁居郊外。很多人就采用租借或者购买的方式住进了农村宅院。尽管对其进行了改建，但是建筑的选址还是延续了巴渝传统民居的选址、布局和建造方式[1]，属于自由散居式[2]的农村宅院。这些名人旧居与布局灵活多样，地形结合紧密，和周围的竹木树林、院坝田地等形成一个完整居住单元。

以位于歌乐山以西的沙坪坝土主镇三圣宫村的张治中旧居为例。基地远离主城区，时至今日，建筑周围仍然是一片田园风光。旧居依山就势，建造于山坡上，与周围起伏绵延的丘陵融为一体，远可遥望歌乐山，近可俯瞰周围乡野农田，是方圆几里地的制高点。建筑坐东朝西，三进院落层层跌落，与地形紧密契合（图4）。

(a) (b)

图4 张治中旧居周边环境（作者自摄）
（a）旧居近景与远山；（b）旧居建筑轮廓线与山势完美契合

2 小结

重庆抗战时期名人旧居，无论是隐匿闹市中，还是依山、临水，或是独处乡间，建筑都与周围环境达到了和谐共生的状态。其选址特征，以及特征背后蕴含的建筑与城市、与自然的关系，都对当今城市规划和建筑设计有重要的借鉴价值，值得进行更深一步的研究。

---

[1] 陈卓，重庆居住建筑，重庆大学，p35。
[2] 陆元鼎，《中国民居建筑》，四川地区 "汉族民居的分布从聚落形态角度可划分为三类，一是县城以上的城镇民居，二是区乡以下的乡场民居，三是广大农村民居。前两类为街坊聚落式，后一类为自由散居式"。

The Site Selection Research on Chongqing Celebrities' Former Dwellings during War of Resistance Against Japan

He Yuan

(Chongqing Real Estate College)

Abstract: Chongqing, as the "war capital" of China during the War of Resistance Against Japan, accompanied by the westward shift of the political, economic and cultural center, many famous people gathered here, leaving a large number of celebrities' former dwellings in the war. Through the research on the characteristics of the site selection, we hope to explore the relationship between celebrities' former dwellings and cities and nature.

Keywords: Chongqing during war of resistance against Japan, Celebrities' former dwellings, The characteristics of the site selection

参考文献

[1] 杨嵩林，张复本. 中国近代建筑统览·重庆篇 [M]. 北京：中国建筑工业出版社，1993.

[2] 隗瀛涛. 近代重庆城市史 [M]. 四川：四川大学出版社，1991.

[3] 重庆市规划局，重庆大学建筑城规学院. 重庆市优秀近现代建筑 [M]. 重庆：重庆大学出版社，2007.

[4] 黄光宇，李和平. 山地历史文化遗产的保护观念——论重庆黄山陪都遗址的保护与开发 [J]. 城市规划，1998，3：44-45.

[5] 杨宇振. 现代城市空间演化的三种典型模式：以重庆近代城市住宅群为例——兼论民间建筑的现代演化 [J]. 华中建筑，2004，3：87-89.

自下而上的城市更新与居住形态演变：以田子坊为例

朱晓宇

(同济大学建筑与城市规划学院城市规划系)

摘 要：居住形态包括两方面内容：一是住区中静态、永久的物质实体；二是居民的行为活动。从城市更新的自发性来看，旧城更新可分为自上而下和自下而上两种模式。以上海田子坊为例，其自下而上的更新模式起源于居民自发出租住宅开设商铺的行为。更新后的田子坊集合了原住居民、商人和艺术家，成为一个利益关系交织的多元化邻里网络。本文以田子坊为例，从人口结构、空间环境、商业发展、商住矛盾四个方面研究了自下而上的城市更新对居住形态演变的影响，提出可持续的自下而上的城市更新策略。

关键词：居住形态学，自下而上的城市更新，田子坊，商住矛盾，"契约化"管理机制

1 研究意义与方法

1.1 城市更新中的居住形态演变

在城市面临转型和重构的背景下，旧区更新成为一个重要议题。旧区集中体现城市文化、空间方面的多样性特征，旧区更新会伴随其居住形态的演变。居住形态包括两方面的内容：一是聚居区中大规模、静态、永久的物质实体，如建筑物、街道、设施、自然环境；二是人的行为活动，如生产方式、社会习俗、社会结构、经济体系等。[1] 在城市更新的过程中，旧区如何改造、居住形态如何改变、原住民何去何从，都是需要慎重考虑的问题。

1.2 自下而上的城市更新特点

从城市更新的自发性来看，旧城更新可分为自上而下和自下而上两种模式。上海的新天地是自上而下城市更新的代表，自上而下统一的改造模式需要大量的资金投入，而居民的利益往往无法在城市更新中得到保障。[2] 与此不同的是田子坊自下而上的更新模式，这种模式起源于居民自发出租住宅开设商铺的行为，让原住民能够自主选择城市地块的更新模式和方向，并从城市更新中获益。自下而上的更新模式下，地区居住形态一方面得到保留，一方面获得更新。

1.3 研究方法与路径

本文的研究方法包括形态分析、问卷访谈、观测统计。研究对象包括田子坊空间与功能、商业业态、当地居民生活状况、田子坊管委会。

研究路径是通过文献检阅、现场调研，分析田子坊空间与功能，访谈当地居民并了解其生活状况，拜访田子坊管委会获取商业运营数据，观测田子坊的每日客流量以研究其旅游接待情况。

2 文献综述

2.1 田子坊的更新背景与历程

田子坊（表1）主要分为两部分，一部分是位于泰康路210弄的弄堂工厂群，即现在的田子坊厂房地区，这部分建筑建于20世纪50年代，由上海人民针厂、上海食品工业机械厂等六家里弄工厂组成。另一部分则是上海传统的里弄住宅区，即现在的田子坊里弄片区，包括泰康路210弄、248弄、274弄的建筑，建于20世纪30年代。

田子坊主要发展历程与阶段（作者自绘） 表1

年份	发展历程	阶段概述
1998	"一路发"文化公司将田子坊工业楼宇整饰一新；开始有少量文化艺术品店铺，其主要分布于210弄	第一阶段：文创公司开始对旧区进行小规模更新改造，艺术家入驻
1999	著名艺术家陈逸飞入驻田子坊	
2004	石库门民居出租，创意产业从工厂衍生到居住区；媒体大量报道民居可能被拆迁	
2005	陈逸飞逝世，众人慕名前来观看艺术家曾经创作的地方；第一家纯工艺品店进入田子坊	第二阶段：除艺术家以外的商业投资者进入田子坊，租金上升
2006	田子坊成为中国最佳创意产业集聚区；第一家酒吧开门迎客；租金开始上涨，初期进入的艺术家开始退出	
2008	田子坊管委会成立，卢湾区政府介入；投资者和外来居民购置田子坊房产的意愿较高；租金继续快速上涨	第三阶段：田子坊知名度不断提升；政府介入田子坊发展；金融资本进入田子坊；原住居民和早期入驻的艺术家迁出
2009	媒体大力宣传，田子坊第一栋民居卖出；更多有实力背景的企业开始在田子坊投资	
2010	琉璃博物馆入驻；被评为国家AAA级旅游景区；发展规模为200弄到274弄；租金维持在高水平，但增速减缓	
2011	本土高端奢侈品牌双妹入住；成为上海市下一步重点推进的都市旅游集聚地；租金继续上升	

2.2 田子坊的更新概况

在历史上，田子坊地区建于租界的"越界筑路"，但其地处租界控制区的边缘，田子坊地区设置有较集中的工厂用地，与里弄住宅并存。该处的里弄建设规模相对较小，包纳多种风格并存的建筑群体，既有里弄住宅主次分明、规矩整齐的格局，又兼容了多转角的多样化空间。[3]

田子坊自2004年11月的首个里弄居民出租房屋作为商铺开始，"居改非"行为就在街道以及商家的推动下开始了。很多原住民就积极推行田子坊的规范化管理，比如加入田子坊业主委员会，引入工厂区的业态准入机制。自下而上模式探索的出发点基于原住民能积极、持续地参与到田子坊的更新中，使田子坊的更新不与城市文脉割离[4]，同时，让居民能获得经济收益和基础设施的改善。

2.3 自下而上的城市更新如何影响居住形态

在人口构成方面，自下而上的城市更新使得田子坊成为一个利益关系交织的多元化邻里网络。个体受利益驱使，本地群众通过一些自发性改造吸引人气，比如引入创意产业，提高社区品位及形象。田子坊内原有671户原住民，现在他们的去向分为多种：一部分居民留在田子坊继续着原本的生活方式；一部分居民迁出原居住地，靠租金获得收入；还有一部分居民自营商店，成为商人。更新后的社区往往集合了原住居民、本地商人、外来商人、艺术家和文化名人。

在空间结构方面，自下而上的城市更新使得田子坊空间的开放、商业化程度增强。城市建成区是城市生产与再生产、消费与循环的物质空间表征，当这些要素发生变化时，城市物质空间也将出现相应的变化。[5] 自下而上的城市更新是由众多个体的小规模改造积聚而成的形态与功能更新。在田子坊街道空间方面，本地店主或租客为了吸引人气，对街道的结构进行适用性改善；在商业功能方面，自发性的更新使得个体对所经营的商业有自主选择权，这让沿街商业更趋多样化；在居住功能方面，主导自发性更新的群体大部分是旧城区的老居民。

3 现状调研与分析

3.1 人口结构与邻里关系的重构

田子坊的邻里关系演变为多元多层次的社会关系。由于房屋租金颇为可观，并且政府出台了"居改非"等支持性政策，大部分居民已将可租赁的房屋出租，近 10 年该地房屋中介业务量大幅提升，租赁对象多为进驻田子坊的商户。活跃的租赁市场对该地区的人口更替产生了重大影响。田子坊的人口变动大体上以社会经济地位相对较高的群体代替社会经济地位相对较低的群体为大趋势。

3.2 田子坊空间结构的演变

田子坊自发性的更新较好地保留了原有的里弄空间格局与风貌，基本保持了上海旧式弄堂"主弄 - 支弄 - 住宅"的空间结构。根据田子坊管委会提供的资料，作者梳理了 2004 ~ 2016 年的田子坊建筑功能演变过程，得出田子坊纯商业功能的建筑比例正不断扩大，商业过度占用居住空间，部分里弄建筑的功能由纯居住变为商住混合，最终变为纯商业，显示出原有居住形态受到商业开发的冲击。值得注意的是，作为田子坊精髓的创意工坊的面积在田子坊发展过程中不升反降（图 1 ~ 图 4）。

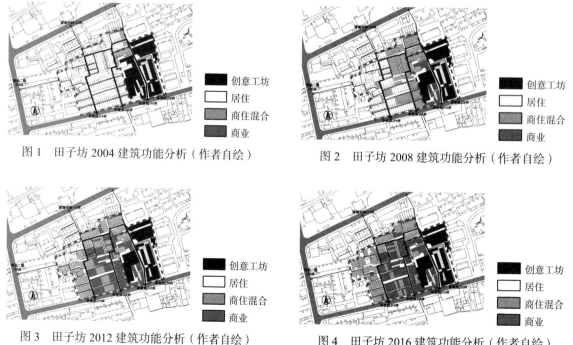

图 1　田子坊 2004 建筑功能分析（作者自绘）

图 2　田子坊 2008 建筑功能分析（作者自绘）

图 3　田子坊 2012 建筑功能分析（作者自绘）

图 4　田子坊 2016 建筑功能分析（作者自绘）

3.3 商业发展的问题

3.3.1 高租金与过度商业化

城市更新推进了创意产业所依附的旧工厂、旧楼宇的改建及公共设施的修缮,改善了创意产业发展的物质空间,同时也带来了租金的快速上涨。在 2008～2016 年间,租金始终维持在高位,2016 年的租金是 2004 年的 10 倍以上。目前,沿泰康路商铺日均租金已达 96 元 /m^2,田子坊内底层石库门的日均租金也已达到 32 元 /m^2。在实地访谈中,几乎所有受访者都认为田子坊租金过高。从历年田子坊建筑功能分析也可知,田子坊商业功能发展较快,其与租金的快速上涨有一定关联性。

3.3.2 经营业态趋向同质化

租金的逐日上涨将商户的进驻门槛抬高,留守商户也急需调整方向,才能使盈利跟上租金的上涨。当前,文创类的商户只占田子坊全部店铺的 17.71%,田子坊的业态主要是服装和手工艺品(占44.09%)以及餐饮食品类(占 38.20%)。在实地访谈中,近 70% 受访者表示,租金上涨使他们盈利变得困难;超过一半的受访者表示,经营种类不得不向市场偏好屈服。坊内租金过高给许多创意工作者放弃创意而追求盈利,这使得田子坊创意氛围淡化,商业发展呈现同质化趋势。

3.3.3 店铺流转频率较高

较高的租金也使得经营者不断调整经营种类,获得更多盈利,直观反应就是田子坊商户的流动率比以前高出许多,许多店铺处于装修阶段。根据田子坊管委会的商铺数据,连续经营 5 年以上的店铺只占 5%,29% 的店铺经营时间不足 1 年,52% 的店铺的租约在 1 年及以下。对于许多初创时期的企业而言,被迫离开田子坊的现象屡见不鲜,客户群可能会因为店铺搬迁而流失(图 5～图 7)。

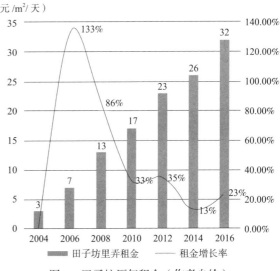

图 5 田子坊历年租金(作者自绘)

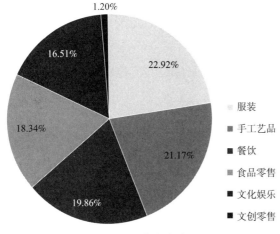

图 6 田子坊业态(作者自绘)

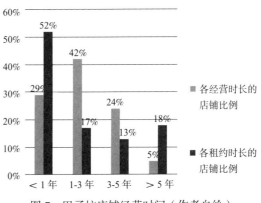

图 7 田子坊店铺经营时间(作者自绘)

3.4 田子坊发展中的商住矛盾

3.4.1 商住混合的空间格局

根据2016年6月第一周的瞬时客流量数据，田子坊的工作日日均客流量达到近2000人，周末则达到近4500人，庞大的游客量给居民日常生活造成一定影响。截至2016年年底，已有约480户居民陆续出租自家住房，居民区出租面积达到近17000m²。现在街区中底层的居住空间大部分已变为商铺。当前田子坊正往餐饮休闲的方向靠拢，违背了其艺术化发展的初衷。

3.4.2 居民利益格局的分化与居住体验的恶化

由于不同地理位置的商业价值不同，可达性高的里弄的租金较高且容易出租，租金水平的不均衡导致了里弄居民利益格局的分化。对田子坊的一部分居民来说，通过居住与商业空间的置换，他们通过租金改善了日常生活。田子坊另一部分居民则继续留在田子坊，他们由于不愿意或不能够将住宅出租给商铺，其生活并未得到改善，居住条件甚至由于商业影响而进一步恶化。

采取随机抽样问卷调研的方式研究田子坊居民的居住体验。调研时间是2016年6月1日（周三）、6月4日（周六）的13：00～15：00。地点选取居住功能较集聚的西片区（泰康路274弄）。发放问卷28份，回收24份，有效问卷率85.7%。结果显示，居民对住在商住混合的街区中感到不满意和非常不满意的在回收问卷样本中共占78%，原因主要有污染、环境嘈杂与生活成本提高等问题（图8、图9）。

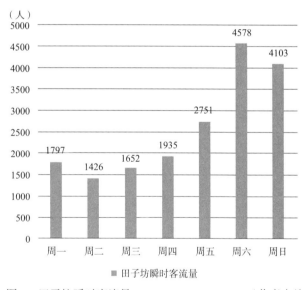

图8 田子坊瞬时客流量，2016.5.30～2016.6.5（作者自绘）

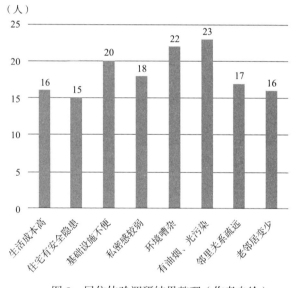

图9 居住体验调研结果整理（作者自绘）

4 反思与规划建议

4.1 "自下而上"城市更新的反思

（1）自下而上城市更新带来地区居住形态变化是非均质的

住宅所处的交通区位决定其商业价值，也决定其被居民自发更新的潜在价值。区位较差的里弄还保留着最初的居住功能，原住民间依然维系着里弄邻里关系网络。田子坊不同区域居民利益格局的分化导致居住形态的非均质变化，居民自发更新行为的内容与程度也有所差别。

（2）在邻里关系层面，自下而上的城市更新并未充分延续原有的居住形态

虽然田子坊里弄的建筑形式被保留，但商业空间的外拓导致商住矛盾突出，居住体验变差，过度商业化使得一些居民被迫迁出田子坊，通过收取租金来改善自身生活。紧随商业开发而出现的原住民迁离导致田子坊原有社会网络的破裂，居民自下而上更新行为的负外部效应较明显。

（3）自下而上的城市更新也会助长内绅化

田子坊城市更新驱逐创意产业以及居民类型的更替是一个人口中产阶级化的过程，这与自下而上城市更新的社会意义背道而驰。中产阶级化反映出大量拥有较高社会经济地位、消费能力的居民在田子坊地区集聚、迁入，他们以外籍人士居多，入住形式多为租赁，排斥了中低收入原住民。

4.2 关注原住民需求，创新解决原住民的安置问题

城市更新表面上看是物质空间形态、功能及使用者的改变，其实是一种利益格局的改变。[6]个体的利益需求是旧区自发改造的发展动力所在，但不同个体的利益需求可能彼此冲突。因此，旧区更新要在了解公众需求的基础上制定引导政策。比如，想将自己房屋出售的居民不在少数，但由于田子坊内房屋都是使用权房屋，使用权房屋只能在本市户籍居民之间转让。政府可从法律制度层面入手，采取直接收购、出面组织他人收购、完善使用权房屋交易条例等方式来加快城市更新的进程。

4.3 完善田子坊的"契约化"管理机制

田子坊管理委员会作为一个民间自治组织，是自下而上城市更新的重要推力。当前田子坊过度商业化导致的商住矛盾、内绅化现象反映出居民在自发更新中趋利的盲目性。为了兼顾原住民的不同利益，应充分发挥田子坊管委会的作用，定期通过多种渠道收集、反馈民意，使得原住民与商户在田子坊的商业发展要求、限制条件等方面达成一定的契约，双方在出租房屋、经营商铺时自觉遵守。"契约化"管理机制的目标是让原住民共享更新红利，体现自下而上城市更新的公平性。针对未能出租住宅而获益、生活受到游客和商家影响的居民，管委会应重视这部分弱势群体的诉求，通过限制商业区向居住区的过度扩张，来保护居民居住空间和生活方式。具体可以控制不同地块的开发时序来实现对居住空间的保护，通过分区块的控制对自发性的租赁和改造行为进行引导。

5 结语

上海田子坊的城市更新是自下而上自发性更新的典范，它克服了政府主导的自上而下城市更新的一些问题，比如老城区的居住空间和场所记忆无法保留、居民原本的生活方式被迫改变等。自下而上的优势在于，更新的决策主体是本地居民，易于互相理解与协作，能通过参与地区公共事务来保障自身权益。为了引导更可持续的自下而上城市更新，街道办、管委会、原住民还需共同完善田子坊的"契约化"管理机制，明确各自的权利和义务，规范商业行为，营造稳定的社区环境。

Bottom-up Urban Renewal and Residential Morphology Development: A Case Study of Tianzifang

Zhu Xiaoyu

(Department of Urban Planning, College of Architecture and Urban Planning, Tongji University)

Abstract: There are two aspects of the residential morphology: one is the static and permanent material entity in the residential area; the other is the behavior of the residents. From the perspective of urban renewal, the renewal of the old city can be divided into two models: top-down and bottom-up. In Shanghai, the bottom-up update model of Tianzifang originated in the behavior of the residents' spontaneous opening and renting shops. After the transformation of Tianzifang, it becomes a diversified network of local residents, businessmen and artists. The paper takes Tianzifang as an example, analyzes the bottom-up renewal mode from four aspects of population structure, spatial environment, business development and commercial and residential contradiction, studies the influence of bottom-up urban renewal on the residential morphology and puts forward some strategies to promote sustainable bottom-up urban renewal.

Keywords: Residential morphology, Bottom-up urban renewal, Tianzifang, Commercial and residential contradiction, Contract management mechanism

参考文献

[1] 宇文娜, 李志民, 沈莹. 城中村居住形态的现状研究 [J]. 西安建筑科技大学学报: 自然科学版, 2008, 40（6）: 824-829.

[2] 郭淳彬. 旧城居住区自发性改造问题研究——以田子坊为例 [G]. 2011 中国城市规划年会: 7413-7425.

[3] 孙施文, 周宇. 上海田子坊地区更新机制研究 [J]. 城市规划学刊, 2015, 1: 39-45.

[4] 朱敦煌, 黄晨虹. "边缘"到"主体": 城市更新背景下原住民角色变化的思考——以上海新天地和田子坊为例 [J]. 建筑与文化, 2015, 8: 172-173.

[5] 邵静怡, 孙斌栋. 创意产业集聚与城市更新的互动研究——以上海田子坊为例 [J]. 城市观察, 2013, 23（1）: 158-168.

[6] 黄晔, 戚广平. 田子坊历史街区保护与再利用实践中商居混合矛盾的财产权问题 [J]. 西部人居环境学刊, 2015, 1: 66-72.

Land Readjustment as A Solution to the Dilemma of Urban Village Redevelopment in China: A Case Study of Yiwu

Yuan Dinghuan, Yau Yung, Li Ruoshi

(Department of Public Policy, City University of Hong Kong)

Abstract: China has been experiencing rapid urbanization in recent decades. Various approaches have been taken to implement urban development and renewal. As far as rural land is concerned, most development projects are still top-down, state-led or property-led. With participation of the affected villagers in the development exercise, their interests often receive inadequate consideration in the decision-making process. Thus resulting in unfairness and some social problems. To avoid the social deadlocks in the process, the existing institutions need to be revamped. This calls for innovative solutions which can achieve socially acceptable and economically efficient outcomes. Focusing on urban village redevelopment, this paper adopts a case-study approach to anatomize a land readjustment project in Yiwu, China. Unlike other land readjustment projects for "old village renewal", the subject project was led by the villagers' committee which was empowered to design the compensation and relocation schemes. In the light of fairer cost contribution and return redistribution, the affected villagers were more willing to participate. At the same time, the local government could also realize the goals of increasing land use efficiency and land value, and providing the basic infrastructure and public spaces without putting in any financial resources in the project. The case study demonstrates that empowerment of villagers' committee is an innovative experiment in urban village redevelopment. Such a bottom-up model which represents the best interests and allows true participation of the rural communities can lead to a win-win outcome to the villagers and local governments.

Keywords: Institutional reform, Empowerment, Land readjustment, Urban village, Urban renewal

1 Introduction

Playing vital roles in exchange, consumption, production and capital investment, land is the foundation of human survival and development[1]. Since 1987, the speed of urban development and expansion has accelerated in China as a result of land, housing and fiscal reforms[2]. The high-speed urbanization has played a major part in China's modernization and economic growth[3,4]. However, the problem of sub-optimal land use prevails in urban villages which are often characterized as institutionally insecure, disorderly, economically under-productive and incompatible with modernity[5]. Renewal of urban village, being one form of urban development, plays an important role in enhancing land value, land use efficiency and quality of living environment[6]. Yet, it is nearly impossible to avoid the issues of "community involvement" or "public participation" in urban village renewal projects[7]. In some cases, land assembly is a time-consuming process, especially when the land ownership rights are highly fragmented[8,9]. The potential holdout problem might be aroused when the landowners seek the opportunity to maximize their own interests. Thus, it becomes a dilemma in the urban development process.[5,10,11].

Since the fiscal reform in 1994, local governments have been empowered to formulate and implement their own urbanization strategies[12,13]. This allows the local authorities to attempt different approaches to design and implement urban village renewal projects for more desirable outcomes. The land readjustment (LR) model, which has been commonly employed for urban planning and redevelopment in many other parts of the world, is usually adopted for redeveloping urban villages in China. Different LR projects in China have been analyzed in academic works[14,15]. Very often, the LR model projects are led by the local governments so they are regarded as top-down in nature[12]. Being the decision-makers of these top-down redevelopment projects, the local authorities go into joint ventures with private developers to execute the projects and seldom pay adequate attention to the interests of the affected households and historical heritage preservation[12]. In this light, villagers are dissatisfied by the redevelopment projects and often choose to hold out the projects. In response to the prevailing conflicts among different parties, some local authorities empower the "villages' committees" (VCs), which are also known as "collective committees", to initiate urban village renewal projects in which the villagers can take charge of their own projects. This bottom-up approach is a product of the decentralization of authorities in China. VC, as a kind of the collective organization, plays an important role in the self-development of villages[16]. Unlike the local governments who have been criticized for making profits at the costs of the villagers during urban village redevelopment, VCs strives to protect the villagers' interests. Another special feature of the bottom-up LR approach is that participating villagers can lead and finance the project costs by themselves.

This bottom-up LR model is an innovative experiment of urban development on rural land in China. Nonetheless, it has attracted little attention in the international academic works. To fill up this research gap, the present paper aims at analyzing the VC-led LR model with the use of a case study in Yiwu. The next section offers an overview of the problems of urban village renewal in China. It is then followed by a description of research methodology. Afterwards, the case study is elaborated and analyzed in detail. The conclusion is presented in the last part.

2 Urban Villages in China and Difficulties in Renewing Urban Villages

Broadly speaking, urban villages are villages engulfed by the extended urban areas. While being located geographically in urban areas of cities, the land on which the urban villages are built is de facto rural land in China[17]. The evolution of urban villages in China can be ascribed to the flawed land tenure, household registration (*hukou*) and housing development systems. Although the living conditions in urban villages are not as good as those of other formal urban areas, urban villages provide affordable accommodations, education and job opportunities for marginal groups such as indigenous villagers and rural migrants[18,19]. In the absence of land use planning or poor planning enforcement for urban villagers, building plot ratios and site coverages are typically very high in urban villages. Besides, illegal structures proliferate in urban villages, along with negative living environmental and social problems, creating negative externalities for the neighborhoods[20]. In this regard, local governments often coin urban villages as "scars" and "urban cancers" and endeavor to eliminate them by redevelopment. Yet, the fragmented ownership of rural land and huge number of villagers involved give rise to very high transaction costs in the negotiation between local authorities and villagers.

Besides, the interests of the affected villagers sometimes warrant unfair consideration in the top-down urban village renewal projects. Hence, land takings often result in some social problems[21]. In this light, a new approach for urban village renewal which is workable and socially acceptable is needed.

3 Design of the Research

This paper takes a case-study approach to analyze the VC-led LR model for urban village redevelopment in China. The redevelopment of Louxitangcun in Yiwu, Jinghua, Zhejiang Province was investigated. Both primary and secondary data were collected in 2015 for the investigation. Primary data came from the in-depth interviews with the VC members and affected villagers while the sources of secondary data included relevant official policy and planning documents, news reports and commentaries.

4 Bottom–up Land Readjustment Project in Louxitangcun: An Anatomy

In order to improve land use efficiency and living environment, the local government in Yiwu started the "renewal of old villages" program (*Jiucun gaizao*) in 1998. The plan targeted to redevelop all urban villages in the city. Renewal projects under the program, however, were predominantly led by the local government and executed by private developers. The outcomes of these projects were not favorable to the affected villages. After the institutional reforms in the early 2000s, VCs were allowed to lead urban village renewal projects pursuant to two policies – Yizhen [2001] No.113 and Yizhenfa [2009] No.84. Such institutional arrangement provides a foundation for the bottom-up LR model. In the model, the scattered and inefficiently used settlement plots were pooled and then repartitioned into three parts: communal space, building plots and streets. The monetary compensation for demolition of the original buildings built upon the land was around RMB100-200/m^2 which was relatively marginal. The size of the returned building plot was calculated according to the settlement radix standard (SRS) set out by the state. As shown in Table 1, the SRS was designed with reference to family demographics rather than size of surrendered land.

SRS based on the family demography   Table 1

Family size	Size of returned building plot
1-3 people	36-108 m^2 (depending on factors like whether the younger generations chose to live with their parents and the marital status of the younger generations)
4-5 people	126 m^2
6 people or above	140 m^2

The conventional SRS favored large families. To motivate villagers who own large original building plots (OBP) to participate in the LR project, the VC in Louxitangcun devised another compensation scheme by taking both the conventional SRS and the size of land inputted for LR into account. The size of the total relocated building plot is calculated according to Equation (1), (2) or (3):

$$STRBP = SSRS \quad \text{for } SOBP-SSRS \leq 0 \tag{1}$$

$$STRBP = SSRS + 0.7(SOBP-SSRS) \quad \text{for } 0 < SOBP-SSRS \leq 200 \tag{2}$$

$$STRBP = SSRS + 140 \quad \text{for } SOBP-SSRS > 200 \tag{3}$$

in which　STRBP——Size of total relocated building plot, m^2;

SSRS——Size of returned building plot according to the SRS, m^2; and

SOBP——Size of original building plot surrendered for LR, m^2.

For instance, if the size of OBP exceeded the size of returned building plot calculated based on the SRS, a bonus which is equal to 0.7 (*SOBP-SSRS*) was offered to the villagers in addition to the SRS-based returned building plot. The total bonus was capped by 140m^2. This innovative plot bonus system extended the consideration to the size of surrendered land and gave strong incentives to villagers with large building plots but small family size to partake in the LR project.

Apart from the bonus system, another innovation of the VC-led LR project in Louxitangcun was the free choice of the new house type. In conventional LR projects led by the local governments, old low-rise structures were commonly replaced by high-rise buildings for higher land use efficiency. Nonetheless, some villagers, especially the elderly couples, were reluctant to reside in the high-rise buildings for various reasons (e.g. cultural beliefs and habitual factors). To encourage participation of this group of villagers in the LR project, a compromise relocation plan was thus devised——the new structures built on the readjusted land comprised high-rise buildings and 4.5-storey houses as shown in Figure 1. The villagers were allowed to choose to get back properties in a high-rise building or a 4.5-storey house in the end of the LR project.

Figure 1　New 4.5-storey houses and high-rise accommodations in Louxitangcun

Since the LR project in Louxitangcun was led by the VC, the local government did not intervene much in the project. Yet, at the same time, there was no financial resources offered by the state to support the project. In other words, the VC had to seek their funding sources to finance the LR project. Instead of selling the development rights of the land to a private developer for cost recovery or going into a joint venture with the development, the VC decided that the project cost were borne by the villagers themselves with an eye to bigger profits in the future. Without the need to sell surplus readjusted properties (i.e. those properties left over after rehousing the villagers) to private developers, the villagers can hold and lease out these surplus properties for steady rental incomes. In spite of the huge profits derived from the LR project, villagers might quarrel about the locations of the returned building plots, impeding their cooperation in the LR project. Everyone would like to choose a property in a prime location or with a better view.

Instead of using lottery for allocating readjusted building plots to the participating households, a novel approach was adopted in the LR project in Louxitangcun. Each household bade for the priority to choose the returned property by submitting a "selection fee" (or *xuanweifei*). More specifically, the household who offered the highest selection fee had the privilege to choose first the property they would like while the household with the lowest bid had to accept the property left over after the property selection by all other households. The selection fees were collected and managed as a temporary common-pool financial resource to fund the costs of providing basic infrastructure and amenities (e.g. roads, public lighting and landscaping). These provisions were vital for improving the quality of the living environment in the village. After financing the infrastructure works, the residue of the common-pool money was shared equally among all households regardless of their contribution shares. This novel financial arrangement pooled capital from villagers by means of selection fee, which is very similar to the fund-crowding mechanism whereby the better-off villagers contribute more while the less well-off ones contribute less. In the LR project in Louxitangcun, the selection fees offered by the villagers ranged from RMB0.57 million to 2.80 million (equivalent to US$81,700–401,400) per household. This innovative design made some sense because those who contributed more funds for the village development or improvement deserved to have a wider selection of property locations in return. Such an arrangement was much fairer to the villagers and fitted the local culture well so no dispute or confrontation was resulted in the property selection exercise. After all households had picked their returned properties, the leftover properties were collectively-owned by the villagers and they were used for generating rental incomes for financing public services.

The project smoothly entered into the construction stage. The villagers were permitted to choose their construction companies to build their residences, albeit there were some requirements for the uniform style and appearance of the houses and high-rise buildings. According to several interviewees, for a building plot of 108 m^2, the construction cost was around RMB750,000–840,000 (equivalent to US$107,500– 120,400). As aforementioned, the villagers chose to finance the LR project by themselves. Yet, it was not easy for the less wealthy households to bear the construction costs. Hence, the local government actively initiated some privileged policies to assist these households. For instance, the villagers could use a building plot of 36 m^2 as a collateral to borrow RMB200,000 (equivalent to US$ 28,700) from the local banks. In addition, they were allowed to sell parts of their returned building plots to the market (at around RMB60,000–70,000/m^2) to raise fund for construction. With these enabling policies initiated by the local government, the financial hurdle for the villagers to participate in the LR project was overcome. After all, the real motivation behind most villagers' voluntary partaking in the project was the potential profits that they could obtain in return. Most households opting for high-rise buildings for relocation got at least six units. As revealed by the interviewed villagers, the annual rental level for one apartment unit of 108 m^2 was around RMB60,000–70,000 in 2015. The rental return for the total investment was attractively high.

With the active participation of all villagers in Louxitangcun, it merely took three months to demolish all the old houses in the village after the project was initiated in 2011. The LR project was finished in June 2014 in the end, with the completion of all resettlement structures. In addition, at the time of investigation, the village has successfully attracted the investment from the woolen industry. Entrepreneurs rented the ground-floor units of the resettlement structures which were properties collectively owned by the villagers. The rental incomes added to a common financial pool to provide the welfare for the villagers. In the opinions of the villagers and local government officials, this innovative VC-led LR project has brought win-win outcomes to different stakeholders. On one hand, without the need for much financial input, the local government achieved its urban development plan in a peaceful manner. On the other hand, the local villagers enjoyed the increased values of their properties and a quality living environment.

5 Conclusion

China has been experiencing rapid urban development in recent decades. Institutional reforms in various aspects have enabled and stimulated local governments to devise and implement their own urbanization strategies. Yet, in the absence of laws or rules governing redevelopment on rural land, the compensation and relocation schemes vary from time to time and from place to place. This is a vivid reflection of the heterogeneity and flexibility of the institutional arrangements across localities. While LR technique has been widely used for renewing urban villages in many different cities in China, a top-down approach are usually adopted. However, in response to their financial constraints, the local governments tend to work with private developers in form of public-private partnership to undertake the LR projects. As a result, urbanization in China has been characterized as property-led[22,23]. Yet, despite many top-down LR projects for renewing urban villages executed by the coalitions between local governments and private developers did serve the public interests, the interests of the affected villagers were sometimes ignored or sacrificed. Villagers are normally forced to partake in the projects for the sake of public interests. They are at the bottom in the ladder of participation and this illusory participation is often ascribed to their powerlessness. In the absence of true empowerment, the villagers' interests can not be fully protected, thus results in some social problems. Therefore, it is time to change and invent new institutions to have the interests of the rural communities duly observed in urban village renewal.

This paper suggests that the VC-led LR model, which is a bottom-up, participative model, is a kind of an innovative experiment in urban village redevelopment. It can offer a win-win solution to the typical dilemma of urban village renewal, as demonstrated by the successful LR project in Louxitangcun. In that project, state involvement was minimal. Villagers chose to shoulder the financial burdens of the project themselves. The VC invented some special arrangements to lure villagers to actively participate in the project. These institutional innovations include bonus building plots for rewarding surrender of large land parcels and selection fees for settling location selection conflicts. As a whole, the best interests of the rural communities received full concern so villagers were willing to take part cooperatively and keenly in the project. At the same time, the local government did not come into any conflict or even confrontation with the villagers for achieving the goals of increasing land use efficiency and land value and providing the basic infrastructure and amenities without actual monetary input.

以义乌为例探讨解决中国城中村改造困境的方案：土地调整模式

袁定欢　邱　勇　李若诗

（香港城市大学公共政策学系）

摘　要：近几十年，中国城镇化实现了高速发展。其中，不同地区采用了不同的模式。而在集体土地上，大多数城镇化发展项目仍然是"自上而下"、"政府主导"或"房地产导向"。但基于此模式的村民参与，并没有使他们的利益在政策决定中得到充分考虑，出现了一些不公平现象，甚至产生了社会矛盾。为避免社会僵局，现有的制度需要改变。亟待建立被社会认可及高效的创新制度。聚焦于城中村改造项目，本文以义乌土地调整模式为例进行剖析。不同于其他土地调整模式，义乌土地调整模式是村民委员会主导并授权探讨补偿安置策略。在相对合理的成本分摊及利润分享的条件下，当地村民积极参与改造。与此同时，义乌政府在没有支出公共财政的条件下也实现了土地集约利用、土地增值、基础设施提供及公共空间整合的目标。本案例显示，授权村民委员会是城中城改造过程中的一个创新实践。自下而上的改造模式能真正代表农民集体的利益，从而实现利于村民和政府的双赢结果。

关键词：制度改革，授权，土地调整模式，城中村，城市更新

References

[1] Keng C K. China's land disposition system[J]. Journal of Contemporary China, 1996, 5: 325-345.

[2] Cheng J, Masser I. Urban growth pattern modeling: A case study of Wuhan city, PR China[J]. Landscape and Urban Planning, 2003, 62: 199-217.

[3] Huang J. Media dilemmas and countermeasures during the citizenization of land-lost farmers[J]. Canadian Social Science, 2015, 11: 197-201.

[4] Lichtenberg E, Ding C. Local officials as land developers: Urban spatial expansion in China[J]. Journal of Urban Economics, 2009, 66: 57-64.

[5] Sargeson S. Violence as development: Land expropriation and China's urbanization[J]. Journal of Peasant Studies, 2013, 40: 1063-1085.

[6] Adams D, Hastings E M. Urban renewal in Hong Kong: Transition from development corporation to renewal authority[J]. Land Use Policy, 2001, 18: 245-258.

[7] Zheng H W, Shen G Q, Wang H. A review of recent studies on sustainable urban renewal[J]. Habitat International, 2014, 41: 272-279.

[8] van der Krabben E, Needham B. Land readjustment for value capturing: A new planning tool for urban redevelopment[J]. Town Planning Review, 2008, 79: 651-672.

[9] Miceli T J, Sirmans C F. The holdout problem, urban sprawl, and eminent domain[J]. Journal of Housing Economics, 2007, 16: 309-319.

[10] Hui E C M, Bao H. The logic behind conflicts in land acquisitions in contemporary China: A framework

based upon game theory[J]. Land Use Policy, 2013, 30: 373-380.

[11] Zhao B. Land expropriation, protest, and impunity in rural China[J]. Focaal, 2009, 54: 97-105.

[12] Cheng Z. The changing and different patterns of urban redevelopment in China: A study of three inner-city neighborhoods[J]. Community Development, 2012, 43: 430-450.

[13] Heikkila E J. Three questions regarding urbanization in China[J]. Journal of Planning Education and Research, 2007, 27: 65-81.

[14] Li L H, Li X. Land readjustment: An innovative urban experiment in China[J]. Urban Studies, 2007, 44: 81-98.

[15] Lin Y, De Meulder B. A conceptual framework for the strategic urban project approach for the sustainable redevelopment of "villages in the city" in Guangzhou[J]. Habitat International, 2012, 36: 380-387.

[16] Sorensen A. Land readjustment, urban planning and urban sprawl in the Tokyo metropolitan area[J]. Urban Studies, 1999, 36: 2333-2360.

[17] He S, Liu Y, Webster C. Social groups and housing differentiation in China's urban villages: An institutional interpretation[J]. Housing Studies, 2010, 25: 671-691.

[18] Lin Y, De Meulder B, Wang S. Understanding the "village in the city" in Guangzhou[J]. Urban Studies, 2011, 48: 3583-3598.

[19] Wang Y P, Wang Y, Wu J. Urbanization and informal development in China: Urban villages in Shenzhen[J]. International Journal of Urban and Regional Research, 2009, 33: 957-973.

[20] Tian L. The chengzhoncun land market in China: Boon or bane?[J]. International Journal of Urban and Regional Research, 2008, 32: 282-304.

[21] Zeng S. Establishing land assembly districts[J]. Frontiers of Law in China, 2015, 10: 690-713.

[22] Cao J A. Developmental state, property-led growth and property investment risks in China[J]. Journal of Property Investment and Finance, 2009, 27: 162-179.

[23] Chen J, Guo F, Wu Y. Chinese urbanization and urban housing growth since the mid-1990s[J]. Journal of Housing and the Built Environment, 2011, 26: 219-232.

日本长期优良住宅认定制度对我国既有居住建筑改造的启示

李翥彬　兰凯斐

（大连理工大学建筑与艺术学院）

摘　要：本文在对日本住宅发展及其面临的主要问题进行概要性论述的基础上，重点就长期优良住宅认定制度提出的背景、主要内容、认定标准及实施成效进行了介绍；并从政府视角出发，讨论了其对我国既有居住建筑改造活动推进体制的启发。对我国未来相关活动的发展方向进行了展望。

关键词：长期优良住宅，既有居住建筑，改造，机制，日本

1　引言

随着我国住宅产业的不断发展，人们居住生活水平不断提升。与此同时，建成于20世纪八九十年代的大量既有住宅由于多年的使用，建筑本体劣化严重，大部分处于弃管状态。由于设计建造标准较低，高耗能问题突出，尤其在我国北方地区问题更为突出。因此，我国北方地区主要城市相继开展了大规模的既有居住建筑改造工程，在提升既有建筑质量以及性能方面取得了一定的成效，但也存在改造方式单一，改造机制不完善等问题。日本同样经历过住宅大量供给的时期并逐步进入存量时代，其经历的发展过程以及面临的主要问题对我国住宅产业的发展具有一定的参考价值。尤其是针对既有住宅建筑的长期优良住宅认定制度对于我国完善现行既有居住建筑改造体制机制，激发市场活力具有一定的借鉴及启发意义。

2　存量时代日本住宅面临的问题

日本大规模的住宅建设开始于第二次世界大战之后，大量的住宅短缺要求政府在短时间内向社会大规模地提供住宅。随着经济的快速发展，在解决了住宅短缺问题后住宅建设量依然以每年100万户左右的速度增长（图1）。截至2014年，日本住宅的总存量已经达到 $5.4 \times 10^9 m^2$。[1] 既往研究表明日本住宅存在多方面的问题与挑战[2]，主要包括由于拆除重建带来的住宅寿命缩短，既有住宅的低流通率，高住宅空置率，随着标准规范提升带来的对于节能以及抗震的新要求等。2016年3月日本内阁决议通过了最新的《住生活基本计划》①，提出了从"居住者""住宅存量""住宅产业与地域"三个视点出发的八个目标，对未来10年间日本的住宅以及居住问题进行了规划。[3] 新时期，日本住宅产业依然面临来自多方面的挑战及问题。首先，在高龄少子化的社会背景下，有孩子的家庭以及老龄人群对居住空间面积提出了更高的要求，需要对三代同居以及邻近居住等问题提供对应方策。其次，住宅存量巨大且

---
① 在人口减少的背景下，日本政府制定《居住生活基本法》（2006），并据此制订了2006~2015年的《住生活基本计划》，以提升住宅性能、居住环境以及居住面积水准为主要目标，其最新一期十年规划于2016年制订并实施。

流通率依然较低。2013年日本市场流通中既有住宅所占比例为14.7%，与欧美国家相比依然处于较低水平。再次，住宅空置问题仍然严峻。目前日本整体住宅存量约6063万户，空置约820万户。空置的住宅中没有租售计划的达到318万户。如何抑制不断增加的空置住宅是日本政府面临的挑战之一。从住宅产业发展的视角来看，除了新建住宅，既有住宅的运营管理、改造、流通以及与之相适应的金融保险制度等都亟待确立。长期优良化住宅认定及推进制度的确立，是日本为解决诸多住宅问题所采取的一种方案。

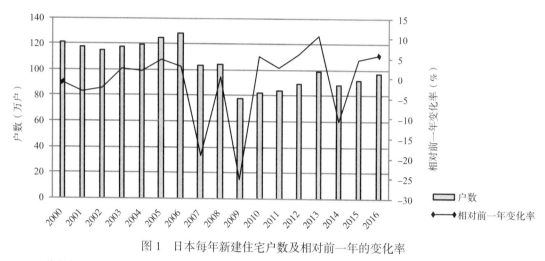

图1 日本每年新建住宅户数及相对前一年的变化率

资料来源：日本国土交通省. 建筑施工统计调查报告[R]. http://www.mlit.go.jp/statistics/details/jutaku_list.html.

3 长期优良住宅认定制度

3.1 缘起及意义

21世纪初，面临日益严峻的高龄少子化以及地球环境问题，日本逐步意识到消费型社会发展方式的弊端，并更加注重整体社会的可持续发展。在此背景下，2006年日本政府制定《居住生活基本法》，明确了日本住宅建设需要由"量"的提升转向"质"的提高。此后，时任政务调查会会长的日本前首相福田康夫于2007年5月提出"200年住宅构想"，其目的是实现住宅作为优良社会资产的可持续利用，在其就任日本首相后作为其住宅政策之一付诸实施。并于2008年12月制定《促进长期优良住宅普及的法律》，以法律的形式加以明确。[4, 5] 依据其基本方针，长期优良制度的重要性主要体现在三方面：第一，减轻环境负担，实现资源的有效利用；第二，减轻国民的负担。将过去用于重建住宅的费用用于增加最新的设备等提升居住生活"质"的方面，有利于创造更加舒适的居住环境。据估算，如果住宅的使用年限延长到当前的四倍，用于建造及维护的必要费用可削减1/3；第三，提升国民资产价值。日本住宅资产不到国家资产的一成，通过长期优良住宅建设，有利于维持住宅的资产价值，提升与国民住宅相关的国家资产比重，也有助于形成重视存量的国民意识。[6]

3.2 认定制度概要

与日本通常使用30年左右即拆除重建的住宅不同，长期优良住宅的主体构造及设备具有能够长期使用的特征。其与传统住宅的差异主要体现在更高的住宅性能，相关的税收优惠以及特有的认定制度。

长期优良住宅性能认定基准包括：构造主体的劣化对策、抗震性、维护管理及更新的容易性、平面的可变性、无障碍设计、节能对策、居住环境、住户面积以及具有维护计划九个方面。其中，劣化对策及抗震性为改造必需项目，其他项目为可选择项目（图2）。针对改造项目内容的不同有不同的补助措施。改造项目劣化对策与抗震性改造必须达到评价基准，其他任一改造项目达到评价基准即可判定为评价基准型，并给予相应财政补贴。改造后住宅性能完全满足长期优良住宅认定标准的住宅为认定长期优良住宅型，获得的补贴更多。同时，进行三代同居改造活动[①]的将获得额外补贴。具体补贴标准如表1所示。截至2015年，据不完全统计，已经有累计超过64万户（图3）取得长期优良住宅认定，其中以独栋住宅为主，集合住宅的改造活动主要集中于公用部分的改造。常见的改造内容如表2所示。经过多年的实施，长期优良认定制度极大促进了日本既有住宅品质的提升，也在一定程度上推动了多方利益主体参与既有住宅的改造活动。

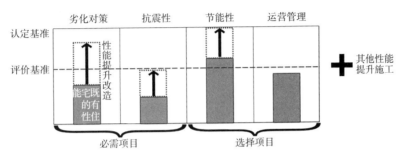

图2　日本长期优良改造住宅性能提升示意（以独栋住宅为例）

资料来源：依据日本国土交通省公开资料改绘。

长期优良认定住宅类型及补贴标准　　　表1

类型	评价基准型	认定长期优良住宅型	高度节能型	提案型
住宅性能要求	劣化对策、抗震性能以及其他的性能项目满足评价基准	获得长期优良住宅认定	在达到前两个要求的基础上，一次能源消费量比节能标准进一步减少20%	提出评价基准及认定基准的其他代替措施
补贴限额（三代同居改造）	100万日元/户（150万日元/户）	200万日元/户（250万日元/户）	250万日元/户（300万日元/户）	根据提案内容100万或200万日元/户（150万日元或250万日元/户）

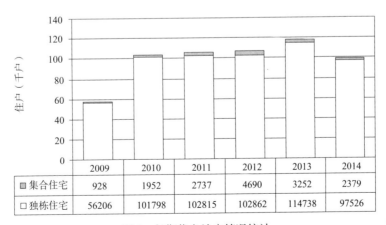

	2009	2010	2011	2012	2013	2014
集合住宅	928	1952	2737	4690	3252	2379
独栋住宅	56206	101798	102815	102862	114738	97526

图3　长期优良认定情况统计

资料来源：日本国土交通省. 长期优良住宅的认定实绩 [R]. http://www.mlit.go.jp/.

---

① 指厨房、浴室、卫生间、玄关的增设施工。

长期优良住宅改造常见施工内容 表 2

性能提升项目	主要施工内容	
	独栋住宅	集合住宅（共用部分）
劣化对策	防腐·防蚁处理 一体化浴室的安装 防水混凝土施工	外墙及屋顶改造 裂纹的修复
抗震性	增设承重墙、抗震板 增设斜撑 增加五金固定件	增设承重墙
节能对策	增加保温隔热层 双层玻璃 高效率热水器	高效热水器 保温隔热改造 开口部隔热处理
维护管理	给水排水管维修	排水管更换
其他	裂纹修补 设置节水型坐便器 外墙涂装	共用部分设置扶手 使用保温浴缸 阳台防水施工

4 我国既有居住建筑改造的背景及问题概况

改革开放以来我国住宅建设取得了巨大的成就，人均居住面积由 1978 年的 3.6m^2 提高到 2012 年的 32.91m^2，基本达到发达国家水平。然而，在经历了快速增长之后，我国住宅施工量于 2014 年迎来转折，并出现了下降趋势（图 4）。新常态下城市住宅建设将面临新的问题与挑战。与新建不同，不同时期建设完成的既有住宅在建筑质量、舒适性等方面无法满足现代生活的需求，同时随着建筑本体的劣化，改造势在必行。尤其是 20 世纪八九十年代建设的住宅，经过 30 多年的使用，问题更加突出，也成为当前改造的主要对象。通过对我国现行改造活动的分析，其存在多方面的问题。我国目前的改造主要集中于住宅的围护结构改造，抗震加固改造及供热计量改造等方面，层次相对较低。

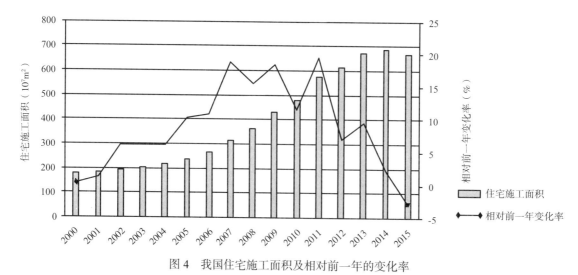

图 4 我国住宅施工面积及相对前一年的变化率

资料来源：中华人民共和国国家统计局．http://data.stats.gov.cn/easyquery.htm?cn=C01.

改造实施机制上，基本由政府完全主导，资金来源途径单一。同时，根据工人素质水平的高低施工质量难以保证，存在重复改造的可能。无论从使用角度还是实施机制角度，现行做法的可持续性较差，需要探索出一种适应我国国情及既有建筑特点的有效改造途径，推进既有居住建筑改造工作向纵深发展。

5 启示

长期优良住宅认定制度的实施在一定程度上缓和了日本社会以及住宅领域存在的矛盾问题，对于提升日本既有住宅的价值，实现住宅的长寿命化起到了积极的推动作用，是现阶段日本社会背景下推动住宅产业发展的一种有效途径。由于国家体制及社会背景的差异，我国既有居住建筑改造不可能完全采用日本模式，但其多年的实施及成效为我国体制机制的创建提供了一种思路。

第一，在制度建立的过程中需要明确政府、住宅所有人等改造活动参与者的角色定位。当前我国既有居住改造活动基本以政府主导进行，某种程度上有提升民生福祉的政绩考量。改造费用由政府完全支付，很难调动社会资本的积极性参与改造活动。长期优良住宅则由住宅所有人或购买人发起，依据自身需求进行改造目标的设定，政府给予财政补贴支持，一方面降低了住宅改造成本，激发了住宅所有人改造的积极性，另一方面政府在改造活动中的职能清晰明确，有利于制度得到贯彻与执行，也有利于形成住宅改造市场，促进相关产业的发展。

第二，摒弃单一的改造模式，构建多层次、多目标的住宅再生体系。当前我国改造基本采取专项改造形式，主要针对住宅外保温、外立面、抗震加固等方面进行有针对性的性能提升，并没有针对不同的住宅产权类型、使用者需求进行不同层次、不同目标的改造。同时，改造多集中于住宅外围，对于建筑内部公用部分的改造有限。日本长期优良住宅实施过程中制定了极具弹性的多目标评价标准，在控制必需项的基础上允许改造活动针对具体情况进行有选择性的提升，大大提高了认定制度的灵活性，也激发了住宅所有人及购买人进行长期优良住宅认定的积极性。

第三，构建既有居住建筑改造相关法律法规体系。日本长期优良住宅的实施有赖于明确的法律法规保障及标准体系建设。相关法律法规的制定先于改造实践展开，使全国范围内开展的相关活动有法可依。反观我国当前的既有居住建筑改造活动基本处于自由开展的阶段，虽然部分政府出台的一些地方性法规但执行力度较弱，同时多种类型的改造活动缺乏统一的流程管理及评价机制，导致改造成效难以明确判定。

6 展望

目前，全国各地针对老旧住宅展开了大范围的改造工程，切实提升了老旧住宅性能及环境，然而也存在多方面的问题。部分地区城市已经意识到并且进行了十分有益的尝试和探索。例如，上海市的"美丽家园"模式，将公众参与很好地融入整个住宅改造流程体系，使广大住户深度参与改造决策、实施及验收，在实施机制创新方面取得了一定成效。[7] 未来我国的既有居住建筑改造工程必然向法制化、规范化发展，改造对象也将逐步由建筑单体改造拓展到住区及街区层面，改造内涵从单纯的物理性能提升到整体区域品质提升。在此过程中，日本长期优良住宅认定制度提供了一种政府视角下的推进机制，值得我国在发展既有居住建筑改造的事业中借鉴参考。

致谢

作者感谢中央高校基本科研业务费专项（项目号：DUT16RC(4)44），国家自然科学基金重点项目（项目号：51638003）以及国家自然科学基金青年项目（项目号：51608090）对本研究的支持。

The Inspirations from Japanese Long-life Quality Housing to Chinese Residential Building Renovation

Li Zhubin, Lan Kaifei

(School of Architecture & Fine Art, Dalian University of Technology)

Abstract: After an introduction to the development and issues of Japanese housing, this paper focuses on the background, contents, standards and effectiveness of Japanese Long-Life Quality Housing program, which is considered referable for China. Then, it is discussed that how to improve the mechanism of Chinese residential building renovation from the perspective of local governments. The future direction of Chinese residential building renovation is also mentioned in this paper.

Keywords: Long-life Quality housing, Existing residential building, Renovation, Mechanism, Japan

参考文献

[1] 日本国土交通省. 建筑物存量统计 [2017-5-5]. http://www.mlit.go.jp/statistics/details/jutaku_list.html.

[2] 椎本浩和,金多隆. 日本の住宅問題と長期優良住宅の関わり. 日本建築学会大会学術講演梗概集，2010，9: 1375-1376.

[3] 浅見泰司，中川雅之，深尾精一，和田康紀. 新たな住生活基本計画について，住宅土地経済，2017，103: 2-15.

[4] 松村秀一. 長期優良住宅普及促進法の成立. 建築雑誌，2009，9: 22-23.

[5] 吴东航，章伟林. 日本住宅建设与产业化 [M]. 北京：中国建筑工业出版社，2009.

[6] 日本国土交通省. 長期優良住宅の普及の促進に関する法律関連情報. 2015 [2017-1-9]. http://www.mlit.go.jp/jutakukentiku/house/jutakukentiku_house_tk4_000006.html.

[7] 古小英. 既有住宅小区宜居综合改造实践与思考 [D]. 中国建筑科学研究院，2017.

存量背景下上海老旧社区更新的价值导向与规划实践

匡晓明[1]　陆勇峰[1]　丁馨怡[2]

（1.上海同济城市规划设计研究院；2.城市中国）

摘　要：在城市更新转型发展和创新社会治理的时代背景下，上海中心城区的老旧社区更新成为改善人居环境、实现社会公平与社会包容及提高社区自治能力的重要落脚点。本文结合笔者团队所参与的上海静安区"美丽家园"社区更新规划经历，回顾整体实践过程，总结更新规划内容与创新探索，提炼出社区更新的 PPP 模式；并从社区更新价值导向和设计理念的视角，提出社区更新规划的"五个价值转变"：从空间逻辑到以人为本、从工程模式到规划引领、从目标导向到问题导向、从空间设计到社区营造、从蓝图规划到行动规划，以期为国内存量社区更新规划提供上海经验和借鉴启示。

关键词：老旧社区，更新，价值导向，规划实践

1　引言

改革开放以来，我国经历了快速城市化的发展阶段，城市化水平从 1978 年的不足 18% 提高到 2016 年的近 55%，年均增长率约 1%。随之也产生了一系列城市问题，特别是城市中心的老旧社区迅速沦为"失落的空间"。1998 年我国城镇住房体系改革以来，城市住宅产业的高速发展进一步助推了城市化进程，当前各大城市商品房价格居高不下，住房保障与居住问题成为最热门的社会焦点和民生话题。城市版图中嵌有大量的棚户区、老旧社区，尤其是老旧社区往往不在市政动迁范畴之内，二次开发缺乏经济利益驱动，成为城市更新和社区治理的难点。基于此，上海静安区自 2015 年起，围绕解决老旧住区的"急难愁"问题，开展了全区美丽家园社区更新。笔者作为社区规划师有幸参与了该项工作，从前期配合政府开展基础研究、到负责社区更新规划实施方案编制及与社区居民沟通协调、再到施工过程的实施指导以及后续相关评估工作的开展等全过程。本文结合美丽家园更新实践，通过具体的规划实践案例介绍，总结更新规划内容与创新探索，提炼社区更新应秉持的价值观和设计理念，以期为国内其他城市老旧社区更新及规划的编制提供经验和借鉴。

2　上海老旧社区更新的时代背景

2.1　国家层面的要求

2015 年 12 月，中央城市工作会议召开，精准把脉了当前城市发展和建设中存在的问题，树立了"人民城市为人民"的价值体系，提出了"一个尊重、五个统筹"的城市发展原则。其中也提到了"要深化城镇住房制度改革，继续完善住房保障体系，加快城镇棚户区和危房改造，加快老旧小区改造"、

"规划编制要接地气,可邀请被规划企事业单位、建设方、管理方参与其中,还应该邀请市民共同参与。要在规划理念和方法上不断创新,增强规划科学性、指导性。要加强城市设计,提倡城市修补和生态修复……"等。政策性的要求为老旧住区的更新和复兴提供了方向性的指引。

2.2 上海城市发展和社会治理要求

上海作为全国社会经济和城市化快速发展的标杆城市,其城市发展从快速的增量扩张时代,开始进入到以存量更新为主线的转型期,并于2015年5月1日,正式发布了《上海市城市更新实施办法》。在新一轮《上海市城市总体规划(2015~2040)纲要》中,明确提出建设用地"零增长"、"负增长",城市发展要从传统的增量拓张向存量提升转型。以往大规模拆除式的旧城改造已不再符合上海城市发展的要求,要以提高城市活力和品质为目标,积极探索渐进式、可持续的有机更新模式,以存量用地的更新利用来满足城市未来发展的空间需求。[1]

2.3 上海老旧社区更新的现实需求

建于20世纪八九十年代左右的老旧住宅小区既是存量用地主角,又是城市建成环境的重要组成部分,但是由于缺乏经济利益的更新驱动,成了城市更新中的痛点。在居住空间环境层面,老旧住宅区普遍存在着基础设施老化、建筑年久失修、交通组织不畅、停车矛盾突出、小区环境差等诸多问题,严重影响了居民最基本的日常生活;社会属性层面,住区居民存在着社区观念薄弱、自治共治意识欠缺、老龄化现象明显、社会阶层分化、社区文化匮乏等现象。老旧社区的居民大多是从传统的市中心等地动迁而来,某种意义上,他们为上海城市建设做出了牺牲和贡献。不论是从空间活化还是从城市人文关怀的角度来考量,这些老旧社区都具备了更新改造的客观诉求和外在动因。

3 静安区美丽家园社区更新规划实践

3.1 项目基本概况

2015年7月以来,上海静安区正式启动老旧社区美丽家园更新建设[2],以下辖的各街镇为实施单位,每个街镇选取若干试点小区分批次有序推进,并在2015年工作基础上,于2016年又进一步开展了美丽家园(升级版)建设。笔者团队有幸参与其中,并承担了静安区彭浦镇美丽家园建设具体工作,包括从前期配合镇政府开展基础研究,到负责社区更新规划实施方案的编制、与社区居民沟通协调,再到施工过程的实施指导以及后续相关评估工作等整个过程。同时彭浦镇也是第一个在静安区美丽家园建设中引入社区规划理念的街镇,这一社区规划模式随后在2016年美丽家园升级版建设中在全区得到推广。期间,笔者团队先后承担了彭浦镇27个住区(2015年)、静安区24个重点住区(2016年)的社区更新规划编制。

3.2 更新规划主要内容

针对老旧住宅小区的实际情况,结合前期的调研基础,以问题导向为主,其物质空间更新改造内容可以概括为"安全维护、交通组织、环境提升、建筑修缮"四个方面。[3、4]

3.2.1 安全维护更新

主要指对小区内的安全设施进行统筹规划，通过增设或维护，实现住区安全全覆盖，主要包括：对小区出入口的门卫岗亭、智能化道闸、安全技防等设施进行综合改造；对小区内的路面、二次供水、排水管网、户外照明等基础设施进行改造、疏通和维修，从而提高住区的安全性和归属感。

3.2.2 交通组织更新

以确保生命通道和消防通道畅通为主要目标，针对老旧住宅区内部存在的行车路线不合理、机动车停车矛盾突出、非机动车停车无序等问题，对住区场所空间进行充分挖潜，因地制宜提出交通组织优化方案、规范划定机动车停车位、增设非机动车停车棚等。优化方案可以是以一个住宅小区为单位，进行内部空间挖潜和组织交通，也可以是以几个规模较小且相邻的小区进行整体统筹布局，打破既有的围墙分割和空间限定。比如很多单位售后公房小区，因历史上隶属于不同的单位建设，导致各住宅地块被围墙分割，内部交通空间和开敞空间局促。规划改造强调"自治共治、共建共享"的理念，打破既有小区的空间壁垒，有条件的小区拆除内部围墙，打开空间整体更新改造、共享公共绿化空间、重新梳理交通流线，对不合理的出入口进行调整，实现人车分流。

3.2.3 环境提升更新

重点从景观功能性、针对性、适用性以及美观性四个方面，对老旧小区公共绿地和活动空间，结合不同小区不同居住人群的实际情况，因地制宜进行提升设计并加以改造，通过景观植物的配置优化、景观设施的改造，以此提升老旧住宅小区绿化布局和绿化品质，为各年龄层居民提供公共交往与健康场所。

3.2.4 建筑修缮更新

针对诸如屋顶漏水、墙面渗水、楼道整治等建筑本身存在的问题，需进行综合梳理，并由专业部门予以落实解决，从而解决居住建筑的功能性与美观性问题。尤其是在空间允许的情况下，针对老旧住区老龄化现象，应尽可能通过改造，增加适老性设施和无障碍设施。

3.3 更新中的实践探索

本次规划实践，除了编制完成若干社区更新的具体方案外，还有效地指导了后续施工建设。在完成传统意义上的设计师任务之余，笔者认为更重要的是在工作中规划团队还做出了如下探索。

3.3.1 提出社区更新 PPP 模式

围绕"存量老旧住区"这一特点，在项目前期研究中结合上海创新治理的时代要求，笔者确定了社区更新开展坚持"整体统筹、规划引领、公众参与、群众满意"的基本原则，并重视其惠民工程性质，强调最终的实施成效。因此笔者将其概括为"社区更新 PPP 模式"，分别指规划（Planning）、公众参与（Participating）、实施（Put-into-effect），即动态规划和自治共治相结合的社区更新理念，并落实具体建设。强调社区更新应以社区居民为核心，依托静安区基层治理中既有的"三会一代理平台[①]"和"1+5+X[②]"自治模式，建立社区更新工作机制，为居民、政府、

[①] 三会一代理：由居委会负责搭建的决策听证会、矛盾协调会、政务评议会、群众事务代理机制。
[②] 1+5+X："1"：居民区党总支书记；"5"：居委会主任、社区民警、业委会主任、物业负责人、群众团体及社会单位负责人；"X"包括住区单位负责人、楼组长、党员志愿者等，引导社会组织实现自我管理。

规划师、建设方搭建一个高效的协同平台，协调各参与主体角色扮演和职责分工，从而积极有效地推动社区更新（图1）。[5]

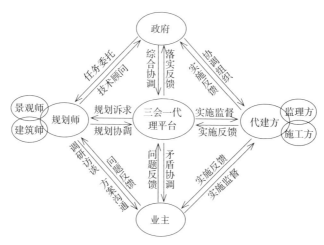

图1　社区更新PPP模式示意框图

3.3.2　社区规划推动社区治理

本次社区规划，重点关注住区空间与环境提升，这也正是老百姓迫切需要的，因此在整个过程中，居民参与度非常高。依托社区规划这一平台，居委会、业委会、物业、楼组长与居民代表等逐渐探索并形成了针对美丽家园建设的居民自治议事平台和工作机制，比如制定每周一次的工程例会制度等。同时笔者团队社区规划师作为专业性的技术人员，全过程参与美丽家园建设，编制和讲解社区规划方案，听取居民意见，解答居民疑问，协调居民的空间矛盾，指导施工单位工程建设等。社区规划作为专业性的规划技术支撑，为社区物质空间环境改造提供解决方案，更为重要的是与"社区治理、居民自治"相结合，成为有效推动基层社区治理、做实公众参与的协同平台。

3.3.3　社区规划师机制的探索

上海之前的存量住宅社区的更新改造，基本都是按照房管局系统下的房屋修缮类工程和要求实施，往往少有先通过规划师编制社区规划来统筹，公众参与也仅仅处于初级阶段。本次彭浦镇美丽家园建设，突破了传统单一的工程思维模式，强调了社区规划在社区更新中的综合作用。社区规划师在该项目中的作用体现为五点：（1）专业技术，易于居民信任；（2）桥梁作用，利于利益协调；（3）设计表达，引导公众参与；（4）成果规范，利于指导实施；（5）实施跟踪，便于后续服务。也正因此，这一"社区规划引领的老旧社区更新"模式被政府部门高度认可，继而在2016年静安区美丽家园建设中全区予以推广，为上海老旧住区的更新改造工作起到了一定的示范作用。

3.3.4　设计理念提升更新品质

老旧住区的更新改造，思路上要从传统的诸如"平改坡"等相对单一的房修类工程改造，向系统化的社区更新转变。在这个过程中，一方面要强调规划对居民公众参与的促进作用，从而推动社区自治能力的提升；另一方面更要强调"设计创造价值"的理念，通过专业的规划、建筑、景观设计团队介入，借助设计师的智慧，引入"生态、健康、智慧、人文、环保"等设计理念，实现低造价、参与式、渐进式的住区有机更新与社区营造，进而提高住区改造的综合品质和社会效益。比如在静安区部分小区更新方案中，设计团队适当地应用了海绵城市、开放、绿色、共享等理念。在彭浦镇海鹰小区的更新规划中,将战争年代遗留的现已废弃的半地下水库,设计改造为兼具雨水花园功能的公共活动空间;在临汾街道760弄小区,更新方案提出通过内部围墙的拆除,实现小区绿化广场的共享、开放,同时在围墙拆除的带状路径上,规划设置了健康步道(图2、图3)。

图2　静安区临汾760弄内部围墙拆除前后对比

图3　静安临汾760弄健康步道建设效果

4　老旧社区更新的价值导向

4.1　从空间逻辑到以人为本

在城市增量扩张阶段,居住区设计围绕的是空间逻辑,政府、开发商、设计师等以空间为对象主导居住区的建设。从设计到建设,人的概念都是抽象意义上假想的未来客户群体,而非具体的居住人群概念。存量更新发展时代,老旧社区更新的核心是以既有居民为本,更新价值强调社区的空间正义,不仅是空间资源分配结果的正义,还包括分配过程的正义。即更新过程要体现多元参与主体间的各种博弈,更新方案要体现社区居民的共同意志,更新结果要集中体现社区居民公共利益最大化,更新目标是为了提高社区居民的满意度和获得感。

4.2　从工程模式到规划引领

老旧住区的更新改造并非是近年来的新词,全国各地也都有各自的成功经验,上海也同样经历了"平改坡"、"二次供水"等单一的工程改造,甚至也探索过老旧住宅通过增加楼层的改造实现改造资金的平衡,比如2005年上海杨浦鞍山新村综合改造。[6] 这些改造虽然从硬件上改善了居民的居住条件,但其更偏向于以房修类为主的工程模式,社区居民处于被动从属的状态,对改造方案缺少了解,更新过程参与度极低甚至缺位。因此,在当前创新社会治理背景下,"社区更新PPP"模式(前文提到)更为行之有效,社区规划、社区规划师的综合作用机制的引领社区治理,推动老旧社区综合复兴。

4.3　从目标导向到问题导向

不同于传统的总规、控规等法定规划,强调远期的目标导向和空间管控,社区更新应该更关注社区现状存在的问题,以解决问题为出发点提出切实可行的更新改造方案。[7] 因此社区更新思维要从生地开发的目标导向转变为存量发展的问题导向。与此同时，除了解决空间环境诸如基础设施老化、建筑年久失修、交通组织不畅、停车矛盾突出、小区环境差等问题之外，还要进一步考虑社区的历史传承和社会生态更新，比如违章搭建的拆除、老龄化现象带来的适老性设计以及提升社区归属感的公共空间设计等。在此前提下，针对问题精准施策，并在调研环节、初步方案、方案草案、实施方案等不同环节进一步锁定问题和细化方案，以提高社区更新的综合效率。

4.4 从空间改造到社区营造[1]

在社区规划引领的机制下，老旧住区的更新要从一次性的空间环境工程改造转向可持续的社区营造。工程改造纵然可以改善空间环境，但不久之后问题会再现。存量社区更新更需要长效的维护机制，需要社区居民主动关心共有的社区环境，因而需要社区营造的概念。社区营造被公认为是现代社会治理中值得提倡的一种社区治理方式，其具备以下作用：（1）促进居民参与解决自己的问题，提高社区居民的社会意识；（2）调整或改善社区关系，减少社区冲突；（3）鼓励居民参与社区公共事务，增强邻里互动来往，促成社区自治；（4）发挥居民的潜能，发掘并培养社区的领导人才，为社区增能；（5）培养互相关怀、彼此互济的美德，建立社区归属感，荣誉感和责任感。上述内容也正是创新社会治理背景下应提倡的价值导向。

4.5 从蓝图规划到行动规划

传统的城市规划更多表现为目标导向清晰的蓝图规划，强调其法定性、约束性和管控性，变更也必须按照严格的程序执行。社区更新规划应该是一种自下而上的主导方式，强调的是政府、利益相关者、规划师或者其他协调者、NGO 等多方参与，针对社区问题共同探寻一种解决之道。社区更新规划更多是一种行动规划，社区规划师需要有沟通、协调、引导、处理问题的综合能力。当然规划方案是随着更新事项的具体开展，结合实时环境变化和新问题的产生，允许弹性的动态优化和完善，社区规划可以有阶段性停止或者完全放弃。比如静安区美丽家园社区更新规划实践中，有的小区在更新方案公示后，社区居民意见又出现了巨大的分歧，短时内也难以达成共识性，最终社区更新终止于方案阶段。因此社区规划作为工程建设依据之外，更大的意义在于与社区自治共治相结合，成为推动社会治理的有效方式。

5 结语

静安区美丽家园社区更新资金以区政府公共财政投入为主，因此依然带有政府主导色彩，但在此过程中，已经显现出了与时代发展、社会发展、现代社会治理相符的转型理念和成功经验。比如彭浦镇的老旧社区更新，创新性地引入了社区规划，推动了社区参与，引领了全区，乃至全市的社区更新模式，改变了以往房修类工程主导的单一逻辑，价值导向上实现了从工程改造到社区更新的转型。同时，这也给予了笔者团队一次全面、系统、深度实践社区规划师的机会，一方面探索了社区规划如何与社区治理相结合，另一方面推动了社区规划师从之前理论层面的倡导走向了真实的规划实践，为上海社

---

[1] 社区营造在维基百科里的定义是："居住在同一地理范围内的居民，持续以集体的行动来处理其共同面对社区的生活议题，解决问题同时也创造共同的生活福祉，逐渐地，居民彼此之间以及居民与社区环境之间建立起紧密的社会联系，此一过程即称为'社区营造'。"

区规划师制度的建立起到了积极的试点作用。对于实践中的一些新问题和挑战，比如社区更新中的审批管理、社区更新人文特色需求挖掘等议题，需要在以后的实践中逐步探索。

The value Orientation and Planning Practice on Old Residential Renewal of Shanghai in the Background of Inventory Planning

Kuang Xiaoming[1], Lu Yongfeng[1], Ding Xinyi[2]

(1. Shanghai Tongji Urban Planning & Design Institute; 2. Urban China)

Abstract: In the context of urban renewal and social governance innovation, the renewal of the old community in the downtown area of Shanghai is an important foothold of improving the living environment, achieving social equity and social inclusion and improving community self-governance. The paper combines the "beautiful home" community updated planning experience in Jing'an District of Shanghai which the author participated in. Systematically reviews the overall practice process, combines the analyses of community update planning case, then extracts the community to update the PPP model. From the perspective of the value orientation of community update and design conception, put 'five changes' into the community renewal planning, from the space logic to the people-oriented, from the project model to the planning lead, from the goal–oriented to the problem–oriented, from space design to community created and from blueprint planning to action planning, hoping to provide Shanghai experience and reference.

Keywords: Old community, Urban renewal, Value orientation, Planning practice

参考文献

[1] 上海市城市总体规划（2015～2040）纲要.

[2] 《中共上海市委关于进一步创新社会治理加强基层建设的意见》（沪委[2014]14号）.

[3] 《静安区关于开展"美丽家园"建设的实施意见》（2015.7）.

[4] 《上海静安区彭浦镇美丽家园社区更新规划暨实施方案》（上海同济城市规划设计研究院 2016.5）.

[5] 匡晓明，陆勇峰. 存量背景下上海社区规划实践与探索. 2016中国城市规划年会论文集[M]. 北京：中国建筑工业出版社，2016.9.

[6] 赵民，孙忆敏，杜宁，赵蔚. 我国城市旧住区渐进式更新研究——理论、实践与策略[J]. 国际城市规划，2010，1：24-32.

[7] 黄瓴，许剑峰. 城市社区规划师制度的价值基础和角色建构研究[J]. 规划师，2013，9：11-15.

触媒理论引导下的社区更新模式探讨：以可食地景为例

徐晓岛

（同济大学建筑与城市规划学院）

摘　要：选取可食景观作为一种社区更新触媒，对触媒理论引导下的社区更新模式进行研究。首先结合国内外对城市触媒的相关研究成果，阐释了更新触媒的内涵以及在社区更新中引入更新触媒的必要性；然后对社区可食景观的定义、作用、类型进行阐述，并结合实际案例，分析社区可食景观的营造模式；最后总结出触媒理论引导下的社区更新模式：选择更新触媒、触媒空间设计、合作经营与管理维护、衍生的社区再更新。

关键词：更新触媒，社区更新，社区营造，可食景观

1　引言

新常态背景下，我国进入趋势性转变时代，城市发展从数量增长为主转向质量提升和结构优化为主，从"大拆大建"的粗放设计向"针灸式"精细化更新转型。社区作为城市的基本单位，在过去30年经历了建设的高潮，但几十年的建设开发过程中，无论是以工人新村为代表的单位制社区还是1970年后建设的商品房小区，都属于"一次性开发"，即开发商建设完毕撤出，交由物业管理公司进行管理；而物业管理公司出于对经济利益的追求，对没有经济收益的社区后期维护积极性较低，社区自行发展过程中随着时间推移逐渐出现空间破败、活力丧失等现象，尤其是老旧居住社区，作为社会矛盾聚焦和体现城市特色的空间载体，如何使社区再活化，成为政府和设计师所关注的焦点。

针对社区更新课题，很多学者设计师从不同角度进行了有益的探索，如从传统保护和历史传承角度研究历史城市中传统社区更新与开发方法；从社会融合角度研究以多元化混合社区为目标的社区更新模式；从社区空间和生态循环角度研究城市"有农社区"的必要性和可行性。此外还有关于社区营造、社区生态改造技术、社区文化景观等的研究。这些探索都为实现可持续的社区更新提供了宝贵经验。

本文结合城市触媒理论及相关研究，探讨可持续的社区更新模式及应用。实践证明，兼具景观生态价值和文化价值的社区可食景观营造是一种积极、有效的社区更新途径，对社区活化、环境更新和景观实用性具有重要意义。因此本文以可食景观营造为例，进一步阐述触媒理论引导下社区更新模式的应用。

2　触媒理论引入社区更新

2.1　城市触媒理论及相关研究

城市触媒理论最早由20世纪末美国规划师韦恩·奥图和唐·洛干在《美国都市建筑：城市设计的

触媒》一书中提出。城市触媒类似于化学反应中的催化剂，作为城市更新植入的新元素能激发一系列相关元素的连锁反应，即带动和激发城市建设与复兴，并促使后续持续、渐进的城市改革发生。触媒理论的核心是新旧元素之间、新元素之间的相互影响与相互作用，以及各元素对城市形式与社会网络的影响。城市触媒的表现形式不限，从构筑物到建筑群、自然景观都可以是物质形式的触媒，而非物质形式的触媒可以是社区活动、城市事件等，具有多样化的形式。

国内外对触媒理论有广泛研究与应用，包含触媒的概念、形式、作用及对城市的影响，且对城市事件触媒、建筑单体触媒和更新触媒有较详细的实例研究。本文聚焦于"更新触媒"，即促进和激发社区可持续更新的触媒。

2.2 更新触媒为社区可持续发展带来契机

社区可持续发展的内涵包含经济、社会和环境三方面的可持续。首先，社区更新触媒作为公共产品，是公共服务设施的末端补充，且能聚集各类型社会群体在此集聚，从而带动基于人流量的商业（如广告、店铺等）市场活跃和土地升值，增长的市场需求使更新范围进一步扩大，且有助于获得进一步更新的资金，从而实现社区经济层面的可持续发展。其次，社区更新触媒具有社会、文化等层面的非物质性价值，成为社区居民的交往场所和精神归属，从而帮助实现社区营造，且社区更新的沟通和实践本身即是化解居民矛盾、促进社区融合的过程，是实现社会层面可持续的精神动力。此外，近年来海绵城市、生态城市等相关理论和技术的研究逐渐成熟，城市利用更新契机进行景观生态化改造，包括屋顶绿化、透水铺装等技术的应用，把原本"硬质"城市环境逐步改造成能有机应对灾害性气候的"弹性"、"韧性"城市。社区层面的更新设计同样是植入生态技术、实现环境可持续的契机，且作为城市的基本单位，是城市生态化改造的构成单元。

3 可食景观作为社区更新触媒

3.1 可食景观的概念

可食景观，又称生产性景观，是指选择可供人类食用的植物种类，用生态园林设计方式设计，构建绿地、花园等场所，使其变成富有美感和生态价值的景观场地。

3.2 可食景观在我国的兴起与发展

可食景观的出现平衡了社区居民种地生产的需求与破坏城市景观的矛盾。我国可食景观的雏形是农业生产，在城乡发展过程中农业与园林景观逐渐分开。近年来，随着空气污染、热岛效应等"城市病"频现，食品安全也频频出现问题，城市环境治理、景观生态化改造和食品安全管控日益受到重视；城市人越发渴望返璞归真，希望回到气候舒适、环境自然、"天人合一"的乡村环境，但由于乡村的公共服务配套不完善等问题和工作等限制，城市人口密度依然与日俱增，只是城市周边农家乐、民宿旅游等得到发展。

当前城市更新背景下，以都市农业理论和朴门永续设计理念为指导，城市中——尤其是社区内，可食景观营造逐渐成为趋势。从每户各自营造的可食阳台，到集体组织下的社区菜园、屋顶菜园等，越来越多的居民在城市环境中也能享受到晴雨耕读的惬意。

3.3 可食景观是良好的社区更新触媒

作为社区更新触媒的可食景观，主要指社区组织的集体共享型可食景观，与居民私家阳台、花园等私有型可食景观概念相对。可食景观营造通常利用社区空地、废弃地，不受场地大小限制，成本较低且符合"3R 理念"——减少原料（Reduce）、重新利用（Reuse）和物品回收（Recycle）。作为生产性景观，可食景观有天然、安全的农作物这项基本产出，成为对社区居民的重要吸引点；农业生产的周期性为可食景观带来视觉上的变化，激发社区持续的活力。城市居民广泛缺乏农业生产的经验，因此必须组织相关教育教学活动，促进社区居民相帮助互学习交流和实践，成为良好的社区营造途径。可食景观的营造过程吸引人流聚集，能有效带动周边商业活力，带来经济效益。

此外，对城市中长大的儿童，可食景观使得他们得以获取关于自然环境和农业的实践知识，树立良好的环境观，具有深远的教育意义。

3.4 社区可食景观的分类

按种植地点分类，可分为阳台和屋顶、小型庭院、社区农园三类。按景观特点分类，可分为农业景观、可食树木与花卉景观、可食菌类景观三类。按植物类型分类，可分为粮食农作物类、观赏蔬菜类、观赏果木花卉类和药草类四个类型。

4 社区可食景观营造的实践

4.1 法明顿可食用的生产性道路景观

历史上纽约法明顿曾经是一片繁荣的农业区。更新前的基地内有五车道的商业大道，但由于人行空间品质低下，商业街逐渐走向没落，地区经济也随之下滑。当地政府意图通过"车本主义"向"人本主义"的转变来更新实现地区复兴。

规划参考了当地 20 世纪曾经繁荣的农业景象，选择可食景观及其相关功能系统为更新触媒，包括可种植瓜果蔬菜的复合型街道景观、果园、农贸市场，以及有标识性的景观步行桥等。

规划构建了地区绿色网络，它既是连接各门户节点的步行导向通道，也是承载可食景观的绿色空间（图1）。整个景观网络包括果树园、盆栽花园等。基于某些植物净化空气和水源的作用，以及另外一些植物具备的营养循环、维护土壤或综合防治病害虫的功能，设计者们将社区景观设计成一个共生的复合生态系统。

图 1 更新后种植食物的复合型林荫道

此外，项目组设计了一个包含公路建设一般要素的"公路生态矩阵"，并根据不断升级的服务水平进行分类。作为非设计人员进行城镇景观规划的理想工具，该矩阵有助于实现公众参与景观设计，从而落实更新触媒的实施保障。

4.2 中成智谷火车菜园

中成智谷火车菜园原为铁路轨道旁堆放建筑垃圾的城市废弃地，周边分布着旧时铁路线板道房、废弃仓库建筑群、堆场和遗留工业构筑物等。企业与设计师自发组织社会人群将该场地改造成极具野趣的可食园圃（图2）。

可食景观作为更新触媒的作用在该案例中具有典型性：火车菜园项目通过网络宣传吸引了社区居民和各类社会人士参与营建，从原本的城市废弃地变成人流聚集的实践活动场地和自然教育基地。基于项目的高人气，企业利用周边废弃仓库改造成火车餐厅，食材主要取自

图2 社会人士在企业和设计师组织下营建火车菜园

火车菜园，节省了餐厅运营成本，也构成餐厅的一个吸引点。通过这一系列活动，企业建立起良好的社会形象和知名度，更顺利地进行周边地区的厂房改造创意园区项目，进一步带动了参观游览活动（如牛仔观光火车）的发展。正是可食景观营造激发了一系列社区更新项目，使原本的城市废弃地成为社区活力场所。

此外，火车菜园的肥料来源于周边创意园区产生的垃圾、边角料的堆肥，以草屑进行厚土堆肥，做到社区部分垃圾的自消化，一定程度上也实现了环境层面的可持续发展。

4.3 五角场创智农园

创智农园原本是创智坊社区内一块有些凌乱的公共用地。社区委托设计师进行绿地改造，需紧密贴合居民生活需求。设计师选择实践朴门永续设计理念，将农业与园艺设计相结合，通过营造可食景观推进社区交流和居民参与，融入食安、自然、可持续的生活方式。

项目中，设计师选择将地块分割成 $1m \times 1.2m$ 的菜地单元，并开放认购，由居民自行种植，避免了传统集体可食景观营造出现的产出归属不清等问题，同时降低了投入成本。依托社区菜园这一更新触媒，创智农园拓展了社区小厨房、食农沙龙、研讨会等促进交往的社区营造活动以及农夫集市等产生经济效益的商业活动，促进了社区更新在社会和经济层面的可持续发展。

4.4 小结

集体性可食景观作为新兴社区更新触媒，能有效地促进社区更新，实现社区再活化。但在实际操作过程中，可能出现问题，如：①产出归属不清，集体耕作成果被个人私摘；②大面积种植一种作物，反而导致生态破坏；③居民劳作积极性不高等。文中介绍的案例给出了良好解决方案：菜园模块化分割，明确产出归属；多样化种植，遵循共生原理；体验导向、教育导向，与活动相结合等。

5 触媒理论指导下的可持续更新模式

结合对触媒理论的研究总结和以可食景观为例的更新触媒应用探索,得出触媒理论指导下的社区可持续更新模式:选择更新触媒、更新触媒设计、合作经营与管理维护。

5.1 选择更新触媒

在地性原则——社区更新触媒设置的类型和位置应与社区整体环境相协调,且应具有问题导向、需求导向特性。如上海虹口区本地文化氛围浓厚,现状区内社区的居民中老年人群体占大多数,区内商业配套设施完善,鲁迅公园、和平公园等绿地活动场地较能满足需求,但缺乏面向老年人的文化场所,相关机构部门在需求调研的基础上结合现状绿地、社区中心等设置若干老年大学,定期开展文娱活动,不仅丰富了区内老年人的文化生活,而且成为虹口区对外交流的一张名片,达到从个人到社区的再活化效果。

经济高效原则——社区更新触媒资金来源分政府出资、公众集资和企业赞助三类,产出往往以精神文明层面如社区再活化、社区营造和环境层面如空间品质提升、环境美化等非直接经济收益为主,即使带来土地价值提升和店铺客流量增大等经济收益,也并非都能精准回馈到投资方。因此社区更新不能像城市初期开发大手笔投资并迅速通过售卖、出租等获得资金回笼,更新触媒应追求经济高效,即以最小的投入成本获得最大的经济社会等收益。如同济景观学系刘悦来教授在社区组织的苔藓花园营造活动,将社区照不到阳光的废弃地作为更新触媒设置场地,仅投入非常低的苔藓种子和木板、颜料成本,通过设计师亲力亲为和组织社区居民共同参与,达到了环境美化和社区营造的良好效果。这样的精细化更新触媒正是社区更新值得推广的。

社会公正公平原则——社区更新触媒具有服务性公共产品的属性,应和其他社区公共设施一样遵循社会公正公平原则,表现为:在位置上,更新触媒应处于服务范围能覆盖整个社区的位置,且具有良好的可达性,便于吸引人流;在开放度上,更新触媒应具有开放性、低门槛特征,避免收费项目、高档会所等,关注低收入弱势群体的需求。

5.2 更新触媒设计

各类型更新触媒的设计应符合相应的应用要求,在具体设计上遵循以下原则:①功能联动:触媒功能选择应与周边地块功能协调,联动发展;②功能复合:触媒本身应具备复合化功能,以确保使用人群多元化和全时性的空间利用;③空间多样化:触媒本身应营造丰富的空间体验,以便开展各类型活动,保证空间活力;④可识别性:更新触媒应当突显特色,成为社区的标识;⑤记忆传承:在空间重塑的更新背景下,城市触媒可在功能上还原场所逐渐消失的功能,或是在形态上纪念曾经的场地特色,作为社区居民共同记忆的载体,强化居民认同和归属感。

5.3 合作经营与管理维护

对于社区更新而言,居民、企业、政府等多方共同参与的更新手段是更新触媒有效的实施保障。对于社区居民,按参与度从低到高分别是:被动、调查、协商、交互和共建,在共建式更新过程中,居民不仅能充分表达更新诉求，监督更新过程，更实际参与更新过程中，促进居民交往和社区营造。此外还包括政府（发起者）、设计师（组织者）以及部分更新触媒可能有的投资方等参与者各司其职，政府和设计师尤其应当做好协调工作，使社区居民成为更新主体和受益者。

6 结语

社区作为城市的基本单位在过去 30 年里经历了建设高潮，但几十年的开发建设都属于"一次性开发"，社区在缺乏后期维护的过程中自行发展，逐渐出现空间破败、活力丧失等现象。在此背景下，引入更新触媒将是社区再活化的高效更新途径。本文探讨了城市触媒的内涵及相关研究，并以可食景观营造为例，阐述了更新触媒理论引导下的社区更新模式：从因地制宜选择更新触媒、针对性触媒空间设计到多方参与的实施保障策略。社区更新应积极应用更新触媒，实现经济高效和社区共赢。

Research on Community Sustainable Renewal Based on City Catalyst Theory: A Case of Edible Landscape Construction

Shyu Shyaodao

(College of Architecture and Urban Planning, Tongji University)

Abstract: Select the edible landscape as a community renewal catalyst to study the mode of community renewal based on city catalyst theory. Firstly, based on the current research situation, this paper explains the connotation of renewal catalyst and the necessity of introducing this theory. Then, the definition, function and type of community edible landscape are expounded combined with actual cases, as well as mode of community edible landscape constructing. Finally, we summarize the community renewal mode under the guidance of the catalyst theory: renewal catalyst choosing, the catalyst space design, the cooperative operation, the management and maintenance, and derived renewal community.

Keywords: Renewal catalyst, Community renewal, Community empowerment, Edible landscape

参考文献

[1] 运迎霞，田健. 触媒理论引导下的旧城更新多方共赢模式探索——以衡水市旧城区更新为例 [J]. 城市发展研究，2012，10：60-66.

[2] 孙乐. 历史街区复兴中的"城市触媒"策略研究 [D]. 同济大学，2008.

[3] 罗秋菊，卢仕智. 会展中心对城市房地产的触媒效应研究——以广州国际会展中心为例 [J]. 人文地理，2010，4：45-49+146.

[4] 荣玥芳，徐振明，郭思维. 城市事件触媒理论解读 [J]. 华中建筑，2009，9：79-81+95.

[5] 金广君,刘代云,邱志勇.论城市触媒的内涵与作用——深圳市宝安新中心区城市设计方案解析 [J].城市建筑,2004,1:79-83.

[6] 蒋爱萍,刘连海.可食地景在园林景观中的应用 [J].林业与环境科学,2016,3:98-103.

[7] 刘长安.城市"有农社区"研究 [D].天津大学,2014.

[8] 杨雨璇,杨洁.旧社区改造更新中的场所重塑——以成都市曹家巷社区改造设计为例 [J].安徽农业科学,2012,35:17193-17196.

[9] 任栩辉,刘青林.可食景观的功能与发展 [J].农业科技与信息(现代园林),2015,10:737-746.

[10] 李和平,杨钦然.促进社会融合的中国低收入住区渐进式更新模式——"磁性社区"初探 [J].国际城市规划,2012,2:88-94.

[11] 洪亮平,赵茜.走向社区发展的旧城更新规划——美日旧城更新政策及其对中国的启示 [J].城市发展研究,2013,3:21-24+28.

[12] 叶炜.英国社区自助建设对我国社区更新的启示 [J].规划师,2006,3:61-63.

"城中厂"的紧凑型居住化改造探索：嘉兴市民丰造纸厂、冶金机械厂的改造经验

邝远霄　李振宇

（同济大学建筑与城市规划学院）

摘　要：在中国，城镇工业用地绝大多数来自政府划拨，这些工业用地往往位于城市中心，有些城市甚至依附大型工业集聚地带而建。随着城市发展，城市地价提升，位于城市中心的工业用地变成了"高投入、高能耗、高污染、低效益"的低效用地，"城中厂"这一称呼便应运而生。"城中厂"作为工业场地的一部分，改造前的去工业化操作是必要的；另一方面在中国城市化的过程中，高密度的生活也是不可回避的议题。正如 2011 年 ICOMOS 通过的《都柏林宪章》里所写的那样：在一些地区，工业场所仍然在生产中，工业化尚处于未完成状态。然而在其他区域，工业场所慢慢成为考古学视野中的要素，旨在证明过去的人类活动与记忆。本文借助嘉兴市两个大型"城中厂"改造项目中的规划策略及建筑改造经验，讨论在快速城市化过程中如何协调"城中厂"的改造与再利用，同时对人口集中与老龄化过程中如何营造宜居的高密度社区提出一些思考与见解。

关键词：城中厂，高密度，工业遗产，居住改造

1　引言

截止到 2010 年，中国城市（镇）体系由 287 个地级市、367 个县级市、1636 个县级城镇和 40000 多个建制或非建制镇组成。中国正处于城市化的快速发展阶段，此时大型城市的建设用地规模已经接近极限，反观改革开放 30 年来的城市建设发展，消费资源式的粗犷发展早已备受指责。[1] 土地资源是社会、经济发展的重要载体，社会和经济发展在很大程度上依赖建设用地增长。而当一个国家或地区发展到一定程度后，都会采取一定的措施，控制建设用地过度增长，优化用地结构[2]。在社会各界力量的推动下，上海市规土局正式发布《上海市城市总体规划（2015～2040）纲要概要》，首次完整披露上海未来 20 年发展目标。其中，规划确定了三个底线约束。最主要是建设用地总量控制在 3200km^2 以内（2014 年已达 3100km^2）。[3] 随着城市逐步转型，当年重要的工业区域逐步变为城市中心区域，使得新经济结构下的城市用地结构不合理：截至 2014 年，上海市集建区外建设用地 780km^2，其中工矿仓储用地 202km^2，农村宅基地 327km^2，约 400km^2 为低效建设用地。新型经济结构下的城市中如果工业用地占比过大，将影响城市土地收益率，阻碍城市发展；"城中厂"与居住区的混杂是那个时代不可避免的，现在由于工业建筑的破旧，工业生产退出，导致环境质量降低，这将影响城市核心地带的价值。针对上述情况，新一轮总体规划将旧城工业用地的改造退出问题放在重要位置。

当超级大城市的人口聚集成为必须理解的现状时，规划师与建筑师应该正视这一其他国家不曾体会过的状况，高密度居住环境下的老龄化、社区精神等问题就成为我们不断探索的方向与目标。本文即从这一角度出发，总结在实际工作中的经验，对利用"城中厂"营造高密度社区这一话题提出自己的见解。

2 "城中厂"相关问题辨析

"城中厂"这一称呼是"城市棕地"的中国化称呼,"棕地"源于英文"Brownfield",这一词语至今没有明确定义,但是囊括工业用地之上的建筑等物质化要素。如今,"城中厂"不仅因为土地上矗立的建筑,还因为存在过的生产关系而受到人们关注,这样的场地往往被称作工业遗存。2011年第17届ICOMOS大会通过的《都柏林宪章》中提到工业遗存由场地、结构、范围和地景以及相关的机械装置、能证明以前或者仍在进行工业化进程的物件以及文本、原材料的提取物、原料转化后的产品、相关的能量及物质转运基础设施所构成。[4]《都柏林宪章》中对于工业遗产的关注不仅仅限于其物质性成分。工业遗产的重要性与价值存在于场地与结构自身的本质状态中,而工业遗产的材料构成、组成、机械装置配置则在工业的地景,以及无形的记忆、艺术和习俗上得以表达。

"城中厂"由于历史、政治及经济等各方面原因常常分布在城市内的"黄金地带",具有良好的基础设施和地理区位优势。造成这种状况的第一个原因是运输,早期的城市对于工业依赖深重,而工业开发对原材料的输入需求非常大,同时对成品的输出需求也很大,造成了工业对于水运的依赖,也成就了"城中厂"沿河靠岸的性质。观察上海的"城中厂"分布可以得出这样的结论,大多数"城中厂"聚集在沿河地带。[5]第二个原因便是行政要素,上海早期的工业发展几乎与租界的进驻同步,工厂常常分布在租界的边缘,那里地价较为低廉,同时能借助租界的优势甚至保护。第三个原因与生产相关,这类"城中厂"基于家庭甚至社区进行小作坊式轻工业生产,产品多为电池、纽扣等日用品,工人来自社区,于是这类"城中厂"与社区有良好的联系,也成为场所精神的重要组成部分。在这三个因素的作用下,"城中厂"在城市的分布常常有很多固定的元素,而随着城市的急剧扩张,原来位于相对边缘的工厂也获得了相对中心的地带,前面提到的沿河靠岸、租界边缘、联系住区就成为现今的商业与办公的黄金地带标准。在对这样的"城中厂"进行再开发的时候,开发商在基础设施建设方面可以节约部分成本,良好的区位优势又能吸引商业。从另外一个角度讲,为控制城市过度平面发展,政府鼓励新增建设用地尽可能使用城市建成区内的土地。"城中厂"再开发符合政府土地管理政策原则,将获得政府政策支持补贴。

上海是全国首个也是唯一一个在省级层面提出全域建设用地减量化的区域。工业用地减量化即是去除低效用地,增加发展空间;削减淘汰落后产能,优化产业结构;降低污染状况,提升环境品质。2013年,上海市规土局《关于印发<郊野单元规划编制审批和管理若干意见(试行)>的通知》,对集建区外的现状零星农村建设用地、低效工业用地等进行减量。然而由于中国工业划拨用地转性等各方面法律法规要素的限制,"城中厂"全面的重生需要假以时日,当前上海的"城中厂"改造以创意产业园为主。创意产业园式的改造在土地转性的过程中出现各种灰色产权,这种模式实际上是违法的,这样的改造模式也逐渐在市场的推动下显示出自己的弊端:特定城市对于创意产业园的需求是有限的,因此主动创造"城中厂"的其他开发模式是一个必然选择。

在所有的改造方向中,"城中厂"改居住将会受到各方面因素制约。"城中厂"的土地污染程度存在大量差异,治理标准不明确,治理结果难控制。同时,工业用地在划拨的时候低价与产权关系是当时时代的产物,这导致了土地转性过程中的模糊产权,也带来巨大的成本。因此,中国土地转性的结果往往远超原土地的容积率,如果成为居住项目,则将从客观上导致高密度社区。

3　从"城中厂"到紧凑城市

皮特·钮万（Peter·Newman）和杰佛里·肯尼思（Jeffrey·Kenworth）曾绘制了一张精彩的能量－人口密度图表，从这张图出发，二人提出了精辟的"紧凑城市（Compact City）"理念。[6]"紧凑城市"作为一种城市发展模式是对北美为主的摊大饼式城市的批判，其重要的体现便是以香港为代表的高密度的亚洲城市。

面对亚洲独一无二的城市化进程中的各种复杂问题，"紧凑城市"是一个很好地回答了亚洲城市共同面对的人多地少问题的模式。在农村人口持续涌入城市的状况下，"城中厂"作为城市中现今存在的大量已建设区域，将其作为紧凑城市营造的基础拥有大量优势。如果能解决好诸如"去工业化"之类的问题，将能获得很好的收益。

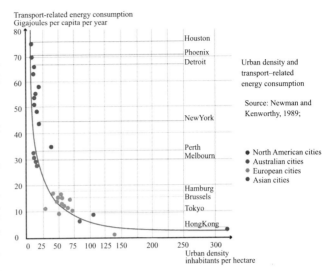

图1　能量－人口密度图表

3.1　Vertical city Asia 2014（Bombay India）

孟买是印度各种意义上的中心，不仅为印度贡献了大量的GDP，而且大约10%的工业坐落于此，为人们提供了大量的就业机会，约25%的工业产品也出自孟买。虽然孟买的IT业等其他行业的发展迅猛，而且是印度不可替代的金融中心，但都市区域仍然体会着经济结构转型的苦难。随着港口优势的退化，工业型基础设施变成了城市的包袱，尽管城市规划了以滨海区景观再造为核心的城市再开发计划，现存的大型工业用地仍然在阻碍着滨海区域与城市中心的联系，东部滩涂区域是现在十几个重度工业污染区和重工业工厂所在，它们是上文提到的"城中厂"。为了完成改造更新的目标，参赛团队希望借助原有的生态系统重构整个城市的肌理。结果将会由现存的、为工业服务的大尺度建筑肌理与街道形态转变成一个生态宜居的新景观。

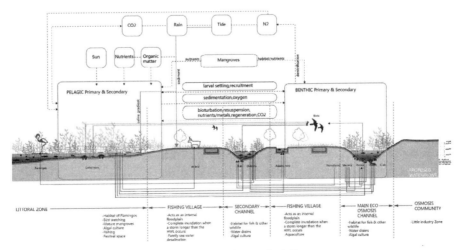

图2　场地去工业化过程

在这个语境下，同济大学参赛团队提出以家庭尺度的产业模式来连接现在的城市中心与"城中厂"。首先，家庭尺度的产业模式恰恰是在贴近自然生产属性的同时，适宜现行多重交通系统的；其次，这一产业结构是孟买当地人所熟知的，也具有与现状的延续性；最后，这种模式是参赛团队希望在整个方案中强调的一种在"生活－工作"状态中的经济单元。家庭尺度手工业因其弥散的形态与渐进式发展的特性，会重新定义城市结构，同时城市中其他基础设施围绕家庭小产业发展而最终与其融合在一起，成为参赛团队所提出的 2050 年孟买的"渗透性城市"。"渗透性城市"即是一种发展的模式，这种模式强调高密度，强调家庭小尺度，强调自发性产业的诞生，同时通过一系列城市网络组织破碎化的工业场地。

在整个竞赛文本中，我们能看到参赛团队对于"城中厂"的高度重视，没有将之视作洪水猛兽完全去除。取舍之中，去除的是落后的工业生产带来的生态环境及地景地貌改变，保留的是"城中厂"这一模式的家庭小产业生产关系。深深扎根于当地在家庭血缘关系基础上的社会结构，使得这一生产关系成为稳定高密度社区的重要基础[7]（亚洲垂直城市竞赛由新加坡国立大学主办，2014 年同济大学参赛团队在王桢栋及董屹老师的带领下获得一等奖）。

3.2 嘉兴民丰造纸厂、冶金机械厂的改造经验

嘉兴市地处浙江省东北部，处在长江三角洲地区杭嘉湖平原的核心地带，是长江三角洲地区重要城市之一。民丰造纸厂及冶金机械厂位于甪里街以北，甪里街位于嘉兴市中心城区东部，南临南湖，西接嘉兴市火车站，东接 S07 省道。甪里街沿线分布有嘉兴市诸多工业建筑，嘉兴工业历史上著名的绢纺厂、冶金厂、造纸厂等工厂均位于甪里街沿线或附近。项目基地占地面积 89.6hm^2，以东塔路为界，西侧为民丰造纸厂，东侧为嘉兴冶金机械厂。作为一座以水而兴的历史文化名城，项目基地所涵盖的街区是较为完整的工业遗产待更新区。基地民丰造纸厂内的历史建筑有：老造纸车间等 10 幢建于 20 世纪 80 年代以前的老厂房、民丰会堂、3 幢民北宿舍楼；基地嘉兴冶金机械厂内的历史建筑有：9 幢建于 20 世纪 60 年代以前的老厂房，平湖塘以南、民丰宿舍楼东侧的 3 幢嘉冶职工宿舍楼。整个冶金机械厂与造纸厂宛如中国那个时代工业与城市关系的博物馆，里面纷繁复杂的空间关系至今诉说着当年全民生产的盛况。

在整个冶金机械厂和民丰造纸厂的改造计划中，建筑设计与规划设计最关注的莫过于如何通过设计延续固有的工业区的格局（这是场所精神的重要体现），同时对建筑本体进行改造使之符合不同的使用要求（这是高密度的社区不可或缺的）。在目标引导下设计团队提出了三个方向：生态型高密度住区、存续工业遗产与可持续的城市更新、"城中厂"更新的建筑类型学探索。针对以上关注点，设计团队提出四个设计目标：

第一是针对空间的，这类目标旨在保护原有工业肌理及单体建筑，通过设计，尊重原有工业区域的肌理，同时梳理其江南水乡的历史地景。在这一设计目标中，如何平衡原工业厂区的大尺度空间与高密度社区中的小尺度甚至步行尺度空间是难点；第二是针对历史的，正如上文提到的，工业时代的记忆由各种工业元素与特定空间承载，如何展示这片场地上的历史元素并以此塑造新的建筑氛围是历史类的难点；第三是针对生态的，在研究了各种生态技术之后，设计团队决定以老城区 LID 技术作为支点，探索"城中厂"遗留地的改善方案，在此基础上需要平衡高密度社区高程与原场地高程的限制；第四是社区类的，现行场地上人口结构不尽合理，社会住宅资源分配失调。设计团队努力调节经济适用型住房（回迁房）与高档住宅之间的配比，植入并探索社区养老的老年公寓、青年公寓及 SOHO 办公等多种住宅形式，利用工业厂房的尺度优势将它们改建为具备社区文化活动中心、市场、商店乃至运动场等各种功能，以此回应高密度的社区营造。

设计中 LID 系统的构建是基于原工业厂区工业用河流的，这些河流本来就是江南水乡的遗存，顺

应地形优势建立更多明暗运河穿插城市之中链接自然水系统与人造水系统。这些水系统将划分城市的框架，以此为基础建立生态湿地系统。在小型单元层面（pocket park）、社区绿地层面、大范围水系层面均建立 LID 系统，以此作为海绵城市的基础，优化城市可持续状态。

工业建筑遗产保护强调的是建筑遗产的各方面价值，而"城中厂"再开发着眼于污染物的处理。在冶金机械厂项目中，设计团队着重于"城中厂"的功能转换，这是老建筑的遗产价值利用；另一方面，虽然以社区为核心，却着眼于城市公共空间的营造，以小尺度街巷路网，构建开放街区。在污水池改造的棕地公园中，设计团队将棕地公园与现有道路水系链接成一个整体，同时链接周围社区配套教育文化设施包括博物馆、多媒体展览和观景平台等，这是城市棕地的污染处理手段的延续。

图 3　项目总平

图 4　LID 系统

对于"城中厂"外观的改造，则首先需要对老旧建筑做出分类评估，需要意识到保留老建筑不仅需要考虑风格问题，还有经济问题的考量。优秀的老建筑原样保留，还有的拆掉改造，但是整个过程保护了原来的文脉肌理。在改建成为居住功能的"城中厂"建筑中设计团队采取七大建筑对策：一、组，新元素与旧元素整合一体，表面冲撞，结构独立，利用工业厂房的独特美学价值，同时为营造高密度社区打下基础，充分尊重"城中厂"的原真性。二、挖，保留"城中厂"的结构框架与立面元素，拆除内部分隔墙甚至楼板。充分利用大尺度工业空间，划分为小尺度的社区空间，并充分利用既有建筑成模数的桁架结构体系。三、贴，新元素与旧元素贴合而建，在街道尺度感与人行视线方向上采用远高近低的手法，使得老建筑不被削弱。在此基础上考虑新旧建筑在功能上的呼应，形成统一整体。四、围，对于特征明显，十分优秀的建筑物采取全面保护，在新旧建筑中穿插联系。保留标志性建筑的显著制高，同时利用这一高处优势作为周边建筑纵向交通功能，物尽其用。五、拆，这部分老厂房需要拆除部分屋顶或立面，以此塑造新的室外空间。这样的手法可以保护现有建筑体量，保护城市界面的完整，亦即保护历史街区的特征。六、插，旧建筑中形成"楼中楼"的格局，插入一个完整的体量，用强烈的材质对比强调不同的时代特征。七、植，保留既有建筑的框架和部分外立面，水平方向植入符合新功能的建筑体块，将老建筑掏空的空间作为室外活动区。

4　结论

许多亚洲城市将高容积率、垂直发展的模式作为限制城市过度扩张的方法，这种模式的优势是为居民创造更加有活力的居所；引入多样性的适当的产业，改善就业状况，提升城市活力。以香港为代表的亚洲高密度垂直城市的发展模式，提供了基于城市活力视野下全新的城市发展理念。在这里，原有场地上的社会关系，生产关系紧凑的城市结构中必要的联系纽带。我们用城市活力的营造审视"城中厂"这一人类工业时代的遗存，发现它不仅是工业时代的产品，也成为工业时代的城市基因。

环顾世界，我们发现还有伦敦巴特西发电站这样的改造案例，虽然这只是一个个案并且有极为深刻的甲方背景，同时不可避免地会有诸如"社会阶层如何和谐相处"这样的问题存在，然而这也预示着"城中厂"的确有不可估量的潜力。我们同样可以看到，由上钢十厂改造而成的"红坊"被再次改造成商业区域，许多案例说明现有的"城中厂"改创意产业园的思路存在问题。在未来，随着大城市建设用地逐渐接近规模极限，"城中厂"在城市中的利用价值将更多地被人们发觉，如何利用"城中厂"的场所要素营造一片适宜人类生活的高密度社区，将是我们不断探索的重点。

致谢

本篇论文的写作由国家自然科学基金项目《长三角地区"城中厂"的社区化更新技术体系研究》资助（项目编号：51678412）。

The Re-habitation of Town Factories and the Construction of High Density Life: the Experience on the Regeneration of Jiaxing Min Feng Paper Factory and Machinery Factory

Kuang Yuanxiao, Li Zhenyu

(College of Architecture and Urban Planning, Tongji University)

Abstract: In China, industrial land is mainly allocated by the government, industrial sites are always located in city center due to several reasons. With the development of city, these industrial lands become of low efficiency, that's basically how these lands become "town factories". For these lands deindustrialization shall be treated properly. On the other hand, with the increasing of urban population, high-density living has become an inevitable topic. Just like what is written on the Joint ICOMOS – TICCIH Principles for the Conservation of Industrial Heritage Sites, Structures, Areas and Landscapes ("The Dublin Principles"), in many places, this heritage is still in use and industrialization is still an active process with a sense of historical continuity, while in other places it offers archaeological evidence of past activities and technologies. How to reuse the town factories and how to create a comfortable high-density residential area in the irreversible population increase and aging process are two correlated issues. This article proposes some thoughts and ideas on these issues based on the experience in the transformation project of Min Feng metallurgical machinery factory and paper mill.

Keywords: Town factories, High-density, Industrial heritage, Residential transformation

参考文献

[1] 孟鹏."经济新常态下土地利用方式转变与建设用地减量化"研讨会在沪召开. http://www.chinalandscience.com.cn/UserFiles/File/shanghaijianlanghua.pdf,2015-10-23/2015-12-03.

[2] 李辉,王良健. 土地资源配置的效率损失与优化途径 [J]. 中国土地科学,2015,29(7):63-72.

[3] 上海市规划和国土资源管理局. 上海市城市总体规划(2015～2040)纲要概要,2015.

[4] ICOMOS. The Dublin Principles. Adopted by the 17th ICOMOS General Assembly,2011.

[5] 黄琪. 上海近代工业建筑保护和再利用 [D]. 同济大学博士论文,2007,37.

[6] (美)爱德华·格莱泽,刘润泉. 城市的胜利 [M]. 上海:上海社会科学院出版社,2012,12:42.

[7] 王桢栋,文凡,陈蕊. 紧密城市基于越南河内的亚洲垂直城市模式思考 [J]. 时代建筑,2014,4:148.

基于领域行为理论的既有住区公共空间改造研究：以苏州为例

胡 莹 汪文韬

（苏州科技大学）

摘 要：近年来，中国快速发展的城市化进程，导致城市人口的骤增。原有老住区的社会交往和良好社区生态随着人口结构的变化而被打破。本文选择苏州典型的老旧住区为研究对象，通过行为观察、居民走访的方式对公共空间的使用状况进行调研，了解在人口结构发生变化以后，公共空间使用中存在的问题。同时运用"领域行为"理论，分析其隐藏在背后的原因。针对这些原因，文章最后提出公共空间混合利用与公共空间领域划分相结合的方法，并针对既有住区得出改造设计策略，旨在提升交往水平、社区公共生活水平以及居民的归属感，达到多元文化共生的目的。

关键词：公共空间，人口结构，苏州

1 领域的研究

1.1 领域的概念

领域在生物学概念中是一种被动物所占有和保卫的空间，这种空间通常具有占有者所需要的资源，这些资源是占有者占有及保护该领域的原因，而占有者在领域中对该领域进行占有和保卫等行为就是领域行为。在建筑上来说，领域可以是一栋别墅，也可以是整个城市。不论领域的大小和领域占有者的多少，领域行为都是普遍存在的。根据奥尔特曼发现，领域的基本分类有三个，主要领域、次要领域和公共领域。主要领域是一个被个人或群体长期拥有且难以动摇、最重要的领域。次要领域的重要程度不及主要领域，但是依旧对个体或群体在生活中有着一定的影响。重要的是，个体或群体对该领域的使用性大于占有性，次要领域的可变性较大，会出现轮换，分享等占有权变化。公共领域则如字面意思，是一个公共使用的领域，领域中的使用者可能对该领域本身没有占有权，但所有符合该领域使用要求的个体或群体都具有使用权，比如公园等。

1.2 苏州既有住区的情况

苏州自20世纪70年代起迫于人口、交通、环境等问题，在古城区及周围修建了大量的住宅楼，在当时看来，这些住区居住形态还算较好。随着时代的发展，既有住区建造时间较早、缺乏严谨的设计等情况引发了诸多问题，其中较为突出的，停车空间不足、公共空间缺乏、环境景观破坏等。同样变化的还有其中的居民，在快速城市化的背景之下，来自农村、外地的流动人口涌入城市之中，由于经济等条件的制约，既有住区成为这些人口居住的首选。外来人口与原住居民存在生活和文化上的差异，对原有的社会交往和社区生态都产生了不同程度破坏。既有住区出现了许多社会问题，居民的社区意识淡漠，邻里衰落和邻里交往危机日益严重。现在既有住区的空间环境早已经不能满足住户的生活要求，这些仅有的公共资源也成为居民争夺的对象。

1.3 住区居民的领域

1.3.1 居民对住区领域的划分

与自身财产相关的空间都视为其主要领域，不论其是否对这个空间具有严格意义上的占有权。主要包括住房和车库以及其周围部分空间等，一楼的住户通常有自己的小型院落以及与其他住户独立分开的单独出入口，他们还会将这个出入口周围的部分空间视为自己的主要领域。有的住户也会私自将一些公共空间视为其主要领域。

除主要领域之外，居民们通过与自身主要领域的距离区分其次要领域和公共领域，将住宅楼中的楼梯走道空间、住宅出入口空间、住宅楼周围的部分空间视为次要领域。通常包括住宅楼旁的桌椅休息空间、机动车或非机动车的临时或公用停车空间、住宅楼旁的绿化空间和其他空间。

对于同一住区的居民而已，他们对于公共领域的划分都相类似，将住区中较大的广场空间、集中活动空间、绿化空间和其他空间视为公共领域。

1.3.2 居民对领域需求

通过居民对领域的划分，不难看出居民对于领域的需求，这些需求都体现着居民的对住区公共空间现在使用情况的满意程度，以及他们理想中的住区公共空间。

（1）交往的心理需求

网络时代，人们对于交往逐渐冷漠，但人的生活始终离不开与他人交往。长时间在家的老人和小孩，他们需要一个交流玩耍的空间，工作一天的父母也希望与家人在住区中散步，正在奋斗的青年下班后在住区中寻找休憩之地，他们对于领域的心理需求都体现在能够交往和放松心情等方面（图1）。居民需要住区公共空间为他们提供进行日常交流的场地，希望这片场地能够成为居民固定的领域，而领域中也应包含满足交流行为的桌子、座椅、遮阳避雨设施等资源。居民在这个领域中进行交往，并形成一致性的群体。在居民相互交往中能够形成固定的人际关系，也能在一定程度上加强住区的安全性。

图1　交往的需求（作者自摄）

（2）运动的生理需求

随着时代的发展，科技的进步，人们越来越关注自身的健康问题，工作、家庭等各方面的压力，也需要用各种方式来释放（图2）。从年轻人的运动手环到老年人的养生之道，都体现着他们需要运动以及运动场地的诉求，住区公共空间中应当包含这些场所。居民需要住区公共空间中用来运动健身的场地，同样这片场地能够促成一个固定领域，领域中包含固定的活动设施场地以及穿梭在住区中的运动步道。居民在这个领域共同进行运动，相互陪同，相互督促，形成一致性的群体。

（3）私人空间扩大的需求

很多既有住区人口密度大，人均占有的空间较少，居民希望增加自己的主要领域和次要领域（图3）。但是每增加一点空间，就对他人的次要领域和公共领域进行侵犯，这是一种不正当的需求。

综上所述，居民需要能够进行交往的领域和能够运动的领域，也有希望增加自己的私有领域的需求。改善住区中的公共空间能够满足居民正当的领域需求，通过其他领域的形成也能削弱居民的对次要及公共领域私有化的不正当需求。

图2 运动的需求（网络）

图3 私人空间扩大的需求（作者自摄）

2 领域行为的研究

2.1 领域行为的概念

人们的领域行为主要有两种，也即侵犯和保护，这两种行为又各自具有几种形式。但是领域行为的褒贬与它的形式无关，侵犯行为可能产生积极的影响，保护行为也可能对领域产生问题。

侵犯的第一种形式是入侵，入侵的目的是夺取领域原有使用者的占有权，使得原使用者丧失对领域的控制，入侵发生在主要领域之中。侵犯的第二种形式是侵害，这种形式的最终目的不是使用者的占有权，而是为了获得领域的某些资源或者为了满足侵害者的某些需求，也可能是让领域中的某些使用者丧失使用权，例如偷盗行为，破坏行为等，侵犯的第三种形式是污染，这种形式通常是不具有占有权的领域使用者在暂时或永久丧失领域使用权时对领域遗留下的不利影响及因素，比如在离开公园后留下的垃圾，弄脏公共厕所的环境等。

领域的保护行为也有几种不同的形式。预防是对可能预知的侵犯行为经行提前的保护措施，比如建立围墙，树立静止标志等行为，希望能在受到侵犯之前能够加以制止。但是预防的作用有限，也无法预防未知的事情，所以保护行为的另外一种形式就是反击，对领域的侵犯者的侵犯行为作出反应。反击伴随着侵犯而出现，没有侵犯也不会有反击。另外领域的占有者对领域的使用者有一些要求或使用要求，对领域边界进行保护，比如会员制、安检等。

2.2 居民在公共空间的领域行为

2.2.1 居民的侵犯行为

侵害行为是居民侵犯行为的主要行为，而居民对于领域的侵害行为通常来自对私人空间扩大的需求，这些需求使得他们通过侵害行为对他人的次要以及公共领域的资源进行占有。有的住户在自己住宅楼边的公共空间中自己搭建私人构筑物或堆砌私人物品形成围合空间供自己使用，有的住户将住宅楼旁的绿地私自改为私人种植地，有的住户将车辆私自停放在活动场地或住区道路上，这些行为都是为了个人利益侵犯整个住区居民的领域（图4）。

在有限的公共空间使用中，不同的使用群体对于同一片场地使用方式不同，也是主要发生侵害行为的情况之一。幼年群体喜欢在场地上进行追逐玩耍，青年群体也有滑板、轮滑等运动的需求，中老年群体喜欢在动感的音乐之下跳广场舞，养宠物的群体也需要一片活动的区域。这些不同的使用人群有各自领域，但在领域对于领域的边界划分或是场地的轮流使用通常得不到合理的分配，进而在有意和无意之中产生侵害行为，占有其他领域的资源。

污染行为虽然没有直接侵害他人的领域，但对他人的领域产生很多不利的影响。如在声音方面，公共空间中进行休憩行为的居民，经常受到附近其他领域正在活动的声音干扰。当活动场地的人群进行交换时，前一个活动的群体产生的垃圾也会影响接下来使用者。随着领域资源不断被消耗，活动设施不断被使用，

图 4　公共空间的侵害行为（作者自摄）

它的损坏情况也日益严重，每一个使用者都在有意无意地损耗设施的耐久性，对下一个使用者不利。

2.2.2　居民的保护行为

居民的保护行为并不一定是正当的行为，有褒贬的情况，有时保护行为的进行甚至是为了满足其侵害行为。在公共空间中，居民为了防止他人的侵犯行为，对自己的领域搭建围墙或篱笆等围合构筑，搭建障碍阻止侵犯领域的停车行为。反击行为在公共空间中更像是报复，在其他群体侵犯领域之后，对侵犯的群体作出回应，这类回应通常对领域保护起不到正向的效果，反而会加重不同领域人群的矛盾。居民的领域保护行为主要特点是无论自身所在的领域是否合理，都对领域进行保护。在公共空间中营造合适的领域能够减少领域群体在领域边界的矛盾，对于资源的合理分配能够减少侵犯行为，从而减少保护行为。

图 5　公共空间的保护行为（作者自摄）

如图 5 所示，在停满汽车的道路旁边用遮阳帐篷和桌椅组成的交流空间是居民的一个重要的交往场所，通过帐篷和周围的石块将这个空间保护起来，防止被占用。

2.3　影响居民领域行为的因素

2.3.1　个人因素

不同的年龄、性别、性格等方面都会影响居民在领域中的行为。男性居民对于领域的范围的要求比女性更大，男性居多的群体在公共空间中的活动通常会占有较大的空间，从而在空间的分配中产生更多的领域行为。老年人由于行动不便以及思想保护等因素，在领域中占有的范围通常较小，青年和幼年的活动群体精力旺盛，思想跳跃，对领域范围的需求较大。当他们在同一时间进行活动时容易产生领域行为。

2.3.2 环境因素

公共空间的大小对居民领域行为有较大的影响，当原本可分配的空间充足时，不同的使用群体为资源的竞争较少，活动场地较大时，不同的活动人群也不易发生争夺场地的冲突。当场地资源较少时，居民会进行各种保护行为来防止自己的领域被侵害，在领域边界筑起不可逾越的围墙来保证自己的领域活动空间，进行不同活动的群体会对其他群体进行侵犯来获得更多的资源。

2.3.3 文化因素

苏州古城区及周围既有住区，有着地理位置优越、房价相对较低的优势，吸引了许多外来人口，从而使得这些住区的人口结构更为复杂。不同地区的文化差异较大，对住区中的领域带来了冲击。如苏州本地居民的领域意识普遍较强，会主动预防来自其他群体的领域侵犯行为。外来人口对于空间的需求更大，相互之间的领域进行侵犯行为更多。对于领域的概念划分也会各有不同，影响侵犯领域时候作出的反应。

3 结论

3.1 公共空间中领域的作用

领域可以组织人的行为，处于同一个领域中的人，有着相似的特征或相同的目的，因为特征相似而行为相同，抑或为了达到相同的目的而行为相同。当居民通过交往相互熟识之后，他们在公共空间中的行为也会更加接近，从而避免个人与个人之间的使用冲突。同样为了运动而出现在健身场地中的居民，用相类似的行为方式使用场地，使得场地的分配更加和谐。领域使得相似行为的人聚在一起，成为这个领域的内部人员，产生一致的领域行为，使得这个领域变得井井有条。在氛围良好的领域中，居民的行为也更加友善，形成一个良性循环。最终通过领域的组织领导来自不同领域的人群也会相互理解和沟通达到和谐的地步。

3.2 解决办法

根据上文的研究，住区的居民依照自己对领域划分的不同，为了争夺公共空间资源而产生领域行为，而这些领域行为就是住区中居民在公共空间使用方面的主要冲突和矛盾。不同的性格、环境和文化都会对领域行为产生影响。只有通过设计手段在公共空间中创造领域，利用领域来引导群体的行为，才能解决住区中所遇到的问题。

A Study on the Transformation of Public Space in Existing Residential Area Based on the Theory of Field Behavior: Taking Suzhou as An Example

Hu Ying, Wang Wentao

(Suzhou University of Science and Technology)

Abstract: In recent years, the rapid development of China's urbanization process, leading to a rapid increase in urban population. The social interaction and the good ecological environment of the old residential areas were broken with the change of population structure. This paper chooses Suzhou typical old residential area as the research object, and surveys public spare usage through the way of behavioral observation and visiting residents, after understanding the changes of the population structure, there are problems in the use of public space. At the same time, it uses the theory of "field behavior" to analyze the reasons behind it. For these reasons, the article finally proposes method of mixed use of public space and public space domain division combination, and according to the existing settlements that design strategy, aims to enhance the communication level, the community public life level and their sense of belonging, to achieve the multicultural symbiosis.

Keywords: Pubic space, Population structure, Suzhou

参考文献

[1] 吉福德. 什么是领域行为?[J]. 力文译. 国外社会科学文摘, 1990.

[2] 郑颖, 谷口元. 从领域性研究的视角论"公"、"私"空间的边界[J]. 建筑学报, 2011.

[3] (美) Paul A B, Thomas C G, Jeffrey D F. 环境心理学 (第 5 版) [M]. 朱建军, 吴建平译. 北京: 中国人民大学出版社, 2009.

语用思维下长影旧址街区的保护与更新

刘 岩 高雁鹏 付艳华 刘生军

（东北大学）

摘 要：书写百年影视传奇，传承千年民族文化。如今的长影如同经过涅槃般重生，与过去10年相比，今日的长影吸引了更多人的关注。而其周边街区的建筑群落，呈现参差不齐的建筑环境现状。各区域的建筑虽与长影旧址毗邻，却缺少与长影相协调的感觉。每个区域风格迥异，将各个区域与长影产生关联性，成为重兴长影旧址活力的必然趋势。长影的特定历史背景使长影具有独有的风情韵味，运用独有的特质，将长影保护与更新成为一处独一无二的影视文化街区。语用思维来自方法论，多运用于哲学，将其运用在保护与更新长影旧址街区中，是因为此方法异于其他方法，是一种从特殊环境中寻找特殊风格的方法，正与本次的保护与更新意图相辅相成。语用思维属于规划学科研究的一个创新思维，此方法前人实少运用，大胆将此方法运用在长影旧址街区的保护与更新中，必将产生前所未有的突破性研究成果。结果认为：通过对长影旧址街区的建筑、道路、景观、设施等进行保护与更新，可以形成一个活力十足的长影旧址街区。

关键词：文脉保护，语用思维，长影旧址街区

1 引言

"长春电影制片厂旧址早期建筑"作为第七批全国重点文物保护单位，不仅仅是"新中国电影的摇篮"，同时也是日本军国主义对中国"文化侵略"的历史见证。流转70年的光影声色的长春电影制片厂旧址，其建筑的保护与再利用，其给人记忆中留下的场所、领域感及文化特征，归落于语用维度上情景与脉络要素上的科学诠释。当具有强烈暗示的历史认同感的长影旧址，身处在文化整体复兴的时代背景下，研究历史文化空间脉络，唤回城市原有特色与地方认同感，成为最具必要性的研究方向。长春旧址街区的尺度使公共空间中脉络暗示和认同感成为保护和更新的重点。注入城市人文情怀的长影旧址的文脉延续，不仅依靠对实体的物质环境保护，更重要的是保护其范围内人们曾经真实的生活文化，张扬传统的文脉和价值观念，在下文中，笔写将详细介绍基于语用思维下，长影旧址街区各区域的保护与更新研究成果。

2 研究背景与目的

随时代进程的不断发展，长影昔日的荣光都已褪去。长春发展形成了长影旧址接近长春市中心红旗街商业圈的现状，这种结构成为长春建设和发展的长影历史文化的受阻点。长影具有强烈文脉传承作用，如何在适应城市发展的同时，有效地完成长影旧址街区的保护和更新，成为此次研究的思考点。虽然全面严苛保护方式在最大限度保护了建筑遗存，但这种毫无推陈出新的陈列只能让建筑遗产成为只可远观而缺乏活力的一种相对消极的存在。对具有文脉传承价值的历史建筑，进行多种形式的合理性利用与再开发，不但可以维系城市历史意向的连续性，还能将建筑遗存再次融合到充满生机与活力

的日常文化生活中。所以从语用思维的维度上，结合长影旧址街区现状，对长影旧址街区形成合理的保护和更新建设意见，激发出街区的潜在活力，是本文研究的目的。

3 研究方法与步骤

在广泛阅读和学习历史文化保护与更新相关理论和案例的基础上，综合运用详细描述法（亦称专家学派）、公众偏好法（亦称心理学派、认知学派）和综合法（亦称心理物理学派）的方法开展研究，具体的研究步骤如下：

（1）运用心理物理学派的方法，请人画心智地图，了解人们心目中的长影的图像。

（2）运用专家学派的方法，请没有来过长影旧址的朋友、同学作为专家，对长影旧址2014年重新开放前后的两组长影旧址照片进行选择和评价。

（3）运用公众偏好法，设计调查问卷对游客和居民进行现场调查和访谈，了解他们的意愿和感受。

（4）在语用思维的维度，对以上三方面的调查结果进行总结、分析、研究，得出初步结论，提出改善措施和建议。

4 基于语用思维维度的研究分析

4.1 受访人群分析

我们于2016年4月2日至4日开展了问卷调查工作，发放并收回有效问卷共158份，其中现场调查访谈110份，网上调查48份。158份问卷中来过长影旧址街区的83人，未来过的75人；年龄主要集中于19～40岁之间，有116人；学历以本科居多，有76人；现场调查问卷发放主要面向长影旧址街区本地居民及活动在长影旧址街区的行人（图1）。

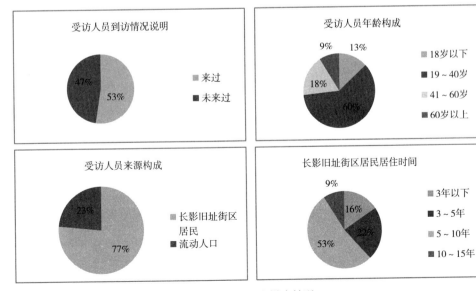

图1　问卷调查样本情况

4.2 语用思维分析

我们请了几位未来过长影旧址的高一学生根据自己脑海中的意象，写出四个他们心中最能体现长影旧址街区的词语，经过分析可以得出，电影影片、电影院、广场、商铺是他们对这个地区的共同意象。由此证明，由于长影自身的历史积淀及其文化传承，在人们心中已经形成了独特的印象，运用语用思维，这种否定一般化，切入特定时间，从特殊结构来寻找特殊意义与关系的研究方式，可以使长影旧址街区的文化价值和场所文脉得到有效的保护和更新。

强调长影旧址自身固有的文化背景、理解能力、个性特质及其信仰，强调了科学诠释的语境、强调长影旧址街区的主体性作用。语用思维是一种真正具有本土性、实践性的和可持续品质的城市设计思维方式。对语用思维的重视让人们意识到空间环境中情境与脉络的重要作用。语用思维与长影旧址街区的保护与更新的融合，使情境与脉络阐明事件，长影的意义在一定程度上能够根据脉络通过语用来解释。在不同的保护与更新要素中，人们的注意力首先被具有特质的要素所吸引，因为这些要素强烈暗示着他们所具有的特殊意义，而这些特殊意义最为本真的表现方式即是具有强烈本土性的语用。语用思维下对长影旧址街区的保护与更新可以归落于建筑、道路、景观、设施等方面。

5 基于语用思维下，多维度进行保护与更新的研究分析

本文对长影旧址街区的范围界定，如图 2 所示。以电影制片厂现实状况为重要依据，主要考虑建筑质量，道路质量，景观质量，设施质量四个方面现状条件，综合其环境与功能等特点加以确定长影旧址街区的范围。范围东北以同德路为界，东南以湖西路东胡同和建昌界连接成边界，西南以长久路为界，西北以红旗街为界。该范围内主要分布了长春电影制片厂旧址、长影世纪村、东煤新村、长春光机与物理研究所第八小区、长影阳光景都、南湖祥水湾、长久家园、星宇长久小区、卫星家园、长春燃气厂等建筑群，以及一些其他使用中的建筑和部分废弃的荒地。

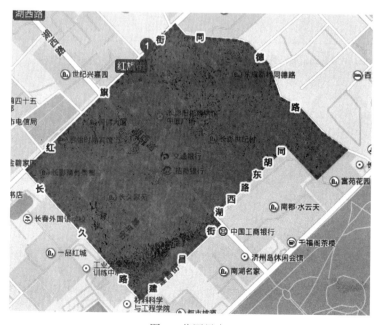

图 2　范围界定

5.1 从建筑质量维度进行长影旧址的保护与更新

长影旧址街区现状建筑质量差别较大。其中,长春电影制片厂旧址2013年被国务院核定并公布为全国文物保护单位,现状建筑质量良好,建筑颜色以棕红色为主色调,建筑风格以复古80年代砖混结构为主。如图3所示,此次保护与更新研究的保护区,包括长影电影艺术馆、长影摄影棚展址、长影电影院、长影音乐厅等建筑;改造区包括长影世纪村、南湖祥水湾、长久家园小区及与道路相邻的沿街商业,现状建筑质量良好,其地理位置与长春电影制片厂旧址紧邻,现状建筑整体风格与长影旧址缺少联系,尤其是沿街商铺的门面布置形式上差异较大,缺少统一的视觉冲击力。此次保护与更新研究中,要着重对这一区域的建筑进行立面改造。更新区主要包括东煤新村、长春光机与物理研究所第八小区、卫星家园小区、长春燃气厂等。其中东煤新村、长春光机与物理研究所第八小区建筑质量一般,需要进行全部外立面改造,改造风格与长影旧址统一,丰富整个街区的整体感,突出长影历史文化。

图3　建筑保护与更新分区

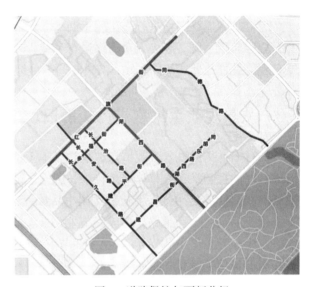

图4　道路保护与更新分级

5.2 从道路质量维度进行长影旧址的保护与更新

如图4所示,研究范围内包括两条次干路,红旗街和湖西路,和七条支路,分别为同德路、长治路、长安路、长久路、多福街、建平街和建昌街,以及多条巷路。由于长影旧址街区地处长春市中心红旗街商业圈,车流量巨大,且因城市历史建设土地性质,导致现状道路存在明显的问题,主要可归纳为四个方面:

(1)承担主要车流的红旗街拥堵现象严重,导致长影活力负效应,减少对参观长影博物馆的积极性。54路、55路有轨电车在红旗街通行,设置车站站点指示导向不明显,导致人行流线混乱。

(2)同德路紧邻万达广场,万达广场现状停车位严重不足,导致同德路道路两侧乱停现象严重,而且同德路是延安大街和红旗街的连接要道,车流量巨大,造成道路拥堵现象严重。同时,同德路两侧商业向人行道方向圈地现象严重,使行人被迫在车型道上行走,影响车行和人行安全。

(3)长治路、长安路、长久路、多福街、建平街和建昌街两侧人行道停放大量车辆,影响人行安全和两侧商业的活力。

(4)湖西路与红旗街交汇路口车流与人流混流现象严重,且交叉口路边存在路边摊位对人流的正常通行造成了影响,应将其取缔。

道路改造表　　　　　　　　　　　　　　　　　　　　　　　　　　　　　　　　表1

序号	道路名称	道路等级	现状红线宽度（m）	规划红线宽度（m）	规划横断面（m）				
					中央分隔带	机动车道	两侧分隔带	非机动车道（辅道）	人行道
1	同德路	支路	12	20		9			5.5×2
2	湖西路	次干路	21	28		16			6×2
3	长治路	支路	11	16		7			4.5×2
4	长安路	支路	11	16		7			4.5×2
5	长久路	支路	12	20		9			5.5×2
6	红旗街	次干路	39	52		22	2×2	7	5+6
7	多福街	支路	11	16		7			4.5×2
8	建平街	支路	12	20		9			5.5×2
9	建昌街	支路	14	24		12			6×2

综上，将道路断面进行表1所示调整，形成流畅的车行和人行空间。同时，为公共交通设置流畅的人流导向指示牌，组织人流有序通行，减少对车行的影响。对乱停车辆进行严格治理，除规划地面停车外、设置一处立体停车楼，解决空间不足但车辆停放量大的问题。

5.3　从景观质量维度进行长影旧址的保护与更新

长影旧址街区现状景观节点缺少长影本土特色，人行流线景观缺少文化感植入。绿植景观带没有形成良好的视觉渗透，整体缺少传承长影文化的创业空间，在改造过程中，将空间以长影独有的文化脉络串联，形成语用维度下长影文化小品景观，激活空间整体的文化认同感；如图5所示。西路为长影文化小品重点更新道路，形成三条主要景观流线，主要以丰富人行流线文化视觉感为目的，浅色虚线节点为长影文化小品节点；浅色实线节点为植物景观视觉观赏中心，对四周形成景观渗透；深色节点为长影旧址博物馆保护的主要景观；其他次要景观节点建设风格均以此为参考。景观保护与更新最终目的是形成长影文化特色明显的文化区，制造文脉场所吸引效应，凝聚人文激发活力。通过更新周边小区的景观特色，丰富空间小品，增加长影旧址街区的独特风格，突出长影特色，使长影旧址街区形成长春独具一格的影视景观文化区。

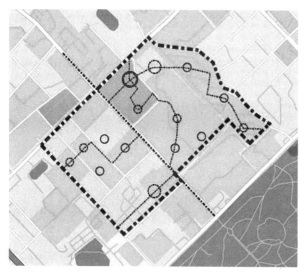

图5　景观保护与更新流线及节点

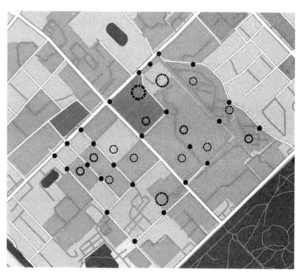

图6　指示牌增设位置

5.4 从设施质量维度进行长影旧址的保护与更新

长影旧址街区的设施相对陈旧,尤其是沿街的道路指示牌、车站站牌、电线走线、垃圾桶摆放位置及数量、雨水排水口质量等。如图6所示,点的位置为指示牌增设位置,此次建设着重将景观指示牌系统丰富,达到行人无论行走在长影旧址街区的任何位置,都能迅速选择自己的最佳路线,以主观意愿通过长影旧址街区,增加长影对本地居民及行人的吸引,从而增加活力激发特色潜质。

6 结语

通过上述分析,语用维度上保护与更新的过程一定要避免粗放性的规划,应进行合理的、符合人本思想的设计。将建筑质量,道路质量,景观质量,设施质量进行改造后,首先,激发出了长影旧址街区公共开放空间的活力,打造出长春旧址街区的"街道眼"。然后,注重公众认识与参与下的保护与更新,强调本土性情景感知下的开放街区。最后提高文脉统合、文脉并置以及文脉的延续性,将自然环境、社会文化、经济技术、人文习俗的综合表型落于实处,表现在社会环境中产生一些特有形态、符号、文化,组成长影所特有的历史文化和建筑形式,也自然形成了其特有的城市形象。然而,历史文脉和场所内涵的延续有限、地段功能复杂、土地区位价值如何完全得到体现、地段城市竞争力怎样变强等都是待思考解决的。客观上说,通过公众的积极参与、政府的合理决策、法规的坚决保障和投资团体的正确认识共同努力协调,日后长影旧址街区必能达到一个更为合理的保护与更新的效果。

The Context of Pragmatic Thinking Projected Changchun Site Blocks' Protection and Renovation

Liu Yan, Gao Yanpeng, Fu Yanhua, Liu Shengjun

(Northeastern University)

Abstract: Changchun film studio has made a century-old legend of film and television, inheriting millennium national cultures. Compared with the past decade, the current Changchun film studio attracts more attention through a life-altering reconstruction. However, the surrounding communities of architecture, stay in uneven built environment. Although the buildings in each region are adjacent to the site, they still lack a sense of coordination with Changchun film studio. Each region has a different style, the key area and projected, become an inevitable trend of revival of Changchun film studio. The specific historical background of Changchun film studio has shaped a unique Changchun feeling. With the unique temperament, Changchun film studio will turn into an unparalleled screen culture block through protection and renewal. Pragmatic thinking is from methodology, and used in philosophy. It is a method for finding the special style from the special environment thus applied in the protection and renewal of Changchun film studio, which exactly complement the intention. Pragmatic thinking is a creative thinking in planning research and rarely used in previous work. Boldly use of this method in the protection and renewal of the site block of Changchun film studio will produce a hitherto breakthrough research results. Conclusion is drawn that protection and renewal of the buildings, streets, landscape and facility in the site of Changchun film studio will turn it into a dynamic screen culture block.

Keywords: Preservation of history and culture, Pragmatic thought, The site of the old Changchun film studio

参考文献

[1] 刘生军，徐苏宁．城市设计思维的意义维度 [J]．华中建筑，2009：32-34．

[2] （德）伽达默尔．真理与方法（上、下卷）[M]．洪汉鼎译．译文出版社，2004．

[3] 王爱因．大规模城市重建环境下的城市文脉保护与开发 [J]．沈阳航空航天大学，2013．

[4] 赵永浩．从历史街区公共空间改造到历史街区活力复兴 [J]．天津大学，2006．

[5] LYNCH K.The Openness of Open Space nature, in City Sense and City Design [M]. MIT Press, Cambridge. MA, 1990.

[6] 王腾飞，陈天，臧鑫宇．中新天津生态城街区尺度公共开放空间规划策略研究 [J]．天津大学，2013．

[7] 李子建．长影旧址街区保护与更新 [J]．吉林建筑大学，2010．

[8] 蔡晓萌．流转七十年的光影声色长春电影制片厂早期建筑的保护与再利用．世界遗产，2015．

社会空间博弈下城市与住房的转型机制研究
——以苏州山塘街为例

郑 玥 胡 莹

（苏州科技大学）

摘 要：2002年苏州政府开始进行山塘街改造工程，随着空间分异程度加剧，城市空间和住房结构产生了相应的转型。本文从社会—空间的视角出发，从东西两段不同的社会、经济和文化背景入手，挖掘出东西两段不同人口结构引发的不同类型问题，通过访谈、参与式倾听的方法，最终得出山塘街东西两段的社会空间在经历了博弈—融合—稳定的过程后所实现的住房与城市空间的转型机制，并为未来历史街道的发展提供借鉴和参考。

关键词：山塘街改造工程，住房转型，社会空间，人口结构

1 背景

苏南地区是吴文化的发源地和核心区域，而苏州又被称为苏南文化的源头，本文选取了其中最有代表性的山塘街道为研究对象。山塘街作为苏州典型历史街道，位于苏州古城边缘，毗邻虎丘山下，东起金阊，西至虎丘，全长约3.5km，因此也被称为"七里山塘"，1200年来一直保留着"水陆并行、河街相邻"的格局，山塘河穿插其间，形成了"街—巷—弄"的苏州传统空间结构肌理。2002年，苏州市政府启动了山塘历史文化保护区保护性修复性修复工程，对不同区域进行功能重组和优化，以新民桥为界将山塘街分为东西两个部分：西段为居住复合型、东段为商业复合型（图1）。

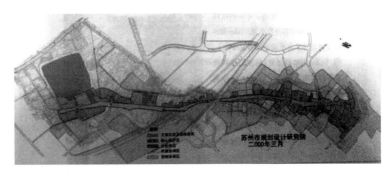

图1 山塘街控制规划图

自2002年政府改造工程启动之后，从高特第纳和亨切森提出的社会—空间的视角来看，东西两段由于城市定位上的差异，在地理位置上产生了居住隔离，再加上时间累积下的人口阶层的分异，共同导致了迁居现象，并在此基础上出现了住房结构和建筑结构的转变，进而影响城市空间的重新划分，而在居民对城市空间的重塑和改造过程中，还受到城市生活的反作用，在居民、游客、经营者三者的利益博弈中，城市社会空间、居住空间分异、居民日常生活三方面寻求到了平衡点，并最终达到了双赢的稳定融合状态。

2 社会空间视角下山塘街城市与住房发展过程与机制研究

2.1 总述

山塘街东西段虽然地处姑苏区，但由于两者的城市定位不同：西段主要为中低端居住区，东段为首个试点开发的历史商业街区，因此相对应，就出现了漏斗形和纺锤形两类人口结构，人口阶层的差异性也反映在居民的日常活动上：一方面，为了满足不同的生活需求进而对住房的空间结构进行改造，出现了西段居住空间的融合与共生以及东段游憩空间的博弈与复合两种结果；另一方面，产生的不同类型城市问题也推动了城市空间的变化，而城市空间的演变过程最终又成为城市发展的制约或促进因素（图2）。城市、人口、空间三者始终保持着这样一个循环往复的关系，而城市也就在这种循环的过程中取得了螺旋式上升。

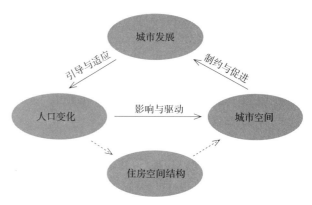

图 2 城市与住房发展动态过程

2.2 居住空间的融合与共生

山塘街西段在保持原住民居住状态的同时，由于居住空间等级较低、租金便宜，外来务工人员作为主要的"入侵者"插入这块城市空间中，两极分化的人口结构打破了原本紧密的邻里关系和人际交往，但是在逐渐适应的过程中，最初的冲突和矛盾由逐渐融合的居住空间所化解，同时两者的共生推动了家庭化商业的产生。

2.2.1 漏斗形人口结构

对这一区域的住户进行人口结构统计时可以发现（图3、图4）（采用连续一周，同一时间段数据平均而得），山塘街西段人口结构呈现出明显的漏斗形两极分化状况，70%以上为本地居民，25%左右为外来务工流动人员，60岁以上年龄段和20～30岁人口占主要部分。前者主要为本地居民，他们长期居住于此，由于形成了自己特定的朋友圈和亲属圈，再加上周围有古城区最大的菜场，因此即使很多生活设施不便，仍不愿意搬迁，而由于多个长期定居的家庭又会在周围形成稳定的交际网络，从而演化成社区型的居民家庭[1]，无形中形成的社会组团又使得年长居民的定居意向更为稳固；年龄较轻的定居者一部分为外来务工人员，他们看中此处租金便宜、生活便利的优点；另一部分为还未成家的本地居民，他们往往与父母居住于此，白天外出工作。通过询问，大部分居民的工作地点集中在周围，采用公共交通工具出行，早出晚归，形成了江南地区最为传统的"2+1"的家庭模式。但是已成家或经济水平较好的居民由于拥挤、生活设施不便、道路过窄等原因，都选择搬离此处，并且不希望下一代继续居住在山塘地区。根据"推–拉理论"，同一区域的相同生活条件对于不同的人口阶层形成了相反的推因素和拉因素，也就产生了人口的迁入与迁出。

---

[1] 在家庭生命周期说和生活方式说中，贝尔（1956）对居民家庭的分类。

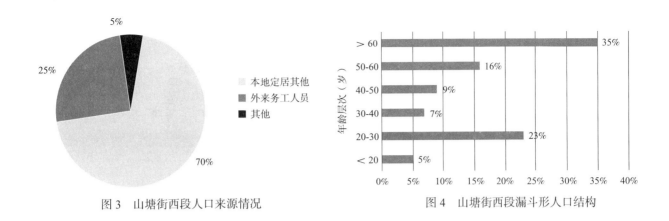

图3 山塘街西段人口来源情况　　　　　图4 山塘街西段漏斗形人口结构

2.2.2 城市居住问题产生

通过实地调研与采访可以发现，山塘街西段由于人口结构的两极分化，在邻里、交通和污染方面产生了相应的问题。

（1）人口阶层差异导致邻里问题。外来务工人员由于房屋租期短、人口变化快、流动性大，工作时间长，70%的娱乐活动在晚上展开，因此造成了作息时间与原本年长的本地居民不一致，会相互干扰。并且由于外来人口多采用群租的形式，因此经常出现空间不足而占用公共空间，同时也存在一定的安全隐患。居民也抱怨和邻居由于方言问题无法聊天，使得原本由本地居民构成的较为紧密的邻里结构遭到了破坏。

（2）菜场等人流聚集点的迁移导致交通问题。由于前半段周围有大量居民区，在山塘街未改造之前有许多便民设施，改造后为了满足东段游览区的要求，原本位于广济桥边的上塘菜场向西挪了300m，而上塘菜场是周边小区居民购买粮油米面的主要聚集区。通过观察可以发现，在山塘街前半段几乎没有自行车停放点，而周围居民又偏向于骑电瓶车或者自行车来购物，这就造成了广济桥下原本就不宽阔的道路被两侧乱停放的车辆占据了大半路面。加之大量的摊贩集中于桥下这个交通节点，使得新民桥的上下人流混杂，阻碍通行。

（3）公共设施不足导致污染和生活不便问题。周围建筑在改造时未考虑到底层的店面，以至于形成了大量移动摊贩，一方面造成了食品卫生隐患，另一方面突出的阳伞和雨棚占据了半幅路面，使得路人在躲避时很容易产生碰擦，激发矛盾。西段路面模仿东段采用了青石铺地，但没有增设排水设施，也没有垃圾桶等基础设施，使得污水和垃圾无法及时排掉，下雨天易形成积水，对周围居民的出行产生了不便。由于现代交通工具的更新，大部分家庭都配有至少一部汽车，但是由于巷子太窄，地面不平等原因，再加上山塘街附近多为老小区，没有规划停车位，很多家庭不得不将汽车停在离家门有一定距离的路边，在雨雪天气尤其不便（图5）。

图5 缺少基础设施

（a）广济桥下交通混乱；（b）摊位乱布；（c）停车远离家门；（d）地面积水严重

2.2.3 城市与住房结构拆解

对山塘街西段的商业业态进行统计可以发现，由于西段核心区为辐射人口 20 万左右的大型菜场，因此周围店铺的目标人群为来此采购的居民，业态也集中在满足居民最底层的生理需求[①]，如水果店、米面粮油和生活用品，店铺以 2 开间以下的中小型店铺为主（图6）。

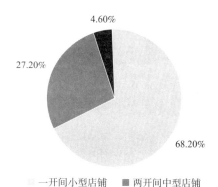

图 6　山塘街西段商铺分布

山塘街西侧基本保留着以家庭为单位的商业运营方式，建筑产权也包括了公房、私房等多种类型，里弄、过道等较多，并且建筑的高度、面宽、进深等也各有区别，因此在建筑肌理方面形成了较为细碎并且密集的城市肌理，这也与此段的人口结构相适应。在住房结构方面，山塘街西段大部分建筑保留了原本的结构类型，只是进行了简单的吊顶和粉刷，未对结构进行大改动，将原本两层的居住功能转化为下店上寝的情况，一楼的入户门改成与店铺大小一致的卷帘门，并增加隔墙划分厨房、仓库、用餐区等，部分商户白天将烹饪区域置于店铺之外，占用部分路面，有极少数住户将二层外墙拆除形成开敞阳台，破坏沿街一致的立面效果（图7）。大部分住宅为一楼相连的 3～4 间店面分租给不同商家，中间有一巷道，几家共用一部楼梯。二楼一部分自住，其余部分划分成若干小间分租给外来人员，由于卫生间、浴室等设施不足，二楼房屋结构较为混乱，而这样的房屋结构也制约了在此居住的人口阶层和人口组团规模，但是在"本地—外地，大空间—小空间"这样的博弈过程中，形成了当下这种人口结构两极化、商业模式单一、住房形式混乱的融合模式，而如果没有外来因素的强制插入，此类居住模式在未来的一段时间内也将保持稳定。

  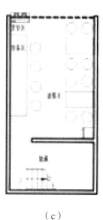

（a）　　　　　　　　　　　　　（b）　　　　　　　　　　　　（c）

图 7　山塘街西段住房改变

（a）山塘街改造前；（b）部分住户二层改造阳台；（c）某馄饨店平面

资料来源：平龙根. 古街新韵：山塘历史街区保护性修复钩沉录 [M]. 江苏：古吴轩出版社，2012.

2.3　游憩空间的博弈与复合

与西段不同，山塘街东段作为山塘地区的开发重点，主街上全部住宅均改为商业建筑，仅在周边

---

① 马斯洛层次理论将人类需求像阶梯一样从低到高按层次分为五种，分别是：生理需求、安全需求、社交需求、尊重需求和自我实现需求。

保留少量民居，商业形式较为多样，并演化出了商业与休憩并存的复合空间，因此东段更多的是游客—居民—经营者三者的领域博弈。东段由于商业经营模式较为新颖、商品较为新潮，同时商铺装修具有苏州特点，因此吸引了大批中青年游客，而年轻的参观者又促进了东段的商业气氛更为活泼和自由，但是在这个过程中，年龄较大的原住民成了一个阻碍因素，如何权衡三者的利益关系成为东段的主要城市问题。

2.3.1 纺锤形人口结构

对山塘街东侧的人口结构进行统计可以发现（图8），与西段呈相反情况，由于政府早在2002年就开始整治东段，大部分居民都已经搬离，因此西段中的本地居民仅占5%以下，超过90%为游客和另有住所的店主。而在山塘街东侧的游客中70%为外地游客，本地游客仅占30%。外地游客中又以偏向于自由行的20～40岁青年人为主，主要包括学生、家长带孩子、妈妈团几类，另一部分则为跟随旅行团出行的60岁以上的老年团；山塘街东侧的店铺老板也趋于年轻化，除了少数老字号外，大部分餐饮和工艺品店铺的员工平均年龄为20～30岁。通过观察可以发现，游客在山塘街东段的游览时间一般都控制在1～2小时内，并且很少在此留宿，因此人员的更新速度非常快。与西侧市井气息不同，山塘街东侧的整体气氛更为年轻和精致。

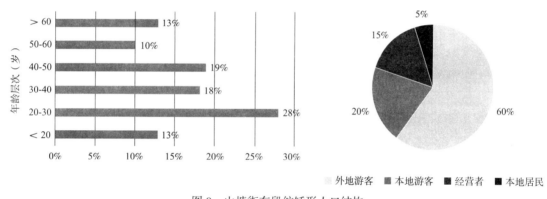

图8 山塘街东段纺锤形人口结构

2.3.2 城市公共及商业问题的产生

东段主要为经营者、游客和少量居民，三者在领域的博弈过程产生了居住安全、商业和交通三方面的问题。

（1）居民生活需求与商业定位不融合。虽然东侧全段为步行街，但仍有一部分住在山塘街西段，留在西段弄堂中的住户仍会选择骑电瓶车穿过前段，这一类人群一般会在后座或车篮里放置大量蔬果肉类，在经过人流聚集区时，容易产生碰擦。由于主街上游客较多，居住于此的年长居民缺失了休息聊天的场所，家长也出于安全考虑不让孩子在主街上玩耍。

（2）商业氛围悬殊。整个山塘街前段共有3座桥可以通往河南侧，但是由于指向性不明确，河南侧的店铺大多以餐饮为主，在非就餐时间对游客的吸引力不大，使得游客只是在桥上欣赏风景，而不会倾向于去河南岸，商业气氛不均，形成了"河北人挤人，河南空荡荡"的场景（图9）。

（3）人流、车流交通压力大。就整个街道的人流量来看，大量排队人群集中在几个餐饮店铺门口，并且店铺处于道路较窄地段，因此会对双向行人造成阻碍。而东段全段仅有一处公共卫生间，在旅游旺季排队的人群往往占据整幅路面。除此之外，东段大量旅游车和私家车缺少疏导和停放区域，因此，大部分车辆选择停在路边，一方面造成安全隐患，另一方面增大了交通压力。

图 9　河两岸商业气氛差异

2.3.3　城市与住房结构整合

由于山塘街东侧主要为游客，店主整体较为年轻也具有活力和创新精神，因此商业业态的分布主要针对 20～40 岁的年轻游客以及 60 岁以上的老年游客（图 10、图 11）：包括传统工艺品、休闲食品、工艺品等，由于人口结构的低龄化，消费等级也从西侧的满足生理需求上升到寻求更好的生活品质。

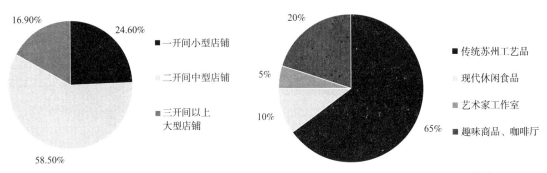

图 10　山塘街东段商铺大小统计　　　　图 11　山塘街东段商铺类型统计

与西侧部分住宅功能不同，东侧房屋基本都由住宅功能转向了商业功能，每家均设置单独楼梯，二层也只供该店铺储藏或店员临时休息、使用而不另外出租，并且不存在多个社会阶层的领域争夺，在发展过程中始终保持了"买—卖"这一单向的商业过程，住房结构的不断优化也是为了更好地达成买卖关系，年轻人对新鲜事物的追求以及物质的迅速更新，决定了东侧的经营形式更为多样化。店铺均为政府所有，而店主向政府租用，店铺整体装修较为精致并且各个店面内部装修差异较大，但外立面基本保持一致，整体规划较为规整，建筑体量均按照一定的模数布局，因此形成了完整的沿街立面。大多数售卖丝绸、刺绣的店铺为两开间店铺，同时增加了具有中式风格的吊顶，内部也基本以木质装饰为主，而 DQ 和星巴克等国外连锁品牌在保留本身店铺特点的同时，在此处的分店均采用了中式风格。另一种售卖奶茶等现代休闲食品的店铺往往只占有一间店铺，不设置座椅，而在临街面设置售卖柜台，店铺后侧则作为厨房以及仓储空间。为了增加游客的停留时间，大多数店铺在售卖空间又增添了休憩空间，如一些售卖苏式点心的店铺因为需要及时烹调或者为了满足游客堂食的需求，往往占据了三间以上的店面，将一层隔墙拆除空出开敞空间放置桌椅等，有的甚至将二层的一部分也作为用餐区域，其余空间作为储藏和员工休息处，这类售卖食品的店铺均在门口处设置了吧台和展示区域，以招揽生意。

3 山塘街东、西段发展机制与转型模式归纳

对山塘街东西两段的转型机制和模式进行归纳（图12，图13）可以发现，由于两者在最初的城市定位上出现差距，导致两者的人口结构出现了漏斗形和纺锤形两种类型，对应出现了交通这个公共问题以及邻里、污染和居住安全、商业两类针对性问题，前者恶化了破碎的城市空间，进而限制了居住型定位的转变；后者只是在空间整合度提高过程中出现的副产物，与商业型定位的进步呈负相关，从侧面促进了城市定位的优化。

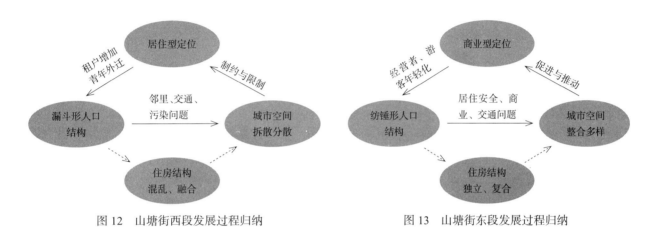

图12 山塘街西段发展过程归纳　　　　　图13 山塘街东段发展过程归纳

4 结论

山塘街东西两段由于人口结构的差异产生了不同的社会活动，继而导致不同类型的问题以及后续引发的住房和城市肌理的改变，而这些改变又反过来成为在此生活的人群的引力和推力，这一循环过程从侧面反映出，"人"作为城市发展中的一个重要因素，主导着城市演变的方向，这与芝加哥学派提出的"不同社会集团在各种人类活动竞争中形成城市空间结构"的社会生态学派理论相一致，而社会—空间视角也为未来的城市规划提供了很好的切入点和立足点。

A Study on the Transformation Mechanism of Cities and Housing under the Social Space Scramble
——A Case Study of Shantang Street

Zheng Yue, Hu Ying

(Suzhou University of Science and Technology)

Abstract: The Suzhou government began to renovate Shantang street since 2002. With the aggravation of spatial heterogeneity, the urban space and housing structure have been transformed correspondingly. From the social-spatial perspective, this paper starts with the different social, economic and cultural backgrounds of the east and west segment of the street to investigate the phenomenon that the two segments of Shantang Street differ in typology due to varies demographic structure. Through interviews and participatory listening, the result manifested that the urban and housing transformation mechanism were achieved from a game-integration-stabilization process after the social-spatial self-renovation of the east and west segments of Shantang Street. The experience provides a reference for the future development of historical streets.

Keywords: Shantang street reconstruction project, Housing Transformation, Social space, Population structure

参考文献

[1] 平龙根. 古街新韵——山塘历史街区保护性修复构成录（第1版）[M]. 江苏：古吴轩出版社，2012.

[2] 王保森. 社会空间视角下的广州大学城和谐发展研究[D]. 同济大学博士学位论文，2007.

[3] 李珊. 社会空间重组与生活方式变迁（第1版）[M]. 北京：知识产权出版社，2011.

保障性住房与房地产市场管理
Affordable Housing and Real Estate Management

台湾地区面向青年人的社会住宅模式供给模式探析
——以新北市为例

郭净宇

(北京大学城市与环境学院硕士研究生)

摘　要：面对快速城镇化已成为当前世界的重要议题，我国台湾地区自1975年城镇化率从六成五到现在近八成，结果面对都市住宅用地紧张与公共资源分配不均，引发激烈社会矛盾与冲突以及大规模的群众抗争，说明了快速城镇化发展不均所产生的严重社会矛盾问题，当前大陆面对快速城镇化趋势，预计2020年达到60%，因此要如何从这样的经验中撷取参考是值得我们思考的议题。面对前述问题，2016年联合国住房和城市可持续发展大会通过《新城市议程》(New Urban Agenda)，强调对于可持续与包容性的概念，提出面对快速城镇化应当同时兼顾资源分配并对不同族群进行潜能投资与开发，期望使用住宅政策消除贫穷及解决社会排除困境，透过城镇化的契机带动经济发展，然而要如何落实？该理念在西方社会福利的发展已非新事，自英国社会学家纪登斯提出第三条路后，将依赖性社会福利政策，转化为兼顾经济发展与福利提升，其中许多概念成为当前发展型福利的关键思维：(1)积极性福利：从直接提供的福利给付，转为强调透过工作满足需求；(2)社会投资：面对能力匮乏者采取人力资本、经济资本等各项资源投注以提升能力；(3)社会包容：任何阶层都不被排斥于主流社会之外。2007亚洲开发银行更提出包容性增长的理念，强调经济成长应兼顾不同阶层皆能融入；(4)混合经济福利：福利不应仅政府承担，可以结合商业等进行多元提供，兼顾分散化与民营化优势。本文试图透过发展型福利架构对台湾地区新北市使用土地开发展权奖励作为青年社会住宅供应模式进行检视，能否在发展型福利的观点下，提出引导方向，提升其社会价值与成效，达成新城市议程期许具有包容性与可持续的社会住宅模式。

关键词：发展型福利，新城市议程，青年住宅，保障性住房，容积奖励

1　引言：快速城镇化引发的居住矛盾与冲突

如何面对快速城镇化已成为当前世界的重要议题，联合国预估2050年世界城镇化率将从当前的50%迈向70%，我国台湾地区则是自1975年城镇化率从约65%到现在近80%[1]，快速城镇化的结果导致都市住宅用地紧张与公共资源分配不均，增长红利未让全民共享引发激烈社会矛盾与冲突，新北市房价收入比曾攀升至远超出国际标准，以致1989年无壳蜗牛运动与2014年巢运等群众抗争，说明快速城镇化下发展不均所产生的严重矛盾问题。面对这样的问题，庞大的社会压力下也催生了台湾地区的社会住宅建设热潮，政府预计于8年内兴建20万户社会住宅，其中新北市的青年社会住宅也是其中一例。当前大陆也面对快速城镇化趋势，截至2015年，中国城镇化率已达到56.1%，并预计将于2020年达到60%。以北京为例，2000～2010年期间[2]，长期移民的数量从268万增加到704万 (19.4%，占城市人口的35.9%)。透过数据表示商品住房平均售价从2001年的5062元/m^2上升到2010年的17151元/m^2，增长240%。2009年北京的价格收入比为13.3，远高于常规可承受水平4～5。因此要如何从这样的经验中撷取参考是值得思考的议题。

2　快速城镇化文献回顾与探讨

2.1　可持续发展与新城市议程

面对快速城镇化所导致的一连串问题，围绕着所谓的可持续概念进行了很多讨论，联合国于巴西里约召开的地球高峰会（Rio+20）中，一致决议以可持续发展目标（Sustainable Development Goals，SDGs）[3]作为未来15年（2016～2030年）的发展议题主轴。这一概念背后的目的是制定一套普遍适用于所有国家而又考虑到各国不同的国情、能力和发展水平，同时尊重国家政策和十七项优先目标和平衡可持续发展的三大支柱分别是环境、社会和经济。而在2016年10月联合国住房和城市可持续发展大会通过《新城市议程》[4]则更具体地强调了对于可持续与包容性的概念在城镇化的应用，说明面对快速城镇化应当同时兼顾资源分配并对不同族群进行潜能投资与开发，期望使用住宅政策消除贫穷及解决社会排除困境，透过城镇化的契机带动经济发展，然而对于追求包容性与可持续发展的概念，要如何在我国台湾地区的青年社会住宅建设落实呢？

2.2　发展型福利观点

追求包容性与可持续发展的概念的实践在西方社会福利的发展中已非新鲜事[5]，从20世纪90年代起由英国社会学家纪登斯（Anthony Giddens）《第三条道路：社会民主主义的复兴》中明确提出，应当以"积极的"或"主动的"福利政策代替目前的传统福利模式，使传统福利国家现代化，对于如何使原本依赖性的社会福利政策，转化为兼顾经济发展与福利提升，提出了各项积极作为主要注重人力资本的培育，期望创造社会投资型国家。为了创造自我实现的条件，社会投资型国家的基本原则是：在可能的情况下尽量在人力资本上投资，而最好不要直接提供经济资助。经济问题与福利问题都可以归结为"人"的问题，所以解决了"人"的问题，提高了人的生存能力，经济问题和福利问题就都解决了。因此，在人力资本上投资才是治本之策。

前者鼓励个人积极创造的福利制度改革方向。发展型福利一种积极福利政策，通过改变福利国家开支的方向，从福利消费支出，改为教育、培训、创造就业机会等社会投资支出。改革原福利体系，将其与经济发展相结合，推动积极福利政策的发展与完善。其中许多概念已成为当前福利的关键思维，如（1）积极性福利（Positive Welfare），扭转过去提供直接的福利给付，而强调透过工作满足需求；（2）社会投资（Social Investment），面对能力匮乏与不足采取各类资本投注以提升其能力，包含人力资本、经济资本与社会资本；（3）社会包容（Social Inclusion）：包容是相对于排斥概念而言，包容性的社会是指社会的任何阶层都不会被排斥于主流社会之外，沦为边缘族群。2007亚洲开发银行更进一步提出包容性增长（Inclusive Growth）的理念，强调经济成长应兼顾不同阶层，并使其皆能融入；（4）混合经济福利（Mixed Economy of Welfare），强调福利提供者不应由政府单一承担，可以结合商业部门与第三部门多元的福利提供，以兼顾分散化与民营化之优势。

其中包容性增长观点是更深入运用包容性与经济发展的理念，其概念如下[6,7]：（1）既强调经济增长的速度，也强调经济增长的方式。长期可持续的经济增长必须基于广泛且包容这个国家弱势劳动力人口；（2）强调以增加生产性投资和生产性就业机会为导向，更倾向透过增加生产性就业机会，而不是直接的收入再分配来实现经济增长和贫困缓解，可以说是更重视的是机会的公平，而非结果的公平；（3）强调对大众能够广泛地参与经济增长并且从中受益，因此注重经济机会的平等以及发展成果的全民共享特质。由此观之，包容性增长理念呼应了前述所提及的包容性与可持续的观点。

透过上述概念，可以发现包容性增长理念与发展型社会福利体系是能够帮助社会成员解决实际生存发展问题的制度化、专业化服务体系，是一种与经济发展水平相适应的、动态的、可持续的福利体系，在解除社会成员后顾之忧的基础上促进生活质量不断提高，并带来实质性的满足感，增进其幸福程度，也是让全体人民共享国家改革发展成果的基本途径。发展型福利强调协调经济发展与社会发展的关系，意味着社会政策并不意味着单纯性的支出，它也是生产力的要素之一，对经济发展有促进作用，并改变了传统社会福利模式对福利主体的维持性救助形式，基本思路是致力于消除或减少那些会使人们陷入不幸或困境的因素，试图促使福利主体的自立自强，将社会福利的被动接受者变为经济与社会发展的主动参与者，而不是事后再向他们提供生活保障。与之相对应，发展型福利模式的对象也不再局限于现实中的问题人群，而是试图寻求一种促进全体社会成员能力发展的社会资源再分配机制。

3 研究方法

今日本文分析是透过发展型福利架构，对台湾地区新北市使用土地开发权奖励作为青年社会住宅供应模式进行检视并提出修正，达成新城市议程所期许的包容性与可持续的社会住宅模式（图1）。

3.1 研究架构

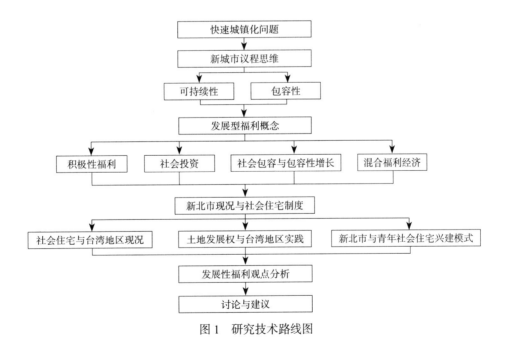

图1 研究技术路线图

3.2 研究对象

3.2.1 社会住宅与台湾地区现况

台湾地区社会住宅推动联盟所谓的社会住宅[8]，在欧洲又称社会出租住宅（Social Rented Housing），而各国实际运作所使用之名称不尽相同，例如美国称之为可负担住宅（Affordable Housing）、日本称公营住宅、香港称公共屋邨（简称公屋）、新加坡与马来西亚称组合房屋（简称组屋）等，我国台湾地区又因为年代不同和地方政府政策施行而有不同名称之社会住宅，例如平价住宅、出租国宅、公营住宅、青年住宅、劳工住宅等，对于大陆则是所谓的保障性住房政策，根据2010年的资料指出台湾地区社会住宅比例仅有0.08%。社会住宅是指政府（直接或补助）兴建或民间拥有之合于居住标准的房屋，并且采用只租不卖模式，以低于市场租金或免费出租给所得较低的家户或特殊的弱势对象的住宅。这包括：（1）绝对经济与社会弱势者；（2）相对经济弱势者，待有能力时再进入资本住宅市场购屋；（3）一般民众，借由社会住宅数量之增加，成为抑制房价之调节机制，进而让大众有适当住宅安居。法定狭义社会住宅之定义则是住宅法第3条：社会住宅为由政府兴办或奖励民间兴办，专供出租之用，并应提供至少10%以上比例出租给具特殊情形或身份者之住宅。政府提出将于8年内兴建大约20万户[9]，缓解台湾地区住宅需求与社会压力。

3.2.2　土地发展权与台湾地区实践

理解土地开发权的概念[10]，应当从土地开发权发源的英国与美国两个国家探索起，其中土地利用的多元化使各国开始重视对土地的管制，通过设立土地开发权来解决管制产生的损益问题。1909年，英国颁布了世界上第一部城市规划法《住宅、城镇规划诸法》，赋予地方政府对正在开发或有可能用于建筑目的的土地进行事先限制和规划的权力；美国于20世纪20年代颁布了《标准州区划授权法》，由各州授权地方政府制订区划条例，将城市划分成各个分区，给予不同的用途、建筑高度、体量以及开放空间面积等的规定。然而规划管制带来了地块或分区之间的土地价值差异，使土地所有者或因允许开发而获益，或因限制开发而受损，因此英国于1947年颁布的《城乡规划法》将土地开发权及其相关利益实行国有化，而美国政府借鉴英国，于20世纪60年代引进了土地开发权概念，将土地开发权的权益私有化，通过市场交易机制，使受损者获得补偿，降低政府征收土地资金压力和诉讼案件的发生。我国台湾地区土地开发权，基本上是依循美国的土地分区用途管制而产生，目前开发权移转主要应处理三种土地使用课题上：（1）辅助都市计划实质建设事业；（2）有关古迹及历史保存区之保存；（3）敏感地区之保护。此外更延伸出以土地开发权给予容积奖励的做法，在原法定的开发量体上，因为对于环境有正面贡献，在一定的限度内给予该土地范围内额外的楼地板空间，新北市相关容积奖励主要依据的是"新北市都市更新建筑容积奖励核算基准"与"都市更新建筑容积奖励办法"等办法，包含经政府指定额外提供公益设施或是兴建社会住宅等。透过容积奖励为引导方式。

3.2.3　新北市与青年社会住宅兴建模式简介

新北市为我国台湾地区最大行政区，约398.04万人，以外来劳动人口为主，新北市15岁以上劳动人口约为194.7万，平均年龄为41岁，65岁以上人口占全市总人口数11.71%，为目前高龄化问题相对较低且外来青年劳动人口较多的区域。新北市政府[11, 12]文件为照顾优秀青年及弱势等族群，得以租得一个优质的安身居所，故以多元化方式推动青年社会住宅政策。其中新北市青年住宅扮演三大角色，分别是（1）提高生育率之配套社会福利政策：透过减轻住屋负担与设置适当社会支持系统；（2）吸引产业投资配套人才引入政策：透过青年就业，推动商业与日间活动强度并以优秀人才吸引产业进驻；（3）社会经济弱势族群之基本照护策略：建构地区社会福利网络系统，就业辅导与托育照护等服务项目。新北市府新修正"都市计划法新北市施行细则"部分条文，调整容积奖励以强化公益性，开发商释出部分楼地板面积做社会住宅、公共托育中心、老人赡养设施、图书馆、活动中心或机关等公益性设施，可获20%容积奖励，20%容积奖励的其中5%，必须是社会住宅，基准容积奖励提高1.5～2倍；民间则以捐赠社会住宅为优先序位者，则可取得1.05～1.2倍的容积奖励。2016年已经完工1480户，约有4200户兴建中，约5200户规划中，新北市计划于2019年前完成7000户社会住宅。主要照顾对象锁定青年及弱势族群与特殊身份比如低收入户、身心障碍者、灾民等，申请条件为年满20岁以上公民，最近一年综合所得在新北市家庭年收入50%分位点以下。当前租金均为市价8折以下，优先户（弱势户）为市价 64 折以下。并以多元方式兴办青年社会住宅，如公办都市更新、公有房舍改建成青年住宅等机制以增加社会住宅单元。

4 研究结果：以发展型福利观点分析新北市青年社会住宅建设模式

以下透过发展型福利可归纳出的四个要点：（1）积极性福利；（2）社会投资；（3）社会包容与包容性增长；（4）混合经济福利。分别对新北市青年社会住宅建设模式进行检视：

4.1 积极性福利

比起传统的依赖性的福利观点，这样选择青年为最主要社会住宅照顾对象，透过对于社会住宅本身的定义之中，青年因为其发展阶段的不稳定性高，所以属于所谓的相对经济弱势者，是希望能够促使这些青年在住宅资源的扶持之下，可以增加其就业能力，免于沦为失业的群体，合乎于积极性福利的理念，无论是促进就业，还是增加其与社会的融合。

4.2 社会投资

虽然青年社会住宅看似是透过住宅费用的减免，算是另类的经济资本的补充与投注资，然而其在地理位置的提供面上则有更多的价值，乃是从资源可达性的观点切入，剥夺放大理论指出，贫穷地区与富裕地区相比资源可达性往往较低，匮乏的资源容易导致原本就已陷入贫穷的住户生活再度雪上加霜。因此好的区段位置所能提供不仅是住宅，而是从属于此地理位置其他资源，如社会资本教育资源等皆是，此外其附属的相关公共设施则可以更具体提升相关资源供给作用，因此这样青年住宅的供给可被视为同时兼具各项资本投注。

4.3 社会包容与包容性增长

当前台湾地区青年人普遍面对青年低薪与近贫，如高生活开销与低起薪的问题，因此透过这样青年社会住宅的供给，是对青年群体减少生活开销，以及增加未来进入较佳的社会地位良好手段，更重要的是让原本因为购屋房价与租房价格问题而被被迫选择到较偏远与次级居住地区，并面对社会排挤的青年人来说，可以享受市中心相关的公共资源与就业机会，确实是实践了社会包容的效果，解决因为经济能力而产生的社会排挤问题，让不同的群体有能力在城市中生存。对于透过容积奖励作为促进青年社会住宅供应的诱因，这样社会住宅的诱因高低会伴随在房价变动，比起原先因为住宅价格高速飞涨因此而被排除在城市核心区域之外的情况，而这样的供应模式会因为经济增长连带促进青年社会住宅的供应，房屋市场的发展成为青年社会住宅供给的诱因，促使了青年人享受到了住宅市场发展的利益，可被视为包容性增长的福利普惠与机会公平体现。

4.4 混合经济福利

此模式体现多元的社会福利供给模式，不仅是新北市政府对于多元方式兴办青年社会住宅的具体体现，同时也因为容积奖励的方法让这样的供给，同时兼具市场机制作用，由市场机制灵活的供给达成了去中心化的作用，乍听之下有所疑问，也就是规模可以创造规模经济，那么为何需要去中心化，原因是中心化容易带来的即是标签化问题，尤其是在早些年来欧美进行社会住宅建设时碰到的窘境，透过大规模的社会住宅建设，虽然在经济方面取得了相对的效应，然而此区域因为相关弱势人口太多，而被标签化与污名化，导致恶性循环，无法达成原先扶助弱势的作用，甚至恶化成为所谓的贫民窟问题。而这样去中心化的作用，则是在区域尺度中，实践了多元的供给者以及社会混居的作用，以促成去标签化及去污名化的效果。此外同样取得了所谓民营化与市场化的效用，与政府的措施相辅相成，借由开发商自主参与，可以使用市场动力与资金，推动青年社会住宅提供。

5 讨论与建议

透过上述讨论，可以发现新北市的青年社会住宅是合于发展型福利观点，然而强调以青年为主的做法，与传统的社会住宅针对狭义弱势者有所区别，也使其面对各类质疑，因此本文进一步思考政策成效与实践过程有什么需要反思之处。此模式并非没有缺陷，其依赖容积奖励的激励措施，然而台湾地区对于透过容积奖励措施事实上检讨声浪不断，虽有激励措施的作用，但破坏原容积规划，本质上挑战了原本规划对于开发强度设定的逻辑，此外青年社会住宅的建设公益性如何与开发商所获得的私人利益，以及开发强度提高而造成公共损害平衡是需要思考的地方。此外虽然是一种提高开发的经济性诱因，然而这样供应的手段也有局限性，如果是有更特殊需求的族群如身心障碍者，那么透过这样机制下提供的社会住宅是否能吻合需求，此外社会混居的落实，本质上也可能成为开发者的负面成本，在当前尚未完全让社会大众接纳这样具有负面标签的群体之前，此开发手段都可能对开发商开发目标带来负面效果，因此成效不佳呢？并在台湾受限于大环境所造成的都市更新与开发低效率，透过这样的供给模式需要多长的时间才能达到合理的水平，都是需要去思考的。因此不应认为此模式是唯一解决之道，这样的开发模式可以作为多样社会住宅的提供方法之一，并在适合的情况下弹性运用。这样手段确实是解决了当前台湾地区地方政府普遍财政情况有限的问题，借由民间与市场推进才有可能促使这样具有发展型福利特色的社会住宅有发展的机会，不失为合理且可实行的手段，并透过这样的手段实践与实现可持续与包容性的城市发展目标及理想，未来发展仍是值得我们观察与期待。

回顾本文最开始所讨论的主题，面对快速的城镇化过程中，我国台湾地区也曾经经历了这样的情况并且产生严重的社会矛盾，而后可看到了新北市推动了青年社会住宅的建设，尤其是落实人居三所提出的新城市议程强调包容性与可持续的理念，然而这样的理念应当要如何落实，是欠缺明确的指引框架与评估标准，因此本文借用社会福利领域中已经行之有年的发展型福利概念，分别是积极性福利；社会投资；社会包容性增长；混合经济福利面向为评估的工具，借此来评估新北市的青年社会住宅其效果为何，然而我们可以发现概念是相当符合，因此我们可以思考未来是否应当推行这样的青年社会住宅的模式，作为面对快速城镇化的应对措施。近年来大陆也面对快速城镇化压力，及快速发展房价和居住困难矛盾，因此是否能够透过发展型福利观点来实践新城市议程，并透过此青年社会住宅作为落实前者的方法呢？可思考透过发展型福利观点，对未来保障性住房建设提供参考与借鉴，落实包容性与可持续发展理念，促进经济发展与社会和谐共荣，透过城镇化促成经济发展与社会进步。

Analysis on the Mode of Supply of Social Housing for Youth in Taiwan——A Case Study of New Taipei City

Kuo Chin-Yu

(College of Urban and Environmental Sciences, Peking University)

Abstract: When faced with rapid urbanization has become an important topic in the current world. Taiwan since 1975, the urbanization rate from 65% to now nearly 80%, The results of the facing of urban residential land tension and uneven distribution of public resources, and cause the rapid urbanization the problem of serious social contradictions arising from uneven development. China is currently facing a trend of rapid urbanization; therefore, it is worthwhile for China to think about Taiwan's experience. In the face of the aforementioned problems, the HABITAT III in 2016 adopted the "New Urban Agenda". That emphasizes the concept of sustainability and inclusiveness and suggests that rapid urbanization should take into account both the allocation of resources and the potential investment and development of the different social class, the expectation of the using residential policies to eradicate poverty and address social exclusion difficulties, the opportunity to drive economic development. However, how to implement these ideas? These ideas have been developed for the social welfare in the West after the British sociologist Giddens proposed the third way, the past dependency-based social welfare policy has changed into both economic development and welfare improvement. Many of these concepts become the key part of current Developmental Welfare, such as 1. Positive Welfare; 2. Social Investment; 3. Social inclusion and Inclusive Growth; 4. Mixed Economy of Welfare. This paper attempts to use the Developmental Welfare as the structure to review the New Taipei City where used the land development rights reward for the youth social housing supply model to implement inclusive and sustainable social housing modle as New Urban Agenda expected.

Keywords: Developmental welfare, New urban agenda, Youth social housing, Low-Income housing, Reward of building bulk

参考文献

[1] 刘克智，董安琪. 台湾都市发展的演进——历史的回顾与展望 [J]. 人口学刊，2004，26：1-25.

[2] Youqin Huang & Chengdong Yi. (2015) Invisible migrant enclaves in Chinese cities: Underground living in Beijing, China[J]. Urban Studies, 2015, 52 (15): 2948-2973.

[3] CSRone 永续报告平台.【2016，永续新禧年】17 项永续发展目标（SDGs）. [2017-01-11]. http://www.csronereporting.com/en-US/topic_2225.

[4] 联合国住房和城市可持续发展大会. 联合国住房和城市可持续发展大会（人居三大会）成果文件草稿. 联合国，2016.

[5] 顾昕. 中国迈向发展型福利国家的路径：增进市场，激活社会 [J]. 澎湃新闻，2016[2017-1-9]. http://www.thepaper.cn/newsDetail_forward_1579340.

[6] 杜志雄，肖卫东，詹琳. 包容性增长理论的脉络、要义与政策内涵 [J]. 中国农村经济，2010,（11）：4-14，25.

[7] 陈家付. 包容性增长与社会公平 [J]. 学术界，2011，（1）: 5-12.

[8] 社会住宅推动联盟. 社会住宅推动联盟为弱势与青年居住权益发声. 社会住宅推动联盟. 2010[2017-1-9]. http: //socialhousingtw.blogspot.tw/.

[9] 徐珍翔. 8 年兴办 20 万户社会住宅有谱:国发会通过这草案，ETNENS 财经，财经焦点. [2017-1-13].

[10] 林坚，吴宇翔，郭净宇. 英美土地发展权制度的启示 [J]. 中国土地，2017，2: 30-33.

[11] 新北市政府. 新北市青年社会住宅. 新北市政府. 2015[2017-1-9]. http: //www.planning.ntpc.gov.tw/webpage/youth-social-housing/.

[12] 新北市政府，新北市政府施政成果网. [2017-01-11]. https: //wedid.ntpc.gov.tw/Site/PolicyDetails/137.

Hong Kong's Public Housing Policy and Social Problems ——A Case Study of Tin Shui Wai New Town

Li Yi

(Mse in Advanced Environmental Planning Technologies, Center for Housing Innovations,
The Chinese University of Hong Kong)

Abstract: Based on past researches in Hong Kong's public housing policy and development process, this paper mainly analyzed relative social problems, and tried to find ways to alleviate current situation in Tin Shui Wai new town as a case study. After the World War II, in order to satisfy housing needs of increasing population, Hong Kong has released a series of public housing policies like Home Ownership Scheme (HOS) emphatically focused on low-middle income group. So far, there is about 47% of population living in public housing provided by the housing authority. Though large-scale public housing has improved housing conditions for low income group, these policies only pay attention to residents' need for accommodation, with their long-term development ignored. Most of public housing estates locate in the New Territories, accounted for about 57%. However, majority employment opportunities and public facilities are provided in Kowloon and Hong Kong island. Moreover, the strict transfer regulation on public housing led to considerable waste of resource and social efficiency. As a result, serious social problems triggered by policies are gradually emerging. Tin Shui Wai, as the 3rd generation new town, has been suffered from various social problems including high unemployment rate, youth problem, social barriers etc. Thus, in this paper, TSW is studied as an experimental case to put forward some strategies for alleviating these problem and suggestions for policy making in the future.

Keywords: Public housing policy, Social problems, Unemployment rate, Social barrier

1 Introduction

The housing policy not only relates to housing itself, but also political and economic issues. Moreover, it is the foundation of social stability as well. Hong Kong's public housing policy is a positive example in the aspect of providing accommodation to approximately half of permanent residents. However, in the process of public housing development, various issues emerged due to developer monopoly and foreign economic force in housing market. Furthermore, enormous public housing limited by "transfer regulation" leads to waste of social resources and efficiency. The aims of this paper are offering some strategies to alleviate the current situation and giving suggestions to the future development of Tin Shui Wai new town.

Programs introduced below were the major Hong Kong's public housing policy during past 60 years. Home Ownership Scheme (HOS) is the only program still in progress today. Resent years, Hong Kong SAR government mainly focuses on the maintenance scheme and the comprehensive redevelopment program to boost the living quality of residents living in private rental housing (PRH) estates.

1.1 Review of Hong Kong's Public Housing Policy Development Process

1.1.1 Resettlement Program

Hong Kong's Dramatical increase in population from 0.6 to 2.3 million (1945-1951) led to squatter area occupying the edge of urban area. The fire happened in the squatter area of Shek Kip Mei made more than 50,000 people homeless overnight, forcing the government to launch the resettlement program immediately to provide temporary shelter to the victims. The resettlement program became the beginning of Hong Kong's public housing policy. It had offered accommodation for more than 1 million residents during 1954 to 1973. However, settlement buildings were criticized for poor quality lower than Hong Kong's living standard at that time, especially compared with private housing estates.

1.1.2 Ten-Year Housing Program

In order to improve the living environment of lower-middle income families, the government announced a Ten-year Housing Program (TYHP) (1972-1982). The goal of TYHP was to provide 1.8 million housing for the public in 10 years and increase the home ownership rate up to 60%. Another TYHP was announced later by Tung Chee Hwa, with the goal of helping 70% of households get homeownership. Besides, the Housing Authority was established to promote development of TYHP and organize construction of public housing estates. These two programs not only improved residents' living condition by providing public rental housing for 1 million people, but also promoted rapid development of new towns such as Tsuen Wan, Sha Tin and Tuen Mun in the New Territories. Unfortunately, the homeownership rate in Hong Kong was only 53.1% at the end of the second TYHP [Wong, Y. (2015)].

1.1.3 Home Ownership Scheme (HOS)

Although TYHP made remarkable achievement, there were still some citizens not poor enough to fulfill the condition applying for public rental housing and not wealthy enough to afford buying or renting private housing. These people were called "sandwich class". Aimed at helping this class, the government put forward the HOS to help lower-middle income families and public rental housing tenants to acquire their own flats. In HOS, change of ownership is strictly restricted. HOS Secondary Market was founded for ownership transaction among specific buyers with special condition including white form holders and green form holders. If owners want to transfer ownership in free market, they have to pay excessively high premium about 30%-50% of market value mostly. Thus the transaction volume of HOS units is extremely limited in free market.

1.1.4 Tenants Purchase Scheme

The Tenants Purchase Scheme (TPS) was launched in 1998, allowing tenants to purchase the public rental housing (PRH) flat they lived at affordable price. This program prominently increased the ratio of home ownership, but it was terminated in 2005.

1.2 Social Problems

Although the public housing policy provides accommodation for lower-middle income families, residents' long term development is ignored. Social issues such as high unemployment rate, economic inequality and rigid policy have also emerged in Hong Kong society. Major social problems were studied in this paper as below.

1.2.1 High Unemployment rate

In Hong Kong, 47.3% of households live in public housing flats, among which 30.8% live in public rental housing (PRH) units and 16.5% in HOS units [Wong, Y. (2015)]. The restrictive tenancy arrangements and requirement to pay excessively land premiums for HOS flats mean that nearly half the population of Hong Kong are forced to stay in the same place the government arranged. Residents' development thus was limited by commuting time, transportation cost to find a job. People living in new territories, Tuen Mun and Tin Shui Wai in particular, are the best examples where high-dense large-scale public housing communities are far from Kowloon and Hong Kong island. The unemployment rate of Tuen Mun and Tin Shui Wai is 7.2% and 9.1% respectively, higher than average unemployment rate in Hong Kong.

1.2.2 Social Barrier

To satisfy people's housing demand, the government began to construct many public housing units in new territories to transfer population away from crowded Hong Kong island and Kowloon area. The percentage of population living in public housing of New Territories (NT) was 57.6% in 2015 (Figure 1). With the development of Hung Shui Kiu new town and Kwu Tung North new town, the percentage of population living in public housing in NT will rise dramatically. In addition to this, disproportion between public housing and private housing happens in areas like Tin Shui Wai where about

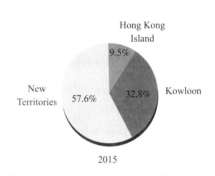

Figure 1 The proportion in public housing

80% of permeant housing is public housing. Obviously, occupants in public housing are low income groups likely. Hong Kong society thus becomes dual city, suffering from economic inequality, leading to social conflicts. The flow barrier of social class is also harmful to social stability in Hong Kong.

1.2.3 Social Inequity

Generally, the public housing policy is an predictable outcome to pursuit social equity, though it still brings social inequity unavoidably because of inflexible rules and regulations. The public housing program has existed more than 60 years, with some flats owned by wealthy household who owns private flats at the same time. Although Housing Authority has implemented "double rent policy" since 1980s, the rental price is still relative low comparing to private market. However, some other private housing tenants from the less wealthy class must suffer extremely high rents. The public rental housing benefits many households, but not all of them are the real people in need.

2 Literature Research

In order to find methods of alleviating these social issues, some researchers have proposed lots of strategies based on social issues related to public housing policy in Hong Kong. According to previous researches, this paper summarized some practical ways to temper current situation.

2.1 From Shelter to Homeownership

Richard Wong (2015) pointed out that the PRH units or HOS flats are only shelters for residents due to strict restriction from free transaction. Low circulation has an impact on employment due to restriction on mobility. Richard Wong suggested that housing authorities should set an affordable price for the whole ownership instead of unrealistic premium to promote join of public housing units in free market. In these cases, People get options to choose the location they live and work, thus reaching more employment opportunities. Moreover, it can also increase the homeownership rate in Hong Kong, which is helpful for social stability.

2.2 Matching Work–Residence in Spatial

Most researchers think that jobs-housing mismatch in some new towns of new territories is the major factor for high unemployment. Joseph Lau suggested that government could afford financial resources and land space to unemployed workers to develop social enterprises, collaborating with local special resources such as natural resources or historical resources to create special industries (Joseph, C.Y.L.2010). Eddie C.M.E and Zhong J,Z described that the PRH and HOS residents have worse work-housing matching than private housing residents in developing new town through relative analysis. They suggested that the government should consider revising the eligibility criteria for public housing to provide these real less wealthy groups with housing assistance, creating economic growth potential of developing new town (Hui, C. M. E., Zhong, J. & Yu K. 2015)

2.3 Social Integration

Hong Kong society has generated obvious social barrier for flowing upward, for residents living in the new territories especially where 57% of them living in public housing estates (Wei C., Li X. & Lai Y. 2016). Generally, the gathering of social disadvantaged groups and isolation from others has negative effect on their living areas, some even becomes slums (Xu Qin, 2008). Jacobs (Jacobs, J. 2006) believed that diversity is the most important condition for a healthy urban environment. Urban diversity means multifunction, and multi-social level. Li Zhigang (Li,Z., Xue,B. &Wei, L. 2007) pointed out that mixed income dwelling is helpful for social integration since this method could promote people from different levels to keep in touch and communicate with each other.

2.4 Improve the Efficiency and Equality of Housing Policy

Strategies suggested to address the problem of unfair subsidy in Hong Kong are double-rent policy for both HOS and the Home Purchase Loan Scheme (HPLS). The HOS and HPLS try to encourage well-off public housing tenants to buy their own house and release more public rental units for the needy people. However, these policies only affect people who are willing to move from public housing; moreover, the incompletes ownership is not so attractive (Yeh, 1990). Yeh suggested that housing authorities could gradually increase rents to the free market level. Then government should provide housing allowances to well-off tenants who need subsidies to pay for the raised rents (Yeh, 1990). While Richard Wong pointed out that the HOS is successful in the aspect of recovering public housing units, the well-off households were still taken care by governments, transferred into the HOS units. He suggested that the Tenant Purchase Scheme should be revived along with public rental housing units available in the open market to increase the circulation. In this case, well-off tenants have enough incentive to release public housing units to satisfy the needs for housing of low income groups(Wong, Y.C.R. 2015).

3 Case Study

3.1 Background

Tin Shui Wai, as one of nine new towns in Hong Kong from a gei wai fish pond area, has developed typical residential area with about 292,000 populations in past 30 years. In the process of development, the policies changed again and again. Instead of developing according to original plan which is a self-contained and balanced community with various function, Tin Shui Wai is regarded as a city of misery with high unemployment rate, high youth crime rate, high suicide rate and a large number of social-disadvantage new immigrants.

3.2 Disadvantages and Advantages

Tin Shui Wai is regarded as a besieged city because of its isolated location. It is located in the northwestern New Territories of Hong Kong, Yuen Long district, far from city center providing job opportunities. In addition, local area can not provide enough jobs because of unrational land use. These have led to high unemployment rate. Imbalanced housing type composition is another critical factor. The ratio of public housing and the private housing is up to 8:2 (gov. 2016). In this case, it could lead to unhealthy gathering of low income groups, generating social barrier mentioned above. Besides, TSW is suffering from other social problems such as high youth crime rate, divorce rate and new immigrants' issues. In short, Tin Shui Wai is a unsuccessful case of new town development and public housing policy.

On the other hand, there are some potential advantages in Tin Shui Wai. Firstly, although it has bad transportation location, the Hong Kong wetland park is on the north, with another travel destination PingShan heritage trail to the south. These travel resources could be special industrial resources to increase jobs opportunities in local area. Specifically, Tin Shui Wai is a "young" community, with about 20% aged between 10-19 and 21% aged between 40-49. It means that it has abundant labor forces, unlike the first generation of new towns faced with the issue of aging population (SWSA. HKU. 2009). Additionally, it is about 10km from Shenzhen bay checkpoint, which could bring some development opportunities for Tin Shui Wai new town. Last but not least, around 80% of public housing units means that reforming public housing policy could be an effective way in this area.

3.3 Strategies

3.3.1 Create More Employment Opportunities

The government should utilize local resources to create more employment opportunities for local residents to temper unemployment issues. The Hong Kong wetland park is a world-class ecotourism park with educational and ecological function. In 2016, the Hong Kong Wetland park attracted around 490,000 visitors. Large amount of visitors could bring some commercial and jobs opportunities. However, due to the lack of supporting tourism facilities such as restaurants, shopping centers and related products shops, most of visitors are more likely to choose Yuen Long or Tuen Mun to have a meal or go shopping after visiting Tin Shui Wai. Ping Shan heritage trail, as another tourist point, also can bring some tourists. In addition, Tin Shui Wai is closed to Shenzhen bay checkpoint where 30,800 passengers pass per day to Hong Kong for shopping, education and traveling. Local government can collaborate these local resources as breakthrough point to upgrade its supporting facilities such as shopping center to accommodate more visitors for shopping or visiting. In this case, instead of long commuting time and high transportation costs to cross-district working, TSW residents can find a job in surrounding areas.

3.3.2 Increase Free Circulation of Public Housing

Low circulation of public housing in free market is a limiting factor for employment since people have to give up some jobs opportunities considering commuting time and costs. In Singapore, all Housing and Development Board (HDB) flats could be rented and sold in the free market after 5 years from the date of purchase. In addition, the owner of HDB flats can "sublet" the unit totally or partly on the open market without repaying the land premium to the government (Kershaw, R., & George, T. 1975). As a consequence, housing-working has been matched more reasonably. People can choose workplace and housing location based on their own actual needs. In Tin Shui Wai, 80% of housing units are public rental housing and HOS flats, with only 8.3% population works in local area (Census, 2011). Government should adopt similar public housing policy of Singapore, with opening the market of public housing units with reasonable conditions such as affordable land premium. Conceptually, these ways could increase circulation of public housing flats on free market. It means that people will not be limited in an assigned location to pursue their long term development.

3.3.3 Mixed Housing

In Tin Shui Wai, imbalanced housing structure and mismatched working-housing make it desperate new town, suffering from the severe social barrier resulting from extremely high percentage of public sector housing units. The government can redevelop Tenant Purchase Scheme to increase the homeownership rate in this area. At the same time, in the future development, pay more attention on the ratio of public housing and private housing. Additionally, in same area, different types of housing should be mixed and integrated rather than separating. The planning of communities also should create more public space to promote people from different level to communicate with each other.

4 Conclusion

In conclusion, although Hong Kong's public housing policy help 47% Hong Kong residents with their housing need, the government only provided shelters while ignoring people's need for long term development. Additionally, current housing policy also causes waste of social resources and efficiency. The lesson from all these is that housing policy must take deep social conflict, and people's long term development into consideration. Besides, policy makers should have vision with correct direction, instead of suggesting unrealistic strategies. Putting people's welfare to the first place should be a must. Through collaboration of every sectors, Hong Kong can achieve a city of prosper, stability, democracy as well as equality.

香港的公营房屋政策与社会问题——以天水围新市镇为例

李 益

（高级环境规划技术理学硕士课程，中国城市住宅研究中心，香港中文大学）

摘 要：基于对香港公营房屋政策发展历程的研究，本文着重分析由公营房屋政策所带来的社会问题，并尝试着寻求缓解天水围目前状况的策略。第二次世界大战之后，为了满足越来越多人口的住房需求，香港颁布了一系列针对中低收入人群的公营房屋政策，如居者有其屋。目前为止，有47%的人口居住在房屋署提供的公营房屋。即使大规模的公营房屋已经改善了中低收入人群的住房条件，但是这些政策仅仅关注与满足居民的住所需求，而人们的长期发展被忽略。大多数的公营房屋位于新界，占全部公营房屋的57%，但是大部分的就业机会及公共设施分布在九龙和香港岛。同时公营房屋有严格的转换限制，随之带来巨大的资源浪费和社会效率的流失。因此一些由于这些公营房屋政策所引发的社会问题逐渐升级。天水围作为第三代新市镇，集中了许多典型的社会矛盾如高失业率、青少年问题、社会隔阂等，本文将它作为典型案例，分析所存在的社会问题，并结合实际情况提出相应对策，以缓解社会问题另外还给予公营房屋政策的制定提出一些建议。

关键词：公营房屋政策，社会问题，失业率，社会隔阂

References

[1] Wong Y. Hong Kong land for Hong Kong people: Fixing the failures of our housing policy / Yue Chim Richard Wong. 2015.

[2] Joseph Cho Yam Lau. The influence of suburbanization on the access to employment of workers in the new towns: A case study of Tin Shui Wai, Hong Kong[J]. Habitat International, 2011. (http://www.sciencedirect.com.easyaccess1.lib.cuhk.edu.hk/science/article/pii/S019739750900054X).

[3] Hui C M E., Zhong J, Yu K. Housing policy, work-residence mismatch and poverty concentration[J]. Habitat International, 2015, 48(8): 198-208. (http://www.sciencedirect.com/science/article/pii/S0197397515000594).

[4] Wei C, Li X, Lai Y. Be in a Dilemma: The Difficulties and Challenges of Public Housing Policy in Hong Kong[J]. URBAN PLANNING INTERNATIONAL, 2016, 31(04): 64-71.

[5] Xu Q. Housing policy and social integration——experience and revelation of foreign. JIANGHUAI TRIBUNE, 2008. http://doi.wanfangdata.com.cn/10.3969%2fj.issn.1001-862X.2008.05.016.

[6] Jacobs, J. The death and life of great American cities; with a new introduction by Jason Epstein and a foreword by the author (50th anniversary ed., 2011 Modern Library ed.). New York: Modern Library. 2011.

[7] Li Z, Xue D, Wei L. Housing mix in European and American cities: theories, application and implication. 2007. 31(2): 38-44. http://doi.wanfangdata.com.cn/10.3321%2fj.issn%3a1002-1329.2007.02.006.

[8] Yeh A. Unfair housing subsidy and public housing in Hong Kong. Environment & Planning: International Journal of Urban and Regional Research, 1990, 8(4): 439-454.

[9] HK. Department of Social Work and Administration & University of Hong Kong. (2009). A study on Tin Shui Wai New Town. Retrieved from http://www.pland.gov.hk/pland_en/p_study/comp_s/tsw/r3.pdf.

[10] Kershaw R., & George, T. (1975). Lee Kuan Yew's Singapore. International Affairs (Royal Institute of International Affairs 1944-). 51(2): 291.

开放住宅体系周期性共享租用模式探究

王春彧　李振宇

（同济大学建筑与城市规划学院）

摘　要：开放式住宅作为一种可变的结构体系，本身便具有改造与出租的灵活性。本文以开放式住宅理论为背景，探讨可能的三类公租房周期性租用模式：卧室分离式分享模式、公共空间平台化共享模式、大空间合同同享模式。本文通过分享、共享、同享这三种模式的概念拓展方案设计分析，基于 SI 体系、开放建筑（Open Building）等理论，结合各国公租房有关经验，总结出利用开放式居住建筑的灵活性进行共享租用以提高空间利用率的完整策略。

关键词：共享建筑，开放建筑，刚需空间，周期性空间

1　引言

近几年来，共享经济发展迅猛。从"Uber"代表的共享出租车到"ofo"为首的共享单车，乃至"Airbnb"创立的共享住宅租住平台，共享经济已经涵盖了人们衣、食、住、行的方方面面。与此同时，年轻一代购房压力骤增使得公租房的需求成倍增长。从 2014 年起，我国的保障性住房体系已经逐渐开始由经济适用房到公租房（廉租房）为主的过渡（范悦等，2008；林立震等，2017）。传统的住宅结构与建造方式存在着结构不可变、建设效率低、可持续性差等问题，不能很好地顺应公共租赁的要求。开放式住宅体系作为集合预制化、装配式、部品化、标准化等特征为一体的、全生命周期价值最大化的结构体系，更加顺应公租房的要求。

现代日常生活中，人们对居住空间的租用需求，从时间跨度上可分为刚需空间和周期性空间两类。刚需空间是指租客长期稳定的空间需求，如一对年轻夫妇的卧室、起居室等；周期性空间是指租客部分时间使用、部分时间闲置的空间，如定期到家里暂住的老人所需的次卧室。周期性空间的闲置带来了社会资源的浪费和住房压力的紧张。如果居住空间可以周期性租用，则将大大提高其利用率。开放式住宅的结构与空间灵活性，可以为周期性租用的实现提供更好的策略。

2　开放式住宅体系对于共享租用的优势

我国的保障性住房类型多样，从属性上大致可分为"出售型住房"和"租赁型住房"两类。"出售型住房"多采用现浇钢筋混凝土体系，技术成熟、成本优势明显，在现今高层、多层住宅中得到了广泛应用。而"租赁型住房"作为一种以政府主导的小面积住宅而非永久性住宅，其周期性特点更加明显，不仅需要符合保障性住房的特点，更要对其建造方式提出新的要求。开放式住宅作为一种灵活可变的体系，相比于传统建造方式，对于共享租用模式有诸多优势。

（1）建设效率高、质量可控、后期易维护

公租房主要面对群体集中在中低收入人群，同时作为政府主导项目，需要一方面具有较高建设

效率，另一方面可以以较高质量完成。开放式住宅在工厂预制生产，可有效地避免天气、环境等因素带来的生产延误，同时标准化、部品化使得质量也更加易于控制。公租房在一个租住周期结束后，管理方可对房屋内装修设施和非结构性构件进行较为方便的更换从而进一步出租。

（2）建造流程满足可持续发展要求

开放式住宅在建筑材料、建造能耗和建造流程上更多考虑环保和可持续的要求。同时，在大规模的交付使用之后，还能顺应未来社会发展情况和周期性共享的需求，根据需要改变其空间结构和功能。

（3）可满足租客"拎包入住"需要

开放式住宅通过"S（skeleton，支撑体）"和"I（infill，填充体、内装体）"有效分离，使得内装体能够在工厂标准化预制。因此内装体可以较为容易达到简单装修水平，满足短期租赁者的基本生活需求，同时也易于简单进行改造，免于二次装修。

3 开放式住宅三种共享租用模式

3.1 卧室分离式分享模式

大部分家庭都会面临家庭结构随着时间调整的情况，比如子女到异地上大学、参军等，这时家庭成员之一的卧室会周期性闲置。卧室分离式分享模式，即把套型中的一间划分出来，当周期性利用的时候房主使用，当周期性闲置的时候对外出租。这种分享模式是现今大部分家庭将周期性闲置房间出租的主要方法，也是共享程度较低的一种。这种模式虽然能够有效利用占套内25%以下面积的闲置空间，但是会存在租客和房主之间互相隐私度低、安全性差、租客可能需要和房主共用卫浴等问题，既降低了租客的体验也较大程度干扰了房主的生活。

开放式住宅具有内装体可变的优点，因此墙体的拆装挪移变得更加容易。基于开放式建筑理论，可提出一种新的卧室分离式分享模式——对于大户型开放住宅，将入口玄关设置两道门，玄关通向一间灵活次卧。当这间次卧周期性闲置的时候，可将其对外分享出租，外层大门隔墙拆除或常开，同时主人的主要居室由内层大门隔离，实现闲置空间的充分利用（图1）。这种模式具有可行性强、拆装作业小的特点，较好地解决了隐私和安全问题。对外出租的次卧如自带卫浴，也可提高租客的生活品质。

这一模式的出租周期涵盖跨度可以以年、月计算。

 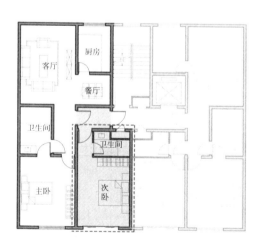

图1 卧室分离式分享模式示意（作者自绘）

3.2 公共空间平台化共享模式

年青一代家庭通常不具备足够的资金实力，因此这部分人群也成为公租房租用的主力军。他们由于预算有限，通常租住的套型并不大，很多单身者或年轻夫妻两人一般倾向于租住仅有一间卧室（或卧室和起居室合一）的小型公寓。但是这些年轻人中有一部分喜爱与朋友在家中聚会、娱乐，因此该人群除刚性空间的租用以外，对空间有额外的周期性需求以容纳更多客人。但周期性的需求不足以让租客有理由负担额外的、可能会大部分时间闲置的一间房间。

公共空间平台化共享模式，就是一种解决小户型的周期性额外空间需求的开放住宅模式——将独立的两户之间预留一间公共房间，双侧开门，通过社区管理网络平台预约使用该共享空间，通过开放建筑体系灵活调整内装体的部品，实现该空间最小化闲置（图2）。

图 2　公共空间平台化共享模式示意（作者自绘）

这种方式相当于将两户所需求的两间房间合并为一，实现了互联网思维下的共享经济，是共享程度较高的一种。这种模式能够节约原本占套内 25%～40% 左右的周期性空间闲置，既高效利用了空间又节省了租客的租金。但是，虽然使用了互联网平台进行预约协调，但是由于共享空间可能存在两方同时需求的小概率冲突，因此仍然有进一步商榷的空间。在冲突之时，遵循互联网思维下"友好协商、先到先得"的原则是一种较好的解决方案。

除两户共同所需聚会用会客空间以外，公共空间平台化共享模式还有更多类似的运用。比如不同进货周期的淘宝店主共用库房、不同时间亲友来访小住的共用卧室等。由于开放建筑部品化的特点，内部家具、空间格局可以随周期性租用者要求而灵活调整。

这一模式的出租周期涵盖跨度可以以时、日计算。

3.3 大空间合并同享模式

当代社会 SOHO 模式的流行，让更多人离开办公室，回归家庭办公的新模式。通常这样的家庭以 1～3 人的小集体为主，在办公时小型会议不需要过大的空间。但家庭办公有时会涉及更多人次的同时讨论，这时需要一些较大空间进行会议或者聚集，而这样的周期性需求往往只占一小部分时间。如果因为周期性大会议室的需求而租用更大的户型空间则造成了较多时间的空间闲置与浪费。

大空间合并同享模式就是针对有周期性会议、聚集等需求的开放住宅的租住模式——相邻两户的公共空间毗邻设置，其间使用可以简单安装的轻质隔墙进行分离，当公共空间需求变大时，可拆除隔墙将二者合并为大空间同享，实现邻里空间利用率的共赢。

这种方式相当于大工作组内两个小工作组的分离与组合。如一个规模为5人的初创公司，分为2人的部门一、3人的部门二，因为容易产生互相干扰的问题，平时大部分时间相对独立为两间工作。当每周一次的例会时，可以将两户之间的轻质隔墙局部拆除或推拉重叠，获得两个小空间相加而来的大空间。空间合并同享不止于2户，在合理条件下，也可推广到3户的合并乃至更多（图3）。这种模式能够将需要额外租用的占原本套内面积40%~60%的大会议室通过小空间整合的方式实现，高效地利用了小空间并且节约了租客的租金，是最高程度的"同享"。当然，空间合并同享模式的可行性也是三种模式中比较低的一种，亦存在着一些操作上的问题，诸如要求相邻两户为同一公司组织，要求开放住宅的结构体在保持声学、力学、热学特性的同时易于改变等。

这一模式的出租周期涵盖跨度可以以时、日计算。

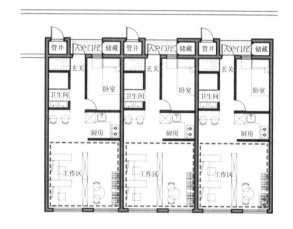 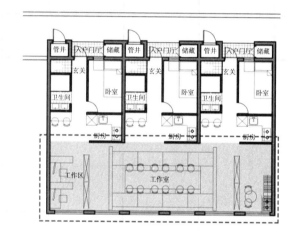

图3　大空间合并同享模式示意（作者自绘）

4　共享租用住宅概念方案拓展设计例析

4.1　项目背景

共享公租房概念设计选择了某创意园片区西南角的地块。建筑以组团形式存在。组团外皆为设有人行道的双向机动车道路，与城市道路自然交接，融为一体。组团内部设置纯粹的步行道及景观，独立封闭管理。商业人流可以直接进入面向道路的商铺，办公人员及住户则通过各单元的出入口进入围合组团内部或通过组团的地下车库进入各户。基地西南侧、东南侧两个人流热点连成一条线，形成主要人流线。

4.2　方案概念设计

共享租用公租房概念设计考虑如今大量周期性使用的空间被闲置或紧缺的现状，基于前述三种共享租用模式（卧室分离式分享模式、公共空间平台化共享模式、大空间合并同享模式），结合开放式住宅的特点，进一步拓展出周期性空间租用的概念模式。

首先，设计中明确了"以类型为原则的刚需空间"——LDK+nB，和"周期性空间"（$15m^2$的空间为基数乘以n）。经过背景调研，一部分租客会选择"适当拥挤"，抑制了周期性需求的合理实现；另一部分租客会选择"追求宽裕"，但会导致周期性的空间闲置。设计中为解决这一问题，以实际调研中发掘的极具代表性的两组家庭为例，公共空间平台化共享模式为基础进行探讨。第一组家庭是一对夫妻，他们的儿子每周五晚至每周日要从寄宿学校回家，这时候需要一间临时的卧室。第二组家庭是一位人声乐团的团长，他在每周二、每周四要组织4～6人的人声乐团排练，需要一间小型排练房。将二者的空间需求列在坐标轴上，发现二者可以互补（图4）。于是选择将两组家庭在平面上并置，中间预留一个约$15m^2$的空间进行共享租用。

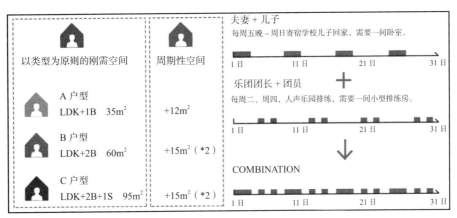

图4　刚需与周期性空间、两组家庭邻里匹配时间轴（作者自绘）

实现方式上，鉴于开放式建筑内装体可变的优势，设计进一步探讨了空间更灵活的可变方法，把"租房间"演绎为"租空间"。将两户之间公共空间预留，每户毗邻公共租用空间的房间有可移动的双层墙楼板盒体。技术性要点一是使用反梁结构将其降板，使得管线和部品贮藏得以良好结合；二是在梁边设置牛腿，将盒体以滑轨和滑轮进行良好支撑；三是干湿分离，可移动部分只涉及电气的转换，设置触点进行连接（林立震等，2017）。

空间共享租用的核心使用场景通过互联网平台手机APP来实现（图5）。相邻两户各自安装应用程序，并以住户身份注册和登录。以"周"周期为例，每周五填写下周的租用意愿并提交、支付租金、完成预约。若相邻两户需求发生偶发性冲突，则相互协商或先到先得。预约成功之后，在下一周可享受空间。

在相邻空间共享的思路下，可以扩展3种不同套内面积和不同周期性租用面积的户型（①基础$35m^2$+拓展$12m^2$，②基础$60m^2$+拓展$15m^2/30m^2$，③基础$95m^2$+拓展$15m^2/30m^2$）。设计中将3种户

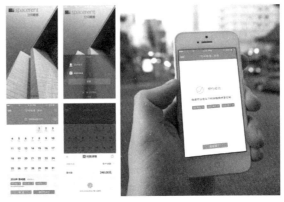

图5　周期性空间租用互联网平台示意（作者自绘）

型结合到一个五开间单元中（图6），形成了一个标准层的原型。每个标准层中的通高空间就是用于共享租用的空间。

图 6 标准层五开间单元（作者自绘）

5 优势与延伸

共享租用公租房开发商易于根据两户的需求计算每月的使用率，结合本身公共空间的租金价，计算两户租用时租金的加权系数收取租金。以 4.2 中的概念设计模型简单地进行理想化计算，原本一个 $15m^2$ 的空间，如定价日租金为 50 元，周期性共享租用时定价为 80 元，则两户每个月各租住 10 天只需要各付 800 元租金，各自节约了近一半租金的同时，开发商也能多获得 100 元的利润。

除了成本与利润的优势，开放式住宅体系也为共享租用带来了可行性与易用性方面的优点。在 3.1~3.3 中陈述的三种方式是对开放式住宅的简单利用，而 4.2 中的概念设计模型则是对开放式住宅特性的更进一步发挥。开放建筑内装体及设备部分与主体结构分离的特性使得户内空间获得更大灵活性以满足以后生活方式变化的适应性，因而墙体的拆装、楼板的滑移，可以让共享租用从简单的房间共享转变为空间的灵活共享。

3.3 ~ 3.3 中的"分享"、"共享"、"同享"三种模式在当前具有较高的可操作性，而在此基础上拓展的 4.2 中的概念设计提出了未来公租房周期性共享租用的创新模型。这一模型在实际推广中仍然会面临一系列问题，如滑动结构复杂易损坏、公共无楼板空间在报批计算容积率时难定义、每户内装体更新周期难统一等问题，这些问题的解决方案在未来仍然具有更深一层的研究意义。

致谢

本篇论文的写作受到国家自然科学基金项目《长三角地区"城中厂"的社区化更新技术体系研究》的资助（编号：51678412）。

Periodic Renting Sharing Mode Research of Residential Open Buildings

Wang Chunyu, Li Zhenyu

(College of Architecture and Urban Planning, Tongji University)

Abstract: As a kind of flexible structure system, open building system has flexibility for renting. This paper discusses three possible periodically renting modes of public housing: bedroom separated sharing, common space sharing, and combined large space sharing. This paper summarizes strategies of periodically renting of residential open buildings to improve space utilization, using conceptual design in Shanghai based on SI and OB theories.

Keywords: Sharing architecture, Open building, Rigid demand space, Periodic demand space

参考文献

[1] 邹经宇，李响. 高密度模式下的人居环境建设策略及新机遇 香港社会型住房的开发及转变 [J]. 时代建筑，2016，6.

[2] 王全良，战晓静，李建海，张伟. CSI 住宅 住宅产业化发展的必然选择 [J]. 住宅产业，2008，11.

[3] 范悦，程勇. 可持续开放住宅的过去和现在 [J]. 建筑师，2008，3.

[4] 林立震,王春彧,李瑜,应亚,张薇."空间租客"基于开放建筑理论的住宅适应性设计 [J]. 建筑技艺，2017，3.

[5] 谢颖，南锦顺. 地方租赁式保障房建设多元化融资模式研究 [J]. 建筑经济，2014，8.

Green Building Understanding Among Public Green Housing Residents: A Case Study in Hong Kong

Ji Jie, Yin Huai

(MSc Advanced Environmental Planning Technologies, The Chinese University of Hong Kong)

Abstract: Chinese Hong Kong has launched a few green building projects among both public and private housing estates. Previous literatures have revealed that the result in Hong Kong is different from the hypothesis that people with better green experiences will have better willingness to pay more for their green experiences. Although Hong Kong SAR Government has propagandized the idea and development of green buildings in Hong Kong, residents thought it was the responsibility for governments to provide the nice residences for citizens and it was easy for them to accept the money-conversion method to calculate the green space and living experiences as a price tag. This study investigated the cognition of green building among public green housing residents to realize the end-users' experiences and understand their thoughts about green buildings. It has been found out that the government propaganda of green building has less effect on influencing people to understand what green building is, regardless of the benefits or spirit of green buildings, which need comprehensive policies to promote in the future.

Keywords: Green building, Public housing, Residents' attachment

1 Introduction

With the development of urban growing, sustainable development policies have been conducted by many region and country to reduce the negative impact of human activities. As a result, performing outstanding in sustainability, green building has been introduced for years into the market. Meanwhile, the residents of these buildings also play a key role when considering about the maintenance, operation and other issues of the green buildings, which related to success of sustainability. Hong Kong is one of the regions that introduced green building into construction market and has its own green building standard called BEAM Plus. With limit personal incomes, about 45% of the Hong Kong population lives in the public house (2015, 香港房屋委员会及房屋署 [1]). Therefore, studies about green building understanding among public green housing residents can have great reference value for the similar cities with high density.

2 Literature Review

According to Chau, Tse, and Chung [2] (2010), residents with green experience would value enhancements on all kinds of environmental performance like energy saving the same as conventional residents. However, green residents were less interested in expanding their landscape, although landscape is a key element that distinguishes green projects from common ones. Nevertheless, in another investigation carried out amongst the residents of Hong Kong, Alex Lo and Jim [3] (2010), most of the respondents would like to pay a notable amount of money to recover the possible loss of urban green spaces, which different from the research of C.K Chau. The possible reasons may be the misunderstanding of the survey questions, high expenditure of personal household landscape and poor policy communication and so on, which need to be further studied.

3 Methodology

This study was led and conducted by a questionnaire survey taken place in late December 2016 in Ngau Tau Kok Upper Estate. The questionnaire was provided by Prof. Norgarsek and her research team and the authors engaged in the on-site community survey. It was a pilot survey to evaluate the general housing experiences in Hong Kong. The respondents were asked to indicate basic data (gender, age, occupation, and marriage) and rate the relative satisfaction of a series of attributes about their living experiences using the six-point Likert scales (6 = Don't know). 20 pilot questionnaires were sent out in Ngau Tau Kok Upper Estate and all surveyors accessed 26 responders to fill in the questionnaires. Authors selected 7 aspects including satisfaction of settlement and community outdoor environment qualities, the inside living efficiency and the understanding of the sustainability to evaluate how the residents understand the green housing schemes according to their own living experiences and the variance of their willingness to pay for the green building experiences.

4 Results Analysis

The total responsive rate of the attributes was relatively low which is 52%. It indicates that only 13 responders answered for each question. Therefore, only simple data generation was processed in this paper to see the trend of residents' choices. Further intensive statistics test will be done if there have more samplings.

4.1 Age, Gender, Occupation and Housing Types Distribution of Responders

The average age of the responders is 44.71 years old. 12%, 42%, 8% 19% of them are under 18 years old, among 19-45 years old, 46-65 years old and over 66 years old, respectively. Another 19% of them refused to provide their ages. The elderly rate (>66) of the responders is 19%. 50% of the responders are male and 38% of them are female. 12% of them did not allow us to record their gender. 8%, 23%, 4%, 19% of the responders are unemployed, employees, retired, students, respectively. 46% of them did not report their occupation. 46% and 19% of them are from public housing and private housing. 4% of them reported no house. 31% of them refused to tell their housing status.

4.2 Satisfaction of Community Surroundings

From the satisfaction of community surroundings aspect (Figure 1), it can be shown that the location and easy transportation of Ngau Tau Kok Upper Estate is the most favored aspect from the residents. And most of them are also satisfied with the safety of pedestrians, arrangements of houses, the appearance of the community, the shops in the community, the close medical service, the greenery and the air quality.

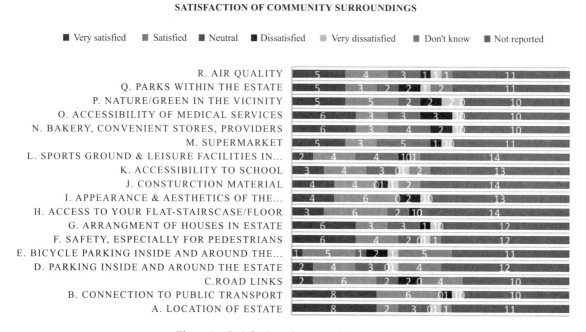

Figure 1 Satisfaction of community surroundings

But the residents are also reported their less satisfactions on the inadequate of sports or leisure area and the inadequate parking areas for bicycles and vehicles inside or outside the community. It indicates that there still have the needs for using bicycles or vehicles to supplement the transportation needs although Ngau Tau Kok Upper Estate has equipped with very intensive public transportation facilities including Ngau Tau Kok Station and Kowloon Bay Station of MTR and 26 public buses services within N.T. and connecting Hong Kong Island and N.T.

4.3　Problems within Housing Estate

The biggest problem (Figure 2) reported from the responders is the inadequate place for households, which was sourced from both genders (4 male, 2 females, 2 unknown gender). The second mostly-reported problems are humidity and noise within and without the community. A lack of playgrounds or sports facilities is also an often-mentioned problem here as mentioned in the previous aspect.

In fact, not only the space for household is inadequate in Ngau Tau Kok Upper Estate. This is a problem often mentioned in every Hong Kong public estates (2015, "Hong Kong Must" [4]). According to the fire control regulation in Hong Kong, the kitchen must be separated as an independent room (2011, Building Department[5]). As a result, the kitchen for households are often small and always multi-functional, which means the kitchen space is not adequate for completing so many households' tasks. Another reason for the complaint may result from the lack of balcony for surveyors observed that many residents put their clothes outside the windows to dry out because the household is too small to dry out the clothes. If the balcony is built, residents can solve the problem. But the balcony building in Hong Kong is recognized as a bonus and luxury item, only the private housing will provide such item to balance the service gap between private housing and public housing.

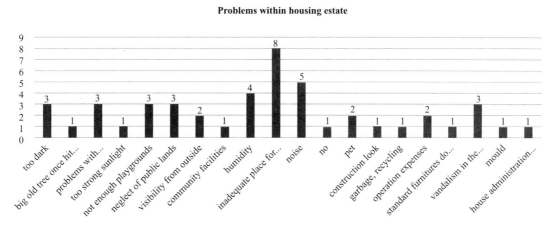

Figure 2   Problems within housing estate

4.4 Housing Space Efficiency

The above figure reveals that the responders are not satisfied with the current apartment space efficiency. Surprisingly, it is favored to have better cost benefit sacrificing the house space despite the house space is already limited, which can be seen that the affordability may be the piority of the other concerns' of the responders during choosing settlement. They have more willingness to pay for the better cost benefit houses. Also, it is satisfied to combine the kitchen and living room together. However, sharing rooms with neighbors are not accepted for most of the responders, which can be seen that the privacy is the concern of the residents (Figure 3).

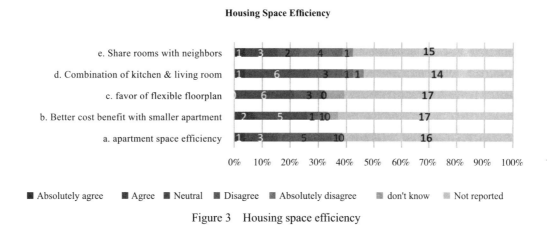

Figure 3   Housing space efficiency

4.5 Sustainability

This saction asked them if their apartment or community is with above statements, whether they will be satisfied with these (Figure 4). The most favored aspects are to have a good thermal insulation, fitting with standard furnitures nicely and estate consuming less energy.

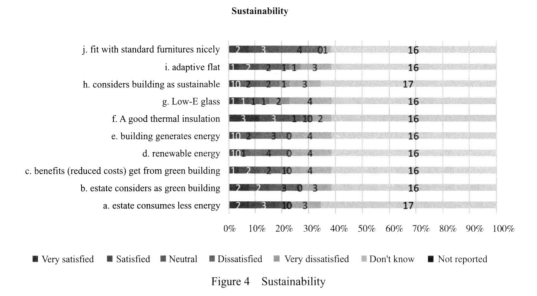

Figure 4 Sustainability

Although the responsive rate is quite low of this saction, it is surprisingly to find that many responders replied unknown to these statements about green buildings and their performances and equipments. The most unknown aspects are applying low-E glass, building generating energy, renewable energy and getting benefits from green buildings.

The responders' age varied from 10-71 and education level varied from primary grade 4 to bachelor degree. But even with a bachelor degree which is in relatively high education level, the responder still replied 5 statements as "don't know", which showed the neglectance of the green building industry. From Hong Kong SAR government website, it can be clearly seen the statements and propagandas to promote the idea of green buildings (2015, "Green Buildings" [6]). But in current development path, the sustainability education in Hong Kong is focusing on the low-carbon emmission for vehicles and natural environment conservation (2011, 香港课程发展议会 [7]19; 2017, 环境运动委员会 [8]). The building aspect or the housing aspect, for residents, whether it is sustainability for environment is not the first priority to consider. Whether they have the chance to get up the train —— to have their own house is usually their first consideration. Not to mention the design and certification of green buildings may become a profit point to increase their housing cost.

5 Discussion and Conclusion

It has to be indicated firstly is about the pilot survey data that is not adequate to illustrate the trend of their willingness to pay for the green experience or the understandings of sustainability theories.

According to the residents, some of their housing has irrational room distribution, such as small kitchen that allows single person's activity, which leads to ventilation and other indoor environmental quality problems and affects their living experience. Therefore, future green building design and construction can improve indoor environmental quality by paying more attention to living experience. On the other hand, to solve the high operation expanse that some residents complain about, a project should conduct a Life Cycle Cost evaluation and apply innovation of cost-efficient strategies to make sure the project can achieve lower cost not only in the long run but also in terms of hard cost.

Additionally, the study is initially to evaluate the propaganda of government for promoting green building theories and green building projects. But it is disappointed to find that the government propaganda of green building has less effect on influencing people to understand what green building is. Even the residents of Ngau Tau Kok Upper Estate, where their living places is a green building community, they still do not understand the rationale of how it developed to have such a performance. Or they even haven't realized that it has an environmental-friendly performance. Green building policy or its development should not be a shrine placing in the realm in the superstructure – the decision makers group, while its benefit and significance to build should get attached to the residents to make them feel that their choices are wise to live in and make contributions to protect the environment. The propaganda materials should not just simply put on a website, but also needs the offline on-site promotions to let the citizens recognize its existence as much as the low-carbon emission and nature conservation.

Of course, these results have limitation because most responders are from public housing and their economic and education level may not be so high to understand these statements or get attached to these aspects of information.

Acknowledgements

This paper is greatly supported by Prof. Nograsek and her colleagues from Graz Technology University, Austria by providing us the pilot questionnaire and its data. Meanwhile, thanks to Prof. Tsou Jin Yeu and Ms. Erica Li for their kindly help and suggestions.

香港公屋居民对于绿色建筑认识：个案研究

季 洁 郫 槐

（香港中文大学高级环境规划技术理学硕士）

摘　要：香港已在公屋和私人屋宇领域都推出了几个绿色建筑项目。然而根据以前的文献，与想象中不同的是，有过较好绿色建筑体验的人并不愿意为绿色体验付出更多金钱。虽然香港特区政府一直在宣传香港绿色建筑的理念和发展，但居民认为政府有责任为市民提供不错的住宅，而且居民们很容易接受以绿色空间和生活体验作为价格标签。本研究调查了绿色公屋居民对绿色建筑的认知，了解住户的体验及其对绿色建筑的想法。我们发现，政府对绿色建筑的宣传很少影响人们对绿色建筑的了解，因此今后需要全面而综合的政策来对绿色建筑进行推广。

关键词：绿色建筑，香港公屋，居民接触

References

[1] 香港房屋委员会及房屋署，房屋统计数字 [M]. 香港：香港房屋委员会及房物署，2016.

[2] Chau C K, Tse M S, Chung K Y. A choice experiment to estimate the effect of green experience on preferences and willingness-to-pay for green building attributes[J]. Building and Environment, 2010, 45(11): 2553-2561.

[3] Lo A Y, Jim C Y. Willingness of residents to pay and motives for conservation of urban green spaces in the compact city of Hong Kong[J]. Urban Forestry & Urban Greening, 2010, 9(2): 113-120.

[4] South China Morning Post. Hong Kong must do more to ensure adequate living space for its citizens[EB/OL].[2017-04-22]. http://www.scmp.com/comment/insight-opinion/article/1833252/hong-kong-must-do-more-ensure-adequate-living-space-its.

[5] Building department. Code of Practice for Fire Safety in Buildings 2011. Section F. 香港：[出版者不详]. 2011.

[6] GovHK. Green Buildings. [EB/OL].[2017-04-22]. https://www.gov.hk/en/residents/environment/sustainable/buildings.htm.

[7] 香港特别行政区教育局. 小学常识课课程指引 [M]. 香港：香港课程发展议会，2011.

[8] 环境运动委员会. 教师手册. [EB/OL]. [2017-04-22]. http://www.eccteachingkit.org.hk/web/teacher_manual.html.

Social Housing in Different Cultures——Comparative Study Western Europe and East Asia: A First Attempt

Wolfgang Dokonal[1], Marlis Nograsek[1], Ernst Dengg[1], Tsou Jin-Yeu[2]

(1. Graz University of Technology,

2. Center for Housing Innovations, The Chinese University of Hong Kong)

Abstract: Based on a mutual research agreement between Graz University of Technology, Austria and the Chinese University of Hong Kong, we have tried to evaluate the living conditions and the living quality of public housing projects in Austria and Hong Kong. The main objective of this research is the comparison of housings and tenants' satisfaction in both countries to be able to learn from each other and identify areas of improvements for both partners based on this information.

Keywords: Housing satisfaction, Public housing

1 Introduction

This research is based on a PhD work of one of the authors of this paper, who based the research on the "Wohnungs-Bewertungs-System" (WBS) or "Flat Evaluation System" which has been established in Switzerland many years ago. The WBS tool served as a planning instrument which allows to assess and compare different residential housings, considering housing quality, their flexibility, and the quality of life in the different housing schemes. The PhD used this system to research the situation in a mid-sized (in European terms) Austrian town and compared it with a case study from sociologists, who had made a survey about housing satisfaction. The result was, that the subjective opinion of the inhabitants did fit together with the measured results from the WBS.

The difficult challenge for us was to find a way to adapt this European system to the very different situation in Asia. We wanted to be able to investigate and compare the tenant's housing satisfaction in Chinese Hong Kong and Austria due to very different conditions in terms of culture, social structure, education and climate. Also size is an issue here —— the city of Hong Kong has nearly the same population as the whole state of Austria. Therefore the system had to be modified to meet the requirements on the Hong Kong housing market due to spatially very confined housing typologies.

It turned out that due to several problems and restrictions and the availability of students for this project we were not able to do the full research in the available timeframe but we managed to test a part of our strategy in two "test runs" —— one in Hong Kong in December 2016 and one in Vienna in April 2017. In these "test runs" we managed with the help of students from Hong Kong and Graz to interview and collect around 70 questionnaires.

1.1 Starting Point of the Research

The main idea was to conduct a resident's survey with the help of a questionnaire. After many discussions with the Hong Kong partners, it was clear that the original idea to send out the questionnaire or put it online to be filled out by the tenants was not possible in Hong Kong situation. Therefore, we decided that students should interview the residents at public housing estates and fill in the questionnaire with them. In December 2016, after several adaptions and amendments of the original questionnaire, we conducted a first attempt as a test run for the wider survey. The test run clearly showed that we had to do some changes to the questionnaire —— mainly because the questionnaire was too long and some questions were too specific for the tenants to understand. Based on these changes the second test run in Austria was conducted in April 2017.

2 The Estates

The area we picked for the test run in Hong Kong —— Upper Ngau Tau Kok, is considered as one of the most livable public housing projects constructed in Hong Kong and is therefore the best match with the more "upmarket" situation in social (public) housing in Austria. The area for the test run in Austria was a part of SeestadtAspern, which is a new development in the city of Vienna. Both projects try to fulfill the principles of Social, Environmental and Economic Sustainability and both won "Green Buildings awards in their countries and had a certain amount of participation during the planning process.

2.1 Upper Ngau Tau Kok Estate, Hong Kong

Some statistical data:
- population: 12.200
- Net site area: 32 200m^2 (3.2 ha)
- Gross domestic floor area: 220 000m^2 (22 ha)
- 6 blocks with 4.584 units
- Average Living Space: > 7m^2 /person
- Landscape area ratio: > 30% of the site area
- Prevailing rents: HK$ 1000 – 2700 (120 – 300 €)

Common provisions:
- Footbridges and shuttle lifts
- A central plaza
- A podium garden on top of the commercial centre
- Children's play areas and a basketball court above the ICYSC
- Extensive plantations and preserved mature trees

Achievements e.g.:
- Green Building Award 2006 organized by the Professional Green Building Council, Hong Kong
- Quality Public Housing Construction & Maintenance Awards 2009

In general this estate has a higher standard than the usual standard of public housing in Hong Kong.

https://www.housingauthority.gov.hk/en/common/pdf/about-us/publications-and-statistics/UNTK.pdf.

2.2 Seestadt Aspern, Vienna

Some statistical data:
- population: 20,000 (estimated for 2028)
- Net site area: 240,000 (240ha)
- Gross domestic floor area:
- townhouses with 10,500 units plus 20,000 work stations
- Average Living Space: > 22.5m^2 /person
- Public space area ratio: > 50% of the site area
- Prevailing rents: € 16/m^2 (135 HKD/m^2)

Common provisions:
- Working Rooms and Music and Rehearsal rooms
- Library and Sauna
- Common Kitchen
- Indoor Playground and Foyer Spaces

Achievements:
- European Green Building Integrated Design Award 2014
- World Smart City Award fürSeestadt-Projekt 2016

General important aspects in the design of the Seestadt Aspern project were: Social sustainability, Environmental Friendliness, Low Energy Standard, Mix of functions and the variety of architecture and the affordability.

3 The "Test Runs"

The first test run in Hong Kong in December 2016 was divided into two timeslots —— one workdays and one on weekend —— to get a better range of different target groups. In Hong Kong situation because of the long working hours, it is hard to be able to interview the "working generation" during a weekday as there is a better chance to reach the target population group on weekends. The aim for this test run of the survey was to figure out if there are difficulties with specific questions, the amount and duration of the interview/ questionnaire and if or to what extend test persons can fill out the questionnaire on their own without the help of a student.

We gathered much useful information about necessary modifications to the questionnaire. Amongst other things, it could be recognized that the duration of the first version of the interview was much too long, technical questions on the building quality cannot be answered due to lack of knowledge and certain questions were simply ignored. A positive finding is, that most of student age to middle-aged test persons could fill out the questionnaire almost independently, in just a few cases they need to ask, which allows to more interviews within a shorter time.

Because of these circumstances, several questions concerning "green topics" had to be cancelled.For the test run in Vienna we had already used the adapted questionnaire. Some parts of these projects included so called "Baugruppen" which means that a group of people already is involved in the design concepts of the estate in a participatory way.We also had some additional question for a research on these kind of design processes and its consequences because of the fact that other researchers were interested in that topic.

4 What Did We Ask —— The Questionnaire

For the test survey in Hong Kong we adapted a questionnaire, which sociologists had created for a case study in Graz, Austria (see [7]).

Their questionnaire had the following chapters:
- Satisfaction with the flat
- Satisfaction with the estate
- Daily Life
- Position to modern architecture
- General important Factors for Housing

We adopted the first three chapters and abandoned the last two because they did not seem relevant for our survey. Instead we added the following additional chapters
- Background and wishes for the future
- Housing Space Efficiency
- Sustainability

and of course, we asked the sociodemographic data.

5 Preliminary Findings from the "Test Runs"

There were some obvious results and some unexpected. The number of parking spaces in the vicinity of the flat is much higher in Seestadt Aspern than in The Upper Ngau Tau Kok Estate. But that doesn't have a negative impact on the satisfaction of the tenants in Hong Kong because there is no need for cars at all(in fact, only one of the people we interviewed in Hong Kong had a car). But it would have had a big influence on the satisfaction in Vienna because, although there are good public transport facilities there, most of the people will have a car anyway that is part of the Austrian lifestyle nowadays. In general, the satisfaction with many aspects e.g. number of rooms, the accessibility of apartments and facilities like school/kindergarten, nature and parks in the vicinity were quite high in Vienna.The urge to move into a different settlement was very low at SeestadtAspern – lower than in the Upper Ngau Tau Kok Estate.

Concerning question that directly addresses the flats we saw a similar picture. In most cases people were more satisfied in SeestadtAspern, than in the Upper Ngau Tau KokEstate. One interesting aspect was that there seemed to be a higher number of conflicts between tenants in SeestadtAspern. Whether this is caused by the fact that different ethnical groups are involved or by the fact that it is a tradition in Vienna to have conflicts with your neighbours even when you have no real reason for that could not be verified through the test runs

Several questions (variables in the statistical evaluation) showed quite significant differences when we compiled them with the help of a statistical program (SPSS) (see Figure 1). Whenever there are such differences, the positive value at SeestadtAspern is higher. This is partly obviously due to the architectural circumstances. But probably there are other underlying factors influencing the outcome of the "test runs" For example, some answers might have been influenced by the fact that people are assembly members and part of the founding movement in Aspern —— they are involved to a certain degree in the design process through participation and that clearly might have influenced the answers. A similar effect could also be a factor at Upper Ngau Tau Kok because there was also a certain degree of participation and we did not ask about this kind of personal involvement in the questionnaire. Other interview effects can also influence the outcome.

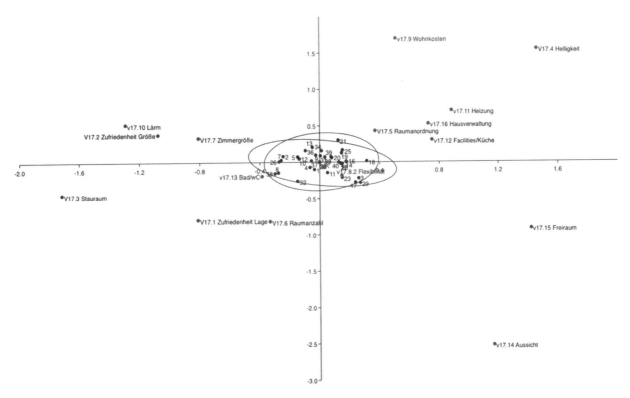

Figure 1   Example of correspondence analysis using SPSS

6 The Comparability of The Survey and Cross——Cultural Influences

In general, where there are differences, satisfaction in Seestadt Aspern is higher. This is quite interesting because normally people in Vienna are not easily satisfied and complain a lot. For the most part, this is certainly due to technical details. But the question of intercultural bias needs to be asked. We tried to avoid some of these problems by having local students – on the one hand Chinese students in Hong Kong and on the other hand Austrian students in Vienna doing the interviews with the questionnaire. But in fact, most of them where not really "local" —— Chinese students often come from mainland china and are not directly from Hong Kong and speak Madarin rather than Cantonese. A certain percentage of Austrian students (also those doing interviews) often come from eastern European countries. Therefore, there is still a slight chance that this fact has a certain influence on the answers. There is also the fact that the so called "social desirability" which is the effect that people tend to present their own situation in a better way than they are.

Some of the most compelling evidence regarding the effects of culture on the survey process comes from studies that have demonstrated that cultural distance between respondents and interviewers sometimes produces varying patterns of responses. In U.S. studies, respondents have been shown to defer to the perceived values of other-race interviewers when answering relevant survey questions (see[8]).

7 Outlook

In future, we will try to conduct the interviews in Hong Kong and Austria on a much bigger scale with the adapted questionnaire. We want to have at least 12 groups with 3 students per group in Hong Kong and a similar number of students in Austria. We plan to do the interviews in different housing estates and have a mix of 60% public housing and 40% private housing in Hong Kong to compensate for the fact that the social housing market in Austria is much more "upmarket" compared to the situation in Hong Kong. For the same reason, we plan to include some estates in Austria with a "lower" social and quality standing. For the test runs the results were clearly influenced by the fact that both test areas are outstanding and rather new examples and don't show the average situation of tenants in public housing estates.

These insights together with recommendations for future developments will be the core of future research within this project.

Acknowledgements

We have to thank Rainer Rosegger for contributing his expertise as a sociologist into the evaluation of this survey. Many Thanks to Prof. Jin Je Tsou for supporting this survey. The following students took part in the survey and did the interviews to fill in the questionnaire:

Hong Kong:
- Cao Xiuan, Amy Liang, Lei Qinghua, Ji Jie and Yin Huai.

Graz/Vienna:
- AntonopoulouAthina, Kougia Maria, Nenadic Alexandra, NuicAnela, Reisenhofer Theresa, Tamandl Laura.

不同文化背景下的社会性住房：西欧与东亚的初步比较研究

Wolfgang Dokonal[1]　Marlis Nograsek[1]　Ernst Dengg[1]　邹经宇[2]

（1. 格拉茨技术大学；2. 香港中文大学中国城市住宅研究中心）

摘　要：基于奥地利格拉茨技术大学和中国香港中文大学的研究合作计划，本研究对奥地利和香港公营房屋中的生活状况和居住质量进行了调查和评价。本研究的主要目的在于通过比较两个地区的住宅和居住者的居住满意度，促进经验的相互借鉴；同时基于此调查和评价结果，了解双方在当前住房发展建设中有待改进的方面。

关键词：住房满意度，公营房屋

References

[1] Bewertungsprobleme in der BauplanungArbeitsberichte zur Planungsmethodik 1 mitBeiträgen von Jürgen Joedicke, Siegfried Maser, Arne Musso, Horst Rittel, Barbara Köhler, Artur Bottling, Horst Höfler, Lutz Kandel, Gunter Kohlsdorf, Eva-Maria Kreuz, Peter Dietze, Karl KrämerVerlag Stuttgart/Bern, 1972.

[2] Faller, Peter, Der Wohngrundriss, Entwicklungslinien 1920-1990, Schlüsselprojekte, Funktionsstudien, Untersuchung im Auftrag der Wüstenrot Stiftung Deutscher Eigenheimverein e.V., Ludwigsburg, Dt. Verlagsanstalt, 1997.

[3] Riccabona, Christof, Wachberger, Michael, Wohnqualität, Bewertungsmodell für Wohnungen, Wohnanlagen und Standorte, Österreichisches Institut für Bauforschung, Wien, 1977Schriftenreihe Wohnungswesen, Band 53, Wohnung und Haushaltsgröße, Anleitungzur Nutzungsanalyse von Grundrissen, Markus Gierisch, Hermann Huber, Hans-JakobWittwer, Bundesamt für Wohnungswesen, Bern, 1993.

[4] Schriftenreihe Wohnungswesen, Band 69, Wohnbauten planen, beurteilen und vergleichen, Wohnungs-Bewertungs-System Ausgabe 2000, Bundesamt für Wohnungswesen, Grenchen, 2000.

[5] Wohnbauten planen, beurteilen und vergleichen, Wohnungs-Bewertungs-System WBS Ausgabe 2015, Eidgenössisches Department für Wirtschaft, Bildung und Forschung WBF, Bundesamt für Wohnungswesen BWO, Grenchen, 2015.

[6] Wohnwert-Barometer, Erfassungs- und Bewertungssystem nachhaltiger Wohnqualität, Manfred Hegger (Hrsg), Bauforschung für die Praxis, Band 90, Fraunhofer IRB Verlag , 2010.

[7] Wohnbund Steiermark, Wohnzufriedenheit und architektonische Innovation in der Steiermark seit den 60-er Jahren. Eine Studieim Auftrag der Steiermärkischen Landesregierung, durchge führt vom Wohnbund Steiermark., Werner Nussmüller, Markus Müller, Winfried Moser, Dieter Reicher, Graz, März , 2000.

[8] Cotter et al. 1982; Anderson et al. 1988; Finkel, Guterbock, and Borg 1991; Davis 1997. Chapter 13 Social Desirability in Cross Cultural Research.

台北都市区家户之居住安排特性研究

徐国城　刘芷妤

（中国文化大学都市计划与开发管理学系）

摘　要：民众由租赁房屋转变为购置自有住宅之行为，系属多元考虑之决策行为，包括：工作稳定性、家庭收入、子女就学、居住环境等考虑。举例而言，租屋主要仅考虑与其就业地点之邻近性、居住环境之便利性等，但一旦欲转为购置自有住宅，则必将房价水平、房贷支出、子女就学、房地产增值与否等更为深入之因素纳入思考，且多数民众在迁就可负担房价的情况下，通常首次购屋多会选择郊区之住宅，如此，长期的通勤成本（包括：金钱与时间）亦将成为购屋决策之重点考虑。因此，本研究思考台北都市区房价高涨，居住在台北都市区的家户，是否因社会经济条件与各项特征的差异，而必须在购置或租赁住宅的决策行为间进行选择。为探究家户居住转换背后的行为模式与影响因素，在实证设计部分，本研究乃透过多项逻辑特模型（Multinomial Logit Model）厘清家户居住安排与不动产市场景气、个人社经特性、整体经济景气氛围之互动关系，进一步了解不同形态的居住转换族群间，如何受到各项社会、经济等影响因素，而在居住安排决策行为上呈现差异之样貌。

关键词：购租屋决策，居住安排，华人家庭动态数据库，多项逻辑特模型

1　前言

快速工业化及都市化的发展，使人口纷纷往工作机会多、薪资所得高的都市区集中，此系为都市区中心之不动产需求增加的初始影响因素（Baharoglu，1996；Oktay et al.，2014），至于地区文化特色、年龄分布、经济能力、经济成长、货币政策、等因素则会对都市区之不动产需求产生长远的影响（Tiwari，2000；Saita，Shimizu and Watanabe，2016）。此外，由于都市地区提供的资源相对较多，吸引外地的高知识族群涌入，教育水平亦提高，一般而言，受教育程度越高者，其收入水平越高，对生活质量即会有较高之期待及需求，愿意支付较高之代价获得一定程度以上的生活空间与质量，此亦成为都市区中心不动产市场蓬勃发展之原因。

归纳林左裕（2014）、卓辉华（2014）针对台湾不动产市场景气发展经历过 1973 年及 1980 年两次全球性的能源危机，及岛内放宽外汇管制、降低关税的政治经济解严造成不动产景气高峰；在亚洲金融风暴及岛内房地超额供给，林肯大郡、921 地震等自然灾害造成台湾不动产泡沫化；2008 年又遭逢美国次贷风暴、全球金融海啸、欧债危机，各国为挽救经济，祭出低利率及增加贷款供给等宽松贷款政策，造成资产价格的膨胀，高房价成为民怨之首。可得知岛内外经济局势变动、政治、不动产政策等，皆影响不动产市场的变化。Ermisch and Salvo（1996）认为，除所得、财富对家户购置住宅有显著影响外，总体经济面因素如住宅价格涨幅程度、贷款利率与失业率等，亦会对家户购屋行为产生显著影响。显示家户的居住安排会牵涉到其自身之主观意愿与客观能力等问题，以及整体环境下的价值观与经济环境之可支配性。此外，人们将购屋视为生活及社会地位象征之目标，并以拥有自有住宅作为终其一生追求的梦想（彭建文、花敬群，2001；Ahn，2001；Garriga et al，2006），连带影响家户必须在居住安排选择上要斟酌思量。

Hughes（2004）认为目前的经济状况让年轻世代难以达到有资格结婚的最低经济门槛。对于结婚

后无法负担长期的经济义务，使得寻求婚配之动机降低（Oppenheimer，1988。引自 Kalmijn，2011）此与部分西方学者提出"结婚需拥有自有住宅，若目前尚无购置住宅之能力，则需等到你具备该能力，才能有结婚之计划"（Mulder and Wagner，2001；Forrest，Kennett and Leather，2001）的社会现象一致，此背后隐含着欲购屋者由于需要花费更长的时间累积财富购屋，而可能排挤结婚或生育的意愿。另外，黄靖容（2011）研究进一步指出结婚与生育，对自有住宅的影响力随世代不同已逐渐减弱，但与父母亲同住的居住倾向却越来越高，对于老人而言，同住是身心状况下降时的较佳选择，对于子女而言，同住则是基于父母能协助照顾小孩，以及减轻生活费用、房屋贷款负担等财务压力所产生的居住安排行为（De Vos and Lee，1993；曾沥仪等，2006），此等现象显示出年轻世代的家户在难以负担购屋所需成本时，除暂时性的租屋选择外，就近照顾父母而选择与父母同住已成普遍现象。更凸显出住宅选择不仅包括购屋或租赁两种，亦有与父母共同居住这一项选择，陈佳欣（2007）即指出，租拥选择在台湾不应只是租或拥，而是租、拥或回原生家庭之多事件决策。综合相关研究对于影响居住安排之论述，能将其分为自有、租赁、父母拥有等三种住宅权属外，亦可以理解，在经济条件方面，家户本身之社会经济资源及负担能力的限制，将会直接影响住宅权属的选择（Painter and Redfearn，2002；Groot，Manting and Mulder，2013）。

此外，在金融政策方面，在住宅贷款、税收抵免的政策帮助下，往往造成少数族群、年轻购屋者与低收入者，在充分利用税收信贷下增加购置住宅的概率（Hempel and Punj，1999；Goodwin and Zumpano，2011；Gan et al，2014）。至于迁移行为方面，租赁者在选择居住空间与通勤时间上较有弹性，使得租赁者的迁移概率高于购置住宅的家户（Boehm，1981；Ioannides，1987）。

基于此缘故，本研究思考台北都市区房价高涨，居住在台北都市区的家户，是否因社会经济条件与各项特征的差异，而必须在购置或租赁住宅的决策行为间进行选择。为探究家户居住转换背后的行为模式与影响因素，在实证设计部分，本研究乃透过多项逻辑特模型厘清家户居住安排与不动产市场景气、个人社经特性、整体经济景气氛围之互动关系，进一步了解不同形态的居住转换族群间，如何受到各项社会、经济等影响因素，而在居住安排决策行为上呈现差异之样貌。

2　研究设计

2.1　数据源说明

本研究探讨影响家户居住安排行为所需之样本数据，系来自于华人家庭动态数据库（Panel Study of Family Dynamics，PSFD）。该数据库以台湾地区之华人家庭成年样本为研究对象，其抽样方式采用分层三段等概率抽样原则抽取合格样本，抽样程序先进行乡镇市（区）抽样，次进行村里抽样，最后选取合格者。此数据库自1998年开始，对华人家庭之经济、社会、心理及习俗等方面，进行全面研究，目前已释出1999～2011年调查资料，逐年亦会因调动问卷内容有些微差异，问卷内容涵盖个人资料、教育经验（生命历程）、工作经验、婚姻与配偶数据、家庭价值与态度、亲属数据、居住安排、家庭决策与支出、性别角色与婚姻态度、家庭关系与和谐、子女生育与教养、工作状况、家人互动关系、家庭经济管理、居住安排及亲子互动、生活照料、个人生活经验及借贷问题等层面。

此外，华人家庭动态数据库的属性为追踪调查数据，亦即调查作业会根据主样本延伸出来的子女等亲属，接续进行追踪访问，此种回溯特性可协助观察家户长期的变化趋势。因此，在数据属性方面，可切合本研究欲探讨在台北都市区发展变迁过程中，家户居住转换行为不动产市场景气、个人社经特性、整体经济景气氛围影响下，借以了解家户居住安排直接或间接影响因素之目的。

本研究考虑欲探讨之主轴，乃将家户居住转换分为换屋、首次购屋、持续租屋、由父母同住转租屋及家户其他情形等五大族群（各家户族群之界定标准，详如表1所示）。家户样本数据选取方面，系2003～2011年的华人家庭动态数据库中之问卷样本内，初步筛选出受访对象为1935～1984年出生之样本（即在2016年时为32岁至81岁之样本），总计18873份；再将受访者现居地不在台北都市区之样本剔除，剩余问卷份数为10083份；接续将2003～2011年间没有居住转换行为的样本予以删除；最后，采用逐笔观察之方式，将问卷中属于本实证分析所需之变量，但受访者未回答之样本予以剔除，获得本研究可用之问卷样本290份。

家户居住转换族群之分类　　　　　　　　　　　　　　　　表1

家户族群	居住转换状况
换屋	已购屋者转购屋换屋者
首次购屋	父母所有者转购屋者、居住宿舍者转购屋者、租屋者转购屋者及配偶所有者转购屋者
持续租屋	租屋转租屋者、租屋者转居住宿舍者、居住宿舍者转租屋者及居住宿舍者转居住宿舍者
由父母同住转租屋	父母所有者转租屋者、父母所有者转居住宿舍者
家户其他情形	父母所有者转父母所有者、父母所有者转配偶所有者、购屋者转子女所有者、购屋者转租屋者及购屋者转父母所有者等

2.2 居住安排之影响因素选取

本研究整理相关研究中有关家户住宅权属选择及决策的影响因素，借以探讨家户之特征差异是否对其居住转换行为造成影响。总计纳入包括通勤时间改变程度、居住转换时有无结婚、居住转换时小孩数、家庭收入改变程度、居住转换有无父母资助、不动产市场景气、房屋坪数改变程度、房间数改变程度等8项影响因素，兹将其详细内容分述如表2所示。

居住安排之影响因素汇整　　　　　　　　　　　　　　　　表2

变数	变量选取说明	变量选取依据
通勤时间改变程度	朱芳妮等（2008）指出区位选择与工作通勤成本有密切关联性，购置住宅前居住区位越接近市中心者，能节省往返工作地点的交通成本，而会继续选择市中心或近郊区位的住宅，已购屋者及购屋搜寻者在区位选择的过程中，当期望的住宅总面积越大，家户越不会选择接近市中心的区位	依据"华人家庭动态数据库"问卷中每天上下班总共需多少交通时间。采用选择前与选择后间之差异，作为该影响因素之数据，以时间数表示，单位为分钟
居住转换时有无结婚		依据"华人家庭动态数据库"问卷中住宅进行转换时的婚姻状况来判定，将居住转换时有无结婚分为居住转换时有结婚及居住转换时没有结婚两类，并以虚拟变量表示。
居住转换时小孩数	彭建文、花敬群（2001）认为国内租赁住宅市场的实质居住环境与租赁相关法令保障长期不佳下，租赁者往往无法获得与拥屋者相同的居住质量与居住稳定性。这种情况，造成未购置住宅之家户为累积充足的自备款压力下，大幅降低生育的意愿（彭建文、蔡怡纯，2012；林佩萱，2015）	系指"华人家庭动态数据库"问卷之受访者的小孩个数
家庭收入改变程度	相关研究（Ioannides, 1987；谢文盛、林素菁, 2000；Painter and Redfearn, 2002；曾喜鹏、薛立敏, 2005；陈佳欣等, 2010；彭建文, 2012；Groot et al., 2013）指出，恒常所得之多寡，系为居住安排决策的重要影响	由"华人家庭动态数据库"问卷中户长每月平均收入及配偶每月平均收入予以加总。采用居住选择前后之差异作为此影响因素的数据
居住转换有无父母资助	陈佳欣（2007）指出财富的累积，除个人储蓄外，父母的赠与或财产移转，亦为重要来源	系指"华人家庭动态数据库"问卷中，在购屋资金调度方面，有否接受父母亲资助或借款。将居住转换有无父母资助分为居住转换有父母资助及居住转换无父母资助两类，并以虚拟变量表示

续表

变数	变量选取说明	变量选取依据
不动产市场景气	彭建文、蔡怡纯（2012）研究中发现，房价攀升对于住宅自有率有正向显著影响，家户虽然认为高房价不合理，但对高房价的增值预期下，担心未来更无能力购置住宅，驱使家户愿意承担高贷款负担而选择购置住宅	系依据"华人家庭动态数据库"问卷中同一受访者样本于2003～2011年分别出现的换屋年份为2003年、2004年、2005年、2006年、2007年、2008年、2009年、2010年及2011年，再依据"台湾房地产景气动向季报"将换屋年份对照房地产景气对策讯号。分为不动产市场景气趋缓、不动产市场景气稳定、不动产市场偏热等三类，并以虚拟变量表示
房屋坪数改变程度	陈彦仲、陈佳欣、吴俊贤（2004）提出房屋坪数、卫浴设施与剩余所得对于家户之效用有正面影响效果，显示家户剩余所得越高，则家户之效用将提升，但房屋坪数在年轻、单身家户及低所得家户的选择模型中显著为负	系参考"华人家庭动态数据库"问卷中房屋坪数。采用居住选择前后之面积差异，作为该影响因素之数据
房间数改变程度		系参考"华人家庭动态数据库"问卷中房间数。采用居住选择前后之房间数差异，作为该影响因素之数据

3 变数基本统计检定

本研究针对问卷所得到的 8 项影响居住安排因素进行基本统计检定，包括相关性分析与允差（TOL）、变异数膨胀因素（VIF）等，借以了解这些因素是否适合纳入多元回归分析，以避免造成模型结果解读的偏误。其中，相关性分析可以呈现两个因素之间的关联程度，一般而言，假如该影响因素的 r 值若是大于绝对值 0.8，就可能存有共线性问题，在校正多元回归分析的时候，就可以考虑将这个指标删除。此外，允差、变异数膨胀因素，则可检定自变量间多元共线性问题，容忍度值低于 0.1，而且变异数膨胀因素值高于 10，就可以代表该影响居住安排因素存有共线性问题，则可以考虑将此一指标删除。

透过表 3 相关性分析呈现的数据与表 4 允差、变异数膨胀因素呈现的数据可知，本研究选取之 8 项居住安排影响因素中，未出现相关系数（Correlation Coefficient）绝对值高于 0.8 的情况，且允差值皆高于 0.1，变异数膨胀因素亦低于 10，代表本研究选取之 8 项影响因素间并无存在共线性的情况，适合纳入后续之回归模型。

家户居住安排因素之相关性分析结果　　　　表 3

相关程度	相关变项	r 值
高度相关 0.80 以上或 –0.80 以下	—	—
中度相关 0.40 至 0.79 或 –0.40 至 –0.79	—	—
低度相关 0.10 至 0.39 或 –0.10 至 –0.39	通勤时间改变程度与不动产市场景气	0.138
	居住转换时有无结婚与居住转换时小孩数	0.287
	居住转换时有无结婚与家庭收入改变程度	0.145
	居住转换时小孩数与家庭收入改变程度	0.117
	居住转换时小孩数与不动产市场景气	0.169
	不动产市场景气与房间数改变程度	0.130
	房屋坪数改变程度与房间数改变程度	0.314

家户居住安排影响因素之允差、变异数膨胀因素结果　　　　　表 4

变数	标准化系数	T	共线性统计量	
			允差	VIF
通勤时间改变程度	−0.061	−1.063	0.972	1.029
居住转换时有无结婚	−0.190	−3.114	0.864	1.157
居住转换时小孩数	0.086	−1.404	0.863	1.159
家庭收入改变程度	−0.029	−0.498	0.945	1.058
居住转换有无父母资助	−0.106	−1.848	0.978	1.022
不动产市场景气	0.068	1.169	0.936	1.069
房屋坪数改变程度	−0.032	−0.535	0.889	1.125
房间数改变程度	−0.144	−2.360	0.860	1.163

4　台北都市区居民之居住安排决策分析

如表 5 所示，经过模型的校估与测试过程，共有 8 项自变量纳入最终模型，包括：通勤时间改变程度、居住转换时有无结婚、居住转换时小孩数、家庭收入改变程度、居住转换有无父母资助、不动产市场景气、房屋坪数改变程度、房间数改变程度。概似比指针（Likelihood-Ration Index）为 0.2396，显示最终纳入模型的应变量组合适合本研究建构之逻辑特模型，因此可信赖其校估结果。下述分别就各个家户族群呈现之特性予以说明。

影响居住安排因素的多项逻辑特模型校估结果　　　　　表 5

变数	换屋之家户族群		首次购屋之家户族群	
	系数值	t 值	系数值	t 值
通勤时间改变程度	−0.34658241**	0.0698	0.35156793E−01*	0.0740
居住转换时有无结婚	−0.58332748	0.9825	0.41318899***	0.0092
居住转换时小孩数	0.25131544**	0.0381	−0.22079719*	0.0845
家庭收入改变程度	−0.39346400	0.7402	0.20412748*	0.0902
居住转换有无父母资助	−0.81364599**	0.0342	−0.41642765	0.1883
不动产市场景气	−0.20994281**	0.0117	−0.14712460*	0.0709
房屋坪数改变程度	0.21805760	0.6930	0.13720832	0.7986
房间数改变程度	−0.47374422	0.1191	−0.30556153	0.2026
变数	持续租屋之家户族群		由父母同住转租屋之家户族群	
	系数值	t 值	系数值	t 值
通勤时间改变程度	−0.36347499***	0.0039	−0.68534452E−01	0.8830
居住转换时有无结婚	−0.48094548	0.7260	−0.83696711***	0.0041
居住转换时小孩数	−0.25856354	0.2410	−0.34989129	0.9453
家庭收入改变程度	−0.41946668**	0.0206	0.32501711	0.6129
居住转换有无父母资助	−0.51045014***	0.0065	−0.65554088	0.1020
不动产市场景气	0.13282246***	0.0074	−0.18264744	0.2203
房屋坪数改变程度	0.11429262	0.1063	−0.70125477**	0.0311
房间数改变程度	−0.27411778	0.5185	−0.56732768	0.5851

注：* 表示 α=0.1 显著水平；** 表示 α=0.05 显著水平；*** 表示 α=0.01 显著水平。

4.1 换屋之家户族群

本研究界定的换屋家户族群,系指原本已在台北都市区拥有自有住宅,于 2003～2011 年间出现换屋行为的家户。由表 5 呈现之模型结果,居住转换时的小孩数此项因素,会对此族群的居住转换行为产生显著之正向影响。本研究推论,家户所拥有的小孩数目越多,所需之居住空间越大,导致原有住宅空间不敷使用的情况出现,因而产生换屋行为。

此外,通勤时间改变程度、居住转换有无父母资助、不动产市场景气等三项因素则是对本族群换屋行为具有显著的负向影响。代表本族群在已拥有自有住宅的情况下,进行换屋决策考虑时,现有住宅的出售所得,在偿还房屋贷款后,一定程度上可以减轻新购住宅的财务负担,故有无父母亲的资金援助此项考虑点相较不重要,且在新购置住宅之区位考虑时,将具有更大的弹性,因此,模型上呈现出通勤时间减少较有可能让此家户族群出现换屋的行为。进一步由换屋的时机点观察,台北都市区之家户族群在已拥有自有住宅的前提下,较没有购置住宅的时间与心理压力,是以,在不动产市场之景气呈现热络趋势时,较不会出现换屋的动作,反之,此族群较偏向在市场景气衰退时进行换屋行为,借由不动产市场景气属于沉寂市场(Dull Market)走向时,以较为划算之价格或购屋条件于台北都市区购置新住宅。

4.2 首次购屋之家户族群

本研究界定之首次购屋家户族群,是指在 2003～2011 年间,家户从与父母同住转为购屋者、居住宿舍者转购屋者、租屋者转购屋者等居住安排出现转换的族群。根据表 5 的模型结果显示,对台北都市区之首购家户族群产生居住转换的显著影响因素有 5 项,包括通勤时间改变程度、居住转换时有无结婚、居住转换时的小孩数、家庭收入改变程度、不动产市场景气等。其中,通勤时间改变程度、居住转换时有无结婚、家庭收入改变程度等 3 项因素,会对此族群之居住转换行为产生显著正向影响;至于居住转换时的小孩数、不动产市场景气等 2 项因素,则会对此族群之居住转换行为产生显著负向影响。

此般模型结果可推论,由于不动产此项财货目标之购置金额相较其他财货庞大,在财务负担上,购置行为产生时需支付头期款,且未来将长达一二十年的时间必须负担房屋贷款。因此,与换屋家户族群最大的差异,在于本族群进行首次购置住宅决策时,除本身积蓄是否足以因应购屋头期款之外,亦必须考虑后续的房屋贷款负担。是故,透过本研究实证模型可发现,此家户族群之家庭收入越增加,越有可能于台北都市区进行首次购置住宅行为。进一步从居住转换时有无结婚此项影响因素来推论,有结婚的家户或许因为属于双薪家庭,储蓄及累积财富的速度将较单身家户来得快,因此于台北都市区产生首次购屋行为的可能性亦会越高。再者,有别于单身家户,有结婚之家户受到中国传统的成家立业观念影响,透过自有住宅的购置行为求得安定的动机会较高。此外,由财务考虑的观点亦可解释为何居住转换时的小孩数此项因素会对家户首次购屋行为产生显著之负向影响。本研究针对纳入最终模型的族群样本进行统计后发现,此家户族群出现居住转换后至今仍未生育小孩的家户,占此家户族群的 56%。推测其原因,主要因为小孩的养育费用将会影响家户整体财务分配,是以,家户小孩数越少,则越能提高首次购置住宅的概率。

至于台北都市区的首次购屋族群在住宅区位的决策考虑方面,由模型结果可发现,通勤时间的改变程度此项影响因素对于此族群的购置住宅行为呈现显著正向影响,代表通勤时间越增加,此家户族群越可能出现首次购置住宅的行为,其原因可解读为,有别于租屋行为在区位考虑时,可选择在市中心租屋,借以邻近就业区位并享受丰富、便利的商业机能,家户首次购屋时,受限于购屋预算及日后的偿债能力，住宅区位的选择多偏好房价水平相对较低的都会区外围区域，因而增加通勤时间与费用。此外，在首次购屋的时间点方面，不动产市场景气此项影响因素，会对此族群之居住转换行为产生显著负向影响，代表不动产市场景气越低迷，台北都市区之家户越可能做出首次购置住宅的决定。

4.3 持续租屋之家户族群

根据表5的模型结果显示，在台北都市区中，会对持续租屋之家户族群的居住转换行为产生显著影响的因素有4项。其中，不动产市场景气这项因素会对这个族群的居住转换行为产生显著的正向影响；至于通勤时间改变程度、家庭收入改变程度、居住转换有无父母资助等3项因素则会产生显著的负向影响。之所以会被归类为本家户族群的样本，主要指家户在2003～2011年间，出现了租屋地点转换、原租屋转换为居住宿舍、原居住宿舍转换为租屋等情况。有别于前两个家户族群，此家户族群虽有进行住宅转换行为，但转换前后的住宅皆是属于租赁，仅出现地点改变的情况。

观察此家户族群的居住安排特征可发现，此家户族群可能因为某些原因（例如：原本住宅的租赁契约届满、换工作、就业地点改变等）而需搬离原本租赁之住宅或宿舍。然而，由于居住转换时，不动产市场景气较为热络，且由于家户的家庭收入并未增加，因此，在以租赁形式满足居住需求会较拥有自有住宅来得轻松的考虑下，此家户族群乃选择维持租赁住宅的形式。再者，此种居住模式不见得会加重家户之财务负担，因此，相较于首次购置自有住宅族群，有无父母的金钱援助此项因素对于此族群在进行住宅租赁行为时系呈现负向的显著影响。进一步探究此家户族群与首次购置自有住宅族群之相异处，由于租赁住宅仅需负担住宅租金，故在寻找租赁住宅区位时，会较首次购置住宅族群更具弹性，也较容易在适切其工作地点的通勤考虑下，选择新的租赁住宅地点。因此，当寻找到可降低通勤时间的租赁住宅时，将因而增加台北都市区之租屋族群进行转换租赁住宅行为的可能性。

4.4 由父母同住转租屋之家户族群

本研究界定之家户由父母同住转租屋族群，是指在2003～2011年间，父母所有者转租屋者、父母所有者转居住宿舍者等居住转换的情况。根据表5的模型结果显示，对此家户族群产生居住转换的显著影响因素有2项，包括居住转换时有无结婚、房屋建坪改变程度等，对于此族群居住转换行为皆呈现负向且显著的影响。

此般结果可推论，在台北都市区中，原本与父母同住的受访者，尚未结婚者较有可能出现搬离父母家，至外面自行承租住宅的可能性，究其原因，子女在没有小孩的照顾考虑与较大的财务压力下，可能会因为希望拥有自有生活空间，或因考虑通勤时间等原因，而产生居住转换的行为。至于在租赁住宅的坪数部分，由于家户搬迁至外租屋后的居住人口数降低，加以此种居住转换行为仅是为能拥有方便通勤、满足基本居住需求的栖身之处，是以，转换后的住宅坪数会较原先与父母同住的坪数小。

5 结论与建议

本研究采用华人家庭动态数据库，其样本回溯特性，将不同居住转换之家户族群予以分类，分为换屋家户族群、首次购屋家户族群、持续租屋家户族群、由父母同住转租屋家户族群及家户其他情形等五大族群，作为研究的对象，借以厘清居住在台北都市区不同形态的居住转换族群，在居住安排影响因素上相互之差异，并参考相关研究文献，建构影响居住安排所带来的正负面转换影响因素，共计列举出 8 项影响因素，包括：通勤时间改变程度、居住转换时有无结婚、居住转换时小孩数、家庭收入改变程度、居住转换有无父母资助、不动产市场景气、房屋坪数改变程度、房间数改变程度，作为建构多项逻辑特模型之基础。以下就各形态的居住转换族群对居住安排因素间的影响差异进行描述。

（1）在通勤时间改变程度影响部分，对换屋及持续租屋这两种家户族群有显著负向影响，则对首次购屋家户族群有显著正向影响。本研究认为，首次购屋有别于租屋区位考虑时，可选择在市中心租屋，借以邻近就业区位并享受丰富且便利的商业机能，家户首次购屋时，受限于购屋预算及日后的偿债能力，在区位决策时，比较有可能选择房价水平相对较低的都市区外围区域，因而增加通勤时间与费用，换屋族群则在已拥有自有住宅的前提下，较没有购置住宅的时间与心理压力，将会较有选择的空间。

（2）在家庭收入改变程度影响部分，可以知道家庭收入的多寡还是能否购置住宅的重要因素。因此，在不动产财货目标购置金额巨大下，除了应付头期款，家户本身需具备一定之储蓄金额外，未来长达一二十年的房屋贷款摊还，则是属于长期、持续的固定财务负担，因此，其家庭收入增加的程度越大，越有可能产生首次购屋的行为，反之，在租赁形式满足居住需求会较拥有自有住宅来得轻松的考虑下，会考虑本身负担能力范围，维持租赁住宅的形式。

（3）在不动产市场景气影响部分，经实证结果得知，在不动产市场景气衰退时，换屋及首次购屋之家户族群会以较为划算的价格或购屋条件购置新住宅，不动产市场景气热络时，对于租屋家户族群亦趋向保守，显示不动产市场景气的波动对于不同形态的家户族群有显著的影响能力。

（4）在居住转换时有无结婚及居住转换时小孩数影响部分，对首次购屋之家户族群，夫妻为双薪家庭，其家庭收入增加的程度越大，越有可能产生首次购屋的行为，另外，家户之小孩数目越少，其育儿的财务支出较少，亦会提高首次购置住宅的概率；从另一个角度来看，换屋族群在所拥有的小孩数目越多，可能会出现原有住宅空间不敷使用的情况，越有可能增加换屋行为的产生，但对于由父母同住转租屋族群，则可能在尚未结婚前，会因为希望拥有自有的生活空间，或因通勤时间过长等原因，而产生居住转换的行为。

A Study on the Characteristic of Household Living Arrangements in Taipei Metropolitan Area

Hsu Kuo-Cheng, Liu Chih-Yu

(Department of Urban Planning and Development Management, Chinese Culture University)

Abstract: The transformation from renting to purchasing house is a decision of multiple consideration, including job stability, family income, children's education and living environment, etc. For instance, only commuting distance and convenience of dwelling environment etc. matters with renting houses, while the housing price, mortgage, children's education, increase in real estate price, etc. would be all taken into consideration for house purchasing. Additionally, most residents tend to choose suburban residential site to purchase the first house due to the housing price. The long-term commuting cost including both money and time also becomes a key problem. Therefore, this study intends to explore that under the situation of soaring house price in Taipei Metropolitan Area, whether the residents have to make a choice between lease and purchase because of the difference of social and economic condition and other various qualities. To figure out the behavior pattern and influence factors behind the transformation, Multinomial Logit Model is applied in empirical design to find out the interaction of household arrangement and real-estate market, individual socioeconomic characteristics and macroeconomic, and to further know about the discrepancy of household arrangements for different morphology of residents and how influenced by social and economic factors.

Keywords：Buy or rent decision, Living arrangements, Panel study of family dynamics, Multinomial logit model

参考文献

[1] 朱芳妮、张金鹗、陈淑美. 已购屋者及购屋搜寻者之购屋需求决策比较分析——兼论显示性偏好及叙述性偏好之差异 [J]. 都市与计划，2008，（35-4）：339–359.

[2] 卓辉华. 房市激荡五十年 [M]. 台湾：财信出版，2014.

[3] 林左裕. 不动产投资管理（第五版）[M]. 台湾：智胜文化，2014.

[4] 林佩萱. 家户购屋与生育行为关系：资源排挤与动机刺激 [J]. 住宅学报，2015，（24-1）：89–115.

[5] 陈佳欣. 家户首次购置住宅与生命历程之关联分析 [D]. 台南成功大学都市计划研究所博士论文，2007.

[6] 陈佳欣、张曜麟、欧阳宇. 台湾地区各世代已婚家户由租屋至拥屋之影响因素 [J]. 嘉南学报，2010，36：672–684.

[7] 陈彦仲、陈佳欣、吴俊贤. 家户之住宅选择模型与住宅之家户竞争模型实证比较分析 [J]. 住宅学报，2004，（13-1）：1–13.

[8] 彭建文. 拥屋相对成本对住宅租拥选择之影响 [J]. 都市与计划，2012，（39-1）：1–23.

[9] 彭建文、花敬群. 住宅租买选择行为之探讨——住宅服务质量差异之影响 [J]. 台湾土地金融季刊，2001，38：89–107.

[10] 彭建文、蔡怡纯. 住宅负担能力与住宅自有率之长期关系——追踪数据共整合分析应用 [J]. 住宅学报，2012，（21-2）：1–28.

[11] 曾喜鹏、薛立敏. 不同类型迁移者之住宅区位与权属选择的实证估计——以台北都会区迁入者为例 [J]. 台湾土地研究，2005，（8-2）：21–48.

[12] 曾沥仪、张金鹗、陈淑美. 老人居住安排选择——代间关系之探讨 [J]. 住宅学报，2006，（15-2）：45–64.

[13] 黄靖容. 台湾年轻家户之住宅权属选择——世代分析 [D]. 台北政治大学财政研究所硕士论文，2011.

[14] 谢文盛、林素菁. 租税效果对住宅租买选择影响之分析 [J]. 住宅学报，2000，（9-1）：1–17.

[15] Ahn N. Age at first-time homeownership in Spain. Documento de trabajo，2001，23：1–19.

[16] Baharoglu D. Housing supply under different economic development strategies and the forms of state intervention: the experience of Turkey. Habitat International，1996，20：43–60.

[17] Boehm T P. Tenure Choice and Expected Mobility：A Synthesis[J]. Journal of Urban Economics，1981，10：375–389.

[18] De Vos S，Lee Y J. Change in Extended Family Living among Elderly People in South Korea，1970-

1980. Economic Development and Cultural Change, 1993, 41: 377–393.

[19] Ermisch J, Salvo P D. Surprises and Housing Tenure Decisions in Great Britain[J]. Journal of Housing Economics, 1996, 5（3）: 247–273.

[20] Forrest R, Kennett P, Leather P. Home Ownership in Crisis? The British Experience of Negative Equity[J]. Journal of Housing and the Built Environment, 2001, 16: 119–121.

[21] Gan C, Hu B, Gao C, Kao B, Cohen D A. An empirical analysis of homeownership in urban China[J]. Journal of Asia Business Studies, 2014, 8: 1–17.

[22] Garriga C, Gavin W T, Schlagenhauf D. Recent Trends in Homeownership. Federal Reserve Bank of Louis Review, 2006, 88（5）: 397–411.

[23] Goodwin K R, Zumpano L V. The Home Buyer Tax Credit of 2009 and the Transition to Homeownership[J]. Journal of Housing Research, 2011, 20: 211–224.

[24] Groot C D, Manting D, Mulder C H. Longitudinal analysis of the formation and realization of preferences to move into homeownership in the Netherlands[J]. Journal of Housing and the Built Environment, 2013, 28: 469–488.

[25] Hempel D J, Punj G N. Linking consumer and lending perspectives in home buying: A transaction price analysis[J]. The Journal of Consumer Affairs, 1999, 33: 408–435.

[26] Hughes M E. What Money Can Buy: The Relationship between Marriage and Home Ownership inthe United States. The Network on Transitions to Adulthood, 2004.

[27] Ioannides Y M. Residential Mobility and Housing Tenure Choice[J]. Regional Science and Urban Economics, 1987, 17: 265–287.

[28] Kalmijn M. The Influence of Men's Income and Employment on Marriage and Cohabitation: Testing Oppenheimer's Theory in Europe[J]. European Journal of Population, 2011, 27: 269–293.

[29] Mulder C H, Wanger M. The Connections between Family Formation and First-time Home Ownership in the Context of West Germany and the Netherlands[J]. European Journal of Population, 2001, 17: 137–164.

[30] Oktay E, Karaaslan A, Alkan Ö, Kemal Çelik A. Determinants of housing demand in the Erzurum province, Turkey[J]. International Journal of Housing Markets and Analysis, 2014, 7: 586–602.

[31] Oppenheimer V K. A theory of marriage timing: Assortative mating under varying degrees of uncertainty[J]. American Journal of Sociology, 1988, 94: 563–591.

[32] Painter G, Redfearn C L. The Role of Interest Rates in Influencing Long-Run Homeownership Rates[J]. Journal of Real Estate Finance and Economics, 2002, 25: 243–267.

[33] Saita Y, Shimizu C, Watanabe T. Aging and real estate prices: evidence from Japanese and US regional data[J]. International Journal of Housing Markets and Analysis, 2016, 9: 66–87.

[34] Tiwari P. Housing demand in Tokyo[J]. International Real Estate Review, 2000, 3: 65–92.

对我国棚户区改造建设管理云平台的研究和实践

陆伟良[1]　李学东[2]　杜　昱[3]　苏　俊[4]

（1. 南京工业大学；2. 南京建普软件有限公司；3. 中国智慧城市咨询网；4. 南京扬子国投资集团）

摘　要：本文首先介绍课题背景，其次论述棚户区改造建设管理云平台三个主要组成：监管平台、工作平台及接口开发等，最后指出推广范围及应用价值等。

关键词：棚户区，改造，云平台，开发，应用

1　引言

当前我国棚户区改造发展迅速，已有不少文献发表。[1~3] 本文介绍的南京棚户区改造建设管理云平台是一个针对我国城市棚户区改造特点开发的涵盖棚户区改造全过程的管理云平台，是一个横跨互联网、政府网和银行内网的既有逻辑关联又有物理隔离的混合云平台，是一个包括国家开发银行、政府职能部门、项目代建、拆迁、设计、施工、监理等所有参与棚户区改造单位共同使用的棚户区改造资金监管、拆迁和建设管理的协同工作平台。

2017年1月10日，江苏省住房和城乡建设厅在南京组织召开的"南京市棚户区改造建设管理云平台"成果鉴定会认为：该课题针对大型城市棚户区改造建设管理特点设计的混合云平台架构以及棚改资金监管智能化引擎具有创新性，适合大中型城市的棚户区改造建设管理，社会经济效益显著，研究成果为国内首创，达到国际先进水平。[4]

2　棚户区改造建设管理云平台体系结构

该平台体系结构如图1所示。

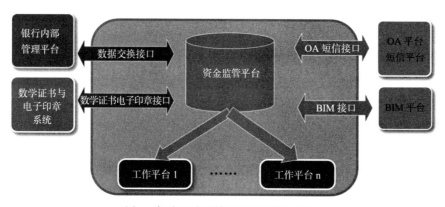

图1　棚户区改造管理云平台体系结构

2.1 棚户区改造建设管理云平台

该平台资金监管平台功能体系图如图 2 所示。

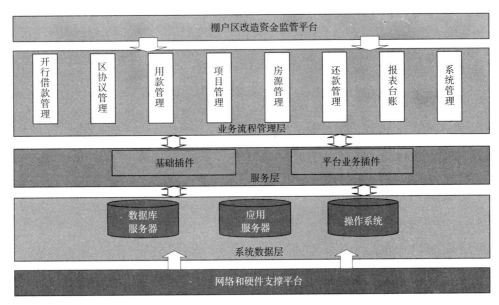

图 2　南京市棚户区改造项目资金监管平台功能体系图

2.2 棚户区改造建设管理云平台工作平台

该工作平台如图 3 所示。

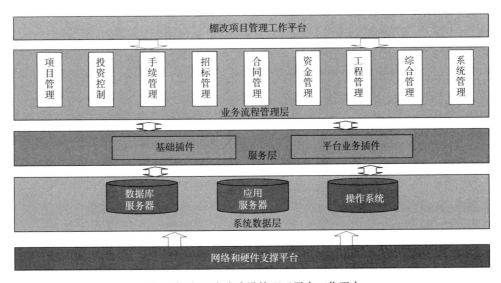

图 3　棚户区改造建设管理云平台工作平台

2.3 棚户区改造建设管理云平台、监管平台与工作平台对接

其对接示意图如图 4 所示。

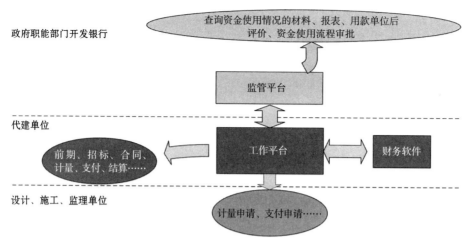

图 4 建设平台、监管平台与工作平台对接示意图

2.4 与相关系统对接管理

2.4.1 与 OA 系统的对接管理

棚改平台中各项资金使用的审批流程任务与 OA 系统对接，可以在 OA 系统的任务中查看到棚改平台的审批任务，通过单点登录的形式实现用户登录，通过点击任务名称跳转到棚改平台处理任务。

2.4.2 与数字证书系统的对接管理

棚改平台用户登录、签字、盖章统一使用的 UKey 形式实现，保障用户账号的信息安全，流程审批中的签字、盖章有法律效应，杜绝了人为伪造平台信息的可能。

2.4.3 与短信平台的对接管理

移动短信平台对接，在任务审批中提醒下一步审批人有任务需要处理，能更快捷地处理审批任务，用户不但可以经常登录系统查看是否有任务需要审批，还可以在每天上班前得到当天有多少条任务需要处理的提醒。

2.4.4 与 BIM 平台的对接管理

该棚改项目采用了 BIM 技术[5]，从设计到施工管理、变更计量都采用 BIM 技术，工作平台支持 BIM 文件的审批，BIM 信息上传到上层平台，使得棚改办和国开行的人可以直观地看到棚改项目的三维展示信息。

3 本课题创新点

3.1 多层次参与、多组织协同

棚改平台设计了监管平台+多个工作平台的混合云平台架构，成功地实现了参与南京市棚户区改造项目建设管理的所有层次所有组织在同一个信息平台协同工作，国家开发银行、南京市参与棚改相关的政府职能部门、各区平台、项目管理单位、现场项目部等多个层次共同参与；业主、设计、施工、监理、勘探、质量检测、材料供应等多个组织协同工作，因为参与棚户区改造的各个层次和组织在平台中有各自的权限，所有必须有一整套完备的权限控制解决方案，才能保证系统的正常运行，本项目是个多层次多组织共同参与的协同工作平台。[6]

3.2 棚改资金全过程监管

由于有平台支撑，棚改资金的监管模式由原来人工监管变成了将监管要求输入系统智能监管引擎，由平台对棚改资金的流向实时监控，对不符规的资金流向实时报警，不仅监控资金的使用，还监管资金的全部走向，包括从开行到市平台、区平台以及各建设单位间资金划拨，同时也监管政府配套资金的到位与使用情况。资金的使用只有在工作平台上最终棚改参与方的支付申请通过审批后才真正发生，极大地提高了棚改资金的使用效率。

3.3 设计了上层监管平台 + 多个有差异化工作平台的混合云平台架构

棚改平台是由棚改资金监管平台和各区棚户区改造工作平台共同组成的混合云平台，其中监管平台主要是国家开发银行、市棚改办、扬子集团（市级平台）以及各区级平台使用，主要功能通过从各区工作平台实时提取棚改工作平台的业务流程数据，对数据分析研判，并实时提供棚改的各种实时分析报表，有问题及时预警，同时支持国家开发银行、市、区两级平台的信息流转审批、协同工作；工作平台主要提供承担棚改区改造管理具体业务的项目管理、设计、施工、监理等干系人使用，具体功能包括拆迁、房源管理、建设程序管理、棚改房建设的投资控制、进度控制、质量安全管理、竣工验收、结算审计等，并实时提供上层监管平台所有数据，在上层监管平台集成大数据平台。混合云平台的体系结构，即满足了工作和监管的要求，又各有侧重，上层大数据平台和下层工作平台数据的冗余，也保障了数据的安全性，同时也避免了个别平台的故障影响全市工作的情况发生。

3.4 集成了电子印章工作更高效

棚改平台目前所有的审批事项已经全部实现线上运行，并且集成了电子印章系统，从参与建设的设计、施工、监理等干系人单位，到各区平台，各区政府、南京市市级平台以及开发银行间，全部通过平台流转审批并采用电子印章，极大地提高了管理效率。特别是远郊的棚改项目，已经不需要为了审批到处跑，在提高管理效率的同时，时效性也有所提高。

3.5 融合了 BIM 数据，管控更精确

平台融合了 BIM 数据，特别是在建设阶段，将 BIM 数据导入平台，不仅起到了设计验证的作用，更重要的是通过对 BIM 数据的跟踪，可以对项目的投资、进度等管得更细更精确，目前在国内，全过程使用 BIM 管理棚改项目的单位还是很少的，我们在这方面做了很好的尝试。

3.6 自主开发智能监管引擎，使用更方便

平台具有自主知识产权的智能监管引擎，引擎可以根据需要，不断增加监管内容，一旦将相关的监管内容输入进去，平台就可以监管相应的行为，目前有项目合规性监管、资金划拨和使用监管、建设程序监管等。

3.7 广域网与客户端零维护

平台是基于广域网运行的，特别适合城市棚户区建设项目管理的特点，因为棚改项目分布广，项目管理干系人多。基于广域网的平台能够让众多管理者协同工作。同时平台的所有软件都部署在服务器上，用户端不需要安装任何软件，使得系统的升级和维护很容易实现。

4 推广范围及应用价值

棚户区改造平台的资金使用，全部在线上进行，资金只有到最终参与方计量支付申请通过后，才真正发生资金的支付，开发银行才会将资金通过网银支付给最终用户，并且所有的审批都是通过电子印章系统在线上进行;同时所有不合规的资金流转，会引起告警，从而保证资金使用的安全性和合规性，极大地提高了资金的使用效率，我们经测算，净利息的节约每年在2000多万元。如果全国棚户区改造都适用本项目的研究成果，每年将产生数以亿计的经济效益。其经济效益十分可观。有关评审专家一致认为，整个平台实用好用，得到不同类型用户一致好评，实现了效益最大化。

因为平台的变更、签证、计量、支付的规范运作，使得项目整个建设期的费用几乎没有漏洞，同时由于项目的每一笔支出的来龙去脉十分清晰，应该获得的费用由平台自动计算出来，项目干系人特别是承包商，已经不需要靠拉关系来收回工程款，对于反腐倡廉也具有十分重要的现实意义。同时，平台的监管引擎，对资金使用的监管、项目合规性监管、建设程序的监管都是实时监管与预警，有效保证了棚改项目的合规性，而且形成的大数据平台及对大数据的研判分析和使用，对全国棚改政策的制定具有决策支持作用，本项目的社会效益和廉政效益十分明显。

本文撰写过程中，得到了住建部科技委顾问、瑞典皇家科学院外籍院士许溶烈博士和东南大学吴乐南教授、江苏省住建厅车黎刚教授级高工、深圳市建筑工务所刘哲高工的指导。在此表示衷心感谢!

限于作者水平，文中错误之处敬请大家批评指正。

The Development of Construction Management in the Shanty Towns Cloud Platform and Application

Lu Weiliang[1], Li Xuedong[2], Du Yu[3], Su Jun[4]

(1. Nanjing University of Technology; 2. Nanjing JPM Software Co., Ltd; 3. Chinese Smart City Construction Consulting Services Net; 4. Nanjing Yangzi Investment Group Co., Ltd)

Abstract: Firstly, this paper introduces topic background, secondly turns shanty towns into new housing areas cloud platform construction and management of three main components: Regulatory platform, work platform and interface development, etc., and Finally points out that the scope of promotion and application value, etc.

Keywords: Shanty town, Transform, Cloud platform, Development, Application

参考文献

[1] 董成珍.棚户区改造建设的项目管理[J].中国城市经济,2011,29.

[2] 宿辉,石磊.吉林省棚户区改造项目管理模式研究[J].建筑经济,2008,7.

[3] 张雷.保障性安居工程专项资金"1+6"监管模式构想[J].财政监督,2014,19.

[4] 许溶烈,陆伟良."南京市棚户区改造建设管理云平台"成果鉴定会鉴定意见.江苏省住房和城乡建设厅,2017,1.

[5] 陆伟良,杨军志,张宜,王铁,杜昱,徐龙.数据中心建设BIM应用导论[J].江苏:东南大学出版社,2016,12.

[6] 南京建普软件有限公司."棚户区改造建设管理云平台"科技查新报告.江苏省科技查新咨询中心(国家一级科技查新咨询单位),报告编号:201632B2510473.2016,12.

长者友善人居环境营造

Age-friendly Human Habitat

基于老年人行为的既有住区环境优化设计研究：
以大连地区为例

于文婷　周　博　周志伟

（大连理工大学建筑与艺术学院）

摘　要：在 2017 年 2 月 28 日颁布的《十三五国家老龄事业发展和养老体系建设规划》中明确指出需要夯实居家社区养老服务基础。这意味着，社区居家养老是未来养老的必然趋势。然而，我国既有住区的存量十分庞大。并且由于建设年代已久，社区内部大部分基础设施以及配建早已不能满足老人生活的需求，既有住区中老人的生活质量很难得到保障。对于这部分住区，全部重新建设不但会是资源的浪费也会带来诸多的社会问题。因此，对既有住区进行适老性改造是当前社会养老发展的必经之路。本论文选取东北地区重点城市大连为研究主体所在地，以大连市星海街社区为研究对象。通过对星海街社区的调研；资料收集、问卷、探访等方式，总结星海街社区环境现存问题，资源利用中的不合理分配的出处以及老年人的行为需求。在调研以及整理资料的基础上，结合已有案例，通过对该社区既有资源进行整合归纳，针对当下既有建筑中老年人以及居民的需求，提出适应该社区的既有住区外环境改造策略优化方法。旨在通过此次研究为北方地区既有住区适老性优化问题提出有益的补充。

关键词：既有住区，适老性，优化设计，行为

1　引言

随着老年人人口比重的不断加大，中国的老龄化问题逐渐成为社会的热点问题。截至 2015 年，中国的老年人口数已经达到了 2.2 亿，占总人口数量的 16%。在北方，由于计划生育政策的实施以及长期的年轻人口外流，老龄化程度已经远远超过了国家的平均水平，特别是在既有住区当中，老龄化现象以及趋势愈加严重（有的已超过 30%）。在 2017 年 2 月 28 日颁布的《十三五国家老龄事业发展和养老体系建设规划》中明确指出需要夯实居家社区养老服务基础。这意味着，社区居家养老是未来养老的必然趋势。

然而，我国的既有住区的存量十分庞大。由于建设年代已久，社区内部大部分基础设施以及配建早已不能满足老人生活的需求，既有住区中老人的生活质量很难得到保障。对于这部分住区，全部重新建设不但会是资源的浪费也会带来诸多的社会问题。因此，对既有住区进行适老性改造是当前社会养老发展的必经之路。

2　既有住区的界定及特色

在 1979~1987 年这 9 年间，大连市有 20 多亿的政府投资用于住宅建设，这期间，新住宅共建 $10.423 \times 10^6 m^2$。大约有 80 万人口、22 万户家庭搬进了新居。这时期的人均住宅达到了 $6.48m^2$，比省人口平均居住面积 $5.1m^2$ 高出约 $1.4m^2/$ 人。截至 1990 年，室内四区的住宅面积总量达到了

$17.7 \times 10^6 m^2$。本文所提到的既有住宅是指建设于这个时段的住宅区。

在这个时期，居住小区规划结构沿用 20 世纪 60 年代形成的"住宅 - 组团 - 小区"的三级结构，在户型方面，通常用"一室户、二室户、三室户"这样的居室数量表示户型的差别，住宅设计相对单调。在外环境上，开始出现了住区以及小区绿化景观的概念，但是还是很不成熟。

3 星海住区基本状况

大连市星海街社区（表1）位于大连市沙河口区中山路附近，有星海街道贯穿其中，社区北部毗邻富国公园，东侧据中山路仅有近百米之隔，并与会展中心，星海广场相望，住区南侧是星海小学。调研的小区站点面积 $0.111 \times 10^6 m^2$，内部有有 10 条路、街、巷，贯穿其中，交通便利，区内共有人口 7000 多人，2500 余户，住区建设在坡地上，区内由东南向西北高差较大。

星海街社区基本信息　　　　表1

属性	基本信息	星海街社区
区位	星海街社区位于中山路沿线，星海广场西侧	
人口状况	人口数	7075 人 /2573 户
	老年人比例	24%
	平均家庭人口数	2.75 人
住区特点	住宅形态	多层单元式以及外廊式，69 栋楼，142 单元
	层数	大多数居民楼为 6～7 层，少数 3～4 层
	单元	一梯 2、3、4、5、6、7、12 户
配套设施	周边设施	市场、超市、诊所、美发店、药店、服装店、棋牌室、建材店等

3.1 社区室外空间状况

3.1.1 室外停车状况

在调研中发现小区内部停车问题比较严重，由于规划指出并没有设计大型的地下停车空间，社区内部车辆大多数沿着街边停放，这给社区内部交通带来了很大的问题，也为人们出行以及社区内部活动带来不便。另外，由于公共空间较少，内部少有的室外活动场地也通常被车位占据（图1、图2）。

3.1.2 室外高差状况

除了室外空间的停车问题，住区内部高差问题也亟待解决，如图所示，标注红色的区域是住区内部高差较大且设置了台阶的地方，可见，很多台阶并没有配合坡道设计，这为老年人出行带来了很大的障碍。由于住区建设在坡地上，因而大部分的住区内部道路都是以坡地的形式出现，我们在对住区老人的调研访谈中了解到，住区内部的坡道形式的高差并没有给老人生活带来太多的不便，反而是楼宇内部的楼梯上下行走起来比较吃力。

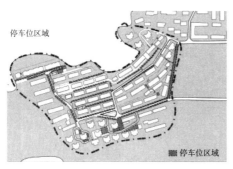
图 1　南石道街小区停车分布图

图 2　室外台阶坡道分布图

3.1.3　室外公共空间及道路状况

住区内部设置着若干公共场地以及绿地，但是数量较少，大部分住宅楼前后均是硬质铺地，并没有设置一些老人休息的空间。为了满足老人们的需求，老人们通常自行搭建娱乐设施。

住区内部道路系统比较完善，但是却不是很通畅，由于很多尽断路的出现，使得人们在住区内部行走的路线非常单一（图 3～图 6）。

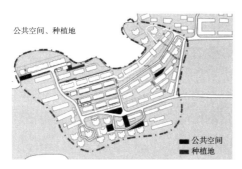
图 3　内部公共空间分布

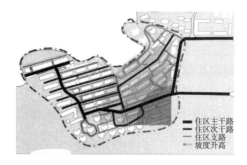
图 4　小区道路分布

图 5　内部公共空间使用状态

图 6　内部停车现状

4　老年人行为需求分析

作者通过定点观察的方法对小区内的老人的行为进行了定点观察，发现在老人室外活动的过程中，出现很多行为特征：在住宅楼的街角，阳光能照射到的有座椅的空地上，老人们喜欢三五个人聚在一起聊天，晒太阳，老人的活动以静态为主。

在社区内部的一些公共活动开敞空间里，由于配备了活动器材，大部分老人们都在使用活动器材，但是，由于数量不足，很多老人处于排队等候的状态，在这个过程中，老人们相互之间会通过聊天发生一些交往的行为。

在社区的主要街道两侧也是老人数量比较多的地方之一，在这里的老人的行为主要体现在活动购物这些目的上，也有部分老人在停留聊天。老人的活动需求主要以动态为主。

5 优化设计方法

5.1 室外活动空间改造策略

老年人在住区环境的活动可以大致分为四种类型：运动健身、娱乐、文化教育以及社会交往。这几类活动所处的场景并不同，因此，在既有住区环境适老性改造时，我们要根据老人不同类型活动的需求，改造相应的室外场所。

5.1.1 社会交往空间

社会交往是老人使用空间的主要目的，因此，将社会交往空间的设计以及改造作为既有住区外环境改造的基本。通过上文调研中发现，老人们最经常发生社会交往活动的地方是距离建筑很近的入口区域，其次是附近的公园绿地，老人们散步的地方。另外，对于很多老人来说，坐在室外观看他人的行为也是其参与社会交往的行为之一。在生活中，住区老人的社会交往空间（表2）分为以下几个部分：

（1）大规模集体交往空间

很多老人喜欢跳广场舞，或者参加类似的集体活动，因为通过这样的集体行为会使老人们获得对退休后孤独生活的弥补。这样的交往空间通常位于住区的中心广场区域，然而，在很多既有住区再设计时，并没有规划核心大型广场区域，因此，很多老人会选择在附近的广场或者街边进行此类活动。在社区环境改造时，尽可能在住区中心区域开放一片开敞的活动区，这片活动区域需要满足社区内居民容易达到，而又避免车辆干扰的安全性的特征。

（2）小规模群体交往空间

在老人的交往活动中，发生最多的行为是三两个老人间进行交往活动，这种活动发生的地点通常在老人居所附近，大部分发生在住宅楼的下面或者楼附近的凉亭中。改造时，应该选择住区内部向阳的场地，避开风口阴冷地方，增加休息座椅以及遮阴凉亭。

老人行为记录汇总　　表2

地点	行为分布	行为特点
住宅楼下有阳光的街角，有座椅		有3~5个老人聚集在座椅上聊天，晒太阳，老人行为以静止的为主
社区内部公共空间		大部分人在使用运动器材，也有一部分老人聚在一起聊天，老人行为已为以健身，交往为主
主要街道		行走的老人居多，也有部分老人停留在路边和人聊天，老人以购物等动态活动为主

（3）私密性活动空间

在既有住区室外空间改造时，要满足老人的私密性活动的需求：许多老人喜欢独自行动，不愿意被打扰。对于这些老人来说，在室外为他们提供一个可以一个人独处的室外活动空间是很必要的。对于这类需求，需要在住区安静之处设置若干独立的小空间，这类小空间需要与主要道路，活动场所有一定的联系，保证老人通过小空间实现交往活动。

5.1.2 景观观赏空间

老年人则喜欢生活在一个与自然接近的居住环境中。所以景观观赏空间的品质能够直接影响到老年人晚年生活的幸福感。良好的景观，如绿植以及花卉等，可以有效消除老年人的消极情绪，使老年人体会到生命的乐趣。景观观赏空间可分为以下两部分：

（1）室外观赏性空间

享受自然，与自然亲密接触，是老年人使用室外活动场所的主要原因。大多数老人喜欢闲暇时在室外散步、欣赏花卉或绿植，放松身心。同时绿植下面的树荫也是老人们夏季室外乘凉以及娱乐的主要场所。

根据上面所叙述的内容，室外观赏性空间设计应满足老年人亲近自然的心理需求以及使用需求，合理规划空间区域，利用树冠的遮蔽作用营造出一种半私密空间，避免草坪面积比例过大，空间过于开阔。可以在住区空地上规划出一片自主种植区，让老年人从事花园的种植活动，这样即丰富了老年人的生活内容，又满足了既有住区绿化的需求。另外社区之间可以利用既有空地建设休闲花园，作为一个区域性有吸引力的空间，为老年人交往提供良好的机会与环境。

（2）从室内观赏的室外空间

对于行动不便的老人或者在寒冷的冬季，从建筑物内观赏室外的景观是老人们很重要的一项活动。在观赏的同时，也鼓励和吸引了老年人到室外参与各种活动。室内外空间环境在视觉上和心理上的联系有利于增强老年人的安全感和参与愿望。

目前很多住区周边环境状况不佳，例如许多坡地住区低层住户从窗内只能看到窗外高大的挡土墙，或是处于商业区的旧房，被高大的办公楼所围困。解决此类问题应从多角度出发，例如合理的区域规划、避免城中村的出现。或是合理改造建筑功能，在景观日照条件不理想的楼层设置库房或停车场等辅助功能用房。尽量通过绿植来美化现有不足，例如挡土墙下种植爬蔓植物，在住宅与办公楼用绿化带分隔等手段解决现有问题，提升老年人窗外观感质量。

5.1.3 健身锻炼空间

对于老年人来说，室外的健身锻炼是必不可少的。适时适量锻炼有助于延缓身体机能的衰老，同时健身活动又与互相交往、观赏景色等活动密不可分，所以在空间的组织改造上也应与交往空间和景观空间相互渗透，形成一个有机整体。

（1）健身场地设置

散步、晒太阳、打太极拳、跳广场舞是老年人的普遍爱好。因此，散步道、活动广场、健身场等内容必不可少，这些场地通过改造可达性较强的社区公共绿地、院落、小广场等公共空间来解决。在改造时应尽量选择平坦开阔的场地，或是局部利用一些坡地，增加老年人锻炼乐趣。场地边缘宜设置长条座椅，方便老年人休息聊天。

（2）健身设施设置

由于老年人健康程度不同，因此锻炼活动设施要多样化，提供多种形式，多个部位的锻炼器材，使之适合老年人使用。设施宜集中设置在离室外有一定距离的地方，并确保这些场所可以被周边的用户看到，以鼓励人们参与进来。健身设施自身颜色应鲜艳些，增加人们的参与感。

6 结语

本研究在中国老龄化背景下，以居家养老为主的养老模式中。基于环境行为学理论在通过对大连市星海街道外环境调研中，总结归纳了既有住区外环境改造策略及方法，期望通过这项研究对于既有住区适老性环境体系建构提供参考。

Research on the Optimal External Environment Design of Old Residential Area Base on the Elderly Behavior——Take Dalian as An Example

Yu Wenting, Zhou Bo, Zhou Zhiwei

(School of Architecture & Fine Art, Dalian University of Technology)

Abstract: The 13th five-year plan of national aging development and retirement system construction promulgated on February 28, 2017 clearly indicates the need to strengthen the foundation of community service for home care of elderly. This means that aging at home is the inevitable trend of future retirement. However, the large stock of domestic existing residential areas which constructed long time ago leads to the situation that most of the infrastructure inside the community can not satisfy the living need of the elderly and their quality of life is hard to guarantee as well. For these residential area, the whole reconstruction will not only be a waste of resources but also bring a lot of social problems. Therefore, transforming the exist residential area to aging-friendly communities it is a necessary way for the development of social retirement. This paper selects Dalian, a key city in the northeast of China, as the research subject area, and Xinghai street as the specific study area. Investigation are conducted by data collection, questionnaire and visit to conclude the environment problems, unreasonable distribution and utilization of the resource as well as the behavioral requirements of seniors in Xinghai Street. On the basis of investigation and sorting data, combined with the existing case, this paper contributes to integrate the existing resources and put forward environmental renovation strategy to adapt to the need of the elderly and residents in current residential area. This paper aims to provide a useful complement to optimizing the aging-friendly design in the northern regions.

Keywords: Old residential area, Elderly, Optimal design, Behavior,

参考文献

[1] 陈喆，胡惠琴. 老龄化社会建筑设计规划——社会养老与社区养老 [M]. 北京：机械工业出版社，2013.

[2] 姚栋. 当代国际城市老年人居住问题研究 [M]. 江苏：东南大学出版社，2007.

[3] 周典,周若祁.构筑老龄化社会的居住环境体系[J].建筑学报,2006,10:12.

[4] 李斌,李庆丽.老年人特别护理福利院家庭化生活单元的构建[J].建筑学报,2010,3:48.

[5] 邓斌."在地安养"模式下城市高龄者住宅室内空间设计研究[D].东南大学硕士论文,2012,5.

[6] 赵晔.老年人居住环境的舒适性研究[D].天津大学,2003.

[7] 贺佳.建成社区居家养老生活环境研究——以上海市S社区为例[D].同济大学,2008,3.

[8] 王江萍.老年人居住外环境规划与设计.[M].北京:中国电力出版社,2009.

生产性适老社区的设计概念初探

吴浩然　张玉坤　贡小雷　郑　捷

（天津大学建筑学院）

摘　要：针对我国愈加严峻的人口老龄化与养老问题，以社区农园为切入点，以适老社区规划设计实践为依托，提出"生产性适老社区"的概念——通过给健康老人提供合适的社区生产机会，满足老年人的身心需求并促进其"自我实现"。本文概述了社区农园与适老社区的关系，从社区农园的空间设计策略，管理模式以及经济、社会和文化价值等方面进行阐述与分析，并结合设计实例对"生产性适老社区"的概念作出初步实践，以期探索较为可行的、可市场化操作的社区建设新模式。

关键词：生产性，适老社区，社区农园，管理模式，设计策略

1　引言

我国老年人口增速快，预计2050年60岁及以上人口将达总人口1/3。[1]这与未富先老、家庭结构小型化、空巢家庭增多等变化趋势相叠加，使得养老问题异常严峻。面对养老事业的家庭与社会成本居高不下，如何推进适老社区的可持续发展成为迫切需要研究的问题。

针对愈加严峻的人口老龄化与养老问题，本文提出"生产性适老社区"概念，试图从生产性老龄化的角度探讨老年人居环境设计。本研究的目的在于充分调动赋闲老年人的生产积极性，使社区成为资源生产消费分布式网络中的单元，使老年群体作为重要的社会资源，对经济社会和文化发展作出积极贡献，一方面增强其内心满足感，促进其"自我实现"，另一方面降低家庭与社会的养老负担，有益于建立一个可持续发展的社区。生产性适老社区的内容涵盖老年人居住、生产及娱乐等多个方面，社区农园是其重要组成部分之一。西方发达国家在社区农园方面已积累了丰硕的理论成果与实践经验，一些西方学者认为老年人的潜在贡献不应被年龄歧视、腐化的组织结构和无效的政策所限制，老年群体作为重要的社会资源，仍可对经济社会和文化发展可作出积极贡献。[2]本研究有益于建立一个可持续发展的适老社区，打破"老年人无用无能"这一迷思，提醒人们广泛关注老年人的能力和他们对家庭、社区作出的宝贵贡献。本文将从社区农园的角度阐述"生产性适老社区"概念。以期为我国适老社区的发展提供参考。

2　社区农园与适老社区

2.1　社区农园研究综述

社区农园（Community Gardens）又称社区花园、社区园圃，是为了让社区居民进行园艺与农事耕作的场地，社区农园鼓励了城市社区的食品安全，让居民们可以种植作物供自己或捐给他人食

用，还可以避免人们在现代城市生活中的互相疏远，通过食物的来源将居民们紧密联系在一起，并通过建立社会团体来打破人们的隔阂。[3] 最早的社区农园可追溯到18世纪晚期的英国的家庭花园（Allotment Gardens），它们由当时的城市化、工业化及农业转型所催生（Warner，1987）。美国的社区农园已有百年历史，其伴随着三项重要的城市农业运动而发展：即早期食物花园；战时农园及现代城市社区园艺运动（Benn. E，2010）。亚洲地区有组织的社区农园发展较为迟缓，香港康乐及文化事务署于2004年开始，分阶段在各区推行社区园圃计划，鼓励市民将绿化活动生活化，积极参与邻里层面的绿化活动及通过体验种植的乐趣来培养绿化环保的意识。[4] 一直以来，社区农园的蓬勃发展基于人们自发性地不断追求更高的生活品质。社区农园的功能性满足了人们消遣娱乐及物质生产的需求，其社会性增强了人们的身份认同及自我价值实现，其象征性体现了一种特定时期特殊文化的空间表达。

2.2 社区农园与适老社区的同一性

社区农园与适老社区的同一性体现在三个层面：

（1）环境功能层面

居家养老和机构养老概念的提出是不断改变的社会关系和社会价值观的结果，其分别把社会化的养老问题交给了老人的亲属和医疗机构。而社区农园作为一种生活方式型功能空间的存在，提供给老人进行休闲生产活动的非正式环境，有助于自身满足感的增加和社会养老负担的降低。这与家庭和养老院等制度化功能空间是不同的，家务活、照料婴儿等产生于制度化环境的工作，有时等同于被强加的义务，拒绝参加这样活动的老人，常被视作难以相处或是不近人情的。对于养老环境功能的设定，如果没有考虑到老人在活动中认知模式和参与的方式，就会导致老年人远离这些活动。社区农园与适老社区的功能性联系在于"增强其信心和生产力"和"满足自我发展"概念的实践和创新，提供给老年人自由选择活动的物质条件，使"自定义老年生活"成为可能。

（2）身份认同层面

人群的身份认同方式是被场所化、空间化的，我们置身所处的环境会传递出大量关于我们是谁的信息（Glenda Laws）。并且，人群具有归属于特定地理区域的模式化刻板印象，这是由于同等强有力的场所的模式化印象所导致的。当退休老人身处于社区农园这一环境中，其社会身份被认同为极具生产力的形象，这与"养老院中老人是失能无助的且需要护理"这种刻板印象所区分；社区农园还会带给老人能够独立地对经济社会和文化发展作出贡献的印象，这不同于"居家养老的人需要亲缘关系的维持才得以健康生存"这种刻板印象。因此，社区农园能够赋予一般适老社区所不具有的身份认同信息，提供给老年人构建新的老龄身份的外部条件。

（3）场所象征层面

场所除了具有其物质性，也是一种象征性的构筑，它充当了在人们的活动中为自身定位的心理构筑物。在总体的建成环境中，某些空间会被赋予比其他空间更为重要的意义（Kontos）。在适老社区中，社区农园会被认为是在老人与社区其他人群之间的象征性"地标"，对于老人来说，他们才是农园活动的主体，社区农园作为集体文化的表征，将集体的兴趣、活动与老人的联系具体化，而对于一般人群来说，其象征价值代表了社区景观绿化的一部分，这无关于在其中发生的活动。建筑师在为老人的社交活动而设计物质环境的同时，应意识到一个空间对于涉及的不同人群具有完全不同的象征性价值。同样，在适老社区的规划设计中也应考虑社区农园等公共空间背后的场所象征意义。

3 生产性适老社区的社区农园

生产性适老社区是以可持续发展为宗旨，以建筑空间承载各项生产要素，是有机整合物质生产、文化生产、空间生产、社会关系生产等多种功能于一体的适合老年社会成员的栖居之所。其生产性体现在物质资源：即食物、能源、工业品的生产；象征资源：即自我实现、身份认同、社会关系的生产；以及空间资源再生产，是一种包含消费的生产过程。随着时间的流逝，特殊的退休文化在这里形成，老年社会成员在这里对其身份进行重构，有助于形成关于晚年生活的新观念。生产性适老社区的核心在于使退休的意义发生根本变化，并肯定老年人在场所意义的个别构建方面的重要性。

社区农园是生产性适老社区公共空间的重要组成部分，其人员特定以老年人为主，通过给健康老人提供合适的社区生产机会，以满足老年人的身心需求并促进其"自我实现"。社区农园作为具有鲜明特色的社区公共空间，提供给农业种植需要的土地资源，生产农作物有助于"本地食物景观型社区"[5]的形成，产生老年合作的社会关系有助于密切的邻里关系的形成，给老人带来精神慰藉，使其保持活力并获得成就感。

3.1 社区农园设计策略

社区农园是塑造社区景观的主体，设立公共菜园，公共厨房、公共餐厅与堆肥处理设施，以在社区内部实现农产品的生产、加工、消费与处理循环。可将果树代替景观树，用农作物种植代替纯景观绿化，利用社区绿地、建筑周边、建筑屋顶等空间开发点状或片状的蔬菜园、果园。社区农园生产区域与儿童活动场地结合布置，便于儿童熟悉农业种植。种植劳作为社区居民提供了新鲜蔬果，为老年群体创造了劳作机会。还能通过公共餐厅烹饪，共同享用劳动的果实与丰收的喜悦。老年人不再只是等待别人的照顾然后无所事事的老去，而是有着自己的工作岗位，为社区作出贡献。

空间结构需清晰明了，可设置多种与农园联系紧密的社区公共活动空间组织社区布局，使不同组团具有易达性与可辨识性。住宅面对具有生产性内容的公共空间，强调社区内部环境的向心性与吸引力。私密与社交、私人与公共的空间平衡与过渡，将共同形成有层次有变化的空间序列，同时老人还可以从住宅的窗户、共享平台、室外座椅等位置看到公共活动区域。

社区农园根据其所处社区位置不同可分为独立式、退台式与屋顶平台式。独立式农园处于建筑之间的空地上，优点是具有较好的连续性和开放性，缺点是与建筑室内空间联系较弱；退台式农园设置在建筑立面的退台处，优点是做到了种植与建筑一体化，缺点是影响建筑室内的采光；屋顶平台式农园位于建筑屋顶，优点是美化了建筑屋顶，缺点是可达性较弱。针对不同的场地应选择适宜的农园形式以确保其存在的价值。在可持续原则的前提下，还可在各户阳台种植小株农作物，改善室内环境，以种植长生菜为例，在阳台开展梯田立体栽培，每年可收鲜菜 $60kg/m^2$。充分利用社区垃圾与雨水回收，建立社区农业生态经济循环系统。社区餐厨垃圾经净化反应，除进入沼气池做燃气能源外，固体废物经过滤处理、添加营养成分生成固体肥料；雨水回收后可用于农作物灌溉。居民生活的废弃物通过社区农业的新陈代新，以养分形式重归自然。[6]

3.2 社区农园管理模式

不论发达国家，还是发展中国家，社区管理模式不外乎三种类型：政府主导模式、社区自治模式和混合模式。[7] "空间是一种社会构筑物"，农园空间的背后隐藏着老人、管理人员及游客之间错综复杂的社会关系。管理模式不应从纯粹功能性的角度来考虑，我们需要创造一种非正式的环境和管理模式，以减少强制性的"角色扮演"情况，老年人不能被单纯地定义为"都市农夫"或"农园生产者"。通过调动老年人参加农园劳作的积极性，可确保其自由地构建新的老龄身份。

首先，要从传统控制型管理向服务型管理转变。社区管理要提供老年群体更多的交流机会，实现互助、陪伴与依靠，缓解老人的孤独感。密切的邻里关系和丰富多彩的老年生活能为老人带来精神慰藉。设置管理用房并作为社区的公共用房，同时设置保健室和康复护理室，并根据需要雇用相关人员，实现医护资源共享并防止突发事件的发生。

其次，建立包含老人、家庭、社工、社团及政府的"五位一体"管理模式。老人作为管理监督的主体实行自我管理及约束，家庭作为赡养老人的主要支柱，社工作为养老志愿服务的提供者，社团作为社区活动及服务的组织者，而政府则扮演催化剂的角色，促进社区的健康发展。只有当社会价值观与社区管理模式所展现的外在条件相符合时，社区农园的积极性才会有所体现。

3.3 社区农园的经济社会及文化价值

（1）经济价值

以社区及其建筑为载体，对老年人的生产性潜力进行大力挖掘，可缓解社会劳动力来源不足的趋势；生产出大量的物质资源，满足社区内部人群的消费需求，降低社会养老成本同时还可增加就业岗位；社区农园作为特殊的公共空间可提升周边的土地价值，丰富城市区域经济繁荣发展。

（2）社会价值

提高老年人生活品质，通过社区内的生产性活动转变养老生活方式，从枯燥的社区生活转变为丰富的都市田园生活；可增强社区凝聚力，促进居民交往，有助于构建熟人社会；有助于赋予一般适老社区所不具有的身份认同信息，提供给老年人构建新的老龄身份的外部条件。

（3）文化价值

非正式农业休闲活动的核心价值在于文化。社区农园作为城市公共空间，不仅给中华传统农业的当代实践提供了契机，也会在老年群体内部形成新的文化圈，其作为中华传统农耕文化的载体，使生产活动、生态理念与传统文化相辅相成。

4 设计案例

选取作者近期设计实例，试图对"生产性适老社区"的概念的作出初步尝试。在实际设计过程中，我们将适老住宅定义为生产性建筑，将适老社区定义为生产性适老社区。生产性系统是一个多层次的系统，是物质生产、文化生产、社会文化资本保护和重建等多功能的整合。

4.1 福建省某生态颐养中心设计

本方案的构思将交通、建筑、农业与退台有机整合，通过生产性元素的置入以组织多种公共活动空间布局，打造适应老年人生活习惯的养老建筑。

策略与特征：

（1）光伏农园

透光光伏结合种植是塑造社区景观的主体，以连续生产性景观代替纯景观绿化，开发点状和片状的蔬菜园、果园。贯通各层的社区农园还是建筑的"第二逃生通道"（图1）。

图1 光伏农园人视图

资料来源：2017台达杯太阳能国际建筑设计竞赛方案（作者自绘）。

（2）连续院落

内部院落空间与风雨廊连续贯通，在保证私密性的同时强调社区内部环境的向心性与吸引力。

（3）绿色技术

对透光光伏薄膜、点状种植砖、木质种植架、电动遮阳百叶、光热屋檐、风力发电等构件进行单项设计，创建适老、健康、舒适、生态、环保的绿色空间。

本方案的重点在于建筑南侧退台式社区农园的空间塑造，老年人居室和退台式农园的灵活交接与穿插，提供了积极活动的可能性，老年人可利用连续而开敞的退台农园自由地进行交往活动（图2）。

图2 南立面效果图

资料来源：2017台达杯太阳能国际建筑设计竞赛方案（作者自绘）。

5 结论

在未来老龄化问题愈加严重的时代背景下，社会将无法负担以休闲活动为主的退休生活。本文以社区农园为切入点，结合适老社区设计实例与前人研究成果，提出"生产性适老社区"的概念，初步探索了社区农园与适老社区的关系与社区农园如何体现适老社区的生产性。

社区农园给我们的启示是：在社会价值观层面，应当为老年人创造丰富的机会和选择并推广老年人的生产性参与，支持他们成为有价值的角色，造福个人、家庭和社会，应当建立以最小的社会成本实现社会价值最大化的公民总体价值观；在建筑设计层面，不应把适老社区看成是一个与其他功能隔离的居住区，应当将其视作具有完整生产、生活、生态功能的系统，以充分鼓励老年人自由而全面发展其晚年人生阶段，发掘其在物质资源、社会资源及文化资源生产方面的潜能。

本研究为当前适老社区的发展提供了新的视角，后续还有大量的工作要做，包括对现有适老社区的调研，进一步的理论探索与项目设计，以期探索更为详尽的生产性适老社区系统方案。

致谢

本文受国家自然科学基金（面上）资助项目：基于生态足迹分析的合作性城市农业社区研究（项目批准号：51578363）资助。

A Primary Study on Concepts of Designing Productive Community for the Elderly

Wu Haoran, Zhang Yukun, Gong Xiaolei, Zheng Jie

(School of Architecture, Tianjin University)

Abstract: In the face of an aging population and an increasing challenge to national retirement problem, This article proposes the concept of a "productive community" for the elderly based on a community design. By means of providing the elderly with opportunities to grow vegetables and fruits, this strategy satisfies the elderly's physical and mental needs and enables them to make full use of themselves in the rest of life. This paper outlines the relationship between community garden and community for the elderly. Moreover, it elaborates and analyzes the community garden's space design strategy, management model and its economic, social and cultural values. Furthermore, this paper makes a preliminary exploration with a specific design to fully explore a feasible model of community construction which allows for a market-oriented operation.

Keywords: Productive, Community for the elderly, Community garden, Management mode, Design strategies

参考文献

[1] 新华网. [2017-3-21]. http：//news.xinhuanet.com/photo/2012-10/22/c_123855681_3.htm.

[2] Morrow-Howell N，Hinterlong J，Sherraden M W. Productive aging : concepts and challenges[M]. Johns Hopkins University Press，2001.

[3] Wikipedia. [2017-3-21]. https：//zh.wikipedia.org/wiki/社区农圃.

[4] 香港康乐及文化事务署网站. [2017-4-1]. http：//www.lcsd.gov.hk/sc/green/garden/index.html.

[5] My food scape. [2017-3-21]. http：//www.myfoodscape.com.

[6] 张玉坤，孙艺冰. 国外的"都市农业"与中国城市生态节地策略[J]. 建筑学报，2010，4：95-98.

[7] 新华网. [2017-3-21]. http：//www.hq.xinhuanet.com/finance/2013-10/29/c_117909838.htm.

[8] Irvine S. Community gardens and sustainable land use planning：A case——study of the Alex Wilson community garden[J]. Local Environment，1999，4（1）：33-46.

[9] Ghezzi P，Santo E D，Sacco S，et al. What are community gardens? A DIY approch to growing food in our cities：discussion sheet（2008）[J]. European Cytokine Network，2000，11（3）：464-469.

[10] Liangtao LI，Lorraine Weller，Yuanyuan TAO，Zhenrong YU. Eco-vegetation Construction of the Community Gardens in US and Its Implications[J]. Asian Agricultural Research，2013，7：92-96.

长远老年建筑设计策略

吕庆耀

(吕元祥建筑师事务所)

摘　要：未来的 20 年内（2017～2037 年），中国将会迎来 2 亿新增的老年人口（65 岁以上）。香港地区的人口老龄化问题更加日趋严重。仅 15 年内（2014～2029 年），香港地区将增加近 100 万的老年人口，占整体人口比例从 15% 增至 26%。在新的医疗科技辅助下，我们预期老年人达到退休年龄后将会有近 20 年（60～80 岁）的活跃且有品质的生活。新一代的老年人以及大幅延长的退休生活，将为老年住宅设计带来新问题和前所未有的挑战。本文探讨其他国家（日本、澳大利亚和加拿大）对老化的不同阶段的分类以及与各个阶段相关的老年人需求。通过对这些国家阶段性养老制度与政策的分析，本文讨论建筑设计如何适应老年人阶段性需求，以香港地区的老年住宅项目作为案例进行分析，提出适应阶段性老年人需求的五个主要设计策略。

关键词：快速老龄化，老年护理，老年住宅

1　中国及香港人口老龄化的趋势

1.1　急速老龄化

中国人口老龄化的趋势日趋明显。学者 Florian Coulmas 曾对日本老龄化社会研究作出了一个定义，一个国家内 65 岁以上的人口，占总人口比例 7% 以上，即称为老龄化社会（ageing society），达 14% 称为老龄社会（aged society），达 21% 称之为超老龄社会（hyper-aged society）。[1]

而且根据世卫组织的人口统计及预测数据，中国内地和香港特别行政区已分别于 2000 年和 1980 年进入老龄化社会，随后经过仅 30 年就从老龄化社会进入老龄社会；中国再进一步成为超老龄社会则仅需 10 年时间（2030～2040 年）。这远超发达国家 20 世纪初开始的老化进程（法国经过了 115 年、瑞典 85 年、加拿大 65 年、英国 45 年从老龄化社会进入老龄社会）。中国老年人口比例增长一倍达到 25% 的超老龄社会仅需 22 年（2010～2032 年）。[2] 根据估算，到 21 世纪中期，中国超过 1/4 人口将会超过 65 岁。而绝对人口数量实属一个相当大的规模，老年人口规模甚至长期处于世界第一位。

急速的人口增长以及巨大的老年人口规模对社会经济意味着什么？从较直观的数据来看，未来的 20 年内（2017～2037 年），中国将会迎来两亿新增的 65 岁以上老年人口，相当于两倍现时日本的总人口。与中国内地整体相比，香港的人口老龄化问题更加日趋严重。仅 15 年内（2014～2029 年），香港将增加近一倍的老年人口；从 2014 年的 100 万，占总人口 15%，迅速增长到 2029 年的 200 万，占总人口 26%。[3] 如何在 10～15 年内为这激增的老年人口提供居所与养老相关社会服务将是中国内地和香港特别行政区都要面对的一个严峻挑战。

1.2　老年期生活的延长

伴随着人口的老龄化，老年期的生活时间也相对地延长。由于在中国一般的退休年龄在大概 60 岁

左右。因此老年人口实际生活的重大转变比生理上进入老年期来得更早。以60岁为界线的低龄老年人口比例的增长较65岁以上老年人口更为急速，最高峰时超过60岁的人口甚至达到接近1/3。[4]再且，中国的人均预期寿命也在持续增长。到21世纪中期中国的老年人口高峰期，人均预期寿命将达到超过80岁。换而言之，未来的老年人口将会有超过20年的老年期生活。

而香港的情况较中国内地整体更加突出。香港从现在到21世纪中期，人均预期寿命将一直处于世界第一位。[5] 2045～2050年香港的人均预期寿命将接近90岁，也即是香港老年人未来有可能面对近30年的老年期生活。延长的老年期生活对养老服务和居所设施也有较以往不同的要求。

2 国外老年人的阶段性护理

2.1 以年龄界定的不同阶段（加拿大）

身体机能的衰退的程度与老年人的护理需求是相适应的，因此根据加拿大卫生局20世纪90年代的定义，60岁以后的老年期养老安排可以分为三个年龄阶段：(1) 独立自理：大致从退休到75岁左右（根据个人情况而异）；(2) 半独立：72岁以上；(3) 全护理：79岁以上。[5]

2.2 各阶段的护理需求及生活辅助设施（日本）

1997年日本制定了老年长期护理需求分级标准——要介护认定标准。通过以护理时间、护理强度的评估体系将老年人生活自理能力分为7个等级，即自立、要支援、要介护Ⅰ～Ⅴ级。2006年日本制定了介护预防政策，将原来的7等级护理修改为8等级护理，自立、要支援Ⅰ、要支援Ⅱ、要介护Ⅰ～Ⅴ级8个等级。其中将护理级别要支援Ⅰ及以上等级的老人认定为有护理需求的人（图1）。[6]

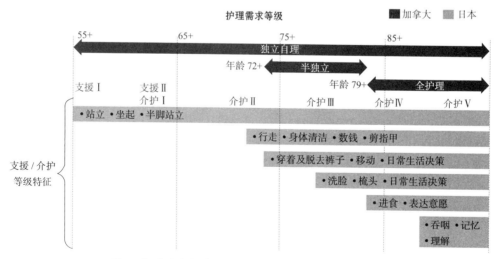

图1 加拿大老年阶段划分以及日本老年护理需求评级

2.3 阶段性的养老制度及政策（澳大利亚）

目前，澳大利亚社区养老护理发展非常全面，并可根据老年人个人需要提供量身定制的服务。老年人因此可以获得更长时间的独立生活期，这缓解了对养老院机构的需求量，相应节约了社会成本。根据护理级别的不同，澳大利亚社区养老提供的服务包括：家庭和社区照料（HACC）；社区养老照料计划（CACP）；和长期居家养老计划。[7]

2.4 现有中国养老政策对阶段性的分类

目前中国《老年人社会福利机构基本规范》对60周岁及以上的人口的护理需求分为三个阶段：自理老人；介助老人和介护老人。根据不同年龄阶段的护理需求，规范提供了服务具体内容的指引。对应不同程度的护理需求，养老设施也分为不同的类型：养老院或老人院；老年公寓；护老院；护养院；敬老院；托老所和老年人服务中心。[8]

3 适应中国的老年生活支援与设计实例

3.1 老年生活支援的原则

3.1.1 养老观念的转型

随着医疗科技的进步以及老年人生理机能的改善，社会对老年期的界定逐渐与生理机能的退化脱节。中国订立50～60岁的退休年龄（特殊工作甚至早至45岁）与实际生理机能退化已经不完全一致。50～60岁的退休人士大部分仍然精力充沛，身体状况也能够继续与青壮年无异地生活甚至继续某程度的工作，而且这种状况很可能持续长达10～20年的时间。

3.1.2 早期老年人的心理与社交需求

和青壮年人一样，老年人除了基本的生存需求以外也有一系列心理需求需要被满足。[9]（1）安全感和情感关顾：得到爱和关顾；（2）社会认同及地位：受到重要的人的尊重；（3）自我价值及自尊：生活能达到理想。在老年化的初期，社会角色的突然改变往往为老年人带来不适。例如退休令他们失去原来的自我价值和社会地位；身体机能和感知能力的减退，以及退休后收入的减少，使老年人逐渐失去安全感；生活上的一些变故，如丧偶，也需要一段适应期去习惯老年的生活。

但是以往着重医疗辅助的养老设施和机构，往往缺乏对老年人心理上的调适和照顾。过早将他们的生活和社交圈子局限于同年龄人甚至高龄老年人，并不利于他们对将来生活的调适。

3.1.3 医疗护理

由于老年人的身体出现状况，其严重性差异相当大，所以一般应该尽快送到附近的医疗机构进行诊治。因此老年住宅对医疗需求的目标应该是一旦出现变化能够在一定时间之内送抵医院，并为医生提供准确而详细的资料。

3.1.4 家居安全与便利

大部分老年人在出现家居意外，例如跌倒后，身体都会受到不同程度的伤害。有些伤害会对他们的身体状况造成非常严重的打击，其恢复也相当困难。因此，住宅的设计重点除了为满足老年人日常所需提供便利之外，更重要的是减少引致家居意外的因素。针对老年人衰退的机能如记忆与感知的衰退或行动能力的减退提供适度的支援。

3.2 老年住宅设计的策略

老龄化社会在中国内地和香港已经成为一个不能回避的社会问题,而老年人口结构和身体状况的新趋势造成传统的养老设施远远未能满足现在甚至未来50年的需求。这些新趋势导致新一代老年人期望有别于一般养老院的养老模式,他们需要能够支援长达10~20年高品质退休生活的老年住宅。老年人在得到适当的支援下,仍然能保持与青壮年时相约的生活模式与品质。原来被忽略的社交心理等需求,应该重新被满足并协助他们适应心理和生理上的变化,顺利过渡到人生的另一个阶段。为适应上述的老年人养老的各项需求,住宅建筑的设计可作出相应的改善,以达到支援高品质养老生活的要求。

(1)私人与社交空间:在保障老年人安全的前提下,尽量让他们享有私人安静的空间,同时透过便利的社交空间满足他们心理上的需要,例如希望有人陪伴,或希望参与社会活动时能够轻易融入社群之中。

(2)舒适称心的环境:住宅建筑使用天然物料如木材以及较柔和的暖色调会营造一个舒适而温暖的环境,减低对老年人的刺激。另外,天然日照、通风以及绿化不但有利于改善室内的卫生,而且接近自然环境也会使老年人感觉安宁与舒畅。

(3)家居便利与安全:由于老年人肌肉力量的不足,在房间通道的墙壁以及公共空间如电梯和走廊处设置站立或轮椅高度扶手;升降机内设置座位,减少因疲累而跌倒的危险;另外,一般家具的尺度都需要适应轮椅的高度而调整,橱柜台面的高度应下调至0.8m,而微波炉及吊柜应在1.3m以下。

(4)简明的家居标志:居室内外的指示性标志要简单而明确。例如每个楼层的数字或逃生出口等标志可采用较大的字体和明显的颜色,以便快速辨认;大门的窥视孔可以设于站立高度和轮椅高度;在走廊或玄关处可设置嵌入式感光夜视灯,老年人在晚间也能看清地面的状况;其他安全设备,如烟雾感应器和火警钟也要额外加设在每个住宅单位内,让听力退化的老年人,不会错失逃生的时机。

(5)畅通的急救通道:居室内设置动态监测器,一旦因突然发病而长时间未有移动,也能够第一时间被发现;浴室及厕所等独处的空间,设置在紧急状况下可以开启而不会触碰到倒地或昏迷的老年人的趟门;住宅的大堂和升降机应可容纳活动式病床或担架,让需要急救的老年人无论处于躺卧或者乘坐轮椅的状态也可直接进入救护车;小区内有便捷的救护车通道以及上落点;为尽快将病者送到医院,老年住宅的选址应该尽可能靠近医疗机构,而交通上也应该作出周全的规划。

3.3 高密度都市环境中的养老社区发展模式

如前所述,中国老龄化社会的发展,对适合老人居住的住宅产生大量需求。要满足这类需求,一种适应高密度都市环境的养老社区模式会比较适合。中国传统文化一直以来将家庭视为社会的基石,家族关系更是社会伦理的基础,而长辈在家庭中的地位尊崇,这种尊老的传统是中华文化的一大特色。在传统的四合院,长辈居住的堂屋和儿孙辈居住的厢房围合成院落。长辈和年青一代各有自己独立的家庭居住空间,同时又通过院落这个共用的活动空间相互联系为一个整体,长者家庭和晚辈家庭可以互相照顾,并获得情感支持和家族的归属感。

时至今日,在高层高密度的发展中,建筑可在垂直方向上形成不同分区,低层区域设计成老人公寓,室内设计特别照顾老人不同需要,更有辅助服务;高层部分则是普通的住宅单位,再配合相关的公共设施。让同属一个大家庭的长者和晚辈家庭可以居住在同一栋大楼的不同分区,既有各自的独立空间,又通过垂直的交通及大楼内的公共空间相互联系、照顾,将旧有的四合院模式垂直化。

另外,在同一小区内,以不同住宅类型配合不同的家庭。如以低层联排住宅作为长者住宅,而已经成家立室的子女,因为家庭成员数目相对较小,所以就可以住在同一个住宅小区内,其他的高层公寓,形成集合多个家庭的现代聚居院落,促进长幼家庭之间的互动和照顾(图2)。

图 2　养老社区发展模式

3.4 案例分析

3.4.1 老幼共融设计——乐融轩

乐融轩位于香港岛筲箕湾，是 2015 年竣工的市区重建发展项目。其中包括一幢综合大楼以及一幢 42 层住宅大厦（图 3）。项目旨在推动老年人与家庭共同生活的养老模式，以适应老龄化的新趋势。住宅大厦约 30% 为出租的老年公寓，其余优先出售予租住低层老年公寓的老年人的家庭成员。以鼓励老年人与家人各自拥有独立生活空间而彼此相邻方便照应。而综合大楼特为老年人的需要而设计，设有零售商店、长者门诊部及长者服务中心。

这种居住状态尽量维持老年人原有的生活与社交模式，包括与家人共聚天伦、与朋友欢聚。这种模式有助于之前提到老年人两个层次的心理需求：家人朋友的关顾以及社会认同与地位。与家人近在咫尺的半独立生活能将老年人的孤独感以及因退休而与社会的日渐疏离减至最低。

图 3　乐融轩低层出租老人公寓与高层私人住宅的"老幼共融设计"

3.4.2 室内家居设计——隽悦

位于香港岛北角的隽悦是香港首个专为退休人士而设的优质生活小区，旨在以一站式的配套，全方位照顾住客的起居，让老年人置身悠然逸乐的生活环境。住宅单位室内家居考虑到老年人的身体状态与生活实际需要加入许多细节设计（图 4）。

图 4　隽悦内多种为老年人而设计的设置与设备

Redesigning Long-term Senior Care Housing Strategy

Bryant Lu

(Ronald Lu & Partners)

Abstract: Over the next two decades, between 2017 and 2037, China will see an enormous increase in its population of senior citizens (people over 65). This increase will result in two hundred million seniors needing to be accommodated. In Chinese Hong Kong, the issue of an aging society is even more critical: in just 15 years, the city will need to accommodate another one million seniors, one-seventh of its current total population. Today's seniors are expected to enjoy a dynamic and high-quality lifestyle for a much longer period of time after they retire. The extended lifespan of these "new generation senior citizens" poses a number of uncertainties and unprecedented challenges in terms of the design of senior housing and the provision of sustainable elements—— these designs need to be adapted to help seniors enjoy their dynamic lifestyle as well as assist them through the aging process. This paper explores how the different stages of life and aging are categorised in different countries and which long-term senior care needs are associated with these categorisations. It also investigates the country-specific regulations and guidelines formulated for the needs of seniors, and discusses how design solutions can facilitate their implementation. Japan, Australia and Canada have comprehensive pension and senior care policies. Their long-term care systems were also studied. Lastly, the paper discusses two senior housing projects in Hong Kong, Harmony Place and The Tanner Hill, as case studies. The paper concludes four design strategies that will help achieve sustainable long-term senior care in housing developments in China and chinese Hong Kong.

Keywords: Rapid ageing, Elderly care, Elderly housing

参考文献

[1] F. Coulmas. Population Decline and Ageing in Japan: The Social Consequences[M]. London, New York: Routledge, 2007.

[2] United Nations Department of Economic and Social Affairs/Population Division. World Population Prospects: The 2015 Revision, Key Findings and Advance Tables. New York: United Nations, 2015.

[3] 香港特区政府统计处. 香港人口推算 2015～2064. 香港: 特区政府统计处, 2015.

[4] 杜鹏, 翟振武, 陈卫. 中国人口老龄化百年发展趋势 [J]. 人口研究, 2005, 29（6）: 90-93.

[5] United Nations, Department of Economic and Social Affairs, Population Division（2015）. World Population Prospects: The 2015 Revision. New York: United Nations.

[6] R D Chellis, P J Grayson, Symposium Farnsworth Trust. Life Care: A Long-Term Solution?[M]. Lexington, Mass.: Lexington Books, 1990.

[7] 张莹. 日本介护保险制度中老年长期护理分级标准研究 [J]. 中国全科医学, 2011, 14（8）: 2544-2545.

[8] 许岩丽, 刘志军. 澳大利亚老年保健服务现况分析及其对我国的启示 [J]. 医学与哲学. 人文社会医学版. 2008, 29（8）: 68-70.

[9] 中华人民共和国民政部社会福利和社会事务司. 老年人社会福利机构基本规范 [S]. 北京: 中华人民共和国民政部, 2000.

应对老年人走失的高密度住区转型研究

卢丹丹　周　博　周志伟　杨岸霄

（大连理工大学）

摘　要：由于生理机能的衰退，对环境的辨识能力下降，如今老年人走失问题已屡见报端。随着我国城市化进程的不断加快，城市人口剧增和土地资源紧张之间的矛盾日益突出，高密度住区成为城市住区建设的主要模式。然而高密度住区中，建筑的密集性、环境的趋同性越发增大了老年人对于建筑、道路和环境的辨认难度。为防止老年人因高密度住区环境而走失，文章选取大连市区内三个有代表性的高密度住区为研究对象，通过对住区中增大老年人辨识难度的不利因素进行分析，试从住区的路网规划、建筑设计及环境景观等角度，提出一些改进思路和建议。

关键词：老年人走失，高密度住区，转型

1　引言

当前我国正处于快速城镇化进程的城市转型期，截至 2015 年，中国城镇化率已达到 56.1%，并预计将于 2020 年达到 60%。在此大背景下，城市人口剧增和土地资源紧张之间的矛盾成为城市建设面临的首要问题，城市住区的高密度发展已经成为我国住区建设不可避免的趋势[1]。截至 2015 年年末，中国 60 岁以上人口达到 2.22 亿，占总人口的 16.1%；65 岁以上人口 1.44 亿，占总人口的 10.5%[2]。由于老年人生理机能的衰退而造成的记忆力衰退、注意力不集中、认知能力和视觉能力下降等原因，导致老年人在高密度的住区环境中对道路、建筑、环境的辨识方面出现困难。因此，为防止老年人走失，在高密度住区转型过程中，适老性的因素是不容忽视的，只有满足各项适老化要求，才能最大限度减少老年人走失问题的发生。

2　大连高密度住区调研情况简述

2.1　调研对象的选择

为了保证调研结果的客观性与代表性，以获得大连高密度住区现状的准确资料，笔者在调研之前走访了很多住区，在综合考虑住区的特点后，选择了比较有代表性的三个高密度住区：大华锦绣华城、中铁·诺德滨海花园和小平岛亲海园，这三个住区规模大小不一，各自特点较为鲜明，能够基本反映出大连高密度住区的现状（图1、图2）。

为了对调研住区有更明确的认知，笔者从住区区位、空间密度指标、建筑样式等方面对三个住区的基本概况和规划特点进行了总结（表1）。

图1 调研对象区位图（作者自绘）

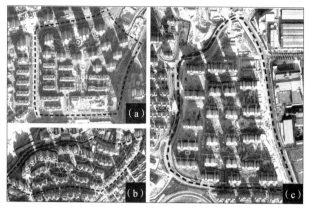

图2 调研对象总平面图（作者自绘）
（a）大华锦绣华城；（b）小平岛亲海园；（c）中铁·诺德滨海花园

调研住区基本概况总结　　　　　表1

	大华锦绣华城	中铁·诺德滨海花园	小平岛亲海园
地理位置	高新园软件园路与红凌路交汇处	高新园区河口国际软件园（东软向北500m）	大连市高新园区河口北疗养院附近
开盘时间	2010年	2011年	2007年
总用地面积	9hm²	23hm²	7.5hm²
容积率	2.5	2.9	3.5
绿化率	45%	55%	40%
住宅样式	别墅、多层、小高层、高层	高层	小高层、高层
住区入口			

2.2 调研过程

调研主要采取走访及发放问卷的方式，分为五个阶段：（1）准备工作，包括确定调研时间、地点选择、资料收集，确定访谈问题等；（2）实地观察，通过对住区的实地走访，观察其规划结构特点，推测住区内可能增加老年人辨认难度的因素；（3）问卷调查，将实地走访中推测出的问题组织成问卷的形式，在住区内随机选取老年人发放调查问卷；（4）访谈，与老年人进行访谈，主要询问是否还有其他影响他们辨认的不利因素，（5）总结，对信息进行处理，并对调研结果进行分析（表2）。

研究方法概述　　　　　表2

调研方法	实地观察法	问卷调查法	访谈法
调研时间	2017年4月6日	2017年4月7日	2017年4月7日
调研对象	大连近几年建成的住区：大华锦绣华城、中铁诺德滨海公园、小平岛亲海园	65周岁以上老年人	65周岁以上老年人
调研内容	新建高密度住区的现状特征：包括路网、建筑布局、绿化环境、指向性标识物等	老年人对于小区辨认难易程度的评价	老年人日常生活的其他不便因素等

2.3 调研结果总结

关于路网规划及其辨识度的问题，由图3a问卷调查结果显示，整体来说，三个小区老年人认为路网混乱的比例较高，其中小平岛亲海园的现象较为严重，认为路网规划清晰的比例为零，大华锦绣华城次之，中铁诺德滨海花园情况较好。

关于住宅楼栋辨认难易度的问题，调查结果如图3b，若只考虑住宅楼栋的相似性，在笔者实地观察中发现，三个小区楼栋的立面都可以用"千楼一面"来形容，为了设计和建筑工艺定型，高密度住宅在结构、建材选择等方面难以创新，绝大部分高层高密度住宅的建筑形式基本雷同，尤其是为保证小区的外观统一性，一般选用相同的外墙面颜色，外观显得单调呆板，缺乏标识性。

如图3c为对三个小区宅前环境的评价结果，可见景观环境设计趋同性很高。

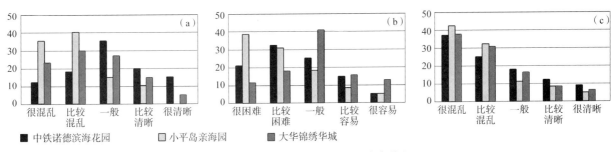

图3 问卷调查评价结果（笔者自绘）

（a）住区路网规划评价；（b）楼栋辨认难易度评价；（c）宅间环境景观趋同性评价

3 增大老年人辨识难度的不利因素分析

结合笔者的实地观察以及调查问卷结果，针对住区路网的规划问题、楼栋的辨识难易程度以及宅前环境景观的趋同性等方面进行了以下分析：

3.1 住区路网规划评价结果及分析

提取三个住区的路网规划图进行分析（图4），可以发现三个住区的路网不同程度地趋于曲线形态设计，亲海园的路网设计最为突出，全小区道路均采用曲线设计，没有一条道路是直线型的，锦绣华城和滨海花园两个小区路网整体上看算是规则的形状设计，但即使是外形大体规则，曲线的因素也占很大的比例。

分析其原因，具体来说，通路的线型越平直，其空间比例和尺度越大，通达性也越强，但其沿路景观的丰富感要差一些；相反，通路的线型越曲折弯曲，其空间比例和尺度越小，通达性也越弱，但其沿路景观的变化感觉会比较丰富。[3] 所以随着时代的发展，

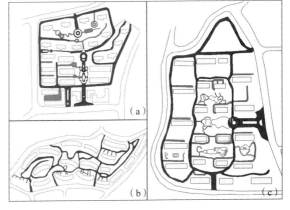

图4 住区路网规划图（笔者自绘）

（a）大华锦绣华城；（b）小平岛亲海园；（c）中铁·诺德滨海花园

人们对居住环境景观的要求越来越高，曲线形的路网设计配以多彩的植物搭配有利于塑造丰富多彩的小区空间形态。

然而对于记忆力、视力等均已不同程度衰退的老年人来说，方向时刻变化的曲线形路网设计加重了他们的辨认难度，对中铁·诺德滨海花园老年居民访谈结果显示，刚搬来小区居住的老年人很难分辨道路方向，找不到自己家的位置，常年居住的老年人情况会稍微好转；若非本小区居民，只是来探望亲朋好友的老年人基本是找不到目的地的。

3.2　住区建筑形态及布局分析

楼栋的辨识难易度的问题除了楼栋的立面，还需要考虑楼栋的数量、布局方式以及建筑类型等因素。小平岛亲海园由于其曲线形路网的影响，采用的是弯曲状半围合的建筑布局方式，规划设计层级不明确，整体建筑组织平铺开来，没有组团的概念，且建筑类型单一，导致其楼栋辨识困难。中铁诺德滨海花园虽然也是建筑类型单一，但其内环状路网设计，使得主次路分明，建筑布局方式简单，楼栋辨识较为容易。大华锦绣华城建筑类型主要分为高层和多层且分区明确，使得建筑辨认较为简单。

在中铁诺德滨海花园访谈中发现刚搬来不久的居民或者探亲访友的人在找住宅楼栋时，都是按照住宅楼栋号进行寻找，所以合理安排楼栋的排序号也是一种降低老人辨认难度的有效方法，但笔者发现住宅楼栋号的标志牌非常小，布置得较高，一般是放置在第四层楼高的位置，且采用的是蓝色，其明度较低，老年人视力衰退，对色彩的感知度不高，何况如今雾霾严重，老年人抬头查找楼栋号牌也是一件很困难的事，而且容易后仰摔倒（图5）。

图5　楼栋标志牌现状（作者自摄自绘）

3.3　宅间环境景观设计分析

随着社会经济的发展，环境绿化工作越来越引起人们的高度重视，与绿化率较低的老旧住区相比，新建的高密度住区对景观绿化的要求越来越高，以便创造更美好的住区生活环境。然而，楼栋间的景观布局设计趋于统一，不同的楼栋前绿化环境基本看不出差别，笔者在锦绣华城不同的楼栋间拍摄的照片（图6a、图6b），若不细心观察，很难发现照片中绿化环境的不同之处。

另一方面，绿化模式和植物树种比较单一，就笔者调研的三个住区而言，基本是较矮的树墙或者在小区内部种植大片草坪，其上种植灌木的绿化设计方案；亲海园建成时间较长，无论是草坪，还是其上的灌木都已长得十分茂盛（图6c）。单一的绿化方式导致整片小区环境就是一片绿色，因为相对于建筑而言，人们对于植物的感知能力并不高，所以楼栋间如此趋同的绿化环境设计进一步加重了老年人对于住区的辨认难度。

图6 住区宅间绿化现状图

(a)(b)大华锦绣华城；(c)小平岛亲海园（作者自摄）

4 关于高密度住区适老化转型的建议

4.1 路网规划简单清晰，曲直形态设置得当

路网的形态应与通路本身的功能要求、通达性要求、交通方式等相适应，并不是所有平直的路网都不好，也并不是所有优美的线型对所有的通路都适合。[3] 在老年群体人数较多的住区中，路网的形态还是应该在满足视觉美观效果的同时，尽量考虑老人的使用需求，若单纯追求视觉美感而采用过度随意自由的线型，如小平岛亲海园的路网规划，会导致居民，尤其是老年人的使用不便。另外，应在适当位置，如道路交叉口或者驻足点等设置清晰的道路指向牌，指向牌的绘制可借鉴旅游区中的指向方法，上面应清楚地展示小区整体路网关系、楼栋的标号以及您现在所在的位置（图7以中铁诺德滨海花园为例）。

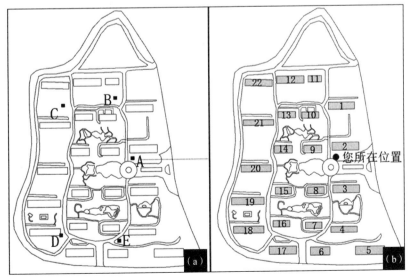

图7 住区指示牌示意图（作者自绘）

(a)指示牌位置图；(b)A处指示牌示意

4.2 建筑组群布局层次分明，适当放大楼号标志牌

住区建筑组群设计的规划布局在满足日照、噪声、通风、消防等功能要求以外，应创造不同的空间形态[4]，避免单一的布局方式造成的不易识别效果。楼号标志牌应尽量放大，以老年人能看到标志牌上的数字为准；研究发现，老人对橙色、红色等暖色系比较敏感，笔者建议，标志牌的颜色不妨多用暖色系，方便查看；标识牌不应设置太高，以老人视线仰角 10° 为宜。

4.3 宅间绿地避免同质化布局设计，增添构筑小品提高辨识度

布局设计上，在注重整体连贯统一的同时，还应注重局部的创新突破，避免同质化的布局设计，营造多样的景观模式，作为各户宅前标志，提高楼栋的可辨认度。树种选植上，可在不同的宅间绿地上种植不同的花树品种，形成不同主题、不同颜色的宅间景观，提高可辨认度。增添主题小品，由于人们对于植物的感知度低于建筑物或构筑物，所以可以考虑在宅前绿地上适当位置设置不同主题的环境小品等构筑物，以方便老年人辨识。

5 结语

未来的 5~10 年是中国为应对人口老龄化高峰到来做好各项准备的重要机遇期和窗口期，与此同时高密度住区已成为我国住区建设的主要模式，推动高密度住区的建设模式向适老化转型，在当今环境问题凸显，雾霾严重的情况下，使高密度住区仍然具有较高的可辨识度，减少老年人的辨识压力，无论是对于防止老年人走失还是住区的长远发展，都具有重大意义。

High Density Residential Transformation Research Dealing with the Old Lost Problem

Lu Dandan, Zhou Bo, Zhou Zhiwei, Yang Anxiao

(Dalian University of Technology)

Abstract: Due to physiological function decline and ability degradation to identify environmental, the problem of the elderly lost repeatedly reported today. With the acceleration of urbanization in China and the contradiction between the increasing of city population and shortage of land resources, high density residential area has become the main mode of city residential construction. However, in high density residential area, building density and the convergence of the environment make more difficulty to recognize the construction, roads and the environment for the elderly. In order to prevent the elderly from being lost in the high density environment, in this paper, three representative high - density residential areas in Dalian are selected as the research objects. By analyzing the adverse factors affecting the elderly identification difficulty in high density residential district, this paper tries to put forward some ideas and suggestions from the aspects of road network planning, architectural design and environmental detail design.

Keywords: The elderly lost, High density residential area, Transformation

参考文献

[1] 陈星. 宜居视角下高密度住区公共空间规划策略研究 [A]. 中国城市规划学会. 城乡治理与规划改革——2014中国城市规划年会论文集（12——居住区规划）[C]. 中国城市规划学会，2014，11.

[2] 周燕珉，秦岭. 老龄化背景下城市新旧住宅的适老化转型 [J]. 时代建筑，2016，6：22-28.

[3] 裴雪静. 路网，居住小区的基本脉络 [J]. 河南城建学院学报，2013，4：13-15.

[4] 赵继龙，陈有川，陈朋，陈仰金. 北方高层住区规划设计中的若干问题探讨——以济南市为例 [J]. 规划师，2011，5：63-68.

苏州姑苏区古建旧民居的适老化更新与再利用

曹修安　华振宁

（香港中文大学住房研究社会科学硕士课程）

摘　要： 面对日益严峻的老龄化问题，基于中国内地庞大的人口数量，首先应该考虑的是改善居家养老环境，倡导绝大多数老年人能够生活在自己的家庭里，发挥家庭养老功能，故对于既有的建筑的适应老龄化的改造是实现居家养老的前提。本文所研究的苏州地区，位于全国老龄化程度较高的江苏，同时，姑苏区作为原平江、沧浪、金阊三个老城区合并而成的城市中心区域，是各级文物保护单位、控制保护建筑群落、旧街巷历史街区集中的区域，同时拥有全市最高的老年人口比重。苏州姑苏区地处历史文化名城中心，由于依照国务院要求认真贯彻落实关于古城的批复精神，对于古城的建筑高度、建筑容量、建筑造型及建筑环境等需要全面控制，并且姑苏区作为各种园林古建聚集的区域每年都吸引这大量的游客，所以在对古建旧民居的适老化更新以及再利用，特别是一些居住性传统历史街区上面临更复杂的问题。基于已有的对于苏州姑苏的实地调研的基础上，本文旨在为老城区的旧民居以及居住性历史街区的适老性更新所面对的，如城市空间布局上旅游与居住的冲突，老旧居住性建筑的一些日常居住功能性空间缺失、生活空间小、采光条件差、无障碍设施不齐全等问题进行分析，在各种矛盾中找到平衡，提出一些可行性优化建议和改造措施。此研究希望能在不对旧城保护造成影响的前提下，既能够保留城市特色甚至更好的创造城市多样性，又考虑并尊重当地老年人的生活习惯及模式，为老城区的老年人口创造更好的私人养老空间、良好的公共交流空间。

关键词： 老龄化，苏州，姑苏区，适老性更新，古建旧民居

1　引言

苏州，作为中国历史文化名城，保留了大量前人遗留下来的古建筑，其中最为著名的，不外是苏州园林。而要说数量最多的，非古建旧民居莫属，1983年公布的"控制保护建筑"就有近250座。这些旧民居，历尽沧桑，大多都已年久失修，对于住在这些老房子内的居民，尤其是大量的老年人来说，生活条件不容乐观。如何在不对旧城保护造成影响的前提下，既能够保留城市特色，又考虑到当地老年人的日常生活，为古城区的老年人口创造更好的养老空间。本文将基于已有对于苏州姑苏的实地调研，对古城区适老化更新及再利用等方面，提出一些可行的优化建议及改造的措施，以改善当地居民，特别是老年人口的生活环境及条件。

2　研究背景

2.1　人口老龄化

按照联合国对于人口老龄化的定义，即60岁以上人口占总人口的10%，或65岁以上人口占总人

口的 7%，结合《苏州统计年检 2016》公布的数据，早在 1982 年，苏州就已经进入老龄化社会。而如今，根据苏州市民政局公布的苏州市老年人口数据，截至 2016 年年底，苏州市户籍人口 6781957 人，其中老年人口（年龄大于等于 60 周岁）为 1708816 人，占户籍总人口的 25.2%，比 2015 年增加了 52235 人，增幅为 3%。这就意味着，苏州已大大超越了国际上对于老龄化社会定义的标准线。而且从 20 世纪 80 年代末开始，苏州市 65 岁老年人口数量就以年均 3% 的速度递增（王雯岚，2016）。另外数据[①]显示，苏州市 60～69 周岁的老年人占全市老年人口总数的一半以上，为 55.7%，较 2015 年增加了 18620 人；70～79 周岁为 49.62 万人，占比 29.04%，比 2015 年增加 23629 人；80～89、90～99 及 100 周岁以上的老年人口数量也都有相应的增加。人口老龄化，甚至是超老龄化，对公共环境、社区环境、居家环境提出了严峻挑战。

2.2 老年居住形式类型

2.2.1 家庭居住

在中国传统儒家思想的影响下，一般老年人都会与自己的子女等住在一起，享几代同堂、子孙绕膝之福。老年人的日常生活通常由家人陪护照料、和老伴相互照顾、自给自足或者雇用护工照看等。在这种模式下，他们可以居住在自己所熟悉的环境中，对整个居住空间有一种归属感和自主权，并保持着独立生活的能力。另外，在与家人更多的接触中，老年人的心理能得到满足。但是家庭养老也有其劣势，其中最主要的是家庭成员之间，由于不同的生活节奏会打扰各自的生活，从而激发代际间的矛盾。此外几代人生活在一起，个人的生活空间会受到挤压，尤其是老年人所需的生活设施会不齐全，比如行动不变的老人所需的扶手等，这对于他们的日常生活会造成不便。

另外，一些地区的年轻人为了生计外出打工，或者无儿无女等特殊情况，导致空巢老人，甚至是独居老人现象的出现。由于没有子女的陪伴，这些老人的日常生活得不到照顾，甚至因此会产生心理失调症状，如心情郁闷、沮丧、孤寂。这对于老人的晚年生活十分不利。

2.2.2 集体居住

集体居住意为，老年人聚集居住在老年公寓、敬老福利院或者护老院等养老机构。在这种模式下，老年人能够得到各种服务，包括食宿、日常料理照顾、专业医疗等。在这些机构内，居住环境一般都是按照便利老年人的无障碍标准建造的。同时，机构还提供专门的老年活动场所来丰富他们的日常生活。还有一个优势是，众多老年人生活在一起，他们之间有共同的话题，相互交流间能排解孤寂感，在一些必要的情况下，机构还能提供专业的心理辅导来安抚老人。但是在集体居住中，老年人可能会感觉到束缚感。由于这些养老机构都是采用类似于"军事化管理"的管理方式，统一安排老人的日常起居，一些老人可能会觉得不自由，而且所有的生活空间都是统一化的，会给老人一种居住在医院病房的感觉。此外，子女认为老人居住在养老机构内，会得到周到的照顾，因此亲自看望的次数也会越来越少，这种亲人的关怀会逐渐缺失，会对老人的身心造成不良的影响。最后，生活在养老机构内，老人与外界的接触比较少，会慢慢地与社会脱节，不再适应快速变化的外部世界。

2.3 苏州古城旧民居现状

经过几十年的变迁，苏州这些以砖木结构为主的古民居大都年久失修，在政府出台的一系列文件，

---

① 数据来源：http://www.subaonet.com/2017/0207/1926774.shtml。

从 2002 年的《苏州保护古建筑条例》，到 2005 年的《苏州市市区依靠社会力量抢修保护直管公房古民居实施意见》，一定程度上对古建的保护起到了促进作用。同时，政府每年都投入 5000 万元以上的资金，但这笔钱只能保证古建筑保护以 10 万多平方米的速度推进，而根据目前的预算，每年仍然有四千多万的资金缺口。

本文主要研究地区位于苏州姑苏区古护城河包围的古城区，其现如今基本保持着水路并行、河街相邻的双棋盘格局，房屋民居密集紧凑。苏州古城区旧民居因保留了原有的结构形式，所以大都有几落几进，围以高墙，并且多有备弄连廊，设有天井、门楼。古城区这一代的建筑在新中国成立前大都为私人的宅第或庄祠，在建国之后政府进行了改造，只有少数一些产权是私有的，其余大部分都归国有，成为直管公房，现在以租赁使用权作为保障性住房提供给居民居住。在调研走访过程中，凡有一定规模的建筑群原先为大户人家的私家住宅，如今一个院落多的有 30 多户人家，在这种居住环境下邻里关系紧密，但是相对应的彼此的生活空间有了交集有时又会互相存在一些干扰。

调研过程中，对平江历史街区的居民进行了走访和交谈，大体上可以把他们分为两类，一种是完全私有性质的住房居民，另一种是直管公房的居民，这些直管公房也同时是苏州的控保建筑。首先，住在私房的居民表示他们现有的住房都经过自己出资进行改造，现有的居住条件尚可，对于日常生活所需的水电设施、独立卫生设施以及厨房都在翻新房改造后配备齐全，只是两三代人共同居住，人均居住面积小以及老年人上下楼梯不便是这类居民中最普遍反映的问题。

然而，对于住在控保建筑中的居民生活条件就不容乐观。1983 年初，苏州市建委、市文管会经市政府批准，公布了古城区控保建筑 252 处。从此，便有了"控制保护建筑"这一全新的概念，此举开中国文物保护之先河，具有苏州地方特色。控制保护建筑是指苏州市政府尚未公布为文物保护单位的具有历史、艺术、科学价值的建筑。控保建筑通过市文物行政部门调查、核定、登记，由市政府向社会公布。苏州控保建筑的用途广泛，种类庞杂，保护难度可见一斑，同时，《苏州市古建筑保护条例规定》中规定："维修古建筑不得任意改变和破坏原有建筑的布局、结构和装修，不得任意改建、扩建"。在控保建筑中生活的居民，无论其房屋性质是租赁的直管公房，或是祖辈传下来的公私合有的房屋，对于这类古建旧民居的改造都有很多限制和规定，向居民了解到最近一次修缮工作是 2007 房管局进行的对屋顶和门窗的修缮。一居多户，人口过剩的居住现状使得老年人口的生活起居更为不便，由于直管公房一直是社会保障性住房，其中的老年居民都没有子女同住，与他们住在同一院落中的有近一半为外来人口，基础的卫生设施需要共享，原有的公共走廊及天井都堆满了杂物及作晾晒用途。午后在小河旁晒太阳的老人表示由于经济条件的制约只能在此度过晚年，因为房屋的进深较深，通风采光都不佳，居住和条件的限制白天基本都会出门在河边坐上一天与街坊聊天。

经调研，旧民居外的公共空间设施条件也需要更多的改善，从而为老年人提供更舒适友好的环境。现保留的一些门槛和台阶，以及公共走道的铺地高低不平加上较多的窨井盖，对老年人的出行造成不便和存在一些安全隐患，无障碍设施在古城区范围内也还未完善。此外，由于历史街区作为旅游业的一部分，络绎不绝的游客占用了很多公共开放空间，而与此同时，并没有新开发和建造的老年休憩娱乐场所来满足他们的日常需求。

2.4 困难与挑战

2.4.1 资金不足

苏州古建筑数量众多，又具有极高的历史文化价值，仅靠政府的资金投入进行修缮和保护，是远远不够的。大量的维修资金除政府出资外，近年来，以市场化为基础筹集资金也是一种趋势。城市商报就曾以名为《苏州民企 2900 万元拍下山塘雕花楼——这是苏州控保建筑拍卖现场成交第一单》的文章报道过：2009年7月13日，控保建筑首例交易成功，苏州山塘雕花楼2900万元正式易主。民营资本介入控保建筑，是苏州市一直主张和推行的政策。因此，在有一定历史价值，政府却又无力保护的矛盾情况下，古城苏州对一部分非文物保护单位的控保建筑选择了"上市"之路，对控保建筑实行"谁使用，谁管理，谁维修"的原则，将文化遗产的产权转让给私人或者一些投资者，并从法律上加以保护，如2002年10月25日公布的《苏州古建筑保护条例》中明确"鼓励国内外组织和个人购买或者租用古建筑"，但从实际情况看，控保建筑的流通渠道仍比较少。

2.4.2 产权性质

产权属于个人的旧民居，由产权所有者自己出资保护，大量的资金投入使得这部分建筑拥有良好的建筑实体形态，同时在政府的监管下，修缮保护工作也没有破坏其历史价值形态，"修旧如旧"并且体现了古城的文化风貌。然而，产权为非私有的古建筑，使用单位为保护管理责任人；作为公房民居使用的，管理单位为第一保护管理责任人，使用者为第二保护管理责任人。苏州古城区的控保建筑中，占比最大的就是直管公房，通过房管局了解到，现居于直管公房的居民五成为外来人口，一方面，有着良好的经济条件的原住民迁出，剩下的居民以及迁入的外来人口，不仅保护古建筑的意识较为薄弱，而且在经济条件上也没有能力出资维修控保；另一方面，剩下的五成中大多数都是受经济条件制约没有迁出的原住民，以不与子女同住的老年夫妇居多。

2.4.3 空间格局

建筑内部，因为保留着原有的建筑结构和布局，原先作为一个建筑整体而建的建筑群，考虑了日照、通风等自然环境，而如今划分给多户，甚至是几十户居民居住，故每家每户的生活空间不足，在隔断改造的同时，整个建筑不再南北通透，出现了采光、通风上的问题。苏州属亚热带季风海洋性气候，四季分明，多雨潮湿，没有制冷采暖措施老年人在夏季和冬季都没有良好的居住条件，夏初的梅雨季节更容易多发关节炎风湿病。旧民居入口也以台阶为主，有限的走道空间因为堆放杂物，若使用轮椅无法顺畅通行。加上存在租户的私拉电线、私搭乱建等行为，又出现很多消防上的安全隐患。

古城的空间格局呈现网状，河网密布，道路与街巷顺应河道而建，老人喜欢沿河坐着与街坊邻里进行日常沟通交流，也少有开放式的公共空地和空间。随着历史街区的商业开发，游客的需求空间与居民生活的日常需求空间出现了重叠，适老化更新过程中，使两者能够更好融合，以最大化利用土地和城市空间，功能上能够逐渐过渡找到一个平衡点，给老年人创造安静隐私的生活空间，也能够提供一个热闹融洽的公共活动区域。

3 可行性建议

3.1.1 对于资金和产权问题

古建旧民居以及其他历史文化遗产在保护和开发利用中所产生的一系列弊端的根源，就在于产权的不明晰。若房屋产权得以明晰，就可以明确政府和产权所有者的责、权、利关系，就可以降低保护过程中的交易成本和扩大保护资金的来源，从而使古建筑的保护、更新工作能更好开展和推进。

房屋产权不明晰的状况是绝大部分旧民居普遍存在的问题，要改变这样的现状，要对各种产权主体进行定位，把使用权、收益权和转让权这三权落实到个人。尤其对于国有的民居建筑，若是仅仅赋予居民和使用者使用权，那就无法实现产权的激励功能，不能提高使用者对古建筑的保护意识，容易产生过度使用甚至破坏的情况，政府出资再多用于维修也只会是无效的投资。

政府用来修缮的古建筑资金总是有限的，通过市场来解决是最有效的。但是，如果产权不能有效的转移，相信很很难会有人愿意花大量资金买一套只有使用权而没有产权的房子。《苏州古建筑保护条例》中明确"鼓励国内外组织或个人购买或租用古建筑"，实行产权多元化、抢修保护社会化、运作市场化，但从实际情况来看"流通"渠道仍比较少，其中重要一点归因于让社会力量进入保护领域，设计的部门众多，办理手续的流程复杂，所以建立产权转移的有效机制可以简化流程，促使更多的力量参与古建筑的保护。

尤其对于控保建筑，这些房子本来大都是用于居住的，政府可以实行产权的有限开放，将一些国家认为需要控制的列入禁售名单，其他的可以拿出来交易，这样有利于使建筑的产权转移到珍惜、热爱古建筑并有能力有效维修和保护古建筑的所有者手中。

同时，政府做好监管工作，保证古建筑的传统风貌不能改变，产权转移变更后建立相应的保护责任奖惩制度，若在产权转移后并没有真正做好保护工作，或者不按照规章乱拆、乱修的，政府有权直接干预；若真正切实履行保护职责的所有者，可经过评定考核，给予税费减免、贴补修缮开支等奖励措施。

3.1.2 对于空间格局的问题

民居建筑在翻新改建的过程中若能有效提高室内地坪，对墙体采取结构上的防潮措施，很大程度上能够缓解梅雨季的潮湿，同时加强夏冬两季室内的保温隔热，加固房屋结构后为居民提供加装空调的条件，将对老年人在家养老的舒适性提供保障。将空间重新设计划分，明确每户的空间将使走道、庭院不再被私人占用，共有的道路更为通畅，在建筑出入口修砌合理坡度的坡道代替现有的台阶，为老年人使用轮椅提供更好的条件。在室内为老年人多加装扶手，尤其是身体重心发生变化的地方。

利用原先拥有较大庭院的民居建筑，将其公共庭院进行优化设计，给邻近老人提供一个聚集交流的场所，除沿河的护栏外，提供一个更为安全舒适的活动空间。基于现有的主街商业趋于饱和，相邻主街的民居可发展成为民宿，兼有商业和居住用途，成为民居和旅游街区的良好过渡。

4 结语

随着社会的进步和经济的发展，人们的生活水平不断提高，与此相伴的是老龄化进程的推进。苏州的古建旧民居，是作为历史文化名城的苏州不可或缺的一部分。然而，不仅要保护好旧民居的历史风貌，同时也要保证居住在旧民居内的年长者的生活需求。本文基于苏州姑苏的实地调研，发现在旧民居更新改造过程中，出现产权不明、资金不足及空间格局规划不合理等问题，提出了在政府监管下把古建筑放入市场、引入社会资金的方式来更新建筑，并提出一些适老化改造方面的建议，希望能够给相关建筑的保护和更新提供有效的帮助，并为老年居民提供一个舒适的养老空间。

The Regeneration and Reuse of Historic Residential Buildings Adapting to Ageing in Suzhou Gusu District

Cao Xiuan, Hua Zhenning

(MSSC in Housing Studies, The Chinese University of Hong Kong)

Abstract: Facing with the increasingly serious aging problem, based on mainland China's vast populations, we should firstly consider how to improve the environment of home-based care for the aged, and advocate that the most elderly can live in their own home. Therefore, it is the premise for home-based care to renewal existing architectures to adapt to the aging population's needs. The Gusu District, Suzhou, has majority of historic buildings and also the highest proportion of elderly residents. Based on the field research data collected in Gusu District, this article will analyze the problems faced by renewal of historic buildings, such as poor living environment and conflicts between tourism and residents, to find a balance and try to put forward some feasible optimized suggestions and renewal measures.

Keywords: Aging society, Suzhou, Gusu district, Regeneration and reuse, Historic residential buildings

参考文献

[1] 黄蓉，叶琦琦，翟宣臣等. 霜鬓尽从容——苏州传统社区公共空间适老化营造 [J]. 城市建筑，2016，14: 378-378.

[2] 张寒，覃丽伊. 刍议城市化进程中居住性历史街区保护与更新 [J]. 城市地理，2015，20.

[3] 周宇. 基于苏州古城老年人居住现状分析的旧民居优化设计研究 [D]. 苏州大学，2015.

[4] 朱茜. 上海市老年人住宅更新模式研究初探 [D]. 东华大学，2012.

[5] 周雪凤. 基于体验式开发的传统民居适应性改造研究——以苏州平江区潘宅改造项目为例 [D]. 东南大学，2012.

[6] Xia J, Wang Y. From the Replacement to the Rebirth: The Protection of the Living Authenticity of the Residential Historic Blocks[J]. Urban Studies，2010.

[7] 龚鸽. 基于老龄化背景下杭州居住性历史街区保护更新研究 [D]. 浙江大学，2010.

[8] 马海东. 近 20 年来苏州古城传统街区保护与更新的研究 [D]. 清华大学，2003.

[9] 许懋彦. 日本小布施町传统街区修景规划与宫本忠长 [J]. 世界建筑，2001，6: 70-74.

[10] Jacobs J. The Death and life of great American cities[M]. Random House，1961.

智慧城市与计算机辅助技术集成应用
Smart City and Computer-aided Technology Integration

BIM平台架构下采光性能模拟的自适应性建筑立面策略与原型研究

陈上元　沈扬庭　何妍萱　吴念瑾

（逢甲大学建筑专业学院研究所）

摘　要：面对气候变迁与能源危机的情势下，建筑物具备自适应性（Adaptability）以响应环境复杂而动态地改变，成为近代智能建筑发展的重要议题。另一方面随着建筑信息建模（Building information modeling，BIM）和可视化编程（Visual programming）界面技术的演进，使得建筑设计迈向智能整合的时代。本文旨在智能建筑与BIM平台的技术支持下，探讨现代自适应性建筑立面构成所需具备的能力。本研究以最佳化策略验证、脚本导向的自动控制，作为整合性架构，探讨设计端和营运端间缺乏联结的困境，提出将建筑全生命周期的设计端与营运端的预先链接的方法流程，测试营运状态及收集场域实测数据，进行反馈评估；并实际建构一自适应性外墙实作，具体的方法从原型设计的角度，以光照作为主要的环境因子，将实作分为"BIM平台的建模与模拟"、"实体模型建构"二阶段，借由两者间的协作，验证其理论的可行性。然而，软件的性能模拟数据和实体环境性能的实测数据之间始终存在着差距，本研究拟以类神经学习系统减少差距，以增进立面的调适能力。

关键词：自适应性建筑立面，建筑信息建模，参数设变引擎，建筑性能模拟，类神经网络

1　缘起与目的

自适应性建筑立面是智能住宅下的环节之一，也是建筑物最直接接触外部环境与使用者的界面。在科技高度发展的现今，建筑立面应脱离既有的思维，以往一般的建筑立面大多采取被动控制的设计，在被动控制的情况下建筑回避了气候信息的复杂性，不能适应不断变化的条件，也缺乏主动响应的机制来满足使用者的需求（Adaptivefacade network-Europe，2015）。[1]本研究的目的，在于探讨现代"基于环境性能模拟的自适应性建筑立面"构成所需具备的能力包括：具备主动控制的能力、BIM设计端到营运端接轨、最佳化策略到达自动化控制的联结。

2　文献回顾

自适应性建筑立面所需具备的目标，即"感知环境能力"以及"响应使用者对于环境需求的能力"。要达成目标就必须拥有控制系统的能力，然而系统的运作牵涉营运管理端的控制能力，因此要使自适应性建筑立面原型，达到虚拟模型与真实驱动的控制能力，则需要搭载在BIM平台上且需透过BIM的性能模拟即自动控制验证能力。BIM的概念着重于建筑各项信息的整合，并透过建筑性能模拟得到最理想的居住环境。将建筑生命周期中各阶段信息及软件操作结果整合，可有效减少设计者在各种软件间转化的数据遗失及错误并可透过计算机协助除错、分析模拟建筑性能（蔡宗玮，2013）。[2]因此，透过联结BIM平台与模拟工具的协作流程，在设计初期的概念阶段就能评估能源使用，避免传统设计

流程方式采用经验法的臆测结果，能提升建筑物的能源效率、建筑性能、增加永续设计的机会。[3, 4]

3 自适应性建筑立面原型的理论与方法

因应环境参数并与环境产生相对应的互动是自适应性建筑立面的主要目的。若要达成自适应性建筑立面有效的营运控制就要透过 BIM 模型的可持续沿用，即需要透过可脚本化的建筑性能模拟（Building Performance Simulation，BPS），以及可对应脚本回应环境变化的自动化控制（Building Automation System，BAS），因此要使设计端与营运端产生有效的联结与沿用就必须透过 BIM 平台执行让脚本可携。[5] 透过 BIM 可以同时承载建筑物的"三维模型资料库"（Revit）、和"脚本资料库"（Dynamo），拟借由此平台达成 BIM 建筑全生命周期之沿用，尤其是设计端至营运端之间的"可持续性运用"。其系统运作的方式则借由 IPO 模型（Input, Process, Output），以感知（Input）、运算（Process）、行动（Output）去定义模拟策略，最后沿用到后端的自动控制系统策略，以建立链接的关键。如图 1 所示，

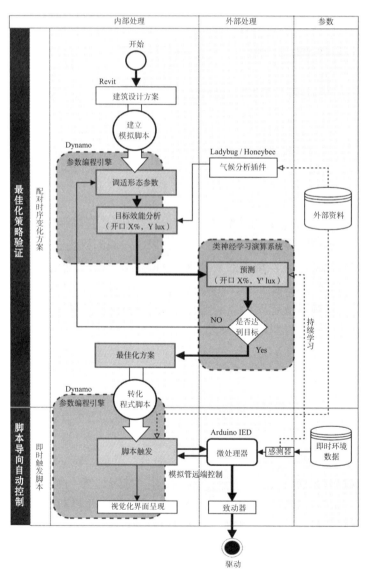

图 1 协助延续设计策略到实际的营运使用场域系统之流程图

在协助延续设计策略至实际营运使用场域系统之流程中，为了实现从设计到营运之间的可持续沿用的影响，垂直轴将其分为"优化策略验证"和"脚本导向的自动控制"两个主要阶段，而水平轴分为内部处理、外部处理、参数资料库三个平台。

- 最佳化策略验证阶段：重点在于虚拟平台上的流程；其中又包含了五个步骤：（1）建立设计方案：旨在基于参数设变引擎（Revit）的立面建模能力；（2）调适形态参数：参数编程引擎（Dynamo）之具备可调适之能力，在于测试自适应性立面的动态效果；（3）目标效能分析：借由性能模拟工具仿真评估趋近于真实之环境信息；（4）预测：数据搜集与学习演算之能力；（5）最佳化方案。
- 脚本导向的自动控制阶段：为使设计端至营运端可以被可持续沿用，其重点在于借由参数编程引擎（Dynamo）将上阶段的优化方案结果转化为程序可读取脚本，透过实际运转的方式进行虚实互动的信息回馈。

3.1 最佳化策略验证

为达到立面的性能最佳化（Optimization），自适应性建筑立面需要一个与传统建筑设计流程不同的设计方法。在寻找最佳化方案的过程中，设计过程和性能模拟是不可分割的一部分，因为性能模拟有助于研究与调查不同的选择和模拟设计策略。而传统的设计工作流程是线性流程，且建模与分析是相互分开的独立作业，如今随BIM平台的开发，能在同一套BIM软件中执行最佳化策略的整体流程。透过本研究之决策循环，更有能力寻找出最佳的解决方案，其中包含三个主要的原因：性能模拟可得到实际的量化数据而不是传统方法常采取的经验法则；使用三维的建筑信息建模来模拟，分析和预测系统行为；可以同时产生多个设计方案进行评估。因此，现代的策略需要透过可脚本化的建筑性能模拟，以及可对应脚本回应环境变化的自动化控制达成有效的BIM模型沿用。本节将设计最佳化策略分为五个步骤：（1）建立设计方案；（2）调适形态参数；（3）目标效能分析；（4）类神经学习演算；（5）最佳化方案。当运用此策略时，我们可以在建筑设计的初期，根据性能分析的各阶段结果，提出建筑设计更多优化的建议，换言之，从建筑设计的阶段就注入可持续的观念，使性能分析在可持续的设计中发挥主导作用。如下分述：

（1）建立设计方案：即是透过"参数设变引擎"（Revit）建立三维信息模型。①建立BIM量体模型项目：定义为设定基地信息、建立建筑量体、建立楼板、定义房间（room）等主要四个操作步骤；②建立BIM组件参数：定义为设定自适应组件。

（2）调适形态参数：旨在运用参数编程引擎平台（Dynamo），关键功能在于建立判断用之脚本，而脚本是透过设计者预先根据使用者的需求而定义的。本阶段是借由可视化的参数编程引擎来实现参数化。

（3）目标效能分析：模拟模型是对现实的近似值。目标效能分析是以性能作为目标的设计模式，旨在建筑设计时间操作的可视化模拟（如采光环境、风场模拟等），有助于建筑设计方案之决策流程，并能根据性能分析结果提出更多最佳化的建议。

（4）类神经学习演算：整合性的设计策略，已经成为建筑师与设计工作者选择与改善设计方案的重要依据。然而在场域模拟时，当优化方案落实至现实环境中，性能模拟软件的仿真数值和实质环境性能的实时数值之间，始终存在着差距，因此旨在说明效能分析结果之数据搜集与学习演算的能力。

（5）最佳化方案：根据上阶段类神经的学习方式使系统具备预测能力后，以预测值 Y' 作为设定目标的比对条件，借以找寻优化的调适方案，加入类神经学习系统的设计决策程序，其"预测值 Y'"会比"效能模拟数值 Y"更为接近实时数值。主要目的在于解决虚拟环境和实际场域的链接，其目标是为协助延续设计策略到实际的营运使用场域达到BIM模型的可持续运用，将最好的方案转换为实际场域可读取的程序脚本进行自动控制的触发。

3.2 脚本导向的自动控制

本阶段研究重点为协助延续设计策略到实际的营运使用场域，提出将最佳化的判断条件沿用至自动化控制，作为建筑立面的维运条件。脚本导向的自动控制阶段，旨在为使设计端至营运端可以被可持续沿用，其重点在于借由参数编程引擎（Dynamo）将上阶段的最佳化方案结果转化为程序可读取的脚本，透过实际运转的方式进行虚实互动的信息回馈。本研究透过 IPO 模型架构建立与自动控制联结的关键。感知（Input）：原于最佳化策略验的形态参数调整端，将手动调整转变成导入实际环境参数，运算（Process）：目标效能模拟结果之最佳方案转变成自动控制之判断条件，行动（Output）：驱动可视化模型和控制真实外部设备原型。

4 实作与讨论

在本研究的策略流程的架构中，分别于虚拟环境和实质环境，建构基于采光环境条件的可调适性的机制；且尝试运用同一 BIM 平台实作，并将其分为（1）最佳化策略验证，即透过虚拟参数设定至参数调控，产生最佳化策略；（2）脚本导向的自动控制，即透过实质参数导入至最佳化策略转为判断式脚本，最后到实体建筑物的控制。在此次实作中由于类神经学习系统持续改进是需要大量的数据和过程去检验的，而本研究此次尚无法达成此部分，因此在没有类神经持续学习的状态下，先产出初步的最佳化策略方案，并以 CNS 照度表作为验证最佳化的依据，将其验证结果转化为自动控制的概念。最后透过实作过程探讨本策略流程的运用及限制（图 2、图 3）。

- 最佳化策略验证：（1）建立 Revit 组件；（2）调适形态参数（Revit、Dynamo）；（3）目标效能分析（Dynamo-Ladybug-Honeybee）。经由模拟结果，透过中国台湾 CNS 照度标准表验证得出一最佳策略，此策略将作为自动控制阶段之判断式依据，透过此结果可以于自动控制的运算端建立范围达到自动控制的参数脚本。
- 脚本导向的自动控制：自动控制（Dynamo、Arduino、Reaction Component）旨在真实取得外部数据并驱动可视化模型和控制真实外部设备原型。

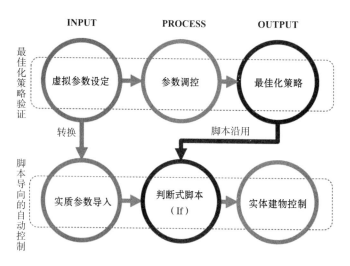

图 2　协助延续设计策略到实际的营运使用场域系统之流程图

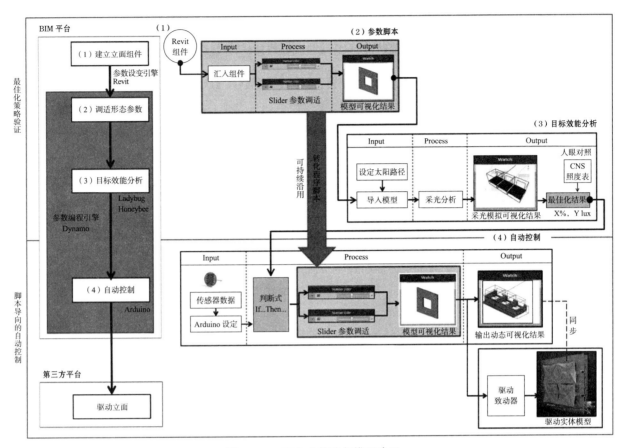

图 3　BIM 平台之策略与模型建置

5　结论

本研究提出一策略流程，针对基于环境性能模拟的自适应性建筑立面原型研究，将设计、模拟与实体控制整合于同一平台，其核心要点为（1）与传统设计方法不同，尝试运用同一套 BIM 工具 Revit 与其插件 Dynamo，联结"设计策略面"与"实际场域面"之平台，并运用参数编程引擎 Dynamo 作为链接两者的关键;（2）发展设计流程为解决虚拟环境与真实环境数据落差的问题，尝试以类神经学习系统作为推论的方法，探索得到最佳方案的可能性。借由以上两者间的协作，验证建筑全生命周期于设计端与营运端的预先链接方法流程和理论的可行性。借由"可持续策略沿用至营运场域流程图"，以接近达成设计端至营运端的联结。

The Research of Adaptive Building Facade Strategy and Prototype Based on Daylight Performance Simulation

Chen Shang-Yuan, Shen Yang-Ting, Ho Yen-Hsuan, Wu Nien-Chin

(Feng Chia University Department of Architecture)

Abstract: Facing the situation of climate change and energy crisis, buildings have adaptability to respond to the complex and dynamic environmental changes, which has become an important issue in the development of modern Smart buildings. On the other hand, with the development of building information modeling (BIM) and visual programming technology, architectural design is moving towards intelligent integrated generation. Under the intelligent building and BIM platform technical support, "The Research of Adaptive Building Facade Strategy and Prototype for Daylight Performance Simulation Based on the BIM Platform Framework" are purpose to discuss the necessary ability of modern Adaptive Building Facade. Through the reviewing of the literature to sort the dimension of composition and required conditions of the adaptive building facade archetypes and to discuss the difficulties. In this research, we will use Optimization strategy validation and script-based automatic control as an integrated frame to discuss the dilemma between the design phase and the management phase. as well as to propose a method of pre-connect between the design phase and the management phase of the whole building lifecycle. Then we will test the operation status and collect the measured field data for the feedback evaluation.

Keywords: Adaptive building facade, Building information modeling, Parametric change engine, Building performance simulation, Artificial neural networks

参考文献

[1] COST ACTION TU1403——ADAPTIVE FACADES NETWORK[D]. http：//tu1403.eu/.

[2] 蔡宗玮. 性能导向之参数式设计于 BIM 整合评估流程 [D]. 成功大学建筑学系硕士学位论文，2013.

[3] Almusaed A.Biophilic and bioclimatic architecture：Analytical therapy for the next generation of passive sustainable architecture. Springer Science & Business Media，2010.

[4] Asl M R，Bergin M，Menter A，Yan W. BIM-based parametric building energy perfrmance multi-objective optimization. Education and Research in Computer Aided Architectural Design in Europe，2014，32：1-10.

[5] Attia S. Achieving Informed Decision-Making using Building Performance Simulation. In Proceeding of the Education and research in Computer Aided Architectural Design in Europe Conference，Delft，2013.

日本智慧型技术在城市住宅中的应用研究

伊藤增辉

（清华大学建筑学院）

摘　要：智能住宅在日本发展至今已经历了将近40年，近年随着网络信息科技的日趋成熟，许多智慧型技术在住宅实用化上取得了突破，日本通过产（企业）、官（政府）、学（学界）的联合研发和推广，令这些技术在城市住宅领域中实现了快速普及应用。在创造"以人为本"的舒适生活空间的同时，实现了环保节能的未来生活理念。目前在智能住宅的技术应用上，已建立起 ZEH 零能耗住宅标准，以 HEMS 住宅能量控制系统为基础设备，结合 IoT 信息平台利用的智能住宅标准型。智能住宅的推广不仅为日本民众带来了环保舒适的家居生活，更重要的是这一领域在未来将为日本的产业带来巨大发展的可能性前景。通过对日本的智慧型技术在城市住宅中的应用调研，明确其技术的发展方向和产业发展的战略思维，这对中国乃至亚太地区城市在未来城市住宅发展上都具有重要的借鉴意义。

关键词：日本，城市住宅，智慧型技术，应用，产业发展

1　绪论

智能住宅是建设智慧城市的重要构成内容，随着智慧型技术的发展和成熟，许多节点技术在住宅实用化上取得了突破，日本通过跨部委的政策制定、跨行业的政企结合的研发和推广，近年在城市住宅中实现了新技术的快速普及应用。这些技术在创造"以人为本"的舒适生活空间的同时，实现了环保节能、安心安全的未来生活理念，因而有 "Smart House" 之称。

自20世纪70年代微处理器（Microprocessor）被发明之后，人类开始尝试将自动化控制技术应用到住宅中，日本的电子企业第一时间跟进了这一技术的应用开发。如在1978年日立和松下便已各自提出了"家居电脑系统"的概念，构思通过电脑自控技术实现舒适、安全的现代化生活。在之后的实践进程中，智能住宅在日本至今已经历了三个质变的发展阶段。第一阶段是由电子企业自身或与住宅开发商合作进行实验性开发，比如1982年由东芝和三井住宅合作的 HOPES-204 实验住宅、1988年松下开发的 HIS 实验住宅等，对之前所构思的各种自控技术进行可行性验证。并在随后的多个被称为"未来住宅"的实建项目中，对这些技术进行了综合的系统化实验性应用。进入90年代，随着互联网在日本的商用化开始，智能住宅的发展进入第二阶段，实践通过联网实现住宅连接外部的各种远程服务和家居设备的信息化管理，比如松下的 eHII House、三洋住宅的 SANFIT 样板住宅、大和住宅工业的 D'sSmartHouse 等。进入21世纪，随着全球范围对环境与资源的重视，对能源利用的可视化管控成为智能住宅中智慧型技术应用的主要部分，技术的成熟促进了市场的形成，市场的扩大反过来也促使了法规制度的制定和产品系统化的完善。从2010左右开始的第三阶段，政府明确将智能住宅定义为：融合住宅与 ICT 形成对能源供给的控制，使居住者得以简便地节能节电，实现更加舒适生活的住居。其中最主要的一个系统是 HEMS（Home Energy Management System），即通过家居能源管理系统对住宅的能源生产、储备、消费、再生循环实现一体化管理的系统，并逐渐演变成今天这个以 HEMS 能源管控系统为基础的 IoT 信息平台 Echonet Consortium。

在以上对日本智能住宅发展历史梳理的基础上，本研究旨在通过对日本的智慧型技术在城市住宅

中的应用调研，分析这些技术成果得以发展起来的市场背景与政策关系，明确其技术的发展方向和产业发展的战略思维，借以从中导出今后中国在发展这一领域上的借鉴意义。

2 智慧型技术在城市住宅上的应用

2.1 技术应用过程中的住宅市场背景与政策意识

在当初制定第三阶段政策的 2009 年，日本全国住宅总数约 4500 万户，年度的新建住宅数量不及 80 万户，加上今后人口的结构性减少，新的智慧型技术如果只考虑在国内新建住宅上的应用，市场是有限的，很显然由此获得的总体节能效果也是极其有限的。故在系统的实验阶段已经考虑到包括现存住宅的所有住宅上的应用可行性。

2011 年发生的"3·11 东日本大震灾"，福岛核电站的泄漏事故引发民众对核能过分依赖的危机意识，连带提升了日本国民对生活节电和能源自给的积极性，从而也推动了以能源自产自销和节电为中心的智能住宅的发展。有些住宅厂家甚至将全线产品智能化，市场呈现飞速扩大的趋势。日本经济产业部在 2012 年的智能住宅标准化研究报告[1]中测算，到 2020 年智能住宅的全球市场将达 12 万亿日元，日本国内市场将达到接近其总量的 30% 的 3.5 万亿日元规模。

从以上的对国内市场，以全住宅为应用对象，在国际市场中定量日本的市场比例，作者认为它们明确体现出日本政企共同对待这一新技术领域的政策意识态度。按现代全球化经济规律，占领全球市场必须建立全球体系标准，树立标准很大程度依赖已成型规模效应。因此在一系列的应用技术开发和实用化过程中，日本政府从经济角度，比如投资补贴，税负减免等给予多种优惠制度，最大限度扶植规模效应的形成。比如国土交通部曾提供"零能耗住宅补助费"[2]，就是一项针对实现了节能、产能的住宅提供补贴的制度，为每个独栋住宅提供最高达 165 万日元的设置补贴资金。还有针对 HEMS（能源管理系统）导入促进事业费的补贴。对获得社团法人环境共创倡导机构（SII）所认证的，导入了 HEMS 系统的住宅，提供最高达 1/2 的这一设备导入费用。[3]对获得同机构认证的，采用固定式锂电池的住宅，提供最高达 1/3 的设备导入费用[4]等。另外，从税负减轻的角度，比如实行住宅取得资金的免税赠与、认证节能住宅取得的贷款减税措施等。

在打消国民取得智能住宅经济顾虑的同时，不断充实相关法规建设，提升技术竞争力。在 2012 年政府策定了现行的 ECHONET lite 并网协议和界面的标准化规格，同年开始实行个体多余电力向电力企业卖电的义务接受条例，并最终在 2016 年 4 月开始实施全国范围的电力零售全面自由化，加速了终端设备的 Smart Meter（智能电表：具备信息联网功能的未来型电表）的普及使用。

2.2 智慧型技术的应用

日本在住宅中应用智慧型技术，建设智能住宅主要目的在于实现舒适、经济、环保这三方面要求。这三大要求都归结到住宅能源的生产 - 积蓄 - 利用上。住宅的能耗主要有建筑能耗和设备能耗两方面，因此住宅的节能既包括建筑自身的隔热性能改善，也包括住宅设备机器的能效提高。日本现行住宅节能标准执行的是由国土交通部住宅局在 2013 年 10 月颁布的《住宅、建筑物节能标准》[5]，将建筑外皮（包括外墙、开口部等）的隔热性能的"一次能源消耗量"标准作为建筑整体节能性能的评价标准。建筑外皮的节能主要通过建材的高性能化来解决，而住宅整体的能耗则主要通过智慧型技术的应用。

2.2.1 建筑标准：ZEH 零能耗住宅

ZEH 零能耗住宅是指"追求大幅度提高建筑外皮等的隔热性能，通过导入高效的设备系统，在达到维持室内环境品质的同时实现大幅度的节能，并且通过导入可再生能源，使整体的年间一次能源消耗量平衡为零的住宅"。[6]

2010 年 6 月，由日本经济产业部、国土交通部、环境部三部委联合设置了"面向低碳社会的住宅与居住方式推进会议"的跨部委组织，其中一个重要的目的就是推动住宅、建筑物的 NET ZERO ENERGY（净能耗为零）化的对策，提出了到 2020 年实现将 ZEH（Zero Energy House）零能耗住宅作为新建住宅的标准型，到 2030 年针对新建住宅在均值上实现这一节能标准。这一内容被纳入日本的《能源基本规划》并在 2014 年 4 月在政府内阁会议上获得通过，成为政府的政策目标加以实施，这一政策在进度上参照了欧美的同类标准实施计划进度，表明了日本在这方面紧跟而上的战略意图（图 1）。

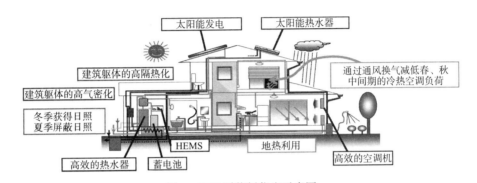

图 1　ZEH 零能耗住宅示意图

资料来源：住宅、建筑物的节能对策．日本国土交通部住宅局，2011．

2.2.2 住宅节能：HEMS 住宅能源管理系统

HEMS 为 Home Energy Management System，即住宅能源管理系统的略称。指通过 IT 信息技术控制住宅中的电力供给、蓄电和消费功能的管控系统。是结合新一代 Smart Grid 供电网应用所开发的构成素子之一，这一系统的全面应用是建设未来智慧社区（Smart Community）乃至智慧城市（Smart City）的基础，日本政府在 2012 年制定了到 2030 年在所有住宅中设置 HEMS 设备系统的政策目标。[7]该系统主要通过将住宅中的设备机器能源消耗的可视化和自动操控，实现节能（电）和舒适的家居环境（图 2）。

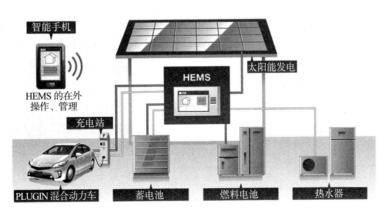

图 2　HEMS 住宅能源管理系统示意图

资料来源：智能住宅标准化研讨会资料．日本经济产业部，DENSO TECHNO．

要实现 HEMS 的能源系统化管控,要求在不同厂家的不同设备之间建立共通的通信规格(并网协议和界面),之前由于这一技术规格没有统一,在相当程度上阻碍了系统功能的普及发展。2012 年日本经济产业部与行业团体共同策定了现行的 ECHONET lite(Energy Conservation and Homecare Network)规格,并将其定位为日本面向国际的规格。之后技术的应用有了迅速推广。比如位于神奈川县的 Fujisawa 可持续智慧小镇项目(住区总户数约 1000 户)中,对所有独栋住宅全部设置了太阳能发电系统和蓄电池,将 HEMS 系统作为标准配置设备,构建每个住户单位的自我产能、蓄能、耗能的能源循环。这类技术的应用,在对应遭遇自然灾害等公共能源被中断时具有积极意义,它确立了一种紧急时的能源自给方式,确保了生活基础条件的可持续性保证。其能源循环主要通过太阳能电池,蓄电池和燃料电池(利用燃气发电和热水供应)三种电池的系统来构建,发电多余的电能可以通过公共电网反向卖电,同时实现居住时 CO_2 排放的大幅度降低。另外基于环保目的,绿色(电力)能源汽车的利用也被纳入能耗计划的基础构成部分,智能住宅中均预置电动汽车充电的设备条件(图 3)。

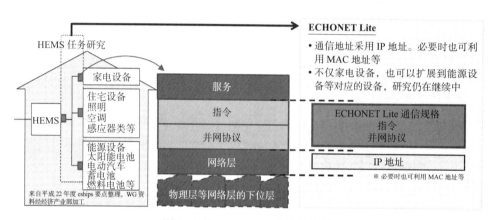

图 3　ECHONET Lite 系统示意图

资料来源:智能住宅标准化研讨会资料. 日本经济产业部,2013.

2.2.3　智能生活:住宅 IoT 平台

建立起了 IoT 信息平台的智能住宅应用可谓前途广泛,虽然目前在实用化上还未成熟,外接服务也只是有限程度,尚未实现大数据的积累和分析利用。[8] 主要有如下几个方面的利用。

远程监控:利用智能手机上的应用软件实现对住宅功能的远程监控。比如通过监控摄像头确认各处门窗的状态及开关操控,控制住宅的电子锁开关,以及其他经过登录认证设备的实时操控等。日本版的微信软件 LINE 便提供部分此类服务。

基于大数据的设备联动自控:通过信息平台收集个人及环境的生活信息,把握个人的作息规律、喜好等,加上对环境特征的认识,自动协调空调、照明等多种住宅设备至最佳的合理模式,在实现舒适居住环境的同时降低能耗。比如通过夏天自动调节遮阳通风的自动控制减少冷气空调负荷,冬天考虑通过日晒采暖减少暖气空调负荷等。

双向信息互动:通过信息平台链接外部,再通过各自的终端设备操作实现远程实时互动的行为。目前得到较多应用的是远程儿童照顾,老年人健康管理,网络课堂教育等。比如地域的医疗看护服务,通过从住宅信息平台所取得的监控健康数据进行诊断,提供适宜的保健事业服务。比如健康服务业的 Finc 在 2016 年 4 月所开始的面向法人客户的健康经营计划,预测未来将扩展到住宅 IoT 平台上的服务等。随着老年化社会的不断深化,将成为解决老年人的医疗看护问题,从而减少财政压力的重要手段。

家务省力化:家务、育儿、老年人看护等是在社会家庭生活中具备义务性质的活动。通过导入智能设备,可以大大降低工作强度,实现省力化。这对于日本未来所面临的深刻的少子高龄化社会具备十分积极的发展意义。得到应用的包括联网厨房家电的自动烹饪、玻璃窗的自动清洗机器人等。生活支援人工智能（机器人）的开发上也实现了日本主导的产品，其安全性标准正逐步成为国际标准。

3 问题与发展趋势

智能住宅虽然已经在加速普及的进程上，但也面临着不少问题。主要有以下几点。一是并网规格的统一。国际上现行网络存在不同的接入协议和界面，不同厂家产品并没有统一的信息标准，故机器设备在并网后无法实现对全系统的控制。日本采用的是自我研发的 ECHONET Lite 规格，而美国是 SEP 规格，欧洲是 KNX 规格[9]，所以未来要实现应用技术市场的国际化，一是要解决规格的连通或统一。在这一问题的对应上，日本动用了产、官、学界的联合力量。二是重点机器及下位层设备机器的系统认证，需要业界共同商定运用和管理方案。三是能源生产中对太阳能的依赖。利用太阳能的能源生产强度依地域地理条件不同而不同，为天气条件所制约。在实际的应用中需要高度结合系统电力（由电力企业提供的公共供电）的互动使用，才能实现能源的高效利用。因此针对现有系统也开始有了改良型的产品出现，比如村田制作所的协调型能源系统产品等。四是实际系统导入时的高费用问题。现阶段通过导入费用的政府补贴、取得目的的税负减免等手段降低导入门槛，但这种最终成为财政负担的做法是无法长期持续的，如不能在预定时期内形成一定密度的覆盖面规模，从而实现产品的价值构筑，通过量产实现价格的低廉化，便可能导致失去市场的风险。

另外前述住宅的节能涉及建筑外皮和建筑整体的一次能耗问题，建筑外皮的节能主要通过高性能建材来实现，整体能耗包括了建筑外皮能耗内容，于是建材开发自然被纳入整体节能对策的构成部分。因此出现了建材厂商与电子企业的联合，比如 2011 年大型住建商的 Lixil 与夏普的合作，大型家电量贩企业的 Yamada 电机通过资产运作收购了住建商 SXL 等。

4 结论及对中国的借鉴意义

综上所述，智慧型技术从建设住宅的能源控制平台 HEMS 入手，通过不断提高产电、蓄电、耗电的能源供给循环效率来完善系统，同时不断扩展平台功能，包括通过并网提供使用大数据的同时取得外部提供的远程服务，基于大数据的居家功能无线监控及操控等。在平台建设及硬件设置的基础上，通过网络不断提供应用软件，就可以获得不断延伸的应用功能，相当于提供了未来极大的扩展空间，最终成为链接家庭与社会的 Gateway（门户）。

作为一个面向未来具有极大发展空间的产业，日本政府在政策层面上对该领域发展予以高度重视，通过牵头组织政企体系共同策定发展环境，建立技术标准，构筑对企业有利的加入环境，同时通过经济辅助手段积极推动技术的普及应用。所瞄准的不只是日本国内的市场，可以推测今后其系统成熟后的国际市场技术输出。政府继 2015 年的"日本再兴战略"后在 2016 年的"新产业结构展望"中明确提出了家居智能化未来将导向第四次产业革命，全球产业结构重组的可能性。[10]

以 IT 网络技术和人工智能技术等为支持的智慧型住宅技术的应用，不仅为日本的家居生活带来了方便，更重要的是其未来的巨大发展前景将为日本的研发和制造产业带来新一轮繁荣发展的可能性，这对中国乃至亚太地区都有重要的启迪意义。当前中国部分产业还徘徊在既存环境下的去库存、去产能阶段，未能系统关注基于大数据支持的智慧型住宅产业，而中国的住宅发展关乎国家发展大计，如能在住宅的智慧型应用技术上取得国际先进地位，不但可以为住宅产业注入新的发展要素，更可以在形成体系的基础上发展对外技术输出，树立行业的世界标准。

A Study on the Use of Intelligent Technology on the Field of Urban Housing in Japan

Ito Masuteru

(School of Architecture, Tsinghua University)

Abstract: In Japan, Smart house has been developing for nearly 40 years. Many intelligent technologies made breakthrough in the practical use of city housing accompanied by the development of internet and information technology, and these technologies are widely used through the promotion by the cooperation of industry, government and academia, During the creation of comfortable living spaces in "people-oriented" way, they are also achieved on making the future living concept of developing an eco and energy-saving environment. Currently for the application of intelligent residential technology, the ZEH (Zero Energy House) standard has been set up, it is based on the HEMS (Home Energy Management System) and take advantage of the IoT (Internet of Things) smart house platform. The promotion of smart house brings Japanese not just about comfortable green lives, more importantly it may bring great prospects for the industry development of Japan. By focusing on the industry developing trend and strategy, with this research, we might learn the significance of developing future city residences in cities in China and even in Asia-Pacific area.

Keywords: Japan, City housing, Intelligent technology, Applied to, Industrial development

参考文献

[1, 9]　日本経済産業部. スマートハウス標準化検討会とりまとめ概要. 日本経済産業部官网, 2012.

[2]　日本国土交通部. 平成26年度住宅のゼロ・エネルギー化推進事業. 日本国土交通部官网, 2014.

[3]　日本経済産業部. BEMS・HEMS補助金についてのお知らせ. 日本経済産業部官网, 2013.

[4]　日本経済産業部. 定置用リチウムイオン蓄電池導入促進対策事業費補助. 日本経済産業部官网, 2013.

[5]　日本国土交通部. 住宅・建築物の省エネルギー基準. 日本国土交通部官网, 2013.

[6]　日本経済産業部. ZEHロードマップ検討委員会とりまとめ. 日本経済産業部官网, 2015.

[7]　日本政府エネルギー・環境会議. 「グリーン政策大綱」の骨子案. 日本内閣官房国家戦略室, 2012.

[8]　日本経済産業部.「新産業構造ビジョン」~第四次産業革命を」リードする日本の戦略~. 日本経済産業部官网, 2016.

[10]　日本経済産業部. スマートホームにおける現状と将来像の実現に向けた検討の方向性について. 日本経済産業部官网, 2017.

An Innovated Smart Home Sensors Integration and Remote Control Solution and Implementation Based on the Mirror Touch Interaction

Li Jixun, Qiu Shenping, Wang Hao, Ye Lei

(Pacific Telecom & Navigation Limited)

Abstract: Smart home is the residential extension of building automation and involves the control and automation of lighting, heating, ventilation, air conditioning (HVAC), and security, as well as home appliances such as washer/dryers, ovens or refrigerators/freezers that use Wi-Fi for remote monitoring[1]. Modern systems generally consist of switches and sensors connected to a central hub sometimes called a "gateway" from which the system is controlled with a user interface that is interacted either with a wall-mounted terminal, mobile phone software, tablet computer or a web interface, often but not always via internet cloud services.The smart home market was worth US$5.77 billion in 2015, predicted to have a market value over US$10 billion by the year 2020[2]. This paper tentatively proposes a method and solution able to cope with smart home solution's existed problems. It is using Smart Mirror as a human-computer interaction platform as well as a management center which can realize centralized information display and intelligent control. The study is important to explore an idea for the integration and remote control of internet of things in smart home.

Keywords: Smart mirror, Control, Integration, Smart home, Open standard

1 Introduction

With the fast development of technology, IoT (internet of things) use in smart home has been taken more and more notice [3].

Smart home solutions on the market are compared firstly. They both have their advantages and disadvantages. After it, theessay compares four kinds of popular communications protocol for products in smart home with their features.

On the basis of the solution, this paper tentatively proposes a method and solution able to cope withsmart home solution's existed problems. And there are significant evidence and implementation experiment to prove that it can overcome the summarized shortcomings of mentioned popular solution. The scheme is using Smart Mirror as a human-computer interaction platform as well as a management center. It can realize smart home centralized information display and intelligent control withthe use of wireless communication technology and cloud computing technology. At the same time, this paper also introduces the implementation process and test results of the proposed smart home solution.

The study is of great importance to explore an idea for the integration and remote control of internet of things in smart home. As aninvestigation of the possible solution for smart home, this study aims to throw some light to both smart home and internet of things to promote more relevant studies.

2 Comparison of Existing Smart Home Solution

Recently the use of smart technology has developed so that almost any electrical component within the house can be included in the system [3,4]. The home network encompasses communications, entertainment, security, convenience, and information systems.In the chapter, I mainly compare three smart home solutions to see their advantages and disadvantages and to summarize the main shortcomings of the existing smart home solution.

2.1 Mi Home

Xiaomi Inc., literally "millet technology", is a privately owned Chinese electronics company headquartered in Beijing.

The advantages of Mi Home solution are these following:

1. Devices type is the most abundant: Xiaomi design and manufacture all its belonging devices. Comparing with other two smart home solution, it has the most abundant devices type. 2. Low in price: It has price advantage of internet of things for Mi home. Xiaomi is responsible for all manufactory part just like computer manufactory Dell, it will reduce the cost of these devices apparently. 3. Allin one app with one standard: All products in mi home are integrated in one standard. It is very easy to use and to install.

And the disadvantages of Mi Home solution are:

1. Function is not useful and powerful. Technology foundation of Xiaomi is not as powerful as others. Sometimes it will manufacture some devices of little use such as electric kettle or rice cooker. The product is weak in function while convenient in control. 2.Weak in extension: Due to its company's strategic plan: one company for all equipment and software themselves. It can hardly cooperate with other devices while they are in different standard.

2.2 Haier U Home

Haier Group Corporation is a Chinese multinational consumer electronics and home appliances company headquartered in Qingdao, China. It designs, develops, manufactures and sells products of white goods.

The advantage of Haier U home are these following:

1. Reliable in quality: Haier now is the largest home appliance brand. It is the powerful in household development and design. With the brand support, it is most reliable in quality of intelligent devices.

2. Extension is good: Haier, based on years of its experience, sets own standard for the solution. It opens the standard for other company meaning any company can develop their own devices integrated into the Haier U home solution.

The disadvantage of Haier U home are these following:

1. Weak in platform management: It opens the standard for other company to take part in. It suffers from weak platform management. 2. Few in cooperated companies: Haier is experienced in product design but not a mature third party company. Although it opens the standard for other company to develop and integration, there are few companies are willing to just act like product provider especially for large companies. So, Haier U home still needs to find a way to attract more company to join its standard.

2.3 Eastsoft Communication

Eastsoft Communication is a company concentrating on power carrier technology area. The main businesses of it are low voltage power line carrier communication products production, sales and service.

The advantage of Eastsoft Communication is: Mature in function: The initial objective for the company is internet of things and power carrier technology. It is most experienced in smart home solution. It already presents a variety of mature solution in home control.

The disadvantage of control 4 are these following:

1. High in price; if only test for some function, the price for Eastsoft are acceptable. But if you want to use it for whole smart home solution, the price is relatively high than other two solutions. 2. Need hardware line patch. It need hardware line patch in house to realize total control of smart home. The whole system is hard to install and deploy.

2.4 Summary

To conclude from all, while there are many competing vendors, there are very few world-wide accepted industry standards[5] and the smart home space is heavily fragmented. Manufacturers often prevent independent implementations by withholding documentation and by suing people.

3 Wireless Technology Comparison

Nowadays, replace cable connection with wireless ones is the trend. After introducing common smart home solution, I will introduce four common wireless communication technology and their features in this chapter.

3.1 Bluetooth

Bluetooth is a wireless technology standard for exchanging data over short distances and building personal area networks. The advantage is it is low in electric consumption (still higher than ZigBee) and cost. But the limitation is the communication distance. It can only connect devices within 10 metres and it can only build network within ten devices. In conclusion, it is a point-to-point, short-distance transmission protocol. The targeted area and situation for is to provide short distance talk communication and private data transmission [6].

3.2 Wi-Fi

Wi-Fi is a technology for wireless local area networking with devices based on the IEEE 802.11 standards.

The advantage is it is fast in transmission speed, low in devices cost and most abundant in life. For users, it is easiest to build smart home based on Wi-Fi. The disadvantage is acting normally in security and stability. And it is also high in energy consumption so it can't be used for some devices requiring low consumption. And like Bluetooth, it is limited to number of connection nodes. It can only connect 16 nodes.

3.3 ZigBee

ZigBee is an IEEE 802.15.4-based specification for a suite of high-level communication protocols used to create personal area networks with small, low-power digital radios [7]. The advantage of it is high in security and lowest in energy consumption. And it can be connected to 65300 nodes, the most in all wireless technology. The disadvantage is it cannot be integrated into mobile devices directly which will require a corresponding router to act as medium. Another is it has some compatibility problem between different company.

3.4 Z-Wave

Z-Wave is a wireless communications protocol used primarily for home automation in residential control and automationarea [8]. The data transmission rate of it is 9.6kbps suitable for narrow bandwidth applications. The shortcomings are mainly three: 1.low in nodes. 2. the tree structure, once the top of the tree is off, the equipment in bottom will not be able to work; 3. Security is poor, vulnerable to attack.

3.5 Summary

ZigBee is not compatible between different companies and Z-wave has few devices with low popularity for its standard [9]. Although Wi-Fi and Bluetooth has some disadvantages due to its design, comparing with others, they are the most suitable wireless protocols at present because of their features of openness and usability.

4 Smart Mirror Solution Introduction

After concluding these problems for present smart home solution, we propose an innovative solution based on an interactive intelligent device to solve the mentioned problems. Smart mirror is a technology defined as Next Generation display which is a promising product used in retailing, smart home, and security area.

The solution is made of three subsystems, and the protocol between them are like Figure 1 shows:

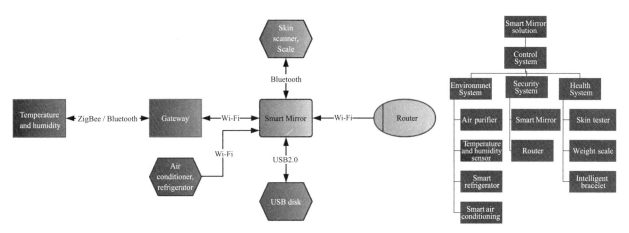

Figure 1 System protocol and solution components

4.1 Home Environment Subsystem

Home environment subsystem can realize home environment monitoring and maintenance, including temperature and humidity sensors, smart refrigerators, smart air conditioning and air purifiers. Air purifier, is responsible for cleaning indoor PM2.5 particles. Smart air conditioning monitor the temperature within the house. Smart refrigerator, can real-time control through app and view refrigerator storage of food. Temperature and humidity sensor, glued to the room records indoor temperature and humidity condition.

4.2 Home Security Subsystem

Home security subsystem is responsible for the family security, includingintelligent routers and Smart Mirror. Smart router is installed in the open space in home, providing Wi-Fi network coverage for the entire residential. Smart mirror is installed in the bathroom and bedroom, as an intelligent terminal for software operation, equipment operation and security camera.

4.3 Home Health Subsystem

Home health subsystem is responsible for the management of residents' health, including three parts: skin tester, weight scale and smart bracelet. These three devices are connected to the mirror through Bluetooth. Skin scanner will detect the user's skin condition, and gives the results and recommendations on smart mirror. The body weight will record the user's weight and record the weight of the history. Walk smart bracelet to record the user on the same day, the consumption of calories and sleep quality, the results displayed in the mirror on.

5 Implementation and Experiment

We already test smart home solution in office. All the mentioned devices can be connected to smart mirror. Smart mirror appearance is shown as Figure 2. Temperature and humidity sensor and air conditioning diagrammatic sketch is shown in Figure 3, as well as skin scanner and weight and PM 2.5 device as Figure 4.

Finally extension is also available for home security as figure 5.

Figure 2   Smart mirror appearance

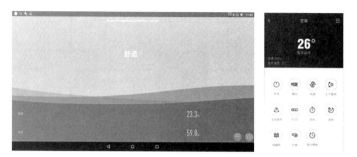
Figure 3   Diagrammatic sketch of temperature sensor and air conditioning

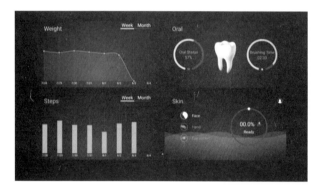

Figure 4   Screenshot of skin scanner and PM 2.5 device

Figure 5   Extension of home security

With all these pictures of experiment to prove that smart mirror solution is realistic with convenience, it is reasonable to believe a wireless centered solution can be ensemble with smart mirror as display and operation device.

6   Conclusion

In summarized, the proposed smart home solution is obviously innovative in these following aspects:

1. Perfectly integration of mirror and touch. When it works, users touch it like the PAD or Tablet; when power off, it's a traditional decorative mirror in home. 2. Open standard. The solution is open in standards,

devices which are compatible with Android can be connected to the mirror for unified management. 3. Easy to install and use. All interactionsarethroughwireless technology, no additional wiring is required. 4.Firm and compact in structure. Smart Mirror, as the main control center,is concise in structure, reliable and durable. Its waterproof design is IP65 with a built-in camera. 5. Cloud services supported.Through the Wi-Fi Internet connection, Smart Mirror can provide any public or private cloud service, cloud computing, apps and various types of business information push as well as other functions.

一种基于镜像交互技术的智能家居传感器集成与远程控制解决方案及实现

李佶逊　邱沈萍　王　浩　叶　雷

（泛太通信导航有限公司）

摘　要：智能家居是楼宇自动化的住宅延伸，涉及照明、加热（如智能恒温器）、通风、空调（HVAC）和安全等的控制和自动化和家用电器如洗衣机/烘干机、烤箱或使用 Wi-Fi 进行远程监控的冰箱/冷柜。现代系统通常由连接到中心集线器的交换机和传感器组成，称为"网关"，系统由用户界面进行控制，其交互可通过壁挂式终端、手机软件、平板电脑或 Web 界面等。2015 年，智能家居市场价值 57.7 亿美元，到 2020 年预计市值将超过 100 亿美元。本文提出了一种能够应对智能家居解决方案存在问题的方法和解决方案。将智能魔镜作为人机交互平台，实现智能家居集中信息显示和智能控制的管理中心。这项研究对于智能家居互联网的整合与远程控制的探索具有重要的意义。

关键词：智能魔镜，控制，集成，智能家居，开放标准

References

[1] https://en.wikipedia.org/wiki/Home_automation.

[2] Lee Won-Jun. When the Future Technology Is Now: Paradoxical Attitudes of Consumer and Evaluation of IoT Service[J]. International Journal of Smart Home，2016，10（6）：115-26.

[3] Risteska Stojkoska，Trivodaliev. A Review of Internet of Things for Smart Home: Challenges and Solutions[J].Journal of Cleaner Production 2017，140：1454-1464.

[4] Li and Yu. Research and Application on the Smart Home Based on Component Technologies and Internet of Things[J]. Procedia Engineering 2011，15：2087-2092.

[5] Chan，Estève，Escriba，Campo. "A Review of Smart Homes——Present State and Future Challenges. Computer Methods and Programs in Biomedicine，2008，91（1）：55-81.

[6] Ricquebourg V. The smart home concept: our immediate future[C]//E-Learning in Industrial Electronics，2006 1ST IEEE International Conference on. IEEE，2006：23-28.

[7] Qinqin Z Y L Z W. ZigBee Wireless Communication Technology and Investigation on Its Application[J]. Process Automation Instrumentation，2005，6：002.

[8] 查珑珑. 浅析物联网智能家居发展 [J]. 科技信息，2012，25：42.

[9] 吕莉，罗杰. 智能家居及其发展趋势 [J]. 计算机与现代化，2007，11：18-20.

轻型钢结构模矩化设计方法论

陈上元[1]　刘泰佑[1]　蔡立伟[2]

（1.逢甲大学建筑专业学院研究所；2.逢甲大学土木及水利工程博士学位学程）

摘　要：全世界发展轻钢结构房屋已有数十年之久，唯其关键技术乃在于建立一个经济、快速、有效的连接系统。本研究利用本文作者自行发明的专利"轻钢构建筑物结构"之C型钢连接系统并导入BIM系统应用于轻钢结构模块化设计，提出轻钢结构最佳模矩化设计方案，自设计端解决制造及施工端所可能发生之问题，降低施工总成本、减少总工期及避免产生的困扰，意即面向制造和装配的设计（DFMA）。再搭配本研究所建立的钢结构施工手册，可作为施工流程之指引及降低人为判断错误之行为，加强施工效益及效率，使其过程符合经济、快速、环保。本最佳模矩化设计方案针对轻钢结构建筑非常实用，可建造使用者满意、维护容易、结构安全之中低楼层建筑。

关键词：轻钢结构，模块化设计，建筑信息模型，装配式建筑，开放式建筑

1　缘起与目的

近10多年来，我国台湾地区应用冷轧型钢于建筑物的情况已相当普遍，冷轧型钢构材使用的范围也相当广泛，如楼板、帷幕墙之支撑系统，建筑物内之轻隔间、工厂、餐厅及一般住宅等。诸如此类的轻钢构建筑，绝大多数系以冷轧型钢材料组合而成，方便、迅速且质量轻，地震发生时所造成的摇晃程度，亦较钢筋混凝土构造轻微，是较有安全感的建筑构造形式。此外，钢构造建筑之耗能量仅为混凝土构造之83%，二氧化碳排放量仅为其71%[1]，就环境保育观点而言，钢构造非常适合在地震带地区推广采用。其研究目的如下：

（1）在全球轻钢构建造日愈大量需求的情况下，建立一个有效的连接系统，将BIM的观念应用此连接系统[2,3]，并导入轻型钢结构模块化设计，透过BIM系统的整合，将提出最佳模矩化设计方案。

（2）应用钢结构具有高强度、高韧性、耐震性佳及施工迅速等特性，由建筑生命周期之推估，从材料生产、施工建造、维护使用及拆除回收再利用，利用建筑模型信息化的特点延伸钢结构组装图（组装程序步骤）。

2　文献回顾

轻钢构（LGS）建筑是一种工业化、轻量化且高质量的绿色建筑工法，从1940年开始广泛使用。美国轻型钢构建筑在推广之初，1992年只有500栋，1998年成长为住宅市场的10%，2000年已达20%。在澳洲市场占有率为15%，且每年均卓越成长。日本为防火、耐震、耐久的高质量住宅，并同时提供较低的火灾、地震保险与房屋税等优惠方法。LGS建筑虽然名为"轻钢构"，但是耐震性能却在一般的钢筋混凝土建筑之上，相比之下，LGS建筑可减少对砂石的需求、施工时期缩短一半，也可减少劳动成本，同时安全性也高，并可减少30%的二氧化碳排放量，在到达使用年限而必须拆除时，主结构可以再回收重新利用。轻钢构建筑运用在新建的建筑里，大多为搭配混凝土结构的形式，而全

模块化的轻钢构件运用于建筑的案例更为鲜见。与混凝土结构相比，轻钢构不仅重量少于混凝土结构的 30%～50%，又因断面较小，可增加建筑有效面积 8%，因此轻钢构建筑可为未来建筑之发展方向。[4]

3 竹节式钢结构概要

本研究之竹节式钢构，旨在利用现有成熟技术及材料规格，其中使用国际标准规格的平头内六角螺栓及拉帽，通过连接器载体将 C 型钢联结成一个系统。此系统具有组装容易且施工性能佳的特点。本研究利用此系统的特点，建立这四种构建的三维信息模型，将杆件结构参数化，并加入模矩数与逻辑判断式（图 1）。

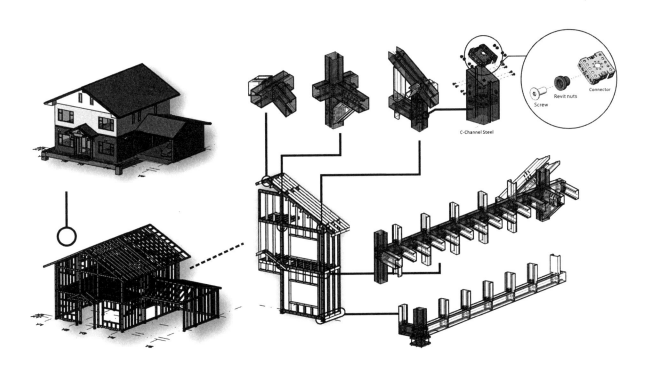

图 1　连接器模矩化设计概要图

- C 型钢特性：金属电镀或热浸镀锌防锈而不可焊接，C 型钢经热卷板冷弯加工而成，壁薄自重轻，截面性能优良，强度高，与传统槽钢相比，同等强度可节约材料 30%。C 型钢广泛用于钢结构建筑的檩条、墙梁，也可自行组合成轻量型屋架、托架等建筑构件。
- 模矩概念：使用模矩，加工容易，组构简单，进而使建物扩建与空间延展弹性强。运用模矩尺寸可使内外封装材互相搭配，达到构件组装容易及省料之目的。

3.1　设计方法与步骤

- 参数共享之设定

本研究采用 Revit 结构杆件的簇群设计方法，簇群是具有共享性质（称为参数集）和一个相关图形表现法的组件群组，因此透过簇群参数能够建立构件与属性数据的关联性。[5, 6] 本研究之系统，包含螺丝、拉帽及连接器载体，皆为单一个体模型，使用共享的设定可让层叠的五金组合构件不致重复计算或遗失（图2）。

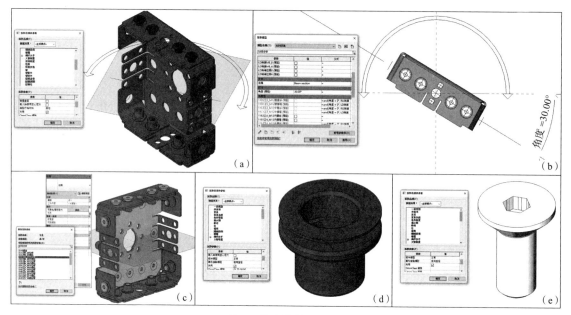

图2　簇群参数之设定

- 结构杆件的设计

结构杆件中有柱、结构框架（梁、椽），使设计与制造精确，最终必须完美产出材料明细表；因此设计单一杆件必须有通用性、真实性、模矩化的规律性。为达到通用性，杆件设计就必须加以逻辑性选择与判断（图3a、图3b）。真实性是让设计过程容易判断设计有无错误或干涉。模矩化的规律性，是杆件可以因长度拉伸改变而自动计算产出（图3c）。

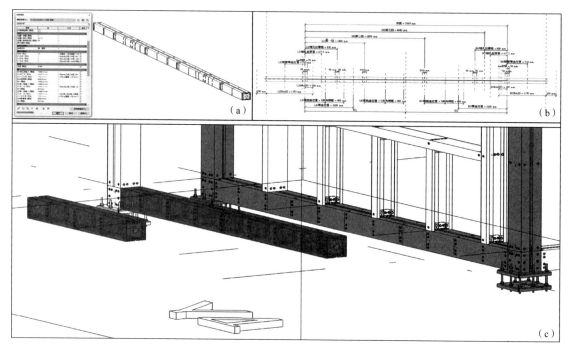

图3　结构杆件的设计

- 模矩式设计

平面：平面模矩安排，须以外墙阳角为计算范围，国际板材尺寸皆以 915mm×1830mm、1220mm×2440 mm 尺寸为主，因此模矩基数会是 305mm。本研究所使用模矩方块外围线即是底板封装完成面，因此实务面柱中心至柱中心就不是模矩倍整数（图 4a）。梁的拉伸起始与结束的连接器必须选择对称（图 4b），因此封板时能将板之缝对接于杆件之上。

立面：在设计立面高度时也尽量让封装底板为 305 模矩数。有此思考模式可形成封板锁装系统，墙面或地板杆件加装拉帽，以模矩点利用锁装容易的锁板弹簧片将板材固定于结构体上（图 4c）

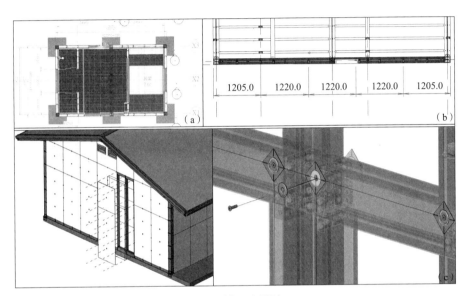

图 4 模矩式设计

3.2 生产设计

快速 C 型钢的生产：所有建筑用材产业中最有效率的生产方式应该就是 C 型钢滚压快速成型（图 5a），C 型钢成型机由装料架、整形系统、成型系统、校正系统、计算机控制系统、液压系统、冲孔、剪切系统组成，所生产的产品广泛应用于钢结构标准厂房及各种简易棚等场合，是制作钢结构单位不可缺少的设备之一。C 型钢机用于将连续的钢管在线切断成预先设定长度的成品管，采用非接触数字传感器，IPC 和 IPC 控制，定尺精度高。

模矩化的设计可产生真实确切的明细表与滚压成型机数字对接而自动化生产，因此要让房屋经济、快速、安全与工业化，生产方式与设计是必须要考虑的。本论与实作中的杆件设计就可很明确在明细表产生（图 5b）。

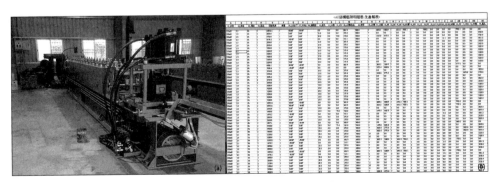

图 5 快速 C 型钢的生产与明细表产生

4 结论与建议

轻钢构建筑对于环境百利而无害，期能尽速制定适合对台湾省环境所需的轻钢构建筑规范，促进市场需求之轻量化建材的研发量产，使其生产过程符合经济、快速、环保，成为使用满意、维护容易之低层耐震建筑主流。从能源再利用的观念，如何以最节约能源、最有效利用资源的方式，在最低环境负荷情况下，提供最安全、健康、效率及舒适的居住空间，并将建筑材料回收再利用，以达到人及建筑与环境共生共荣、永续发展。本研究提出以下结论：

（1）本研究将建造服务透过 BIM 的整合，建造过程信息化、透视化，使建造团队与业主进行最紧密沟通与减少矛盾与错误点。一般业主鲜少是接受过读图与识图的能力，唯有透过快速的 APP 信息提供业主 3D 与实境虚拟，才能达到客户最精准的需求。

（2）钢构材远胜于其他建筑方式的构材；而钢构材中又以 H 型及 C 型钢构建材为最可能回收利用，将 H 型及 C 型钢有系统计划地推展于低层建筑，对全省整体自然环境，减少资源的浪费，以加速绿色建筑的推广。

4.1 建议

轻钢构建筑的运用在发达国家已甚为普及，如美、日等多国政府亦制定其相关的规范，而省内虽然已有轻钢构建筑，却无相关规范，以至于产生适法上的问题。由本分析得知，轻钢构建筑对于环境百利而无害，期能尽速制定适合对台湾省环境所需的轻钢构建筑规范，促进市场需求之轻量化建材的研发量产，使其生产过程符合经济、快速、环保，成为使用满意、维护容易之低层耐震建筑主流。也希望此种构造与容易组装的形式，成为开放式建筑的主流架构，让建屋不再是困难之事，让年轻人期许着一个比较轻松的家庭营建过程。

The Design Methodology of Light Gauge Steel Structure Modular

Chen Shang-Yuan[1], Liu Tai-Yu[1], Cai Li-Wei[2]

(1. Feng Chia University Department of Architecture; 1. Feng Chia University Department of Architecture; 2. Feng Chia University Department of Civil and Hydraulic Engineering)

Abstract: The LGS structure building technology has been developing worldwide for decades. The critical technology of the LGS structure building is to develop an economic, fast, and effective connection system. In this study, the author uses the C channel steel connection system of his own invention patent "LIGHTWEIGHT STEEL CONSTRUCTION" for an LGS modular design program study, in which the BIM system technology is introduced. This paper proposes an optimal design program for LGS structure modular, which from the design stage can solve all the issues that may happen during the manufacture and construction stages, i.e., Design for Manufacturing and Assembly (DFMA), to save cost, time, and troubles. In addition, the use of the developed LGS structure construction manual in this paper is to guide the construction process which can reduce the human errors and enhance the construction benefit and efficiency to achieve an economic, fast, and environmentally sound process. This proposed optimal modular design program is very useful for the LGS structure construction of the low to medium-rise buildings that are customer satisfying, easy maintenance, and structurally safe.

Keywords: LGS, Modular design, BIM, Prefabricated construction, Open building

参考文献

[1] 陈瑞玲，林宪德.建筑产业生命周期二氧化碳减量评估应用之研究，2008：5-17.

[2] Dongping Cao, Guangbin Wang, Heng Li, Martin Skitmore, Ting Huang, Weiyu Zhang. Practices and effectiveness of building information modelling in construction projects in China. 2014：113-122.

[3] Farzad Jalaei, Ahmad Jrade. Integrating building information modeling (BIM) and LEED system at the conceptual design stage of sustainable buildings. 2015：95-107.

[4] Steel and Composite Structures, Research on cold-formed steel connections[J].A state-of-the-art review, 2016, 20 (1): 21-41.

[5] Hyun Woo Lee, Hyuntak Oh, Youngchul Kim, Kunhee Choi. Quantitative analysis of warnings in building information modeling (BIM). 2015：23-31.

[6] Mehmet Yalcinkaya, Vishal Singh. Patterns and trends in Building Information Modeling (BIM) research：A Latent Semantic Analysis. 2015：68-80.

整合建筑信息建模参数编程引擎与嵌入式系统的智能化城市住宅研究

沈扬庭　吴念瑾

（逢甲大学建筑专业学院）

摘　要：本研究提出"智能化适性建筑"的概念，倡议在环境友善的高效能建筑趋势下，建筑信息模型（BIM，Building Information Modeling）将出现应用端的典范转移，从现行运用于设计与施工的位阶，进入到建筑生命周期的最后一哩路——"维运使用阶段"，以绿色智能管理者的角色介入到建筑物的维运使用，成为建筑物与所在环境互动调适的思考核心。本研究所发展的智能化适性建筑描绘出一套能与真实环境互动调适的智能维运机制和系统，以（1）监控层：感知化的效能分析；（2）剧本层：互动化的智能系统；（3）控制层：调适化的设施管理三者共构的整合性流程，使得建物能够执行有效的数据源整合，进行互联的信息同步交换，以达到绿色的智能建筑生命周期管理和自动化决策，进而促成与环境共生的绿色智慧城市。

关键词：建筑信息模型，参数编程引擎，智能维运，适性建筑，嵌入式系统

1　引言

根据报告指出 1950～2005 年间，全球城市化水平从 29% 升至 49%，同时焚烧化石燃料产生的二氧化碳排放量增加了 500%，城市化的发展导致气候状况不利于生态环境发展；2030 年预计发展中国家的城市人口、土地面积扩张三倍，将会导致一连串严厉的考验。我们所居住的传统建筑仅提供人类遮风避雨功能，现今面对气候条件多变下，建筑的形态逐渐朝向与环境互动的形式发展，衍生例如智能建筑、智能表层等多项功能。Mitchell 教授于 e-Topia 提到形态随机能转，机能随程序转（Form Follow Function，Function Follow Code），转变为程序代码的方式设计，并随着嵌入式系统、传感器等互动技术在不同层面的应用下，将与传统的建筑思维产生极大不同。BIM 的出现更会传统建筑产业造成影响，未来建筑将须面对在建造后、改造中所面临的各种问题，被动式的维护管理已无法满足动态环境的变化，需开发出一套能与真实环境作互动的新机制，才能在这迫切的条件下改善气候环境。

2　文献回顾

2.1　环境友善的智能建筑

城市化的高度发展下，人类对于居住空间的需求量增加，其中建筑所产生的能耗高达全球能源的 35%，根据联合国 2016 世界城市化报告指出 2050 年将增加超过 60% 的人口生活在都市中。当今

这波城市化的发展已导致气候变化剧烈，极端气候频繁，使自然生态负载着超过自身平衡系统，无论再如何强调低碳或环保都无法忽视对于环境所产生的冲击，因此我们需要建立更前瞻的思维。[1] 1973 年美国生态学家 Holling（C.S.Holling）以韧性一词描述当生态系统受自然或人为扰动后是否有自身快速恢复能力。然而建筑物的出现对生态系统本身便是一种扰动，如何使建筑的介入为生态系统演变为另一种新的循环，使建筑具有调整、复原能力的可适应行为[2]是我们所需面对的挑战。鉴于现今永续生态等议题的出现，使人类思量着城市、住宅与环境间的关系，自然界的生物体与系统具备着互动性（Interactive）及灵敏性（Environment-Sensitive）的形态自我调解；1970 年 Charles Eastma 发展出可适应建筑、Nicholas Negroponte 的可响应建筑及 Michael Fox 所提出的互动建筑，为更聚焦建筑与环境间的互动、回应、适应等调适的功能。

20 世纪 80 年代美国开始把智慧的概念引入建筑，主要是因为信息发达使得建筑设施可以遥控，自动减少资源耗损，同时加上对舒适生活环境的要求，才衍生出智能建筑[3]，但随着时代的改变演变为智能建筑强调于建筑的结构、系统、服务以及跨领域间管理，为使用者设计环保节能的建筑[4]，且依据使用者为导向需求[5]，增加学习能力及顺应使用环境反应而具备实时调整功能。[6] 将智能建筑由时代的转变可划分为：（1）自动控制时代（1960～1990 年）：Nicholas Negroponte 提出自动控制学（Cybernetics）于建筑的应用，主张整合计算机运算与建筑设计；（2）物联网时代（1990～2000 年）：与 1991 年 Mark Weiser 于《The Computer for the 21th Century》一文当中提出"最深奥的科技，最终要与生活结合，并令人感觉不到它的存在"，叙述着计算机会与我们生活紧密结合，成为无形的计算机（Invisible Computers）无所不在的运算（Ubiquitous Computing）；（3）永续互动时代（2000 年至今）：Michael Fox 教授提出互动建筑的概念，认为借由人与环境间的互动行为，将互动建筑视为一种空间和对象，于单元与设施中嵌入运算、可动装置。当 21 世纪永续成为建筑物的主流价值，智能建筑开始朝向永续的方向发展，一个因地制宜、能自主调适、主动反映气候变迁的智能建筑体[7]，成为建筑的新方向。

2.2　建筑信息模型应用于维运使用阶段

1970 年由 Charles Eastman 等人开发出建筑信息模型（Building Information Modeling，BIM）。Charles Eastman 教授在《Building Product Models》一书中，以介绍建筑物的组件信息模型组构原理，揭示 BIM 概念。《BIM Handbook》一书中叙述着 BIM 一词为建模技术及一组相关于此技术的，用以产生、沟通与分析建筑模型的流程。[8] 近几年 BIM 的使用如雨后春笋般地大量涌现，大多数应用于前中期阶段，只有少部分用于后期使用阶段。建筑的全生命周期（Building Lifecycle Management，BLM）可分成规划、设计、施工、营运使用四阶段，BIM 的导入在建筑全生命周期中，各自在前期、中期以及后期使用阶段扮演着不同的角色，建筑物在设计、施工端所花费建造的时间仅有几年；而完工后的使用时间可长达数十年以上，在未来 2050 年的城市中，我们所居住 80% 以上的建筑物是由现在住宅所延续使用的，以友善环境的角度介入思考是不可忽视的问题。

美国国际设施管理协会（International Facility Management Association，IFMA）对于设施管理之定义为"一项借由整合人、环境、过程与科技之职业，并且执行规范以确保建筑性能正常。"[9] 目前设施维护管理可分为营运管理、维护管理，主要着重于建筑物的设施功能以及运作是否正常等，少数能有与环境互动并产生调适的应用。而目前位于中国 - 北京的银河 SOHO 以能源管理平台涉及环境、感测、能源、机电通风、空调、照明、电梯等系统，例如环境管理 - 感测各公共区域的温度，以可视化的界面呈现不同色点得知温度高低，结合其他系统共同调整，以实时响应感测到的信息。

3 BIM智能维运系统设计架构

本研究以提出"智能维运系统",倡议在环境友善的高效能建筑趋势下,以绿色智能管理者的角色介入建筑物的维运使用,开发出智能化适性建筑能与真实环境互动调适的智能维管机制,成为建筑物与所在环境互动调适的思考核心。主要目的以互动调适提高建筑性能,以主动控制适应微气候环境对建筑进行调节。[10] 透过BIM的导入使应用端的出现典范转移,BIM如同建筑物的大脑般,使建筑能以互动调适进行控制,依循着IPO模式进行感测环境数据、参数编程引擎的运算、控制改变。[11] 运用嵌入式系统设备组成,以连接实体空间进行建筑立面开口部的调整。本研究的智能维运系统架构如图1,以(1)监控层;(2)剧本层;(3)控制层三大层面作为设计的整合架构原则。

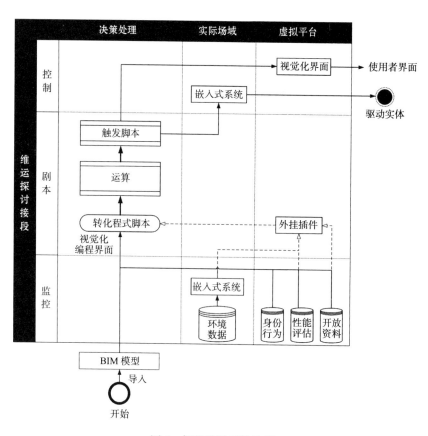

图1 智能维运系统流程

(1)监控层

以嵌入式系统(Embedded system)连接实体,系统包括微处理器Arduino、传感器及输出设备。其中微处理器Arduino如同嵌入式系统的大脑,可编程建立程序语言。1981年Michael Davies提出建筑表层构想具有反应器、过滤器、传输器等多功能的建筑表层,这样的概念已开发出智能建筑上的表层系统。运用传感器检测到的环境微气候数据对建筑皮层做往复的传递与调整以适应多元的环境变化,使建筑达到实时动态反应。[12] 除此之外能从开放数据得到数据例如天气预报,或于规划设计时间所仿真的性能评估数据,且利用身份行为能辨识用户身份、位置,以监控撷取设计者或用户所需的数据。

（2）剧本层

主要目的是与环境互动调适的决策关键。剧本层的定义由设计者事先定义好参数的决策范围，借由传感器检测环境数值，再由计算机端去判断与决策的能力。[12] 以 BIM-REVIT 的参数编程引擎 Dynamo 为核心运算，参数编程引擎为可视化编程（Visual Programming，VP）工具，可为使用者提供互动剧本的撰写、自定义节点、Python。其中 Python 可提供实现脚本撰写程度高，以编写条件语句（if/then）及循环等，可以延伸参数编程引擎的功能，可借此使用程序代码来取代许多节点。[13] 剧本层在参数编程引擎中的决策处理分为（1）汇入；（2）运算；（3）驱动三部分，主要将检测到的环境参数，汇入参数编程引擎并转化为程序脚本，并以脚本运算处理后触发相对应的剧本，驱动实际场域、虚拟平台。智能环境下建筑物会随着环境、位置以及用户的需求做改变，而其后端的智能系统则如同建筑的大脑般，不仅须具备接收信息以及运算剧本的功能，还需考虑自然环境变动与人类活动等两种涵构信息。[14]

（3）控制层

控制层主要应用于实际场域与虚拟平台。驱动后实际场域由嵌入式系统调适建筑表层，为建筑物与其所在环境之间的接口，以调整建筑立面开口部以适应多样性微气候变化，其中动力构建的设计是模块化以便覆盖建筑表层。虚拟平台则以控制 BIM 模型以可视化接口呈现连动，提供给使用者或管理者所需对应的工作站平台，例如屏幕展示、中心监控、远程监控、行动装置。

4 实作

本研究的智能维运系统实作，以嵌入式平台 Arduino 的感测模块检测阳光、空气、湿度三项环境因子感知环境，进行依用户导向需求的脚本设计，且触发驱动实体进行建筑表层的改变。为延续 IPO 模式运用参数编程引擎 Dynamo 作为剧本层的决策处理，以（1）汇入：汇取环境数据；（2）运算：依照用户导向的复杂条件脚本设计；（3）驱动：以触发的脚本驱动实体、虚拟平台两端。三阶段的实作说明。

（1）汇入

此阶段撷取从嵌入式平台所检测到的环境参数，作为参数编程引擎端口数据的汇入依据。于参数编程引擎中可由节点控制链接嵌入式系统的端口开启与关闭；以布尔数据形态（Boolean）的 True 与 False 节点，以取得 Arduino 的端口编码作为后续调控。并将已撷取到的端口编码以链接形式于 Arduino node 作为开始端，则会得到于真实环境中传感器的参数。本研究以读取阳光、空气、湿度三种模拟数据，读取后并于传感器中所对应的脚位写入，以联结节点进行真实端的数据汇入且读取。

（2）运算

运算端为本研究的实作核心重点，以 python 作为撰写复杂条件的脚本设计。接续上一阶段中所读取到的环境因子数据，需进行数据转换。借由转换值的节点做范围区分，原因是每个传感器所赋予的数值都不尽相同，须将不同的数值转换成相同区间值后才能进行脚本设计。转换后的数据值将以判断是否为紧急状态，若是脚本则进入紧急模式，若否则进入一般模式。

（a）紧急模式

进入紧急模式后，则不做规则式的运算直接驱动实体。此模式可能发生的情况例如：台风、水灾、雾霾等以不危急使用者为优先。

（b）一般模式

进入一般模式后，透过权重排序进行规则式运算。此阶段为 python 进行撰写脚本，故首要条件为环境因子假定为程序所能使用的值。本研究的环境因子有阳光、空气、湿度三种，设定的数值代码为空气以 air、阳光以 sun、湿度以 h 表示。再进行依照以用户需求为导向进行权重的排序。并设定数值以对应区间,本实作以 30～60～90 三区间数值的界定,作为环境数据严重程度的比较,以 0～30 区间内的数值表示此项目环境因子优良,30～60 区间值内则表示普通,60～90 或超过 90 的区间值则表示严重。当撰写脚本的过程中设计者须设定好剧本的思考逻辑,得以套用阶段脚本的运算(图 2)。

以下将进行情境空间、使用者权重排序的剧本说明:使用者所处在的空间为个人工作室,使用者认为三个环境因子中空气质量的需求对于他而言是最重要的,故权重为最高排序、其次为阳光、最低为湿度。

(i)剧本 A——当三项环境数据进入运算阶段中,可以逐级判断进行处理。假如目前 air 数值小于 30,则进入 sun 的层级做判断;若 sun 数值也小于 30,则进入 h 层及做判断;若 h 数值也小于 30,此时则驱动电动机转动至最大角度开窗。此逻辑思考为透过权重排序将数值依次进行判断,若符合则进入下一层级的判断,可知此阶段的数值接小于 30,所以可得知气候状况为空气良好、阳光小、湿度低,故驱动实体将开窗角度转至最大。

(ii)剧本 B——假如目前 air 数值小于 30,进入 sun 层级做判断后得知 sun 的数值大于 30,则进入 30-60 的数值区间进行判断 sun 数值是否符合此区间,是的话则进入 h 层级判断数值是否小于 30 区间值内;若否 h 则再次判断是否介于 30-60 区间内,是的话则驱动至相对应的开窗角度。以此类推脚本的规则。

(3)驱动

以脚本触发后驱动实际场域及仿真平台。实际场域:触发脚本后以伺服电动机驱动实体,使开口部转动至脚本所触发的对应角度,实时回应以产生真实环境中的调适。而虚拟平台:触发脚本后则连动 BIM 中的模型以可视化接口呈现给用户实时查看变化,能借由脚本的触发同时观看模拟状态(图 3)。

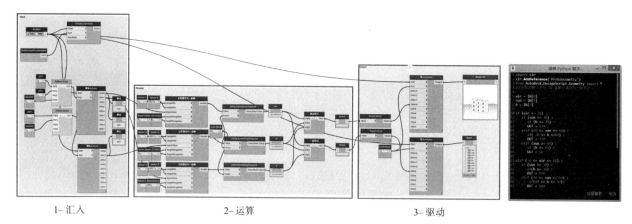

1- 汇入　　2- 运算　　3- 驱动

图 2　以 Dynamo 作为智能维运系统运算

图 3　驱动实体模型

5 结论与建议

本研究以智能化适性建筑，提出 BIM 在建筑物维运使用阶段时出现应用端的典范转移，开发出一套与真实环境互动调适的智能维运系统。利用主动控制动态响应环境，以 BIM 的参数编程引擎 Dynamo 作为撰写脚本且利用嵌入式系统 Arduino 与环境传感器、致动器作为应用平台工具。运用感知模块检测真实环境数据以 Python 编程作为交互式的脚本，设计出规则以及用户需求导向的权重排序运算处理，并触发相对应的动态脚本，以可视化界面实时连动 BIM 模型做互动，调适性使实体模型产生建筑表层的变化。以改变建筑表层的开口部大小改变，响应真实气候环境以有效调解住宅的生活质量。

根据文章中智能维运系统所构成的模式，本研究已完成剧本层中参数编程引擎的脚本运算编写，以复杂条件作为本系统的核心重点。在实作过程中以初步尝试利用不同材料作为建筑表层的驱动实体[15]，以成功达到驱动伺服电动机进行触发脚本的相对应角度进行转动，目前正在进行下一阶段建筑表层实体模块的实际构筑。未来城市中我们所居住的住宅将会负载着各种建筑信息数据，以提供智能维运系统能依据环境以及用户的需求做动态的互动调适，住宅将以智能化的发展进行下一步城市发展。

The Research of Smart Urban Housing via Integrating BIM-based Parametric Programming Engine with Embedded System

Shen Yang Ting, Wu Nien Chin

(School of Architecture, Feng Chia University)

Abstract: This research proposes the smart adaptive building which interacts with its environment during the operation stage. The build with BIM-based management system becomes the green manager to operate eco-friendly. There are three layers to achieve BIM-based management system including (1) monitor layer: sentient performance analysis; (2) script layer: interactive smart System; (3) control layer: adaptive operation management. The BIM-based management system uses parameter-based programming engine and embedded system to operate the interactive adaption of building. It facilitates the automatized green building operation to realize the eco-friendly smart city.

Keywords: Building information modeling, Parameter-based programming engine, Intelligent operation, Adaptive building, Embedded system

参考文献

[1] 沈扬庭. 从仿生建筑到韧性城市的智慧生态地景革命 [J]. 智慧化居住空间，2015.

[2] Sterk T. Using actuated tensegrity structures to produce a responsive architecture. Annual Conference of the Association for Computer Aided Design In Architecture. 2003: 80-93.

[3] 林元兴. 市地利用应加强环境的维护——再论智慧建筑 [J]. 土地问题研究季刊, 2011, 10（1）: 14-28.

[4] Arkin H, Paciuk M. Evaluating intelligent building according to level of service system integration. Automation in Construction, 1997, 6（5-6）: 471-479.

[5] Wigginton M, Harris J. Intelligent Skin[M]. Routledge, 2013.

[6] Yang J, Peng H. Decision support to the application of intelligent building technologies[J]. Renewable Energy, 2001, 22（1）: 67-77.

[7] 郑泰升. 有感觉、会思考与可调适的感性建筑 [J]. 成大研发快讯, 2008: 2（10）: 1.

[8] Eastman C, Teicholz P, et al. BIM handbook: A guide to building information modeling for owners, managers, designers, engineers and contractors[M]. John Wiley & Sons, 2011.

[9] International Facilities Management Association（IFMA）. 2001. https://www.ifma.org/.

[10] Yang Ting Shen, Pei Wen Lu. Development of Kinetic Facade Units with BIM-Based Active Control System for the Adaptive Building Energy Performance Service. The 21st International Conference on Computer-Aided Architectural Design Research in Asia. 2016, 3: 517-526.

[11] Yang Ting Shen, Tien Yu Wu. Sync-BIM: The Interactive BIM-Based Platform for Controlling Data-Driven Kinetic Façade. The 18th International Conference on Human-Computer Interaction, 2016, 7: 445-450.

[12] 陈上元, 沈扬庭, 何妍萱. 发展适性调节皮层应用于环境友善住宅之研究 [G]. 2016 年住宅学会年会暨论文研讨会, D2 不动产居住, 2016, 1.

[13] Dynamo.2017. http://dynamoprimer.com/en/.

[14] 潘晨安. 智能机器建筑的动态表层研究 [D]. 成功大学建筑学系学位论文, 2015.

[15] 沈扬庭, 吴念瑾. 电致变形聚合皮层应用于可调适建筑立面之研究 [G]. 都市计划与空间信息研讨会, 2016, 4.

以网络数据为主体的空间句法模型对城市中心的识别与分析——以吉林市轨道交通项目为例

杨振盛 盛 强 刘 星

（北京交通大学）

摘要：城市的发展离不开轨道交通的支持，轨道交通又反过来促进城市中心的进一步发展提升。网络数据可以从数量、位置等多个角度反映商业。本文以吉林市轨道交通路线的站点选址项目为例进行研究，首先采集网络数据和建立道路网络模型，然后对吉林市城市中心进行识别与分析，最后探讨了城市中心的识别对轨道交通发展的促进作用。本方法可以预测轨道交通路线变化引起的空间参数变化，分析现有站点布局方案并为站点布局提出建议。

关键词：网络数据，空间句法，城市中心，识别，轨道交通

1 引言

随着城市经济的发展，在城市中高强度的集中开发区域，形成了经济活动密集的城市中心，在城市中工作生活和居住的人口不断增多，城市开发区域不断扩大，城市也从单中心向多中心不断发展演变，在发展过程中城市各中心呈现出不同服务职能、不同等级规模以及不同的服务范围，城市各中心之间相互联系，互为补充，统一构成"城市中心体系"。[1] 人是社会活动的主要群体，换言之，城市中心的发展离不开大量的人口支持，没有了大量的人口流动与聚集,城市中心就难以维持长久的稳定发展。而将城市各中心以及城市中心与人联系在一起，最基本的就是城市内部的道路交通系统。道路拥堵的出现，使地铁和轻轨交通的高效便捷优势日益明显，很多城市开始规划布置轨道交通线路。没有良好的道路交通网络，人们无法便捷地到达城市中心接受商业服务，城市中心地区慢慢就会失去它的中心地位，因此可以说轨道交通路线可以支撑和引导城市中心的发展变化。本文主要研究对吉林市城市中心的识别，并指导建议轨道交通站点的选址以促进城市的发展。

随着网络时代的到来、网络数据平台的开放使用以及数据挖掘技术的普及，很多学者开始利用网络数据进行城市中心的识别。郑晓伟基于开放数据对西安的城市中心体系进行识别并提出了相应的优化调整建议，该学者所采集的大众点评网数据，涵盖了城市级和社区级两个不同级别的服务业。[2] 陈蔚珊以面向公众服务的商业机构兴趣点（POI）数据为研究对象，运用核密度法和局域 Getis-Ord G* 指数法识别城市尺度下零售商店分布的集聚区域和热点地区。[3] 米瑞华以现实第六次人口普查常住人口街道（乡镇）数据为基础，同时结合西安市建设用地类型，借助 Arcgis10.0 软件进行人口密度分析，研究识别城市主副中心数量和位置。[4] 钮心毅以移动电话使用过程中所生成的包含个人空间、时间尺度上的行为数据为基础，对上海中心城的城市空间结构进行识别分析。[5] 以上学者借用不同的数据源进行城市中心的识别与分析，相比实地调研采集数据，网络数据可以在短时间内获得大量丰富的数据，但数据库数量的庞大并不代表数据精确性高，周新刚在城市中心识别过程中，以手机定位数据为例探讨了动态数据在进行空间分析时存在的不确定性问题。[6] 对城市中心的识别经常用核密度分析法，核密度分析法是基于功能点的数量关系进行分析，忽视了店铺之间的真实路径连接关系，在实际生活中

必须经过道路网络联系各个功能店铺而不是直线连接。

空间句法是一种用来描述和分析空间的方法,空间句法关注的不是空间本身,而是空间之间的联系,空间句法依赖数学方法寻找空间与各种社会活动之间的关系。空间句法软件 depthmap 依据道路网络建立空间模型,并进行相应的计算自动生成空间分析参数。在针对空间本身分析的基础上,还可以结合餐饮店等实际社会活动数据进行空间相关性分析,对空间与功能进行研究。

2 数据与研究方法

2.1 常用网络数据的对比

在建筑规划领域的研究中,目前常用于科研的网络数据主要包括大众点评网数据、POI 数据、移动用户数据(手机数据、微博数据、定位数据)以及政府公开的普查统计数据(表1)。

常用网络数据对比　　　　　　　　　　　　　　　　　　　　　　　　　表1

数据类型	数据量	等级分类	经纬度地址信息	使用后评价数据
大众点评网	大	一般	有	详细
POI 数据	大	明确	有	无
移动数据	不断增长	不明确	有	无
政府公开数据	小	不明确	很少有	无

大众点评网最具有研究价值的数据是消费者反馈到网站表达主观感受的评分数据,包括人均消费、星级评价、评论数以及各类服务评分等。POI 数据相对大众点评网数据来说,分类等级更明确,数据涵盖范围更广。本研究主要应用了 POI 数据。

2.2 研究方法

首先建立基础模型,本项目团队建立了大区域尺度范围的路网空间模型,涵盖了吉林市及其周边村镇约 5800km² 的广大范围,共计 65104 条街道段。

本研究从两条不同的路径识别城市的中心:一条路径基于 POI 数据在 Arcgis10.2 软件中的空间落位进行核密度分析;另一条路径基于空间道路网络,统计分析每条街道线段上 400m 范围内的商业数量,进而进行城市中心的识别,并借助识别结果对吉林市轨道交通站点的布局方案进行分析(图1)。

图 1　研究流程图

3 吉林市城市中心的识别与分析

3.1 核密度分析法识别城市中心

在本次研究中采集了零售、办公、宾馆、购物这四类 POI 数据。其中零售类 POI 数据 18750 个，数量最多，餐饮类 POI 数据点 16319 个，宾馆类 POI 数据点 1467 个，办公类 POI 数据点 1804 个。分别用以上四类 POI 数据在 Arcgis10.2 软件中进行核密度分析识别城市中心，核密度分析结果会输出密度大小分析图（图2），在本研究中将城市中心分为 A、B、C 三个等级，其中 A 等级城市中的商业店铺密度最高，C 等级店铺密度最低。

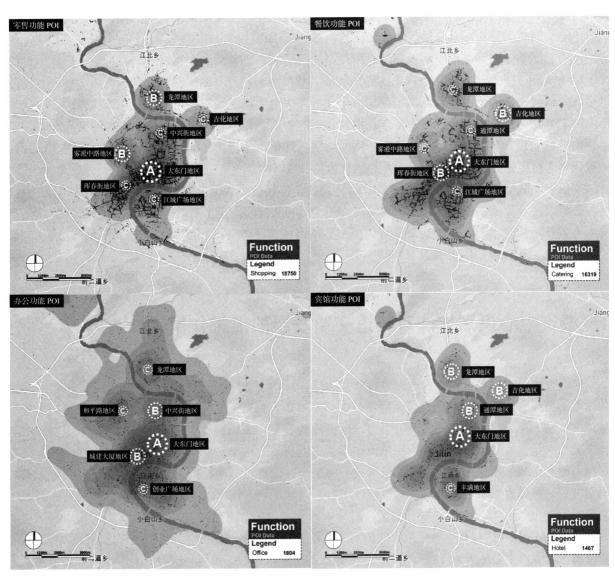

图 2 核密度分析对城市中心的识别

将以上结果进行汇总（表2），大东门地区在各类功能的密度分析中均为最高密度区域，因此识别大东门地区为吉林市的城市主中心，汇总四类功能的密度分析，将龙潭地区，吉化地区、雾凇中路地区、龙潭地区、珲春街地区、通潭地区识别定义为城市副中心，将丰满地区识别定义为第三等级城市中心。

核密度分析城市中心识别汇总表　　　　　　　　　　　　表 2

POI 类型	A 等级	B 等级	C 等级
零售	大东门地区	雾凇中路地区、龙潭地区	吉化地区、珲春街地区、中兴街地区、江城广场地区
餐饮	大东门地区	珲春街地区、吉化地区	龙潭地区、通潭地区、雾凇中路地区、江城广场地区
宾馆	大东门地区	龙潭地区、通潭地区、吉化地区	丰满地区
办公	大东门地区	城建大厦地区、中兴街地区	龙潭地区、和平路地区、创业广场地区

3.2 均匀化方式识别分析城市中心

仅仅以 POI 数量进行核密度分析识别城市中心，会由于高密度 POI 点提升所处地区的密度，比如一个美食城有大量的餐饮店铺会在 Arcgis 的核密度分析中将该美食城地区识别为城市中心甚至高等级城市中心，而对于分布相对分散的美食街而言，如果还用以往的分析方法，将不会被识别为相应等级的城市中心。基于这种城市中心识别途径所存在的问题，本研究团队在路网空间模型中，依靠软件统计了每条线段周围一定半径内的 POI 数，depthmap 软件会根据计算结果赋予每条线段不同的颜色，颜色由红到蓝代表着数值由高到低。这种均匀化分析方法由于每条线段的数值都表达该线段周围一定半径内的 POI 数量，所以相邻线段一定半径均匀化后的数值差异不会很大，基于整体路网引入 POI 一定半径内的均匀化分布结果，当某一片区的路网均呈现红色以及橙黄色等表达高数值的颜色时，该片区即被识别为城市中心，进一步对比 POI 的加总数量对城市中心等级进行分级。

本研究团队结合吉林市路网模型以 400m 为均匀化半径进行分析，城市中心的识别结果如图 3 所示。这种分析方法也反映了实际生活需求，比如 A 地点 400m 外的街道上有餐馆或是购物店铺，当 A 地点的人有餐饮购物需求时，他不会介意只能按照某条路径去往 400m 外的目的地进行活动，这也从侧面表达了 A 地点所在线段的吸引力。

4　城市中心识别方法对轨道交通发展的促进作用

轨道交通路线以各个站点为基础进行联系，当在规划交通路线的站点落位时，会考虑将有限的站点尽可能落位在人流量大的地方。无疑城市中心是城市人口聚集和流动的中心，城市中心区域的 POI 是该区域高人流量高车流量的最大吸引力，也正是基于 POI 去识别城市中心，这也保证了识别方法与轨道交通目标的一致性。成功的识别城市中心，可以有效地指导站点落位在有需求的地理位置上，有效地引导和疏散城市中心的流量，反过来良好的交通又促进城市中心的进一步发展。同时结合未来的规划发展，将站点设置在目前开发程度较低但有着近期规划发展需求的地理位置，将会促进这类地区的迅速发展。

在本次实践项目中，根据城市中心的识别结果将会在大东门地区、珲春街地区、吉化地区、龙潭地区、通潭地区、雾凇中路地区、江城广场地区设置站点疏解城市中心人流量，同时也会考虑在丰满地区设置站点促进该地区的进一步发展。空间句法模型可以从不同尺度预测路网改变以后的空间参数变化，借助模型预测站点的设置是否会提升站点附近区域路网的空间参数，根据以往的研究经验，小尺度的整合度和大尺度的穿行度与人流量和车流量的关联性比较高，因此可以对比轨道交通站点设置前后各个站点区域的整合度与穿行度空间参数的变化情况来评判现有站点布局方案，进一步指导修正站点布局。

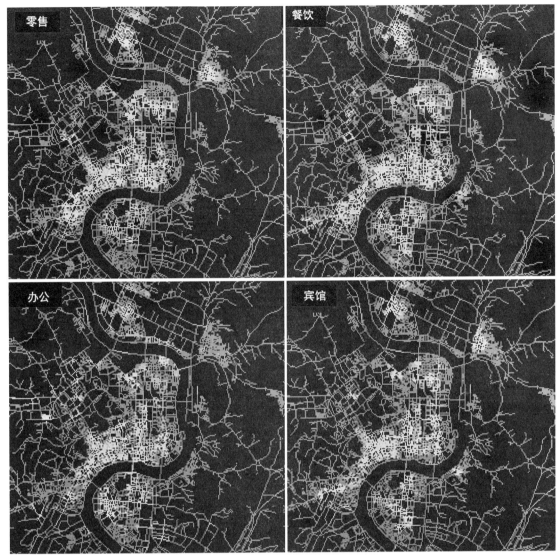

图3 400m半径均匀化对城市中心的识别结果图

The Identification and Analysis of the City Center by the Space Syntax Model Based on Network Data——Jilin's Rail Transit Project

Yang Zhensheng, Sheng Qiang, Liu Xing

(Beijing Jiaotong University)

Abstract: The development of the city is dependent on the support of the rail transit, and the rail transit promotes the further development of the urban center. Network data can reflect business from multiple angles, such as quantity, location, etc. This paper takes the analysis of the Jilin metro station placement as an example. Network data and space syntax model is established first, and then identify and analysis Jilin's city center, finally discusses the effect of the identification of city center on the development of rail transit. This method is used to predict the new parameters caused by the change of rail transit route, analyze the existing site layout plan and make suggestions for the layout of the site.

Keywords: Network data, Space syntax, Urban center, Identification, Rail transit

参考文献

[1] Peopoins J, et al. Street Connectivity and Urban Density: Spatial Measure and Their Correlation [C]. Istanbul: The 6th International Space Syntax Symposium, 2007.

[2] 郑晓伟. 基于开放数据的西安城市中心体系识别与优化 [J]. 规划师, 2017, 1: 57-64.

[3] 陈蔚珊, 柳林, 梁育填. 基于POI数据的广州零售商业中心热点识别与业态集聚特征分析 [J]. 地理研究, 2016, 4: 703-716.

[4] 米瑞华, 石英. 基于常住人口分布的城市主副中心识别方法——以西安市为例 [J]. 陕西师范大学学报（自然科学版）, 2014, 3: 97-102.

[5] 钮心毅, 丁亮, 宋小冬. 基于手机数据识别上海中心城的城市空间结构 [J]. 城市规划学刊, 2014, 6: 61-67.

[6] 周新刚, 乐阳, 叶嘉安, 王海军, 仲腾. 动态数据空间分析的不确定性问题——以城市中心识别为例 [J]. 武汉大学学报（信息科学版）, 2014, 6: 701-705.

社区居民社会聚集的影响：对北京街区公共空间的空间句法分析

刘 星 杨振盛

（北京交通大学建筑与艺术学院）

摘 要：社区户外环境对居民的社会聚集起着重要作用，而空间因素同样也是一个重要原因。本文选取北京胡同和多层住宅两类街区的四个代表性案例，实地调研记录了 2016～2017 年夏、冬两个季度平时和周末户外空间交往状况，并应用空间句法软件对其空间分布机制进行量化性研究。其成果表明，在夏天胡同类街区能更好地支持社会聚集，但是在冬天却恰恰相反。在各街区内部，拓扑肌理相对复杂的道路能更好地支持社会聚集，在胡同街区表现得最为明显。

关键词：社会聚集，公共空间，关联性因素，空间句法

1 研究背景

自与国际接轨以来，中国现代化、工业化的迅猛发展，城市化的进程也大幅度向前迈进。伴随着经济与科技的提升，城市的人口密度与建筑密度都达到了最高点，而更为人性化的设计因素却时常遭忽略，如何在当代城市背景下建设出符合大众心理的、适宜居民使用的公共空间是一项重要任务。社区公共空间，作为城市居民日常生活的起居室，对促进社会交往和提升社区质量方面有至关重要的作用，而社区居民的聚集活动能在很大程度上反映了居民和社区公共空间的关系。探求社区居民的聚集行为和公共空间的关系，提高社区公共空间的使用率是人性化社会亟待解决的问题。

在理论研究领域，对公共空间的户外聚集影响因素的分析一直是环境行为学的基础议题。扬·盖尔在《交往与空间》中便把户外空间活动划分为三种类型：必要性活动、自发性活动和社会性活动，本研究则是对自发形成的社会聚集进行探索分析。近十几年来环境行为学方向的研究者积累了大量基础实证研究。扬·盖尔和怀特提出社会活动很大程度上依赖于户外空间质量[1,2]，他们认为阳光、绿地、基础设施、道路的宽度与铺装等对居民的社会聚集产生影响。在此研究发现的基础之上，又有其他学者对环境因素进行了更细致的研究分析。[3,4]这些研究都很好地证明了户外环境质量对社会聚集的影响。

然而，社区的居民聚集往往不仅受到局部环境因素的影响，作为运动的载体，社会聚集也在很大程度上与运动流产生关系。Hanson 指出，对于设计来说，对空间组织和社会生活的联系认知是最基本的。[5]对于社会活动的空间分析，一方面，纽曼提出空间私密性对于人的空间归属感和社会交往有促进作用[6]，而另一方面，荷兰学者 Maartin Hajer 和 Arnold Reijndorp 提出"阈限型空间"的理念。[7]以上著论对社会活动交往和空间的关系起到很大的推动作用，但缺乏的是对交往行为定性定量的分析方法。Trova 对街区聚集案例进行过分析，其结论大都证实作为驻留行为的社会聚集人群的流动分布具有相似的空间规律。[8,9]经多年的科研积累，空间句法已在运动流量有可观的实证基础研究，被证明空间句法模型能很好地模拟人流运动，以上的研究虽采用了定性定量的分析方法，很好地证明了人流与空间活力的关系，但对数据的收集与细分程度却有不足，本文以空间句法作为理性量化的分析工具，通过大规模的调研与数据的筛选，对公共空间居民交往进行研究。

2 研究方法介绍

2.1 研究区域介绍

本研究的案例社区包括具有明显历史价值的胡同地区，以及新中国成立后建造的多层住宅街区。选择这两类街区主要是因为以下两个方面：首先，胡同作为典型的北京式街道，虽然具有很高的历史价值，但很少用于改造参考，研究其空间逻辑与居民聚集的关系有利于文化的继承。其次，从街区类型来看，胡同街区和多层住宅街区肌理结构相差很大，便于展开分析，以更好地解析空间与社会活动的关系。进而选取了北京街区中比较有代表性的前门大栅栏街区、白塔寺街区此种胡同类街区，以及人定湖周边街区和百万庄街区的大院类四个案例作为研究对象，如图1。大栅栏街区和白塔寺街区为北京传统的胡同地块，人口居住密度较低，居住类型多为低层的四合院。百万庄街区多为苏式老建筑，规划形式和建筑风格统一，多数为多层住宅，少量高层住宅，街区空间更为开放和外向，最为主要的是百万庄地区的小区类型丰富，在街区内部可量化分析其差异。而与百万庄街区相比较，人定湖周边街区住宅类型更加混合，各小区划分更明确。

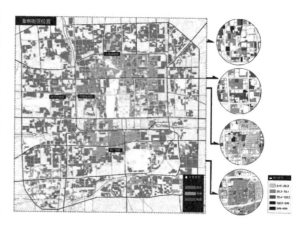

图1 案例街区位置（作者自绘）

2.2 研究方法介绍

本研究以现场行为注记法加快照法为主，访谈法为辅对上述四个案例街区展开户外聚集调研。为弱化偶然因素的影响，本研究在夏季和冬季均选取平时和周末两天中四个时间段（8:00~9:00，10:00~11:00，14:00~15:00，16:00~17:00）进行记录。需要特别说明的是，为了避免既有空间句法研究中快照式调研导致"街上人多则聚集人也多"的问题，本研究在现场记录中排除了必要性的聚集，诸如街道清洁工、商贩或店员、在公交站等车的人群和等待办事的人群，从而过滤出所谓"净"居民的社会聚集。但是，商铺的店员、厕所的清洁工等街头工作者由于在本地长时间的户外工作，与周边居民非常熟识，也往往成为社会交往的催化剂，可以被认为是居民的一分子。因而本研究在进行数据处理的时候，将户外人群分为两类，含与居民交往的工作人员聚集和净居民的社会聚集，如图2。

图2 数据分类方法（作者自绘）

基于上述方法，本研究在2016年夏季以拍照和地图标注方式记录了四个案例区域中共2037个聚集位置，共计6101人次的社会聚集空间分布数据，在2016～2017年冬季记录了450个聚集位置，共计1931人次的社会聚集空间分布数据。

2.3 街区非关联性因素整理

根据各街区的道路形态和住宅类型，将四个案例街区分析整理成为20块地段，记录了各个地块的居民活动情况，如图3。以调研获得的各个区块的居民数、住宅类型、区块面积、街道长度和聚集人数等数据为基础，分别计算了夏季和冬季聚集人口占比，并且计算了单位面积聚集人数和单位长度街道聚集人数，以客观比较各区块的户外空间的使用情况。

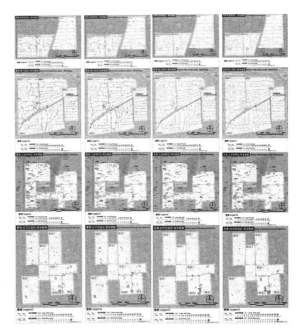

图3 街区社会聚集

2.4 街区关联性因素分析方法

根据城市路网结构，应用depthmap软件建立了深度达到宅前路的细化空间句法线段模型进行量化分析。整合度（integration）的算法含义是计算某条线段到一定几何距离可达范围内所有其他线段的最短拓扑距离（以综合折转角度为定义），它反映了该线段到其他线段的中心性。选择度（choice）算法含义是计算某条线段被一定几何距离可达范围内所有其他任意两条线段之间最短拓扑路径（同样以综合折转角度为定义）穿过的次数。基于这两个基本指标，2012年年底，Hillier、杨滔和Turner提出了标准化角度选择度（简称穿行度，缩写NACH）与标准化角度整合度（缩写为NAIN）这两个指标[10]，其意义在于进一步消除了线段数量对分析效果的影响，实现不同尺度范围和复杂程度空间系统的比较。

3 非关联性空间因素影响分析

以调研数据为基础，将各街区的居住人数、居住面积以及街道长度分别与户外聚集数量做了相关分析（图4），可看出20个地块的居住人数与户外聚集最为相关，所以进一步的研究则以两个季节户外聚集人数占比作为街区公共空间活力的衡量标准进行了分析。

通过对胡同类街区和大院类街区夏季和冬季的空间聚集情况进行比较（图5），显然夏季的居民户外聚集占比要高于冬季，综合比较也可得出，夏季传统的胡同类街区的净聚集人数占比要高于大院类街区。然而，冬季所呈现的数据恰恰相反。产生这种现象的原因，是由于夏季街区的公共空间更多发生的是"外向型"居民聚集，居民活动范围更广，胡同类街区的较开放空间和大院类街区的小区内部公共空间都能很好地支持户外聚集的发生。而在冬季则多数为"内向型"户外空间聚集，由底层住宅组成的胡同类街区的聚集由街道转向了室内，只在更为固定的街道空间发生聚集现象，由多、高层住宅组成的小区内部空间，则受季节的影响小。

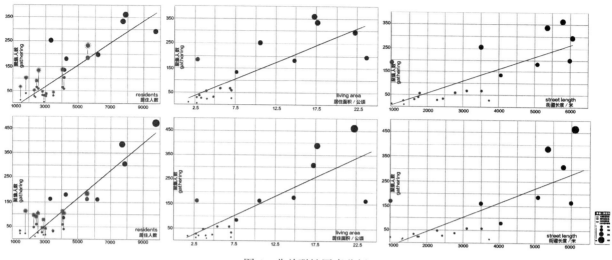

图 4　非关联性因素分析

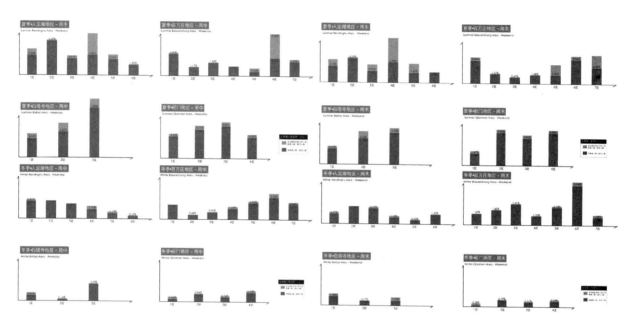

图 5　社会聚集占比分析

进一步分析夏季和冬季两类街区的户外聚集情况，更细部分析 20 个划分的区块，人定湖 2 区块的聚集占比很高，这块区域为高层住宅，得出高层住宅小区的公共空间使用效率较高，并且需要指出的是，百万庄的 4 区块也多为高层住宅，但聚集占比则较低，究其原因是这块区域所提供的经设计的公共空间较少，所以应加强对高层住宅的公共空间建设。人定湖街区的 4 区块、百万庄 6 区块也有很高的聚集占比，但从图表可观察到其提升是由于与工作人员和当地居民发生交往所产生的聚集，如图 6。这个区块内部有更多的小商业据点，促进了户外聚集的发生。相对于大院类，胡同类街区在夏季的户外聚集各区块更为稳定，产生差异也更多是因为商业的影响，例如夏季白塔寺地区的 2、3 区块，要明显高于 1 区块。而冬季 2 区块的聚集人数占比骤减，一是由于调研时天气情况的影响，二是冬季商业对户外聚集的促进作用减弱。

再对冬季的户外聚集情况进行细化研究，发现不同季节两种街区所呈现的现象有相同之处，在胡同类街区和大院类街区都能看出这一现象。在冬季具有可供居民使用的户外公共空间的高层住宅也有很高的户外聚集占比，但不同的是，冬季抑制了商业带来的聚集增长，如白塔寺 2 区块，冬季的聚集

图 6　街区商业占比（作者自绘）

人数占比骤减，还有一部分原因是调研时天气情况所导致。需要进一步剖析的是，在大院类的百万庄街区内，区块 6、7 对户外聚集有很好的支持作用，对比区块肌理能直观看出这两个小区是更开放的组团结构。综合分析得出，在大尺度上，夏季开放式的传统胡同街区要比大院类街区能更好地提升户外聚集的数量，而冬季则是在更小的尺度上体现这一规律，反映出开敞的街区利于居民的户外交往，提升公共空间使用效率，即"开"比"闭"好。

4　关联性空间因素分析

4.1　大尺度分析：对胡同街区和大院类街区整合度和穿行度的分析

在四个街区尺度上，应用加权统计宏观分析了社会聚集的空间逻辑，将户外聚集分为 6 种规模，分析各规模的空间位置在不同尺度半径穿行度和整合度上的统计规律，并比较了不同季节公共空间居民聚集的差异。基于前文四个案例街区的数据整理成果，本部分研究将对各个街区和案例地点内进行各聚集点聚集规模的高精度空间分析，试图发现街区内微观尺度上的公共空间居民聚集规律。图 7 中的表格显示了各案例地区从 3 人以内到 20 人以上，共 6 个级别人数规模的聚集点在空间中的分布情况，其中分整合度和穿行度两类参数列出了各个聚集点位置超过北京全城各半径空间参数平均值的百分比。其超出的比例越高，则说明该级别的聚集对该类空间参数的依赖程度越高。

从图 7 表格统计数据可直接看出，在聚集规模上，冬季和夏季户外的主要差异体现在中等规模聚集数量的不同，受季节的影响大，聚集规模夏季要多于冬季。从大院类街区空间统计数据分析，小规模聚集虽然更多地表现为短暂性停留交往，但小规模聚集所处的公共空间的参数值变化不大，冬季和夏季均发生在小半径范围内空间连接较好的户外空间。大规模聚集的位置和人数都更固定，不随季节的变化而减少。胡同类街区中前门地区虽然聚集数量减少，但聚集点的空间位置连接性提高，发生在更外向的空间。

而从整体来看聚集空间的参数值，夏季和冬季大院类街区的户外活动的整合度半径都很小，传统胡同类街区的要高于大院类，尤其是白塔寺地区。从穿行度的分析结果来看（排除了线段数量影响），两类街区均指向了对小尺度范围高穿行度街道段的依赖，但整体上来看，大院类街区的聚集空间的穿行度要高于胡同类街区。这个结果说明白塔寺和前门胡同区的聚集空间相对于人定湖和百万庄而言更为外向。对比前门与白塔寺，由于前门的外向空间（大半径整合度值高的街道段）多被城市商业占据，社区交往不得不更加深入街区的内部。而在大院类的社区中，人群聚集则更趋向街区深处短距离半径出行路径的汇集路段。

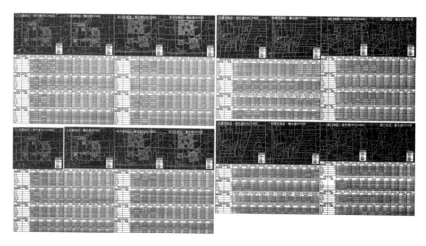

图 7 街区整合度和穿行度分析（作者自绘）

4.2 小尺度分析：在街区尺度内部对标准化整合度的分析

图 8 为对这四个案例的标准化整合度参数分析，该参数能够排除整合度受绘图精度（即线段数量）的影响，更有效地度量道路肌理形态的复杂性。不同于上文在大尺度的宏观分析聚集的空间参数，从更小尺度，各个案例街区内部对社会聚集和公共空间的关系进行了解读。图中各区块标出了该区域内所有街道 800m 半径 NAIN 参数的平均值，通过夏季和冬季总体的统计可以看出，从夏天的数据看，道路肌理相对简单，并且通达性好的公共空间，社会聚集占比更大。而冬天这一规律在更小尺度的单个街区内部被发现。这个初步的发现暗示了街区的空间形态与交往强度有一定的关系，但并不是简单地呈线性的关系，在一定范围内促进户外聚集，易形成户外活力空间，但超过一定数值则会减弱。

图 8 街区标准化整合度分析分析（作者自绘）

5 结论与讨论：走向量化的街区空间活力与交往模型分析

通过对四个地区的夏季和冬季调研统计数据的整理与分析，公共空间对社区居民户外聚集的影响可总结为以下几点内容：

本研究以北京胡同和大院两类街区的四个街区为例，基于对街区居民聚集的实地调研，分析了两个季节户外公共空间居民聚集的差异，从数据统计的结果来看，夏季户外聚集人数要高于冬季，尤其在胡同类街区表现得极为明显，此外中等规模的居民聚集减少最多，并且相对于夏季、冬季的商业据点对户外聚集的促进作用不明显。从空间角度来看，在大规模的街区尺度或更小尺度街区的内部，公共空间的道路肌理较复杂，通达性越好，与外部道路连接越好，则能更好地支持街区居民社会聚集。简言之，通达性通过对外部人流的引入，提升了空间活力，并且单个小规模街区的空间逻辑与多个街区组成的大规模街区有相似的空间逻辑。而未来针对这种形式的量化研究需要在两个层面上继续深入：一是将高精度人口数据落位到更小的空间单元中，引入本地居民密度的参数；另外需要考虑案例周边其他类型商业服务业功能的权重，更为精确地分析对外出行行为空间轨迹分布对聚集的影响。

The Influence of Outdoor Gathering of Community: Space Syntax Analysis on the Public Space in Beijing's Neighborhoods

Liu Xing, Yang Zhensheng

(Architecture and Art Institute of Beijing Jiaotong University)

Abstract: Community outdoor environment plays an important role in residents' gathering, however, the spatial factor is also a leading reason. This paper analyses four case areas which represent two kinds of neighborhoods in Beijing: Hutong and Mega-courtyard composed by multi-story social housing. The research is based on the detail fieldwork mapping of social gatherings in both weekday and weekend in summer and winter of 2016-2017. It also uses space syntax as a main tool to analysis the impact of street pattern. The results show that in the summer, Hutong area can generally support more social gatherings, yet, it is different in winter. While within each type of neighborhood, comparing with the simple rules texture, the street whose topology is relatively complex can better support the social gathering, especially in Hutong area.

Keywords: Social gathering, Public space, Relevance factor, Space syntax

参考文献

[1] Jan Gehl. Life between buildings: using public space[M]. 1987.

[2] Whyte, and william Hollingsworth.The social life of small urban spaces[M].1980.

[3] Zacharias John.Microclimate and downtown open space activity, environment and behavior[J]. 2001, 33.2（2001）: 296-315.

[4] Liu Qinqin. The Relationship Between Community Ambient Environment And Spontaneous Activities of Residents——A Case Study of "DangDai Homeland" community[M]. DeiJing University, 2015.

[5] Hillier, Bill, and Juliene Hanson.The social logic of space[M]. Cambridge: Cambridge university press, 1989.

[6] Newman Oscar. Defensible Space: Crime Prevention through Urban Design[M].New York: Macmillan, 1972.

[7] Hajer M Reijndorp A. In Search of New Public Domain[M]. Rotterdam: NAi Publishers, 2001.

[8] （Manuela Ribeiro）urbanity in brasilia's superblocks [C]. in 10th International Space Syntax Symposium.

[9] Trova V, Hadjinikolaou E, Xenopoulos S, Peponis J, THE STRUCTURE OF PUBLIC SPACEIN SPARSELY URBAN AREAS[C].Proceedings of the second Space Syntax Symposium, Vol.II, Brasilia, 53.1-12.

[10] Hillier, BYang T Turner A. Advancing DepthMap to advance our understanding of cities: comparing streets and cities, and streets to cities[C]. in Eighth International Space Syntax Symposium, 2012.

探讨深度学习在智慧城市中的应用方法：以 AI 风水助手为例

杨金泽[1]　李秋明[2]　邱仁钿[2]　谢尚贤[2]

（1.重庆大学土木工程学院；2.台湾大学土木工程学系）

摘　要：深度学习，即多层人工神经网络，是机器学习的分支。它在智慧城市中的应用潜力巨大，因智慧城市具备深度学习应用的要素，即海量资料和高速计算能力；同时，智慧城市又对于"智慧"有需求，尤其是从大量的时间序列资料或是非结构化资料中提取特征，而深度学习在这个方面已经展现了优异的表现。为了降低深度学习应用于智慧城市的难度，本文提出了一种架构于已有深度学习成果之上的客制化修改方法，它具有易上手、自由度高、适合前期探索的特点。本文将借自制的房屋风水评价深度学习模型 AIFS 雏形做案例分析，详细讲述该方法的操作流程和实作要点。在未来，AIFS 将能够针对更多元的房屋信息进行处理，以得到更全面而准确的评价；另外，AIFS 有望与 BIM 的设计流程做整合以达到前端预测或是后端模拟的效果，进而实现 BIM 的智慧化发展。本文的贡献在于提出了一种架构于已有深度学习成果之上的客制化修改方法并加以实证；制作了 AIFS，可经由户型图评价房屋风水的状况。

关键词：智慧城市，人工智能，深度学习，风水

1　深度学习与智慧城市

深度学习是指多层的人工神经网络，是机器学习的分支。近年来，随着海量数据的存储和处理方式更新，计算机硬件的快速发展，依赖大量数据和高速计算的深度学习在越来越多的领域崭露头角。例如 AlphaGo 击败世界顶尖围棋选手，无人车试验成功，IBM 人工智能 Watson 拯救白血病患者，这些成功案例不仅展示了深度学习的强大威力，更激励着来自其他领域的研究者继续挖掘深度学习的潜在能量。

智慧城市的核心理念是利用新一代信息技术改进政府、企业和居民相互交往的方式，以达到对城市运行中出现的各种需求做出快速、智能的响应，提高城市运行效率，为居民创造更美好的城市生活的目的。[1] 事实上，深度学习与智慧城市有着很好的契合点，其原因有二：第一，在作为"智慧城市大脑"的大数据分析部分中，深度学习有着得天独厚的能力与优势。深度学习最适合于数据庞大、参数之间关系复杂的情况，它已在海量数据的模式识别和趋势预测上表现出了优异成绩。谭娟、王胜春[2]利用大量的道路监测数据配合深度学习制作了交通拥堵预测模型，平均预测精度可达85%；吕启等人[3]利用深度置信网络制作了遥感图像分类模型，经验证其比支持向量机（SVM）及传统的神经网络（NN）方法有更好的分类效果；Elhenawy 等人[4]采用道路传感器回传的数据训练深度学习模型有效预测了司机的紧急刹车反应时间。第二，物联网数据库是深度学习出色发挥的保障。物联网数据库虽然庞大且复杂，但它的数据类型多数为时间序列型。针对这种数据类型的处理，深度学习已初见成效。Peng 等人[5]提出了"识别多时间尺度中互动模式内在动态"方法，这种深度学习模型的每一层捕捉一个具体时间尺度的相关模式。它有望解决诸如水资源分配优化、检测水的渗流、最小化能源需求等问题。深度学习在智慧城市中的应用模式[6]经作者改画为图1，它直观地显示了深度学习在智慧城市中扮演的角色。

深度学习的成绩举世瞩目，但想要引入智慧城市的研究中却并不简单，这其中的挑战之一就是掌握深度学习的使用方法，但是现有的文献中很少有从实用角度讲述深度学习的使用方法。选用已公开

的深度学习成果做客制化修改是一个易上手、速度快、自由度高、适合前期探索的方法，本文将重点讲述这种方法。此外，现在网络上已有足够多的开源模型可供使用，这也使得本文讲述的方法极具实用价值。

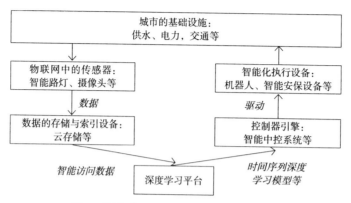

图 1　深度学习在智慧城市中的应用模式

　　本文将采用案例分析的方式，以自制的房屋风水评价深度学习模型 AIFS 为例，详细讲述深度学习模型客制化的方法及流程。AIFS 以中国古典风水理论中"藏风纳气"的部分[7, 8]作为理论基础进行风水评价，其运作的流程如图 2 所示。AIFS 采用自建的户型图数据集进行训练。在深度学习模型的部分，本文选用 Linux、Torch、Caffe 和 NVIDIA 1070 GPU 作为实作的软硬件环境，使用 UC Berkeley 提出的 R-CNN[9] 和牛津大学提出的 VGGNet-16[10] 作为基础进行训练。AIFS 于测试阶段确实能够给出较准确的房屋风水信息。

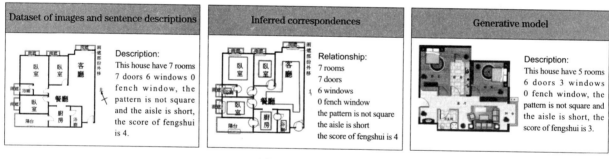

图 2　AIFS 概览图

AIFS 的输入是户型图数据集和对应的图片描述（左），它首先去学习图片与描述的对应关系（中），然后学习去生成新的描述（右）

2　AIFS 实作

2.1　模型分析

　　本次选题"利用户型图辨识风水"，作者先期判断其适用于深度学习技术，原因如下：

　　首先，住宅风水与房屋的户型关系紧密，根据中国经典风水理论中"藏风纳气"的原则，房屋的坐向、空间布局、大门方向、窗户的数量与方向等都直接影响房屋中的气，进而影响风水；其次，识别住宅风水是难以用算法的方式表述清楚的复杂问题。由于判别风水规则的多样性以及边界条件的模糊性,导致风水很难用具体的、硬性的规则去表达;第三,户型图的网络资源丰富,各大房屋交易网站上均能找到,其理论资料量足够大。这样的议题使用深度学习比较当对。

2.2 模型设计

AIFS 明确使用深度学习技术,实现功能是找到户型图和风水描述的内在关系。该模型应使用户型图和风水描述进行训练,学习模式为有监督学习,数据类型为图像和文本,模型的应用模式是分类。由于我们的方法是基于已有的深度学习成果进行客制化修改,因此据此分类的信息在针对深度学习的资源中进行搜索。

2.3 模型实作

AIFS 系统的实作流程如图 3 所示,接下来之后是针对该流程的具体描述。

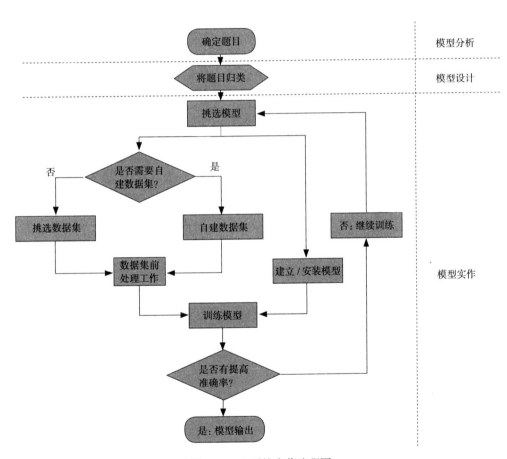

图 3　AIFS 系统实作流程图

2.4 挑选模型

本文使用的是来自 Stanford 计算机视觉团队研发的 Neuraltalk2。[11] Neuraltalk2 是一款"看图说话"的深度学习模型,它使用 VGGNet-16 辨识图片,使用 R-CNN 预测句子中的单词来完成一句话描述。此模型采用 Torch7、Caffe 作为软件框架,使用 Linux 和 GPU 作为实现的软硬件环境。鉴于 Neuraltalk2 在影像描述测试中的优秀表现和基于批处理与 GPU 训练的速度提升,本文选择使用 Neuraltalk2 作为训练用模型。由于模型并非软件，没有成熟的应用市场和完善的安装包可用，因此需要在特定的范围内进行搜寻。现在已有的较成规模的模型库有 Caffe Model Zoo[12]，TensorFlow Models[13]，在这里有经过精选的基于 Caffe 或是 Tensorflow 的深度学习模型可供使用。另外，在全球最大的开源代码库 Github 里面也会找到相当多的模型，但是质量需要读者作进一步辨别。

2.5 建置 / 安装模型

为了阐释清楚安装模型过程中的软件层次关系，本文制作了一个深度学习的层次关系图 4。由于各方软件对 Framework 和 Library 的定义是模棱两可的，为了避免歧义造成读者对此图的误解，本文在此说明他们的不同：需要依赖别的框架 / 库运行的叫作 Library，反之则叫作 Framework。通过考察常用的框架或是库的功能和使用环境，读者会更容易理解两者的区别。另外，在硬件部分，深度学习对 GPU 或 CPU 的要求非常高，视数据量大小要使用一块到多块的处理器才能在短时间完成运算，目前自用计算机最理想的配备是拥有一块具有 CUDA 架构的 NVIDIA GPU。

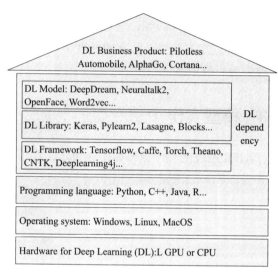

图 4 深度学习的软硬件层次关系图

3 模型训练与测试

3.1 数据集的建立与使用

数据集指的是用于训练模型和测试模型的数据集合，它的大小与质量直接决定了模型的训练效果和最终表现，因此对于数据集的建立和使用需要重视。在本研究中，户型图和风水评价需要做为训练用数据，但现在网络上并没有相关的数据集可用，因此作者选择自建数据集进行训练。在数据集的建立方法上，本文选择仿照相似的知名数据集进行自制。本文以微软的 MScoco[14] 为模板，建立了一个拥有近 2000 张户型图的风水标注数据集，其中户型图以 jpg 格式存储，风水描述以英文书写在 json 档案中，与户型图通过档案名进行匹配。

在建立标注的方式上，给上千张的户型图进行标注是一个大问题。通过拜访资深的建筑师，我们初步选择了几条简易判别风水原则：1. 房屋方正为吉；2. 没有狭长走道为吉；3. 房屋通风状况良好，没有正对的门窗为吉。通过这三条规则，作者使用人工生成对风水的关键描述，再利用机器补足其他部分，最终形成的户型图与风水描述的样例如图 5 所示。这种方式实为折中之举，也从一个侧面凸显出建筑相关数据集的缺失情况。

图 5 数据集中的内容与存储形式

3.2 模型的训练与测试

在训练部分，本模型的表现采用"损失函数"来评估。模型每训练 2500 次就会进行一轮评估，一次评估的图片数量为 50 张，若准确率有上升则将模型输出一次。

在测试部分，作者将测试户型图分为了相似与相近两类，每类 50 张图片。其中相似户型图与训练用图来源相同，相近户型图则来自于其他网络资源。为了得到较为准确的评估结果，除了整段的风水描述，它还被分解为三句和五句两种形式，其中三句的形式全部是对门窗、房间数量的描述，五局描述还另外包含房屋方正和狭长走道的判断。通过人为评估单个评价的对错，再除以所有评价的数量，我们得到如下的准确率条形统计图，如图 5。

从测试结果能够看出，AIFS 不论在哪种情况下都能得到超过 40% 的准确率，说明它确实具有一定的风水判别能力；仔细来看。AIFS 在进行综合性判断时效果较好，在进行单一的数量分类效果不如前者，这很可能是由于原模型并非是设计来计数的。另外，AIFS 对于与训练数据相差较悬殊的户型图表现也十分出色，这也初步展示了 AIFS 对于风水评估的泛化能力。碍于现有训练集的不足，目前达到的准确率并不令人满意，但是随着数据集的加大，准确率会逐步上升。根据原模型的测试数据[11]，其准确率有望达到 65%，如图 6。

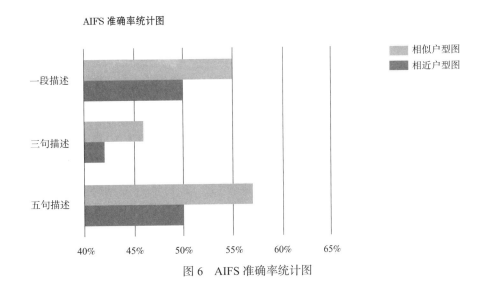

图 6　AIFS 准确率统计图

4　结论

本文建立了一套深度学习模型客制化使用流程，通过实作 AIFS 详细讲解了其中诸多难点，并给出解决建议。文章重点着墨于模型的挑选和数据集的建立部分，以帮助读者利用已有的算法处理自有数据。结果测试部分，AIFS 确能具备一定的评判能力，且其建置速度快，上手难度小。文章通过 AIFS 的表现和 AIFS 建立过程证明了该方法的有效性和快速、轻量的特性。

在研究不足和未来展望的部分，由于本研究缺乏标准的数据集，因此测试结果难以衡量好坏。在研究进行中作者深刻体会到数据集的重要性，以及自建数据集的难度。囿于现实，本研究只能使用较少量的粗糙数据进行训练，其准确度和泛化能力非常受限。因此，在未来作者将会致力于数据集的量质改善，以期得到更好的表现。

此外，本研究只是采用了户型图作为评判风水的依据，这在传统风水学来看是不够全面的。想要将风水判断得全面且具体，判断的依据除了房屋户型外还需要囊括房屋周遭的地理环境，甚至使用者本身的命格特性，因此想办法增加输入的信息类型是 AIFS 继续发展的方向。BIM 的出现给了我们改进信息源的启发，现在 BIM 可以与 GIS 地理信息系统做结合，其几何模型信息可使用 XML 格式，非几何信息可使用 json 格式进行导出。结合这些数据，AIFS 将能"思考"得更全面，更智能。

同样的，以 AIFS 为代表的深度学习的成果也将对 BIM 的智能化起到促进作用。通过将深度学习模型应用在 BIM 系统设计的前端或者后端，它可以实现对 BIM 的前置性预测或是后置性优化。以 AIFS 为例，通过学习房屋信息与风水的关系，AIFS 最终可以根据业主的风水需求预测出 BIM 模型的周遭环境、内部布局等；或是将设计完成的 BIM 模型导入深度学习模型进行评价或是模拟，以此得到优化方向或改善建议。

致谢

感谢蔡亮廷在模型训练上的帮助；感谢杨懿、张引玉、萧中荣在数据集制作中的支持；感谢萧中荣提供的科学风水评价标准；感谢张泽中的爬虫程序。

Customize Deep Learning for Smart City: AI-based Feng Shui Assistant as An Example

Yang Jin-Ze [1], Lee Chiu-Ming [2], Chiou Jen-Dian [2], Hsieh Shang-Hsien [2]

(1. Chongqing University; 2. Taiwan University)

Abstract: Deep learning, or deep neural network, is a sub-discipline of machine learning. It has big potential on Smart City issues for two reasons. First, Smart City has the foundation of big data resources and parallel computing capacity to afford deep learning technology. Second, Smart City needs to extract smartness from the features in the time sequence data and unstructured data the city owns, and deep learning has shown good performance on this aspect. In order to ease the use of deep learning for Smart City, this paper presents a method to customize deep learning model for Smart city issues. This method can help users build up their own deep learning model quickly and freely fit their needs. To investigate and demonstrate the applicability of this method, this paper performs a case study with reconstructive deep learning model AIFS, which can give Feng-Shui comments on given floor plans.

Keywords: Smart City, Deep learning, Artificial intelligence, Feng-Shui

参考文献

[1] 巫细波，杨再高. 智慧城市理念与未来城市发展 [J]. 城市发展研究，2010，11：56-60+40.

[2] 谭娟，王胜春. 基于深度学习的交通拥堵预测模型研究 [J]. 计算机应用研究，2015，10：2951-2954.

[3] 吕启，窦勇，牛新，徐佳庆，夏飞. 基于 DBN 模型的遥感图像分类 [J]. 计算机研究与发展，2014，9：1911-1918.

[4] Elhenawy，M，El-Shawarby，I，Rakha，H. Modeling the Perception Reaction Time and Deceleration Level for Different Surface Conditions Using Machine Learning Techniques. Advances in Applied Digital Human Modeling and Simulation[M]. Springer International Publishing，2017.

[5] Peng，H K，and Marculescu，R. Multi-Scale Compositionality：Identifying the Compositional Structures of Social Dynamics Using Deep Learning[M]. PloS one，2015，10（4）：e0118309.

[6] Prateek，J. Deep Learning For Smart Cities，2016. https：//prateekvjoshi.com/2016/07/05/deep-learning-for-smart-cities/ [Accessed on 2017-4-20].

[7] （明）王君荣. 图解阳宅十书 [M]. 北京：华龄出版社，2012.

[8] 于希贤. 现代住宅风水. 北京：现代知识出版社，2010.

[9] Girshick R，Donahue J，Darrell T，Malik J. Rich Feature Hierarchies for Accurate Object Detection and Semantic Segmentation. Proceedings of the 2014 IEEE Conference on Computer Vision and Pattern Recognition，2014：580-587.

[10] Simonyan K，and Zisserman A. Very Deep Convolutional Networks for Large-Scale Image Recognition[J]. Computer Science，2014.

[11] Karpathy，A.，Li，F. F.，Deep Visual-Semantic Alignments for Generating Image Descriptions. IEEE Transactions on Pattern Analysis & Machine Intelligence，2014：3128-3137.

[12] Lin T Y，Maire M，Belongie S，Bourdev L，Girshick R，Hays J，Perona P，Ramanan D，Zitnick C L，and Dollar P. Microsoft COCO：Common Objects in Context. 2015，8693：740-755.

[13] Caffe Model Zoo，2017. http：//caffe.berkeleyvision.org/model_zoo.html [Accessed on 2017-4-20].

[14] TensorFlow Models，2017. https://github.com/tensorflow/models [Accessed on 2017-4-20].

附 录

第十二届中国城市住宅研讨会论文全文收录列表

Appendix

List of Full Papers Included in the 12th China Urban Housing Conference

注释： 因图书出版的页数考量，本论文集纸质书部分仅包含部分收录的论文全文。获第十二届中国城市住宅研讨会收录之所有论文的电子全文已载入本书附配光盘中。所有收录论文之标题和作者已列入本论文集纸质书附录。

Annotation: Considering the limitation for book pages, this book only includudes part of the accepted full papers. The CD-ROM attached with this book contains the electronic text of all the accepted papers. Title and author information of all accepted papers is listed in the appendix.

特 邀 论 文
Invited Paper

共享、特色、节约：保障性住房创新设计的探索
Sharing, Characteristic and Saving: Exploring the Innovative Design of Affordable Housing
李振宇　孙二奇
Li Zhenyu, Sun Erqi

我国既有住区建筑居住品质问题研究与实践概观
The Conspectus of Research and Practices on Residential Building Qualities in China
范　悦　董　丽　李翥彬
Fan Yue, Dong Li, Li Zhubin

多元文化视角下的城市回族社区居住空间形态研究：以济南北大槐树回族社区为例
Study on the Living Space of Urban Hui Nationality Community from the Perspective of Multiculturalism: Taking Jinan Beidahuaishu Community as An Example
曾　鹏　李若冰　浦　钰
Zeng Peng, Li Ruobing, Pu Yu

传统村落人居环境营建的生态智慧探讨
The Ecological Wisdom on the Construction of the Human Settlements for the Traditional Village
曾　卫　朱雯雯
Zeng Wei, Zhu Wenwen

中美城市居住区步行友好性比较研究——武汉与奥斯汀的六个居住区实证研究
Comparative Study on Neighborhood Walkability between Chinese and American Cities——Empirical Study on Six Neighborhoods in Wuhan and Austin
彭　雷
Peng Lei

隔热涂料在建筑中应用的节能评价方法探讨
Discussion on the Energy Saving Evaluation Method of Heat Insulating Coatings Used in the Buildings
范宏武
Fan Hongwu

Building E-pathy City from an Age-friendly Unit
从长者友善单元建立同理城市
Chang Ping Hung Wallace
郑炳鸿

Travel in Tin Shui Wai as A Housewife
师奶的天水围之旅
Wang Danning
王丹凝

基于 BIM 的主动式防灾通知系统之即时通信架构设计
Communication Framework Design for a BIM-based Proactive Security Messaging System
郭韦良　李秋明　吴轩竹　谢尚贤
Kuo Wei-Liang, Lee Chiu-Ming, Wu Hsuan-Chu, Hsieh Shang-Hsien

SENS project: A User Experience Approach for Smart Energy Environment
SENS：以使用者经验探讨智慧电能环境之互动体验模式
Chang Teng-Wen, Huang Hsin-Yi, Sambit Datta
张登文　黄馨仪　Sambit Datta

建筑屋顶绿化对于顶楼空间降温效益的评估研究：以高雄市建筑为例
The Evaluation of the Roof Greening Benefits for the Roof Space Floor Cooling: A Case Study of the Building in Kaohsiung City
程达隆　李彦颐　张七斗　林嘉雄
Cheng Da-Long, Li Yen-Yi, Chang Chi-Tou, Lin Chia-Hsiung

住区规划、设计与住宅类型研究
Residential Planning, Design and Housing Typology Research

上海围合式住宅理想模型设计研究
Research on the Ideal Model of Shanghai Enclosed Housing
卢　斌
Lu Bin

北方家属楼的特征性演变：以哈尔滨职工住宅为例
Characteristic Evolution of Northern Family Building: Cases of Harbin Staff Housing
顾　闻　李振宇
Gu Wen, Li Zhenyu

住宅通用化设计之课题与实践——以台北市兴隆公共住宅为例
The Subject and Practice of Universal Design in Residential Projects: Taking Taipei Xinglong Public Housing Project as An Example
高文婷　郑人豪　陈雅芳
Kao Wen-Ting , Cheng Jen-Hao, Chen Ya-Fang

Housing As Urban Design
住房作为城市设计
Genasci Donald
Genasci Donald

从开放社区到三维都市：中国当代社会住宅建筑设计趋势与方法研究
From Open Community to Three-dimensional City: Research on the Tendency and Methods of Social Housing Design in China
孙二奇

Sun Erqi

以 Upside-down 体系为核心的住宅适应性设计研究
Research on the Adaptability Design of Residential Buildings Based on the Upside-down System
欧阳文　甘振坤　张　超　陈婉蓉　倪晨辉　陈　旭
Ouyang Wen, Gan Zhenkun, Zhang Chao, Chen Wanrong, Ni Chenhui, Chen Xu

基于"紧缩居住"理念的高层住区交往空间重塑
Reshaping the Communication Space of High - rise Residential Buildings Based on the Idea of " Tightening Dwelling"
黄梓薇　项星玮　沈　杰
Huang Ziwei, Xiang Xingwei, Shen Jie

外廊式集合住宅中外廊空间邻里交往研究——广州深圳 6 个典型案例的比较分析
Residential Neighborhood Communication Space in the Veranda Style House——A Case Study of Six Typical Gallery House in Guangzhou and Shenzhen
郭　萌　杜宏武
Guo Meng , Du Hongwu

中外文化的交融在近代闽南侨乡民居中的体现
The Blending of Chinese and Foreign Culture in the Houses of Overseas Chinese in South Fujian
卢汀滢　边如晨
Lu Tingying, Bian Ruchen

大连市既有坡地住区实例调研及剖面构成方式研究
Study on Realistic Research and Sectional Configuration of Existing Hillside Residence in Dalian
沈莉丽　范　悦　姚小虹　李　曼　刘梦潇　王　翔
Shen Lili, Fan Yue, Yao Xiaohong, Li Man, Liu Mengxiao, Wang Xiang

共享园林"园中园"创意与营造实践
Creative Concept and Practice of Shared Garden Space
吴永发　张　玲
Wu Yongfa , Zhang Ling

基于空间布局形态的住栋环境要素分类研究
Research on the Classification of Environmental Factors Based on the Layout Pattern between Buildings
张明科　范　悦　高　莹　赵　涛
Zhang Mingke, Fan Yue, Gao Ying, Zhao Tao

日本资源循环型住宅长寿命技术研发及其启示
Discussion about the Long-life Technology System of Resource-recycling Housing in Japan
朱启东　范　悦　李国鹏
Zhu Qidong, Fan Yue, Li Guopeng

The Integration of Traditional Chinese Building Concepts with Contemporary Ecological Design Considerations: Wood High-rise Buildings
融合中国传统建筑概念与现代生态设计：木质高层建筑
Zhuo Xiaoying, Shane Ida Smith
卓晓瀛　Shane Ida Smith

基于性能差异的既有住区建筑层级化初探
Preliminary Study on the Hierarchy of Existing Residential Buildings Based on Performance Difference

赵　涛　范　悦　王轶鸥　李汀蕾
Zhao Tao, Fan Yue, Wang Yiou, Li Tinglei

北京四合院建筑形制和气候适应性中阴阳关系的解读
The Interpretation of Yin Yang of the Forms and Climatic Adaptation in Beijing Courtyard House

郭　聪　王惜春　戴　俭
Guo Cong, Wang Xichun, Dai Jian

大连市既有住宅功能性品质提升目标与策略的思考
Thinking on Target and Strategy in the Functional Quality Improvement of Urban Existing Residential Buildings in Dalian

吴新杰　索　健　范　悦
Wu Xinjie, Suo Jian, Fan Yue

维也纳社会住宅的可持续整合性设计策略：以 **Mautner-Markhof** 为例
Sustainable Integrated Design Strategies of Social Housing in Vienna

胡裕庆　李振宇
Hu Yuqing, Li Zhenyu

既有住区底层开放空间的功能构成及布局研究
Research on the Function Composition and Layout of the Bottom Open Space in the Existing Residential Area

王轶鸥　范　悦　赵　涛　李汀蕾
Wang Yiou, Fan Yue, Zhao Tao, Li Tinglei

开放社区的规划设计途径——由"打破小区围墙"引发的思考
Design Methods for Planning of Open Communities——Based on the Thought of "Breaking Walls of Communities"

谢淑姣　陈鹏远
Xie Shujiao, Chen Pengyuan

密度视角下城市住区公共空间环境特征研究初探
Research on the Public Space's Environmental Features of Urban Residential Area Based on Density Perspective

鲍　莉　湛　洋　詹佳佳
Bao Li, Zhan Yang, Zhan Jiajia

碎片整理：针对未来租赁住房的开放建筑新模式
Defragmentation: Open Building as A Strategy for Future Rental Housing

姚严奇　李振宇
Yao Yanqi, Li Zhenyu

The Study of Seating Space in Public Rental Housing Community in Hong Kong
香港公屋休憩社区休憩空间的探索
Li Jiayu
李嘉瑜

寒地城市住区室外公共空间居民使用受限情况改善——以沈阳浑南新区新建居住片区为例
The Improvement of the Situation that the Use of Outdoor Public Places Restricted by Residents in Cold Urban Residential District ——A Case Study of A New Residential District in Shenyang Hunnan New District

张东潇　高智慧　刘玥彤　胡　帅

Zhang Dongxiao, Gao Zhihui, Liu Yuetong, Hu Shuai

城市交界空间激活策略初探

Study on the Activating Strategy of Interface Space between Urban Quarters

袁成龙　鲍　莉

Yuan Chenglong, Bao Li

基于当代社会低活力背景下的新型集合住宅公共交往空间探索

The Public Communication Space of Collective Housing Based on the Low Vitality Background of the Contemporary Society

韩赟聪

Han Yuncong

城乡规划与人居空间设计
Urban-Rural Planning and Human Habitat Design

An Evaluation of Effectiveness of Overall Land Use Planning on Urban Growth——A Case Study of Nanjing City, China

城市增长视角下土地利用总体规划的效果评价——以南京市为例

Chen Zhe, Shen Suyan

陈　哲　沈苏燕

通用设计理念应用于台北地下步行街的评价研究

Application of Universal Design Concept for Evaluating Underground Pedestrian Street in Taipei

黄媖露　许伟深

Huang Yinglu, Xu Weishen

雨水花园在居住区景观设计中的应用——以石家庄淳茂生态城为例

The Rain Garden Application in Residential Area Landscape Design——Take Shijiazhuang Chunmao Eco-city for Example

高力强　白洁媛　文瑞琳

Gao Liqiang, Bai Jieyuan, Wen Ruilin

洮南市城市收缩的表现特征及精明成长策略研究

Research on Performance Characteristics and Smart Development Strategy of Shrinking Cities——Taonan City as An example

何邕健　杨　琳

He Yongjian, Yang Lin

城市滨水区步行环境使用后评价（POE）研究：以天津城市主中心海河沿岸为例

Post Occupation Evaluation on the Pedestrian Environment of Urban Waterfront: A Case Study of Haihe River in Tianjin

梁　晨　曾　坚　张雅鹏

Liang Chen, Zeng Jian, Zhang Yapeng

城乡关系重构背景下村落人居环境提升策略研究：以柳州环江村为例

The Integrated Strategies Research for Improving the Rural Human Settlements Environment under the Reconfiguration of Urban-Rural Relation: A Case Study in Huanjiang Village of Liuzhou City

张　恺　李　乘　沈　杰

Zhang Kai, Li Cheng, Shen Jie

Village Planning Adapted to China Planning System and Urban Rural Integration

适应中国规划体系和城乡统筹的村庄规划

Zheng Shujian

郑书剑

新常态背景下社区精明增长理论与实践研究：以武汉市钢花社区为例

Research on the Theory and Practice of Community Smart Growth under the Background of New Normal: Wuhan City Steel Community as An Example

陈　笛

Chen Di

From Gentrification to Studentification: A Case Study of HEMC in Guangzhou, China

从绅士化到学生化的演变——基于中国广州大学城的案例研究

Liu Yongshen

刘永深

可持续城市规划的水系统规划——构建现代城市水利系统关键技术探索

The Core System Research for the Sponge City——Study on Key Technologies of Modern Urban Water System

文　艳　徐辉荣　刘海洋

Wen Yan, Xu Huirong, Liu Haiyang

EPC-PPP 模式下建构小城镇全域旅游体系的探索与实践：以开化县域的整体营造为例

Exploration and Practices through Reconfiguration of Region-based Tourism System in Small Towns under the EPC-PPP Model: A Case Study of Comprehensive Construction in Kaihua County of Zhejiang Province

李　乘　沈　杰　唐玉田

Li Cheng, Shen Jie, Tang Yutian

产城融合路径下大城市边缘区人居环境提升的规划策略：以天津市西青区为例

The Urban Settlement Improvement Planning Strategy in Major City Fringe with Combination of Industry and City Approaches: A Case Study of Xiqing District

赵紫含　李津莉　鲁世超

Zhao Zihan, Li Jinli, Lu Shichao

Pro-growth Coalition of the Local Political Economy and the Contemporary Upsurge of Sustainable Urbanism in China: Three Cases in Shenzhen

城市增长联盟与可持续城市化策略：以深圳三个新城建设为例的研究

Fu Yang, Zhang Xiaoling

符　阳　张晓玲

小城镇绿色基础设施的现状问题及其规划对策探讨：以浙江海宁市盐官镇为例

Discussion on the Present Situation and Planning Strategies of Green Infrastructure in Small Towns: A Case Study of Yanguan Town, Haining City, Zhejiang Province

胡鹏宇

Hu Pengyu

Communities Inside the Ruins: A study of the Nature of Communities in Abandoned Buildings in Manila as An Alternative Housing Solution for Urban Areas

废墟内的社区：作为城市地区替代住房解决方案的马尼拉废弃建筑物性质研究

Mar Lorence G. Ticao

Mar Lorence G. Ticao

绿色建筑与可持续环境设计
Green Building and Sustainable Environment Design

空调影响下的室内环境分析及改良措施研究:以 8 号公寓一宿舍为例
Research on Indoor Environment Analysis and Improvement Measures under the Influence of the Air Conditioning: Case Study of A Room in Apartment 8
程佳伟 夏海山
Cheng Jiawei, Xia Haishan

A Study of the Energy Conservation Potentials of Earth Sheltered Housing for Purposes of Urban Scale Developments
覆土建筑的节能潜力在城市开发尺度的研究
Jideofor Akubue, Liu Suya
安 赛 刘素雅

应对雾霾——人口结构变迁下的城市旧有住宅的弹性转型与有机更新
Responding to the Fog —— The Elastic Transformation and Organic Renewal of the Old Residential Buildings under the Changing Population Structure
田 昊 周 博
Tian Hao, Zhou Bo

The Study on Land Population Carrying Capacity Based on Comprehensive Evaluation of Ecological Sensitivity: A Case of Hangzhou Downtown
基于生态敏感性综合评价的杭州市土地人口承载力研究
Gao Yanfei, Zhang Yuanzhi
高燕飞 张渊智

基于家庭尺度的混合形态社区居民碳排放影响因素研究:以天津为例
Study On Influencing Factors of Family Carbon Emissions from Mixed Form Community
亢梦荻 杨 琳 陈 天
Kang Mengdi, Yang Lin, Chen Tian

基于最小干预度原则的既有多层住宅节能改造模式研究
Energy-efficient Mode of Existing Multi-story Residential Based on the Minimum Interference
常 艺 宋 昆
Chang Yi, Song Kun

基于 LEED ND 绿色社区认证体系的新区慢行交通系统构建:以成都天府新区科学城为例
The Construction of Walkable Streets in New District Based on the Certification Standards of LEED ND: Take Chengdu Tianfu New Area Science City as An Example
曾 晶 郝桐平 吴亚芯
Zeng Jing, Hao Tongping, Wu Yaxin

从居民需求视角反思既有居住建筑节能改造:以大连市为例
A Rethinking of Residential Building Renovation in Terms of Occupant's Needs: A Case Study of Dalian City
刘昕宇 李翥彬 兰凯斐
Liu Xinyu, Li Zhubin, Lan Kaifei

小区型高楼住宅配置水绿规模改善热岛效应策略之仿真研究

Simulation Study on the Strategy of Equipped with Water and Green Areas on Alleviating the Heat Island Effect of the Scale of Residential Buildings

王文安　董思伟

Wang W.-A., Tung S.-W.

低层住宅改变楼板与开口规模对通风降温舒适度效益之研究

Study on the Effect of Changing the Floor and Opening Scale on the Comfort of Ventilation and Cooling in Low-rise Residential Buildings

王文安　董思伟

Wang W.-A., Tung S.-W.

动态建筑屋顶：可回应式智能建筑应用于室内外空气品质环境自动调节之研究

Kinetic Building Roof: Research on the Application of Intelligent Response Building to Indoor and Outdoor Air Quality Adaption

沈扬庭　林佳汶

Shen Yang-Ting, Lim Chiawen

居住区能耗总体平衡模式研究——以瑞士 More than housing 住区为例

Overall Energy Consumption of Living quarters: Take A Living Quarter in Zurich as An Example

韩鹏瑞

Han Pengrui

Comparison of the Guidelines for Heat Island Countermeasures in China and Japan

中日城市热岛应对技术标准的比较分析

Li Qiong, Yoshida Shiji

李　琼　吉田伸治

热带城市私人住宅的被动式设计方法研究：以越南岘港市为例

Passive Design Methods of Private House in Tropical Climate: Danang City, Vietnam

鲍　莉　Duc Vien LE

Bao Li, Duc Vien LE

中国大陆性气候下大进深内室住宅的多重适应性研究

Study on the Multi-adaptability of Deep-plan Residential Building with Inner Rooms for China's Continental Climate

吕爱民　宣　湟

Lv Aimin, Xuan Huang

浅谈导光管采光技术在城市住宅地下空间中的设计和应用

The Design and Application of Tubular Daylighting Technology in the Underground Space of Urban Residence

严文婷　李俊领

Yan Wenting, Li Junling

Thermal Profiles of A High Density City

高密度城市热剖面

Maing Minjung

孟玫廷

Urban Heat Island Effect (UHI) Analysis of Hangzhou Based on Remote Sensing

杭州市城市热岛效应初探
Wang Siqiang, Xiang Meng, He Yanan, Zhang Yuanzhi
王思强 向 萌 何亚男 张渊智

Urban Impervious Surface Extraction Using Satellite Images in Shenzhen
深圳市城市不透水面遥感研究初探
Zhang Yuanzhi, Yu Qing, Li Yu
张渊智 余 青 李 煜

人居环境更新、改造与历史活化
Renewal, Transformation and Activation of Human Habitat

重庆抗战时期名人旧居选址特征研究
The Site Selection Research on Chongqing Celebrities' Former Dwellings during War of Resistance Against Japan
何 媛
He Yuan

自下而上的城市更新与居住形态演变：以田子坊为例
Bottom-up Urban Renewal and Residential Morphology Development: A Case Study of Tianzifang
朱晓宇
Zhu Xiaoyu

大连市既有住宅节能改造项目实态及问题研究
Research on the Status and Problems of Energy-saving Renovation Project of Existing Residential Buildings in Dalian
王 翔 范 悦 赵 涛
Wang Xiang, Fan Yue, Zhao Tao

Land Readjustment as A Solution to the Dilemma of Urban Village Redevelopment in China: A Case Study of Yiwu
以义乌为例探讨解决中国城中村改造困境的方案：土地调整模式
Yuan Dinghuan, Yau Yung, Li Ruoshi
袁定欢 邱 勇 李若诗

日本长期优良住宅认定制度对我国既有居住建筑改造的启示
The Inspirations from Japanese Long-life Quality Housing to Chinese Residential Building Renovation
李翥彬 兰凯斐
Li Zhubin, Lan Kaifei

基于集成体系的既有住宅室内空间改造可视化研究
Visualization Research of Existing Residential Interior Space Transformation Based on the Integration System
王 悦 范 悦
Wang Yue, Fan Yue

存量背景下上海老旧社区更新的价值导向与规划实践
The value Orientation and Planning Practice on Old Residential Renewal of Shanghai in the Background of Inventory Planning
匡晓明 陆勇峰 丁馨怡

Kuang Xiaoming, Lu Yongfeng, Ding Xinyi

城市更新过程中：住宅建筑遗产的真实性修复与节能策略平衡
Urban Regeneration: Balance Ways between the Residential Built Heritage's Authenticity Restoration and Energy Saving Strategies
朱晓敏
Zhu Xiaomin

触媒理论引导下的社区更新模式探讨：以可食地景为例
Research on Community Sustainable Renewal Based on City Catalyst Theory: A Case of Edible Landscape Construction
徐晓岛
Shyu Shyaodao

"城中厂"的紧凑型居住化改造探索：嘉兴市民丰造纸厂、冶金机械厂的改造经验
The Re-habitation of Town Factories and the Construction of High Density Life: the Experience on the Regeneration of Jiaxing Min Feng Paper Factory and Machinery Factory
邝远霄　李振宇
Kuang Yuanxiao, Li Zhenyu

精明增长下的旧城区铁路沿线立体空间混合功能开发研究——以北京市通州老火车站地区为例
Study on Mixed-use Development of Three-dimensional in Railway Space in Old Downtown under the Smart Growth Theory——Take Old Railway Station of Tongzhou as An Example
龙林格格　甘振坤　张大玉
Long Lingege, Gan Zhenkun, Zhang Dayu

基于领域行为理论的既有住区公共空间改造研究：以苏州为例
A Study on the Transformation of Public Space in Existing Residential Area Based on the Theory of Field Behavior: Taking Suzhou as An Example
胡　莹　汪文韬
Hu Ying, Wang Wentao

语用思维下长影旧址街区的保护与更新
The Context of Pragmatic Thinking Projected Changchun Site Blocks' Protection and Renovation
刘　岩　高雁鹏　付艳华　刘生军
Liu Yan, Gao Yanpeng, Fu Yanhua, Liu Shengjun

社会空间博弈下城市与住房的转型机制研究——以苏州山塘街为例
A Study on the Transformation Mechanism of Cities and Housing under the Social Space Scramble——A Case Study of Shantang Street
郑　玥　胡　莹
Zheng Yue, Hu Ying

保障性住房与房地产市场管理
Affordable Housing and Real Estate Management

台湾地区面向青年人的社会住宅模式供给模式探析——以新北市为例
Analysis on the Mode of Supply of Social Housing for Youth in Taiwan——A Case Study of New Taipei City
郭净宇

Kuo Chin-Yu

基于居民住房可支付能力的公租房租金差别化定价研究：以南京为例

Study on the Differential Pricing of Public Rental Rent Based on the Affordability of Residents' Housing——A Case Study of Nanjing

唐　焱　邢一丹

Tang Yan, Xing Yidan

住房成本对武汉郊区农业转移人口定居地选择的影响

The Influence of Housing Costs to the Choice of Settlement for Wuhan Suburban Transferring Agricultural People

高永波　耿　虹

Gao Yongbo, Geng Hong

Hong Kong's Public Housing Policy and Social Problems——A Case Study of Tin Shui Wai New Town

香港的公营房屋政策与社会问题——以天水围新市镇为例

Li Yi

李　益

开放住宅体系周期性共享租用模式探究

Periodic Renting Sharing Mode Research of Residential Open Buildings

王春彧　李振宇

Wang Chunyu, Li Zhenyu

Green Building Understanding Among Public Green Housing Residents: A Case Study in Hong Kong

香港公屋居民对于绿色建筑认识：个案研究

Ji Jie, Yin Huai

季　洁　鄞　槐

Seeking Sustainable Housing Solutions: China and Iraq from Convergence to Divergence

寻求可持续住房解决方案——中国与伊拉克从融合到分歧

Sivan Al Jarah, Zhou Bo, Liu Mengxiao

西婉月　周　博　刘梦潇

农地"三权"抵押贷款对农民进城购房驱动力影响因素研究：以重庆市606个样本农户为例

Study on the Influence Factors of the Farmland, Forestry and Homestead Mortgage Driving Force for Farmers Real Estate Purchase: In A Sample of 606 Farmers in Chongqing as Example

王　杰

Wang Jie

供给侧改革对重庆市商品住宅市场的影响研究

The Influence of Supply Side Reform on Chongqing City Commodity Housing Market

王婉瑜

Wang Wanyu

Social Housing in Different Cultures——Comparative Study Western Europe and East Asia: A First Attempt

不同文化背景下的社会性住房：西欧与东亚的初步比较研究

Wolfgang Dokonal, Marlis Nograsek, Ernst Dengg, Tsou Jin-Yeu

Wolfgang Dokonal　Marlis Nograsek　Ernst Dengg　邹经宇

台北都市区家户之居住安排特性研究

A Study on the Characteristic of Household Living Arrangements in Taipei Metropolitan Area
徐国城　刘芷妤
Hsu Kuo-Cheng, Liu Chih-Yu

基于PPP模式的城镇棚户区改造项目利益分配及其对策研究
Study on the Benefit Distribution and Countermeasure of Urban Shantytowns Renovation Project Based on PPP Mode
赵　琰　赵翠芹
Zhao Yan, Zhao Cuiqin

对我国棚户区改造建设管理云平台的研究和实践
The Development of Construction Management in the Shanty Towns Cloud Platform and Application
陆伟良　李学东　杜　昱　苏　俊
Lu Weiliang, Li Xuedong, Du Yu, Su Jun

长者友善人居环境营造
Age-friendly Human Habitat

新城镇绿色养老住宅合作居住模式与适宜技术
Study on the Cohousing Pattern and Appropriate Technologies of Green Senior Residence in New Town
李珺杰　夏海山
Li Junjie, Xia Haishan

养老服务统筹下既有住区户外空间适老性优化初探
Preliminary Study on the Old Fitness Optimization of the Outdoor Space in the Existing Residential Areas under the Pension Service Overall
周志伟　周　博　卢丹丹
Zhou Zhiwei, Zhou Bo, Lu Dandan

基于老年人行为的既有住区环境优化设计研究：以大连地区为例
Research on the Optimal External Environment Design of Old Residential Area Base on the Elderly Behavior——Take Dalian as An Example
于文婷　周　博　周志伟
Yu Wenting, Zhou Bo, Zhou Zhiwei

生产性适老社区的设计概念初探
A Primary Study on Concepts of Designing Productive Community for the Elderly
吴浩然　张玉坤　贡小雷　郑　捷
Wu Haoran, Zhang Yukun, Gong Xiaolei, Zheng Jie

长远老年建筑设计策略
Redesigning Long-term Senior Care Housing Strategy
吕庆耀
Bryant Lu

应对老年人走失的高密度住区转型研究
High Density Residential Transformation Research Dealing with the Old Lost Problem
卢丹丹　周　博　周志伟　杨岸霄
Lu Dandan, Zhou Bo, Zhou Zhiwei, Yang Anxiao

重庆市机构养老市场供需现状调查研究
Research on the Current Situation of Supply and Demand of Aged Pension Market in Chongqing
刘继壮
Liu Jizhuang

苏州姑苏区古建旧民居的适老化更新与再利用
The Regeneration and Reuse of Historic Residential Buildings Adapting to Ageing in Suzhou Gusu District
曹修安　华振宁
Cao Xiuan, Hua Zhenning

绿色养老社适宜技术探讨
Appropriate Technology Investigation in Green Retirement Community
徐善梅
Xu Shanmei

智慧城市与计算机辅助技术集成应用
Smart City and Computer-aided Technology Integration

BIM平台架构下采光性能模拟的自适应性建筑立面策略与原型研究
The Research of Adaptive Building Facade Strategy and Prototype Based on Daylight Performance Simulation
陈上元　沈扬庭　何妍萱　吴念瑾
Chen Shang-Yuan, Shen Yang-Ting, Ho Yen-Hsuan, Wu Nien-Chin

日本智慧型技术在城市住宅中的应用研究
A Study on the Use of Intelligent Technology on the Field of Urban Housing in Japan
伊藤增辉
Ito Masuteru

An Innovated Smart Home Sensors Integration and Remote Control Solution and Implementation Based on the Mirror Touch Interaction
一种基于镜像交互技术的智能家居传感器集成与远程控制解决方案及实现
Li Jixun, Qiu Shenping, Wang Hao, Ye Lei
李佶逊　邱沈萍　王浩　叶雷

轻型钢结构模矩化设计方法论
The Design Methodology of Light Gauge Steel Structure Modular
陈上元　刘泰佑　蔡立伟
Chen Shang-Yuan, Liu Tai-Yu, Cai Li-Wei

整合建筑信息建模参数编程引擎与嵌入式系统的智能化城市住宅研究
The Research of Smart Urban Housing via Integrating BIM-based Parametric Programming Engine with Embedded System
沈扬庭　吴念瑾
Shen Yang Ting, Wu Nien Chin

以网络数据为主体的空间句法模型对城市中心的识别与分析——以吉林市轨道交通项目为例
The Identification and Analysis of the City Center by the Space Syntax Model Based on Network Data——Jilin's Rail Transit Project
杨振盛　盛强　刘星

Yang Zhensheng, Sheng Qiang, Liu Xing

社区居民社会聚集的影响：对北京街区公共空间的空间句法分析

The Influence of Outdoor Gathering of Community: Space Syntax Analysis on the Public Space in Beijing's Neighborhoods

刘　星　杨振盛

Liu Xing, Yang Zhensheng

探讨深度学习在智慧城市中的应用方法：以 AI 风水助手为例

Customize Deep Learning for Smart City: AI-based Feng Shui Assistant as An Example

杨金泽　李秋明　邱仁钿　谢尚贤

Yang Jin-Ze , Lee Chiu-Ming, Chiou Jen-Dian, Hsieh Shang-Hsien